CHINA AND BEYOND
BY VICTOR H. MAIR

CHINA AND BEYOND
BY VICTOR H. MAIR

A Collection of Essays

Compiled by
Rebecca Shuang Fu, Matthew Anderson,
Xiang Wan, and Sophie Ling-Chia Wei

Amherst, New York

Copyright 2013 Cambria Press

All rights reserved
Printed in the United States of America

No part of this publication may be reproduced, stored in or introduced into a retrieval system, or transmitted, in any form, or by any means (electronic, mechanical, photocopying, recording, or otherwise), without the prior permission of the publisher.

Requests for permission should be directed to:
permissions@cambriapress.com, or mailed to:
Cambria Press
University Corporate Centre, 100 Corporate Parkway, Suite 128
Amherst, NY 14226

This book has been registered with the Library of Congress.

China and Beyond by Victor H. Mair: A Collection of Essays / Rebecca Shuang Fu, Matthew Anderson, Xiang Wan, and Sophie Ling-Chia Wei.
p. cm.
Includes bibliographical references and index.
ISBN 978-1-60497-889-6 (alk. paper)

Table of Contents

List of Tables vii

List of Figures ix

Acknowledgments xiii

Preface
   Matthew Anderson, Rebecca Shuang Fu, Xiang Wan, and
   Sophie Ling-chia Wei xv

Chapter 1: Scroll Presentation in the T'ang Dynasty 1

Chapter 2: The *Sacred Edict* 39

Chapter 3: *Chiang-Ching Wen* 93

Chapter 4: India and China 121

Chapter 5: The Word *$^*m^yag$* in Old Sinitic 155

Chapter 6: Cheng Ch'iao's Understanding of Sanskrit 185

Chapter 7: Buddhism and the Rise of the Written
   Vernacular 207

Chapter 8: Southern Bottle Gourd (*hu-lu*) 283

Chapter 9: Ma Jianzhong 327

Chapter 10: Xie He's "Six Laws" of Painting and Their Indian
   Parallels 353

Chapter 11: Horse Sacrifices and Sacred Groves 405

Chapter 12: What Is *Geyi*, After All? 449

Index 499

LIST OF TABLES

Table 1: Interpretations and Paraphrases of the *Sacred Edict* 77

Table 2a: Glossary (Part 1) 260

Table 2b: Glossary (*Continued*) 261

Table 2c: Glossary (*Continued*) 262

Table 2d: Glossary (*Continued*) 263

Table 2e: Glossary (*Continued*) 264

Table 2f: Glossary (*Continued*) 265

Table 2g: Glossary (*Continued*) 266

Table 2h: Glossary (*Continued*) 267

Table 2i: Glossary (*Continued*) 268

Table 3a: The Six Laws of Xie He 357

Table 3b: The Six Laws of Xie He (*Continued*) 358

Table 4: Six Laws by Zhang Yanyuan 361

Table 5: S binomials of each of his laws with one of the Six Limbs 383

Table 6: Parallels between the S binomials of the Six Laws and the Six Limbs 384

Table 7: Comparison between *wu jie* (*pañca śīlāni*) and *wu chang* 474

Table 8: Abbreviations 481

List of Figures

Figure 1: Shell Carved Head (T45:2) from Chou-yüan. *Wen wu* 1 (1986): 46 157

Figure 2: Shell Carved Head (T45:6) from Chou-yüan. *Wen wu* 1 (1986): 47 157

Figure 3: Bone carving of a human head from Anyang 159

Figure 4: Aramean from Urartian relief at Zincirli 160

Figure 5: A version of the magic ring of Solomon 167

Figure 6: Sigil 168

Figure 7: Medieval Vernacular Sinitic written in Tibetan transcription 214

Figure 8: Imperial Decree [of June 17, 1389] to the Buddhist Monk Irinjin Dzangbu (in Tibetan Rin-č'en bTsang-po) 221

Figure 9: Opening page of the preface to *Hunmin chŏng'ŭm* (Corrected Sounds for Instructing the People) by King Sejong (1397-1450) 249

Figure 10: Opening page of an article on writing from *Hsi-tzu ch'i-chi* (The Miracle of Western Letters) (1605) by the Jesuit priest, Matteo Ricci (1552-1610) 252

Figure 11: A page from *I-mu liao-jan ch'u-chieh* (First Steps in Being Able to Comprehend at a Glance) by Lu Chuang-chang (1854-1928), who had close ties with Christian missionaries 256

Figure 12: T'ieh-kuai Li ("Iron Crutch Li"), one of the Taoist Eight Transcendents 307

Figure 13: Inverted bottle-gourd visage based on the traditional Peking Opera mask of Liu T'ang, known as the "Redhaired Devil." 308

Figure 14: A stamp issued by the Republic of China 309

Figure 15: "The Bottle-Gourd Immortal" by Shen Chou 310

Figure 16: Fei Chang-fang inside of his utopian calabash 311

Figure 17: The Perfect Symmetry of the Six Limbs (Roman numerals) and the Six Laws (Arabic numerals). The central pair is at the top in both cases 389

Figure 18: Reconstruction of a seventh-century (Iron Age) horse sacrifice over a sacred bog at Lejre, Denmark 430

Figure 19: Reconstruction of a memorial service among the old Türks of the eastern Altai. 431

Figure 20: Altaic sacrificial setup with stuffed horse pelt, including head and hooves. 432

Figure 21: "Oirot" horse sacrifice 433

List of Figures   xi

Figure 22: Drawing of a sacrificial scene on a shaman's magic drum from the Altai region 434

Acknowledgments

This project has been two years in planning, but two months in the making. It could have never been undertaken without those who have given me their support. Many people have collected materials, provided suggestions, answered questions, and helped in different ways. Here I would like to express cordial gratitude to those individuals who contributed to the completion of this collection:

Tansen Sen, Associate Professor at Baruch College, the City University of New York, and a senior fellow student of Prof. Mair, for his instructive counsel in the whole process of making this collection, as well as sharing his experience compiling the 2006 Festschrift for Prof. Mair, usually dispensed over delicious meals in Singapore and New York City;

The staff of Cambria Press, including Toni L. Tan, Director at Cambria Press, who was always willing to answer my questions at any time;

Daniel Boucher, Associate Professor at Cornell University, and Neil Schmid, for their compiling the Festschrift in honor of Prof. Mair's sixtieth birthday (see *Asia Major* [2006]) with Tansen, which provided us a good model to follow when we put this collection together;

Matthew Anderson, Xiang Wan, and Sophie Ling-chia Wei, who are my classmates at Penn and the best co-workers ever, for their enthusiasm and two months of painstaking work in making this project;

Yunshuang Zhang, Ph.D. student at the Department of Asian Languages and Cultures, UCLA, and also my good friend since college, who helped find a rare copy of Mair's 1986 article in *Chinese Studies*, as well as making a high-quality PDF file to facilitate our OCR work;

Zhichen Zhao, my husband and best friend, who took wonderful photos of Professor Mair for this collection, and helped to edit and proofread certain chapters with his characteristic meticulousness and patience.

I would also like to extend special thanks to Professor Mair, as well as the following journals, presses, and institutions for kindly granting us permissions to republish content for the compilation of this book: University of California Press (Berkeley), Center for Chinese Studies (Taipei), *Journal of the Asiatic Society* (Calcutta), *Early China*, Institute of Chinese Studies at the Chinese University of Hong Kong, Cambridge University Press, *Journal of Chinese Linguistics*, University of Hawai'i Press (Honolulu), *Ou ya Xue kan* (Journal of Eurasian Studies), and State University of New York Press (Albany).

Rebecca Shuang Fu

Preface

*Matthew Anderson, Rebecca Shuang Fu,
Xiang Wan, and Sophie Ling-chia Wei*

泰山不讓土壤，故能成其大；
河海不擇細流，故能就其深。
Mount Tai never gives up a soil [particle], and therefore
  achieves its grandness;
Rivers and Oceans are never choosy among minute streams,
  and therefore accomplish their depth.
    Shiji 史記, "Li Si liezhuan 李斯列傳" (Biography of Li Si)

Our mentor, Victor H. Mair, Professor of Chinese Language and Literature at the University of Pennsylvania, has continuously produced a vast number of scholarly works, which have been influential and well known for their broad scope. The essays which make up this collection neither include much of his newest work,[1] nor do they include his most influential pieces. Instead, we have taken care to select some articles which date back to the earliest phases of his career, and others which might be less well-known or less easy to find.

Using the first chapter of this collection as an example, "Scroll Presentation in the T'ang Dynasty" (originally published in the *Harvard Journal of Asiatic Studies* in June, 1978) was written before Professor Mair embarked on his career at the University of Pennsylvania; its origins can be traced back to the time when he was still a student at Harvard University. Other examples include Chapter 2, originally published in 1985, and Chapter 3, originally published in 1986, which are among his earliest publications.[2] Some of the other papers have either not been circulated widely, or are currently unavailable electronically; these include Chapter 8, which originally appeared in a conference volume published in Taiwan, and Chapter 6, first published in Hong Kong as part of a Festschrift produced in honor of Professor Jao Tsung-I's 饒宗頤 seventy-fifth birthday, which brings us to the time of this publication, as we take the opportunity to present this collection in honor of Professor Victor H. Mair's seventieth birthday. Just as Professor Mair wrote the paper to celebrate a great scholar's birthday, we have assembled this collection of his essays to honor another great scholar on his birthday. How could we miss such an opportunity?

This collection was assembled with the intention of connecting a number of pieces from disparate phases of Professor Mair's career, following its trajectory in order to present a picture of its development. Professor Mair's early articles collected in this collection, Chapters 1 to 3, reflect his comprehensive and interdisciplinary training in Chinese literature and Indology at the School of Oriental and African Studies in London and at Harvard University. This quality is evident in all his academic works. Chapter 1 examines a Tang Dynasty (618-907) political/literary phenomenon called "presenting/warming scrolls," which resulted in the creation of a large array of poems, both good and bad. Chapter 2 focuses on the exegesis by scholars or officials on the meaning of the so-called *Sacred Edict* of Emperor Kangxi of the Qing Dynasty and details how orthodox ideology was transmitted and modified. The article published in 1986, Chapter 3, centers on medieval Chinese Buddhist culture and its Indian origins in literature (*jiang jingwen* [*chiang-ching-wen*, sūtra lecture]). It is noteworthy that it was during this period that Professor Mair was writing one of his most influential monographs, *T'ang Transformation Texts: A Study of the Buddhist Contribution to the Rise of Vernacular Fiction and Drama in China* (Cambridge, Mass.: Council on East Asian Studies, Harvard University, 1989).

Though these earlier works certainly included discussion of interactions between China and other cultures, beginning with Chapter 4, this collection shifts its focus to the theme of exchange between China (and to a wider extent, East Asia) and its neighbors--primarily India (Chapters 4, 6, 7), but also Iran (Chapter 5), ethnic groups to the South of China proper (Chapter 8), and even the Western World (Chapter 9); this overall theme has been perhaps the most fruitful in Professor Mair's academic career. These interactions (which went in both directions) resulted in significant changes to Chinese (and East Asian) language and literature—chronologically, from Literary Sinitic to medieval vernacular, and on to Modern Mandarin. The topics cover cultural borrowing from India into China over a variety of types of literature and performing art (Chapter 4); Iranian elements in pre-imperial Chinese aristocratic culture (Chapter 5); the awareness and understanding of Sanskrit alphabetic spelling in medieval China (Chapter 6); the spread of Buddhism in catalyzing the emergence of written vernacular as precursors of national languages in East Asian countries (Chapter 7); the appropriation of Southern Chinese myth into Taoism (Chapter 8); and the first modern Chinese effort to establish a systematic grammar, Ma Jianzhong's *Ma shi wentong* (Chapter 9).

Another conspicuous transition of Professor Mair's research focus occurred during the turn of the twentieth and twenty-first centuries, when he convened two renowned international conferences at the University of Pennsylvania in 1996 and 2001[3] and coauthored with J. P.

Mallory the milestone work *The Tarim Mummies: Ancient China and the Mystery of the Earliest Peoples from the West* (London: Thames & Hudson, 2000). This was followed by a third international symposium at Penn in 2011. Starting from this period, Professor Mair extended the scope of his works beyond language and literature.

The last three chapters of this collection represent his new exploration. Chapter 11 deals with the horse, a medium not only of material but also cultural transmission from the West to China, among the northern nomadic peoples interacting with the ethnic Han. Professor Mair has branched out from philology to make significant research contributions in art, archaeology, and philosophy. While his earlier monograph *Painting and Performance: Chinese Picture Recitation and Its Indian Genesis*, published in 1988, as well as Chapter 4 of this collection, demonstrates his expertise in the art of Asia and the world, Professor Mair has further pursued theories of Indo-Chinese painting, notably the transformation of the Indian concept of Six Limbs (*Ṣaḍaṅga*) into the Six Laws of Xie He (Chapter 10). In tandem with Professor Mair's persistent effort in interpreting and introducing Chinese philosophy (e.g, his translations of the *Tao Te Ching* in 1990, the *Zhuangzi* in 1998, and the *Art of War* in 2007), Professor Mair also meticulously studied the hermeneutics of early medieval Buddhism by scrutinizing the concept of *geyi*, making use of a transnational, historical perspective (Chapter 12).

In the preface to an earlier Festschrift for Professor Mair, published in *Asia Major* in 2006, his former students Daniel Boucher, Neil Schmid, and Tansen Sen presented a full account of Professor Mair's major research methods and the influence he has had over his students. Professor Mair's unique teaching methods and brand of scholarship have naturally been critically important influences on our scholarship, and his spirit and drive have perhaps been even more important in encouraging us and furthering our development. Our research interests are quite diverse, ranging from the relationship between China and the West from late prehistoric times through to the early imperial era, with a focus on the introduction of the horse and wheeled vehicles and the transmission of bronze metallurgy; medieval Chinese literature and history, especially that of manuscripts, often written in the vernacular, from Dunhuang and Turfan; the history of translation in China, especially during the Ming and Qing dynasties, including translation by the Jesuits of the Chinese classics, as well as the much earlier translation into Chinese of Buddhist texts; and the early development of Chinese writing and the complicated ways in which writing and spoken language intersect. Professor Mair's transregional, interdisciplinary approach; his focus on vernacular literature as it appears in manuscripts; his enormous network of valuable contacts; his in-depth research into Buddhist scriptures; his broad research into languages and translation, including his production of his own translations, which reflect the fact that translation is a major strategy in crossing borders and bridging the gap between cultures; and his neverending investigations into the nature and development of Sinitic languages and the Chinese writing system, together with, not least, his boundless enthusiasm, have been an inspiration to all of us.

To take the pieces collected in this book as examples, it is clear that Professor Mair easily and skillfully moves among the cultures of China, India, Central Asia, and, indeed, many other locales, while at the same time weaving together the disciplines of philology, literature, religious studies, philosophy, linguistics, archaeology, and art history, to name but a few. His research in languages and translation also inspires the next generation of scholars to regard the Sinitic languages from brand new perspectives and instills new energy into many disciplines. From the point of view of scholarship, these pieces embody Professor Mair's particular border-crossing methods; additionally, they help to open up the horizons of our own scholarship and keep us continuously excited about our work. The essays in this collection illuminate Professor Mair's limitless curiosity towards the unknown and his boundless passion for exploring anything that might be of interest. On top of this, he is always skeptical of accepted knowledge, making the point through his work that questions that appear answered deserve to be explored further, often with insightful results. Through his writings, he informs that--with the world as big as it is, and the sources of its cultures as deep as they are--scholarship is, and should be, continuously fascinating. Additionally, his acknowledgments for these essays are very telling because they showcase his work and cooperation with his colleagues and scholars from a dizzying variety of fields. He enthusiastically explores fields with which he is not yet familiar, unhesitatingly consulting specialists in these fields, and is always ready to cooperate—indeed he truly leads by his own example. Professor Mair is always extremely generous with his talents —he is not only ready to help scholars in his field, but he is also always gracious in assisting scholars from other fields and many other individuals from a wide spectrum of diverse backgrounds. This generosity in helping others and furthering scholarship are clearly evident in the work of his long-running journal, *Sino-Platonic Papers*, and with many of his other projects; for example, he is editor for the ABC Dictionary series (published by the University of Hawai'i), which includes not only a landmark alphabetized Chinese-English dictionary but a variety of other works, including the first true etymological dictionary of Chinese (Axel Schuessler's *ABC Etymological Dictionary of Old Chinese*; 2007) and W. South Coblin's *A Dictionary of 'Phags-pa Chinese* (2007), among others. Most recently, Professor Mair launched the Cambria Sinophone World Series (published by Cambria Press), which is already home to groundbreaking works, such as *The Classic of Changes in Cultural Context: A Textual Archaeology of the Yi jing* by Scott Davis, *Gao Xingjian: Aesthetics and Creation* by Gao Xingjian (translated by Mabel Lee), *A Study of Two Classics: A Cultural Critique of The Romance of the Three Kingdoms and The Water Margin* by Liu Zaifu (translated by Shu Yunzhong), *Rethinking Chineseness: Translational Sinophone Identities in the Nanyang Literary World* by E. K. Tan, and *Confucian Prophet: Political Thought In Du Fu's Poetry (752–757)* by David K. Schneider.

Although the essays in this collection represent only a small portion of Professor Mair's extensive works, they form a bridge over the past several decades of Professor Mair's work which continues to inspire younger scholars to follow in his footsteps. He has not been satisfied simply to build on the foundations created by previous scholars, but he has forged to open up new fields of research. He stands out in all the fields upon which he has touched, such that the spirit of his scholarship continuously moves us onward and upward. With this commemorative collection of brilliant essays, we respectfully pay tribute to Professor Victor H. Mair's unending dedication and contributions to scholarship, knowing that he still has much to contribute and will be a benchmark for many generations of scholars as he guides us in advancing scholarship.

> *Instead breaking an endnote, // is used to denote a new line within the endnote.

Notes

1. Represented by, to name just two works, *Sacred Display: Divine and Magical Female Figures of Eurasia* (written with Miriam Robbins Dexter; Amherst, N.Y.: Cambria Press, 2010), which won the Sarasvati Award for the Best Nonfiction Book in Women and Mythology, and *Secrets of the Silk Road* (the catalog for an important exhibition which appeared at both the Bowers Museum and the Penn Museum, edited by Professor Mair; Santa Anna, Calif.: Bowers Museum, 2010).
2. Professor Mair is an extremely productive scholar, and these are only some among his many early publications.
3. See his edited works *The Bronze Age and Early Iron Age Peoples of Eastern Central Asia* (Washington, D.C.: Institute for the Study of Man in collaboration with the University of Pennsylvania Museum Publications, 1998) and *Contact and Exchange in the Ancient World* (Honolulu: University of Hawaiʻi Press, 2006).

China and Beyond
by Victor H. Mair

CHAPTER 1

SCROLL PRESENTATION IN THE T'ANG DYNASTY

Source: Adapted from "Scroll Presentation in the T'ang Dynasty," *Harvard Journal of Asiatic Studies*, 38.1 (1978): 35-60.

The T'ang dynasty saw the refinement of the examination system and unofficial practices related to it.[1] Although the examination questions were largely on literary subjects,[2] candidates were somewhat constrained by the rigidly prescribed form of the answers. Consequently, they frequently felt the need to supplement their performance on the examination with other, less circumscribed, types of written expression. One of the most interesting and appealing aspects of the position-seeking competition was the use of poetry in gaining admittance to the offices or residences of powerful political personages. Although the custom frequently degenerated into pure formalism–the poetry becoming a mere adjunct of the calling card–we can be thankful for this peculiar species of corruption[3] for it has left us a large number of excellent poems and a wealth of humorous stories as well.

A related practice in T'ang times was the submission of letters by aspiring public servants to influential figures. In such letters, direct appeals were made for assistance at all levels of the selection, recommendation, examination, and position-seeking process. These appeals were usually couched in the most effusive, sycophantic language. The present paper deals with a more subtle method of influence purchasing. To wit, it examines the notion that a candidate might, by the force or beauty of his compositions, move a well-known person to proffer political assistance. In an attempt to put scroll presentation during the T'ang in proper perspective, the practice as it existed in the Sung is also described.

An early twelfth-century account of office-seeking in the T'ang reveals a tensely competitive pursuit by large numbers of candidates for a comparatively small number of places.

> During the time of Emperor Hsüan-tsung (r. 713–55), there were large numbers of scholars. Those *chin-shih* (Advanced Scholars) who went to the capital each year were often no less than a thousand and some. Students in the academies went about making calls one after another and formed cliques so as to wrest power from other factions. These were called *p'eng* 棚 ("tents" or "canopies") and would elect their more prestigious members as *p'eng-t'ou* 棚頭 ("boss of the tent"). No one of power or influence was left unvisited by them. In this way, they would confuse the senses of the examiners. Those who did not pass would most likely make noisy accusations against which the Bureau for the Investigation of Merits[4] was defenseless.[5]

In a section of the late-T'ang work, *T'ang Gleanings*,[6] entitled "Sheng-ch'en hou-chin" 升沉後進 (The Power to Make or Break Junior Scholars), there are illustrations of the need to establish for oneself the correct image with the right people.[7] "Chih-chi" 知己 (Patrons), in the same chapter, also gives one an idea of the frantic race which political aspirants entered to gain the favor and patronage of those officials who were, at the moment, in the ascendant. In such an environment, any

Scroll Presentation in the T'ang Dynasty

device which would enable the candidate to make himself noticed was valuable.

As evidenced in the following passage from the dynastic history of the T'ang, the blame for the circumvention of the examination system ultimately lay with the Emperor himself:

> The T'ang regulations governing the selection of candidates for government service were, for the most part, based upon old Sui models, the essentials of which were three: nominees from the schools and academies were called "pupils," those from the prefectures and districts were called "local contributions." All of these candidates were recommended to the civil authorities who would promote or demote them....[8] Those who were personally summoned by the Emperor were called "imperial designees," which category was reserved for those of extraordinary ability.[9]

If the Emperor could make appointments without regard to performance on the examinations, certainly others might be tempted to follow suit. According to Li Chao 李肇 (fl. 806–20), they did:

> Han Yü (768–824) made introductions for scholars of the younger generation who were seeking to pass the examinations. There were many who would send in letters to him asking for further instructions and they were called "Han's disciples" by the people of the time. Later, when Han Yü attained high office, he no longer performed this service.[10]

A modern student has made the following assessment of the considerable power of fine writing in the T'ang dynasty:

> When T'ang scholars were preparing to take the examinations, they would invariably present letters to men of influence at the court and to well-known figures among those who had already achieved success in their official careers. These men of influence at court would then independently commend those scholars whom they had chosen to the examiner. After the results came out, the examiner would yet have to inquire of the Prime Minister

whether he had anyone to recommend. Only then was the pass-list posted.

The Prefects and Governors would also generally make it their business to encourage and promote poor scholars. In the event one single poem were appreciated, it would immediately be passed on and recited far and near. And when its author went to the capital, no sooner had he unpacked than people invariably began calling at his door. As a result, there were no talented scholars during the T'ang who complained about having no one to assist them.[11]

It is clear that those in positions of authority were willing to lend a helping hand, but those who needed that helping hand had first to make themselves known. Among the most popular ways of accomplishing this were the presentation, circulation, and "warming" of scrolls (*t'ou chüan* 投卷, *hsing chüan* 行卷, *wen chüan* 溫卷) containing one's compositions.[12] In the twelfth-century *Yen-fan-lu* 演繁露 (The Thick Dews Extended),[13] there is preserved a description of the physical characteristics of the presentation scrolls:

During the T'ang dynasty, candidates who were attempting higher degrees were compelled to "circulate scrolls" by which is meant that they would record their writings on sealed scrolls for presentation to the chief examiner. For the format used, see the *Collected Works of Li I-shan,* "Preface to the New Letter" (chapter 7) which states: "The paper-maker generally uses ink for the borders of each strip. (This is nowadays commonly called a 'dividing line.') A sixteen line layout is employed. (That is to say, each strip is divided by ink borders into sixteen lines.) Generally, each line has no more than eleven characters. (This format has fallen into disuse in the present dynasty.)"[14]

The recipients of the scrolls were important literary and political figures. If a candidate received the support of such a person, his success on the examination was assured. The test thus became an empty exercise, even the rankings being determined beforehand. This state of affairs was particularly true of the mid-T'ang. During the reign of Empress Wu (r. 684–705), reliance on the examination was strict due to the institution of coded examination papers (*hu-ming chih* 糊名制). And, in the late T'ang, party strife led to the loss of power by the literati to the eunuchs and military commanders. Thus, the majority of illustrations in this paper will relate to the eighth century and the first quarter of the ninth century.

A few modern Chinese scholars have attempted to make the case that this practice of the literati was intimately related to the development of the short story in the T'ang. They claim that the need for attractive material to fill the scrolls served as a stimulus to the writing of fiction. The genesis of the theory was Tschen Yinkoh's (Ch'en Yin-k'o 陳寅恪) brief but pregnant article entitled "Han Yü and the T'ang Novel."[15] Ch'en's hypothesis was taken up and expanded by Liu K'ai-jung 劉開榮 in a chapter of his book on T'ang dynasty fiction.[16] The evidence supporting such a hypothesis is both scant and unconvincing. Only two sources appear to give direct support to the argument that the presentation of scrolls directly fostered the growth of fiction during the T'ang. The first, only the beginning of which is generally quoted in this regard, is from a Sung work entitled *Yün-lu man-ch'ao* 雲麓漫鈔 (Rambling Notes from the Clouded Foothills). When the entire passage is examined, however, it is difficult to maintain that Chao Yen-wei 趙彥衛 (fl. 1195), its author, was attempting much more than an educated guess. This is a criticism which has already been levelled by Huang Yün-mei 黃雲眉 and others.[17] Certainly, the focus of Chao's remarks is more on poetry than on prose.

> T'ang dynasty candidates, relying upon an illustrious contemporary, would first have their names brought to the attention of the chief-examiner and would later present some of their writings to him. After several days had passed, they would again present some of their writings and this was called "keeping the scrolls warm." *Record of the Gloomy and the Strange*,[18] *Transmission of the Unusual*,[19] and the like were all used for this purpose. Possibly

this sort of literature embraces a variety of styles and can be used to demonstrate historical talent, poetic flair, and expository skill.

When it comes to the Advanced Scholars, most of them used poetry for presentation pieces. Today there are several hundred different collections of T'ang poetry current which were used for this purpose. Wang An-shih (1021–86) gathered them together and, omitting the poorer ones, made the *T'ang Poems by One Hundred Authors* (*T'ang po-chia shih* 唐百家詩). Some say that, during the period of selection, Wang would mark with pieces of paper those items which he wished to have copied and would then hand the manuscripts over to the scribes. But the scribes were cowed by those poems which were of enormous length and so substituted poems of two or four rhymes for them. Wang did not read them a second time.

I have obtained and examined poems by these authors and not only were the longer pieces for the most part of a poor quality, all the others were rough, extemporary exercises used as presentation pieces. None was the product of inspiration and thus, though there is an abundance of them, they are trivial and weak.[20]

The second item adduced[21] has no real bearing on the subject in question.[22] Leaving aside these problems of literary criticism, let us return to other sources which touch upon "warming scrolls" and related practices. While references to the presentation and circulation of scrolls are numerous, I have discovered only a few which specifically mention the characters *wen-chüan* 溫卷. Among these, a poem by Lu Yu 陸游 (1125–1210) entitled "Writing Out My Feelings during an Autumn Rain" almost equates "scroll-warming guests" with being active in political circles.

> I have newly hulled brown rice[23] and fresh-picked vegetables,
> As long as my stomach is full, I have never wished for more;
> For a long time now, there have been no "scroll-warming guests"
>   outside my gate,
> On my shelves, how could there be any letters from
>   ardent officials?
> Not putting aside my unstrained wine, I sip it from time to time,

Scroll Presentation in the T'ang Dynasty

And my short hair still needs to be combed every day;
I laugh at myself for retaining these youth-like airs,
But the misty rain which covers the river truly depresses me.[24]

秋雨書感

新春赤米摘新蔬　　一飽從來不願餘
門外久無溫卷客　　架中寧有熱官書
濁醪未廢時時飲　　短髮猶須日日梳
自笑少年風味在　　滿川煙雨正愁予

Other Sung sources, such as *Sheng*[25]-*shui yen-t'an lu* 澠水燕談錄 (A Record of Casual Talks by the Sheng River) would seem to indicate that, though the name "warming scrolls" survived, it did not necessarily indicate the actual presentation of one's compositions as it had in the T'ang:

> At the beginning of our dynasty, most of the customs of the literati during the latter part of the T'ang dynasty were retained. The candidate would, upon going to see someone who had already achieved success in his official career, first send in his calling card. This was called "requesting an audience." If the audience were granted, on another day, the candidate would again send in a note which was called "thanking for the audience." After another few days, he would again hand in a note and this was called "keeping the scrolls warm." Whether his superior would write to him thanking him or would extol him, the candidate would promptly compose a separate note in which he would express his thanks in an ingratiating manner and request yet another audience. Such was the respect shown by candidates toward their superiors.
>
> In recent years, this sort of etiquette is no longer observed. And it is also rare for higher officials to commend their juniors.[26]

The notion that the presentation of scrolls during the Sung was but an atrophied holdover from the T'ang is reinforced by a passage in *Liang-hsi man-chih* 梁溪漫志 (Rambling Notes from Liang Stream):

> When previous generations observed the practice of "circulating scrolls," they would always send in their scrolls together with their calling cards. This was most likely done so as to allow the host to read the compositions first and then to receive their author.
>
> During the Hsüan-ho years (1119–25), when Hu Te-hui of Ts'ang-wu[27] met with Liu Yüan-ch'eng, this practice was still followed. In recent years, it is usual to wait for an interview at which time a written note is personally delivered. In general, these are requests for political appointments, supplications for personal recommendation letters, petitions for favors, entreaties for sympathy, and the like. According to custom, the host makes an evasive acknowledgement and tucks the note into his sleeve. After the suppliant has retired, he reads a bit of it. But seeing that it consists largely of the sort of thing mentioned above, he seldom finishes reading such scrolls.
>
> The host roundly detests these petitions for favors. How could he be expected to extol the suppliants? The literati treat themselves lightly, and so the tradition that those who have already achieved success in office should extend favors to them has by now been swept into oblivion.[28]

Although scroll presentation was somewhat time-worn during the Northern Sung and completely out of fashion by the beginning of the Southern Sung dynasty, the following elaborate description shows that it was still observed during the Five Dynasties. On the basis of this contemporary report, however, it would appear that the practice had already hardened into a ritual. The exuberance of the T'ang is noticeably absent.

> My late father once remarked that, for the most part, the examinees of recent times wear "pansy" purple[29] gowns.[30] The horses they ride are outfitted with saddles and caparisons made of tiger and leopard skins. When they pay a visit to some important person they do not, as one would expect, consider a letter of intro-

duction to be a necessary preliminary. Often, they do not have academic gowns with broad sleeves,[31] which is quite unspeakable.

I shall not presume to discuss this by citing incidents out of the distant past. I only remember that, in the time of Ming-tsung (r. 926–33) of the Later T'ang, the high-ranking ministers and leading officials were all old literati of the T'ang Imperial House who were devoted to ceremonial rites and regulations. In those days, Advanced Scholars and Exegetes of the Classics would all dress in ramie academic robes with Prussian blue sashes. They wore boots and rode upon donkeys, taking with them both a letter-holder and a bag to carry their brushes, ink-slab, paper, and ink. Each time one of them visited the gate of a high-ranking minister, he would dismount from his donkey while he was still several paces away. Having adjusted his clothes and cap, he would gather his attendants[32] together and then go in person before the gate. There he would beg the steward to send in his letter of introduction and visiting card and to request an audience for him. Having obtained this audience, on another day he would again send in a note which was called "thanking for the audience." It was only after another few days that he would place inside his sleeve a scroll of his writings to give to the steward or gatekeeper but he would not request a further audience. Once again, after another few days, he would hand in a note and this was called "keeping the scrolls warm."

In general, audiences were not to be repeated frequently. To repeat them frequently was to be overfamiliar. Where there was overfamiliarity, there would be laxity in regard to the etiquette which governed the making and receiving of calls. However, should the leading official have written an inscription on the scroll expressing thanks, or should the caller have heard elsewhere that there were words of praise for it, he would compose an additional note in which he would circuitously express his gratitude. Only then could he once again seek an audience.

In those days, each Advanced Scholar would hand in no more than one or two scrolls of writings in his special field. But when it came to his poems, rhymeprose, and words for songs and old tunes, he would select from among them his very best for presentation.[33] To circulate two scrolls was called "double delivery" and would have been considered a bit much. The late Sang Wei-han, Honorary Duke of Wei (d. 946), circulated only five of his rhymeproses, and the Minister Li Yu of "White Sands"[34] (d. 935) circulated only five of his poems.[35] But they were able to attain great fame and gain high office. What, then, is the necessity of putting so much emphasis on quantity?

The Omissioner,[36] P'ei Yueh (fl. 906),[37] circulated only nineteen of his pentasyllabic poems. Come the next fall, he again circulated the same scroll. When someone ridiculed him for doing so, P'ei replied: "These nineteen poems alone were composed with difficulty, yet they have not been appreciated by anyone. What good would it do to circulate a different scroll?" Persons of discrimination considered these to be words of wisdom.

The late Vice-Minister of the Army,[38] Wang Hu (c. 945–c. 1008),[39] was the son of Wang Ch'e who graduated first in the examinations for Advanced Scholars the same year that Sang Wei-han passed them.[40] Though Hu was orphaned while still a child, his writing showed genius. Just after he had turned twenty, he handed in an announcement to Sang Wei-han, the text of which was made up of several thousand words. No sooner had Sang read it than he was greatly struck with admiration. As a result, Hu's fame spread throughout the capital. From this account, it is quite understandable that "he who intends to convince the mind values cogency."[41] And still more can this be seen as evidence that "it's not how many scrolls you circulate that counts."

In his later years, Ming-tsung came to set such store by luxury that he was misled by a group of petty people. Arms were raised against the palace, causing great alarm and disturbance among the citizens of Loyang. It was more than ten days before calm returned and, even then, the markets did not open. The residents, not daring to go outside, kept their doors closed. From time to time, a few examinees, with black gauze caps upon their heads and wearing white gowns which opened wide at the thighs,[42] would ride back and forth on their donkeys along the main street. There were no residents who saw them that did not laugh at them. From this we can understand that esteem for elegance may be a fine thing in times of peace. At a time of crisis, however, one can use it to divine whether a society will remain ordered or will fall into chaos. How much more so with other things![43]

This lengthy description shows that at least some people during the Sung had both an exalted notion of the nature of scroll presentation in the T'ang and Later T'ang as well as an unhappy recognition of the degeneration of the practice in their own dynasty. The transitional nature of the Five Dynasties—looking back to the T'ang but presaging the Sung—in regard to literati practices is also noteworthy.

The usual attitude of later generations of critics toward the circulation and warming of scrolls was harsh. Such practices were often contemptuously viewed as hypocritical abuses of the examination system, an impropriety unworthy of scholars. A thirteenth-century commentator censured the behavior of T'ang scholars with these words:

The corruption of public morals reached its nadir in the T'ang. Princes, dukes, and other high officials, complacently ensconced in the knowledge that they had "arrived" first, majestically lorded it over others. No longer did they seek out the best scholars. As a result, the scholars of the realm went about in teams and droves, wearing tattered caps and mounted on lame asses. Before they were within a hundred paces of an important person's gate, they would hastily dismount, offer up their calling cards and presents, and prostrate themselves twice before the majordomo in order to gain entrance. They would then hand in their writings and this was called "seeking for someone who is sympathetic." If, after all this, there was no response, they would repeat the process as described above and this was called "keeping the scrolls warm." If, after this, there was still no response, they would bring gifts to present to the worthy when he was out on horseback. They would then introduce themselves saying, "So-and-so pays his respects."[44]

> Alas, that public morals should have fallen to such an extreme! This not only shows how despicable the scholars were: one can also learn from it the disordered state of the time.[45]

A critic writing in the mid-twelfth century voiced this complaint against favor-seeking in the T'ang:

> There have long been prohibitions against bringing books into the examination hall and passing answers. I submit, then, that it was odd for Li K'uei (711–84), as examiner, to make a great display of the classics and histories in the courtyard and to allow the students freely to look at them. Likewise for Ho Ning (898–955), when he was chief examiner, to open the doors and dismiss the guards, allowing the students to do as they pleased. Given these conditions, who could distinguish true virtue and real ability?
>
> I know the reason for this. It is that, since the T'ang, the examiners have emphasized the candidates' established reputations. As a result, as soon as the examination arena opened, there would be a flurry of passing calling cards and poems. The candidates' success or failure is thus inevitably determined. Although the bringing in of books and the passing of answers are prohibited, what good is it?
>
>> In the morning, they prattle to people of high rank,
>> In the evening, they prattle to people of high rank;
>> Who was it that said the tuning fork
>> Has been transformed into a gentlemen's tongue?
>
> This was Meng Chiao's (751–814) plea for political patronage and Lu Wei accepted it.
>
>> Contemplating a move is like being adrift at sea,
>> These words seem but a poetic exercise;
>> My whole life has been devoted to my benefactors,
>> In time to come, what else will there be for me to do?

Scroll Presentation in the T'ang Dynasty

This was Tu Hsün-ho's (864–904) plea for patronage and Fei Chih (d. 905) accepted it.

> Below the wall, the iris and orchid freshly cover the path,
> In front of the gate, the peach and plum
>   have long cast their shade;
> But do consider the grass by the river's edge,
> As it pours forth its tiny heart in the spring mists.

This was Cheng Ku's plea for patronage and Liu Tz'u accepted it.

The candidates make their pleas beforehand and the examiner gives them their passing grades thereafter. Where is there any justice in it?[46]

Even in the early T'ang, there were outcries against this particular abuse of the examination system. Sometime during the year 691, the Remonstrator of the Left, Hsüeh Teng 薛登 presented a memorial in which he trenchantly criticized the hypocrisy of making "poetry calls":

> Today's candidates for higher degrees... who scheme to pass the examinations noisily contest in the prefectural government offices. Bowing and scraping endlessly, they beg for favors.
>
> Or, again, as soon as an Imperial Proclamation calling for an examination to search out and extol the most talented literati is delivered, they go scurrying about the government offices and make calls on influential persons. They display their poems and hand up memoranda, hoping to be granted a few kind words; they wear themselves out from head to foot, desiring the favor of a promotion....[47]

Occasionally, the improprieties which resulted from such abuses of the examination system were discovered and corrected:

> In the early part of the Ch'ang-ch'ing reign period (821–24), Ch'ien Hui was the chief examiner. Cheng Ming and thirty-two other candidates were selected. But, because of an impro-

> priety in the manner of selection, Po Chü-i was called upon to repeat the examination, this time using "Rhymeprose on the Flute of Disjunct Bamboo." None of those who were examined knew to what the allusion referred.[48] Consequently, eleven individuals were dropped. And Ch'ien Hui was degraded to the post of Governor of Chiang-chou....[49]

And then there is the cynic's view, here represented by Liu Tsung-yüan 柳宗元 (773–819) in his preface to a "Poem Given to the Scholar Wei Ch'i after He Failed in the Examinations and Sought Out Helpful Friends":

> Nowadays, there are several hundred scholars every year who come up from the prefectures and commanderies and go to the examiner's place seeking advancement. For the most part, they come bearing compositions they have written and in which they expound upon things modern and ancient. They compete in preciosity, strive for voluminousness. The examiner might, on a given morning, receive manuscripts amounting to several million words of which he could not even read one-tenth. He is soon forced by exhaustion to lie down, so bleary-eyed that he has no desire to see anything. Abandoning heart, he has no wish to carry on with the reading.
>
> For things to come to such a pass and yet for them to say "I don't overlook anyone" is sheer hypocrisy.[50]

In spite of the absurdities inherent in the practice, a large number of T'ang anecdotes attest to the efficacy of scroll presentation. Even discounting a considerable portion of these tales as apocryphal, one is struck by their assumption that poetry was so effective. Three examples, all from twelfth-century sources, are the following:

> When Niu Seng-ju (779–847) went to the capital, he left his lute and books between the Pa and Ch'an Rivers,[51] then straightway went to call upon Han Yü and Huang-fu Shih with some of his writings. The two worthies opened up his scroll and found that at

its head were two poems entitled "On Music." Before reading the words, they suddenly asked: "Well, then, what are clappers for?" "They are for musical punctuation," Niu replied.

The two worthies looked at each other, greatly pleased, and said, "This man's literary ability must certainly be high!"
Whereupon Niu mentioned that he had to arrange for housing. Han Yü and Huang-fu Shih remained silent for quite some time before saying that he could put up at a temple courtyard in the nonresidential section of the city. Niu did as they advised. The two worthies had further instructed him that, on a certain day, he should make an excursion to Green Dragon Temple and return towards dusk.

On that day, Han Yü and Huang-fu Shih rode together to the temple where he was staying and, before returning, wrote in large characters on his door: "Han Yü and Huang-fu Shih together came to pay a visit on our 'senior'[52] but missed him."

On the following day, people in imperial chariots and famous literati all went to see the characters on the door. And, from that time on, Niu Seng-ju's fame burned bright.[53]

On the strength of some songs and poems which he presented, Li Ho (790–816) sought an audience with Han Yü when the latter was a Doctor of the Imperial Academy serving as an Assistant Censor. Han Yü had just come back from seeing off a guest and was very tired. After the gateman had handed over Li Ho's scroll to him, he loosened his sash and began a hasty reading of it. The first piece was "Prefect of Goose Gate March":[54]

Black clouds press upon the city walls, almost crushing them,
Catching the sun's[55] rays, their armor flashes like golden fish scales.

Han Yü loosely tied his sash and ordered that Li Ho be welcomed.[56]

When Po Chü-i ("Live-in-Ease" Po) first went to the capital to sit for the examinations, he sought an audience with the Redactor Ku K'uang on the strength of some poems which he presented. K'uang read his name and, eyeing him carefully, said: "The price of rice at this moment is high. Your life will not be an easy one." Whereupon he opened the scroll, the first poem of which read:

> The grasses on the Hsien-yang plain,
> Each year wither, each year flourish;
> Prairie fires cannot burn them away,
> Vernal winds blow—they spring back to life!

Ku K'uang sighed in appreciation and said, "That's quite a singular expression you have there. Your life will soon be easy." It was on account of this that he extolled "Live-in-Ease" Po whose fame accordingly spread.[57]

There is a story about a man named Lu Ch'u 盧儲 which tells how he presented his scrolls in an effort to gain an audience with Li Ao 李翱 (772–841). The latter accepted the scrolls but put them aside on his table. This afforded his eldest daughter the opportunity of reading them. After doing so, she commented to her young maid that the author of the scrolls would certainly someday rank first in the imperial examinations. The young lady undeniably was possessed of good judgment. Li Ao invited Lu Ch'u to become his son-in-law and he did, indeed, receive top honors in the palace examination the following year.[58]

It is not, of course, to be assumed that the circulation of scrolls was a *sine qua non* for gaining favor with one's superiors:

> When the minister, Yüan Chen was at O-chou where Chou Fu was an assistant administrator, he would often write poems and command those in attendance at his court to compose matching pieces. Chou Fu, wearing his cap-clasp and carrying a jade tablet, went to have an audience with Yüan Chen.

"By chance," he stated, "I have travelled with Your Honor the paths[59] which run between the gates of important families. It was because of this that I passed the examination. This is absurd, of course, for I can write neither poetry nor rhymeprose."

Yüan Chen was pleased and said, "By forthwith telling me the truth, you have shown yourself to be more worthy than those who can write poetry."[60]

But, assuming that one were capable of writing something resembling a poem, there was still the great and thorny problem of the doorkeeper. The question was: would he transmit one's offering to the master of the house?

There was a T'ang scholar who was unsuccessful in handing in his calling card so he presented a poem which included these lines:

> Though I am penniless, I implore Han Yü's gateman,
> My name paper grows fuzzy-edged—it never is sent in.

Later, there was a certain Wan T'ung-yün[61] who had been befriended by the Assistant Grand Tutor Po.[62] On a journey to Tzu-chou,[63] he was repeatedly obstructed by a gateman whereupon he made a presentation of his poetry. The Board President, Lu Hung-hsüan, was angry with the gatekeeper and treated Wan T'ung-yün politely. His poem read:

> I wipe my tears with my lotus shirt,[64] how many times
>   have I pierced it!
> I wish to call at the vermilion gate but that is as hard as
>   ascending to heaven;
> It is not that the President despises his humble guest,
> But that the uncouth fellow has nothing to give to
>   Wang Ch'üan.[65]

Su Ch'in (d. 317 B.C.) said that "The appointments secretary is as difficult to see as Heaven Almighty."[66] Having to see the

Almighty through the offices of a ghost is something which has been lamented since antiquity.[67]

I stated at the outset that, even during the T'ang, the circulation of scrolls sometimes degenerated into pure formalism. To be sure, it went at times even beyond that and descended (or ascended) into the realm of comedy:

> Hsüeh Pao-hsün was fond of circulating enormous tomes and so styled himself "the adamantine cudgel."[68] Now, between the years of 827 and 835, there were no less than a thousand and some graduates of the preliminary examinations. Scrolls were piled in heaps at the gates of high-ranking officials. Mostly they were sold by the gatekeepers and servant-women for "candle[69]-money." On account of this, wags would remark, "If it's Hsüeh Pao-hsün's scrolls, their take is double what it normally is."
>
> The year that the Vice-President, Liu Yün-chang, was in charge of the examinations, he put up a notice-board in the southern courtyard which read: "Advanced Scholars are not permitted to hand in more than three scrolls." Liu Tzu-chen heard this and purposefully handed in forty scrolls.[70]

It is difficult to determine whether Liu was intentionally trying to draw attention to himself by offering such an outrageous number of his writings or whether he thought that forty scrolls would actually be in line with the responses of his peers to the three scroll limit. The former possibility seems the more likely.

With such a vast quantity of poetry scrolls inundating the houses of established scholars, there must have been a problem of handling and storage. One clever solution is indicated in the following passage from *T'ang Gleanings*:

> Cheng Kuang-yeh and his brothers owned a large leather trunk. Whenever their associates would present some writings, those which were laughable they would toss into the trunk. They called it the "sea of sorrow." At their leisure, the brothers would use it

as a source of entertainment. They would order two servants to place the trunk in front of them and each would read one of the pieces. They never failed to enjoy themselves thoroughly before putting it away.[71]

In this same vein, there are amusing accounts of "scholars" who simply purchased the scrolls which they circulated and, much to their chagrin, would occasionally present them to the wrong person:

> When the Minister of Works, Lu Chün (776–862) was serving as Prefect of Ch'ü-chou with the rank of Secretary,[72] an Advanced Scholar bringing a presentation scroll came to call upon him. When Lu opened the scroll and read the ten or so pieces which made up its contents, he found that they were all his own compositions.
>
> "Where did you obtain these writings?" he questioned the Advanced Scholar.
>
> "They are the result of my hard work during 'summer exercises.'"[73]
>
> "But," Lu said, "These writings are my own. I can still recite them." The guest then prostrated himself and said, "When I obtained these writings, I didn't know the name of the author. I had no idea it was you who had written them."[74]
>
> Li Pò,[75] with the rank of Senior Secretary, was administrator of Ch'i-chou, A student, also surnamed Li, brought some poetry and came to call upon him.
>
> "These are scrolls which I circulated before I passed the examination," remarked Li Pò.
>
> "Recently when I was in the capital," replied the student, "I purchased these in a bookstore for one hundred cash. I have been roaming the area between the Yangtze and Huai rivers for

more than twenty years and had hoped to be fortunate enough to receive your favor."

Li Pò, consenting to this, thereupon inquired, "Where are you headed?"

"To Chiang-ling to visit an uncle of mine, Board President Lu," was the reply.

"You're wrong again, sir," said Li Pò. "Lu is *my* uncle."

The student, mortified, rushed forward bewilderedly saying, "It is just as you say. They are for my uncle in Ching-nan."[76] Hastily, he begged to take back the poems, bowed twice, and went out.[77]

The purchase and plagiarism of poems for the purpose of presentation must have been so widespread that it was tolerated even by its victims—so long as certain gentlemanly bounds of propriety were not exceeded:

> The T'ang poet, Yang P'ing (fl. 788), had a cousin who stole a scroll of his poems and thereby succeeded in passing the examinations. When Yang learned of this, he was quite upset and angrily asked his cousin: "Was the line 'One after another, the cries of the cranes fly up to heaven' among those you used?"
>
> "I knew that you were most fond of that line," replied the cousin, "so I refrained from stealing it."
>
> "Then I suppose you may be forgiven," said Yang, his ire somewhat diminished.[78]

Not only the manner of presentation but the poetry itself was sometimes of a rather questionable nature:

> Chu Ch'ing-yü (fl. 826) received the understanding support of the Senior Secretary of the Board of Water, Chang Chi. The latter asked Ch'ing-yü for his works from all periods and, of these, he selected twenty-six pieces which he endorsed by keeping them in the folds of his robes. Because of Chang Chi's respected name, his

contemporaries all copied down and recited the poems. Consequently, Chu passed the examinations.

One of the pieces which Ch'ing-yü had presented was a boudoir poem which read:

> Last night in the nuptial chamber when the red candle
>   had burned out,
> I waited for the morning meeting with his parents in front
>   of the hall;
> After finishing my makeup, I asked my new husband
>   in a low voice,
> Have I pencilled my eyebrows too light? too dark?
>   Do I look fashionable?"

Chang Chi's poetic reply was:

> The fresh adornment of the maiden from Yüeh comes
>   from the heart of the mirror,
> Self-conscious of her bright beauty, she fusses and frets
>   all the more;
> All the fine silks of Ch'i do not match the high esteem
>   men hold her in,
> One water-caltrop tune of hers is worth ten thousand
>   pieces of gold.

Henceforth, Chu's poems were famous throughout the land.[79]

With such esthetic standards current in high places, much of the poetry on presentation scrolls was bound to be of poor quality. Yet, there were works produced which were of genuine literary value and were appropriately honored:

> I was formerly in possession of the scroll which Ch'in Kuan (1049–1100) presented to Lü Kung-chu (1018–89). Chang Chang-wen entered a note at the end of the scroll in an obscure place which said, "I have seen many of Ch'in Kuan's presentation scrolls. 'Rhymeprose on Yellow Tower' and 'Threnody for a Bell' are on everyone of them.[80] May we not assume that these are the writ-

ings with which he was most satisfied? Throughout his life, Ch'in Kuan wrote little. But every single piece is exquisite and worthy of transmission. When he was dwelling beyond the southern passes, he continued to write from time to time. This scroll was presented to Lü Kung-chu. Now it is being kept at Lü Pen-chung's place. Lü Pen-chung is fond of the writings on this scroll and brought it out to show me. I read the scroll and it made me sorrowful. Second month of the first year of Ta-kuan (1107)."[81]

But whether their poems were appreciated or not made little impression on these zealous office-hunters. The persistence of some of the "scroll-warmers" is legendary and awe-inspiring:

Ou-yang Hsieh, grandson of 'Four Doors,'[82] was a poet of modest ability and had been appearing in the examinations for nearly twenty years. President of the Imperial Secretariat[83] Wei[84] was then in office[85] and Hsieh would go to his gate to present his writings. Altogether, this went on for ten years. He did not once see Wei, yet Hsieh was never remiss in his attentions, whether the occasion was joyous or sad.[86] Although Wei never mentioned Hsieh, he was fond of him at heart.[87]

Even that paragon of honor, Han Yü, was not immune to swallowing his pride and returning to the same gate time after time. This is evident in his letter, "Twenty-nine Days Later, I Again Write a Letter to the Grand Minister." This letter follows two earlier epistles to the same person,[88] the first of which concluded with these words:

Your servant dares not presume to congratulate himself on what he has written. He has rashly chosen several of his poems which are passable and copied them onto a separate scroll. It is his hope that you will condescend to favor him by looking at them. For having grievously offended Your Honor, he lies prostrate awaiting punishment. Yü twice does obeisance.[89]

The closing section of the third letter includes the following remarks:

It has been more than forty days now that I have been awaiting your command. I had sent a second letter to you but my wish was not fulfilled. Three times my footsteps reached your gate but I was rejected by the gatekeeper. It is only that I am so obtuse that I do not know enough to keep myself out of sight. So again, I bring up the business of the Duke of Chou....[90] Hence, I push myself forward time after time yet know no shame. I am constantly writing to you and frequently come to your gate but do not know when to stop. Yet could I just let things go at this? I am deeply concerned that I may not receive Your Excellency's patronage and I only hope that you will extend me a modicum of consideration.[91]

So compelling was the belief that literature's primary function was to enhance one's political standing that it came to mean, in the minds of some, that writing had no other value. Li Shang-yin 李商隱 (812–58) had gone to the capital seeking success on the examination and the assistance of someone in a position of power. Unfortunately, as his "Letter to the Advanced Scholar T'ao" ("Yü T'ao chin-shih shu" 與陶進士書) indicates, no one appreciated his writings sufficiently to take an interest in him. Invariably, when he presented his compositions, the recipient would either put them aside because he had no leisure even to glance at them, let alone recite them aloud, or, granting that he did attempt to read them, he would be so insensitive as to miss the point of the composition altogether. Li Shang-yin lamented his fate:

> Consequently, after the year 833, although I yet wished to take the examinations, I simply did not do any writing except for letters of congratulation to those who were getting married, letters of condolence to those who had been bereaved, and some hack work for others such as fancy notes, notices, inscriptions, and memorials. Since I have not even taken up my writing again, how could I ever imitate others by circulating my scrolls?[92]

Similarly, in his "Letter Presented to Ts'ui Kuei-ts'ung" ("Shang Ts'ui Hua-chou shu" 上崔華州書), Li Shang-yin feels it unusual that "I have spent five years without once tucking my compositions up my sleeve and going off to call on some influential person who might befriend me."⁹³ Even so, there are numerous examples in Li Shangyin's collected works and in his official biography⁹⁴ of his "going with his works to pay a call" on influential figures.

In spite of the pervasiveness of scroll presentation, a few scholars looked upon it as a point of honor not to engage in such exercises. There is, for example, Li Shan-fu's 李山甫 (fl. 860–74?) "Congratulations to a Friend on Having Graduated":

> A dragon which has found its environment and a fish out of water,
> With this consciousness, we face each other—what do we feel?
> I dare to reject the "circulation of scrolls" so necessary today,
> Would rather wait till some later year for a recommendation letter.⁹⁵

賀友人及第

得水蛟龍失水魚　此心相對兩何如
敢辟今日須行卷　猶喜他年待薦書

While there may be differences of opinion regarding the morality of the matter, it is undeniable that the T'ang custom of presenting and "warming" scrolls was responsible for the creation of a significant number of good poems and an avalanche of bad ones. Condemned by some as a vicious form of political corruption and devoutly subscribed to by others as an essential rule of etiquette, scroll presentation is, to say the least, one of the most colorful forms of campaigning ever devised.

Acknowledgments

I am grateful to Professor Lien-sheng Yang for providing me with important bibliographical references and for suggesting a number of changes in the early drafts of this article.

Notes

1. For a catalogue, with short definitions, of a number of these practices, see Li Chao 李肇 (fl. 806-20), *T'ang-kuo shih-pu* 唐國史補 (Supplemental Materials for a History of the T'ang Empire) (Shanghai: Ku-tien wen-hsüeh ch'u-pan she, 1957), C. 55-56. In his preface, Li states that the materials which he has collected cover the period from K'ai-yüan down to Ch'ang-ch'ing (713-823). Cf. *Ssu-k'u ch'üan-shu tsung-mu t'i-yao* 四庫全書總目提要 (Synopsis of the General Catalogue of the Complete Library in Four Branches of literature) (Taipei: Commercial Press, 1971), 140.2885.
2. This was particularly true of the examination for the coveted *chin-shih* 進士 degree, less so of the *ming-ching* 明經 examination which was oriented more towards the classics. Occasionally the answers were of such high quality that they were preserved in the candidate's collected works. See, for example, Arthur Waley, *The Life and Times of Po Chü-i, 772-846 A.D.* (London: George Allen and Unwin, 1947), pp. 16, 20f.
3. Indeed, we may not be entitled to disparage this practice unduly since, in many instances, it functioned as an important accessory to the examination and selection process. The presentation of poems and essays served to inject an element of personal judgment into the process without which even an astute examiner might have overlooked a brilliant candidate. Nevertheless, the danger of favoritism attendant upon such a procedure was obviously very great.
4. Robert des Rotours, *Traité des Fonctionnaires et Traité de l'Armée*, Bibliothèque de l'Institut des Hautes Études Chinoises, Vol. VI (Leiden: Brill, 1947), pp. 59-71.
5. Wang Tang 王讜 (fl. 1101-10), *T'ang yü-lin* 唐語林 (Forest of T'ang Tales) in *Ts'ung-shu chi-ch'eng ch'u-pien* 叢書集成初編 (Assemblage of Collectanea—First Series), (Shanghai: Commercial Press, 1935-40), *ts'e* 2756-59, 8.221.
6. Wang Ting-pao 王定保 (fl. 900), *T'ang chih-yen* 唐摭言, in *Assemblage of Collectanea—First Series*, *ts'e* 2739-40, 7.62-63.
7. Cf. Hans H. Frankel, "T'ang Literati: A Composite Biography," in *Confucian Personalities*, ed. Arthur F. Wright and Denis Twitchett (Stanford: Stanford Univ. Press, 1962), pp. 67-68: "Another important aid in getting an appointment was recommendation by an influential patron. This is

reported in twenty-one of the ninety-six biographies [in the "Garden of Letters" ("Wen-yüan 文苑"), *chüan* 190 of the *Old T'ang History*] that register an official T'ang career."
8. Here follows a list of the various categories of scholars within the civil service system.
9. "Hsüan-chü chih" 選舉志 (Treatise on the Selection of Officials), *New T'ang History* (Po-na ed.), 44.1a.
10. Li Chao, *Supplemental Materials*, C.57.
11. Wei Yüan-k'uang 魏元曠 (early 20th century), *Chiao-an sui-pi* 蕉盦隨筆 (Literary Ramblings from the Plantain Hermitage), *chüan* 3. Wei's *Collected Works* 魏氏全集, in which these notes are published, was not available to me; I have had to rely on the passage as quoted in Li Shu-t'ung 李樹桐, *T'ang-shih hsin-lun* 唐史新論 (A New Discussion of T'ang History) (Taipei: T'ai-wan chung-hua shu-chü, 1972), p. 57.
12. The precise nature of these practices will become apparent in the course of the discussion which follows. Several of the passages which are discussed later were noted by Ch'en Tung-yüan 陳東原, "Sui–T'ang te k'o-chü" 隋唐的科舉 ("The Examination System in the Sui and T'ang Dynasties," section 7), *Hsüeh-feng* 學風 (Scholarly Trends), 2.8 (1932), 8–25, and by T'ai Ching-nung 臺靜農, "Lun T'ang-tai shih-feng yü wen-hsüeh" 論唐代士風與文學 ("The Spirit and Literary Achievement of the Tang Scholars," section 2), *Kuo-li T'ai-wan ta-hsüeh wen-shih-che hsüeh-pao* 國立臺灣大學文史哲學報 (Bulletin of the College of Arts, National Taiwan University), 14 (1965), 1–14. For a thorough description of the T'ang bureaucracy, see Tsukiyama Jisaburō 築山治三郎, *Tōdai seiji seido no kenkyū* 唐代政治制度の研究 (Studies on the Political Institutions of the T'ang Dynasty) (Osaka: Sōgensha, 1967). The classic treatment of the examination system, particularly as it developed in the Ch'ing dynasty, is to be found in Miyazaki Ichisada 宮崎市定, *Kakyo* 科挙 (The Civil Service Examination System) (Osaka: Akitaya, 1946).
13. Ch'eng Ta-ch'ang 程大昌 (1123–95), *Yen-fan-lu* (Shanghai: Commercial Press, 1938 [facsimile of the Sung edition formerly kept in the Yüan-pi lou of Mr. Liu]), 7.7b. All parenthetical expressions in this passage are commentaries originally in the text. The reader will search in vain for the "Preface to the New Letter" in the various extant collections of Li Shang-yin. The *Li I-shan chi* 李義山集 itself is not listed in the *Ssu-k'u Catalogue*. However, the existence of this passage in *The Thick Dews Extended* was not overlooked by the later editors of Li Shang-yin's writings. It is listed in the "Lost Passages" 逸句 section at the end of the *Fan-nan*

wen-chi hsiang-chu 樊南文集詳註 (Li Shang-yin's Collected Prose with Detailed Annotations), ed. Feng Hao 馮浩 (1719–1801) (*SPPY* ed.), 8.37a.

14. For another description of the physical characteristics of a scroll (this time, one that was put together hurriedly), see the end of Han Yü's "Letter to the Grand Secretary of the Imperial Chancellory, Ch'en Ching" 與陳京給事書, in *Ch'ang-li hsien-sheng wen-chi* 昌黎先生文集 (Complete Prose of Han Yü) (Shanghai: Han-fen lou, 1918 [facsimile of the 1200 ed.]), 17.10b.
15. Although written originally in Chinese, the article was published first in English in a translation by James R. Ware, *HJAS*, 1.1 (1936), 39–43. The English version was later translated into Chinese by Ch'eng Hui-ch'ang 程會昌 and appeared in various journals, including the *Kuo-wen yüeh-k'an* 國文月刊 (Chinese Literary Monthly), No. 57 (1947), 25–26.
16. The chapter, entitled "Chin-shih k'o-chü yü ch'uan-ch'i hsiao-shuo te ch'an-sheng" 進士科舉與傳奇小說的產生 ("The Examination System for Advanced Scholars and the Birth of the Classical Short Story"), appeared in Liu's *T'ang-tai hsiao-shuo yen-chiu* 唐代小說研究 (Studies on T'ang Fiction) (1947; rev. ed. Shanghai: Commercial Press, 1955), pp. 33–37.
17. "Tu Ch'en Yin-k'o hsien-sheng lun Han Yü" 讀陳寅恪先生論韓愈 (On Ch'en Yin-k'o's Discussion of Han Yü), originally published in *Wen-shih-che* 文史哲 (Literature, History, and Philosophy), 8 (August, 1955), 23–36; appended to "Han Yü wen-hsüeh te p'ing-chia" 韓愈文學的評價 ("An Appraisal of the Literature of Han Yü"), in *Han Yü Liu Tsung-yüan wen-hsüeh p'ing-chia* 韓愈柳宗元評價 (An Appraisal of the Literature of Han yü and Liu Tsung-yüan) (Tsinan: Shantung jen-min ch'u-pan she, 1957), pp. 67–100, esp. 92–95; reprinted in *Han-Liu wen-hsüeh yen-chiu ts'ung-k'an* 韓柳文學研究叢刊 (下) (Collection of Research Articles on the Literature of Han Yü and Liu Tsung-yüan, Vol. 2), ed. Chou K'ang-hsieh 周康燮, in *Chung-kuo wen-hsüeh yen-chiu ts'ung-pien* 中國文學研究叢編 (Compilation of Research Articles on Chinese Literature), second series (Hong Kong: Lung-men shu-tien, 1969), pp. 67–100, esp. 92–95. Wu Keng-shun 吳庚舜, "Kuan-yü T'ang-tai ch'uan-ch'i fan-jung te yüan-yin" 關于唐代傳奇繁榮的原因 ("Concerning the Reasons for the Flourishing of the Classical Short Story during the T'ang Dynasty"), in *Wen-hsüeh yen-chiu chi-k'an* 文學研究集刊 (Collected Literary Studies, I) (Peking: Jen-min wen-hsüeh ch'u-pan she, 1964), pp. 70–100, esp. 74–79 and 98–99, calling into question the reliability of Chao Yen-wei's *Rambling Notes from the Clouded Foothills,* is critical of those

who use it to draw conclusions about the rise of the classical short story. Feng Ch'eng-chi 馮承基, "Lun *Yün-lu man-ch'ao* so shu ch'uan-ch'i yü hsing-chüan chih kuan-hsi" 論雲麓漫鈔所述傳奇與行卷之關係 ("On the Relationship between the Classical Short Story and the Circulation of Scrolls Mentioned in *Rambling Notes from the Clouded Foothills*"), *Ta-lu tsa-chih* 大陸雜誌 (The Continent Magazine), 35.8 (Oct. 31, 1967), 8–10, also subjects to intense scrutiny the theory that there is a connection between the presentation of scrolls and the rise of the classical short story. Feng finds the theory untenable, chiefly on the grounds that the period when, according to him, scroll presentation ought to have been most popular (627–755) came before the flowering of the classical short story. However, since the dates of most of the actual examples of scroll presentation which I have assembled here coincide with the period when the classical short story was at its height, Feng's objection must be overruled. Also see Y. W. Ma, "Prose Writings of Han Yü and *ch'uan-ch'i* Literature," *Journal of Oriental Studies*, 7.1 (Jan. 1969), 195–220, esp. 204–5, n.37, who reviews Feng's article and finds it not entirely convincing. For a general discussion of related matters, see Wang Yün-hsi 王運熙, "Shih lun T'ang ch'uan-ch'i yü ku-wen yün-tung te kuan-hsi" 試論唐傳奇與古文運動的關係 ("A Tentative Discussion of the Relationship between the Classical Short Story of the T'ang Dynasty and the Old Style Prose Movement"), in *Wen-hsüeh i-ch'an* 文學遺產 (Literary Heritage), No. 182 (Nov. 10, 1957); reprinted in *Wen-hsüeh i-ch'an hsüan-chi* 文學遺產選集 (Selections from Literary Heritage), Vol. III (Peking: Chung-hua shu-ch'ü, 1960), pp. 321–32.

18. *Yu-kuai lu* 幽怪錄. This was originally entitled *Hsüan-kuai lu* 玄怪錄 (Record of the Dark and the Strange) but was altered because the first character of the title appeared in the name of a T'ang emperor (Hsüan-tsung, r. 713–55).

19. *Ch'uan-ch'i* 傳奇. For references to this and the previous collection as specific works rather than genres, see Ch'en Yin-k'o, "Han Yü and the T'ang Novel," p. 40, nn. 11 and 12. T'ai Ching-nung, "Spirit and Achievement," p. 8, also considers these to be specific collections. For bibliographical references, see Ma, "Prose Writings of Han Yü," pp. 196–97, n. 7, and 204, n. 35.

20. *Yün-lu man-ch'ao* (Rambling Notes from the Clouded Foothills) (Peking: Chung-hua shu-chü, 1958), 8.111.

21. Mentioned by Liu K'ai-jung, *Studies*, p. 34.

22. This is from Po Chü-i's (772–846) "Letter to Yüan Chen (779–831)" ("Yü Yüan Chiu shu" 與元九書), in *Po Hsiang-shan chi* 白香山集 (Works of Po Chü-i) (Peking: Wen-hsüeh ku-chi k'an-hsing she, 1954), 28.28. And, furthermore, I have lately heard it said among my friends that the Board of Rites and the Board of Civil Office use my test papers, rhymeprose, judgments, and biographical notices as standards and that the rest of my poetic lines are often on people's lips. All of which makes me uncomfortably embarrassed so that I gave it no credence.[20] Liu K'ai-jung contends that this passage matches perfectly the passage in *Rambling Notes from the Clouded Foothills*. "Rhymeprose," he claims, is equivalent to "poetic flair," "documents" to "expository skill," and "biographical notices" to "historical talent." Po, however, was discussing his own popularity and the official standards held by the two boards responsible for the selection of government officials. There is no indication that the government *endorsed* the "circulation of scrolls." The universality of the practice means only that it was countenanced.
23. *Ch'ih-mi* 赤米 "red rice" (also called "peach blossom rice" and "red cloud rice") is a coarse strain of rice especially well suited to upland fields.
24. *Chien-nan shih-kao* 劍南詩稿 (Draft Collection of Poems by Lu Yu) (*SPPY* ed.), 72.9b.
25. There is a Min or Mien River 湎河 in Honan but, since Wang P'i-chih 王闢之, the Sung author of this work, was from Ch'ing-chou 青州, this character is better read *sheng,* as it is pronounced in reference to the Sheng River 湎水 in Shantung.
26. In *Chih-pu-tsu chai ts'ung-shu* 知不足齋叢書 (Awareness of Insufficiency Studio Collectanea), (1872), *ts'e* 86, 9.11b. This passage is copied in Chiang Shao-yü 江少虞 (Sung), comp., *Huang-ch'ao lei-yüan* 皇朝類苑 (Categorized Encyclopedia of the Imperial Court), of which I have used the edition in the *Sung-fen shih ts'ung-k'an* 誦芬室叢刊 (In Praise of Fragrance Chamber Collectanea) (1916–22), *ts'e* 12, 61.4b.
27. In Kwangsi. Hu Ch'eng's 胡珵 place of origin is Chin-ling 晉陵 (in Kiangsu). He fled to Ts'ang-wu when he found himself being attacked at court.
28. Fei Kun 費袞, fl. 1192 (Shanghai: Commercial Press, 1920), 3.4a.
29. Since deep purple gowns 紫皁衫 (子) were the dress of prostitutes and singing-girls, there are implications of jaded effeminacy when men are said to wear gowns of this color. See *Yüan tien-chang* 元典章 (Yüan Regulations) (Peking: Fa-lü kuan, 1908), 29.8b. In general, the darkest colors of clothing were for merchants, soldiers, butchers, and

the like, other colors were for officials of rank, and white (plain) was for commoners. See Chü Hsüan-ying 瞿宣穎, comp., *Chung-kuo she-hui shih-liao ts'ung-ch'ao* 中國社會史料叢鈔 (A Compilation of Materials on Chinese Social History), Series A, Vol. 1 (1936; rpt. Taipei: Commercial Press, 1965), 1.12, 80, 81 and Shang Ping-ho 尚秉和, comp., *Li-tai she-hui chuang-k'uang shih* 歷代社會狀況史 (A History of Social Conditions during Successive Dynasties) (n.p., n.d.), 5.20b, 22b, 26b–27a.

30. 衱 = 衫. See Nagashima Toyotarō 長島豊太郎, *Kojisho sakuin* 古字書索引 (Index to Archaic Characters) (Tokyo: Nihon Koten Zenshū Kankōkai, 1959), p. 1559, citing Shōjū 昌住 (fl. 891–900), *Shinsen jikyō* 新撰字鏡 (Newly Compiled Mirror of Characters) (Osaka: Zenkoku Shobō, 1944; facsimile of Tenji [1124–26] ed.), 12.28b.5 (p. 780).

31. I am uncertain as to what to do with 襴鞹 "academic robe–(depilated) hide." Perhaps, since the T'ang and Sung academic robes had enormous sleeves, we may emend 鞹 *k'wâk* to 廓 *k'wâk*. Cf. *Shuo-wen t'ung-hsün ting-sheng* 說文通訓定聲 (Phonological Glosses on the Shuo-wen Etymological Dictionary) (Shanghai: Shih-chieh shu-chü, 1936), p. 401, entry under 郭, which indicates the possibility of a word-class implying "large," "sheath-like." At any rate, the author's chief complaint is that the examinees of his day were not properly attired since the regulations stipulated that they should wear academic robes of fine white cloth. 襴衫以白細布爲之...進士及國子生州縣生服之. See "Treatise on Carriage and Dress" in the *Sung History* (Po-na ed.), 153.18a.

32. 馭 = 御, "charioteer," here used loosely to mean "groom."

33. An abbreviated version of this passage, as given in Ch'en Ku 陳鵠 (fl. 1216), *Ch'i-chiu hsü-wen* 耆舊續聞 (More Tales Heard by an Old Man) in *Awareness of Insufficiency Studio Collectanea*, ts'e 71, 8.6b–7b, has 之 instead of 擲.

34. The text has 白少. This should be emended to 白沙 for two reasons: (1) Li Yü owned a villa called "Po-sha" (*New History of the Five Dynasties* [Po-na ed.], 67.9a); and (2) his collected writings were known as *Po-sha chi* 白沙集 (see *Wu-ti hsien-chih* 無棣縣志 [Gazeteer of Wu-ti District, rev. ed. of 1924, printed in 1925], 10.1b).

35. The text has 五首 which might ambiguously *refer to the fu* 賦 "rhymeprose" just above. The abbreviated version in *More Tales Heard by An Old Man*, which I follow, has 五首詩.

36. des Rotours, *Fonctionnaires*, pp. 151 and 187.

37. See T'an Cheng-pi 譚正璧, *Chung-kuo wen-hsüeh-chia ta tz'u-tien* 中國文學家大辭典 (Biographical Dictionary of Chinese Authors) (Hong

Kong: Shanghai yin-shu kuan, 1961; facsimile rpt, of Shanghai: Kuang-ming shu-chü, 1934), No. 1767.

38. Chang Fu-jui, *Les Fonctionnaires des Song: Index des Titres* (Paris: Mouton, 1962), p. 188.
39. The character in the note which is incorrectly carved as *yu* 祐 should be *hu* 祜.
40. Cf. Hsü Sung 徐松 (1781–1848), *Teng-k'o chi k'ao* 登科記考 (A Study of the Record of Those Who Passed the Examination) (1888; facsimile rpt. Taipei: Ching-sheng wen-wu kung-ying kung-ssu, 1972), 25.14a.2 (p. 1607).
41. The quotation is taken directly from Lu Chi's 陸機 (261–303) "Wen-fu" 文賦 (Rhymeprose on Literature). See the annotated translation by Achilles Fang, *HJAS*, 14.3–4 (1951), 535: "Hence, he who would dazzle the eyes makes much of the gorgeous; he who intends to convince the mind values cogency" 故夫　誇目者尚奢　愜心者貴當.
42. 袴 = 胯 / 骻. "Treatise on Carriage and Dress," *New T'ang History*, 24.9b: "The name for an item of dress which is open at the waist is 'slit-thigh gown.' It is worn by commoners" 開骻者名曰骹衫，　庶人服之.
43. *Huang-ch'ao lei-yüan* (Categorized Encyclopedia of the Imperial Court), 61.4b–5b, from which this selection is taken, ascribes it to *Li hsüeh-shih chia-t'an* 李學士家談 (Family Talks of the Scholar Li). I have not been able to locate any extant work bearing this title. *Hsüeh-shih* was an official designation in the Sung, see Chang Fu-jui, *Fonctionnaires*, p. 57.
44. *Shang-yeh* 尚謁 is a technical term which means "(to hand in one's calling card and) request an audience." It is used in this sense as early as the biography of Chang I 張儀 in *Shih-chi* (Records of the Grand Historian) (Po-na ed.), 70.1b.
45. Ma Tuan-lin 馬端臨, *Wen-hsien t'ung-k'ao* 文獻通考 (Thorough Examination of Documents) (Shanghai: Commercial Press, 1936), 29.274.1, citing a Mr. Hsiang 項氏 of Chiang-ling (in modern Hupeh).
46. Ko Li-fang 葛立方 (d. 1164), *Yün-yü yang-ch'iu* 韻語陽秋 (Critique of Verse), in *Assemblage of Collectanea—First Series*, ts'e 2553–54, 18.152.
47. In Tu Yu 杜佑 (735–812), *T'ung-tien* 通典 (Encyclopedia of Statutes) (Shanghai: Commercial Press, 1935), 17.94.3. Also, slightly modified, in *Old T'ang History* (Po-na ed.), 101(51).3a.
48. See *Chou-li* 周禮 (*SPTK* ed.), 6.4b: 孤竹之管，　雲和之琴瑟, translated by Edouard Biot as "on joue de la flûte faite en bambou solitaire, on pince les harpes et guitares *Kin* et *Che* du Mont *Yun-ho*." See *Le Tcheou-li* (Paris: Imprimerie Nationale, 1851), p. 34.

49. Ko Li-fang, *Critique*, 18.152–3.
50. *Liu Ho-tung chi* 柳河東集 (*Collected Works of Liu Tsung-yüan*) (Shanghai: Chung-hua shu-chü, 1958), 23.398–99. Perhaps Liu came to hold this opinion because of an unhappy personal experience for we know that he did present his writings to important officials. Cf. "Shang Ch'üan Te-yü pu-ch'üeh wen-chüan chüeh chin-t'ui ch'i" 上權德輿補闕溫卷決進退啓 ("Announcement Presented to the Omissioner, Ch'üan Te-yü [759–818], to Keep Warm the Scrolls and Decide whether I Advance or Retreat"), *Works*, 36.564–66.
51. Two rivers which join near Ch'ang-an and flow into the Wei 渭 River.
52. There is here a carefully calculated use of the intimate reference to Niu's *p'ai-hang* 排行 (ranking of seniority among brothers) to gain the maximum publicity from the visit of these two distinguished scholars. Niu Seng-ju's ranking was "two" which either the two worthies or, more likely, the person who recorded this story was unaware of and hence used the unspecified "number so-and-so," *chi* 幾. *Kuan* 官 is a polite appellation, comparable to *lang* 郎 or *yüan-wai* 員外. For numerous examples of similar usage, including the words *hsien-pei* 先輩 "senior," see Ts'en Chung-mien 岑仲勉, *T'ang-jen hang-ti lu* 唐人行第錄 (A List of Seniority Rankings within Clans of T'ang Dynasty Chinese) (Peking: Chung-hua shu-ch'ü, 1962), *passim*.
53. Yu Mao 尤袤 (1127–94), *Ch'üan-T'ang shih-hua* 全唐詩話 (Complete Poetic Anecdotes of the T'ang), in Ho Wen-huan 何文煥 ed., *Li-tai shih-hua* 歷代詩話 (Poetic Anecdotes throughout the Ages) (Taipei: I-wen, 1959), 3.1b–2a. This anecdote also appears, in expanded form, in *T'ang Gleanings*, 7.63. In several instances, I have had to rely on the longer version for an understanding of the text. Ch'en Tung-yüan 陳東原, *Chung-kuo chiao-yü shih* 中國教育史 (History of Chinese Education), 2nd. ed. (Shanghai: Commercial Press, 1937), p. 187, says that this passage occurs in Lu Yu 陸游, *Lao-hsüeh-an pi-chi* 老學庵筆記 (Notes from the Old-age Learning Hermitage), *chüan* 5. The copy which I have examined (Shanghai: Commercial Press, 1920) does not contain it. Niu Seng-ju's luck in presenting his scrolls was not always so good as it was on this occasion with Han Yü and Huang-fu Shih: "In the autumn, when Niu Seng-ju went up for the examinations, he was invariably slighted by his colleagues. But when he actually rose and passed them, none was his equal. He once presented some of his writings to the Omissioner, Liu Yü-hsi (772–842). Liu unrolled the scroll in front of his guest and, with flying brush, deleted and corrected what he had written." Needless to

say, Niu was much peeved at this and remembered the incident many years later. Recorded in Fan Shu 范攄 (fl. 877), *Yün-hsi yu-i* 雲溪友議 (Friendly Discussions at Cloudy Creek) (Shanghai: Ku-tien wen-hsüeh ch'u-pan she, 1957), B.48–49.

54. For the full poem, see Li Ho's *Collected Poetry* 李賀詩集, ed. Yeh Ts'ung-ch'i 葉蔥奇 (Peking: Jen-min wen-hsüeh ch'u-pan she, 1959), 1.23. There is listed in the *Yüeh-fu shih-chi* 樂府詩集 (Collected Ballads), ed. Kuo Mao-ch'ien 郭茂倩 (Sung) (Peking: Wen-hsüeh ku-chi k'an-hsing she, 1955), 39.3b–6a (pp. 1090–95), an old ballad of the same title. Li Ho's poem, along with four others in the collection, are given as imitations of it.

55. The poem as given in *Collected Ballads*, 39.5b, has 月 "moon['s light]" instead of 日.

56. *Forest of T'ang Tales*, 3.82.

57. *Forest of T'ang Tales*, 3.82. The story also occurs, slightly modified, in Chang Ku 張固 (?–853 ?), *Yu-hsien ku-ch'ui* 幽閑鼓吹 (Muffled Pipe and Drum), in *Hsüeh-hai lei-pien* 學海類編 (Categorized Compilation of the Ocean of Learning) (Shanghai, 1920), *ts'e* 67, 2b–3a. Arthur Waley, *The Life and Times of Po Chü-i*, p. 218, contends that this story is apocryphal.

58. Tsang Li-ho 臧勵龢 et al., *Chung-kuo jen-ming ta tz'u-tien* 中國人名大辭典 (Chinese Biographical Dictionary) (Shanghai: Commercial Press, 1927), p. 1598. This story originally appeared in *T'ang-shih chi-shih* 唐詩紀事 (Anecdotes of T'ang Poets) (Shanghai: Chung-hua shu-chü, 1965), *ch*, 52, II, 797.

59. For the term 還往 (or 往還), see Li Chao, *Supplementary Materials*, C. 56, where it is defined as "to enhance one's reputation" 激提聲價.

60. *Muffled Pipe and Drum*, 7a.

61. The only other mention I have found of Wan T'ung-yün 萬彤雲 is in *Ch'üan-T'ang shih* 全唐詩 (Complete T'ang Poetry) (Shanghai, 1887 lithograph), 17.67b where this story is recorded. The editors identify their source as *Friendly Discussions at Cloudy Creek*, C.75.

62. des Rotours, *Fonctionnaires*, p. 19, translates *t'ai-shih* 太師 as "le grand précepteur" and *t'ai-fu* 太傅 as "le grand maître" both of which amount to Grand Tutor. This is a reference to Po Chü-i who retired in his seventy-first year as *shao-fu* 少傅.

63. Modern San-t'ai 三臺 district in Szechwan.

64. The "lotus shirt" may actually have been a shirt woven of lotus leaves or, metaphorically, the clothes of a high-minded person. For an extensive entry, see Morohashi, 31000.1.

65. Also an elusive character, I have found a person with this name in the *Ch'in-ting ch'üan-t'ang wen* 欽定全唐文 (Imperial Recension of Complete T'ang Prose) (1814; facsimile rpt, Taipei: Hui-wen shu-chü, 1961), 516.3b–4a (p. 6648), where it is mentioned that he was President of the Court of Ceremony for the Reception of Aliens 鴻臚卿 during the Chen-yüan 貞元 years (785–805). Neither the dates nor the office disqualify him for the reference here.
66. *Chan-kuo ts'e* 戰國策 (Record of the Warring States) (*SPTK* ed.), 5.6ab.
67. Chu Meng-chen 朱孟震 (fl. 1582), *Hsu yü-ssu shih-t'an* 續玉笥詩談 (Continuation of the Jade Hamper Poetry Conversations), in *Hsüeh-hai lei-pien* (Categorized Compilation of the Ocean of Learning), *ts'e* 61, 16a.
68. 金剛杵, Vajra, the club wielded by Indra.
69. 脂燭, see Morohashi, 29463.18, where it is explained as being a lamp made of fine pine shavings or paper dipped in oil.
70. *T'ang Gleanings*, 12.114.
71. *T'ang Gleanings*, 12.117. By the Ming dynasty, the expression "sea of sorrow" 苦海 had come simply to mean "doggerel." Patrick Hanan has pointed out to me that the seventh section of Feng Meng-lung's 馮夢龍 (1574–1646) *Ku-chin t'an-kai* 古今譚概 (A Digest of Old and New Chitchat) (Peking: Wen-hsüeh ku-chi k'an-hsing she, 1955 [facsimile of a Ming woodblock edition published by Yeh K'un-ch'ih 葉昆池]), pp. 303–43, is entitled "Sea of Sorrow" and that it contains numerous examples of glaring poetic miscarriages. The introduction to this section of Feng's *Digest* begins with the anecdote about the leather trunk from the *Gleanings*. Although the latter thus represents the *locus classicus* for this meaning of "sea of sorrow," our appreciation of the subtle wit involved is heightened by the knowledge that the expression was originally Buddhist and that it referred to the misery and suffering of mundane existence (*duḥkha-arṇava* in Sanskrit).
72. des Rotours, *Fonctionnaires*, p. 667, n. 2.
73. Li Chao, *Supplementary Materials*, C.56: "To retire and practice one's trade is called 'spending the summer.' Actively to engage in one's trade and enter society is called 'summer exercises'" 退而肄業，爲之過夏。執業而出，謂之夏課。
74. *Forest of T'ang Tales*, 7.196–97.
75. *Pò* 番, not *pó* 白 as in the name of the famous T'ang poet.
76. Which is the crowning drollery of this piece, for both Chiang-ling and Ching-nan refer to the same place, Ching-chou 荊州 (in Hupeh).

77. *Complete Poetic Anecdotes of the T'ang,* 3.37b. The *Wan-yu wen-k'u* 萬有文庫 (Universal Library) (Shanghai: Commercial Press, 1937), p. 64, text of this particular anecdote is corrupt at several crucial points.
78. Wang Shih-chen 王士禎 (1634–1711), *Hsiang-tsu pi-chi* 香祖筆記 (Orchid Notes), in *Wang Yü-yang i-shu* 王漁洋遺書 (Collectanea Assembled by the Yü-yang Mountain-Man) (K'ang-hsi ed.), *ts'e* 67, 6.10b.
79. *Complete Poetic Anecdotes of the T'ang,* 3.34ab. This story also occurs elsewhere, including Li Fang 李昉 et al., *T'ai-p'ing kuang-chi* 太平廣記 (Extensive Register of Great Tranquility) (Peking: Jen-min wen-hsüeh ch'u-pan she, 1959), 199.1495, where it is cited as being taken from *Friendly Discussions at Cloudy Creek,* C.79. Other notables were more discriminating in their judgment as to what constituted acceptable material for presentation: "Ts'ui Hao (d. 754) had an excellent reputation. Li Yung (678–747) wished to have a meeting with him and so prepared a hall in which to entertain him. When Ts'ui arrived, he presented some of his writings. The opening piece read: 'As a lass of fifteen, I was married to Wang Ch'ang (a man of legendary handsomeness).' As he got up to leave, Li scolded him for being an 'impolite whippersnapper' and refused to receive him." Recounted in *Supplemental Materials,* A.15.
80. See *Huai-hai chi* 淮海集 (Collected works of Ch'in Kuan) (*SPTK* ed.) where "Rhymeprose on Yellow Tower" is on 1.2a–3a and "Threnody for a Bell" on 31.1b–3b.
81. Lü Pen-chung, *Tzu-wei shih-hua* 紫薇詩話 (Tzu-wei Constellation Poetic Anecdotes), in *Ying-hsüeh hsien ts'ung shu* 螢雪軒叢書 (Fireflies and Snow Study Collectanea) (Aoki Sūzan Dō, 1892), *ts'e* II, 10b. The correct form of the second character of the title is 微. See *Ssu-k'u Catalogue,* 39.4359.
82. Ou-yang Chan 歐陽詹 (fl. 785) who was an assistant professor in the College of Four Doors. For *ssu-men* 四門, see des Rotours, *Fonctionnaires,* pp. 452–53.
83. *Chung-ling* 中令 = *chung-shu-ling* 中書令.
84. Shan-ho 善和, which I have left untranslated, is most likely a place-name designating Wei's hometown 善和鎮 in Kansu?
85. Perhaps, in this case, in the role of examiner.
86. The *SPPY* text, 10.3a, has 澥慶弔 instead of 慶澥弔 which makes little sense.
87. *T'ang Gleanings,* 10.89. Cf. *T'ang-shih chi-shin* (Anecdotes of T'ang Poets), *ch.* 67, II, 1004–5.

88. The first letter, accompanied by a selection of Han Yü's writings, was sent on the twenty-seventh day of the first month in the year 795, the second "nineteen" (actually eighteen) days thereafter on the sixteenth day of the second month, and the third "twenty-nine" (actually thirty) days later on the sixteenth day of the third month. The three *tsai-hsiang* 宰相 in this year were Chao Ching 趙憬, Chia Tan 賈耽, and Lu Mai 盧邁. Cf. Ma T'ung-po 馬通伯, *Han Ch'ang-li wen-chi chiao-chu* 韓昌黎文集校注 (Collated Edition of Han Yü's Prose) (Shanghai: Ku-tien wen-hsüeh ch'u-pan she, 1957), p. 89. I have not been able to determine to which of these three the letters were addressed or, indeed, whether they were intended for a past minister such as Cheng Yü-ch'ing 鄭餘慶 (748–820) to whom Han Yü had written in the years before 792 seeking help on the Board of Civil Service examination which he had failed four times in succession.
89. See note 91.
90. Han Yü is referring to the famous story which tells how the Duke of Chou was concerned lest he neglect any of his callers to such a degree that he was never able to finish his bath or meal uninterrupted. The Duke of Chou's attentiveness to those who sought his favor is the insistent theme of this letter and is employed in an attempt to embarrass the recipient into helping him.
91. For the three letters together, see the *Ch'ang-li hsien-sheng wen-chi* (Complete Prose of Han Yü), 16.1a–10a.
92. *Fan-nan wen-chi hsiang-chu* (Li Shang-yin's Collected Prose with Detailed Annotations), 8.5a.
93. *Ibid.*, 8.4a.
94. Cf. *Old T'ang History* (Po-na ed.), 190C(140C). 19ab.
95. *Shan-fu shih-chi* 山甫詩集 (Collected Poetry of Li Shan-fu), in *T'ang-shih pai ming-chia ch'üan-chi* 唐詩百名家全集 (Poems by One Hundred Famous T'ang Poets) (preface 1708), *ts'e* 53, 8a. Only the first half of the poem is quoted here. The analogy of the examination candidate in need of patronage to a dragon in need of water is carried to extraordinary lengths in Han Yü's "Letter Written (to Secretary Wei) at the Time of Going up for the Examinations" 應科目詩與 (韋舍) 人書 (written in 793), *Complete Prose*, 18.4a–5a. In brief, Han Yü is at pains to point out that the dragon is incapable of obtaining the essential water by itself but, at the same time, is too proud to ask for help. Assuming that T'ang scholars really were in such a predicament, and so they appear to have been, it is understandable that Han Yü would have felt compelled to write

such a pathetic piece. For a translation, see Ma, "Prose Writings of Han Yü," pp. 212–13.

CHAPTER 2

THE SACRED EDICT

LANGUAGE AND IDEOLOGY IN THE WRITTEN POPULARIZATION

Source: Adapted from "Language and Ideology in the Written Popularizations of the *Sacred Edict*," in *Popular Culture in Late Imperial China*, ed. David Johnson, Andrew J. Nathan, Evelyn S. Rawski (Berkeley: University of California Press, 1985), 325-59.

So that the correct doctrine may be
known to every family and household
(*chia yü hu hsiao*)
—Stock expression of orthodox propagandists—

"Ouang-iu-p'uh
on the edict of K'ang-hsi in volgar' eloquio taking the sense down to the people."
—Ezra Pound[1]

TEXTS

From its promulgation in the latter part of 1670 until the end of the Ch'ing dynasty, the hortatory *Sacred Edict* (*Sheng-yü*) of the K'ang-hsi emperor was widely recognized as the most concise and authoritative statement of Confucian ideology. At the time he issued the *Sacred Edict*, K'ang-hsi was sixteen years old and in the ninth year of his reign. The edict consisted of sixteen maxims, all seven characters in length and possessing an identical grammatical structure that is evident even in translation:

1. Esteem most highly filial piety and brotherly submission, in order to give due importance to the social relations.
2. Behave with generosity toward your kindred, in order to illustrate harmony and benignity.
3. Cultivate peace and concord in your neighborhoods, in order to prevent quarrels and litigations.
4. Recognize the importance of husbandry and the culture of the mulberry tree, in order to ensure a sufficiency of clothing and food.
5. Show that you prize moderation and economy, in order to prevent the lavish waste of your means.
6. Give weight to colleges and schools, in order to make correct the practice of the scholar.
7. Extirpate strange principles, in order to exalt the correct doctrine.
8. Lecture on the laws, in order to warn the ignorant and obstinate.
9. Elucidate propriety and yielding courtesy, in order to make manners and customs good.
10. Labor diligently at your proper callings, in order to stabilize the will of the people.
11. Instruct sons and younger brothers, in order to prevent them from doing what is wrong.
12. Put a stop to false accusations, in order to preserve the honest and good.
13. Warn against sheltering deserters, in order to avoid being involved in their punishment.
14. Fully remit your taxes, in order to avoid being pressed for payment.

15. Unite in hundreds and tithings, in order to put an end to thefts and robbery.
16. Remove enmity and anger, in order to show the importance due to the person and life.²

Here were, so to speak, the bare bones of Confucian orthodoxy as it pertained to the average citizen. It was not long, however, before the need was felt to flesh them out. Within a few years of the issuance of the *Sacred Edict,* adaptations, commentaries, paraphrases, and exegeses began to appear. What is most interesting about these derivative works is that many of them were written in the colloquial language. Who wrote these versions and why? Who read them? And what significance did they have for Chinese society in the eighteenth and nineteenth centuries?

The tradition of explicating classical texts in written colloquial versions seems to have grown up during the Yuan period.³ Hsü Heng (1209-1281) wrote a *Chih-shuo Ta-hsüeh yao-lüeh* (Directly Expounded Essentials of the *Great Learning*), a *Ta-hsüeh chih-chieh* (Direct Explanation of the *Great Learning*), and a *Chung-yung chih-chieh* (Direct Explanation of the *Doctrine of the Mean*). These were still a bit bookish, and served as lecture outlines for the Mongol emperors. After Hsü Heng and inspired by him, in the year 1308, Kuan Yun-shih (1286—1324) prepared a *Hsiao-ching chih-chieh* (Direct Explanation of the *Classic of Filial Piety*). This was written in fluent colloquial and, according to its preface, was intended to educate the masses. But there also seems to have been a close connection between the appearance of the *Direct Explanation of the Classic of Filial Piety* and the presentation to the Mongol princes of copies of the *Classic of Filial Piety* itself the year before.⁴ Another Yuan work of this type is Wu Ch'eng's (1255-1330) *Ching-yen chin-chiang* (Lectures Presented by the Interpreter of the Classics). During the Ming, Chang Chü-cheng (1525-1582) wrote a *Ssu-shu chi-chu chih-chieh* (Direct Explanation of the *Four Books* and Collected Commentaries) and a *Shu-ching chih-chieh* (Direct Explanation of the *Book of Documents*).⁵ Aside from the fact that these colloquial-language explications constitute a clear precedent for the various popularizations of the *Sacred Edict* in the Ch'ing, it is noteworthy that all of them were written by members of the elite.[6]

An even more explicit model for the Ch'ing popularizations is Chung Huamin's *Sheng-yü t'u-chieh* (Illustrated Explanation of the *Sacred Edict*), dated 1587.[7] Chung, whose choice of personal name is conspicuous since it means "transforming the people," was the *ch'a-ma ssu* ("tea and horse administrator") for Shansi and elsewhere. The *Sacred Edict* referred to here was not K'ang-hsi's but the Ming *Liu-yü* (Six Maxims), usually ascribed to the emperor T'ai-tsu. It may be translated as follows:

> Be filial to your parents.
> Be respectful to your elders.
> Live in harmony with your neighbors.
> Instruct your sons and grandsons.
> Be content with your calling.
> Do no evil.

Chung's work consisted of the following parts: (1) a moral precept in classical Chinese; (2) a prose development on the precept that varies from highly colloquial to easy classical; (3) a poem ("song") on the same theme in language more purely classical; (4) a picture with a caption; and (5) a story about the picture in vernacular Chinese with a slight admixture of classical. It will be well to remember this format, because we shall see elements of it cropping up in the Ch'ing popularizations. We should be particularly mindful of the incorporation of materials written in different language levels, because it is typical of the later efforts to make the message conveyed accessible to people of varying degrees of literacy. Also pertinent is the obvious effort of Chung to make his *Illustrated Explanation* widely available, ideally to every household in the empire. According to its inscription, the stele on which the *Illustrated Explanation* was cut was meant to serve as a huge lithographic printing block from which copies could be taken. These were to be distributed to magistrates having administrative responsibility for *chou* (subprefectures or departments) and *hsien* (counties or districts). The local officials were in turn directed to make blocks from which to print additional copies. These would be distributed to each family (ten sheets per tithing [*chia*]). The elders of each district and the heads of the village associations (*pao*) were to lecture on the maxims twice a month (on the first and the fifteenth). It is clear that the broadest possible exposure of the maxims throughout the populace was envisaged, though we cannot be certain that these measures were faithfully executed in all areas.

Around the beginning of the K'ang-hsi reign period, presumably in connection with the 1652 promulgation, a *Liu-yü yen-i* (Elaboration of the Hortatory Edict of Six Maxims)[8] was composed by Fan Hung of Li-ch'eng in Honan. The village lecture system described in the postface was not yet highly formalized. Fan Hung suggests that his book be used for discussions among brothers, officials, village association members, and so on. Furthermore, it is important to note that, at this time, heterodoxy is not really an issue, being referred to only in passing. Fan's attitude toward Buddhism and Taoism, particularly the former, is that they have their legitimate place.[9]

The language of the *Elaboration* is decidedly colloquial but embraces many classical elements (e.g., the use of *tz'u* instead of *che*[a] for "this," *yun* instead of *shuo* for "say," *wei* [*-ts'eng*] instead of [*ts'ung-lai*] *mei* [*-yu*] for "have/has not/ never," *ho* instead of *shen-me* for "what," *che*[b] instead of *te* as nominalizer, the frequent use of *erh* as an adversative, etc.). There is, furthermore, an unvernacular tendency toward a four-six prose rhythm and other classical cadences. The treatment of each maxim includes extensive quotations from the Ch'ing legal code in classical language and concludes with twelve lines of heptasyllabic verse rhyming AABACADAEAFA.

Thus, by the time of the K'ang-hsi emperor, there already was a well-established tradition for the popularization of imperial apothegms. It is not surprising that the vulgarizers soon directed their attention to the *Sacred Edict*. Throughout the Ch'ing period, they issued a constant stream of exegetic and metaphrastic texts based on it. The first of these works to consider is the *Sheng-yü ho lü chih-chieh* (Direct Explanation of the *Sacred Edict* in Combination with the Laws). This was published in 1679, just nine years after the appearance of the *Sacred Edict* itself. The *Combination* was compiled from extant glosses (*yen-shuo*) and edited by the Manchu governor of Chekiang, Ch'en Ping-chih, who had copies printed and distributed to villages throughout the empire.[10] Provided with prefaces by the lieutenant-governor of Chekiang, Li Shih-chen, and another high official, Ch'eng Ju-p'u, the work was divided into two sections: a general survey of the *Sacred Edict,* and discussions of each of the sixteen maxims with examples of applicable legal guidelines. The following extract from the first section will give an idea of Ch'en's approach:

> Since taking up our post, we have observed that, among you commoners, there are quite a lot who are good but there are also not a few who are bad. You have a penchant for litigation and like to get in quarrels. This is ruinous for local customs. Since it is true everywhere, the village lectures that have been held must not be concrete and detailed enough. Now we shall take these sixteen maxims of the Imperial Edict as the text of our lecture. We shall begin with a brief overview of the gist of the sixteen maxims for you to listen to carefully.

The language used throughout is natural and familiar. A rather polished style of the vernacular, it still would have been easily understood by the average listener. There can be little doubt that the explanations in the *Combination* were meant to be delivered orally at the official semimonthly lectures on the *Sacred Edict.* Ch'en repeatedly states that he and his representatives are "lecturing [on the maxims] for you to hear" (*chiang yü ni-men t'ing che*). The prefaces and postface are also very clear on this point. A sizable proportion of the material for presentation consists of songs with word-by-word indication of musical notes. Ch'en displays no particular animus against Buddhism and Taoism, and even goes so far as to admit that they thoroughly illuminate the mind and personality. His emphasis in the discussion of the seventh maxim (a scant two and one-half pages long in contrast to his seven-and-one-half-page lecture on the first maxim) is on the positive qualities of orthodox Confucianism. But Ch'en is wary of unrecognized sects (*tso-tao*) and says in the general survey that they are "most hateful."[11] His greatest effort seems to go into explaining in apprehensible language how the laws work. Accordingly, he devotes fourteen and one half pages to the eighth maxim.

Two years after the appearance of Ch'en Ping-chih's *Combination*, in 1681, the *Sheng-yü hsiang-chieh* (Illustrated Explanations of the *Sacred Edict*), a large work in twenty fascicles, was published by the magistrate of Fan-ch'ang County in Anhwei, Liang Yen-nien. The original edition probably did not circulate much beyond the confines of Liang's own district but, more than two hundred years later, it was twice reprinted by one En-shou and, as I shall show below, was broadly disseminated.

The *Illustrated Explanations* adopts the following format: (1) citation of the maxim; (2) a straightforward explanation of it in easy classical language with punctuation; (3) a finely engraved picture; (4) a caption description of the picture in classical Chinese; and (5) a discussion of the maxim in relation to the picture written in a semiclassical style (i.e., midway between classical and colloquial). Altogether there are 248 pictures, most of them based on well-known personalities and incidents from history. Liang Yen-nien's "General Principles" (*fan-li*) declare that the pictures were intended to stimulate those who did not know how to read. It is possible that the pictures may have been shown to small groups of onlookers. The format of the original edition, retained by Yeh Chih-hsien (b. 1779) of Han-yang (Hupei) in his 1856 reprinting, is quite large: 6 1/4" x 9 3/8" for the printed portion of each page (as opposed to 4 7/8" x 7 1/8" for the editions published by En-shou). The following quotation from Liang's discussion of the thirteenth maxim shows that it was probably meant to serve as the basis for an actual lecture:

> Think of it yourselves, O people. Where can you best enjoy repose, —in the sandy desert of the frontier regions, or in the village in the

country amid its ancestral trees? Which is more comfortable,—to dine on the wind and sleep beneath the rain, or to get up in the morning and go to bed at night in your own homes? Which is the more pleasant, to be supporting your aged and leading your young as they trudge along the weary road, or to know that you have plenty with which to serve the former class and to nourish the latter? Which is the preferable life,—to hear your wives weeping and you and your children wailing or to be free from all trouble and embarrassment? Even if the runaways were your own relations and acquaintances, you ought sternly to repel them; for even a fool would not plunge after another into a deep well to try to rescue him; and how can you involve yourselves and your neighbours, and run such risks for worthless parties, whom you know nothing about?[12]

Liang Yen-nien and his associates definitely saw themselves as operating in a long tradition of popularization. In his preface, Kung Chia-yü (1622-1685) records that

[of] old, when Feng K'ang (744-809) was administering Li-ch'üan, he wrote *Yü meng shu* (A Book of Parables for Beginning Learners) in fourteen chapters. In it, he taught the people to devote themselves to the fundamental occupation of agriculture. As a result, Li-ch'üan was well governed. When Chang Tsai (1020-1077) was administering Yun-yen, on the first of every month he would prepare wine and food and invite the villagers to a meeting in his court, where he instructed them in the principles of caring for parents and serving elders. As a result, Yun-yen was well governed.[13]

The author of the *Illustrated Explanations* is not opposed to Buddhism and Taoism as such but to the abuse of their doctrines. Writing in 1681 or earlier, he is not at all preoccupied with heretical sects. This is in stark contrast to the later paraphrasts, whose chief concern is often the suppression of heresy ("discrepant doctrines" [*i-chiao*]). Indeed, as we shall see below, individuals responsible for the publication of various versions of the *Sacred Edict* after the eighteenth century often view it as being in direct competition with religious movements.[14]

En-shou twice reprinted the *Illustrated Explanations,* once while he was the governor of Kiangsu and a second time while he was the governor of Anhwei. As stated in his "General Principles," he reprinted the *Illustrated Explanations* following the original edition of Liang Yen-nien. There were no revisions or modifications—except in the one transcription that was presented for imperial inspection. Even the original typographical errors were repeated. En-shou specifically states that this procedure was adopted to ensure the rapid completion of the project. All that was done to improve the original was to append a list of eleven errata in the 1902 edition (it is omitted from the 1903 edition).

En-shou had submitted to the throne a copy of the *Illustrated Explanations* with a memorial requesting that it be reprinted and distributed throughout the land. Both the memorial and the imperial response are recorded at the beginning of the 1902 edition. The imperial rescript recognizes that the *Sacred Edict* is "the basis for transforming the people and reforming customs. Every household throughout the land, whether of scholars or commoners, surely already knows it." The rescript further recognizes that the simple and clear language of the explanations that accompanied the pictures was "calculated to allow all women and children to understand easily and thoroughly. It is indeed a worthy supplement to the *Sacred Edict* for educating the ignorant and the benighted." Following the suggestion of En-shou's original memorial, the decision was made—from the throne itself—to reprint the book by lithography and to send copies to each of the provinces. There the governors-general and the governors would instruct their subordinates in the prefectures, subprefectures, departments, and counties to see that it was made available in each school.

En-shou's memorial had been prompted by repeated directives from the empress dowager to take some active steps with regard to the system of education that would stop the rampant spread of heterodoxy. It was agreed that there was an urgent necessity to influence the students during the initial stages of the learning process so that they did not stray onto unwelcome paths.

The *Illustrated Explanations,* En-shou claims, is even more effective in reaching the people than were Li Hsi-yü's *Chung hsiao t'u* (Pictures of Loyalty and Filial Piety), written during the T'ang, or the *Wai-p'ien* ("Outer Chapters") of Chu Hsi's *Hsiao-hsüeh* (Minor Learning), written during the Sung. Unfortunately, the work has had only limited circulation and minimal influence. Consequently, En-shou proposes that three thousand copies of the book be lithoprinted and distributed to all primary and middle schools throughout the country. His proposal was approved and this lengthy work was consequently reprinted in a run of three thousand copies. We cannot say with any certainty how many copies were made of the 1903 edition, for it simply reprints all of the prefatory materials of the 1902 edition without adding any new information.

One of the most prolific popularizers of the *Sacred Edict* was Li Lai-chang (1654-1721), a native of Hsiang-ch'eng in Honan. He became a provincial graduate (*chü-jen*) in 1675. After having been involved with several academies in his home province, both as lecturer and administrator, he was assigned to the magistracy of Lien-shan (literally, "connected mountains") County in Kwangtung. It took him more than four months to reach the place, so isolated and distant was it. The county included a population of approximately ten thousand Yao tribesmen as well as a lesser number of the Han race (seven villages consisting of two thousand individuals). The Yaos lived together in clusters ranging from five to less than twenty families. It was a mountainous district with dangerous paths and very little arable land (one-tenth, by Li's estimate). Moved by the difficult environment, Li is reported to have said,

> "Though the Yao are a different type of people, they possess a human nature. I ought to treat them with sincerity." Whereupon, following the legacy of Wang Yang-ming of the Ming period, he daily received the elderly and inquired about the sickness

and suffering of the people. He summoned to him those who were deserters, encouraging them to open up new lands, and lessening their taxes. Furthermore, he went straight into their hovels and engaged teachers for them, impressing them with his utter sincerity. He founded the Lien-shan Academy and wrote its academic rules. He had the people come to him daily so that he could teach them. The superior members of the Yao tribes, too, responded to this opportunity for learning. The sound of people reciting books filled the precipitous valleys.[15]

Judging from this brief sketch of a part of Li Lai-chang's life, it would have been quite in character for him to provide texts that would facilitate the dissemination of the ideals of the *Sacred Edict* among even the lowest levels of society.

There are three works by Li Lai-chang dealing with the *Sacred Edict*. They are the *Sheng-yü t'u-hsiang yen-i* (Illustrated Elaboration of the *Sacred Edict*) in two fascicles, the *Sheng-yü yen-i san-tzu-ko su-chieh* (Vernacular Explanation of the *Trimetrical Song* from the Elaboration of the *Sacred Edict*) in one fascicle, and the *Sheng-yü hsuan-chiang (hsiang-pao) i-chu/t'iao-yüeh* (Regulations/Usages for Lectures on the *Sacred Edict* [by Village Elders]) in one fascicle.[16] Some copies were given away at government expense to inhabitants of Lien-shan County who Li thought could profit from them personally or, more often, could use them to teach others. In all of Li's popularizing, there is an evident wish to contribute to the sinicization of minority peoples.

The *Illustrated Elaboration,* preface dated December 22, 1704, treats each of the sixteen maxims with the following apparatus: (1) a picture; (2) an elaboration in stilted Mandarin; (3) examples of suitable behavior in the same style; (4) pertinent extracts from the Ch'ing code in legalistic classical language; (5) a "popular" song; and (6) instructions for the Yao written in easy classical with some colloquial elements. Li claims that he did not devise this arrangement himself but was following earlier examples. He further states in the preface that he has "used the literary language with an admixture of the local dialect, the elegant and the vulgar presented together." Li declares that he wrote the *Illustrated Elaboration* because he feels that the teachings of the sages are so deep that not even learned scholars can be sure to understand them fully. He basically treats his auditors as children. His attitude toward Buddhism and Taoism is that they confound the people, are replete with useless customs, and hence are "not to be believed in overly much." But heretical sects are a menace to society, a genuine source of chaos and are "not to be believed in mistakenly."[17]

The *Trimetrical Song*, patently an attempt to duplicate the popularity of the famous and influential *Trimetrical Classic*, was written within the first year of Li's arrival in Lien-shan County. He then made it a part of the *Illustrated Elaboration* but has here printed it separately with a colloquial commentary, without which it would be virtually unintelligible to the average citizen. In his preface, dated the summer of 1706, Li justifies his use of the vernacular by referring to the practices of the Sung Neo-Confucians. He states that his *Illustrated Elaboration* was so successful in the semimonthly lectures on the *Sacred Edict* that he was prompted to extract the song portion of it and provide it with annotations and explications "in the local dialect." The commentary, however, is written neither in Yao nor in Cantonese but rather in slightly pompous Mandarin. What Li must have meant is that, during the lecture, the Mandarin text was extemporaneously rendered into the local dialect. There is an occasional tendency for the text, which is punctuated, to lapse into the four-six rhythm of parallel prose. Li maintains that he wants "to make it as thoroughly understandable as daily speech." Indeed, the song is fully interpreted for the reader, very little being left to the imagination. There are even a few pronunciation notes for difficult words in the song. Each maxim of the *Sacred Edict* has forty-eight lines of verse devoted to it, and these are commented upon a quatrain at a time. Here is the first of the twelve quatrains on the first maxim, together with its commentary:

> [To be] freed [from] bosom's care,
> [They] must [wait] three years;

[The] kindness [of] father [and] mother,
[Is] equal [to] Vast Heaven.

These four lines say: after a father and a mother give birth to a child and for the next one or two years, how concerned they are about feeding and nursing him! In the winter months, they only fear he will be cold; in the summer months, they only fear he will be hot. And, even when they go to work in the fields or gather firewood, they strap him on their backs and take him along with them. They are unwilling to leave him alone in the house. How hard it is! Only after three years, when he can talk and walk, are they freed somewhat from the labor of caring for him in their bosoms. The great kindness of a father and mother is as that of Heaven Above. "Vast Heaven" means "Heaven Above."[18]

The *Regulations for Lectures on the Sacred Edict,* bearing a preface dated 1705 and newly recut in that year, was printed from blocks kept in the Lien-shan County *yamen.* It offers complete instructions on how to carry out a lecture ceremony on the *Sacred Edict*: where to hold the lecture (different in city, town, and country); how to purify the site; where to place the incense, candles, and flower vases; how to wrap and store the *Sacred Edict*; where various groups of the auditors are to stand; what furniture is required; when the musicians are to play; what is the appropriate time for the cantor's singing; when the drums and clappers should be hit; and when the auditors should kneel, bow, kowtow, and so on. There can be no doubt that Li and others like him were attempting to provide a ritualistic setting for the liturgical text embodied in the *Illustrated Elaboration.* As a matter of fact, Li stipulated in the *Regulations* that a copy of the *Elaboration* was to be kept on the altar during the *Sacred Edict* lecture service. Four record books were to be placed on the altar as well. As Li traveled from village to village to lecture on the *Sacred Edict,* he would order the local headmen to record the behavior of the villagers in these four registers or ledgers.[19] In the books were recorded instances of good behavior (subdivided good, better, best), bad behavior (likewise subdivided bad, worse, worst), repentance for misdeeds leading to improved behavior, and amicable settlement of conflict through arbitration by respected members of the community. Li would use these records to gauge the effectiveness of his preaching and would also give rewards or mete out punishment where appropriate. Li says that, after he had published and distributed the *Regulations,* they were widely used as the basis for the twice monthly lectures on the *Sacred Edict* in all parts of his county, no matter how remote. This represented a deliberate attempt to extend the *Sacred Edict* lecture system beyond the towns and cities, where it was a simple matter to organize because of the presence of centrally appointed personnel, into the villages and countryside.

Li Lai-chang's complex apparatus for lectures on the *Sacred Edict* described in his *Regulations* and presented in his *Illustrated Elaboration* would seem to have allowed for ready adjustment to different types of audiences. We know that other officials from around this time who were actively engaged in popularizing the *Sacred Edict* did take into account the level of sophistication of their audiences. While Chang Po-hsing was governor of Fukien (1707–1710), he used one version of the *Sacred Edict* "embellished with classical allusions for the literati, one illustrated with popular sayings for those of medium intelligence and scholarly ability, and one with memorable jingles for the simple country folk."[20]

In the second year of his reign (1724), the Yung-cheng emperor issued the *Sheng-yü kuang-hsün* (Amplified Instructions on the *Sacred Edict*), consisting of approximately ten thousand characters. He was evidently concerned that the K'ang-hsi emperor's sixteen maxims were so concise as to be incomprehensible to the common man. Yung-cheng's preface begins with a justification by ancient example: "Every year in the first *month* of spring, the herald with his wooden-tongued bell goes along the roads, proclaiming...."[21] It is clear that, within the confines of the literary language, he was aiming at lucidity: "Our text attempts to be clear and precise; our words, for the most part, are direct and simple."[22] The prose is easily understandable for someone with a modicum of training in the literary language.

A statistical study of the frequency of graphs in the *Amplified Instructions* in comparison with a standard list for classical Chinese is revealing.²³ There is a close correlation for most of the graphs, particularly those that function as grammatical particles. It is striking, however, that the *Amplified Instructions* has such an extraordinarily high number of occurrences for "people" (*min*) and "soldiers" (*ping*). These two graphs do not occur until much farther down on the standard list. Conversely, the standard list has "Heaven" (*t'ien*) and "ruler" (*chün*) among the first twenty graphs, but they are not so prominent in the *Amplified Instructions*. It is obvious to whom the Yung-cheng emperor was directing his remarks. Unfortunately, his intended audience was unable to comprehend him because he wrote in a language that was alien to its members. Yung-cheng's failure to communicate with the bulk of his subjects and the urgent necessity his officers felt in seeing that he did so led to the repeated vernacular paraphrasis of his *Amplified Instructions*.

The *Amplified Instructions* was eventually also issued in a Manchu version.²⁴ A trilingual (Chinese, Mongolian, Manchu) edition of the text, the *San-ho Shengyü kuang-hsün,* was published no later than the Ch'ien-lung period.²⁵

By far the most influential and best known popularizations of the *Sacred Edict* are a series of related texts emanating from Wang Yu-p'u (1680-1761), who, when he composed the original work on which they are based, was serving as assistant salt controller in Shensi Province. Wang Yu-p'u was a man of Tientsin. He attained the advanced scholar (*chin-shih*) degree in 1723 and subsequently became a Bachelor in the National Academy. The highest rank he achieved was first-class subprefect of Lu-chou prefecture.²⁶

It seems odd that Wang chose not to mention the paraphrase in his autobiography, especially since he is best known for having written it, although he did have a minor reputation as a scholar of the *Book of Change*. Wang completed the autobiography on March 9, 1761, not long before he died, clearly waiting for his end and using the autobiography to assess the course and import of his life. He stated that, in writing it, he would "hide nothing, whether good or bad."[27] He also gave a fairly complete list of his writings. Why, then, did he avoid the paraphrase altogether? The answer is, quite probably, that he simply did not wish to be remembered for this work of *basse vulgarisation*. Nor did his biographers in the *Gazetteer of Tientsin Prefecture*[28] and the *Ch'ing History*[29] think the paraphrase worthy of mention. They were wrong; Wang Yu-p'u's place in history is assured for no other reason than that he was ultimately responsible for the most widely circulated vernacular paraphrase of the *Sacred Edict*.[30]

Wang Yu-p'u's paraphrase has a rather complicated history. It was originally written in 1726, just two years after Yung-cheng issued the *Amplified Instructions*. The original title of the work would appear to have been *Chiang-chieh Sheng-yü kuang-hsün* (Discussion and Explanation of the *Amplified Instructions on the "Sacred Edict"*).[31] When it was republished, with minor modifications, by various officials here and there throughout the empire, it came to be known as *Sheng-yü kuang-hsün yen* (Elaboration of the *Amplified Instructions on the "Sacred Edict"*). This is also the title it bears in Wang Yu-p'u's *Collected Works*.[32] Later, when the text was subjected to major changes and distributed still more widely, it was entitled *Sheng-yü kuang-hsün chih-chieh* (Direct Explanation of the *Amplified Instructions on the "Sacred Edict"*).

Baller's translation[33] of Wang Yu-p'u's *Direct Explanation* went through no less than six editions between the years 1892 and 1924. It was sold widely in general bookstores and had a sizable influence. The original purpose for bringing out this publication was to provide authentic material for the study of Mandarin by Protestant missionaries. Yet, in the end, the work had a much deeper impact upon the foreign community than its sponsors could have imagined. The British magistrate in Weihaiwei, for example, was fond of citing the *Direct Explanation* "in delivering judgments in both civil and criminal cases."[34] He vigorously defended this practice in spite of the fact that a local missionary pointed out to him that he could have found a "far more appropriate text" for his purpose in the Bible.

My impression is that roughly half of the *Direct Explanation* was taken over intact from the *Elaboration* and much of the rest of it follows closely. But there are telling differences, partly due simply to the persistent classicizing tendency in the *Direct Explanation* to avoid prolixity and partly due to a harsher, more condescending attitude toward its audience. Where Wang Yu-p'u tells the people that the government collects taxes to pay the officials who "take care of your affairs," the *Direct Explanation* says that it does so to "control you, the populace."[35] There are also fewer explicit references in the *Direct Explanation* to the solicitude of the K'ang-hsi emperor for the people. Where the *Direct Explanation* simply tells its auditors to use the money they have left over from paying taxes "to buy some things," the *Elaboration* has the more solicitous "to buy some nice things."[36] Yung-cheng had advised the scholars that "the books which you read should all be proper." Wang Yu-p'u displays a keen sense of the real state of affairs when he counsels that "what you read must all be proper books. Don't look at so much as a single line of those lewd lyrics and short stories." The editors of the *Direct Explanation* bring the admonition back more closely to Yung-cheng's formulation with the dull "you must read some proper books."[37] In an attempt to pare down Wang Yu-p'u's smoothly flowing, expansive prose, the *Direct Explanation* editors sometimes construct ungrammatical sentences. For example, they rewrite *Chei-ke ch'ien-liang tsui shih yao-chin-te* ("This tax revenue is most important") as *Che ch'ien-liang tsui shih yao-chin.*[38] The *Direct Explanation* has a greater tendency to use monosyllabic nouns and verbs than does the *Elaboration,* and its handling of colloquial particles and complements is less fluent and assured. The *Elaboration* is an almost flawless masterpiece of natural, colloquial prose. The *Direct Explanation,* on the other hand, is awkward in many instances where it departs from the *Elaboration.* There are other subtle distinctions between the two texts. The *Elaboration* relies more on persuasion to cajole and coax the people, while the *Direct Explanation* is somewhat peremptory and threatening. Both texts are condescending to their auditors but the *Direct Explanation* is more so. It calls the people "stupid," "doltish," "ignorant," "idiotic," "dullards," and "imbeciles."[39] The *Direct Explanation* cites large segments of the Ch'ing code in classical Chinese but the *Elaboration* does not.

There is little doubt that both the *Elaboration* and the *Direct Explanation* were intended to be read aloud *to* the people. There are frequent direct addresses to a listening audience: "You masses of the people," "you soldiers and civilians," "I ask you," "you look," "you just think," "you who are sons," and so on. Rhetorical questions abound: "Do you mean to say . . . ?" "Is it not . . . ?" "Examine yourselves—how can you do it in all conscience?" "What is filial piety?" "Since you know the kindness of your parents, why are you not filial to them?" and so forth. The recurrence of the words "lecture" (*chiang*) and "hear" (*t'ing*) is another indication of the purpose of these texts. Both also display a fondness for proverbs and popular sayings that would have been an effective element in public lectures.

The *Direct Explanation* and the *Elaboration* are explicit in identifying their intended auditors: "Although these remarks are addressed to the soldiers and civilians, we still wish you country squires, men of rank, elders well up in years, graduates in letters, and leading men in the community, first of all to set an example of concord: then you will be able to educate the ignorant people."[40]

It would, admittedly, have been impossible for an official in Canton or Fukien, say, simply to read off Wang Yu-p'u's Mandarin (Chihli) paraphrase and expect the local denizens to comprehend it. This difficulty was obviated by the fact that, "in reading, the orator deviates considerably from the printed copy; supplying what he thinks needful to render the sense perspicuous to the hearers, and altering the phraseology to suit it to the idiom of the spoken language of that particular province, or district."[41] This, of course, is premised upon the ability of the orator to speak the local dialect. In many cases, the centrally appointed officials were not linguistically equipped to speak to the people in the districts they administered.

The problem of language barriers comes up again in a report of Wang Chih (Advanced Scholar, 1721), like Wang Yu-p'u, also from Chihli. While serving as magistrate of Hsin-hui in Kwangtung Province, Wang Chih wrote a *Shang-yü t'ung-su chieh* (Popular Explanation of the *Imperial Edict*). Although Wang Chih refers to the work he paraphrased as the *Imperial Edict,* because of his mention of the *Amplified Instructions,* it is clear that he means the *Sacred Edict.* He explains how he had come to write this work in the following words:

> Formerly I had developed a method of explaining the *Imperial Edict,* using colloquial language to paraphrase the text of the *Amplified Instructions.* I ordered the lecturers to preach in the native dialect. Listeners were able to understand and appreciate quite well. The Overseer of Hsin-ning, Wang Chün-sung, whenever he lectured on one of the maxims himself, would [make the people] understand by going over it again and again. Because my accent was not right, I could not do that.
>
> Upon arriving at the place where the village lecture was to be held, I ordered elderly inhabitants over eighty or ninety to sit behind the gentry. All were served tea; but none [of this privileged group of listeners] was permitted to report on public affairs. Commoners were ordered to stand and listen during the village lectures.[42]

The frank admission of a language barrier is revealing; Wang Chih was unable to address the people of the county in which he was the highest ranking government officer. Wang Yu-p'u reveals his own ambivalence toward colloquial speech when he speaks derogatorily about the "local dialects in the various parts of China."[43]

Several of the editors and publishers of Wang Yu-p'u's famous paraphrase have provided helpful information about how they came to know of it and why they decided to undertake the responsibility for making it available to others. Shortly after 1808, the acting viceroy of the province of Canton, Han Feng, was shown a copy of the *Discussion and Explanation* (i.e., the *Elaboration*) by Wang Hsun-ch'en, the superintendant of land revenue. "Having received and read the explanation," he confesses, "I couldn't help liking it. Therefore, I ordered the officer in charge of instruction to select, from among the fourth class of the literary candidates, four persons whose teeth and mouth were formed for clear and distinct utterance; that on the first and fifteenth of each moon, they might proclaim the original text in the Canton dialect." It is obvious that oral interpretation was an essential part of the presentation, for it would have been impossible simply to read off Wang Yu-p'u's northern dialect *Elaboration* in Cantonese. Apparently it was easier to interpret orally from the *Elaboration* than to translate directly from Yung-cheng's classical *Amplified Instructions* into Cantonese. Han Feng, not without exaggeration, declares that the lectures were a success and then goes on to describe his instructions to subordinate officials:

> I accordingly distributed it throughout the districts; gave it to the local officers, the pastors of the people, ordering that they should widely proclaim the Edict; and not leave a single person, even in the huts thinly scattered along the shores of the ocean, ignorant and disobedient. Should we at a future time receive your imperial order to remove to other places, we will teach the same in the dialects of those places to all the people... .[44]

Judging from these and other remarks, the publication and distribution of vernacular paraphrases of the *Sacred Edict* were dependent upon the individual initiative of officials outside the capital.

In the statement of the Canton editor of the *Elaboration*, Wang Hsun-ch'en, we find the following passage:

> From the time that your Imperial Majesty began to reign until now, you have earnestly commanded all statesmen and officers to hold lectures in accord with precedent so as to encourage and guide the ignorant villagers. We, your ministers, have not failed, each in the vulgar dialect of his own district, by various methods,

to lead on the people to the knowledge of the *Edict.* But our lectures are only occasional and we fear that they may not reach everyone. Hence I have searched out the *Discussion and Explanation of the [Amplified] Instructions on the Sacred [Edict]* published by the Assistant Salt Controller of Shensi, Wang Yu-p'u.[45]

Wang Hsun-ch'en would seem to believe that publication of the *Discussion and Explanation* would allow the *Sacred Edict* to reach a greater audience than he and his colleagues could in the course of their own lectures. But he does not entertain any serious expectation that the common people would actually read the *Sacred Edict,* even in this popularized form. He simply thinks it his duty as an official to make it more widely available, probably to local literates, because "the sense of the discussions and explanations is easily understood and is truly beneficial to the ignoramuses who *hear* them."[46] With this in mind, he "accordingly reprinted Yu-p'u's text and distributed it to the prefectures and counties so that it might be known to every family and household and that they would comment on and explain it to each other."[47] Wang Hsun-ch'en's statement closes with a challenge to the "good civil authorities" to animate and encourage the people without wearying and by a variety of methods.

On June 21, 1815, the judicial commissioner of the province of Shensi, Chi-ch'ang (a Manchu bannerman who had become a provincial graduate [*chü-jen*] in 1800), finished his *Sheng-yü kuang-hsün yen-shuo* (Glosses for the *Amplified Instructions on the "Sacred Edict"*).[48] It is obvious that this text is an abridged adaptation of the *Direct Explanation.* Entire sentences and even paragraphs are left out, while others are rearranged and rewritten. The language, though still fluent colloquial Mandarin, is less assured than that of the *Direct Explanation,* not to mention the *Elaboration.* It is also less graphic and earthy. In short, *Glosses* is an assiduous but unsuccessful attempt to camouflage wholesale plagiarism from its famous predecessor. But it is more than just that, for *Glosses* also evinces a different attitude and tone. Where the *Elaboration* and *Direct Explanation,* in decrying the growth of heretical sects, declare that such sects are prone to "do bad things,"[49] *Glosses* warns that they "do rebellious things until they are discovered, exposed, and attacked from all sides by soldiers and officials."[50] *Glosses* is more threatening than the *Direct Explanation,* partly through greater emphasis on specific punishments cited from the Ch'ing code,[51] partly through increased insistence on the necessity for individuals to "mind their own business" (*shou-pen-fen*), as it were.[52] There is also more frequent reference to the "stupidity" and "ignorance" (*yü-mei, wu-chih*) of the people.[53]

The most telling indication of Chi-ch'ang's intentions in issuing this paraphrase, however, is to be found in the conclusion to his own postface:

> Fearing that the stupid men and women are not fully acquainted with the profound meaning of [the Emperor's] writing [in the *Sacred Edict*] and still cannot completely comprehend it, I have respectfully elaborated the royal words in common language. Thus the twice-monthly explications in the various prefectures and counties as well as the propagandizing (*hsüan-ch'uan*) by instructors in each village and community will be intelligible to the ear of women and children while the recalcitrant and the craven alike will be moved with enthusiasm. It is hoped that the officials who guide the people will carry out these orders without being remiss. They will be endlessly supportive and protective[54] in order to achieve for our country the blessing of peace and harmony and in order to assist the sage Son of Heaven in the task of enlightening the people through emulating his ancestors and making them submit for all time. May this be of some assistance.[55]

Toward the end of the Tao-kuang reign period (1821-1850), heretical sects were proliferating wildly. It was thought that a large part of the responsibility for this unrest lay with the local officials, who were supposedly too lax in combating them. Consequently, study of the *Sacred Edict* in all schools and academies was required as a corrective. The editor of the 1850 edition of the *Direct Explanation* expresses a deep concern about the increasingly overt activities of illicit religious groups:

Recently, heterodox doctrines have been transmitted to all the provinces and are spreading across them. At first, it was only a matter of burning incense, collecting money, and stirring up doubt in the minds of the stupid people. Gradually, we have come to a situation where crowds gather and disturbances are incited. This is all because the local officials are ineffective in their daily guidance of the people. Furthermore, the seniors and leaders among the people are unable to teach and enlighten them from time to time so that the ignorant might be governable and fear punishment and, hence, not be confused by heterodox pronouncements.

Not wanting to be blamed as an irresponsible official, the editor chose to reprint the *Direct Explanation* as his contribution to the struggle against heresy.

The same concerns inform the preface of the 1865 edition of the *Direct Explanation*, which I quote in full:

Of old, the people were made up of four classes; now there are six classes of people. Of old, there was but a single doctrine; now there are three.[56] The more these doctrines diverge, the more confused people become. Divergence multiplies upon divergence until the oppression of the masses caused by these heterodox pronouncements exceeds that of Yang-tzu, Mo-tzu, Buddha, and Lao-tzu.[57] The damage they cause cannot be told in words.

Our Sacred Ancestor, the Benevolent Emperor [K'ang-hsi], himself having been given great authority by Heaven, was disposed to display his sympathy for the benighted. He expressly promulgated the *Sacred Edict* composed of sixteen items to constitute forever a method of indoctrination. Our Epochal Progenitor, the Exemplary Emperor [Yung-cheng], in turn, composed the *Amplified Instructions* in ten thousand words. He also instituted study halls and lectures on the first and fifteenth of each month.

The Plans of the Sages are far-reaching and bright as the sun and the moon. Now the Son of Heaven, at a moment when the empire's fate turns, brings about restoration by diligently seeking order. The Silken Words of the Emperor repeatedly disseminate clear explanations as he lectures on the essentials of the old statutes. Truly this is an important way to transform the people and to reform custom. However, his language is literary and his purport is deep. The learned doctors who proclaim his words and elaborate upon them may perhaps not fully elucidate their meaning. The dull and slow-witted people of the villages and lanes cannot fathom the instructions of the classics nor can they apprehend their profundity, so they do not fully see the intent of the Sages. This is not the way to propagate the Supreme Doctrine.

Formerly, when I was serving as an official in the capital, I heard that in Kiangsi, Hupei, and other provinces, there had been printed a book called the *Direct Explanation*. The authorities, out of respect for the Excellent Teaching of the Court, probably hoped that thereby a part of it might be known in every household. I regret that before I had had a chance to see it, I went to fill a post in Anhwei. It so happened that military matters were quite pressing and I was no longer able to think of the *Direct Explanation*. Today, fortunately, the ravages of the soldiers have abated somewhat.

I deeply maintain that, in order to inculcate the doctrine of propriety, we must cause the eyes and ears of the people to be steeped in it so that it is easy for them to know and follow. By chance, in a conversation with the former Commissioner of Education, the Academician Ma Yü-nung, the subject of this book came up. He brought out from a chest a copy that he owned and showed it to me. I read it carefully and savored its details. This book respectfully adheres to the *Amplified Instructions on the Sacred Edict* by explaining its import in language that young and old among the people can understand and hence become thoroughly conversant with its message. Going over them again and again renders the instructions perspicuous and makes them clear as speech. This causes the auditors to take them to heart actively without wearying of them. For the ignorant and the uneducated, it is quite beneficial. So, having borrowed the book, I took it back to my own place. There I copied it down and re-edited it with the intention of broadening its circulation.

Perhaps someone might say, "When there is great disorder in society, one must first alleviate suffering. Before you have been able to rescue the people from the clutches of death, what leisure have you to cultivate ceremony and righteousness?[58] What are you doing with these writing materials?" He who asks this does not realize that great disorder in society arises in the hearts of men. If the hearts of men are not changed, the disorder in society will not soon abate. Today the area south of the Yangtze is somewhat settled and the people are gradually being relieved of their distress. Everybody is saying, "Peace and order have already been achieved!" Yet those who employ violence presume on their harsh threats; those who are accustomed to cunning abuse others with opportunistic tricks; those who work at being unconventional detest ceremony and law; those who insist upon obstinacy unleash their obtuseness. What is there to be happy about? With words becoming confused and affairs disorderly, once again unfounded heretical pronouncements incite the people. The flames leap higher and higher, as though there were a blazing fire, until they become worrisome indeed.

The printing of the *Direct Explanation* is for the very purpose of elaborating and spreading the fine civilizing influence of the *Amplified Instructions on the Sacred Edict* so as to bring rectitude to the hearts of men. Accordingly, I have brought forth this book to be distributed in the various prefectures and counties. Each of our officials and outstanding citizens ought in all sincerity to do his best to realize this measure. May they daily have the young and the old come to them so that they can instruct them in the meaning of filial piety and subordination, disseminating the Virtues of the Ruler among his subjects. Thus, to a degree, the laws may be restored, the people renewed, and the evils of heresy not arise. Is this not the basis for assisting China to be greatly distinguished in the Way for eons? Is this not the basis?

—Autumn, ninth month, 1865.
Respectfully inscribed by Ho Ching,
Financial Commissioner of Hupei,
retained as Acting Financial
Commissioner of Anhwei.

The *Sacred Edict* and two separate *Amplified Instructions* are mentioned in the introductory essay of Huang Yü-p'ien's well-known antiheretical work, *P'o hsieh hsiang-pien* (A Detailed Refutation of Heresies, Preface 1834). The date given for the first *Amplified Instructions* is 1724, so this is obviously Yung-cheng's original text. The date given for the second is 1797. From the description provided by Huang, it would appear that the text in question is one or another edition of the *Direct Explanation*[59]: "Written completely in everyday colloquial language of the people to set forth and comment upon [the *Amplified Instructions*]. All local officials, on the first and the fifteenth of each month, respectfully use it for lectures so that the ignorant people too can understand thoroughly and with ease. The rectification of the laws and the renewal of the people lie in this." In the preface, Huang writes of his own work: "Because the ignorant people in the villages who recognize characters are few, it is hoped that the gentry in each village read this book [i.e., *Disputation*] until they are thoroughly familiar with it and then transmit it extensively to the broad masses."[60] Presumably, a similar process of transmission was used for the *Amplified Instructions*. The purpose of the *Direct Explanation* thus would have been to provide the gentry or other responsible individuals with a ready-made lecture in the colloquial language that they could adapt to their own needs and tastes.

Who the purchasers of these texts were might be partially deduced from the prices asked for them. In 1847, the *Elaboration*, on good paper, could be bought in Canton for the equivalent of two shillings and sixpence.[61] In Canton, this amount of money, in the same year, could have bought about 40 pounds of rice or a pair of trousers and a jacket.[62]

This was surely within the realm of possible purchase by the literati but it would have been a luxury for the common man. Perhaps there were cheaper editions available, although I do not know what their price might have been. Even at half the price, buying this text would still have been a big investment for the average person.

A most curious production is the small volume called *Sheng-yü ch'u-yen* (Plain Talk on the *Sacred Edict*), by Chien Ching-hsi. This work would appear to be the product of a local group of intellectuals who gave themselves quaint names (Chien, for example, styled himself "The Woodcutter of Cassia Village" [*Kuei-ts'un ch'iao-che*]). The production also seems to have had a limited budget and, hence, limited circulation, perhaps because it did not receive any official backing. The printing on the pages of the text is close set, as though the intention was to save space and hence paper. The carving is clear but by no means distinguished. While not an expensive publication, it has manifestly been lovingly and carefully executed. I have used the 1893 recutting done at Yüshan, Chekiang. The two prefaces, dated 1887, are in the neat calligraphy (one regular script, one cursive) of two of the sponsors of the publication and are helpful in understanding the origins and purpose of the *Plain Talk*. The prefaces are full of amusingly self-congratulatory sentiments. Chien, it would seem, was a rather successful lecturer on the *Sacred Edict*. He was probably a member of the gentry who had been tapped by a county magistrate for this purpose.[63] Some of his friends who read his lectures in written form were so delighted with them that they decided to publish and distribute them. In his preface, one of Chien's friends, Huo Chen, makes rather grand claims about the extent of the influence they hope it will have ("everyone within and without the Four Seas will know how to establish the Way").

The *Plain Talk* may be said to be "plain" only in the sense that it provides straight exegesis of the *Amplified Instructions*. It is insipid and dull; without considerable embellishment, it could hardly have stirred its auditors to follow the teachings of the sages. After quoting each maxim, it mechanically begins with the words "The *Sacred Edict* of the August One Above would have us..." or a similar formulation. Each section ends with a sentence to the effect that "The ____th maxim of the *Sacred Edict* means precisely this." The author is quite condescending to the people, calling them by such endearing epithets as "inferior ignoramuses." On the other hand, he servilely flatters the emperor. He is strongly against secret societies and "religious bandits" but would appear to have no overt quarrel with Buddhism and Taoism. Huo Chen's preface claims that when Chien used his *Plain Words* to lecture on the *Sacred Edict*, he made "the resplendent, imperial language of the *Amplified Instructions* suitable for women and children." But he could not have done so without utilizing some mechanism of oral interpretation, for, although the *Plain Words* does not employ arcane allusions, only an audience with several years of training in the classical language could have understood the text were it read aloud.

The *Sheng-yü kuang-hsün chi-cheng* (Collected Verifications of the *Amplified Instructions on the Sacred Edict*), in two fascicles, bears an inscription by Shih Chih-mo[64] of Yang-hu in Kiangsu dated the sixteenth day of the eleventh month of the year 1878. The blocks for the edition I have used were recut in 1900 and kept at Wu Yin-sun's place in Kiangsu. Wu was from I-cheng County, also in Kiangsu, and brought out the *Yu-fu tu-shu-t'ang ts'ung-k'e* (Good Fortune Library Series) of which the *Collected Verifications* is the first title. In his preface, Wu says that his family owned more than seven thousand books. Of these, 50-60 percent were trade publications and 40-50 percent were old or rare editions. The Wus were obviously avid collectors and they frequently had interesting titles, some still in manuscript form, sent to them. They were also publishers and keenly aware of the intense competition in the reprint-series field. Wu had several times begun to publish a series but soon stopped in each case because he was uncertain of its potential success. He emphasizes that he had to think of some distinctive theme for the series. Ultimately, he decided to choose *easy-to-understand* works of solid moral content that had been overlooked by other publishers. We thus have the

Wu family's entrepreneurial spirit to thank for the preservation of the *Collected Verifications*. It is also significant that a market for this type of material existed and that it was sufficiently large to attract competing publishers.

The nature of the market may, to a certain extent, be understood by examining the *Collected Verifications*. This book consists of stories illustrating the maxims that had been used by lecturers on the *Sacred Edict*. The treatment of each maxim conforms to the following pattern: a general introduction, illustrative stories, and a recapitulation. The latter section often effectively compares and contrasts the moral issues raised by the illustrative examples. A number of the stories are from the Shanghai area but a few come from as far away as Shansi. Some of the stories are historical but most are contemporary. To lend veracity to the accounts, the compiler supplies dates and places, with the result that the reader almost begins to feel that the *Collected Verifications* represents a species of reporting. On the one hand, as might be expected in such a situation, sensational tales of murder are vividly recounted but, on the other hand, there are also a couple of charming stories about animals (the filial calf and the filial kitten). Surprisingly, the compiler has been able to link up such disparate items into fairly coherent and persuasive arguments.

Linguistically, the *Collected Verifications* is a hodgepodge of styles. The first sentence of each section is in the classical language but there is often a gradual shift into an impure colloquial (*chih* for *te, ch'i* for *t'a, hu* instead of *ma, tz'u* for *che^a*, and so on). Some stories are entirely in simple classical and this leads me to suspect that the compiler may merely have been following his sources without making any serious effort toward stylistic unity.

Buddhists are said to be "only preoccupied with purity and cleanliness, calmness and extinction," while Taoists "let things take their natural course so that no harm will come to the people."[65] Elsewhere, the compiler displays a certain sympathy for such Buddhist concepts as retribution and reincarnation. But the millenarian cults are an entirely different matter. Like all the other literati popularizers, he is completely opposed to the ideas and activities of such groups.

LECTURES

To give some idea of the institutional setting in which the Ch'ing popularizations of the *Sacred Edict* appeared, it may be helpful to provide a brief chronology of related government actions. In 1652, the *Six Maxims* were promulgated throughout the land.[66] Following Ming precedent, an imperial directive was issued in 1659 establishing a system of village lectures (*hsiang-yüeh*) to elucidate the *Six Maxims* in plain and simple language on the first and fifteenth of each month.[67] It was this system that was carried over subsequently for use by lecturers on the *Sacred Edict* and continued, with varying degrees of vitality, to the end of the Ch'ing dynasty.[68] Kung-chuan Hsiao refers to it as a method of popular indoctrination.[69] Pei Huang states that later, during the Yung-cheng period, "all the variant forms of intellectual restriction... were channeled toward the same end—the enforcement of orthodox ideology." There was a determined attempt to make this orthodoxy the pattern for the political behavior of everyone within the empire, not just the ideological standard for the literati.[70] Numerous official measures relating to the propagation of the maxims of the *Sacred Edict*, including successive refinements of the village lecture system, were an integral part of this ideological enforcement. Chung-li Chang agrees that the purpose of the semimonthly lectures on what he calls the "politico-moral maxims" of the *Sacred Edict* was "to indoctrinate the masses with the official ideology."[71]

In 1729, it was decreed that, in all larger towns and villages where there were dense concentrations of people, places for lectures on the Yung-cheng emperor's *Amplified Instructions* were to be established.[72] The following year, Yung-cheng agreed to sanction special educational procedures for the children of aboriginal peoples in remote parts of

Chien-ch'ang prefecture (Szechwan) who had submitted to Chinese rule but were unacquainted with Chinese notions of propriety. It was decided that village tutors (*shu-shih*) ought to be invited to instruct them. The problem was that these children did not understand Mandarin (*kuan-yü*) while the tutors were not at ease in the local language.[73] In order to overcome this difficulty, it was suggested that exemplary first-degree licentiates from Szechwan be hired to establish training centers on the model of the free schools in Han areas. The aboriginal children were to be sent to schools not far from their own homes together with Han children so that gradually the culture of the latter would rub off on them. The first text mentioned for study was the *Amplified Instructions on the Sacred Edict.* Only after this work was thoroughly mastered would they turn to the recitation and study of the classics. A similar procedure was suggested in 1732 for instructing the children of the Miao people in six villages of the Yung-sui area.[74] For the instruction of the Li and Yao peoples in Kwangtung Province, the emphasis was on securing linguistically talented teachers and, as in the Miao case, the selection and advancement of the most capable aboriginal children for further study. There were also the obligatory semimonthly lectures on the *Amplified Instructions* and explanations of the legal code.[75] Reading through the government regulations on the subject, one gains the clear impression that the problem of the education of non-Han subjects represented but an extreme form of the difficulties inherent in transmitting the values of the elite to the rest of the population. It is noteworthy that, in both circumstances, the *Sacred Edict* was considered to be the best vehicle for the transmission of these ideals.

By 1736, measures were taken to extend the lecture system to all villages without restrictions on size.[76] Additional measures were to be taken in following years to ensure that copies of the *Amplified Instructions* and abridged legal codes would be available to chief and assistant lecturers throughout the empire. Furthermore, these lecturers were not to look upon their task of speaking on the *Amplified Instructions* and the legal code as a mere formality but were to take it with the utmost seriousness. In 1737, it was specifically stipulated that the main provisions of the imperial code be explained at the end of each lecture session on the *Sacred Edict*.[77] This order had a direct impact on authors and editors of written popularizations of the *Sacred Edict*, who began increasingly to append relevant passages from the code to their discussions of the maxims. In 1753, the emperor ordered that officials be strongly encouraged, in addition to giving the regular semimonthly lectures on the *Sacred Edict*, to instruct the villagers in Confucian moral precepts whenever they could, employing local dialects and colloquial speech so that those present might understand what they were hearing.[78] A directive of 1758 declared that "it would do no harm to explain [the *Amplified Instructions*] clearly in local dialects and with common sayings."[79] This directive was especially concerned with bringing a halt to the spread of heterodox sects. The laws forbidding such doctrines were to be printed and posted widely. By the time of the Tao-kuang emperor (r. 1821-1850), the government seems to have become almost paranoid about the activities of secret and unsanctioned religious groups. Considering the events of the second half of the nineteenth century, however, perhaps their fears were justified. At any rate, from about 1750 on, there is always a close connection between the village lecture system and the suppression of heresies. The increasing emphasis during the Ch'ing on the prevention of socially disruptive behavior and unlawful conduct can be seen clearly by comparing the *Six Maxims* with the *Sacred Edict* and the *Sacred Edict* with the *Amplified Instructions* and its commentaries.[80]

One account of the prescribed ritual for lecturing on the *Sacred Edict* is as follows:

> Early on the first and fifteenth of every moon, the civil and military officers, dressed in their uniforms, meet in a clean, spacious, public hall. The superintendent or Master of Ceremonies (*li-sheng*) calls aloud, "Stand forth in files." They do so, according to their rank: he then says, "Kneel thrice, and bow the head nine times." They kneel, and bow to the ground, with their faces towards a platform, on which is placed a board with the Emperor's name.

The *Sacred Edict* 71

> He next calls aloud, "Rise and retire." They rise, and all go to a hall, or kind of chapel, where the law is usually read; and where the military and people are assembled, standing round in silence.
>
> The Master of Ceremonies then says, "Respectfully commence." The orator (*ssu-chiang-sheng*), advancing towards an incense-altar, kneels; reverently takes up the board on which the maxim appointed for the day is written, and ascends a stage with it. An old man receives the board, and puts it down on the stage, fronting the people. Then, commanding silence with a wooden rattle which he carries in his hand, he kneels, and reads it. When he has finished, the Master of Ceremonies calls out, "Explain such a section, or maxim, of the *Sacred Edict*." The orator stands up, and gives the sense.[81]

The following extract from a letter, dated Shanghai, September 23, 1847, and written by a foreign resident gives a perhaps truer picture of the manner of proclamation of the *Sacred Edict*:

> I have just returned from hearing *Chinese preaching,* or what answers to preaching better than anything else I have yet seen among the Chinese. You know that on the 1st and 15th of every month, the local officers throughout the empire are required to repair to the municipal temples, and then, after having worshiped the deity enshrined therein, and the emperor, are there to have the Sacred Edict brought out in state, and read to the assembly of the people and soldiers. This ceremony I have just had an opportunity of seeing.
>
> At a quarter past 5 o'clock this morning, in company with some friends, I started for the *Ching-hwáng miáu* (i.e., ch'eng-huang miao), the residence of the tutelary god of Shánghái. Entering the city by the Little South gate, and by the way calling for three other gentlemen, we all reached the temple some time before six o'clock. A multitude of devout idolaters had already collected, and most of them were busily engaged in performing their religious rites—making prostrations, offering incense, &c., &c. The officials not having arrived, we strolled through the different apartments of the temple, upstairs and downstairs, among all sorts of shrines

and images. This temple is not only the largest in Shánghái, but has the reputation of being inferior to none of the kind in the whole empire.

In a little while the chief magistrate arrived with his retinue, and was soon followed by the colonel, accompanied by three subalterns, who all repaired immediately to the presence of the presiding divinity, in the centre of the great hall, and on their hassocks went through with the three kneelings and nine knockings of head. As soon as they had retired into a side apartment, a broad yellow satin curtain was suspended in front of the god whom they had worshiped, and under it, projecting forward, a small altar was erected upon a table. Before this little altar, a small yellow satin screen was placed, designed, as I suppose, to hide from vulgar eyes something intended to represent imperial majesty. In front of the small yellow screen were placed pots of burning incense, and close behind them was a small box. These things being arranged, the same was duly announced to the officers, who returned and repeated the ceremonies which they had already performed. Then, while they were still standing before the representatives of imperial power, an aged man, dressed in official robes, came forward, and with all becoming gravity took up the little box from the table, raised it as high as his chin in both hands, and then turned and carried it out of the temple, and laid it on an elevated table in front of the great hall. Another man now came forward, mounted the platform, opened the box, and took out a small volume. This was the *Sacred Edict*, and he the appointed orator for the morning. He commenced and read on most unconcernedly, the officers having retired and a rabble gathered around, attracted evidently more by the presence of half a dozen foreigners than by the eloquence of the orator, or the importance of his subject.

...Anxious to see and hear, and imitating the forwardness of the Chinese, I mounted the low platform and took my position close behind the orator, and the man who bore the little box—both of whom were standing. In this position I had a good opportunity of hearing and, witnessing the *effects* of the eloquence. It was *reading*, and nothing more, in a rapid and distinct, but not very elevated tone of voice. The number of listeners could not have exceeded sixty, though the temple and court in front of the hall were thronged.

Neither the officers, nor their principal attendants were present to *hear* the reading, but were enjoying themselves with tea and tobacco in one of the side apartments. The five classes—scholars, soldiers, farmers, merchants, and mechanics—were all in turn addressed by the orator, for so it was written in the book; but few or none of them were present. The audience consisted almost wholly of vagrants, idle people who were loitering about the place, beggars, and truant boys. The sentence selected for this morning was the tenth, ... Mind your-own business, to settle the people's will: or, in other words, "let each one attend to his own profession, so that the minds of the people may be fixed, and each one remain quiet and contented in his own sphere." Reading the paraphrase on it occupied the orator about ten minutes, when the book was closed, put in the box, and that replaced again on the table before the little screen; the officers in attendance immediately took leave of each other, and returned to their chairs, we at the same time making our exit.[82]

Another report, from the year 1832, corroborates the impression that the official reading of the *Sacred Edict* had already fallen into desuetude by that time: "At present the public reading of the *Sacred Edict* is kept up in the 'provincial cities,' but is neglected in the country towns, or *heen* (*hsien*) districts. The people rarely attend this *political* preaching of the 'mandarins.'"[83] Indeed, the consensus of all foreign observers is that, by 1850, the official lectures on the *Sacred Edict* were largely meaningless exercises.[84] This is partially borne out by the following notice from the *Canton Court Circular* for April 30, 1836, which was the fifteenth of the third lunar month: "Their excellencies went early in the morning to the temple of the god of war, and offered incense; and then repaired to the 'hall often thousand years' (consecrated to the worship of the emperor), and there attended to the reading of the *Sacred Edict*. Seven criminals were brought in for the assizes."⁸⁵ The reading of the *Sacred Edict* here seems to have become a rather routine part of government business.

Apart from the officially sanctioned twice-monthly lectures, there were also Confucian-minded performers whose oral renditions of didactic tales illustrating the *Sacred Edict* must have been truly entertaining. In Kuo Mo-jo's autobiography, we find the following extraordinary description:

> Lecturers on the *Sacred Edict,* who told stories about loyalty, filial piety, and fidelity from the morality books (*shan-shu*), often came to our village. These morality books were for the most part made up of folktales. The form of the narration was a combination of spoken and sung passages, making it seem a lot like that of "strum lyrics" (*t'an-tz'u,* i.e., ballads with string accompaniment), yet it was not exactly the same. If someone had been willing to collect these things and then put them in order and spruce them up, he could probably have produced some ready-made folk literature.
>
> At a street corner, they would set up a dais composed of three square tables, one placed atop the other two. On the dais, incense and candles were lit as offerings to the plaque of the *Sacred Edict.* On top of the right-hand table was placed a chair. If two people performed together, then a chair was placed on each of the side tables.
>
> When it came time for the lecturer on the *Sacred Edict* to preach, he, dressed as though going to have an audience with the emperor, would knock his head audibly on the ground four times as he faced the plaque of the *Sacred Edict.* Then he would stand up again and, drawing out his voice, would recite the ten [*sic*] maxims of the *Sacred Edict.* After that, he would get back up on the platform and start telling stories. His method of delivery was to chant the text⁸⁶ in a very simple manner. Whenever he came to a part that was to be sung, he would draw out his voice as he sang and, especially when there was something sad, it would be tinged with the sound of weeping. Some of the lecturers would accompany themselves

The *Sacred Edict* 75

> with bells, fish-shaped woodblocks, bamboo clappers, and the like to help their tunes along.
>
> This type of simple storytelling was a form of entertainment that people in the villages liked to listen to very much. They would stand before the platform of the *Sacred Edict* and listen for two or three hours. The better storytellers could make the listeners weep. It was easy to make the villagers cry; all you had to do was draw out your voice a bit at the sad parts and add a few sad sobs.
>
> Before I had begun my schooling, I was already able to understand the morality books of these lecturers on the *Sacred Edict*.[87]

This account indicates that preaching on the *Sacred Edict* had given rise to a form of popular entertainment that was probably detached from the semimonthly system of lectures described above. Kuo's lecturers on the *Sacred Edict* actually were more akin to storytellers. Furthermore, it should be noted that they may very well have been itinerants, since they are said to *come* to the village and not to live there. In fact, there is strong confirmation for Kuo Mo-jo's description in the observation of F. R. Eichler for Canton in the early 1880s:

> The *Sacred Edict* is preached nearly every day, yet at many places the orthodox Confucian preacher, under the pretext of expounding the Shing-yü to the people, tells them all kinds of stories that are likely to captivate their fancy, or at the best, betakes himself to the history of the empire in order to entertain the crowd.[88]

That the *Sacred Edict* was "preached nearly every day" shows conclusively that this type of performance was no longer a part of the official twice-monthly ceremonies. In my estimation, the individuals described by Kuo and Eichler were operating at the level of the cultural facilitators and brokers whom James Hayes discusses in chapter 3 of this volume. There can be no doubt that the diffusion of Confucian ideals was far more efficiently accomplished through this type of grass-roots activity than through the pompous, ritualistic, and often lifeless ceremonies presided over by local officials.[89]

CONCLUSIONS

We have examined a number of interpretations of the *Sacred Edict*. Table 1 brings them together for easy comparison. The one-word characterizations are naturally inadequate and are intended only to call to mind other facets of these texts. Essentially, the message in all is the same: be good and dutiful subjects. The individuals who wrote and published these interpretations had a real stake in the maintenance of order and public security. Distasteful as it may have been for them to address *hoi polloi*, there were compelling reasons for doing so. They were both responsible for and stood most to benefit from the inculcation of Confucian values in the populace. Every written popularization of the *Sacred Edict* known to me was the work of a member of the literati. The people themselves were neither equipped nor motivated to undertake such an endeavor. This is a clear case of the bearers of high culture consciously and willfully trying to mold popular culture.

It is remarkable that, without a single exception, all prefaces and postfaces to every version of the *Sacred Edict* mentioned in this study were written in the literary language. If these texts were truly addressed to a popular *reading* audience, what would be the point of providing them with prefaces and postfaces that were impenetrable? The prefaces and postfaces, on the contrary, are always addressed to fellow scholars and officials or other educated individuals who were able to read the literary language, never to a presumed mass reading public.

There were various motives for publishing these texts. The *Collected Verifications* was part of a commercial venture; there was a group of moderately literate persons who enjoyed reading the didactic stories it presented and who were willing to pay for the opportunity to do so.

Table 1. Interpretations and Paraphrases of the *Sacred Edict*.

	Attitude	Tone/Style	Method	Language
Sacred Edict 1670	Imperious	Sententious	Commands	Highest classical
Combination 1679	Benign	Straightforward	Instructs	Cultivated colloquial
Illustrated Explanations 1681	Advisory	Expository	Describes	Mixed
Illustrated Explanations 1704	Magisterial	Methodical	Stipulates	Mixed
Trimetrical Song 1706	Pedagogic	Terse verse, verbose prose	Teaches	Classical verse, vernacular commentaries
Amplified Instructions 1724	Paternal	Laconic	Demands	Classical
Elaboration 1726	Avuncular	Diffuse	Reasons	Colloquial
Direct Explanation c 1729	Judicial	Admonitory	Exhorts	Colloquial
Glosses 1815	Bureaucratic	Peremptory	Declares	Colloquial
Verifications 1878	Raconteurial	Rambling	Explains	Jumbled
Plain Talk 1887	Seignorial	Patronizing	Dictates	Classical

Source: Adapted from "Language and Ideology in the Written Popularizations of the *Sacred Edict*," in *Popular Culture in Late Imperial China*, ed. David Johnson, Andrew J. Nathan, Evelyn S. Rawski (Berkeley: University of California Press, 1985), 356.

The *Plain Talk* was issued by and for local gentry who were peripherally involved in the lectures on the *Sacred Edict*. The *Amplified Instructions* was obviously directed only at the elite; it was up to them to convey its message to those who were not conversant with the classical language. Those popularizations of the *Sacred Edict* written entirely in the demotic language, ironically, were not meant to be read by the common man. A constant refrain in these texts and in their prefaces is that they are to be presented *orally* to the ignorant populace. They were essentially guidebooks for literate specialists that told them not only *what* to say to the people but, more importantly, *how* to say it. Their own ideological predispositions made the first function somewhat superfluous. The distancing effects of social and linguistic stratification made the second function a necessity if there was to be any meaningful communication between the rulers and the ruled. It is for this reason that the vernacular versions of the *Sacred Edict* were such a tremendous boon to local authorities.

In spite of the fact that the *Sacred Edict* and its interpretations cannot be shown to have been read by the vast majority of the populace, their impact was nevertheless considerable. This was accomplished by making the written *Sacred Edict* or one of its amplifications available to virtually everyone who could read and, further, by strongly encouraging this literate segment of society to verbalize its teachings for the nonliterate or semiliterate. In one form or another (including examination essays, school texts, and lecture handbooks as well as boards, strips, and placards to be displayed in public places, etc.), the *Sacred Edict* must have been written down or printed hundreds of thousands of times during the Ch'ing dynasty. The remarkably prolonged stability of the eighteenth-century reigns may, in some measure, be attributed to the effectiveness of formal lectures and informal homilies on the *Sacred Edict* in propagating a uniform ideology. It is noteworthy, as I have pointed out, that this system had largely begun to collapse by around 1850. Yet, even as late as the 1870s, it was possible for anti-Christian forces in Canton to mobilize against the preaching of missionaries by founding a society to hold lectures on the *Sacred Edict* in various meeting halls.[90] Giles was of the opinion that the widespread dissemination throughout China of the *Sacred Edict* "proved a serious blow to the immediate spread of Christianity."[91] In *The Gallant Maid,* a novel in Peking dialect written during the Tao-kuang period by a Manchurian bannerman, the *Sacred Edict* is referred to in a manner that indicates it had indeed become a household word. It is used in an oath to convince another person of one's honesty: "By the resplendent *Sacred Edict,* how could I tell you a lie?"[92]

The local units of the Ch'ing government at the end of the dynasty included 214 prefectures, 75 independent departments, 54 independent subprefectures, 139 departments, 57 subprefectures, and 1381 counties.[93] With 3000 books available from the 1902 printing of the *Illustrated Explanations,* each unit could theoretically have been issued at least one copy, though we cannot assume that this actually happened. If the 1903 printing also amounted to 3000 copies, each of the 1920 local units of government or schools within their jurisdictions could have received three. In its many editions, the *Direct Explanation* must surely have been issued in far greater numbers. And, as I have shown, numerous other popular versions of the *Sacred Edict* were published on a local or regional scale. Taken all together, there can be little doubt that— from about 1750 to the close of the dynasty—the guardians of the people were saturated with handbooks for proclaiming the *Sacred Edict* to their charges in comprehensible language. Still, there is very grave doubt that the common people themselves ever acquired these books in significant numbers. I have found no evidence indicating that the vernacular versions of the *Sacred Edict* and the *Amplified Instructions* were read by the common people on their own initiative (if at all, except in a few government-sponsored schools), whether out of duty, for pleasure, or for edification. These texts are popular or vernacular chiefly in their level of literacy. But they are actually pseudovernacular or pseudopopular[94] in terms of their social standing, for their origin did not lie in any segment of the masses, but rather rested squarely with the ruling classes.

Admittedly, large numbers of the populace were exposed to and, in some cases, thoroughly familiarized with the *Sacred Edict* through the village lecture system. Expositions of the *Sacred Edict* were, however, by no means limited to the officially sanctioned semimonthly lectures. In the hands of talented storytellers who operated outside that system, oral renditions of the *Sacred Edict* were a welcome form of entertainment for certain segments of the populace. There is an enormous gulf between the exalted, sententious maxims of the K'ang-hsi emperor and the minds of the peasants and soldiers for whom they were ultimately intended. The transfer of doctrine from the one level to the other was an exceedingly complicated process and involved many different types of people. Most of the individuals involved in this process of transmission were able to perceive, however dimly, the close interconnections among language, ideology, and politics. Their perceptions of these matters determined, to a great extent, the nature of the written popularizations of the *Sacred Edict*.

Notes

1. *The Cantos of Ezra Pound* (New York: New Directions, 1975), canto 98, p. 688. For studies of Pound's extensive knowledge and application of the *Sacred Edict*, see Caroll F. Terrell, "The *Sacred Edict* of K'ANG-HSI," *Paideuma* 2.1:69-112 (Spring 1973); David Gordon, "Thought Built on Sagetrieb," *Paideuma* 3.2:169-190 (Fall 1974); and David Gordon, "Pound's Use of the *Sacred Edict* in Canto 98," *Paideuma*, 4.1:121-168 (Spring 1975). I am grateful to Achilles Fang for this information.
2. Slightly modified from James Legge, "Imperial Confucianism," *The China Review* 6.3: 150a-b (1877).
3. This is not the place to go into such forerunners of popular *oral* education in China as the Han institution of the "Three Elders" (*san-lao*), Six Dynasties and T'ang Buddhist lectures for laymen (*ch'ang-tao* and *su-chiang*), or Sung village association (*hsiang-yüeh*) instructional methods.
4. See *Yuan-shih* 元史 (History of the Yuan) (Kaiming 開明 ed.), *chüan* 22, p. 6184, col. 1, and *Hsin Yuan-shih* 新元史 (New History of the Yuan) (Kaiming ed.), *chüan* 160, p. 6927, col. 2.
5. Lü K'un (1534-1616), an important Ming scholar-official, was noted for his popularizations of classical texts. Cf. Joanna F. Handlin, "Lü K'un's New Audience: The Influence of Women's Literacy on Sixteenth-Century Thought," in *Women in Chinese Society*, ed. Margery Wolf and Roxane Witke (Stanford: Stanford University Press, 1975), pp. 13-38 and 277-283.
6. Most of the information in this paragraph is drawn from Ōta Tatsuo 太田辰夫, *Chūgoku rekidai kōgobun* 中國歷代口語文 (Colloquial Chinese Texts from Successive Dynasties) (Tokyo: Kōnan shoin 江南書院, 1957), pp. 70-71. Wm. Theodore de Bary discusses Hsü Heng's vernacular interpretations of basic Confucian texts in his *Neo-Confucian Orthodoxy and the Learning of the Mind-and-Heart* (New York: Columbia University Press, 1981), pp. 137, 141-144.
7. Ed. Chavannes, "Les saintes instructions de l'empereur Hong-wou (1368-1398); publiées en 1587 et illustrées par Tchong Houa-min," *Bulletin de l'École Française d'Extrême-Orient* 3:549-563 (1903). In 1901-1904, when Berthold Laufer led an expedition to China for the American Museum of Natural History (New York), the original stela was still located in the Confucius Temple at Sian. See entry no. 1066 in

Hartmut Walravens et al., eds., *Catalogue of Chinese Rubbings from Field Museum*, Fieldiana Anthropology, n.s., No. 3 (Chicago: Field Museum of Natural History, November 30, 1981), p. 256 Monika Übelhör, who provided me with the reference to Chavannes's article, has also kindly read and commented on an earlier version of this paper.

8. I have used the text reprinted in Ogaeri Yoshio 魚返善雄, ed., *Kago kanbun Kō-ki kōtei Sei-yu kōkun* 華語漢文康熙皇帝圣諭廣訓 (Classical and Vernacular Versions of the *Amplified Instructions on the Sacred Edict* of the K'ang-hsi Emperor) (Osaka: Yagō shoten 屋號書店, 1943). The edition I have used is available in *Chin-tai Chung-kuo shih-liao ts'ung-k'an hsu-pien* 近代中國史料叢刊續編 (Materials for the Study of Recent Chinese History, Continuation), seventh series, no. 61, pp. 139-205.

9. See his discussion of the sixth maxim.

10. Suerna 素爾納 (18th c.) et al. comp., *Ch'ing-ting hsüeh-cheng ch'üan-shu* 欽定學政全書 (Imperial Commissioned Complete Book of the Directorate of Education) (1774), reprinted in the *Chin-tai Chuang-kuo shih-liao ts'ung-k'an* 近代中國史料叢刊 (Materials for the Study of Recent Chinese History), thirteenth series, no. 293, 74.3a; *Ta Ch'ing hui-tien shih-li* 大清會典事例 (Precedents for the Combined Regulations of the Great Ch'ing Dynasty) (1899 lithograph), 397.3ab, under the year 1679. The *Combination* appeared together with Wei Hsiang-shu's (1617-1687) *Liu-yu chi chieh* (Collected Explanations of the *Hortatory Edict of Six Maxims*) as *Shang-yü ho lü hsiang-yüeh ch'uan-shu* (Complete Book of the Village Lectures on the *Imperial Edict* in Combination with the Laws). The *Combination* was also referred to in various prefaces (dated 1670, 1679) and in a postface (dated 1678) to this edition as a "direct explanation" (*chih-chieh*) or an "annotated explanation" (*chu-chieh*). It was reissued during the year 1693 under the same title in a crudely printed edition of one fascicle without Wei's *Collected Explanations*. In their stead, we find three pieces of moral encouragement (on agriculture, general diligence, and the proper behavior of women) by Wang Tseng-yuan, the county magistrate of Han-tan County in Kuang-p'ing Prefecture of Chihli Province. Wei's *Collected Explanations*, provided with a 1678 postface by the magistrate of Hai-ning County in Hangchow Prefecture, Hsu San-li, is particularly interesting because of the musical notations provided for the songs that end the treatment of each maxim. I have used a copy of the 1679 edition of the *Combination* kept in the library of the Institute of Oriental Culture, University of Tokyo (Tōkyō Daigaku Tōyōbunka Kenkyūjo).

11. *Combination*, 4a.
12. James Legge, trans., in "Imperial Confucianism," *The China Review* 6.6:365b (1878).
13. *Illustrated Explanations*, 2a.
14. The religious dimensions of the village lecture system were present from its inception. In a fascinating article pointed out to me by Evelyn Rawski after I had completed this study, Ōmura Kōdō 大村興道 shows how the aim of the village lectures gradually changed from being one of prompting cooperation among the local people during the Sung to that of propagating the teachings of the emperor during the Ming and Ch'ing. The ritualistic, incantatory aspects of the lectures also became increasingly evident, especially during the Ch'ing. It is significant that, in some early Ch'ing lectures on the *Sacred Edict*, the presence of Buddhist monks and Taoist priests was required. "Mei-matsu Shin-sho no senkō zushiki ni tsuite" 明末清初の宣講図式について (A Study of the Figures of Xüan Jiang at the Turning Point of the Ming and Ch'ing), *Tōkyō gakugei daigaku kiyō* 東京学芸大学紀要 (Bulletin of the Tokyo University of Arts), 2, Jinbun kagaku 人文科学 (Humanistic sciences), 30:193-203 (1979).
15. Kuo-fang yen-chiu-yuan *Ch'ing-shih* pien-tsuan wei-yuan-hui (Editorial Committee for the *Ch'ing History* of the National Defense Research Institute), ed., *Ch'ing-shih* (Ch'ing History) in *Erh-shih-liu shih* (Twenty-six histories) (Taipei: Ch'eng-wen ch'u-pan-she, reprint of 1961 ed.), *chüan* 479, p. 5152a. The compilers of the *Ch'ing History* have drawn heavily on Li's own prefaces in writing his biography; most of the statements made here about the education of the Yao are corroborated in them.
16. All of these are preserved in Li's collected works, which are poorly printed and on bad paper. *Li-shan yuan ch'üan-chi* 禮山園全集, vols. 25-26, 27, and 28 respectively.
17. Maxim 7.
18. *Sheng-yü yen-i san-tzu-ko su-chieh*, 1a. The translation is deliberately crude. Cf. *The Chinese Repository* 1: 244-246 (May 1832-April 1833), where it is incorrectly stated that these songs are taken chiefly from Wang Yu-p'u's paraphrase. This is impossible, since the *Trimetrical Song* was written at least twenty-two years before the *Discussion and Explanation* (see below).
19. Compare the Ming "Ledgers of Merit and Demerit" discussed by Tadao Sakai in his "Confucian and Popular Educational Works," pp. 342-343 of

Self and Society in Ming Thought, ed. Wm. Theodore de Bary (New York: Columbia University Press, 1970), pp. 331-366.
20. Jonathan Spence, "Chang Po-hsing and the K'ang-hsi Emperor," *Ch'ing-shih wen-t'i* 1.8:3-9 (May 1968), esp. 5; quoted in Evelyn Sakakida Rawski, *Education and Popular Literacy in Ch'ing China* (Ann Arbor: University of Michigan Press, 1979), p. 15.
21. *Book of Documents*, "Hsia-shu," 4.3, trans. James Legge, *The Chinese Classics*, vol. 3, pt. 1 (London: Trübner, 1865), p. 164. Fan Hung had also quoted this sentence in his postface to the *Elaboration of the Hortatory Edict of Six Maxims*.
22. My translation follows that of A. Théophile Piry, trans, and annot., *Le Saint Édit: Étude de littérature chinoise* (Shanghai: Bureau des Statistiques, Inspectorat Général des Douanes, 1879), p. 7. William Milne, trans, and annot., *The Sacred Edict, Containing Sixteen Maxims of the Emperor Kang-he, Amplified by His Son, The Emperor Yoong-ching; Together with a Paraphrase on the Whole by a Mandarin* (London: Black, Kingsbury, Parbury, and Allen, 1817; second ed. by American Presbyterian Mission Press, 1870), p. xxii, is mispunctuated.
23. Based on data supplied by a chart in Piry, *Le Saint Édit* and from the classical lists in E. Bruce Brooks and A. Taeko Brooks, *Chinese Character Frequency Lists* (Northampton, Mass.: SinFac Minor, 1976), pp. 6-7.
24. "Translations are available in Russian and in Italian. A. Agafonov, trans., *Manzhurskago i Kitaiskago Khana Kan'siya Kniga* ... (St. Petersburg, 1788; reissued in 1795 with a different title) and Lodovico Nocentini, trans, and annot., *Il santo editto di K'añ-hi, e l'amplificazione di Yuñ-ceñ*, 2 vols. in one (Florence: Successori Le Monnier, 1880-1883). For various editions of the Manchu text, see Wang Yun-wu 王雲五, ed., *Hsu-hsiu ssu-k'u ch'üan-shu t'i-yao* 續修四庫全書提要 (Continuation of Abstracts of the Complete Collection of Books in Four Categories) (Taipei: Taiwan Commercial Press 臺灣商務印書館, 1971), vol. 10, pp. 1048, 1050-1052, including one work that significantly dealt exclusively with the seventh maxim (against heterodoxy).
25. Ogaeri, *Kago* (cited n. 8), p. 6.
26. Wang Yu-p'u's autobiography (the *Chieh-shan tzu-ting nien-p'u* 介山自定年譜), in one fascicle, is available both in his collected works (the *Shih-li t'ang ch'üan-chi* 詩禮堂全集, also called *Wang Chieh-shan hsien-sheng ch'üan-chi* 王介山先生全集, published in 1751) and in a Republican period reprint series published by Chin Yueh 金鉞 (*Ping-lu ts'ung-k'e* 屏廬叢刻, 1924). The same is true of his *Shih-li t'ang tsa-tsuan* 詩

禮堂雜纂 (Compilation of Miscellaneous Materials), in two fascicles, which has been useful in determining Wang's own views on a number of matters touched upon in his famous paraphrase of the *Sacred Edict.* Chin Yueh's interest in Wang Yu-p'u was due largely to the fact that he, too, was a native of Tientsin. The *Ping-lu ts'ung-k'e* consists of materials that had been brought together by the bureau charged with the compilation of the Tientsin gazetteer.

27. *Autobiography,* preface, 1 a.
28. Shen Chia-pen 沈家本 and Hsu Tsung-liang 徐宗亮, comp., *T'ien-chin fu-chih* 天津府志 (Taipei: T'ai-wan hsueh-sheng shu-chü, 1968 rpt. of 1899 ed.), 43.14b (p. 3840).
29. *Ch'ing shih lieh-chuan* 清史列傳 (Biographies from the Ch'ing History) (Taipei: Chung-hua shu-chü 中華書局, 1962), 68.25b.
30. Wang Yu-p'u was by no means the only person to write a "direct explanation" of the *Amplified Instructions.* One Lü Shou-tseng also wrote a work entitled *Sheng-yü kuang-hsün chih-chieh* (Direct Explanation of the *Amplified Instructions of the Sacred Edict*) in one fascicle. This is mentioned in Liu Chin-tsao 劉錦藻, comp., *Ch'ing-ch'ao hsu Wen-hsien t'ung-k'ao* 清朝續文獻通考 (Continuation of the Comprehensive Examination of Documents relating to the Ch'ing Dynasty) (Commercial Press, Wan-yu wen-k'u ed.), 269.10129b.
31. Ogaeri, *Kago* (cited n. 8), postface, p. 3.
32. Outside of the *Collected Works,* the oldest extant copy of the *Elaboration* known to me is that consisting of four volumes printed in Canton (after 1808) from crudely cut blocks. It is available in the typeset edition of Ogaeri, *Kago,* pp. 1-101. I have also used a rare copy of this text, in one volume, that is kept in the University of Pennsylvania Van Pelt Library. There are a few small differences between the Canton text of the *Elaboration* and that appearing in Wang's *Collected Works* (vols. 37-38). One of the most noticeable is the consistent use of "His Majesty" (*wan-sui-yeh*) to refer to the Yung-cheng emperor in the former as opposed to "Epochal Progenitor" (*Shih-tsung huang-ti*) in the latter. The *Elaboration* continued to be reprinted as late as 1876, when it was recut at the request of the Censor of Yunnan Circuit, Wu Hung-en. In his postface, Wu states that he used a "presentation copy" of the Ying-chou (in Anhwei) Prefectural Director of Schools, Hsia Hsing, as the basis for his reprinting.
33. F. W. Baller, *The Sacred Edict with a Translation of the Colloquial Rendering* (Shanghai: American Presbyterian Mission Press, 1892; later editions published in Shanghai by the China Inland Mission and issued

in London, Philadelphia, Toronto, and Melbourne by the Religious Tract Society of London). The citations in this study are to the sixth edition (1924). Baller also published a lengthy study aid entitled *A Vocabulary of the Colloquial Rendering of the Sacred Edict* (Shanghai: American Mission Press, 1892). It is somewhat unfortunate that Baller chose the *Direct Explanation*, which was usually issued in two volumes, as the basis for his English translation. The choice was unfortunate, as we shall see below, because the *Direct Explanation* was a slightly classicized adaptation of the *Elaboration*, which was written in unadulterated colloquial. Milne (cf. note 22), working in Malacca toward the end of 1815, did follow the *Elaboration* in his English translation of Wang Yu-p'u's paraphrase. Since Baller's rendition of the *Direct Explanation* is commonly known and widely available in this country, however, it will be convenient to refer to it in many cases instead of to the *Elaboration*. Furthermore, Baller provides the Chinese text of both the *Amplified Instructions* and the *Direct Explanation* whereas Milne's translation, itself rare and difficult to obtain, includes neither. I have also examined three Chinese editions of the *Direct Explanation*. The first is a rare edition from the Yung-cheng period printed by movable wooden type. The second is a block print of 1850 and the third a reprinting of 1865 with an added preface dated 1876. Many other editions of the *Direct Explanation* were published. Legge, "Imperial Confucianism" (cited n. 2), p. 149a, states that the *Direct Explanation* was sold everywhere in China. One edition was printed entirely in vermilion ink by the archivist of Soochow Prefecture sometime during the Kuang-hsu reign period (1875-1908). See Ogaeri, *Kago*, plate 6.

34. R. F. Johnston, *Lion and Dragon in Northern China* (New York: E. P. Dutton, 1910), p. 123. It is possible that Johnston knew of the *Direct Explanation* apart from Baller's rendering because one passage he quotes from it (about fellow-villagers quarrelling) is in his own distinctive translation (cf. Baller, *Sacred Edict*, p. 31).

35. Ogaeri, *Kago*, p. 82; Baller, *Sacred Edict*, p. 149.

36. Baller, *Sacred Edict*, p. 151; Ogaeri, *Kago*, p. 83.

37. Baller, *Sacred Edict*, p. 193; Ogaeri, *Kago*, p. 33; Baller, *Sacred Edict*, p. 65.

38. Ogaeri, *Kago*, p. 82; Baller, *Sacred Edict*, p. 149. Current usage would prefer *Chei-ke ch'ien-liang shih tsui yao-chin-te*.

39. See, for example, Baller, *Sacred Edict*, pp. 85, 93, 95, 137, 153, 177, and *passim*.

40. Baller, *Sacred Edict*, p. 38, cf. p. 48; Ogaeri, *Kago*, p. 17.

41. William Milne, "Bibliotheca Sinica," *The Chinese Repository* 16:504 (1847). For sample translations of the *Amplified Instructions* into various dialects, see S. Wells Williams, *A Syllabic Dictionary of the Chinese Language,* rev. ed. (Tung Chou: North China Union College, 1909), pp. xlii-xlvii.
42. Hsu Tung 徐棟, comp., *Mu-ling shu chi-yao* 牧令書輯要 (Compilation of Essential Documents Relating to the Shepherds of the People), ed. Ting Jih-ch'ang 丁日昌 (Kiangsu shu-chü 江蘇書局, 1868 rev. and printed, preface 1838), 6.18a. Cf. Kung-chuan Hsiao, *Rural China: Imperial Control in the Nineteenth Century* (Seattle: University of Washington Press, 1960, second printing, 1967), p.619, n. 51.
43. Baller, *Sacred Edict,* p. 83; Ogaeri, *Kago,* p. 41.
44. Translations of this and the preceding quotation (with slight alteration) are by Milne, *Sacred Edict,* pp. xxvii-xxviii.
45. Ogaeri, *Kago,* p. 100; cf. Milne, *Sacred Edict,* p. xxv.
46. *Elaboration* (cited n. 32 above), italics mine.
47. Ogaeri, *Kago,* p. 100
48. I have used a rare copy preserved in the Gest Library of Princeton University. It is bound together with a standard edition of the *Amplified Instructions* published by Chu Hsun (from Kiangsu), the Governor of Shensi, a post he assumed in 1813. The two texts retain their separate paginations, 1a-54a for the *Amplified Instructions* and 1a-93b plus 1a-2b (postface) for the *Glosses.* On the cover is a seal indicating that the bound volumes were once owned by a Wang I-ch'ang 王義昌.
49. Ogaeri, *Kago,* p. 43; Baller, *Sacred Edict,* p. 84.
50. *Glosses,* p. 36a.
51. E.g., pp. 5B-6a, 36b-37a; cf. Ogaeri, *Kago,* pp. 6-7, 42-43, and Baller, *Sacred Edict,* pp. 16-17, 85-86.
52. See, for example, p. 39a, and contrast Ogaeri, *Kago,* p. 45 and Baller, *Sacred Edict,* p. 88.
53. See pp. 6b, 33a, 34a, 34b; cf. Ogaeri, *Kago,* pp. 7, 37, 38, 39, and Baller, *Sacred Edict,* pp. 18, 74, 76, 78.
54. Based on a passage in the *Book of Change* 易經. See *Shih-san ching chu-shu* 十三經注疏 (Taipei: I-wen yin-shu kuan 藝文印書館, 1965 reprint of 1815 [1896] ed.), 3.7a (p. 59a).
55. *Glosses,* 2ab.
56. The four classes are scholars, farmers, artisans, and merchants; the six classes are these four plus monks and priests. The single doctrine is, of

course, Confucianism; the three doctrines are Confucianism, Buddhism, and Taoism.
57. Representing Hedonism, Universal Love, Buddhism, and Taoism, respectively.
58. This is based on *Mencius*, 1.7. Cf. James Legge, *The Chinese Classics*, vol. 2 (London: Trübner, 1861), p. 24: "In such circumstances they only try to save themselves from death, and are afraid they will not succeed. What leisure have they to cultivate righteousness?"
59. Ogaeri, *Kago*, p. 15 of postface, mentions a one-volume edition of the *Direct Explanation* that was labeled on the outside simply as *Sheng-yü kuang-hsun* (Amplified Instructions on the *Sacred Edict*). On the title page, it carried the additional annotation, "with appended citations from the legal code."
60. Sawada Mizuho 澤田瑞穗, ed. and annot., *Kōchū Haja shōben* 校注破邪詳辯 (A Detailed Disputation against Heterodoxy, with Collocations and Commentaries) (Tokyo: Dōkyō kankō-kai 道教刊行會, 1972), p. 8 and preface, p. 7. I am indebted to Professor C. K. Wang of National Taiwan University for this reference and for the citation in note 88.
61. William Milne, "Bibliotheca Sinica," *The Chinese Repository* 16:502 (1847).
62. Computed from figures available in *The Chinese Repository* 16:56, 297, 318 (1847), and Osmond Tiffany, Jr., *The Canton Chinese: or, The American's Sojourn in the Celestial Empire* (Boston: J. Munroe, 1849), p. 222.
63. In some localities, respected members of the gentry were called upon to help in expounding the *Sacred Edict*. See Chung-li Chang, *The Chinese Gentry: Studies on Their Role in Nineteenth-Century Chinese Society* (Seattle: University of Washington Press, 1955), pp. 15, 65.
64. Shih Chih-mo must be the brother or cousin of Shih Chih-kao 史致誥 (d. 1854), also of Yanghu in Kiangsu. For the latter, see Ch'en Nai-ch'ien 陳乃乾, comp., *Ch'ing-tai pei-chuan wen t'ung-chien* 清代碑傳文通檢 (Finding-List for Texts of Stele Biographies) (Peking: Chung-hua shu-chü 中華書局, 1959), p. 36.
65. *Collected Verifications*, 1.18b.
66. Suerna, *Complete Book* (cited n. 10), 74.1a.
67. *Ibid.*, 74.iab.
68. The *Six Maxims* continued to play an important role in the village lectures alongside the *Sacred Edict* during the first half of the Ch'ing.
69. *Rural China*, p. 185. Hsiao devotes an entire chapter, which he entitles "Ideological Control: The *Hsiang-yüeh* and Other Institutions" (pp. 184-258), to this subject. T'ung-tsu Ch'ü also considers the lectures on

the *Sacred Edict* to be a form of indoctrination. See his *Local Government in China under the Ch'ing* (Cambridge, Mass.: Harvard University Press, 1962), p. 162.
70. *Autocracy at Work: A Study of the Yung-cheng Period, 1723-1735* (Bloomington: Indiana University Press, 1974), p. 188. Cf. John R. Watt, "The Yamen and Urban Administration," in G. William Skinner, ed., *The City in Late Imperial China* (Stanford: Stanford University Press, 1977), pp.353-390, esp. pp. 361-362.
71. *The Chinese Gentry*, p. 65. Perhaps the most extensive treatment of the *Sacred Edict* in English is to be found in Leon E. Stover, *The Cultural Ecology of Chinese Civilization: Peasants and Elites in the Last of the Agrarian States* (New York: Mentor, 1974). Stover has structured much of his discussion around the *Sacred Edict* in a way that is pertinent to many of the papers in this book.
72. Suerna, *Complete Book*, 74.4a.
73. See *ibid.*, 74. 10b-11a for the need to translate the *Amplified Instructions* and parts of the Ch'ing legal code into aboriginal languages. It was recommended that interpreters accompany officials into the aboriginal settlements expressly for this purpose.
74. *Ibid.*, 73.4ab.
75. *Ibid.*, 734b-5a.
76. *Ibid.*, 74.5a-6a.
77. Hsiao, *Rural China*, p. 190.
78. *Ibid.*, p. 186.
79. Suerna, *Complete Book*, 74.11 ab.
80. Hsiao, *Rural China*, p. 188.
81. Adapted from Milne, trans., *The Sacred Edict*, pp. ix-xi, who has based his account on a local gazetteer from Kwangtung province. Most other gazetteers include a similar description. For one such elaborate account, see Sun Hao 孫灝, et al., *Honan t'ung-chih* 河南通志 (General Gazetteer of Honan) (1882), 10.4a. Huang Liu-hung 黃六鴻 has provided a wealth of detail on the prescribed method for reading and expounding the *Sacred Edict* in his 1699 *Fu-hui ch'uan-shu* 福惠全書, tr. By Djang Chu as *A Complete Book Concerning Happiness and Benevolence: A Manual for Local Magistrates in Seventeenth-Century China* (Tucson: University of Arizona Press, 1984), pp. 530-35.
82. *The Chinese Repository* 17:586-588 (1848).
83. Review of Milne, trans., *The Sacred Edict*, in *The Chinese Repository* 1:299-300 (1832).

84. S. Wells Williams, *The Middle Kingdom: A Survey of the Geography, Government, Education, Social Life, Arts, Religion, &c., of the Chinese Empire and its Inhabitants* (New York: John Wiley, 1859, 4th ed.; 1st ed., 1848), vol. 1, p. 554, and Thomas Francis Wade, *Hsin ching lu* (Hong Kong, 1859), p.47.
85. *The Chinese Repository* 5:47 (1837).
86. Literally, "to intone according to a text" (*chao pen hsuan-k'o* 照本宣科). The phrase *chao pen* implies that these lecturers ultimately based their oral renditions of stories on written texts. Whether or not they actually referred to a book during performance is problematic, though it would have been effective as a prop in any case and would have lent an air of authority to the proceedings. *Gwoyeu tsyrdean* 國語辭典 (Dictionary of the National Language) clearly defines the expression *hsuan-k'o* (q.v.) as the chanting or intoning of priests or scholars. This and other aspects of Kuo's characterization suggests that the *Sacred Edict* storytellers he heard as a boy were wont to assume the persona of Confucian officiants.
87. *Shao-nien shih-tai* 少年時代 (The Time of My Youth), in *Mo-jo wen-chi* 沫若文集 (Collected Works of Kuo Mo-jo), vol. 6 (Shanghai: Hsin wen-i ch'u-pan-she 新文藝出版社, 1955; originally published in 1947 by Hai-yen shu-tien 海燕書店 of Shanghai), pp. 29-30. I am grateful to Milena Doleželová-Velingerová for bringing this passage to my attention; cf. her article, "Kuo Mo-jo's Autobiographical Works," in *Studies in Modern Chinese Literature*, ed. Jaroslav Průšek (Berlin: Akademie Verlag, 1964), pp. 45-75, esp. pp. 52-53. David Johnson went out of his way to send me a copy of the original Chinese text and kindly pointed out a number of interesting features about it.
88. "The K'uen Shi Wan or, the Practical Theology of the Chinese," *The China Review* 11.2: 94-95 (1882).
89. It cannot be denied, however, that the government actively and repeatedly encouraged frequent explanation of the *Sacred Edict*. This is evident from numerous edicts preserved in *Precedents for the Combined Regulations of the Great Ch'ing Dynasty*, fascicles 397 and 398. Note particularly the exhortations to use local dialects and homely proverbs (398.9a, in 1746; 398.9b, in 1758).
90. Legge, "Imperial Confucianism," p. 148a. The same spirit was exhibited by the famous general Tso Tsung-t'ang when he was sent in 1868 to control Islamic unrest in Chinese Turkestan. Tso firmly believed that distribution of a Uighur version of paraphrases on the *Sacred Edict* would help to restore order. See Chu Wen-djang, *The Moslem Rebellion in North-*

east China, 1862-1878: A Study of Government Minority Policy, Central Asiatic Studies, V (The Hague: Mouton, 1966). Albert von le Coq obtained several copies of this book during his early twentieth-century archeological expeditions in the area. One of these is edited and translated by him as "Das Lī-Kitābī," *Körösi Csoma-Archivum*, 1:439-480 (1921-1925). A Russian translation of *Lī-Kitābī* was made by Nikolai Fedorovich Katanov and published in Saint Petersburg in 1902. Wolfram Eberhard also saw a copy at the Türkiyat Enstitüsü in Istanbul. His observations on the text may be found in "Bemerkungen zum 'Li Kitabi,'" on pp. 123-127 of his *China und seine westlichen Nachbarn: Beiträge zur mittelalterlichen und neueren Geschichte Zentralasiens* (Darmstadt: Wissenschaftliche Buchgesellschaft, 1978).
91. Herbert A. Giles, *Confucianism and Its Rivals*, The Hibbert Lectures, second series (London: Williams and Norgate, 1915), p. 254.
92. Wen K'ang 文康, *Erh-nü ying-hsiung chuan* 兒女英雄傳 (The Gallant Maid) (Shanghai: Ya-tung t'u-shu-kuan 亞東圖書館, 1932, fourth ed.), chap. 18, p. 29. Widespread familiarity with the *Sacred Edict* is also evidenced by the fact that many of the early attempts to create an alphabet for Chinese used it as a sample text. For examples, see the reproductions on the outside back covers of *Shin Tarng*, 2 (January 1983), *Shin Tarng*, 3 (April 1983), and *Xin Talng* 4 (November 1984).
93. H. S. Brunnert and V. V. Hagelstrom, *Present Day Political Organization of China*, rev. by N. Th. Kolessoff, trans. from the Russian by A. Beltchenko and E. E. Moran (Shanghai: Kelly and Walsh, 1912; reprinted. Taipei: Ch'eng Wen, 1971), p. 426. For earlier periods, when the numbers were slightly smaller, see T'ung-tsu Ch'ü, *Local Government in China under the Ch'ing*, p. 2.
94. Cf. Charles J. Wivell, "The Chinese Oral and Pseudo-oral Narrative Traditions," *Transactions of the International Conference of Orientalists in Japan* 16:53-65 (1971).

CHAPTER 3

CHIANG-CHING WEN

ORAL AND WRITTEN ASPECTS OF CHINESE SŪTRA LECTURES

Source: Adapted from "Oral and Written Aspects of Chinese Sūtra Lectures (*chiang-ching-wen*)," *Han-hsueh yen-chiu* 4.2 (1986): 311-34.

Among the tens of thousands of manuscripts that were discovered at Tun-huang (in Kansu province, far northwest China) around the turn of the century was a small group of stories that have come to be known as *pien-wen* 變文 ("transformation texts"). Written in an early vernacular language, they are of the utmost importance for the study of the development of popular literature in China. But because they had been buried away for almost a thousand years, many difficult problems surround them. After nearly a century of scholarly endeavor, there is still no consensus on such basic matters as the meaning of the term *pien-wen*, the extent of the corpus, and the relationship of *pien-wen* to other genres of popular literature discovered among the Tun-huang manuscripts.[1]

One of the major problems with the hazy nomenclature applied to Tun-huang popular literature in the past has been the blurring of distinction between transformation texts and sūtra lectures (*chiang-ching-wen*). A direct instance of the confusion that can result is manifest in this type of frequently encountered statement: "In the structure of *pien-wen*, there is a peculiar phenomenon which is the frequent use of a short passage from a sūtra and, after that, an elaboration based on this sūtra passage."[2] It is obvious that the reference is to *chiang-ching-wen*, not *pien-wen*. Kenneth Ch'en twice[3] refers to a "*Vimalakīrti pien-wen*" when he should have called it a Vimalakīrti *chiang-ching-wen*. That Ch'en's error was not an accident but a symptom of the general obfuscation surrounding Tun-huang literature studies is apparent from his assertion that "the modified versions of the sūtras preached in these popular lectures were designated *pien-wen*."[4] Lai Ming's statement that "the development of Chinese fiction can be traced from the popularized versions of Buddhist sūtras, which was what *pien-wen* was,"[5] while displaying a degree of perceptiveness in seeing the influence of Buddhism on Chinese fiction, is guilty of the same imprecision. Irwin falls into the identical trap when he speaks of "the early vernacular interpretations of Buddhist scriptures (i. e., sūtras), known as *pien-wen*."[6] Even more mystifying is Chou I-liang's contention[7] that *pien-wen* were somehow derived from *chiang-ching-wen*. According to Fujino Iwatomo, there are over forty *pien-wen*.[8] This figure implies that he includes under the genre both genuine *pien-wen* (approximately twenty manuscripts are known to exist) and *chiang-ching-wen* (about the same number of manuscripts are extant). Indeed, he does refer to the Vimalakīrti sūtra lecture as a *pien-wen*. Because *pien-wen* are still almost universally lumped together with *chiang-ching-wen*, it is necessary to sharpen our understanding of the latter genre.

A fascinating and vivid fictionalized account of a sūtra lecture given by the renowned monk, Tao-an 道安 (d. circa 387 at age 72), before an enormous crowd with surprising consequences is embedded in *A Tale about Hui-yüan of Lu Mountain* (*Lu-shan Yüan-kung hua* 廬山遠公話).[9] Study of this account and comparison with the literary references to transformation performances that I give in chapter six of *T'ang transformation Texts* are helpful in revealing the different purposes and forms of the two genres.

Just as it is possible to identify genuine transformation texts by the occurrence of the standard verse introductory formula, "this is the place where X [happens], how does it go?" (X ch'u jo-wei ch'en-shuo X 處若為陳說, or variations thereof),[10] it is possible to distinguish sūtra lecture texts by the presence of the quotative formula ch'ang chiang-lai 唱將來 (or variations thereof). The meaning of this formula, in most cases, is "Please begin singing," addressed to the assistant or cantor (tu-chiang 都講), assuming that one is present. In early Chinese colloquial, chiang-lai usually functions as a quasi-inchoative grammatical verb ending, hence "verb x chiang-lai" stands for "begin/start/initiate x-ing."[11] But it is apparent from the variations (ch'ang-ch'ang lo 唱唱羅, ch'ang chiang-lo 唱將羅, ch'ang chiang-lo-lo 唱將羅羅, etc.) of this quotative formula in the single lecture on the Vajra[-cchedika] -prajñāparamitā-sūtra (Pelliot [hereafter P] manuscript 2133v) that it also sometimes functions as a gentle imperative or optative: "Let us sing" or "[Won't you] please sing." Also note ch'ang k'an-k'an 唱看看 (T502.7)[12] and ch'ang chiang-lai 唱將來 (T504. 6,505.12, etc. in the lecture on the Saddharmapuṇḍarīka-sūtra (P2133); and note especially ch'ing wei ch'ang chiang-lai 請為唱將來 (T574.1) in one of the lectures on the Vimalakīrti-sūtra (S3872) and ch'ing ch'ang chiang-lai 請唱將來 (T547.12) in another (S4571) where the invitation is made explicit by the addition of the word ch'ing ("please").[13] Another point of interest is that the word ch'ang 唱 also clearly is used in these texts as a adjunct meaning "unit to be sung" (e.g., T436.7, 437.5 and 13, 441.3 and 10, 443.2, 497.14, 499.10, 637.12, 672.3ff, etc.). The function of the quotative formula is to introduce a short passage of scripture. After that is done, the lecture then proceeds to elaborate, sometimes at very great length, upon the quoted passage. This function is obviously very different from that of the pien-wen verse introductory formula which refers to a place (ch'u 處) on a picture.

The only text from Tun-huang known to me that actually has in its title the generic designation chiang-ching-wen is the "Sūtra Lecture Text for the Festival of Welcoming the Sage[14] to the Hall of Restoration in the Year 933 (Ch'ang-hsing ssu-nien Chung-hsing tien ying-sheng chieh *chiang-ching-wen* 長興四年中興殿應聖節講經文, P3808)". It is ironic that this particular text is atypical of the overwhelming majority of sūtra lectures. Only twice in the introduction does the standard formula *ch'ang chiang-lai* 唱將來 occur. The division of the sūtra[15] into sections for discussion is also more perfunctory than in the typical sūtra lecture. After the introduction and a brief exposition of the sūtra, the remainder of the text is given over to poems of praise for the reigning emperor.[16] This latter, in fact, seems to be the main business of the text as we now have it.

Among the Tun-huang manuscripts recently published in Taiwan in the highly commendable form of large, photographic reproductions is one identified by the editors as "*Mu-lien chiu-mu pien-wen (Pien-wen on Maudgalyāyana Rescuing His Mother)" 目連救母變文.[17] Pan Chung-kwei also hazards that it may be a *pien-wen*.[18] This is an extremely important document but it is, unfortunately, not a *pien-wen*. There can be no doubt that this is a sūtra lecture (*chiang-chiang-wen*) since it includes the formula by which such texts may be identified, i.e., "Please begin singing" (*ch'ang chiang-lai*),[19] and is divided into sections according to the portion of the sūtra being explicated. Regardless of its genre, however, Taiwan 32 is one of the most significant Tun-huang manuscripts yet published for it was almost certainly used as the text of an actual sermon or is the record of one. The sense of immediacy it affords the student of T'ang Buddhism is utterly captivating. I know of no other preserved Tun-huang manuscript comparable to it in this respect. The manuscript is quite sloppy and bears numerous corrections and notes. In some places, it even gives the distinct impression that last minute changes were made, as would be natural with the text of a lecture or sermon. Although this manuscript therefore deserves far more complete and careful attention than I am here able to afford it, as an indication of the nature and purpose of a prototypical sūtral lecture, it is worthwhile to examine it in some detail. I have also chosen to discuss this particular sūtra lecture because it has not previously been studied in depth and because of certain essential characteristics it embodies that have broad implications for the theoretical study of folk and popular literature.

The lecturer seems to begin with an introductory exploration of the meaning of the title. Since part of the opening is missing, it is not clear precisely how he goes about this. It is evident, nonetheless, that a platitudinous preview of the subject of the upcoming lecture (viz. the Buddhist saint, Maudgalyāyana's filial devotion and the Buddha's encouragement of such conduct through the founding of the feast for hungry ghosts) occupies a prominent place. It also seems evident that the lecturer is not inclined to embark upon a philological excursus as the more sophisticated sūtra lecturers are.[20] At the close of the introduction, he refers to the sūtra in question as the *Yü-lan ch'ing-ching ching* (Sūtra of Purity and Cleanliness[21] for the Relief of Spirits in Purgatory) 孟蘭清淨經[22] and, in the title given at the end of the work, as the *Yü-lan p'en ching* (Sūtra of the Sacrificial Feast for the Relief of Spirits in Purgatory) 孟蘭盆經.[23] Thus it appears that the putative basis of this lecture was the well-known apocryphal sūtra of the latter name supposedly translated by Dharmarakṣa (active 266-317).

The succeeding piece on the scroll is a "Hymn of the *Abhidharmakośa-śāstra*" (*A-p'ita-mo-chü-she lun sung* 阿毗達摩俱舍論頌),[24] not mentioned by the editors. The impression one gains from the juxtaposition on the same scroll of two such works obviously intended for use in religious services is that the manuscript was prepared for and preserved by a preacher or sermonizer as a handbook or manual.

After the introductory explanation of the meaning of the title, the lecturer declares: "[I] shall explain this sūtra in three major sections" 將釋此經大分三段.[25] He then goes on to state how he will proceed: "I will briefly tell you, my disciples, one item at a time;/ Below, following the sūtra, I lay it out step by step." 略與門徒分別說/向下依經次第（二第）陳.[26] This indicates that the text had a direct relationship to an actual oral setting. Further indication of the high degree of orality of this sūtra lecture occurs repeatedly throughout it.

Not only did he do this, in the first instance, for Maudgalyāyana, He did it also for those of you who are this morning below my pulpit.
不獨當初為目[?] 運/兼為今朝座下人.²⁷
Among these, the three kinds of enlightenment²⁸ are beyond conception; On another day, I will broadly distinguish them for you my disciples. Today, for the moment, I briefly elucidate the subtle dharma.
扵（於）中三覺不思議；別日與門徒 庻（廣）分別/今且略明 役 (=微) 妙法.²⁹
Each of you reverently join his hands, as I ask the cantor to sing of Maudgalyāyana's attainment of the way.
各各 度（虔）恭合掌着/目蓮得道唱將來。

The lecturer (or, perhaps more precisely, recorder of the lecture) skips about wildly. He cannot manage consistently to produce heptasyllabic lines in the verse portions even though he clearly intends from the format (by arbitrary divisions of each column into two sections) to do so. Nor is he capable of providing a sequence of legitimate rhymes. Furthermore, he commits innumerable *non-sequiturs* and hopes to patch up the situation by belatedly adding a verse now and then or by drawing lines to rearrange the sequence. He makes notes to himself to delete words or joins a tiny radical to an already written character. Since many of the revisions are in a second hand, the conclusion that the lecturer or a second auditor is reviewing the recorder's work seems almost inevitable. Yet, in spite of the revisions, the lecture remains, at times, totally incoherent. Whenever the train of thought of the lecture breaks down altogether, the lecturer (or recorder) conveniently resorts to the addition of a "Son of Buddha" 仏學.³⁰ Sometimes he does this with conviction (e.g., p. 273b5 and 10), sometimes timidly, almost as though it was an afterthought, not even managing to add the 子.³¹ It reminds one of a country preacher punctuating his sermon with "Amen," "Praise the Lord," or "Hallelujah" and being answered in chorus by the congregation. To impress his audience, he gratuitously displays his knowledge of the

Chiang-Ching Wen

most basic Sanskrit ("In the Brahmanic language of the western parts, his name is the Buddha" 西方梵語名佛陁). He resorts to platitudes which surely must have stirred the hearts of his listeners to their very depths:

> It is just like the person of a mother in the world,
> If she can raise up a real son and he attains an official position,
> When his authority over people is such that everyone fears him,
> And he volunteers to share the worries of the Emperor
>   by supporting the Great T'ang Dynasty;
> But suddenly he remembers his (literally "my") father and mother,
> And hastens home to wait upon them attentively
> With the ~~money~~ [sic] wealth he has gained, he buys ~~nice things~~ [sic] gems,
> And takes them to present to his ~~kind~~ [sic] respected parents ....
> 恰似世間慈母身
> 養得子時登官位
> 䢤 (威)勢人間皆惣怕
> 自出分憂佐大唐
> 忽然憶着我 耶 (=爺)孃
> 取向本州專(replaces an illegible character)侍奉
> 所得XX財物買XX珠瑱
> 將來奉獻我X尊親³²

This, then, is the constant theme of the lecture-filial piety. To ensure that the members of his flock abide by its dictates, he urges them:

> I exhort you, my disciples, to bestir a faithful heart,
> Not to be lascivious and unfilial.
> 奉勸門徒 㧻 (發) 信心
> 莫作好斯（→ 色）不孝順.³³

He orders them:

> You must surely be filial and not flippant to your parents!
> 大須孝順 莫因循 [=循] 阿耶孃.³⁴

And he threatens them:

> If you do not repay their kindness, you are unfilial,
> And will fall onto the evil paths of the three mires.³⁵
> 不報其恩不孝順
> 墮向三塗惡道中³⁶

And, just in case all of this is insufficient, after having completed a recitation of ten types of parental kindness that it is hard for a child to repay, he invites his flock:

> If you, my disciples, want a detailed explanation,
> First be highly reverent, then act accordingly.
> You below my pulpit³⁷ must(?) be expectant and fervent.³⁸
> 門徒 若（若）要細分別
> 先生 敨（敬？）重後依行
> 坐（→座？）下 䓬 (illegible 須？) 生渴印（→仰）心³⁹

In short, Taiwan 32 is an atrociously written sermon, but one which should strike a warm (or, in some cases, hot) spot in the memory of anyone who grew up in a small town and went to church there. This sūtra lecture bespeaks, at every turn, on-the-spot interaction between a minister and his flock. Thus it would appear possible that at least some sūtra lecturers in the T'ang period employed lecture notes, just as many modern ministers do, but there is no clear evidence that tellers of transformations (*pien*) resorted to promptbooks any more than do storytellers today.

Another valuable manuscript of a sūtra lecture is S6551 which deals with the *Amitābha-vyūha-sūtra*. From a reference to the Holy, Divine Khan of the Great Uighur Kingdom⁴⁰ and other details in the text, we know that it was written by a monk who was living in Khotan⁴¹ when it was under the control of the Uighurs,⁴² i.e., ninth century or later. The first two-thirds of the manuscript in its present condition is an engagingly forthright sermon in a very conversational tone. The opening part accurately conveys the quality of the whole lecture:

Having ascended the platform, first recite a gāthā,[43] burn incense,
and invoke the names of the various Buddhas and Bodhisattvas.
Ever since the World-Honored One of Great Enlightenment
    founded the Buddhist school,[44]
By explaining its religious doctrine at the Deer Park and on the
    Spirit Vulture Peak,[45]
The Five Classes and Three Vehicles[46] are kept on all the
    oceans' shores,
Having been transmitted throughout the world, everyone receives
    their benefit.
Monks, nuns, and the four orders[47] have come into
    the monasteries,[48]
Like rushing clouds, carrying flowers and holding parasols;
Since today you can rid yourselves of the torments of the world,[49]
Be quiet for a moment and listen to the text of the sūtra.
The holy teachings of the Three Vehicles are surely
    worth hearing,
Every word can be taught for they lighten the burden of *karma*;[50]
Not only in the future will you attain the Buddha-fruit,[51]
For eon upon eon the mountains of your sins will surely crumble.
But day after day, all you fret about are your family affairs,
When have you ever, even for a day, listened to the sūtras?
Would everyone present[52] join your palms for a moment,
And listen to the Law with one heart, can you?[53]

The lecturer then proceeds to give a brief biographical account of himself in which he describes how he became a teacher, his travels in China, pilgrimages he has made and planned, and why he stopped at the place where he is lecturing on account of illness. He utters paens of praise for the Uighur Khanate and exhorts all and sundry to support it. Then he gives fearsome account of the perilous conditions most men live in and the need for immediate repentance.

"Oh, you my disciples! Since you have come to this worship service today, you must greatly exert yourselves, joining your palms with one heart."[54] With this encouragement, the lecturer then shrives the members of the congregation of their sins. Once the filth is washed away, he says, they will have pure hearts and, in future rebirths, can be reborn in the Pure Land, there to see Amitābha Buddha. "Do you want to?" he asks them. "Can you? Excellent! Excellent!"[55] He assures his congregation that, if only they will be repentant, they will all achieve Buddhahood. On the other hand, he knows that so and so among those present from time immemorial have been doing bad things such as committing adultery, harming insects, and being discourteous to monks and nuns. But he allows, "if this day, if this hour, facing the Buddhas of the ten directions, facing the Boddhisattvas of the ten directions, facing the sūtras of the Three Vehicles, facing the monks of the ten directions, facing all those present, you dare no longer conceal [your misdeeds] and determine to be repentant, I hope that your sins will be annihilated. Say thrice."[56]

Having finished with the repentance, the preacher moves on to instruct in the precepts, that is the Three Refuges and the Five Commandments.[57]

> You must accept the Three Refuges in order to avoid sinking into evil ways. By taking refuge in the Buddha, you avoid falling into hell; by taking refuge in the dharma, you avoid becoming a ghost; by taking refuge in the saṅgha, you avoid being reborn as a beast. Oh, my disciples, accept these three refuges. Can you? Do you want to?—Invoke the name of the Buddha. *Buddha-putra.*[58]

After calling out several times words which mean approximately the same thing as "Hallelujah," the preacher then asks (and answers) a remarkable question that is most revealing of the problems Buddhist evangelists faced in Central Asia and, to a lesser degree, in China:

> Oh, my disciples, when I say "take refuge in the Buddha," which Buddha should you take refuge in? Neither is it the Manichaean Buddha, nor is it the Persian Buddha, it is also not the Zorastrian Buddha. Rather, it is the clear, essential Buddhahood,[59] the

perfect body of reward,[60] the myriad-fold[61] transformation body[62] of Śākyamuni Buddha.[63]

The three correct refuges (in the Buddha, the Dharma [his Law], and the Saṅgha [the community of monks]) having been explained and accepted, the preacher now moves on.

> Recite [the name of] the Buddha—Next, I invite the Buddhas of the ten directions to act as great witnesses while you accept the five commandments. Oh, my disciples! Can you? Do you want to? Excellent! Excellent![64]

But, before embarking upon a detailed explanation of each commandment, the lecturer engages in a most curiously eclectic interpretation of the significance in there being five commandments:

> In the heavens, they are named the five planets;[65] on the earth, they are named the five sacred mountains;[66] in Taoism they are the five phases;[67] in Confucianism they are the Five Emperors;[68] in Buddhism they are the five commandments.[69]

The preacher then proceeds, in verse, to illustrate each commandment with concrete examples of infraction and their consequences.

Having thus communicated to his auditors through this ceremony the Three Refuges and the Five Commandments, he has formally initiated them as male and female devotees. He indicates that he would like to expatiate endlessly upon these precepts but that it would take him many kalpas (eons) and he still would not finish. "Next, I wish to sing about the sūtra for you, oh my disciples. Can I? Do you want me to? Recite [the name of] the Buddha three or four times— *Amitābha-vyūha-sūtra*. I shall explain this sūtra in three sections ..."[70] But there are still things to do before he gets down to the business of the lecture itself. Now he must pronounce an introductory eulogy on the wondrous merits of the sūtra as a whole and Mahayana Buddhism in general.

As a teacher of the Law hereupon,[71] with several gāthās and eulogies, absolve men of their sins of commission. What follows, then, is the lecture on the sūtra. Will you listen to it, congregation? Can you? Do you want to?[72]

The preacher finally restates the title of the sūtra in preparation for beginning the lecture proper. From his questionable handling of Sanskrit in this section,[73] it appears that the lecturer's (or recorder's) knowledge of Indian languages was derived through Buddhicized Central Asian languages such as Khotanese. The explanation of the title is highly prolix and unenlightening.

Yet our lecturer still cannot bring himself to begin the long-awaited lecture. Now we must hear him out on the meaning of the "T'ang (i.e., Chinese) words 'Kingdom of Unlimited Life,'" for which he offers a delightfully simplistic explanation.[74] He enumerates four other names for this land but leaves off shortly, because "there is such a host of different names that I cannot say them all."[75] But, regardless of what it is called, the lecturer's description of this marvelous land is ever so much more enchanting than the place itself could possibly be. In the Pure Land, there is no sickness, no punishment, no noxious beasts, insects, nor birds. Here, "there are no women; everyone is a man!"[76] There is no torment, for everyone is a Bodhisattva. No one has to suffer the pain of rebirth, not even chickens and salamanders, for it is all accomplished by "direct metamorphosis."[77] The vision is fanciful and utopian, but one which must have spoken with tremendous force to the common people who listened. In the Land of the Buddha of Unlimited Life,

> There are no soldiers, and no slaves. No one takes advantage of anyone else. There are no famines. There are neither kings nor officials, only Amitābha Buddha is King of the Realm, Avalokiteśvara and Mahāsthāmaprāpta Bodhisattvas are his Prime Ministers, Bhaiṣajyasamudgata and Bhaiṣajyaguruvaiḍūrya-prabhāsa his Military Administrators,[78] and directly metamorphosized[79] youths are the population. There's no paying taxes with corn,

wheat, wine, and cloth. There is only donation of flowers and incense in the mornings and presentation of Brahmanic eulogies in the evening. Men[80] don't have to go on campaigns elsewhere......[81]

The preacher rambles on aimlessly about what is pure and impure for six or seven hundred more characters, pausing at one point to interrupt himself with these words: "I'd like to say more about it, but I'm afraid of wasting time."(!)[82] Even when the manuscript breaks off, the loveable old chatterbox has still not explained a single word of the sūtra proper. One can only imagine the great length of the entire service!

Another intimate religious discourse, strictly speaking not a *chiang-ching-wen*, is the so-called "Lecture on the *Inconstancy Sūtra*" (P2305). It ends with the lecturer telling his parishoners not to be put off by the somewhat tedious business of listening to the sūtras for it is that which will lead them to salvation. He encourages them to come often to the lecture hall (*chiang-yüan* 講院), and to be constant even in hot weather. Since he still has several more mornings to spend on the present text (if the donations do not fall off too drastically), he enjoins his listeners, "reciting the name of the Buddha, each to return to your own home and come back tomorrow to accompany me."[83] The orality of this lecture text is also evident in the abbreviation of parts of a line that recur (T663.8, 10, 12, 14, 16).

The intimate immediacy of other Tun-huang popular religious texts used in conjunction with lectures for laymen is humorously evident in such passages as the following:

> What the monk said just now is true;
> Pious disciples, do not dilly-dally,
> Each of you; reciting the Buddha's name, return to your home,
> If you come late, don't make the old lady angry![84]
>
> The day is late and you must hurry back,
> The old lady is at home waiting to scold you.[85]

> What the Master of the Law said this morning is true;
> You who are assembled beneath my pulpit to listen,
> > don't dilly-dally,
> Reciting the name of the Buddha, return to your homes,
> If you return late, the old lady'll be angry![86]

There are at least two plausible explanations for the frequent inclusion of such obvious expressions of immediacy as we have seen in the passages presented above. The first is that someone recorded the lecture on the spot with near-stenographic rapidity. The individual who performed this task may have been a novice, a scribe, or simply an interested person. Given the long, drawn-out style of delivery of Buddhist psalmody (as can be witnessed in Chinese, Japanese, Thai, Ceylonese, and Tibetan services even today), the sung portions, at least, would not actually have required much rapidity in the recording. Furthermore, as I have shown elsewhere,[87] even where strictly oral literature is involved, the verse portions tend to be relatively stable and reproducible *verbatim ac litteratim*. The frequent corrections and additions on the manuscripts could be taken as evidence that someone else familiar with the lecture or even the lecturer himself recalled portions missed or misrecorded by the scribe.[88] The other possibility is that the lecturer wrote out the manuscript ahead of time to serve as notes. The corrections, deletions, and additions could then be taken as last minute changes or notes added subsequent to delivery. But this seems rather less likely than the former possibility, particularly since many of the corrections are clearly written in a second hand. The likelihood that sūtra lecture manuscripts with many indications of immediacy were written ahead of time by the lecturers themselves is further diminished when we consider the implications of a lecturer who instructs himself in advance to punctuate his address with such "spontaneous" interjections and exclamations as "Hallelujah!" and "Amen!" and "Praise the Lord!"

Regardless of whom, and depending on the nature of the various manuscripts, someone did take down these lectures[89] *before*, *during*, or *soon after* their delivery. Probably there are manuscripts which, to a certain degree, represent all three types of procedure although there is no easy way to differentiate them. The conclusion that someone was present who recorded and/or revised the lectures *during their making* seems unavoidable. Several of the colophons also clearly point to this conclusion.

It must also be emphasized, however, that many other sūtra lectures (particularly those that are relatively more polished) present little or no prima facie evidence of immediacy. Their existence and nature can be explained as due to any of the following reasons: they may be literary productions by relatively learned monks; their orality may have been refined out of them by several stages of copying after the first written exemplar of a lecture; they may represent composite literary works based on repeated hearings of the same lecture by an individual or by several individuals who consulted each other in writing them down.

Whenever it is mentioned in a colophon that the text to which it is appended has been "copied" (*ch'ao* 抄), we know for certain that such a text is not primary. It has to have been preceded by at least one earlier exemplar of the work in question. There is no assurance that the earlier exemplar is itself necessarily primary in the sense of having been a direct recording of a storytelling session or religious lecture.

Most of what has been said in the preceding paragraphs concerning the orality and literality of sūtra lectures could with equal justice be asserted of the transformation texts (*pien-wen*) found at Tun-huang. The greater the number of corrections, additions, and deletions on a given manuscript ("degree of messiness") and the more frequent the obvious evidence of immediacy, the higher the likelihood that such a manuscript is closer to being the original written exemplar, or one of the first written exemplars, whether derived from a unique oral event or a repeated series of similar oral events. By "oral event," I intend here the performance of a transformation (i.e., picture recitation) or the delivery of a sūtra lecture before an audience. Naturally, there is no way to quantify this information sufficiently that it may be used as an objective criterion in the study of popular literature. At best, it may serve as an impressionistic indicator of the origin of a given manuscript.

The changes and revisions found on typical transformation text manuscripts are fewer than those found on such sūtra lectures as Taiwan 32 and S6551. Where there is a small number of such emendations on the manuscript of a given transformation text, they might still be ascribed to readers who had themselves attended transformation performances and hence had their own opinion regarding the correct reading of a passage even though the manuscript in question already represented a stage of literary transmission at several removes from the original oral event(s).

When I talk about "degree of messiness" as one indicator of derivation from an oral source, I do not mean the physical condition of the manuscript (whether torn, waterstreaked, and so on), nor the "grassiness" of the calligraphy. The messiness of which I speak refers primarily to corrections and revisions *by second and third hands.*

It may be objected that the manuscript of an author who writes a literary work in his study, completely devoid of any direct or indirect contact with an audience, may be fairly messy. They often are, as a journey into archives of any major university or library will demonstrate. The chief differences between the revisions on the manuscript of a wholly literary text and a manuscript of popular literature from Tunhuang, for example, which has direct or indirect ties to an oral event or events, are two: 1.) those on the latter, more often than not, are from hands other than the primary scribe, whereas those on the former are the marks of deliberate consideration by a single individual. 2.) The popular, orally related manuscript represents an effort, often undertaken by more than one person, to determine the approximate shape and content of an actual performance or group of performances that were completed at some point in the past. Subsequent modifications of a text based on an actual performance or performances represent different opinions regarding what really transpired there. Revisions on the manuscript of a literary creation by a single author represent work-in-progress. In a sense, the work is never definitely completed until it is presented to the public. And even then, the author or his editor(s) may-in unusual circumstances-decide to change it for future editions. The orally generated "text" is completed at the moment of delivery. What happens later is an attempt to recapture it with the utmost accuracy. Of course, this is never entirely achievable because any oral event is composed of too many variables to be described perfectly. Another characteristic of orally derived written texts is that, in the early stages of transmission, they often include unmistakable references to the presence of an audience. In later generations, they develop the apparatus of a "simulated [oral] context"[90] even though it is then patently a fiction.

Many transformation texts, such as those on Maudgalyāyana (S2614) and Wang Chao-chün (P2553), are actually fairly neat and regular in appearance. And, indeed, the Śāriputra transformation text formerly owned by Hu Shih is in a moderately good hand. The extended narrative poem on Tung Yung 董永 (S2204), however, is less neat than any of the transformation texts just mentioned. Such manuscripts as S2614, P2553, and Hu Shih's have all the markings of being kept for purposes of reading, not as notes for or from oral recitation. Yet there are transformation texts, such as that on Chang Huai-shen 張淮深, which are notoriously difficult to read and which show origins of not having fully achieved fixed form as written literature.

Those Tun-huang narratives that exist in booklet form,[91] regardless of their genre, are relatively free of significant variants (although those which were used as copybooks by students may still be very messy and have many teacher's corrections and changes). This is true of the "Transformation on the Han General, Wang Ling" (P3627 and S5437), "The Story of the Crown Prince of the Liu House in the Former Han" (S5547), and "The Story of the Capture of Chi Pu" (S5439). This would seem to indicate that texts which had been transmitted long enough to end up as booklets were relatively stable as written literature and that readers did not feel compelled to bring to bear on them, in the form of major revisions, their own recollections of oral renditions.

When advancing the idea of the amount of untidiness of a manuscript as one possible indicator of the degree of its orality, I restrict this criterion solely to popular narratives and lectures, together with attendant prefaces and eulogistic verse. Many seat-settling texts (*ya-tso-wen* 押座文 [prologues for sūtra lectures], e.g., those on S2440) have relatively numerous corrections, which I take to be an indication of their unstable form as written literature. On the other hand, there are many and diverse reasons why a loan contract or other local document among the Tun-huang manuscripts might present a very untidy appearance, but these have no bearing on the difficult issue of how and why oral literature came to be written down. Occasionally, some canonical and commentarial literature from Tun-huang can also be fairly slovenly. But, here again, the reasons for this slovenliness are unrelated to the question with which we are dealing. The rather unneat commentary on the *Vajracchedikā-prajñāpāramitā-sūtra* (copied in 764) reproduced by Yabuki,[92] for example, has markings for emphasis. Other Buddhist commentaries and sūtras I have seen present an irregular appearance because of added explanations, annotations, or interpretations--seldom do they express a difference of opinion regarding how a sentence or passage should read.

It is significant that most of the classical Chinese literary texts found at Tun-huang (*Analects, Chuang-tzu*, etc.) are comparatively free of emendations by hands other than the original copyist. This is understandable, for such texts had long histories as stable written entities. The same holds true for such texts as *A Record of Researches into Spirits* (*Sou-shen chi* 搜神記; S525) which can be demonstrated to have had an existence in written form before the T'ang period. In other words, for such texts there no longer are numerous controversies over the wording of phrases and sentences. There is more likely to be disagreement on the number of sections or fascicules which properly belong to a given title and their proper order.

There is also available one other gauge of the distance of a text from its ancestral oral performance. Where there are multiple copies of a given transformation text in which the language is noticeably similar or even largely identical (the Maudgalyāyana manuscripts are the best example of this), we may aver that such affinal groups are several generations removed from the original oral event or events which were their parents. It is improbable that more than one scribe would be simultaneously involved in taking down a single performance. And, even if there were, the results would be likely to show a greater amount of variation than exists among the copies in the sort of groups to which I am referring. The relatively high degree of uniformity among them is, rather, more correctly ascribed to the growth of a written tradition in which a standard text gradually comes to be established. This development would not, however, entirely preclude the possibility that readers of the later texts who were also familiar with oral renditions of the theme might feel qualified to make occasional changes in them.

Uncorrected phonological and/or graphical errors are not sufficient proof in themselves that a given manuscript has immediate oral derivation. Since folklorists have already demonstrated this,[93] I need not dwell upon it here. I will only mention some correlated evidence drawn from our experiences with the written English language. How many times as we were growing up did we agonize over whether ("weather"?) to write ("right"? "rite"? "wright"?) "to," "too," or "two," whether "bow" or "bough" is correct and why we cannot spell ("*spele," "*spal," "*spel,' etc.) "*nite" instead of "night" or "knight"?[94] And why is it necessary for secretaries, editors, and *writers* to keep on their desks books which list those words which are most often misspelled? The answer is obvious. These difficulties, furthermore, are magnified tremendously for those who are forced to use a morphographic writing system. Such a system, after long years of evolution, includes thousands of characters which give only the barest phonological clues and whose shapes appear largely to be arbitrary to anyone not deeply learned in philology. Therefore we may not ascribe immediate orality to a Tun-huang manuscript when it has *lieh* 烈 ("burning") means *lieh* 列 ("series"), has *mu* 募 ("enlist") when it means *mu* 慕 ("be fond of"), *p'ei* 陪 ("accompany") when it means *pei* 倍 ("increase") and so on.

Nor is use of colloquial language in a written text necessary grounds for declaring that text to have a particularly close relationship to an oral presentation. Colloquial language, rather than literary Chinese, is used as the vehicle of written literature more for sociological reasons than for any presumed attempt to capture for posterity a specific oral event. Someone chooses (or is forced) to write in colloquial either because he has insufficient training to write proper literary Chinese or because, though able to employ literary styles, he wishes (perhaps only temporarily) to identify with or ridicule those who are incapable of doing so.

The study of *chiang-ching-wen* (sūtra lectures for laymen)[95] leads to an examination of many questions that are of interest to the theorist and historian of oral literature. Consideration of such issues as the use of formulae (to be distinguished from formulaic language) in simulated context, the relationship between written manuscript and oral event, the nature of impromptu additions to sermon notes, and so on, helps to illuminate similar topics in research on secular and more purely diversionary oral literature. Most importantly, our investigations of *chiang-ching-wen* have shown that oral composition is not devoid of links to written texts, regardless of the degree of (il)literacy of the speaker.

Notes

1. In a series of studies undertaken over the last decade and more, I have attempted to clarify these and many other issues relating to the study of *pien-wen*. These studies include *Tun-huang Popular Narratives* (Cambridge: Cambridge University Press, 1983); *T'ang Transformation Texts* (Cambridge: Harvard University Press, 198X); *Chinese Picture Recitation: Origins, Analogues, and Development* (forthcoming from University of Hawai'i Press); "The Narrative Revolution in Chinese Literature: Ontological Presuppositions," with an accompanying symposium, in *Chinese Literature: Essays, Articles, Reviews*, 5.1 (July 1983 [actually published in 1985]), 1-27; "Lay Students and the Making of Written Vernacular Narrative: An Inventory of Tun-huang Manuscripts," *Chinoperl Papers*, 10 (1981), 5-96; and so on. The bibliographies of the first two books list a large number of additional works on this subject by myself and others. Since this article is about sūtra lectures, it does not address the extremely complicated questions of the meaning, corpus, origin, form, and performance of *pien-wen*.
2. Shih Wei-liang 史惟亮, *Yin-yüeh hsiang li-shih ch'iu cheng* (A Study Of Music Seeking Verification from History) 音樂向歷史求證 (Taipei: Chung-hua shu-chü, 1974), p. 20.
3. Kenneth K.S. Ch'en, *The Chinese Transformation of Buddhism* (Princeton: Princeton University Press, 1973), p. 252 and *Buddhism in China: A Historical Survey* (Princeton: Princeton University Press, 1964), p. 288.
4. *Chinese Transformation*, p. 252.
5. Lai Ming, *A History of Chinese Literature* (New York: John Day, 1964), p. 254.
6. Richard Gregg Irwin, *The Evolution of a Chinese Novel: Shui-hu-chuan* (Cambridge: Harvard University Press, 1953), p. 23.
7. Chou I-liang 周一良, "Tun-huang pi-hua yü Fo-ching (Tun-huang Wall-paintings and Buddhist Sūtras)" 敦煌壁畫與佛經, *Tun-huang wen-wu chan-Ian t'e-k'an* (Special Number for the Exhibition of Cultural Artifacts from Tun-huang) 敦煌文物展覽特刊, *Wen-wu ts'an-k'ao tzu-liao* (Research Materials on Cultural Artifacts) 文物參考資料, 2.4 and 5 (1951),105 (of 90-106).

8. Fujino Iwatomo 藤野岩友, *Chūgoku no bungaku to reizoku* (Literature and Ritual Customs of China) 中國の文學と禮俗 (Tokyo: Kadokawa shoten, 1976), p. 165.
9. This is Stein (hereafter S) manuscript 2073, published in Wang Chung-min 王重民 et al., ed. *Tun-huang pien-wen chi* (Collection of pien-wen from Tun-huang) 敦煌變文集, 2 vols. (Peking: Jen-min wen-hsüeh ch'u-pan-she, 1957), vol. 1, pp. 167-193. This collection of Tun-huang popular literary texts is hereafter referred to as T (line numbers are separated from page numbers by a dot). The account of Tao-an's sūtra lecture may be found on pp. 185ff. A partial translation is given in Arthur Waley, tr., *Ballads and Stories from Tun-huang* (London: George Allen and Unwin, 1960), pp. 97-123. Unfortunately, Waley summarizes or skips the parts that are most interesting for the purposes of this article.
10. See *Tun-huang Popular Narratives*, appendix and *T'ang Transformation Texts*, chapter 4.
11. James I. Crump, "On Chinese Medieval Vernacular," *Wennti Papers*, ed. George A. Kennedy, vol. 1 (New Haven: Yale University Press, 1953), pp. 69-70 (of 65-74).
12. Also on T697.5.
13. Cf. also T684.15 and 443.10.
14. The Emperor's Birthday, that is.
15. The *Prajñāpāramitā-sūtra of the Benevolent King Who Protects His Country* 仁王護國般若波羅蜜多經.
16. Ming-tsung 明宗 of the Later T'ang.
17. *Tun-huang chüan-tzu* (Tun-huang Scrolls) 敦煌卷子, 6 vols. (Taipei: Shih-men t'u-shu kung-ssu, 1976), vol. 2, pp. 273a-277a, text no. 32. See also P'an Ch'ung-kuei 潘重規, ed. *Tun-huang pien-wen chi hsin shu* (New Collection of *pien-wen* from Tun-huang) 敦煌變文集新書, *Tun-huang-hsüeh ts'ung-shu* (Tunhuangology Series) 敦煌學叢書, no. 6, 2 vols. (Taipei: Chung-kuo wen-hua ta-hsüeh Chung-wen yen-chiu-so, 1983-84), vol. 2, pp. 1344-1351.
18. Pan Chung-kwei (P'an Ch'ung-kuei), 潘重規 "Kuo-li chung-yang t'u-shu-kuan so ts'ang Tun-huang chüan-tzu t'i-chi (An Annotated List of the Scrolls of Tun-huang Conserved in the National Central Library at Taipei)" 國立中央圖書館所藏敦煌卷子題記, *Tun-huang hsüeh* (Studies on Tun-huang) 敦煌學, 2 (1975), 12-13 (of 1-55). Pan first formally identifies it as a T'ang copy of the *Yü-lan p'en ching* (Sūtra of the Sacrificial Feast for Souls in Purgatory) 盂蘭盆經. In the *Tun-huang pien-wen chi*

hsin shu, vol. 1, pp. 487-496, Pan has edited the text and correctly labeled it as *Yü-lan-p'en chiang-ching-wen*.
19. E.g., pp. 273b3, 274a7, and 274b10.
20. E.g., T412.7ff.
21. Sanskrit *pariśuddhi* or *viśuddhi*.
22. P. 273a9a. I have not seen this name elsewhere that I can recall.
23. P. 276b8. For a discussion of and references to important scholarly opinions on this perennially difficult title, see my *Tun-huang Popular Narratives*, p. 224. A brief entry is given in William Edward Soothill and Lewis Hodous, *A Dictionary of Chinese Buddhist Terms with Sanskrit and English Equivalents and a Sanskrit-Pali Index* (London: Kegan Paul, Trench, Trubner & Co., 1937), pp. 274-275.
24. P. 277a1.
25. P. 273a9.
26. P. 273a11-12. Compare the transformation text verse introductory formula: "How should I explain it (literally, 'lay it out')?"
27. P. 273a5-6. Here and below, characters in boxes represent my reconstructions of missing or damaged portions of the text.
28. For self (*arhat*), for others (Bodhisattva), perfect enlightenment and accomplishment (Buddha).
29. P. 273b7-8. The reading of the last character is uncertain. It is a correction of <%14> which has been crossed out.
30. *Buddha-putra* 仏子.
31. Compare the more regular use of this refrain at the end of each quatrain in a seat-settling text (T829-830).
32. P. 274a9 and 12. I have tried to reproduce the essential features of the passage as they appear on the manuscript.
33. P. 276b4.
34. P. 275a10b. The characters in the smaller hand have been written very hurriedly.
35. The *gatis* which lead to the fiery hell, the bloody hells, and the hells full of swords.
36. P. 276b3.
37. If the proposed emendation is not accepted, perhaps we should understand "sit down [and] ...."
38. The smaller characters are meant to replace the larger ones which someone, not surprisingly, must have thought made no sense. I am not certain that I have grasped the meaning of either of the two possibilities for the last line.

39. P. 275b5-6.
40. T461.1.
41. An ancient Central Asian Kingdom populated by people who spoke a Middle Iranian language.
42. A Turkish-speaking people of Central Asia. See Hsiang Ta's note 3 on T479. Monks from many Buddhist countries came to China to spread the *dharma*. For an example of one, see the poem (S4654v) by the famous Tun-huang cleric, Wu-chen 悟真, in which he mentions a monk from India who lectured on sūtras from the *Triyāna* 三乘 ("Triple Vehicle"). Many of these foreign monks learned Chinese and gave their lectures in that language. Their limited fluency and partial literacy in Chinese made their task difficult, as did the various dialects they encountered.
43. Buddhist strophe.
44. Literally, "Ever since [He of] supreme *bodhi* opened the abstruse gate."
45. Literally, "By turning the wheel of the law (*dharma-cakra*) at Mṛgadāva and Gṛdhrakūṭa (sacred Buddhist sites in India where the Buddha began his career as a preacher)."
46. That is, "The major sects of Buddhism and their chief sūtras."
47. The four varga: *bhikṣu, bhikṣunī, upāsaka,* and *upāsikā*. The first two are actually monks and nuns, the second two are male and female devotees.
48. Literally, "gold[-covered] grounds." This is an allusion to the famous story of the purchase of Jetavana monastery. See my *Tun-huang Popular Narratives,* pp. 52ff and relevant notes.
49. Literally, "the burning house," from the well-known parable in the *Lotus Sūtra*.
50. Sanskrit *karmāvaraṇa*, the screen of *karma* which hinders the attainment of *bodhi* (enlightenment).
51. Sanskrit *buddhaphala*.
52. Sanskrit *mahāsaṅgha,* i.e. the congregation.
53. T460.1-9. I have omitted the Chinese characters for this and all succeeding texts that are published in T. The *Tun-huang pien-wen chi hsin-shu* was not available to me until after I had completed this article so I have not provided specific citations to it. All future research on Tun-huang popular literature should certainly rely on it as a standard reference.
54. T462.15.
55. T462.16.
56. T463.9-10.
57. *Triśaraṇa* or *śaraṇa-gamana* and *pañca veramaṇī*.

58. T464.3-4.
59. *Dharmakāya.*
60. *Saṃbhoga-kāya.*
61. The image derives from the iconographical tradition of a thousand-petalled lotus throne for Locana Buddha, each petal being a transformation of Śākyamuni Buddha.
62. *Nirmāṇakāya.*
63. T464.8-10. Śākyamuni Buddha is the historical Buddha. There are numerous other Buddhas of the past and future.
64. T465.2.
65. Venus 金, Jupiter 木, Mercury 水, Mars 火, and Saturn 土.
66. T'aishan 泰山 in the east; Hengshan 衡 in the south; Huashan 華 in the west; Hengshan 恆 in the north; and Sungshan 嵩 in the center.
67. The metallic, the liqueous, the aqueous, the igneous, and the telluric. It is interesting to note that the five phases are identified particularly with Taoism since this cosmological concept came into existence long before religious Taoism.
68. Greatest Heavenly Emperor 太昊, Flaming Emperor 炎帝, the Yellow Emperor 黃帝, Lesser Heavenly Emperor 少昊, and Correct Concentrator 顓頊.
69. T465.4. The commandments are against slaying, stealing, lusting, speaking lightly, and eating meat or drinking intoxicants.
70. T471.2-3.
71. *Dharma-bhāṇaka* or *dharma-kathika.*
72. T473.11-12.
73. T473.13. "Brahmanic language *mᵫu:* [na/] *d'iᵫ:* 母 [那 mistakenly written for] 陀 [Sanskrit *mṛta* 'dead' or 'deceased,' hence 'corpse' in Buddhist usage] [in] T'ang language is called *b'i̯uət* [Bud(dha)]," The speaker must have intended 母馱 = 佛陀. The faulty analysis of the word Amitā[bha] ("Boundless Light") on T474.6-7 is even more striking, but it is too involved to detail here except to say that the participial ending of *apramīta* ("unbounded, unmeasured" from *a-pra-√mā* "not to measure, not to mete out") is said to mean "longevity"!
74. Han [founder, house] / Kingdom→ man [ruler] / borders ← Unlimited Life [Buddha] / Kingdom
75. T475.9.
76. T475.11. This sort of gross male chauvinism was by no means invented by our sūtra lecturer. Cf. Saul Lieberman, *Tosefta Ki-Fshuṭah* (A Comprehensive Commentary on the Tosefta), *Zeraim* (New York, 1955), pp.

120ff; Diogenes Laertius, *De vitis philosophorum* (Lives of Eminent Philosophers), tr. R.D. Hicks, Loeb Classical Library, 2 vols. (New York: G.P. Putnam's Sons, 1925), I, 34-35; David Winston, "The Iranian Component in the Bible, Apocrypha and Qumran: A Review of the Evidence," *History of Religion*, 5.2 (Winter 1966), 183-216. I am grateful to my colleague, Judah Goldin, for providing me with these references. See also Isidore Lévy, *Légende de Phythagore de Grèce en Palestine*. Bibliotheque de l'École des hautes études; sciences historiques et philosophiques, vol. 250 (Paris, 1950), pp. 261-262 and Lionel Giles, "Two Parallel Anecdotes in Greek and Chinese," *Bulletin of the School of Oriental (and African) Studies*, 2 (1922-23), 609-611.

77. *Aupapadāka* or *aupapāduka*. There are four types of birth (*catur-yoni*): *jarāyuja* (viviparous); *aṇḍaja* (oviparous); *saṃsuedaja* (moisture-born); and *aupapādaka*.
78. Literally, "Plum Appointee[s]" (梅錄 [→ 祿]), the title of a T'ang military official for the northern reaches.
79. See note 77.
80. I do not feel the emendation (男 → 更) suggested by Chou I-liang in T479n24 is necessary.
81. T475.13-15.
82. T476.3.
83. T670.12. At end of several sections in this text, the lecturer mentions that it is late in the day (T659.6-7, 660.8-9, and 661.11-12).
84. P3128 and Peking manuscript 6780, see T298.9-10 and 315n211.
85. T657.3.
86. S2440, see T828.2-3. The phonemes in these passages which I have translated as "old lady" are *a-p'o* 阿婆. It is conceivable that these two characters can stand for an entirely different person, i.e., "me" 阿僕, an equation that was current in the T'ang period. However, because of the context and because I have elsewhere seen 阿婆嗔 (as in these instances) used in a T'ang text to mean "the (old) wife gets angry," I have rendered the expression this way. See Chang Tsu 張鷟 (c. 660-741), *Ch'ao-yeh ch'ien-tsai* (Inclusive Register for Court and Countryside) 朝野僉載, in Ch'en Lien-t'ang 陳蓮塘 (Ch'ing period), ed., *T'ang-tai ts'ung-shu* (T'ang Dynasty Collectanea) 唐代叢書 (Shanghai: Chin-chang t'u-shu-chü, 1921 [?], lithograph), *ts'e* 1, 9b, line 10 and cf. 10a, line 17. Also see S4274v for the name 阿婆子.
87. See the latter part of chapter four in *T'ang Transformation Texts*.

88. It is still possible to document this process of stenographic technique in Taiwan now, although in a very different context, by observing the relationship between spirit medium (*târng-ki* 童乩) and amanuensis who takes down his trance-oracles or between the wielders of the planchette (*fu-chi* 扶箕, also 扶乩 or, 扶 [飛] 鸞) and the scribe who writes down entire scriptures on the spot from the scratchings of the spirit-seat in the sand.
89. I refer, of course, only to those manuscripts with pronounced evidence of immediacy (see the next paragraph).
90. For a discussion of this concept, see chapter five of *T'ang Transformation Texts*.
91. All the other manuscripts cited in this article are in scroll form.
92. Yabuki Keiki 矢吹慶輝, *Meisha yoin* (Rare and Unknown Chinese Manuscript Remains of Buddhist Literature Discovered in Tun-huang) 鳴沙餘韻 (Tokyo: Iwanami shoten, 1930), no. 22.
93. See, for example, Carl Wilhelm von Sydow, "Folktale Studies and Philology: Some Points of View," in *The Study of Folklore*, Alan Dundes, ed. (Englewood Cliffs, New Jersey: Prentice Hall, 1965), pp. 219-242.
94. Data taken from the second and third grade homework of my son and his pals, written exercises of students in freshman English classes at Bhojpur College (Nepal) and Tunghai University (Taiwan), and notes from night janitors in several buildings where I have worked. Comparably literate segments of T'ang society were undoubtedly prone to even greater difficulties with the complicated written Chinese language.
95. Throughout this article, I have used the expression *chiang-ching-wen* ("sūtra lectures [for laymen]") in the strict, technical sense of a religious, exegetical text that cites passages of a given sūtra with the quotative formula *ch'ang-chiang-lai*. This usage is actually a modern convention, but one which is consistent in that it specifies an identifiable genre and a coherent corpus. For some examples of the complexities involved in its application, see my "Inventory" (cf. note 1 above), numbers 173, 440, and 441. There were many other types of Buddhist religious discourses, both popular and ecclesiastical, during the T'ang period. At a bare minimum, we should exercise caution in applying the term *chiang-ching-wen* to any texts which lack the identifying quotative formula as well as to those texts such as Inventory #440 which, though possessing the formula, have a different generic title. Similar cautions must be exercised in the use of the word *pien[-wen]*.

Chapter 4

India and China

Observations and Cultural Borrowings

Source: Adapted from "India and China:
Observations on Cultural Borrowing,"
Journal of the Asiatic Society (Calcutta)
31.3-4 (1989): 61-94.

During the past decade and more, the author has been engaged in an intensive research project on a genre of Chinese popular literature called "transformation texts" (*pien-wen* 變文) [1]. All of the extant manuscripts constituting this genre were discovered around the turn of the century in a wailed-up cave at Tun-huang 敦煌, Kansu province, northwest China. The manuscripts date to the T'ang period (618-906) and the Five Dynasties period (906-960).

Transformation texts were derived from an oral tradition of picture recitation and were the first prosimetric, vernacular narratives written in Chinese. My research has shown that the origins of this genre may be traced through Central Asia to India.

This long-term research project therefore posits the transfer of a cultural phenomenon (prosimetric picture storytelling) from one country to another. Hence, to a certain degree it subscribes to the theory of cultural diffusion. The purpose of this article is to answer the charges of skeptics who, on nationalistic grounds, deny that transformation texts could possibly have come from abroad because they hold that a society invents all of its own cultural property and that nothing of significance ever really passes its borders.

Anthropologists have long recognized the inevitability of cultural borrowing. As stated by Alfred L. Kroeber,

> When something new has been evolved in a culture, whether a tool or an idea or a custom, there is a tendency for it to be passed on to the culture of other societies. This is much like the passing on of culture to the younger generation within the evolving society, except for being foreign-directed instead of domestic. In other words, new culture is transmitted geographically as well as chronologically, in space as well as time, by contagion as well as by repetition. The spread in area is generally called *diffusion*, as the internal handing on through time is called *tradition*[2].

If, as we now know was indeed the case, storytelling with pictures was a popular form of religious instruction and entertainment in India from at least two centuries before the beginning of the international era, it would seem impossible that it would not have been exported to China (where this form was unknown before the T'ang period) along with all the other paraphernalia of Buddhism.

There are two major fallacies that used to be perpetuated by many scholars studying China: one is that her culture developed *in vacuo*, immune to any influence from outside, the other is that all good and new things came from abroad. Neither of these approaches is acceptable because neither of them is true. In studying any civilization, it is imperative that all such biases be set aside. My view of history which denies the creativity and viability of Chinese civilization is bound to be fraught with distortion. Likewise, any view of history which sees China as hermetically sealed off from the rest of humankind—as though it existed in isolation from time immemorial—is a false one.

To deny cultural influence where it is obvious is simply to ignore reality. The *yang-pan-hsi* 樣板戲 ("model plays") of the Cultural Revolution had their origins both in Peking opera and in borrowings from Western ballet. To pretend that they were wholly Chinese in origin is to be hopelessly obtuse; to claim that they were made wholly out of foreign cloth is sheer folly. In the same vein, the student of twentieth-century French art needs to be informed about Japanese woodcuts and the historian of twentieth-century American cuisine must not be ignorant of Chinese and Indian culinary arts. My plea is simply that we should face up to the implications of the inescapable fact of cultural borrowing. In the particular area of scholarship which concerns me most, I hope that no student of Chinese literature will remain entirely ignorant of Indian and other neighbouring traditions. We ought not arbitrarily rule out the possibility of Indian influence upon the development of popular Chinese literature. To do so would imperil our efforts to construct an objective and truthful history of Chinese civilization. On the other hand, we should never claim foreign influence unless it can be demonstrated. Mere coincidental similarity is no test of relatedness.

In this regard, the cautionary note[3] of Y. V. Maretin on cultural borrowing, transmission, and crossing must be taken seriously into account. In actuality, there is never really any outright borrowing, of course, since the mere implantation of anything in a new cultural setting is bound to modify it more or less profoundly. It scarcely needs to be pointed out that all borrowing is done upon a pre-existent cultural base. If there is no such base, obviously no borrowing can take place. And, precisely because there is such a base, any borrowing that occurs will inevitably involve a certain amount of adaptation. Hence no cultural artifact is ever accepted in toto and without modification by a recipient society. This is particularly true of literature, where language exercises such an enormous shaping power[4].

One general observation which may be made regarding literary influence is that forms are far more easily transported across borders than is content. Shakespeare's sonnets are sublimely English even though their form was borrowed from the Italian poet, Petrarch. Similarly, transformation texts may be characteristically Chinese and *wayang bëbër* is quintessentially Indonesian, even though both have their roots in ancient Indian narrative picture scrolls (those of the *mankhas, gauriputrakas, yamapatikas*, etc.). The cultural categories "English," "Chinese," and "Indonesian" were enlarged, but not in any sense destroyed, during the process of the absorption of these new literary forms. This perception makes understandable Rabindranath Tagore's remark uttered in 1927, while he was visiting Indonesia. "I see India everywhere, but I do not recognize it."[5] Hence, though we know that batik was India, we cannot say that, as it is practiced in Indonesia, it is any longer simply an Indian transplantation. The technical terms, the designs, the uses to which it is put—all are Indonesian.[6] Exactly the same situation obtains with regard to *wayang bëbër* (and, for that matter, to transformation texts in China).

The vicissitudes of a cultural product can be prodigiously complicated. The basic tenets of Communism, for example, were established by a German Jew who was living in England, and now "communists" in Russia and in China despise each other. But the complications involved should not deter us from attempting to clarify the historical development and geographical spread of Communism. In like fashion, the intricate interrelationships among Indian *saubhikas,* Chinese *pien-wen,* Indonesian *wayang bëbër,* and Japanese *etoki,* etc. should not force us to throw up our hands in despair. We must patiently attempt to fit as many of the pieces of the puzzle together as possible.

A landmark essay that provides excellent background for the subject of this article is Hu Shih's "The Indianization of China: A Case Study in Cultural Borrowing." It should be required reading, not only for every student of Indian civilization and Chinese civilization, but for all who are interested in cultural history in general. Central to Hu's thesis is that

Buddhism was the vehicle of the Indianization which was so pervasive for the past two millennia. One of Hu Shih's most remarkable statements in the essay is germane to our study here:

> ...The whole Indian imaginative power, which knows neither limitation nor discipline, was indeed too much for the Chinese mind. Indigenous China was always factual and rarely bold in imagination. "Extend your knowledge, but leave out those things about which you are in doubt." "Say you know when you really know, and say you don't know when you really don't know—that is knowledge." Such were the wise instructions of Confucius on knowledge. This emphasis on veracity and certainty was one of the most marked traits of ancient Chinese literature, which is strikingly free from mythological and supernatural elements. Confucius once said, "I have devoted whole days without food and whole nights without sleep, to thinking. But it was no use. It is better to learn [than to think in abstract]." This self-analysis on the part of one of China's greatest sages is of peculiar significance in showing the suspicion with which Chinese thinkers regarded the unbridled exercise of thought and imagination. It must have been very difficult for Chinese readers to shallow down all that huge amount of sacred literature of sheer fancy and imagination. It was probably this native detestation of the unbridled imagination which led the first Chinese leaders of anti-Buddhist persecution in the fifth century to declare that the entire Buddhist tradition was a myth and a lie.[7]

It may be objected that, already before the introduction of Buddhism, China had at least an underground current of imaginative thought. This was reflected in various myth fragments and in a few collections of political, philosophical, and historical apologues. The full extent of this long-neglected and oft-despised minority tradition is only now, with the help of archeology and modern methods of textual analysis, gradually being recovered. Nonetheless, students of Chinese literature who ignore the points which Hu Shih makes here about the orthodox, majority mind-set are liable to have a fatally distorted understanding of the true nature of their subject.

The impingement upon the Chinese mind of such quintessentially Buddhist notions as *nirmāṇa* ("transformational manifestation"), *nirvāṇa* ("utter extinction"), *māyā* ("illusion"), and *sunyatā* ("emptiness") surely had a profound effect on the way fiction was written. The effect, in fact, can be measured or judged by various factors, such as the ability to sustain narratives of greater length, an increased propensity for fantasy, and the abandonment by the writer of any pretense that he is reporting events which actually occurred. All of these modifications—not to mention other more linguistic, formal, and genre changes—took place after the introduction of Buddhism.

Many aspects of Chinese culture were profoundly influenced by India.[8] It is impossible, for example, to overlook the enormous impact of Buddhism upon Chinese art and architecture: the pagoda, sculpture, landscape painting, figure painting, etc. were all affected by this Indian religion.[9] Even in art theory, the resemblance between Vātsyāyana's (third or fourth century I.E.) Ṣaḍaṅga ("Six Limbs") and Hsieh Ho's (Southern Ch'i [479-501]) *liu-fa* "Six Canons" 謝赫六法 are too great to be ignored.[10] And no study of Neo-Confucianism is adequate unless it takes into account the impact of Buddhist philosophy upon it. The educational establishments that helped to sustain neo-Confucianism were also inspired by Buddhism. According to Liang Ch'i-ch'ao, "...the academies which flourished since the Tang (T'ang) dynasty cannot be other than Buddhist in origin."[11] In the area of science and technology, one needs only to read through the pages of Joseph Needham's *Science and Civilisation in China* to appreciate the vast amount of exchange between China and India that went on throughout history. One interesting proof of this exchange is a Tun-huang manuscript (S6107) which lists 30-odd names of medicinal plants with their Sanskrit names in transcription.[12] Even certain common diversions, upon investigation, are revealed to have non-Chinese origins. The Ming writer, Hsieh Chao-chih, has this to say in his *Miscellanea in Five Parts*: "The people in the south like puppetry and the people in the north like swinging, yet both are Serindian amusements."[13] And Wolfram Eberhard lists some of the sports—such as soccer, wrestling, polo, and horse-racing—borrowed by the Chinese from Central Asian peoples.[14]

I should like now to turn to the subject of drama as a case study of the mechanics of cultural borrowing.[15] There seems—from earliest times—always to have been a close connection between Buddhism and drama.[16] The famous Jogīmāra cave of Rāmgarh was perhaps used as a theater hall during the fourth and third centuries before the international era.[17] Aśvaghoṣa, the author of the beloved *Buddhacarita-Kāvyasūtra* 佛所行讚經 also wrote a Buddhist drama called *Śāriputraprakarana* which Lüders unearthed in Sinkiang.[18] Aśvaghoṣa's patron was Kaniṣka, the Indo-Scythian ruler of Gandhara who was the greatest *caskravartin* ("royal patron of Buddhism") after Aśoka.

But there has also been, in China, a more general linkage between religious establishments and drama that is not necessarily solely Buddhist inspired. Justus Doolittle, writing in 1865, perceived that the theater in China was intimately connected with religion:

> ...Playacting is exceedingly often an act of worship, and is generally employed on important festive celebrations. *Theatrical exhibitions are very commonly connected with rendering thanks to the gods for favors believed to have been received from them by the Chinese.* Hence the use of temples for the purpose, where the acting is done in the presence of the idols. The reputed birthdays of the gods are almost invariably celebrated by the performances of plays before their images. Actors are also often employed to perform in a temple in consequence of a vow on the part of the employer. On the occurrence of the marriage of a son, or the birthday of the aged head of a rich family, or on the occasion of successful competition for literary honor at the regular examinations, a company of actors is frequently employed to perform a play, if the expense can be afforded. Festive and joyous occasions are most commonly celebrated by theatrical exhibitions.[19]

John Shryock has posed a number of questions regarding this linkage:

An interesting question which I have never seen discussed is the relation of the theater to religion in China. Four temples in Anking.... have stages over the entrance, facing the main hall across the courtyard. Plays were formerly given there at the New Year and the birthday of the god, but the custom seems to have died out or been forbidden by the officials because of the disorder it created. These plays were not religious, though gods sometimes appeared among the dramatic personae. I do not believe that there are any extant plays with a religious purpose. The ordinary explanation is that the plays were given in honor of the god, that he might enjoy them as any spectator would, and be amused, but this is superficial, of course. How did these plays come to be connected with religion, not only in the temples, but in the trade and provincial gilds? Why do some temples have them and others not? Why is a theatrical performance part of the harvest festival in the country, and why are prayers offered before the play? Such questions will probably await a closer study of the T'ang, Sung, and Yuan Dynasties, when so many new ideas were introduced into China.[20]

Some of the answers to Shryock's questions may be found by further examination of the symbiotic relation between entertainment and evangelism in the T'ang and Five dynasties periods extensively documented in my publications.

The first to declare that Chinese drama had received direct influence from India was Hsü Ti-shan, who in 1927 published in the *Hsiao-shuo yueh-pao* (The Short Story Magazine) 小說月報 (no. 17 [special issue 13] entitled *Chung-kuo wen-hsueh yen-chiu* [Studies of Chinese Literature] 中國文學研究, ed. Cheng Chen-to 鄭振鐸 pp. 379-414) an article entitled "Fan-chü t'i-li chi ch'i tsai han-chü shang te tien-tien ti-ti [The Conventions of Sanskrit Drama and Their Pervasive Evidence in Chinese Drama]) 梵劇體例及其在漢劇上底點點滴滴. Hsü's evidence was primarily based on the striking similarities with regard to conventions and characters between southern forms of Chinese drama and Sanskrit plays. The correctness of Hsu's declaration of Indian influence was impressively confirmed by the discovery of a Sanskrit manuscript with lines from Kālidāsa's *Śakuntalā* and other Sanskrit plays in the Country's Purity Monastery on Mt. T'ien-t'ai 天台山國清寺 by Hu Hsien-su 胡先驌.[21] The location of the discovery is extremely significant, for this internationally famous Buddhist mountain is not far from Wen-chou 溫州. Not only was Wen-chou an important port of call for Indian trading ships, having been designated during the Northern Song (960-1126) as an official port for the collection of maritime customs (*shih-po-ssu* 市舶司), it is also generally acknowledged to be at the very center of the area in which southern drama (*nan-hsi* 南戲) developed.

Chu Wei-chih is of the opinion that southern drama did indeed develop along the southeast coast of China and that it doubtless did receive Indian influence in its formative stages.[22] Since there was such flourishing intercourse between China and India across the oceans, it is likely that cultural exchange was unavoidable. But Chu goes on to say that drama is a complicated form of art and, therefore, that the reasons for its occurrence and growth cannot be explained by Indian influence alone. It could not have been imported entire but must have had some base within China upon which Indian influence could build. Surely all but the most fanatic cultural diffusionist would concede Chu's point.

The major formative influences for the development of southern drama came from India by the sea-route. This was a separate importation and one of a quite different character from that which came to China via Central Asia. The latter must, of necessity, have come by stages: it literally travelled from oasis to oasis and this resulted in a much more attenuated Indian impact. For each stage of the journey entailed the modification or adaptation of the Indian forms, either to suit local audiences or because individuals from the various localities themselves actually became performers. At the very least, many different languages were involved in the Central Asian transmission of literary forms to China.[23] The importation of Indian drama to the southeast coast of China was done more, as it were, "at one fell swoop." Regardless of how long those who were carrying the Indian dramatic forms might be at sea, they had very little contact with people on shore. Thus it is not at all surprising that lines from the Sanskrit text of the *Śakuntalā* by India's greatest dramatist, Kālidāsa, were found in a temple at the epicenter of the area where southern drama was born. Indian drama was imported far more as an integral art form to southern China than it was to northwestern China. In the northwest, it filtered and trickled in with folk performers who followed the caravans. In the south it was brought, more or less intact, by learned scholars who were capable of reading and writing the classical Indian language as well as by merchant patrons who supported them. Consonant with the results of my own studies is Cheng Chen-to's conviction[24] that northern drama during the Yüan (1200-1368) probably developed under the influence of the puppet and shadow theaters while southern drama, which preceded it, was inspired directly by Indian theater. During the Ming (1368-1644), these two traditions fused in the characteristic dramatic forms of that period.

An art form as complex and varied as Chinese drama could not possibly have been imported from abroad and deposited without any change in China it is obvious that, at the very least, one of the Chinese languages must be employed to present intelligently a literary work in China to a sizable audience. This in itself is already a substantial modification of any foreign literary influence which finds its way to China. But it is equally wrong to assume or assert that China was impervious to all foreign literary influence. For the evidence of widespread literary influence from abroad is overwhelming; drama was no exception.

According to Liang Ch'i-ch'ao, Indian influence upon Chinese language and literature can be broken down into five main headings:

> 1. The increase of the Chinese vocabulary by more than 35,000 items.
> 2. Modifications of grammar and literary form (e.g. the Zen adoption of colloquial Chinese as a written medium) that were revolutionary in scope.

3. The development of a new zest for pure (i.e. imaginative and fictional) literature.
4. The introduction of musical drama.
5. The creation of a phonetic spelling system.

Hu Shih refers to three great contributions:

1. The decision of the great translators of the Buddhist sutras to use colloquial styles of Chinese in their work.
2. The liberation of the Chinese imagination (leading to the development of the chaptered novel) brought about by exposure to Buddhist literature, which is supremely fecund in this respect.
3. The prosimetric form.[25]

It seems to me that it would be impossible to deny altogether the literary and linguistic influences to which Liang Ch'i-ch'ao and Hu Shih have alluded, though one may wish to minimize their importance. Even basic theories of literary criticism were profoundly affected by Buddhist metaphysics.[26] In spite of Lu K'an-ju's violent denunciation[27] of Hu Shih for having suggested that India and Indian Buddhism in particular, may have had some significant influence on the development of Chinese literature, the simple and inescapable fact remains that they did. Positive Indian influence can be identified from at least the fourth century B.C.E. in the "Heavenly Questioning" 天問.[28]

In discussing the impact of written Indian literature on other Asian countries, we must not lose sight of the fact that it was, for the most part, either overtly religious in nature or transmitted by individuals who had religious inclinations.[29] Thus the bearers of Indian culture abroad, even its secular aspects, presented it to others in the context of a religious world-view. As Prabhat Mukherji writes,

> The Hindu (i.e., Indian Buddhist) monks did not merely carry Sanskrit books across the mountains and deserts, but they carried a culture to China; they not only translated the Sanskrit works

into the Chinese language but grafted Hindu culture in the Chinese stem.[30]

Those who are interested in the rise of written vernacular Chinese ought to scrutinize carefully the works of Kumārajīva and other great translators from Sanskrit, for it is in their works that we see unmistakably a massive reworking of the written language.[31] Indeed, in two most significant articles[32] on historical linguistics, E. Zürcher has shown forcefully that vernacular elements were already being used in the earliest known (i.e. Eastern Han [25-220]) Buddhist translations. What is even more suggestive is Zürcher's conclusion that these new and distinctive features of written Chinese were due to the social and ideological milieu in which these scriptures were produced.[33] The largest part of the new, written idiom was created by drawing on what Zürcher calls the "Late Han vernacular, metropolitan (Lo-yang) dialect." But part derives from syntactic and grammatical distortion caused by the Sanskrit or Prakrit original, such as the awkward rendering of the vocative ("and so Śāriputra, all dharmas."... 如是舍利弗一切諸法) and the probable use of *ku* 故 to render the casual ablative in certain circumstances.[34]

Chou I-liang, too, has demonstrated[35] the direct influence of the Sanskrit language on Chinese grammar in the use of the particle *yu* 於 between a transitive verb and its object. This usage began to appear frequently in the Chinese language from the Six Dynasties[36] on and is quite common in Tun-huang texts.

Samuel Cheung, in a creative paper entitled "Perfective Particles in the *Bian-wen* (i.e. *pien-wen*) Language," has suggested that the development of sentence-final indicators of the perfective aspect in Chinese was a result of accommodation to Sanskrit grammatical strictures:

> Buddhism reached one of its most sophisticated stages of development in the Tang (T'ang) Dynasty. Massive translations of Sanskrit canons were made by earnest devotees, who often aimed at capturing the spirit of the texts by following the original style as closely as possible. In so doing, they introduced

into Chinese an unprecedented style of prose-verse combination, many new words in transliteration, and, perhaps, some grammatical patterns.

It is suggested here that under the influence of Sanskrit, a sentence-final *liao, yi,* or *qi* (*ch'i*) was used to mark a perfective aspect. In Sanskrit, the perfective form for a gerundial verb is, marked by the suffix *tvā*. As the language is verb-final in its word order, the perfective suffix invariably appears at the end of a gerundial sentence. In rendering such a case into Chinese, translators, consciously or unconsciously, placed a particle at the end of the sentence for the same purpose. Although this practice might seem foreign to the Chinese language, it must have enjoyed great popularity among Buddhist scholars in the late T'ang. Not only translations but also discussions on religious topics record such a usage. The *bian-wen* (*pien-wen*), a genre originally fostered in a religious environment, also abound with cases of this nature.

Furthermore, it is interesting to note that in almost all the examples in the *bian-wen* (*pien-wen*), the perfective marker is limited to a subordinate clause, which relates the temporal setting to the main clause representing the event in focus. In view of the fact that the Sanskrit suffix *tvā* is used to mark the adverbial use of a gerundial verb, the similarity in function lends great support to the hypothesis of a relationship between the two forms.[37]

That Chinese languages are susceptible to the influence of foreign grammatical structures should come as no surprise to those who have studied their development during the course of the twentieth century. For example, the frequent use of *te* 的 as a marker for relative clauses is imitative of European languages, as is the now obligatory inclusion of *shih* as a copula in sentences with a substantive predicate. Historians of Chinese languages must, therefore, follow the lead provided by Buddhologists and carry out a systematic investigation of the influence of Sanskritic (and other Indo-European languages such as Tocharian, Khotanese, etc.) syntax and grammar on the development of the written vernacular.[38]

In phonology, until the Ch'ing period (1644-1911), nearly every major development starting with the invention of the "cut and splice" (*fan-ch'ieh* 反切) system of[39] spelling around the beginning of the sixth century was either invented by Buddhist monks or inspired by their work.[40] It is natural that their interest in psalmody would stimulate them to pay a great deal of attention to this aspect of language. Buddhists outside of India have always been much exercised by the problem of how to approximate in other languages the sacred and powerful sounds of Sanskrit. A Buddhist monk at the end of the T'ang named Shou-wen 守溫 even devised an "alphabet" of 36 letters 三十六字母. Though Sung phonologists adopted its principles in their analyses, it is unfortunate that full-scale alphabetization of Chinese languages failed to materialize.

Music, too, was profoundly affected by influences from beyond the borders of the Central Kingdom. Several modes which later became a part of the Chinese musical system were imported from India and Indianized Central Asia during the T'ang period.[41] Such well-known instruments as the "balloon guitar" (*pi-pa* 琵琶), the hand-harp (*kung-hou* 箜篌), and the "two-stringed Serindian fiddle" (*erh-hu* 二胡), as their bisyllabic names alone should indicate, were not native inventions.[42]

The whole question of the origins of "lyric verse" (*tz'u* 詞) needs to be re-examined carefully in terms of the massive influx of foreign music during the T'ang dynasty.[43] There can be no doubt that Buddhist imported tunes were a significant factor in the rise of *tz'u*. To name only a few of the Buddhist cantos which were later adopted as lyric meters, there were "The Brahman" 婆羅門, "The Hymn of Siddham" 悉曇頌, "Śāriputra" 舍利弗, "The Buddha" 浮圖子, and "Vaiśravaṇa" 毗沙子. During the T'ang period, "Let Us Return (i.e. Take Refuge)" 歸去來 was an explicitly Buddhist canto but, by the Sung, it had been adapted (e.g. by Liu Yong 柳永) as a secular lyric meter.[44]

Hsüan-tsung's 玄宗 (r. 712-756) famed "Rainbow-Skirt and Feather-Blouse Canto" 霓裳羽衣曲 was actually an adaptation of "Brahman's Canto" 婆羅門曲. The probable Indian origins of the tune were still known in the Sung period even though the name had long since been changed. In the ninety-ninth section of his *Dream Brook Essays*, Shen Kua (1030-1094) says that "Now on the lintel of the Tower of Leisure in P'u[45] there is some horizontal writing [in contrast to Chinese vertical writing] in a Devanāgari-like script by a person of the T'ang. It is reported that it is the score for the 'Rainbow-Skirt'."[46] But since no one in Shen Kua's day was capable of reading it, people were not sure just what it was. This is but one of the numerous examples which could be cited that illustrate how rapidly the Indian and Central Asian origins of many important elements of Chinese culture could be utterly obscured. There are even occasions where Chinese authorities, by governmental fiat, required the wholesale renaming of foreign tunes with Chinese-sounding titles. Given this sort of atmosphere and mentality, it is not at all surprising that the alien-sounding name *pien-wen* would seem somehow mysteriously to disappear at the beginning of the Sung dynasty. The actuality, of course, is not that *pien-wen* disappeared in the Sung but that it was so thoroughly and effectively absorbed and Sinicized. As I have demonstrated elsewhere, orally performed expository tales (*p'ing-hua* 平話 or, more precisely, the oral antecedents of written *p'ing-hua*) were not really so different from orally performed *pien* (i.e., the oral antecedents of *pien-wen*), except that they had a different name and favored different stories.[47]

Hsü Chia-jui has made a brief but compelling statement of the crucial significance which the music of "the Western Regions"[48] holds for the development of Chinese literature. He argues, for example, that strum lyrics (*tan-tz'u* 彈詞) were not created by Chinese musicians but were imitative of translated Indian literature. Hsü then proceeds to explain how this could have happened and how to deal with it by mentioning four general points for consideration:

> A. Chinese literature was never free of foreign influence, particularly that of the Western regions.
> B. Chinese literature was never free of the influence of music.

> C. The compilation of literary history ought to focus on music, thereby establishing a musical literary history.[49]
> D. The ten divisions of T'ang music were formerly looked down upon as foreign music. Yet among them, the Kuchean produced the later cantos and the Indian produced the later strum lyrics. Their relationship to Chinese literature is thus exceedingly great. There are still the eight other sections which no one has studied, I believe that, among them, there are certainly quite a few secret gems.... Therefore, I advocate that later, in compiling literary history, we should first compile the history of music. And, in compiling the history of music, we should first compile the cultural history of the Western Regions.[50]

Hsü's points are very well taken. No adequate history of Chinese literature can be written which ignores the profound impact of foreign culture upon it. Some progress has already been made in the direction advocated by Hsü. A large part of the system of Chinese music (including many individual tunes and the majority of instruments) from the T'ang period on has been demonstrated to have a foreign origin. This has been conclusively proven by such eminent authorities as Kishibe Shigeo, Tanabe Hisao, Hayashi Kenzō, Curt Sachs, and Laurence Picken. And Edward Schafer has studied the means by which foreign music was adopted at court:

> But of all the specialists of ambiguous social status who were sent to China by a foreign government, the most popular and influential were the musicians—instrumentalists, singers, and dancers—and the instruments and musical modes they brought with them.... For many centuries the music of the West had its admirers in China, but under the Sui emperors there was a great vogue for it, which continued into T'ang times. As Western nations were brought under Chinese control, their music was "captured", as it were, and subsequently was demanded as "tribute" from them. Foreign orchestras were incorporated into the mass of court employees and were required to perform for courtiers and vassals in "informal" palace entertainments. "Formal" ceremonies,

in contrast, required traditional tunes, played on ancient Chinese instruments, especially bells, stone chimes, and zithers.⁵¹

The massive influence of Indian and Central Asian culture upon the life of the T'ang dynasty capital has been carefully documented by Hsiang Ta in his long essay entitled "Chang-an during the T'ang Period and the Civilization of the Western Regions (T'ang-tai Ch'ang-an yu Hsi-yü wen-ming)." The fourth section, "The Serindianization of Ch'ang-an around the Time of the Incipient Origin Reign Period (713-741) (K'ai-yüan ch'ien-hou Ch'ang-an chih hu-hua 開元前后長安之胡化)," and the fifth section, "Schools of Art and Dances to Music Transmitted from the Western Regions (Hsi-yü ch'uan-lai chin hua-p'ai yü yüeh-wu 西域傳來之畫派與樂舞)," are especially helpful in understanding the nature and magnitude of this cultural impress.

The fact that Indian influence in China reached a peak in the seventh and eighth centuries may bear importantly on the question of why transformations (*pien*) seem to have come into being at about the same time. As C. P. Fitzgerald puts it, India during the T'ang "was probably better known to the Chinese.... than it has been at any subsequent period until modern times. Ch'ang An (the Chinese capital) was in regular diplomatic contact with the more important states of Northern India, and even interfered in Indian politics on more than one occasion"⁵² Confronted with the mass of evidence of foreign (especially Indo-Buddhist) influence on virtually all aspects of culture during the T'ang, we should not arbitrarily reject a partially foreign origin for transformation texts (*pien-wen*) if the evidence available points overwhelmingly in that direction.

Tetragraphs (fang-k'uai-tzu 方塊字) for "India and China: Observations on Cultural Borrowing"

By Victor H. Mair

1. 變文

2. 敦煌

3. 樣板戲

4. 謝赫六法

5. 佛所行讚經

6. 小說月報

7. 中國文學研究

8. 鄭振鐸

9. 梵劇體例及其在漢劇上底點點滴滴

10. 天台山國清寺

11. 胡先驌

12. 溫州

13. 市舶司

14. 南戲

15. 天問

16. 如是舍利弗一切諸法

17. 故

18. 於

19. 反切

20. 守溫

21. 三十六字母

22. 琵琶

23. 箜篌

24. 二胡

25. 詞

26. 婆羅門

27. 悉曇頌

28. 舍利弗

29. 浮圖子

30. 毗沙子

31. 歸去來

32. 柳永

33. 玄宗

34. 霓裳羽衣曲

35. 婆羅門曲

36. 平話

37. 彈詞

38. 開元前后長安之胡化

39. 西域傳來之畫派與樂舞

40. 向達

41. 敦煌佛教藝術之淵源及其在中國藝術史上之地位

42. 水天明

43. 伏安英倫，仆仆大漠——談向達教授對"敦煌學"的貢獻

44. 敦煌學輯刊

45. 常任俠

46. 中印文化的交流

47. 中國古典藝術

48. 藥名譜

49. 侯寧極

50. 陶穀

51. 陳蓮塘

52. 唐代叢書

53. 謝肇淛

54. 五雜俎

55. 胡

56. 鄭振鐸

57. 插圖本中國文學史

58. 朱維之

59. 沙恭達拉與宋元南戲

60. 福州協和大學學術

61. 盧前

62. 中國戲曲所受印度文學及佛教之影響

63. 中國戲劇概論

64. 萬鈞

65. 佛教與中國文學

66. 現代佛教學術叢刊

67. 許地山

68. 林培志

69. 李滿桂

70. 抹泥

71. 貼淨

72. 腳色

73. 木笡

74. 莫鞊

75. 旦

76. 黎薔（李強）

77. 試論梵劇，回鶻劇與中國戲曲

78. 糜文開

79. 印度文學欣賞

80. 三民文庫

81. 胡適

82. 白話文學史

83. 饒宗頤

84. 劉勰文藝思想與佛教

85. 劉勰

86. 般若

87. 嚴羽

88. 王國維

89. 境界

90. 陸侃如

91. 批判胡適的白話文學史

92. 文學遺產

93. 光明日報

94. 現代漢語選擇問句法的來源

95. 中央研究院歷史語言研究所集刊

96. 周一良

97. 中國的梵文研究

98. 魏晉南北朝史論集

99. 思想與時代月刊

100. 論佛典翻譯文學

101. 這

102. 遮

103. 寒山

104. 陳治文

105. 近指指示詞"這"的來源

106. 中國語文

107. 小西甚一

108. 四聲および反切考

109. 文鏡秘府論考

110. 龍笑雲

111. 反切起原考略

112. 學風

113. 謝無量

114. 佛教東來對中國文學之影響

115. 梵音入中國以成沈約四聲及駢文律詩之發展

116. 律詩

117. 近體詩

118. 趙蔭棠

119. 等韻源流

120. 郁龍斜

121. 從沈括的《夢溪筆談》看中印古代文化交流

122. 南亞研究

123. 徐嘉瑞

124. 近古文學概論

125. 聞汝賢

126. 詞牌匯釋

127. 吳藕汀

128. 詞名索引

129. 蒲中

130. 沈括

131. 夢溪筆談校證

132. 胡道靜

133. 西域

134. 朱謙之

135. 中國音樂文學史

Notes

1. For background and bibliography on this subject, see Victor H. Mair, *Tun-huang Popular Narratives* (Cambridge: Cambridge University Press, 1983); *T'ang Transformation Texts: A Study of the Buddhist Contribution to the Rise of Vernacular Fiction and Drama in China*, Harvard-Yenching Monograph Series, 28 (Cambridge, Massachusetts: Harvard University Council on East Asian Studies, 1989); *Painting and Performance: Chinese Picture Recitation and Its Indian Genesis* (Honolulu: University of Hawaii Press, 1988); "Lay Students and the Making of Written Vernacular Narrative: An inventory of Tun-huang manuscripts," *Chinoperl Papers*, 10 (1981), 5-96; "The Narrative Revolution in Chinese Literature: Ontological Presuppositions," *Chinese Literature: Essays, Articles, Reviews*, 5. 1 (July, 1983), 1-27; and "A Partial Bibliography for the Study of Indian influence on Chinese Popular Literature," *Sino-Platonic Papers*, (March, 1987) (iv + 214 pages).
2. *Anthropology: Race, Language, Culture, Psychology, Prehistory* (New York: Harcourt, Brace, 1923; rev. ed. 1948), p. 411.
3. "Indian Influences on Bali Culture", in *The Countries and Peoples of the East: Selected Articles* (Moscow: Nauka Publishing House, 1974), pp. 266-285. Originally appeared in *Countries and Peoples of the East*, issued by the Oriental Commission of the Geographical Society of the U.S.S.R., Vol. 5 (*India—The Country and People*) (Moscow, 1967), pp. 129-148.
4. But even language itself (as we shall see later in this article) is shaped by cultural contact: witness the enormous number of Japanese loanwords in modern Chinese and the enormous number of English loanwords in modern Japanese. It need not be emphasized that loanwords themselves (as well as other types of lexical borrowings) are changed radically by their absorption into a new linguistic setting.
5. Quoted by Claire Holt, *Art in Indonesia: Continuities and Change* (Ithaca: Cornell University Press, 1967), p. 63.
6. B. Schrieke, "Eenige opmerkingen over ontleening in de cultuur-ontwikkeling," *Djawa*, 7.2 (1927), 94-95 (of 89-96).
7. In *Independence, Convergence, and Borrowing in institutions, Thought, and Art*. Harvard Tercentenary Publications (Cambridge, Massachusetts: Harvard University Press, 1937), pp. 229-230 (of 219-247).

8. See Hsiang Ta's 向達 general remarks in "Tun-huang Fa-chiao i-shu chih yüan-yüan chi ch'i tsai Chung-kuo i-shu shih shang chih ti-wei (The Origins of Tun-huang Buddhist Art and Its Position in the History of Chinese Art) 敦煌佛教藝術之淵源及其在中國藝術史上之地位." Appendix (pp. 121-123) to Shui T'ien-ming 水天明 "Fu-an Ying-lun, p'u-p'u ta-mo -- t'an Hsiang Ta chiao-shou tui 'Tun-huang hsüeh' te kung-hsien (Head Bowed over His Desk at the British Museum, Plodding through the Great Desert: a Discussion of Professor Hsiang Ta's Contributions to Tunhuangology) 伏安英倫, 仆仆大漠--談向達教授對'敦煌學'的貢獻' Tun-huang-hsüeh chi-k'an (Journal of Tunhuangology) 敦煌學輯刊, 2 (1980-81 [?]), 117-123. Ch'ang Jen-hsia 常任俠 has discussed Indian cultural influence in the arts under the headings of music, dance, sculpture, and painting. See his article entitled "Chung Yin wen-hua te chiao-liu (Cultural Exchange between China and India)" 中印文化的交流, Chung-kuo ku-tien i-shu (Chinese Classical Arts) 中國古典藝術, 6 (Shanghai: Shanghai ch'u-pan kung-ssu, 1954), 120-144.
9. For an overview of this subject, see René Grousset, *The Civilizations of the East: China*, tr. from the French by Catherine Alison Philips (New York: A. A. Knopf, 1935; originally published in Paris in 1930), chapter 2, "Buddhist influence in China", pp. 147-278. Cf. Frits Staal's remark ("What is Happening in Classical Indology? —A Review Article", *Journal of Asian Studies*, 41.2 (February, 1982), 276 (of 269-291) that "The Indianization of Asia is wider and deeper than is generally acknowledged".
10. See Percy Brown, *Indian Painting* (Calcutta: Y.M.C.A. Publishing House, 1953), pp. 21-23 and William Acker, tr. and annot., *Some T'ang and pre-T'ang Texts on Chinese Painting*, vol. 1 (Leiden: E.J. Brill, 1954), vol. II, parts 1 and 2 (Leiden: E.J. Brill, 1974), pp. xlviii-xlv (of vol. I). The Ṣaḍaṅga actually occur in Yaśodhara's thirteenth-century commentary to Vātsyāyana's *Kāmasūtra*, but he is surely quoting much older sources.
11. *China's Debt to Buddhist India* (New York: The Maha Bodhi Society of America, 1927 [?]), p. 13.
12. Cf. also P2337, P2665v, and P2703. A concrete example of the influence of Buddhism upon pharmacology in China is the *Yao-ming p'u* (A List of Names of Medicines) 藥名譜 by Hou Ning-chi 侯寧極, revised for publication by T'ao Ku 陶穀 (902-970), in Ch'en Lien-t'ang 陳蓮塘 (Ch'ing period), ed., *T'ang-tai ts'ung-shu* (T'ang Dynasty Collectanea) 唐代叢書 (Shanghai: Chin-chang t'u-shu-chü, 1921 [?] lithograph), *ts'e* 7, *chih* 76. T'ao Ku's introduction shows that this list of medicines is of Buddhist origin. The majority of the 190 types mentioned are derived

from plants. Many of the drugs listed have fanciful names which even the editors found difficult to identify. In this article, I focus primarily on literature (especially fiction and drama) and only touch upon language, music, religion, philosophy, medicine, and painting. For a more comprehensive view of early Sino-Indian cultural relations, the reader may consult such general works as the following: Prabodh Chandra Bagchi, *India and China: A Thousand Years of Cultural Relations* (Bombay: Hind Kitabs, 1950, second rev. and enlgd. ed.; first published 1944); H.G. Quaritch Wales, The *Indianization of China and of Southeast Asia* (London: Bernard Quaritch, 1967); and Suniti Kumar Chatterji, "India and China: Ancient Contacts—What India Received from China," *Journal of the Asiatic Society* (Calcutta), I. 1 (1959), 89-122.

13. Hsieh Chao-chih 謝肇淛 (Advanded Scholar 1602), *Wu tsa-tsu* (Miscellanea in Five Parts) 五雜俎 (Peking: Chung-hua shu-chü, 1959), ch. 5, p. 147. For a rich fund of information on the foreign origin of much of Chinese popular entertainment, see James T. Araki, *The Ballad-Drama of Medieval Japan* (Berkeley and Los Angeles: University of California Press, 1964; Rutland, Vermont and Tokyo: Charles E. Tuttle, 1978). The word translated as "Serindian" (*hu* 胡) might more accurately (though clumsily) be rendered as "Turco-indo-iranian."

14. "Sport bei den Völkern Zentralasiens, nach chinesischen Quellen," in his *China und seine westlichen Nachbarn: Beiträge zur mittelalterlichen und neueren Geschichte Zentralasiens* (Darmstadt: Wissenschaftliche Buchgesellschaft, 1978), pp. 128-142.

15. See also Mair, "The Contribution of Transformation Texts to Later Chinese Popular Literature" (forthcoming).

16. For an early reference to dramatic representations in Buddhism, see Jacob S. Speyer, ed., *Avadānacataka*, Bibliotheca Buddhica, 3 (St. Petersburg: Commissionnaires de l'Académie Impériale des Sciences, 1906-1909; reprinted 's-Gravenhage: Mouton, 1958 and Osnabrück: Biblio Verlag, 1970), vol. 2, section 75, pp. 29-30, esp. p. 29, I. 11 where there is mentioned *Bauddam nāṭakam* ("Buddhist dance/drama/pantomime").

17. See A. Berriedale Keith, *The Sanskrit Drama in its Origin, Development, Theory, and Practice* (Oxford: Clarendon Press, 1924), pp. 80-85 and cf. Étienne Lamotte, tr. *Le Traité de la Grande Vertu de Sagesse de nāgārjuna (Mahāprajñāpāramitaśāstra) avec une étude sur la Vacuité*, vols. 2 and 4, Bibliothéque du Muséon, 18 and Publications de l'Institut Orientaliste de

Louvain, 2 and 12 (Louvain: Bureaux du Muséon, 1944 and Université de Louvain, Institut Orientaliste, 1976), vol. 2, pp. 621-649.
18. Heinrich Lüders, ed., *Bruchstücke Buddhistischer Dramen*, Königlich Preussische Turfan-Expeditionen, 1, Kleinere Sanskrit-Texte (Berlin: Georg Reimer, 1911), p. 41 and note 6 on that page. 19. *Social Life of the Chinese* (New York: Harper and Brothers, 1865; reprinted Taipei: Ch'eng Wen, 1966), vol. 2, p. 298 (italics in original).
19. *Social life of the Chinese* (New York: Harper and Brother's, 1865; reprinted Taipei: Ch'eng Wen, 1966), vol. 2 p. 298 (italics in original).
20. *The Temples of Anking and Their Cults: A Study of Modern Chinese Religion* (Paris: Librairie Orientaliste Paul Guenthner, 1931), p. 32.
21. Mentioned in Cheng Chen-to 鄭振鐸, *Ch'a-t'u pen Chung-Kuo wen-hsüeh shih* (Illustrated History of Chinese Literature) 插圖本中國文學史 4 vols., continuous pagination (Peking: Tso-chia ch'u-pan-she, 1957; originally 1932), p. 568. Cf. also the two articles by Lois Finot and Sten Konow entitled "Kālidāsa in China," *Indian Historical Quarterly*, 9.4 (December, 1933), 829-834 and 10.3 (September, 1934), 566-570.
22. Chu Wei-chih 朱維之, "Sha-kung-ta-la yü Sung Yüan nan-hsi (Sākoontalā and Southern Drama of the Sung and Yüan Periods)" 沙恭達拉與宋元南戲, *Fu-chou hsieh-ho ta-hsüeh hsüeh-shu* (The Foochow Union University Studies) 福州協和大學學術 3 (1935), offprint. For Indian influence on the development of Chinese drama, see also Lu Ch'ien 盧前, "Chung-kuo hsi-chü so shou Yin-tu wen-hsüeh chi F'o-chiao chih ying-hsiang (The Influence of Indian Literature and Buddhism upon Chinese Drama)" 中國戲曲所受印度文學及佛教之影響 in his *Chung-kuo hsi-chü kai-lun* (Outline of Chinese Theater) 中國戲劇概論 (Shanghai: Shih-chieh shu-chü, 1934), pp. 6-9. Wan Chün 萬鈞, "Fo-chiao yü Chung-kuo wen-hsüeh (Buddhism and Chinese Literature)" 佛教與中國文學, in *Fo-chiao yü Chung-kuo wen-hsüeh* (Buddhism and Chinese Literature) 佛教與中國文學, Hsien-tai Fo-chiao hsüeh-shu ts'ung-k'an (Modern Studies of Buddhism) 現代佛教學術叢刊, 19 (Series 2, no. 9) (Taipei: Ta-ch'eng wen-hua ch'u-pan-she 1978), p. 3 (of 1-6) says flatly that Chinese drama comes from India (as stated, this is an extreme formulation of a complex issue) and refers to studies by Hsü Ti-shan 許地山, Lin, P'ei-chih 林培志, Li Man-kuei 李滿桂, which document this (see the bibliography by Mair cited in note 1 for references). In a conversation of May 5, 1982 and in a letter of June 8, 1982, Elling Eide has told me of his growing conviction that several Chinese theatrical terms may be traceable to the vocabulary or conventions of ancient Indian drama. He suggests that *mo-ni* (male

lead), *ching* (the villain), and even the word *chiao-se* (role) itself might all be best explained as make-up terms deriving from some regional observation of conventions such as those found in works like Bharata-muni's Nāṭyaśāstra. See the translation by Monrnohan Ghosh (Calcutta: Royal Asiatic Society of Bengal, 1951, rev. second ed.), vol. 1, ch. 23, 4. 72-83, 89-108 where "painting the limbs" (*aṅgaracanā*) is discussed. Construed in this light, the *mo-ni* (read 抹泥) would be "the one who puts on the paste or mixed colors," *the ching* (also called *t'ieh-ching* 貼淨) would be "the one who applies the pure or primary colors," and *chiao-se* 腳色, the word for "role" would be, quite literally, "the color of the limbs." As for the *tan* "female lead," Eide accepts the identification with *mu-tan* (木笪, T'ang *muktân-* or *muktât*) or *mo-ta* (莫靼, T'ang *mwâk-tât*), attested in T'ang sources, and suggests that this might derive from a Sanskrit or Prakrit word for the "the ingénue (mugdhā)". See, for example, George Hass, tr., The *Daśarupaka* (New York Columbia University Press, 1912), 2.2b:

> The inexperienced [kind of wife] (mugdhā) has the desire of new youth, is coy in love and gentle in anger. *mugdhā navavayaḥkāmā ratau vāmā mṛduḥ krudhi.*

An alternative etymology would be *mukta* which means "dissolute woman", an interpretation of *tan* 旦 advanced by several Chinese commentators. Eide further suggests that the Tocharians (the "Kucheans"), who apparently had a rich dramatic literature, may have been the intermediaries for the transmission to China of some terms and conventions that were Indian in origin, but he notes that his evidence for this is presently limited to the fact that the Tocharians and the Chinese seem to have preceded the Indians in the convention of regularly indicating a tune, mode, or raga title before the sung verse passages in their dramas. See also Eide's "Foreign Influences on the Chinese Performing Arts: A Selection of Thoughts and Festerings," appendix to his "Li Po's 'Up into the Clouds Music'," presented to the members of Chinoperl at the thirty-fifth annual meeting of the Association for Asian Studies, March 25-27, 1983, San Francisco.

23. Li Ch'iang 黎薔 (李強), "Shih-lun fan-chü, hui-ho chü yü Chung-kuo hsi-ch'ü (Tentative Discussion of the Relationship between Sanskrit Drama, Uighur Drama, and Chinese Plays)" 試論梵劇、回鶻劇與中國戲曲. Paper presented at the August, 1985 Conference on Tun-huang and Turfan Studies held at Urumchi, Sinkiang. This is a careful analysis of

the resemblances between Sanskrit and Chinese drama, together with a look at old Uighur drama. Li pays particular attention to actual historical contacts. There was, of course, also a long tradition of performing arts in the north, going back through various T'ang theatricals, song-and-dance routines imported from the Western Regions during the Six Dynasties, Han entertainments (many also from abroad), and even earlier indigenous thaumaturgical performances. Yet none of these, obviously, constitutes drama, in the full sense of the word. This is a subject I explore in great detail in my article entitled "The Contributions of T'ang and Five Dynasties Transformation Texts (*pien-wen*) to Later Chinese Popular Literature" which is soon to appear in *Sino-Platonic Papers*.

24. *Ch'a-t'u pen Chung-kuo wen-hsüeh shih*, pp. 567ff. and 633.
25. The views of Liang and Hu are summarized by Mi Wen-k'ai 糜文開, *Yin-tu wen-hsüeh hsin-shang* (An Appreciation of Indian Literature) 印度文學欣賞 San-min wen-k'u (Three People's Library) 三民文庫, 17 (Taipei: San-min shu-chü, 1967); pp. 8-9. Also see Hu Shih 胡適, *Pai-hua wen-hsüeh shih* (A History of Chinese Vernacular Literature) 白話文學史, vol. 1 (Shanghai: Commercial Press, 1934, second ed., first ed. 1928), pp. 169-170.
26. See for example, Jao Tsung-i 饒宗頤, "Liu-Hsieh wen-i ssu-hsiang yü Fo-chiao (The Literary Thought of Liu Hsieh and Buddhism)" 劉勰文藝思想與佛教, in *Fo-chiao yü Chung-kuo wen-hsüeh* (see note 22), pp. 33-39. There is great need for a history of Buddhist influence on Chinese literary criticism from Liu Hsieh 劉勰 (c. 465-c. 522), who used the word *prajñā* 般若 ("transcendent wisdom") in reference to literary inspiration, to Yen Yü 嚴羽 (twelfth century), who was deeply influenced by Zen thinking, to Wang Kuo-wei 王國維 (1877-1927), one of whose basic concepts was *ching-chieh* 境界, i.e. viṣaya, artha, gocara ("sphere, realm, mental projection").
27. Lu K'an-ju 陸侃如, "P'i-p'an Hu Shih te *Pai-hua wen-hsüeh shih* (Criticism of Hu Shih's History of Vernacular Literature)" 批判胡適的白話文學史, *Wen-hsüeh i-ch'an* (Literary Heritage) 文學遺產, Section of the *Kuang-ming jih-pao* (Kuang-ming Daily) 光明日報, 54 (May 15, 1955).
28. Chi Hsien-lin, "Indian Literature in China," *Chinese Literature*, 4 (July-August, 1958), 123-130.
29. See Probhat K. Mukherji, *Indian Literature in China and the Far East* (Calcutta Greater India Society, 1931), p. 1.
30. *Ibid.*, p. 203.

31. This has actually already been done to very good advantage by I. S. Gurevich in *Ocherk Grammatiki Kitaiskogo Yaz'ika tretego-pyatogo vv.* (Moscow: Nauka, 1974). Tsu-lin Mei, in his study of the origin of the disjunctive question in modern Chinese, has stressed the importance of Buddhist materials; see his "Hsien-tai Han-yü hsüan-tse wen-chü fa te lai-yüan (The Origin of the Disjunctive Question in Modern Chinese)" 現代漢語選擇問句法的來源, *Chung-yang yen-chiu-yüan li-shih yü-yen yen-chiu-so chi-k'an* (Bulletin of the Institute of History and Philology, Academia Sinica) 中央研究院歷史語言研究所集刊 49.1 (1978), 17n5 (of 15-36)."
32. "Late Han Vernacular Elements in the Earliest Buddhist Translations," *Journal of the Chinese Language Teachers Association*, 12.3 (October, 1977), 177-203 and "Buddhist Influence on Early Taoism," *T'oung Pao*, 66.1-3 (1980), 84-147.
33. "Late Han Vernacular," p. 177.
34. Zürcher, "Late Han Vernacular," pp. 195n3 and 199n45.
35. Chou I-liang 周一良, "Chung-kuo te fan-wen yen-chiu (Sanskrit Studies in China)" 中國的梵文研究, in his *Wei Chin Nan-pei-ch'ao shih lun-chi* (Collection of Essays on the History of the Wei, the Chin, and the Northern and Southern Dynasties) 魏晉南北朝史論集 (Peking: Chung-hua shu-chü, 1963), pp. 314-322 of (323-338); originally appeared in *Ssu-hsiang yü shih-tai yüeh-k'an* (Thought and Time Monthly) 思想與時代月刊, 35. Chou had also discussed this usage in "Lun fo-tien tan-i wen-hsüeh (On the Translated Literature of the Buddhist Canon)" 論佛典翻譯文學, in *Fo-chiao yü Chung-kuo wen-hsüeh* (see note 22), pp. 314-322 (of pp. 335-344). For other remarks of a general nature on the subject of linguistic influence, see the introduction to my *Tun-huang Popular Narratives*.
36. Zürcher, "Late Han Vernacular," p. 190, noticed this usage already in the earliest Buddhist translations. Cf. Thomas Watters' remarks of nearly a century ago in chapter eight of his *Essays on the Chinese Language* (Shanghai: Presbyterian Mission Press, 1889), which deals with the representation of Sanskrit cases by Chinese particles.
37. "Perfective Particles in the *bian-wen* Language," *Journal of Chinese Linguistics* 5 (1977), 66 (of 55-74).
38. This extends even to such features as demonstrative pronouns. *Che* 這 (cf. *tsia* 遮), for example, was not used as a demonstrative until early in the T'ang period. It is found frequently in Tun-huang texts and in the works of such Buddhist poets as "Cold Mountain" 寒山 Cf. Ch'en Chin-

wen 陳治文, "Chin-chin chin-shin-tz'u 'che' te lai-yuan (The Origins of the proximate Demonstrative che)" 近指指示詞"這"的來源, *Chung-kuo Yu-wen* (Chinese Philology) 6 (cumulative 133) (December 22, 1964), 442-444. One wonders whether it is only a coincidence that the demonstrative pronominal adjective in Khotanese is *sa*. See R. E. Emmerick, ed. and tr., *The Khotanese Surangamasamadhisutra* (London and New York: Oxford University Press, 1970), glossary, p. 130. Much important work remains to be done in order to make clear the full impact of Sanskrit and Prakrit on the development of Han languages.

39. On the Indo-Buddhist origins of the fan-ch'ieh system of spelling, see Konishi Jinichi 小西甚一, "Shisei oyobi hansetsu kō (An Examination of the Four Tones and the fan-ch'ieh System of Spelling) 四聲および反切考" in his *Bunkyō hifuron kō* (An Examination of the Discussions from the Secret-Storehouse of the Mirror of Literature) 文鏡祕府論考 (Kyoto and Tokyo: Ōyashima shuppan kabushiki kaisha and Dai Nippon yūben-kai kōdansha, 1948-1953), vol. 1, chap. 3, pp. 143-554; Lung Hsiao-yun 龍笑雲, "Fan-ch'ieh ch'i-yüan k'ao-lüeh (A Summary Investigation of the Origins of the *fan-ch'ieh* System of Spelling)" 反切起源考略, *Hsüeh-feng* (Trends in Scholarship) 學風, 2.8 (September, 1932), 26-29; Hsieh Wu-liang 謝無量, "Fo-chiao tung lai tui Chung-kuo wen-hsüeh chih ying-hsiang (The Influence of Buddhism's Eastward Movement on Chinese Literature)" 佛教東來對中國文學之影響, section one, "Fan-yin ju Chung-kuo i ch'eng Shen Yüeh ssu-sheng chi p'ien-wen lu-shihchih fa-chan (The Entrance of Sanskrit Phonology into China Leading to Shen Yüeh's (441-513) Four Tones and the Development of Parallel Prose and Regulated Verse)" 梵音入中國以成沈約四聲及駢文律詩之發展, in *Fo-chiao yü Chung-kuo wen-hsüeh* (see note 22), pp. 15-20 (of 15-36), and many other articles listed in Paul Fu-mien Yang, comp., *Chinese Linguistics: A Selected and Classified Bibliography* (Hong Kong: The Chinese University of Hong Kong, 1974) pp. 77-78, entries 1179-1198. Tsu-lin Mei and I are preparing for publication a joint article on the origins of "Regulated Verse" (*lü-shih* 律詩) or "Recent Style" (*Chin-t'i-shih* 近體詩) prosody which will conclusively demonstrate its Indian origins.

40. Lo Ch'ang-p'ei, "Indian influence on the Study of Chinese Phonology," *Sino-Indian Studies*, 1.3 (April, 1945), 115-126; A. von Rosthorn, "Indischer Einfluss in der Lautlehre Chinas," *Sitzungsberichte, Akademie der Wissenschaften in Wien*, 219.4 (1942); Chao Yin-t'ang 趙蔭棠, *Teng-yün yuan-liu* (The Sources and History of Rhyme-Group Classification) 等

韻源流 (Shanghai: Commercial Press, 1957). See also Yu Lungyu (Yü Lung-yü) 郁龍余, "Ts'ung Shen Kua te *Meng-hsi pi-t'an* K'an Chung-Yin ku-tien wen-hua chiao-liu (Shen-kuo's 'Meng-Xi-Bi-Tan,' Study of Cultural Exchange between India and China)" 從沈括的《夢溪筆談》看中印古代文化交流, *Nanya Yanjiu* (South Asian Studies) 南亞研究 2 (1981), 103-104 (of 102-106). Yu discusses other aspects of Indian influence as well (astronomy, music, dance, etc) and provides a useful bibliography of Chinese studies on Indian civilization.

41. Paul Pelliot, review of *Hobogirin*, second fasc., *T'oung Pao*, 28 (1931), 95-104.
42. See the studies by Hayashi Kenzō, Tanabe Hisao, Curt Sachs, and Lawrence Picken (Mair, "Bibliography" [note 1 above]).
43. For an overview of the pervasive influence of foreign music during the T'ang which contributed to the growth of *tz'u*, see Hsü Chia-jiu 徐嘉瑞, *Chin-ku wen-hsueh kai-lun* (Outline of Literature since the Middle Ages) 近古文學概論 (Shanghai: pei-hsin shu-chu, 1947), pp. 73-118. Two recent studies of the early history of the *tz'u* within China are by Kang-i Sun Chang, *The Evolution of Chinese Tz'u Poetry: From Late T'ang to Northern Sung* (Princeton: Princeton University Press, 1980) and Marsha Wagner, *The Lotus Boat: The Origins of Chinese Tz'u Poetry in T'ang Popular Culture* (New York: Columbia University Press, 1984). The first mentions T'ang emperor Hsuan-tsung's active encouragement of the introduction of Serindian music into the court. The second focuses on the popularization of songs by singing girls and their adaptation by literati poets. These are commendable histories of the early *tz'u*, we are still in great need of a pre-history of the *tz'u*. For an offer of extensive research materials relating to proto-*tz'u*, see Mair," Bibliography," p. ii.
44. See Wen Ju-hsien 聞汝賢, *Tz'u-p'ai hui-shih* (Glossary of Lyric Titles with Explanations) 詞牌彙釋 (Taipei: by the author, 1963), pp. 739-740 and Wu Ou-t'ing 吳藕汀 *Tz'u-ming so-yin* (*Index of Lyric Names*) 詞名索引 (Peking: Chung-hua shu-chü, 1958), p. 182.
45. 蒲中. I have been unable to locate this place with any degree of definiteness.
46. Shen Kua 沈括 (1030-1094), *Meng-hsi pi-t'an chiao-cheng* (Collated Dream Brook Essays) 夢溪筆談校證, issued 1086-1091, ed. Hu Tao-ching 胡道靜 (Shanghai: Shanghai ch'u-pan kung-ssu, 1956), p. 235.
47. See the "Introduction" to my *Painting and Performance*.
48. *Hsi-yu* 西域, a vague designation for Central Asia and adjacent areas to the west and south.

49. A very good start at such a history is Chu Ch'ien-chih's 朱謙之 *Chung-kuo yin-yueh wen-hsueh shih* (A History of Chinese Literature Set to Music) 中國音樂文學史 (Shanghai: Commercial Press, 1935).
50. *Chin-ku wen-hsueh kai-lun*, pp. 119-122.
51. *The Golden Peaches of Samarkand: A Study of T'ang Exotics* (Berkeley: University of California Press, 1963), pp. 50-51.
52. *China: A Short Cultural History* (London: The Cresset Press, 1958), p. 326.

CHAPTER 5

THE WORD *M^{y}AG IN OLD SINITIC

*M^{y}AG, OLD PERSIAN MAGUŠ, AND ENGLISH "MAGICIAN"

Source: Adapted from "Old Sinitic *m^{y}ag, Old Persian maguš, and English 'Magician,'" *Early China* 15 (1990): 27-47.

The recent discovery at an early Chou site of two figurines with unmistakably Caucasoid or Europoid features is startling prima facie evidence of East–West interaction during the first half of the first millennium Before the Current Era. It is especially interesting that one of the figurines bears on the top of his head the clearly incised graph ✚ which identifies him as a *wu* (<*m^{y}ag*).[1]

In the autumn of 1980, archeologists working on the remains of the Western Chou palace complex at Fu-feng 扶風 in Shensi province, a bit over sixty miles west of Sian and within the general area of Chouyüan 周原 (the birthplace of the Chou dynasty), discovered two small heads carved from mollusk shell. The heads have been dated to the early eighth century B.C.E. and given catalog numbers 80FCT45:2 (fig. 1) and 80FCT45:6 (fig. 2).[2] The first is only 2.9 centimeters in height and the second 2.8 centimeters. Both have sockets .6 centimeters in diameter drilled into their bottoms reaching approximately half way through to the top. In the cavity of T45.2 remain fragments of what appears to be the stem of a bone pin; thus, it is assumed that the two little heads were used as ornamental tips for hairpins. This is a reasonable assumption in light of both the size of the heads and their somewhat flattened backs,[3] which features are comparable to the tips of other early Chinese hairpins that have been archeologically recovered. On these grounds, I am inclined to believe that the two Caucasoid/Europoid heads were products of local manufacture, rather than imported figurines adapted for local use.

Both of the heads are obviously dolichocephalic in stark contrast to usual human facial representations from the Western Chou period, the vast majority of which are brachicephalic. Both have long and large noses, roundish eyes in deep sockets, thin lips, wide mouths and strong jaws, quite unlike the short and flat noses, shallow almond eyes, thick lips, narrow mouths, and smoothly curved jaws of most Western Chou faces. The sculptor(s) who created these distinctive figures must have been particularly taken by the sharply etched cheeks of the individuals they were portraying because they emphasize this aspect of their physiognomy with raised ridges in one case (T45:2) and comma-shaped indentations in the other (T45:6). Both figures are equipped with similar headgear, slowly tapering truncated cones with closely spaced vertical striations that hug the forehead, temples, and base of the skull, showing neither hair nor ears,[4] except that it slopes evenly from front to back on T45:6 whereas it bends angularly about halfway along the side of T45:2.

It has been asserted that these caps identify the two figures as Sakas.[5] This would be wonderful if it were true, for it would complement the linguistic evidence I shall adduce below regarding the racial identity of the figures depicted. Unfortunately, the typical pointed Saka cap is quite different from that of the two Western Chou figurines: it is not striated, is much more steeply peaked, falls all the way to the nape of the neck, and, above all, is tied beneath the chin.[6]

The Word *m^{y}ag in Old Sinitic 157

Figure 1. Shell Carved Head (T45:2) from Chou-yüan. *Wen wu* 1 (1986): 46.

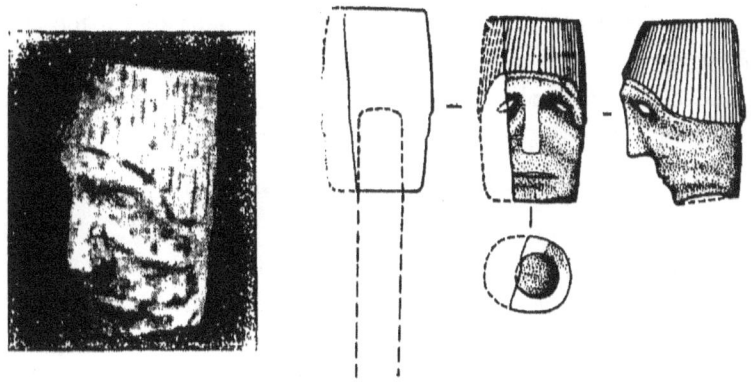

Source: Adapted from "Old Sinitic *myag, Old Persian maguš, and English 'Magician,'" *Early China* 15 (1990): 29.

Figure 2. Shell Carved Head (T45:6) from Chou-yüan. *Wen wu* 1（1986）: 47.

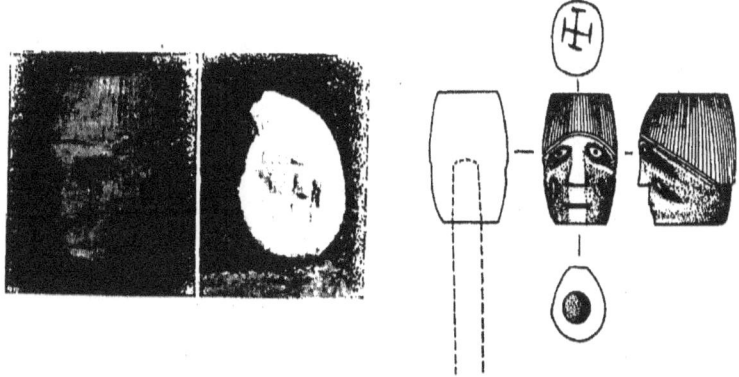

Source: Adapted from "Old Sinitic *myag, Old Persian maguš, and English 'Magician,'" *Early China* 15 (1990): 29.

Suggestions concerning the racial identity of the two figures range widely, from Scythians to Huns, from Proto-Tibetans to Bactrians, and from Tocharians to Wu-sun.[7] Some of these groups appear too late in the historical record to be considered seriously while others are either ethnically or geographically inappropriate. The scholarly consensus, in any event, is that the individuals depicted are Europoid.[8]

I have also found a strikingly similar bone carving of a human head that was unearthed at Anyang earlier in this century (fig. 3).[9] Here the physiognomical features are exaggerated almost to the point of caricature, although the piece evinces an overall realism that is haunting. We have in this Shang piece the same sharply etched cheeks (compare the ridge line with that of T45:2, but here it is even more raised), exceedingly pronounced round eyes that are deeply recessed in enormous sockets, a very long, straight nose extending high to the base of the forehead, thin lips, wide mouth, and square, jutting jaw. There can be little doubt that this Shang piece and the two Western Chou pieces belong to the same category of foreign residents in China.[10] The major differences are that the nose of the Shang head is slightly hooked at the bottom and has more widely flaring nostrils (but this might be attributable simply to the finer modelling of the piece in general), the ears are visible, and the vertical striations (which correspond closely both in number and in spacing with those of the Western Chou heads) converge at the top of a smooth, round dome giving the impression more of a Beatle-ish mop of hair than a skullcap.

Among comparable headcoverings (whether of hair or cap) elsewhere in Eurasia during the time period in question, one finds similar domed striations on the head of an Aramean portrayed in an Urartian relief at Zincirli in the middle late Hittite style dating to the period 832–810 B.C.E. (fig. 4).[11] Temporally and spatially this would be appropriate as a source for the three foreign figures found in China. The Urartian kingdom, initially centered around Lake Van, arose in the ninth century B.C.E. against the background of the Hurrian communities of eastern Anatolia.

Figure 3. Bone carving of a human head from Anyang.

Source: Adapted from "Old Sinitic **myag*, Old Persian maguš, and English 'Magician,'" *Early China* 15 (1990): 32. After Carl Hentze, *Funde in Alt-China: Das Welterleben in ältesten China*, Sternstunden de Archäologie (Gottingen Musterschmidt, 1967), Taf. XV.

Figure 4. Aramean from Urartian relief at Zincirli.

Source: Adapted from "Old Sinitic *myag, Old Persian maguš, and English 'Magician,'" Early China 15 (1990): 32. Ekrem Akurgal, Urartäische und altiranische Kunstzentren (Ankara: Türk Tarih Kurumu Basimevi, 1968), plate 26c.

As we shall see later in this article, this seems to be the region whence the chariot began its long journey c. 1500 to China.[12] Although Vannic (the language of Urartu) was non-Indo-European, its speakers were in a position where they could have been in contact with the Iranian-speaking Sakas, whom, as we shall find, appear to have transmitted the words for "mage" and "chariot" to China. Unfortunately, the pronounced Semitic features, full beard, and long, tightly braided hair of the Zincirli Aramean suggest that this is irrelevant for the three Shang and Western Chou heads.[13]

For the moment, I must admit that I simply do not know the precise ethnic and geographic origins of these three mysterious figures. However, the rulers of the Shang and Chou dynasties must have been sufficiently impressed with them to have their artistic representations made and preserved in the royal precincts. The unusual physical features of their foreign faces were depicted somewhat exaggeratedly during the Shang but with greater familiarity in the Chou. There are many possible avenues for further research on the ethnic identification of these three individuals, but my own impression is that archeologists, art historians, and ethnogeneticists should look very hard at the Andronovo culture as a probable source.

The Andronovo culture covered a huge area from the Urals to Lake Baikal and southwest into Ferghana. It originated during the period between 1800–1500 and developed from the earlier agricultural communities of the region.

> The Andronovo culture was fully bronze-using, obtaining tin from the Altai Mountains and tin and copper from the Urals and the mountains of Turkestan. Bronze-working was developed still further in the succeeding Karasuk phase, which began in about 1200 BC. The development of the Karasuk bronze industry demonstrates that for the first time Steppe culture was oriented towards China rather than the west. Bronzes from the Steppes have been found in Shang China: knives with ringed or ram's head butts from the Karasuk area, and socketed axes and spearheads from as far west as the Urals. One important result of this contact was probably the introduction, in the later Shang period, of the two-wheeled chariot into China—either from or via Central Asia.[14]

The route from the Caspian Sea to Lake Baikal was occupied by people sharing essentially a single culture. These were Indo-Iranians, the same type of people who served in later ages as superb transmitters of cultures among other groups occupying the less central areas of the Eurasian landmass. To the west lay the Pontic region where the horse was first domesticated and ridden and which had close connections with Europe and the Mediterranean. To the southwest were farming groups of Iranian origin, such as the late Namazga culture in which Zoroastrianism developed. To the southeast lay China. Travel across the northern steppes and along the eastern edges of the Gobi Desert to Anyang would have presented no extraordinary obstacles. This is probably the route taken by the individual who was the model for the Shang period head discussed above. An alternative route would have been to follow the foothills of the Altai and the western Celestial Mountains (T'ien-shan) down through the Kansu Corridor to Shensi. This was most likely the route for the models of the two Chou period figures. A less hospitable, but still traversable, route would have been to hop from oasis to oasis along the southern slopes of the Celestial Mountains and thence to the Kansu Corridor. Modern archeology is demonstrating with increasing clarity that China was open to cultural exchange from the very earliest periods. The second millennium was certainly no exception. Indeed, there are excellent grounds for believing that writing, certain types of agriculture, and other aspects of civilization developed through communication with cultures to the west and the south. But these are subjects for future research. In the remainder of this article, I shall focus exclusively on the word *$m^y ag$ incised on the top of T45:6, and its probable Iranian origin.

It has been customary for students of Chinese civilization to translate *$m^y ag$ as "shaman," but this is wrong on several counts. In the first place, the shaman was the leading representative of a specific type of religious system practiced by Siberian and Ural-Altaic peoples.[15] Perhaps the most characteristic feature of this tradition was the shaman's ecstatic trance-flight to heaven during initiation and other rituals. The shaman also served the community as a whole by retrieving the errant souls of sick people and escorting the spirits of the dead to the other world. This is in contrast to the *$m^y ag$ who were closely associated with the courts of various rulers and who were primarily responsible for divination, astrology, prayer, and healing with medicines.[16] Since all that we know of the *$m^y ag$ markedly distinguishes their role in Shang and Chou society from that of shamans in the communities where they were the most important spiritual leaders, it would seem that we should seek a new translation of the term. I should like to propose that an exact equivalent of *m^yag is "magician" or, better still, "mage" (to differentiate this ancient specialist from the modern prestidigitator).[17] This proposal is based on etymological, phonological, paleographical, and functional grounds.

Most readers will already have observed that *m^yag bears a strong resemblance to the word "magician" itself. I believe that English "magician" or "mage" and Modern Standard Mandarin *wu* ultimately derive from the same Indo-Iranian word. Whereas the word "shaman" is now held to be of Tungusic (more specifically Evenki) origin and means "he who knows" (*šamán*),[18] "mage" and "magician" come to us through Latin *magus* from Greek μάγος and ultimately Old Persian *maguš*. The plural of Latin *magus* is *magi*, the designation for the wise men of the East with whom we are all familiar from the story of Jesus' birth.

The Old Persian word has also apparently made its way into Semitic languages, witness Talmudic Hebrew *māgōsh* and Aramaic *amgushā* ("magician") as well as Chaldean *maghdim* ("wisdom and philosophy"). From the first century, Syrian *magusai* were notorious as magicians and soothsayers. One of the earliest references to derivatives of Old Persian *maguš* may be found in Jeremiah 39.3, which enumerates among the retinue of King Nebuchadnezzar upon his entry to Jerusalem the Rab Mag ("Chief of the Magi")[19] named Nergalsharezar. It would appear from this record that the Persian Magi must have exercised considerable influence upon the Babylonian court by around 586 B.C.E.

The geographical and temporal spread of the Magi was by no means restricted to Mesopotamia and the Levant around the middle of the first millennium. We find them also in Parthia, Bactria, Chorasmia, Aria, Media, among the Sakas, in Arabia, Ethiopia, Egypt, and throughout Asia Minor.[20] They were known to have been resident in India not later than the first century B.C.E.[21] The Greeks were certainly well acquainted with the Magi quite early because Herodotus (c. 450) speaks of them frequently.[22]

The celebrated trilingual (Elamite, Old Persian, and Akkadian) Behistun inscription of Darius I ("The Great," 550–486 B.C.E., r. 522–486) describes how the king put down a revolt of the Magi. This indicates that they must have had substantial numbers, influence, and organization in Persia during the sixth century B.C.E.[23] In fact, I suspect that the Magi were already firmly entrenched in ancient Iranian politics and religion at a much earlier date. Many Greek and Latin sources affirm that the Magi were followers of Zarathustra or even that Zarathustra himself was a Maguš.[24] According to T. Burrow, the lowest possible date for the founding of the Zoroastrian religion was 1100 B.C.E.[25] This puts us back at a period of time compatible with the $*m^{y}ag$ who are mentioned fairly frequently in the oracle bone inscriptions.[26] The Caucasoid/Europoid figurine from Anyang discussed above also lends credence to the presence of magi in China during the Shang period and their possible involvement with court ritual or other types of royal activity. Considering the diversity of peoples among whom and the far-flung places where the Magi were active, I see no necessary bar to their travelling to China and becoming employed there as well for their special knowledge and skills.[27]

If the Magi were not limited to any narrow geographical region, nor were they partial to any particular religion. As Ilya Gershevitch puts it, "The Magi were a professional priesthood to whom Zarathuštrianism was merely one of the forms of religion in which they ministered against [i.e., for] payment, much as a professional musician earns his living by performing the works of different composers...."[28] The Magi were technical experts available to all rulers who might contract with them for their services. It is not surprising, then, that Chinese texts dating from or describing the situation during the Eastern Chou show that the $*m^{y}ag$ were present in nearly all of the contending states.[29] What is more, the services the Magi actually performed overlap with the known activities of the *m^yag*. They interpreted dreams, practiced divination, explained omens, chanted hymns and prayers, made astrological calculations, and sacrificed upon the sacred altars.[30] Among the Persians themselves, the rulers called upon the Magi for assistance in carrying out sacrifices and other religious rituals. Most authorities, both ancient and modem, assert that it was virtually impossible to carry out the necessary rituals of state without the assistance of the Magi. Our understanding of the politico-religious foundations of the Shang and Chou may be enhanced by examining in greater detail the role of the *m^yag* as well as parallels between their beliefs and practices on the one hand and those of the Magi on the other.

Perhaps the Magi had the name they did because they were thought to possess general spiritual or occult power. The Indo-European root of Old Persian *maguš* is *magh-*. This means basically "to be able, to have power" ("mighty" is another English derivate from the same root). Another Indo-European root that may be related to *magh-* is *magĥ-* which means "to fight" and yields words having to do with martial activity (e.g. Greek *makesthai* ["to fight"] and Old Iranian *ha-maz-an-* ["the warrior"] where *ha-* means "the," by inference from Greek Αμαζων). This is reminiscent of the close resemblance between *m^yag* ("magician," i.e, "the able/potent one") and another Old Sinitic word *m^yag^x* 武 ("martial," Modem Standard Mandarin *wu*).[31]

Regardless of a possible deep connection between Indo-European *magh-* ("to be able, to have power" > Old Persian *maguš* ["magician"]) and *magĥ-* ("to fight" > "mighty") on the one hand and Old Sinitic *m^yag* ("magician") and *m^yag^x* ("martial") on the other, it is noteworthy that the symbol for magicians in the West is the ancient Cross Potent (also known as the Teutonic Cross, Jerusalem Cross,[32] and Kruckenkreuz). It would appear that the most basic characteristic of the magician was presumed to be his power, hence the name of his symbol.

The most intriguing thing about the Cross Potent for our purposes, however, is that its shape is identical to the earliest form of the Chinese graph for *m^yag ("magician"): both are written ✚. This can hardly be attributable to sheer coincidence or chance independent origination, for ✚ is a highly specific arrangement of lines that stands for a similar complex of ideas in Shang-Chou civilization and in the long Western tradition of magic. Whereas in China ✚ was subsequently replaced by 巫 as the sign for *m^yag, in the West the Cross Potent remained the symbol of the magician through the Middle Ages until the present time (see fig. 5).

The Cross Potent was particularly evident in the magician's handbooks known as grimoires (see fig. 6). Many of these date from the sixteenth through the eighteenth century, but they preserve much older material.[33] The great seal of one of the most renowned men of the Elizabethan age, John Dee (1527–1608), has dozens of ✚ on it.[34] Dee was a philosopher, mathematician, technologist, antiquarian, alchemist, and astrologer, but above all a magician. The Cross Potent appears prominently in Rembrandt's etching of a magician (c. 1632) that has been used as an illustration for Goethe's *Faust*.[35]

The phonological and semantic similarity between Old Persian *maguš* and Old Sinitic *m^yag alone stands as convincing evidence for the identity of the preeminent Shang-Chou religious specialists and the Magi. When we add to this evidence the discovery at Chou-yüan of the two Caucasoid/Europoid figurines, the equation between *maguš* and *m^yag becomes difficult to deny.

But how do we account for this apparent cross-cultural contact in light of the development of Chinese civilization as a whole? For the past several decades, there has been a presumption (sometimes expressed rather vehemently) that Chinese civilization arose essentially in isolation from all other civilizations.[36] Given that the *m^yag would appear to have been situated at the heart of Shang politico-religious activities and institutions, this position seems no longer to be tenable.

Figure 5. A version of the magic ring of Solomon.

Source: Adapted from "Old Sinitic *myag, Old Persian maguš, and English 'Magician,'" *Early China* 15 (1990): 41. David Carroll, *The Magic Makers: Magic and Sorcery Through the Ages* (New York: Arbor House, 1974), 120.

Figure 6. Sigil

Source: Adapted from "Old Sinitic *myag, Old Persian maguš, and English 'Magician,'" *Early China* 15 (1990): 32. (linear representation of the archangel Gabriel from the Grimoire of Armadel in the Gerald Yorke Collection. *Encyclopedia of Magic and Superstition: Alchemy, Charms, Dreams, Omens, Rituals, Talismans, Wishes* [London: Black Cat (Macdonald), 1988; first published 1970-1971], 235.)

Since such an ostensibly key office in the Shang court as that of the *m^yag had connections with Indo-European peoples, it would seem odd if there were not other instances of such ties. Although this is neither the place nor the time to enter into a full discussion of these matters, I believe that there is massive linguistic evidence of Sinitic and Indo-European cultural exchange from at least the late Neolithic, exchange that has continued without interruption until the present.[37] My accumulated research notes include hundreds of more or less obvious borrowings between Old Sinitic and Proto-Indo-European or its daughter languages. It is significant that these words tend to fall in precisely the areas of human endeavor we would expect to be influenced by cross-cultural contact (technology, animal husbandry, crafts, and politico-religious institutions and ideas), but not in basic vocabulary (numbers, primary colors, the main body parts, kinship terms, the words for "I," "you," "he," etc.).

We should bear in mind that not all of the traffic was from West to East, but rather that there was a two-way exchange from very early times. For example, Chinese silk has been discovered in Celtic burials at Hochmichele and Hochdorf (Eberdingen) of the European Halstatt culture dating to the sixth century B.C.E. Silk has also been found for a comparable time period at the Kerameikos cemetery in Athens.[38] Still earlier, at Sapalli-tepe in Northern Bactria, silk was identified as the material clothing the skeletons in four graves dating to around 2000 B.C.E.[39] and it has also been found at other sites in Soviet Central Asia dating as far back as the sixteenth century B.C.E.[40] These findings should encourage us to examine intently the words for silk in Old Sinitic (*$s^y\partial[g]$) and Indo-European languages (Greek σηρικον, Latin *sericum*, Italian *seta*, Spanish *seda*, Old Irish *sila*, Welsh *sidan*, Breton *seiz*, Old Norse *silki*, Old High German *sida*, *serih*, or *silecho*, Lithuanian *šilkai*, Lettic *zids*, Church Slavonic *šelku*, etc.; cf. Korean *sir*, Manchu *sirghe*, and Mongolian *sirkek*). This is assuming that both the object and the name for it may have been passed across the breadth of Asia by the same types of Iranian-speaking individuals who occupied the Asian heartland as they did in later centuries. It is curious, however, that Avestan lacks a cognate word for silk.

Another important example of this type of East–West contact is the chariot, for which there is hard archeological evidence to corroborate the linguistic data. To the best of my knowledge, almost all specialists now agree that the chariots discovered in the Shang royal burials of the twelfth century B.C.E. shared the same technology as chariots excavated in the Caucasus that date to around the fifteenth century B.C.E.[41] Not only would such a revolutionary and complicated piece of technology as the chariot require the introduction of new words to describe it, it would bring in its wake a whole series of social and institutional changes that would also require new words in order to cope with them. Here I wish only to discuss briefly the Old Sinitic word for "chariot" itself, namely *ch'e* (<**kl^{y}ag*[42]), more literally "wheeled vehicle."

The fact that there are two velars and an *l in **kl^{y}ag* suggests that it has some connection with Indo-European * *k^{w}ék^{w}lo-*[43] ("wheel") which also has two labiovelars and an *l. In Tocharian B (*kokale*) and Tocharian A (*kukäl*), or perhaps more likely in their parent language which we may refer to as Proto-Tocharian, this word acquired the meaning of "chariot." Ideally, the word borrowed into Sinitic should have come from some language that had delabialized the labiovelars. Since Tocharian did that only rather late,[44] it would seem not to be an appropriate source. Indo-Iranian did delabialize the labiovelars quite early. Considering the dominant groups in Central Asia who would probably have been responsible for the transmission of this new device, an Iranian source seems likely. The Proto-Iranian stem, attested in Avestan, was **čaxra-* ("wheel"), but various later Iranian languages metathesize the consonants. For example, the related Farsi word is *čaerx*. The Ossetic word is *calx* (where *c* is phonetically [ts] but regularly reflects an older Proto-Iranian *č).[45] The Ossetes, now living on the northern slopes of the Caucasus—the apparent source of the Chinese chariot—are definitely descendants of the medieval Alans and perhaps of the ancient Scythians, the one group of Iranians most likely to have reached the borders of China by circa 1200 B.C.E.[46] I shall return to the phonology of **kl^{y}ag* after discussing the Indo-European antecedents of **m^{y}ag*.

That *m^yag was borrowed into Sinitic from an old Iranian language and not from some other member of the Indo-European family may be deduced from the relevant entry on Proto-Indo-European *magh- ("to be able, to have power, to help") in Pokorny's *Indogermanisches etymologisches Wörterbuch*.⁴⁷ Among the dozens of reflexes in various Indo-European languages listed there, the only word that means "magician" is Old Persian *maguš* (from suffixed Iranian *magh-u); all the other reflexes are verbs meaning "be able" or derived nouns and adjectives meaning "power," "powerful," and so forth. Thus the meaning "magician" must have developed within Iranian and does not go back to Proto-Indo-European. This fits well our historical and hagiographical knowledge about Zoroaster and his associates as innovators in matters magical. It follows that it must have been the Iranian word, and no other, that was borrowed into Sinitic.

This conclusion is supported by what is known of the early historical development of Magianism; viz., that it was a purely Iranian invention. The Sanskrit word for magian, *maga*, which was borrowed from Old Persian, also lends credence to this conclusion. Sanskrit lexicons define the word as indicating "a priest of the sun" and state that such individuals were also called Śākadvipins; i.e., people from Śākadvipa or Central Asia, including Iran. Śākadvipa means "land of the Śāka people." Śāka is the ethnonym of the ancestors of the Khotanese and is related to the word Scyth. Once again, we find ourselves in the orbit of the Central Asian Iranians who for millennia have served as *Kulturvermittlers* par excellence.

The path from Proto-Indo-European *magh- to Old Sinitic *m^yag might be as follows: 1. Proto-Indo-European has a verb *magh- meaning "be able," etc.; 2. Iranian inherits it through regular native language learning; 3. Iranians form a word *maghu or *maguš* ("magician"; that is, an "able [specialist in ritual])"; 4. Iranian-speaking individuals, among them probably a few powerful mages, reach the borders of China; 5. Chinese rulers, impressed with their skills, enlist the aid of the newcomers and borrow *maghu or maguš as *m^{y}ag (hence the meaning of the Chinese word).

The archeological and linguistic evidence for the hypothesis that Old Sinitic *m^{y}ag was borrowed from Old Persian maguš or, more precisely, its Iranian predecessor, is impressive enough by itself. When combined with the archeological and linguistic evidence for the hypothesis that Old Sinitic *kl^{y}ag (or *kr^{y}ag) was borrowed from Iranian čaxra- (or one of its descendants), we enter a whole different level of argumentation. Both Iranian words have short a in the root syllable and both Old Sinitic words contain *^{y}a in the corresponding position. In other words, there is a consistent pattern of sounds associated with these linguistic borrowings. The hypothesis about "magician" and the hypothesis about "chariot" thus support each other. It is not likely that this phonological congruity is the result of chance; rather, it probably reflects a specific (and fairly unitary) historical sequence of events that can be located in time and space. We have moved, then, from the realm of hypothesis to that of regularly verifiable laws. The data here established may be severely limited, but they are a reliable start. Future investigations of Old Sinitic and its relationships with other languages have been placed on a more solid footing because of the synergism of the *m^{y}ag and *kl^{y}ag hypotheses.

I have also been able to equate the Old Sinitic words for other chariot parts, horses, bovines, and speckled bovines—to name only a few examples—with specific Indo-European words and plan to present my findings on these and related matters in the not-too-distant future. In the meantime, I hope that the combined archeological, linguistic, paleographical, and historical information concerning Old Sinitic *m^{y}ag and Indo-European magicians presented herein will convince scholars of early Chinese civilization that East–West contacts at the dawn of history were both real and non-trivial.

Notes

1. The original inspiration for this article was a manuscript by Jao Tsung-i entitled "New Light on *wu*" A revised version of Professor Jao's paper will appear in the next issue of *Early China*. It will treat in more detail many of the larger paleographic and religiocultural issues concerning *wu* that are only touched upon in the present work, the primary purpose of which is to discuss the philological and linguistic implications of the Old Sinitic reconstruction of *wu*. In the meantime, Professor Jao has published a brief but important article on the West Asian connections of ✢ in which he suggests the possibility that such symbols may have influenced the origins of writing in China. See his "Ssu-ch'ou chih lu so yin-ch'i te 'wen-tzu ch'i-yüan' wen-t'i (The Question of 'The Origins of Writing' Brought about by the Silk Road)" 絲綢之路所引起的「文字起源」問題, *Ming-pao yüeh-kan* 明報月刊 25.9 (September, 1990), 47–50, an English version of which is forthcoming in *Sino-Platonic Papers*. Modern Standard Mandarin transcriptions are in Wade-Giles romanization. For Old Sinitic I follow chiefly the tentative transcriptions of Li Fang-kuei and Axel Schuessler given in the latter's *A Dictionary of Early Zhou Chinese* (Honolulu: University of Hawai'i Press, 1987), but also take into account those of Bernhard Karlgren, Tung T'ung-ho, and Chou Fa-kao given in the latter's *A Pronouncing Dictionary of Chinese Characters in Archaic and Ancient Chinese, Mandarin and Cantonese* (Hong Kong: The Chinese University of Hong Kong, 1973). While Li reconstructs a final voiced velar stop for *m^yag, Schuessler omits it. For the significance of this discrepancy, see note 42. I wish to thank my colleague Donald A. Ringe, a specialist on Indo-European historical linguistics, for helping me with the reconstruction of the word for "wheel[ed vehicle]." Participation in the National Endowment for the Humanities institute, "Perspectives on the Ancient Indo-European World," held at the University of Texas (Austin) from June 18 to July 20, 1990, served to sharpen my understanding of many of the issues raised in this article. I am grateful to Edith Porada, Boris Marshack, Irene Winter, Renata Holod, Judith Lerner, G. Azarpay, Parviz Varjavand, and the other authorities on Middle Eastern art and archeology who responded to my requests for assistance in identifying the headgear of the Chou-yüan figures. However, I alone am responsible for all interpretations of the material herein.

2. Yin Sheng-p'ing 尹盛平, "Hsi-Chou pang-tiao jen-t'ou hsiang chung-tsu t'an-so" 西周蚌雕人頭像種族探索 (Investigation of the Racial Affinity of Two Western Chou Human Heads Sculpted of Shell), *Wen-wu* 文物 (Cultural Relics), 1986.1, 46–49; Ch'en Ch'üan-fang 陳全方, *Chou-yüan yü Chou wen-hua* 周原與周文化 (Chou-yüan and Chou Culture) (Shanghai: Shanghai jen-min ch'u-pan-she, 1988), p. 20.
3. The flattened design was presumably intended to enable the pins to lie smoothly along the surface of the user's hair, but is perhaps merely a function of the limitations of the material from which they were made. The shape of the mollusk shell may also help to account for the truncated tops of the heads.
4. The drawings of these pieces supplied by Yin Sheng-p'ing and Ch'en Ch'üan-fang (see note 2) show no trace of ears. The available published photographs of the two pieces are insufficiently distinct to determine with certitude whether ears are present or not.
5. Yin Sheng-p'ing, "Hsi-Chou pang-tiao jen-t'ou."
6. Ellis H. Minns, *Scythians and Greeks: A Survey of Ancient History and Archaeology on the North Coast of the Euxine from the Danube to the Caucasus* (Cambridge: Cambridge University Press, 1913), p. xxxvii (fig. O) and passim; *From the Land of the Scythians: Ancient Treasures from the Museums of the U.S.S.R. 3000 B.C.–100 B.C.* (N.p.: The Metropolitan Museum of Art and The Los Angeles County Museum of Art, distributed by New York Graphic Society, n. d.), color plates 17–18 (the celebrated fourth-century B.C.E. golden vase from the tomb at Kul Oba near Kerch in the Crimea), also reproduced in J. P. Mallory, *In Search of the Indo-Europeans: Language, Archaeology and Myth* (New York: Thames and Hudson, 1989), plate 6, and Christine Flon, ed., *The World Atlas of Archaeology*, translated from *Le Grand Atlas de l'archéologie* (Encyclopaedia Universalis, 1985; rpt, New York: Portland House, 1988), p. 217 (a Central Asian Saka delegation from Persepolis). Among the 3,000 human figures depicted with great realism and fine detail on the monumental reliefs of Persepolis (520–c450 R.C.E.), there are dozens of different hair and hat styles, including those of Sogdians, Ionians, Ethiopians, Lydians, Babylonians, and Scythians, but none of them resemble the headgear of the Chou-yüan figures. One must assume, therefore, that the latter did not fall within the range of those who paid tribute to the Achaemenid kings of Persia. See Donald N. Wilber, *Persepolis: The Archaeology of Parsa, Seat of the Persian Kings* (1969; rev. Princeton, N.J.: Darwin, 1989).

7. All of these are mentioned in Yin Sheng-p'ing, "Hsi-Chou pang-tiao jen-t'ou," p. 47 and Ch'en Ch'üan-fang, *Chou-yüan*, p. 20.
8. *Ibid.*
9. Carl Hentze, *Funde in Alt-China: Das Welterleben im ältesten China*, Sternstunden der Archäologie (Göttingen: Musterschmidt, 1967), Taf. XV. The presence of actual Europoid individuals—not just their artistic representations—in China during the Shang period is proven by a couple of skulls (one virtually indistinguishable from that of a modern Englishman born in America) recovered from the cemetery at Hou-chia-chuang 侯家莊. These skulls were apparently deposited in sacrificial pits along with a large number of Mongoloid skulls and a somewhat lesser number of Eskimoid and Oceanic Negroid skulls as well as an unclassifiable fifth group of small crania. The circumstance of their discovery makes it difficult to draw any firm conclusions concerning the racial composition of the Anyang population as a whole, still less of the ruling elite. See Li Chi, "Notes on the Physical Anthropology of the Yin-Shang Population," in his *Anyang* (Seattle: University of Washington Press, 1977), pp. 255–264 and Kwang-chih Chang, *Shang Civilization* (New Haven: Yale University Press, 1980), pp. 331–335. My thanks to Emma Bunker for these two references. For the present, the safest view is probably that of Li Chi (*Anyang*, p. 264): "From the very beginning, the north China plain was a meeting place of many different ethnic stocks and it is partly from the mixture of these groups that the early Chinese population was formed, although we must not forget that the dominant group among these stocks was indubitably the Mongoloid group," The status of Europoid individuals within Shang society as a whole remains to be determined.
10. The tremendous dissimilarities of these pieces from typical early Chinese representations of human faces are vividly brought home by comparing them with the examples illustrated at Chang, *Shang Civilization*, p. 330, fig. 89.
11. Ekrem Akurgal, *Urartäische und altiranische Kunstzentren*, Türk Tarih Kurumu yayınlarından, series 6, no. 9 (Ankara: Türk Tarih Kurumu Basımevi, 1968), plate 26c.
12. See the discussion of the word for chariot near the end of this article and the notes thereto.
13. Surprisingly, the headgear of Celtic warriors depicted on the silver Gundestrup cauldron bear a conspicuous resemblance to those of the Shang and Western Chou figures. The cauldron, however, is much too

late (La Tène III, around 80–50 B.C.E.) to take seriously into account in our present investigation. See Garrett S. Olmsted, *The Gundestrup Cauldron: Its Archaeological Context, the Style and Iconography of its Portrayed Motifs, and Their Narration of a Gaulish Version of Tain Bó Cúailnge*, Collection Latomus, 162 (Brussels: Revues d'Études Latines, 1979), p. 9; Mallory, *Indo-Europeans*, plate 20. Cf. the warrior's helmet with projecting horns shown in Anne Ross, *Pagan Celtic Britain: Studies in Iconography and Tradition* (New York: Columbia University Press, 1967), fig. 88. This bronze figurine from Grevensvaenge, Zealand, which is dated to c. 1250 B.C.E., bears an intriguing resemblance in its facial features to the Western Chou figures.

14. *Past Worlds: The Times Atlas of Archaealogy* (Maplewood, N.J.: Hammond, 1988), p. 148.
15. See Mircea Eliade, *Shamanism: Archaic Techniques of Ecstasy*, tr, from the French by Willard R. Trask, Bollingen series 76 (Princeton: Princeton University Press, 1964).
16. For a general anthropological study of the *wu* ("mage") in ancient Chinese society, see Liang Chao-t'ao 梁釗韜, *Chung-kuo ku-tai wu-shu —tsung chiao te ch'i-yüan ho fa-chan*中國古代巫術──宗教的起源和發展 (Ancient Chinese Magic: The Rise and Development of Chinese Religion) (Canton: Chung-shan University Press, 1989).
17. In claiming that "mage" *is* a more accurate translation of $*m^yag$ than "shaman," I wish not to detract from the vital ongoing debate between David N. Keightley and K C. Chang regarding the significance of the $*m^yag$ for the alleged theocratic foundations of the Chinese state and the possibility that the king himself may have been the head $*m^yag$. Chang's position is presented in his *Art, Myth, and Ritual: The Path to Political Authority in Ancient China* (Cambridge, Mass.: Harvard University Press, 1983). Keightley's response may be found in "Royal Shamanism in the Shang: Archaic Vestige or Central Reality?" prepared for the workshop on Chinese divination and portent interpretation, June 20–July 1, 1983 (University of California, Berkeley) and "Shamanism in *Guo Yu*? A Tale of *Xi* 覡 and *Wu* 巫" prepared for the Center for Chinese Studies Regional Seminar, April 7–8, 1989 (University of California, Berkeley). I have no view on whether or not there may have been a separate, indigenous tradition of shamanism in China before the introduction of magianism, There is, however, good evidence that the role of king and $*m^yag$ coincide in the crucial matter of the interpretation of the cracks in oracle bone divination. A typical notation would consist of preface (crack-

making *pu* 卜 on [stem]-[branch] day), charge (divination *cheng* 貞), prognostication (the king, reading the cracks, said *wang chan yüeh*王占曰), and verification which records what really transpired later on. See David N. Keightley, *Sources of Shang History: The Oracle-Bone Inscriptions of Bronze Age China* (Berkeley: University of California Press, 1978), pp. 40–44. Hayashi Minao 林巳奈夫, "Chūgoku kodai no shinfu" 中国古代の神巫 (Shamanistic Gods in Ancient China), *Tōhō Gakuhō* 東方学報 (Journal of Oriental Studies), 38 (March, 1967), 199–224, p. 211 cites examples of early prognostications which begin *wu yüeh* 巫曰 ("the *m^yag* said"). Considering the fact that, like the Shang king himself, the *m^yag* was responsible for the very important task of interpreting the divinatory cracks, was sacrificed to after death, and was closely associated with *Ti* (the high god, also a prefix for deceased royal ancestors), his position at court must have been quite exalted. Or perhaps the king was indeed the chief *m^yag*.

18. I reject the old etymology of "shaman" which traces it back through Tocharian ṣamāne to a Prakrit samaṇa or Sanskrit śramaṇa. The ascetic practices of the Buddhist śramaṇa are quite at variance with the ecstatic spiritualism of the shaman.
19. This explanation of Rab Mag was commonly accepted by most biblical commentators until it was disputed by E. Benveniste, *Les mages dans l'ancien Iran*, Publications de la Société des "Études Iraniennes, 15 (Paris: Librairie Orientale et Américaine G.-P. Maisonneuve, 1938), "Appendice," pp. 28–30. Benveniste would derive it from Babylonian *rab mu-gi* which is presumably a military title meaning "Master of the Horse" (Magister Equitum). His attempt to account for the phonetic discrepancy by positing an intermediary Aramaic stage strikes me as unnecessarily strained. For the traditional interpretation, see such standard works as C. F. Keil and F. Delitzsch, *Commentary on the Old Testament in Ten Volumes*, vol. III, *Jeremiah, Lamentations* by C. F. Keil, translated from the German by James Kennedy (Grand Rapids, Michigan: William B. Eerdmans, 1978 rpt.), p. 117; A. W. Streane, *The Book of the Prophet Jeremiah together with the Lamentations* (Cambridge: Cambridge University Press, 1913, revised version), p. 237; and J. R. Dummelow, ed., *A Commentary on the Holy Bible by Various Writers* (New York: Macmillan, 1936), p. 476.
20. R. C. Zaehner, *The Dawn and Twilight of Zoroastrianism* (New York: G. Putnam's Sons, 1961), p. 163.

21. Christian Lindtner, "Buddhist References to Old Iranian Religion," in *A Green Leaf: Papers in Honour of Professor Jes P. Asmussen*, Hommages et Opera Minora, 12 (Leiden: E. J. Brill, 1988), pp. 433–444, esp. p. 442.
22. *Herodotus*, with an English translation by A. D. Godley, 4 vols. (1921–1922; Cambridge: Harvard University Press, 1957), *passim*. It is most interesting that some of the activities of the Magi described by Herodotus correspond very closely with those of the *m^yag in early China. For example, in Book VII.191 (vol. 3, pp. 508–509 of Godley's edition), we find the following passage: "For the storm lasted for three days; and at last the Magians, by using victims [cut up in pieces and offered to the manes, εντομα] and wizards' spells on the wind, and by sacrificing also to Thetis and the Nereids, did make it to cease on the fourth day...." Compare note 27 below.
23. Arthur Darby Nock, *Essays on Religion and the Ancient World*, selected and edited, with an Introduction, Bibliography of Nock's writings, and indexes, by Zeph Stewart, 2 vols. (Oxford: Clarendon, 1972), p. 309. Nock's essay "Paul and the Magus" (pp. 308–330) is the best study of the word *magus* in Greek.
24. Giuseppe Messina, *Der Ursprung der Magier und die zarathustriche Religion* (Rome: Pontifico Istituto Biblico, 1930), pp. 1, 64, and passim. See also James Hope Moulton, *Early Zoroastrianism*, Lectures Delivered at Oxford and in London, February to May 1912; The Hibbert Lectures, second series (London: Williams and Norgate, 1913), pp. 118, 197, 323, and 410; Zaehner, *Dawn and Twilight of Zoroastrianism*, p. 165. According to Zolar, *Zalar's Encyclopedia of Ancient and Forbidden Knowledge* (New York: Prentice Hall, 1986), p. 193, Zoroaster was traditionally held to be "the presumable inventor of all magic."
25. See T. Burrow, "The Proto-Indoaryans," *Journal of the Royal Asiatic Society* (1973), 123–140, esp. p. 139. Gherardo Gnoli, *Zoroaster's Time and Homeland: A Study on the Origins of Mazdeism and Related Problems*, Istituto Universitario Orientale, Seminario di Studi Asiatici, Series Minor, 7 (Naples, 1980), pp. 10–11 and 160–161, strongly supports this view and includes the Magi as part of the Zoroastrian complex of religious beliefs, practices, and institutions. Without specifying a specific upper limit, Mary Boyce also opposes the low date of the seventh century B.C.E. for Zarathustra in her *A History of Zoroastrianism*, 2 vols. (Leiden/Köln: E. J. Brill, 1975–1982). The position of Burrow, Gnoli, and Boyce has recently received a measure of archeological confirmation from the recent discovery of a spectacular temple complex at Togolok-21 in

the southeastern Karakum desert of Turkmenia, an area known to the ancient Persians as Margush and to the Greeks as Margiana. This ritual center, built circa 1000 B.C.E., preserves evidence of the usage of soma (referred to as *haoma* in the Avestan hymns) and has structural characteristics which suggest that Margiana was the homeland of Zoroastrianism; see Victor Sarianidi, "Where Was Zoroaster Born?" *Sputnik*, 3 (March, 1990), pp. 96–101, esp. p. 98. Even if it cannot be proven that Zoroaster himself was the center of the cult at Togolok-21, current scholarly opinion holds that the site was at least associated with proto-Zoroastrianism: see Asko Parpola, "The Coming of the Aryans to Iran and India and the Cultural and Ethnic Identity of the Dasas," *Studia Orientalia*, 64 (Helsinki, 1988), 195–302, esp. pp. 236–238 and the copious bibliographical references cited there.

26. Jao Tsung-i's paper (see note 1) cites dozens of occurrences of *$m^y ag$ in the oracle bone inscriptions. His analysis shows that they were involved with animal (chiefly canine but also ovicaprid) sacrifice and libationary ritual and that they were associated with earth deities of the four directions. Hayashi Minao (see note 17) cites oracle bone inscriptions where *$m^y ag$ are associated with porcine sacrifice, praying for rain, and other tasks that were central to the functioning of the Shang court.

27. Hsü Chin-hsiung 許進雄, *Chung-kuo ku-tai she-hui: Wen-tzu yü jen-lei-hsüeh te t'ou-shih* 中國古代社會──文字與人類學的透視 (Ancient Chinese Society: From the Perspective of Writing and Anthropology) (Taipei: Taiwan Commercial, 1988), pp. 387, 440–441 states that the *$m^y ag$ were thought to be capable of calming the winds and that this is often reflected on the oracle bones. He also holds that the *$m^y ag$ were healers, but this view is based on post-Shang sources and supposition. Hsü interprets 十 as a pictograph of an implement used by the *$m^y ag$ in ritual ceremonies. There is, however, no paleographical or archeological evidence to support this interpretation. A more convincing suggestion is that of Ch'en Meng-chia 陳夢家, *Yin-hsü pu-tz'u tsung-shu* 殷虛卜辭綜述 (A General Account of Oracle Bone Inscriptions from the Wastes of Shang), K'ao-ku-hsüeh chuan-k'an chia-chung 考古學專刊 甲種 (Archeological Monographs, Series A), No. 2 (Peking: K'e-hsüeh, 1956), p. 579 who believes that 十 symbolizes the four directions. This is a reasonable interpretation because of the clear associations of the *$m^y ag$ with the four directions in the oracle bone inscriptions. For other religious and ritual practices of the *$m^y ag$ during the Shang period, see pp.

575–578, 590, of the same work. Ch'en cites one sacrifice which required nine canine victims.
28. Ilya Gershevitch, "Zoroaster's Own Contribution," *Journal of Near Eastern Studies*, 23 (January–October, 1964), 12–38 (on p. 25).
29. Cited in Jao Tsung-i, "New Light on *wu*."
30. Maurice Bouisson, *Magic: Its Rites and History*, translated from the French by G. Almayrac (London: Rider, 1960), p. 17.
31. It has long been asserted that there is some connection between the word *m^yag* 十 ("mage") and *m^yag* 舞 ("make postures to musical accompaniment, dance"). For example, L. C. Hopkins attempted to show that the graphs for *m^yag* ("mage"), the negative *m^yag* 無 ("not have, not, no, don't"), and *m^yag* ("dance") "can all be traced back to one primitive figure of a man displaying by the gestures of his arms and legs the thaumaturgic powers of his inspired personality"; "The Shaman or Chinese Wu: His Inspired Dancing and Versatile Character," *Journal of the Royal Asiatic Society* (1945), 3–16, p. 5. See, too, Hopkins' earlier article "The Shaman or Wu 巫: A Study in Graphic Camouflage,' *The New China Review*, 2.5 (October, 1920), 423–439 plus 1 plate, which follows Bruno Schindler, *Das Priestertum im alten China*, 1. teil: *Königtum und Priestertum, Einleitung und Quellen* (Leipzig: Spamer, 1919), pp. 14–29. There are several objections to this type of graphemic analysis. The first is that it is based on the erroneous identification of the various oracle bone graphic forms for *m^yag* ("not") and *m^yag* ("dance")—which are indeed graphically related—as being equivalent to that of *m^yag* 十 ("mage"). The second is that it confuses word with script. In the study of Sinitic etymologies, phonology should always take precedence over graphology. This is clear from the fact that graphs are frequently borrowed to write homophonous or near-homophonous words that are semantically completely unrelated (e.g. *$mlag$* ["Wheat, i.e. *Triticum aestivum*"] as the written form of *$mlag$* ["come"]). Furthermore, the origin of Sinitic languages antedates the rise of the Chinese script by many centuries. Hence the latter must be regarded as secondary and the former as primary, an observation so painfully obvious that it is often forgotten.
32. Knights of the religious military order known as the Templars, founded circa 1118 at Jerusalem by the Crusaders, had a large Cross Potent woven into the right breast of their robes. For an illustration, taken from a twelfth-century manuscript in the Universitätsbibliothek at Heidelberg,

The Word *m^yag in Old Sinitic   181

of one such Crusader see *The American Heritage Dictionary of the English Language* (1981), p. 1325.

33. The most influential of the grimoires is the *Key of Solomon*, published under the title *Clavicula Salomonis* c. 1456 but probably composed during the fourteenth or fifteenth century; see *Encyclopedia of Occultism & Parapsychology*, 3 vols., ed. Leslie Shepard (Detroit: Gale Research, 1984), vol. 2, p. 718b. A Greek version of the *Key* in the British Museum is held to date from the twelfth or thirteenth century. "Solomon enjoyed a great legendary reputation as a powerful magician and a worshipper of strange gods, and as far back as the 1st century AD the Jewish historian Josephus referred to a book of incantations for conjuring up demons, supposedly written by Solomon. The *Testament of Solomon* (not the same as the *Key*) dating from c 100 to 400 AD, lists the names and powers of demons which Solomon had subdued with his magic ring. In the 13th century Roger Bacon, himself a reputed magician, knew of magical works attributed to Solomon and c 1350 *Le Livre de Salomon*, containing methods of evoking demons, was burned by order of Pope Innocent VI." *Man, Myth, & Magic: The Illustrated Encyclopedia of Mythology, Religion and the Unknown*, 11 vols. plus index, ed. Richard Cavendish (New York, London, and Toronto: Marshall Cavendish, 1983), vol. 5, p. 1181. The antiquity of the essential contents of the grimoires is further evidenced by the strong influence they received from the Hebrew Kabbalah (Jewish tradition of mystical speculation passed on primarily by word of mouth). The most important collection of Kabbalistic knowledge is the massive *Zohar* (*Sefer ha-Zohar* [Book of Splendor]), written for the most part during the late thirteenth century in Spain, in all likelihood by Moses b. Shem Tov de León of Guadalajara, a small town northeast of Madrid. A notable precursor is the *Sefer Yetsirah* (Book of Creation) probably written sometime between the third and sixth centuries C.E. Another ancient source for the grimoires was Babylonian astrological lore, especially as elaborated by the Chaldeans who ruled for nearly a century until they were overthrown by the Persians in 89 B.C.E. Finally, the magical papyri stemming from the large numbers of Greeks who settled in Egypt starting around the fourth century B.C.E. represent perhaps the most significant early textual bases for the grimoires. They were also important sources for the Kabbalah; see Gershom Scholem, *Kabbalah* (1974; New York: Dorset, 1987), p. 185. The more substantial of the Greek magical papyri date from the late third through fifth centuries C.E. but some of the smaller texts derive from as early as the second century. The

classical scholar Arthur Darby Nock was of the opinion that the longer texts were actually handbooks used by practicing magicians while the shorter ones were extracts designed for sale to nonprofessionals who desired them for specific needs and occasions; "Greek Magical Papyri," *The Journal of Egyptian Archaeology*, 15 (1929), 219-235, esp. p. 220. Prominent among the signs on the Greek magical papyri was the Cross Potent (especially in its Pomee variety with knobs at the ends of the arms instead of bars—as it frequently occurs in the grimoires—often tilted). For examples, see Karl Preisendanz, ed. and tr., *Papyri Graecae Magicae: Die Griechischen Zauberpapyri*, Sammlung Wissenschaftlichen Commentare, 2 vols. (1928-41; rev. ed, Stuttgart: B. G. Teubner, 1973- 74), vol. 2, pp. 140, 170-171. For an excellent brief introduction, see the article on "Magical Papyri" by B. R. Rees in Cavendish, ed., *Man, Myth, & Magic*, vol. 6, pp. 1689-1691.
34. Dee's seal is preserved in the British Museum as Sloane MS 3188, fol. 30. See also the mandala-like *Sigillum Dei Aemeth* illustrated in Francis King, *Magic: The Western Tradition* (London: Thames and Hudson, 1975), fig. 15. Complicated sixteenth- and seventeenth-century magical diagrams feature the Cross Potent as a protective device for those who employ the esoteric practices described in the grimoires; see King, *Magic*, fig. 37. It is also very closely linked with names for God and other symbols of power; King, *Magic*, figs. 6, 9-13.
35. King, *Magic*, fig. 36.
36. The classic statement of this view is by Ping-ti Ho, *The Cradle of the East: An Inquiry into the Indigenous Origin of the Techniques and Ideas of Neolithic and Early Historic China* (Hong Kong: Chinese University of Hong Kong and University of Chicago Press, 1975).
37. Compare Robert Shafer, "Eurasial," *Orbis*, 12 (1963), 19-44, also "The Eurasial Linguistic Superfamily," *Anthropos*, 60 (1965), 445-468, and Edwin G. Pulleyblank, "Prehistoric East-West Contacts Across Eurasia," *Pacific Affairs*, 47.4 (Winter, 1974-1975), 500-508. The most complete presentation of Indo-European influence on the formation of Chinese civilization to date is that of Chang Tsung-tung, "Indo-European Vocabulary in Old Chinese: A New Thesis on the Emergence of Chinese Language and Civilization in the Late Neolithic Age," *Sino-Platonic Papers*, 7 (January, 1988), 56 pages. Chang is currently working on a book that will greatly expand his treatment of the subject.
38. Information from Bernard Wailes and *Past Worlds*, p. 190.

The Word *m^{y}ag in Old Sinitic 183

39. Philip L. Kohl, *Central Asia: Palaeolithic Beginnings to the Iron Age* (Paris: Éditions Recherche sur les Civilisations, 1984), p. 155. Kohl notes (p. 157) that millet was also found at Sapalli-tepe and suggests that this too indicates a Bronze Age link to the east. My thanks to Barbara Stephen for this reference.
40. Colin Campbell writing in the *New York Times* (February 17, 1986), 10. I am grateful to Edward L. Shaughnessy for this reference. See also the recent report by Li Hsi-kuang 李希光 in *Jen-min jih-pao* 人民日報 (People's Daily), overseas edition (August 22, 1990).
41. See Edward Shaughnessy, "Historical Perspectives on the Introduction of the Chariot into China," *Harvard Journal of Asiatic Studies*, 48 (June, 1988), 189–237, and "Western Cultural Innovations in China, 1200 B.C.," *Sino-Platonic Papers*, 11 (July, 1989), 8 pages.
42. The initial *k in this transcription might conceivably be aspirated and the *l might be an *r. Also, as in *m^{y}ag, the presence of the final velar might be disputed. None of these adjustments would require a rejection of the relationship between Indo-Iranian and Old-Sinitic with regard to the words for "magician" and "wheel[ed vehicle]" that I am proposing. So long as the correspondences between Indo-Iranian and Old Sinitic are regular, the differences between them may be attributable to their phonotactic constraints. Nonetheless, it is frustrating that the reconstructions for Old Sinitic are still so crude. This makes linkages with alphabetical languages whose archaic phonology is more accurately worked out all the more urgent. Naturally, because historical linguistics is inductive (in principle), it is essential to continue to refine the entire system of Sinitic reconstructions so that they are both increasingly accurate and internally consistent.
43. Tomas Gamkrelidze and Vyachislav Ivanov have noted that Indo-European *k^{w}ék^{w}lo- resembles words for "vehicle" in Sumerian (*gigir*), Semitic (**galgal*-), and Kartvelian (i.e., Transcaucasian *grgar*), indicating that the Proto-Indo-Europeans may have been in contact with these other language groups during the fourth millennium B.C.E. when wheeled vehicles were invented; see Mallory, *Indo-Europeans*, p. 163.
44. George Sherman Lane, "The Indo-European Labiovelars in Tocharian," in *Indogermanica (Festschrift für Wolfgang Krause)*, eds. Hans Hartmann and Hans Neumann (Heidelberg: Carl Winter, 1960), pp. 72–79, esp. pp. 72 and 75; Rudolf Normier, "Tocharisch ñkät/ñakte 'Gott'" *Zeitschrift für Vergleichende Sprachforschung*, 94 (1980), 251–281, esp. p. 263.

45. Wsewolod Miller, *Die Sprache der Osseten: Grundriss der iranischen Philologie*, eds. Wilhelm Geiger and Ernst Kuhn, Anhang zum ersten Band (Strassburg: Karl J. Trübner, 1903), p. 26.
46. For pre-Ossetic loanwords in Tocharian, see Werner Winter, "Baktrische Lehnwörter in Tocharischen," *Donum Indogermanicum: Festgabe für Anton Scherer*, ed. Robert Schmitt-Brandt (Heidelberg: Carl Winter Universitätsverlag, 1971), pp. 217–223, and for the same in Eastern European languages, see V. I. Abaev, *Istoriko-Etimologicheskii Slovar' Osetinskogo Yaz'ika*, 3 vols. (Moscow and Leningrad: Akademii Nauk SSSR, 1958–1973).
47. Julius Pokorny, *Indogermanisches etymologisches Wörterbuch*, 2 vols. (Bern and Munich: Francke, 1959–1969), vol. 1, p. 695.

CHAPTER 6

CHENG CH'IAO'S UNDERSTANDING OF SANSKRIT

THE CONCEPT OF SPELLING IN CHINA

Source: Adapted from "Cheng Ch'iao's Understanding of Sanskrit: The Concept of Spelling in China," in *Festschrift in Honour of Professor Jao Tsung-I on the Occasion of His Seventy-fifth Anniversary* (Hong Kong: Institute of Chinese Studies at the Chinese University of Hong Kong: 1993), 331-41.

In his valuable collection of essays on the Siddham script and related matters,[1] Professor Jao Tsung-i has shown clearly that the concept of spelling (but not spelling itself) was present in China not long after the arrival of Buddhism there.[2] Since, as David Diringer,[3] I.J. Gelb,[4] and others have demonstrated, the alphabet was a powerful and efficient script that rapidly spread to virtually every other literate civilization in the world, one wonders why it did not become popular in China and the East Asian countries which fell within the Chinese cultural orbit. As a matter of fact, the alphabet has now displaced pictoideographic, logographic scripts even in Korea, Vietnam, and partially in Japan. It is only in China that the sinographs (*han-tzu* 漢字), also called tetragraphs (*fang-k'uai-tzu* 方塊字), persist unadulteratedly. Simplification (*chien-hua han-tzu* 簡化漢字) and romanization (*Han-yü Pin-yin* 漢語拼音) have yet to alter the basic configuration of the Chinese writing system, although technological, social, and international considerations will inevitably cause tremendous adjustments during the coming decade.

The survival of an archaic picto-ideographic or logographic (more precisely morphosyllabic) script in China cannot be due to any peculiarity of Sinitic languages. Many other languages in the Sino-Tibetan family (such as Tibetan and Burmese) are written alphabetically and, indeed, it has been customary to write certain languages of the Sinitic group (e.g., Cantonese, Taiwanese, Hokkienese, Amoyese, etc.) primarily in romanization rather than in sinographs. The claim is often made that the Sinitic group of languages are forced to rely on the sinographs because of their allegedly monosyllabic nature. This assertion, however, is false since the Sinitic languages, especially the living vernaculars as opposed to the classical book language, are not really monosyllabic at all.[5] Hence, there are no convincing linguistic grounds for continued usage of the sinographs. China's attachment to the characters is due, rather, to political and cultural reasons. Thousands of years of familiarity with the morphosyllabic tetragraphs, moreover, has made it difficult for Chinese scholars to comprehend the completely different premises upon which phonetic spelling operates. The problem may be illustrated by my own personal experience.

When I began to study Sanskrit, I was immediately struck by the enormous complexity and specificity of the grammar; the writing system presented no great challenges. I began to work on Chinese in earnest a few years later and was overwhelmed by how tremendously difficult the writing system was, whereas the grammar was unimaginably simple and diffuse in comparison with virtually all the other languages I had encountered previously or have encountered since that time. My impressions of the extraordinary obstacles one faces in trying to master the sinographs have only deepened as I learn more about Sinitic languages and Chinese society. This has led me often to wonder whether any early Chinese scholars, perhaps through contact with Sanskrit or other alphabetically written languages, may have had the same perception as I of the sinographs as being unwieldy. There is no doubt that, since the last quarter of the nineteenth century, thousands of Chinese language reformers have expressed themselves in no uncertain terms on this subject. Yet the late Ch'ing script reform movements may have come about as a result of the activities of missionaries such as Matteo Ricci (1552-1610), Nicolas Trigault (1577-1628), and their Catholic and Protestant successors who introduced the romanization of various Sinitic and non-Sinitic languages to China. I wanted to discover whether any Chinese had previously come by themselves to the conclusion that the sinographs were somehow inadequate or clumsy. So I set out looking for the closet script reformers who lived before the Ch'ing period. I thought that I had found one in Teng Su 鄧肅 (1091-1132).[6]

In his *Ping-lü chi* (Coir Palm Collection) 栟櫚集, Teng Su makes the following comparison:

> The skillfulness of the peoples to our north and east lies in the simplicity of their writing; because it is simple, they are quick. The plight of the Chinese lies in the complexity of our writing; because it is complex, we are slow.
> 夷狄之巧在文書簡；簡故速。中國之患在文書煩；煩故遲。[7]

I have provided the tetragraphs for this passage because there is a controversy over their interpretation. Teng Su was a Sung scholar-official who served as an emissary to the Chin (Jurchen) court, so he may have had first-hand experience with the Jurchen script. The above comparison occurs in the context of a memorial to the throne submitted by Teng. In the context of the memorial, it is clear that the statement refers to the superfluity and verbosity of Chinese documents, not to the nature of the script per se. Teng Su is not explicit about whether he considers the Chinese script itself to be a drawback, although his statement has often been cited to that effect by modern Chinese language reformers. Furthermore, the script which the Jurchen were using when Teng Su engaged in-negotiations with them was the Great Khitan script which had been adopted by them in 1119. The Great Khitan script was obviously based upon the Chinese script and was probably every bit as hard to use as the latter. The Jurchens wisely submitted the Great Khitan script to a thorough simplification in 1138, such that it came to be a large syllabary with only a small number of ideographs and was called the Little Khitan script. The Great Khitan script continued to be preferred for most official purposes such as political correspondence until as late as 1180.[8] It is therefore impossible that Teng Su would have been exposed to the Little Khitan script, since he died in 1132 and since the Little Khitan script was not even invented until 1138 and did not come into official favor until much later.

Although Teng Su cannot be credited with a true appreciation of the virtues of phonetic writing, some earlier Chinese were certainly aware of the existence of alphabetical scripts and had a rough understanding of their principles. Furthermore, there can be no doubt that they linked the introduction of these principles to Buddhism. In the "Ching-chi chih (Bibliographical Treatise)" 經籍志 of the *Sui-shu* (History of the Sui) 隋書, we find the following statement:

> After the Later Han when the Buddha's Law circulated in China, we obtained the "barbarian" writing of the Western Regions 西域胡書. With its fourteen letters, all sounds can be encompassed. Although the script is spare, the meanings it can express are vast in number 文省而義廣. It is called "Brahmanical Writing" 波羅門書. It is quite different from the eight styles and six types [of graph formation of the Chinese script].[9]

It is not unlikely that the author of the "Bibliographical Treatise" is here referring specifically to the Brahmi script which has 35 basic letter forms plus a few additional elements for use in spelling. The number "fourteen" 十四 surely must be a transposition of "forty" 四十, approximately the number of elements in the Brahmi script. No Central or South Asian alphabet from the period in question could get by with so few as fourteen letters. Be that as it may, Chang-sun Wu-chi 長孫無忌 (d. 659), the compiler of the "Bibliographical Treatise," had only the vaguest notion of the actual mechanics of alphabetical writing. In my estimation, the pre-Ch'ing scholar who came closest to realizing the true nature of alphabetical scripts was probably Cheng Ch'iao 鄭樵 (1104-1162).

A native of P'u-t'ien 莆田 in Fukien, Cheng Ch'iao was one of the most famous scholars of the Sung dynasty.[10] There are, however, numerous aspects of his career that mark him as having an unusually independent cast of mind. Chief among these is the fact that he never took the civil service examination, something almost unthinkable for an aspiring Confucian literatus, Instead, he lived reclusively, studying diligently and accumulating vast knowledge in almost every area of learning. He assiduously examined antiquities and rareties, taking a particular interest in difficult paleographical problems such as the inscriptions on the ancient stone drums (*shih-ku-wen* 石鼓文). When necessary, Cheng was willing to travel extensively, inasmuch as he emphasized first-hand investigation rather than empty theorizing. As a synthesizer of information, Cheng considered himself the equal of Liu Hsiang 劉向 (77-6 BCE) and Yang Hsiung 揚雄 (53 BCE-18 CE). He also had a passionate concern for historiography, modeling himself after Ssu-ma Ch'ien 司馬遷 (145-90?) and Liu Chih-chi 劉知幾 (641-721).

The crowning glory of Cheng Ch'iao's scholarship is his *T'ung-chih* (Comprehensive Treatise) 通志, an enormous encyclopedic history of institutions in 200 fascicles that was completed in 1161.[11] Pride of place within the *T'ung-chih* was occupied by twenty monographic studies designated as *lüeh* ("compendia") 略. Five of these treated subjects that had never been systematically discussed in China before: family and clan, philology, phonetics, political subdivisions, and flora and insects. The other fifteen compendia dealt with subjects that had been presented in earlier works, but not so thoroughly and clearly as in the *T'ung-chih*.

The most unique feature of Cheng Ch'iao's intellectual orientation is his deep preoccupation with language and script. Perhaps no other individual in China before the advent of evidential learning (*k'ao-cheng-hsüeh* 考證學) during the Ch'ing period, which arose partly under the impact of Western learning brought by the Jesuits and others, was able to make so many critical and penetrating observations about the relationship between writing and speech. Dealing as he did with massive amounts of data in different fields, Cheng was concerned with the question of how to organize knowledge and dimly recognized that script had an important bearing on this issue.[12] He even wrote a "Chiao-ch'ou lüeh (Compendium on Collation)" 校讎畧 which may be viewed as a kind of forerunner of librarianship.[13]

It would seem that the chief reason Cheng Ch'iao was able to make such estimable progress in theoretical studies on the nature of writing was his serious contemplation of Sanskrit. By no means do I wish to imply that he attempted to learn Sanskrit. Rather, he clearly thought long and hard about the manner in which Sanskrit functioned as a written language in comparison with the manner in which the tetragraphic Chinese script functioned. In fact, as I shall demonstrate below, Cheng Ch'iao probably had not the lightest command of any Indian language whatsoever.

Judging from the wording of certain passages in his "Liu-shu lüeh (Compendium on the Six Categories of Sinographs)" 六書畧, Cheng Ch'iao must have been initially exposed to fundamental notions about the Sanskrit alphabet through some such text as *Fa-yüan chu-lin* (Grove of Pearls in the Garden of Dharma) 法苑珠林. In its ninth fascicle, *Fa-yüan chu-lin* has a brief account of the origin and nature of various Indic scripts in comparison with Chinese tetragraphs.[14] Actually, Tao-shih 道世, who finished his compilation of *Fa-yüan chu-lin* in 668 CE, was almost certainly basing himself on Seng-yu 僧佑 (445-518) since he follows the latter almost verbatim.[15] Although Seng-yu himself had only an obscure comprehension of how Sanskrit really operates, he was enormously learned and was able to gather a wealth of useful information on Indian languages.¹⁶ The likelihood of Cheng Ch'iao's encountering Sanskrit through Seng-yu's writings is great since the latter offered his pregnant comparisons of Sanskrit and Sinitic in his *Ch'u San-tsang chi-chi* (Collection of Records on the Issuance of the Tripiṭaka) 出三藏記集. Given that Cheng Ch'iao was a bibliophile and a noted bibliographer in his own right, he certainly would have been well acquainted with Seng-yu's famous catalog of the formation of the Chinese Buddhist canon.

Whereas Seng-yu gave a detailed critical description and explanation of early Sinitic translations of Indian texts, Cheng Ch'iao pondered far more profoundly on the significance of the fundamental differences between Sanskrit and Chinese writing for the dissemination of ideas. The most succinct presentation of Cheng's views on this extremely important topic may be found in section 5 of his Compendium on the Six Categories of Sinographs which is entitled "Lun Hua Fan (On Chinese and Indian Scripts) 論華梵," which I here translate in its entirety:

On Chinese and Indian Scripts

A. The scripts of the various non-Chinese peoples differ, but they are mostly based on Indian writing. I suspect that even the interpreters and the embellishers in the office of the Chamberlain for Dependencies¹⁷ would not be able to understand them completely. This is something that must be discussed.

Indian writing begins¹⁸ at the left and goes toward the right; Chinese writing begins at the right and goes toward the left. Chinese texts are composed of upright and perpendicular strokes; Indian letters are formed from deflected and entwined lines. In Chinese, one syllable is equal to one graph; in Indian languages, one word may be strung together from several sounds. Chinese reads from the top straight down; Indian writing is horizontally connected. Chinese has pictographic characters and so does Indian writing. The word for "tail" (尾 *miuəi/wěi*) is written 𠙸 which shows a tail hanging down. The word for "bind" (縛 *b'uâ/fú*; transcribes Skt. *pa, ba, va*) is written 犮, which has a tightly wrapped shape. Chinese has abbreviated graphs and so does Indian writing. The word for "ground" 地 (*d'i/ti*) was originally written 𠂤, but it is also abbreviated as 𭕄. "Bind" (縛 *b'uâ /fú*) was originally written 𠤎, but it is also abbreviated as 𭕄. The word for "to carry on the back" (馱 *d'â/tò*; transcribes Skt. *dha, dhya*) was originally written 𠂤, but it is also abbreviated as 𭕄. Chinese uses homophonic borrowings and so does Indian writing. The word for "wilds" (野 *ia/yěh*) is 𭕄, while that for "also" (也 *ia/yěh*) is likewise 𭕄. "Carry on the back" (馱 *d'â/tò*[!]) is 𭕄 and "a declivity" (陁 *d'iɛ/t'ó*; transcribes Skt. *t, th, d, dh, ty, dy, dhy*) is also written 𭕄. Chinese has near-homophonous borrowings and so does Indic writing. "Small, minute" (微 *miuəi/wéi*; transcribes Skt. *vi, bi*) is 𭕄 and "tail" (尾 *miuəi/wěi*) is also 𭕄. Sat [*tva*] (薩 *sât/sā*) is also written 𭕄 and "disperse" (散 *san/sǎn*; transcribes Skt. *sam, san*) is also written 𭕄. In Chinese texts there is a sign for repetition. For example, in the *Old History of the Han Dynasty* (*Chiu Han-shu* 舊漢書), "the people rested" (*yüan-yüan hsiu-hsi* 元元休息), the second 元 is marked only by the graph for "two" (*erh* 二, i.e., "duplicate"). In the stone drum inscriptions and on the stele of Mt. I 嶧山碑,[19] all the repeated characters are noted 二. In Indian texts, repeated sentences or a phrases are merely marked 𭕄, but in Chinese texts, every character that is repeated is noted. In Indian texts, if one word is repeated or a phrase is duplicated, it is marked 𭕄. If three or four words are repeated, or three or four phrases are duplicated, they are just marked 𭕄.

This is probably because **Chinese is transmitted visually, therefore it must be explicit in its written form. Indian texts are transmitted orally, as though they were musical scores.** One can only gain a general overview of them from their written, form. In Chinese, the variant pronunciation of a graph is an exact reading but, with Indian scripts, variant pronunciations are approximations. For example, the graphs for "history" (史 *ṣi/shǐh*) and "zither" (瑟 *ṣiĕt/sè*) are both written 𭕄. The graphs for "teacher" (師 *ṣi/shīh*), "history" (史 *ṣi/shǐh*), "emissary" (使 *ṣi/shih*), and "zither" (瑟 *ṣiĕt/sè*) are harmonizations of [the note] *re* (商 *śiang/shang*). The graphs for "emperor" (帝 *tiei/ti*; transcribes Skt. *t*) and "pendulous" (癉 *tâ/tŏ*) are both written 𭕄. "Low" (低 *tiei/tī*; transcribes Skt. *ti*), "bottom" (底 *tiei/tǐ*; transcribes Skt. *t, d, dh*),

Cheng Ch'iao's Understanding of Sanskrit   193

"emperor" (帝 *tiei/tì*), and "pendulous" (觶 *tâ/tŏ*) are also harmonizations of [the note] *re* (商 *śiang/shang*). "Saunter" (娑 *sâ/sō*; transcribes Skt. sounds beginning *s*, *ś*, especially *sa*, *sā*) and *sat* [*tva*] (薩 *sât/sā*) are both written 𑖭 and this too is a harmonization of [the note] *re*. "To hum" (誐 *ngâ/é*; transcribes Skt. *ga*) and "consequences of sin" (孽 *ngiat/nièh*) are both written 𑖐 . This is a harmonization of [the note] *mi* (角 *kok/chiăo*).

B. Looking at today's rhyme handbooks that are organized according to the seven sounds, we find that they come from the Western Regions. The seven sounds correspond to the strings of the lute and are produced by the pipes of heaven. Consequently, the horizontal and the vertical, the upright and the inverted are laid out to become a chart. The pattern is all quite natural and extremely detailed. They cannot be compared with the usual sort of rhymebooks that are merely divided into the level, rising, falling, and entering tones. Scholars need to do research on the learning of the seven sounds. **Chinese has sounds that are combinations of two elements but has no graphs that show such combinations. Indian languages have sounds that are combinations of two, three, or four elements and they also have letters to represent them.** Among Chinese books, only lute scores are comparable and this is likely due to the emphasis on sound in lute playing. It is difficult to equate one sound with one graph. The shapes of several graphs must be combined in order to capture an expression made up of several sounds.

An expression composed of two sounds requires two shapes. For example, "saunter" (娑 *sâ/sō*) is written 𑖭 and "to bind" (縛 *b'uâ/fú*) is written 𑖪 . When the two are combined as *sâ-b'uâ*, one takes the bottom portion of "bind" and brings it together with "saunter", the result being the graph 𑖭𑖾 . Or, for example, the graph for "to prattle" (囉 *lâ/lō*; transcribes Skt. *ra* sounds) is written 𑖨 , that for "to carry on the back" (馱 *d'â/tò*) is 𑖠 , and that for "bag" (囊 *nang/náng*; transcribes Skt. *na*) is 𑖡 . When the three are combined as *lâ-d'â-nang*, one takes "prattle" for the top part, "carry on the back" for the middle part, and "bag" for the bottom part, yielding the graph 𑖨 . Or, for example, the graph for "to know thoroughly" (悉 *siĕt/hsī*; transcribes Skt. *si*, *sa s*, *śr*) is written 冽, that for "bottom" (底 *tiei/tǐ*) is 人, that for the final particle 哩 (*liəɣ/lǐ*) is 丂, and that for "wilds" (野 *ia/yěh*) is 夕. When the four are combined as *siĕt-tiei-liəɣ-ia*, one takes "know thoroughly" for the top part and "wilds" for the bottom part, including "bottom" and the final particle as incidental parts of the pattern. "Bottom" and the final particle do not need to be given in their entirety. Hence, the combined graph is 竕.

There are, however, combinations of two elements that yield a single sound from the combination of a pair of sounds. For example, the nominal particle 者 (*tśia/chě*) and the final particle 焉 (*ian/yēn*) are paired sounds, but "silken banner" (旃 *tśiän/chān*; usually transcribes Skt. *can*, rarely *śan, ṣan, cin, kim*) is the resultant single sound. The nominal particle 者 (*tśia/chě*) and the conjunction 與 (*iwo/yü*) are paired sounds, but the pluralizing prefix 諸 (*tśiwo/chū*) is the resultant single sound. Similarly, "to saunter" (娑 *sâ/sō*) and "to bind" (縛 *b'uâ/fú*) are paired sounds, while "to search" (索 *sak/sō*; transcribes Skt. *sa*) is the resultant single sound. "To saunter" (娑 *sâ/sō*) and "pendulous" (嚲 *tâ/tǒ*) are paired sounds, whereas *sat* [*tva*] (薩 *sât/sā*) is the resultant single sound. Why, in these latter two cases, is not "to search" (索 *sak/sō*) alone sufficient? Why use the combination of "to saunter" and "to bind" when *sat*[*tva*] by itself would be sufficient? Why use the combination "to saunter" and "pendulous" at all? My reply is that **Chinese sounds emphasize reading pronunciations.** It is necessary that each item which is pronounced be one sound [i.e., a single syllable]. Thus, even though we begin with the nominal particle 者 (*tśia/chě*) and the final particle 焉 (*ian/yēn*), the resultant combination may be read independently as "silken banner" (旃 *tśiän/chān*). Even though we begin with the nominal particle 者 (*tśia/chě*) and the conjunction 與 (*iwo/yü*), the resultant combination may be read independently as the pluralizing suffix 諸 (*tśiwo/chū*). Although we may refer to single sounds in the recitation of Indian languages, within these single sounds there are high and low accents or stresses. Therefore, "to saunter" (*sâ/sō*) and "to bind" (*b'uâ/fú*) cannot be read as "to search" (*sak/sō*), "to saunter" (*sâ/sō*) and "pendulous" (*tâ/tǒ*) cannot be read as *sat*[*tva*] (*sât/sā*). There is indeed a subtle linkage that draws the two parts together.

When we speak of a combination of two elements in Indian writing, we do not mean that it is either one or two sounds. When we speak of a combination of three elements in Indian writing, we do not mean that it is either one, two, or three sounds. When we speak of a combination of four elements, we do not mean that it is either one, two, three, or four sounds. But when we speak of a combination of two elements, its sound is easy to differentiate, whereas when we speak of combinations of three or our elements, their sounds are progressively difficult. **In general, we may say that Chinese people are not good at sounds. When Indian monks pray for rain, the rain responds; when they invoke a dragon, the dragon appears. This takes place in an instant, following the transformations of their voices. Although Chinese monks try to imitate their voices, their requests are not fulfilled. The real reason for this is that they have not yet achieved proficiency in the way of sounds and control of the voice.**

C. The Indians' ability to distinguish sounds lies in their emphasis upon sounds instead of upon graphs. The ability of Chinese to distinguish graphs lies in their emphasis upon graphs instead of upon sounds. Consequently, Indian writing is very simple, consisting only of a few bends and angles.[20] The variations in their script are few and their writing does not constitute a literary style. Yet they have an unlimited number of sounds. Chinese are encumbered by their inability to distinguish sounds. Phonological studies were completely unknown before the Han period and, indeed, they entered the Central Realm from the Western Regions. Therefore, the followers of Buddhism are, for the most part, able to discuss rhyme charts and the like, whereas Confucians are ignorant of their basic premises because the fountainhead of the charts lies elsewhere.

Chinese writing is extremely dense in the construction of its graphs, what with their extremely numerous dots and strokes. Indian writing, by comparison, is truly sparse. Therefore, Indian writing has an unlimited number of sounds whereas Chinese writing has an unlimited number of graphs.[21] The sounds of Indian writing have a marvelous significance, but its graphs are devoid of literary grace. Chinese graphs display a rich variety, but lack even a smidgen of phonology. The Indians are adept at phonology and what they acquire is gained through listening. Thus they say such things as "The substance of the true doctrine is this: purity (pariśuddhi, viśuddhi) lies in the sounds one hears." "My former samādhi (perfect concentration, an advanced meditational state) was completely dependent upon what I heard." They also have the theory that the merit (puṇya) of the sense of sight is small, whereas the merit of the sense of hearing is great. The Chinese are adept at philology and what they acquire is gained through seeing. Therefore all those under heaven who are literate are considered to be learned sages while those who are illiterate are considered to be simple and stupid.[22]

The last section of "On Chinese and Indian Scripts" is very revealing, for it shows that Cheng Ch'iao believed literary excellence to be somehow dependent upon the visual intricacies of the Chinese script itself. This is, of course, a fallacy because calligraphic complexity and beauty are completely unrelated to literary achievement. If anything, the necessity to devote most of one's attention in writing to the mastery and control of an exacting script results in a corresponding lack of attention to diction, structure, euphony, image, metaphor, and all the other ingredients of fine literature, such that there may well exist an inverse ratio between the complexity of a script and the ability of an author who relies on that script to produce good literature.

In the first paragraph of "On Chinese and Indian Scripts," Cheng Ch'iao makes an explicit comparison between the traditional seven note musical scale and the seven different types of sounds (labials, linguals, velars, dentals, guttarals, semilinguals, and semidentals) in the analytical systems of phonology which he declares were brought to China from the

Cheng Ch'iao's Understanding of Sanskrit   197

Western Regions. Cheng carries this line of thinking to great lengths in his "Ch'i-yin lüeh (Compendium on the Seven Sounds)" 七音畧. While this confusion of the musical and the phonological is fundamentally erroneous, Cheng as usual offers many penetrating insights with terribly imprecise data. The entire "Compendium on the Seven Sounds" is full of interesting ideas about the nature of language (some of them, unfortunately completely wrong), but many of Cheng Ch'iao's most prescient comparative statements occur in concentrated form in the Preface to that work, a portion of which I translate here:

Preface to the Seven Sounds

Han literati only knew how to analyze graphs with the *Explanation of Script*,[23] but they did not know that there were vowels and consonants[24] in writing. Words originate with Vowels, and consonants are subordinate to vowels. They did not distinguish between consonants arid vowels, so they failed to understand the principle of the composition of words. The four tones are the warp and the seven sounds are the woof. Literati from south of the Yangtze River knew that, on one plane, there were the four tones called "level," rising," "falling," and "entering" but, on another plane, they did not know that there were seven sounds called *do, re, me, so, la, hemi-so,* and *hemi-do.*[25] The first plane becomes the warp and the second becomes the woof. Because they did not interweave the warp and the woof, they failed to discover the basis for the establishment of rhyme categories.[26] The organization of rhyme categories according to the seven sounds arose in the Western Regions and from there was transmitted to the various parts of China. Therefore foreign Buddhist monks, wishing to propagate their doctrine throughout the world, wrote this book (i.e., *The Seven Sounds*). Although their texts are translated and re-translated hundreds of times to places so remote that they are unfamiliar with a single word of the original, still the sound and sense can be conveyed.

Chinese Buddhist monks, following their methods, devised a syllabary consisting of 36 initials[27] which preserved their distinctions of accented and unaccented, voiced and voiceless. The sounds of all the myriad things of heaven and earth are reproducible through these means. Though it be the cry of a crane, the voice of the wind, the crow of a cock, the bark of a dog, the crash of thunder which startles heaven, the buzz of a tiny insect passing by your ear, all can be rendered into written words. How much more so can human speech! As a result, whenever the light of the sun and moon shine, those desirous of transmitting Buddhist texts rely on the chart of the seven sounds to communicate their meaning through a hundred successive translations.

Now, the writings of Confucius travelled as far east as Korea, as far west as Kansu, as far south as Annam, and as far north as Inner Mongolia. All of these were our ancient feudatories. His writings did not reach beyond these ancient feudatories. How is it that Gautama Buddha's books can penetrate the various parts of China but Confucian writings cannot reach the Airavati River? It is because there are obstacles to the passage of tones and sounds. This is the fault of scholars who came after Confucius! Wherever boats and carts can arrive, there too words and their meanings can extend. Why are there places where boats and carts arrive today but Confucius' words and their meanings do not extend?

Now I have taken the *Seven Sounds* and edited it as a compendium with the intent of enabling scholars to propagate their learning fully whereupon they can thoroughly disseminate Confucian writings in all regions where there are human beings. The so-called "application of Chinese civilization to transform barbarians" begins with this.[28]

It is ironic that, with their superior alphabetical scripts, the "barbarians" (viz., Indian and Central Asian Buddhists) were actually able to change Chinese civilization profoundly and irrevocably. Cheng Ch'iao is thus to be credited for accurately perceiving the power of phonetic writing. In his frustration over the poor showing of Confucianism outside of China and its immediate environs, he blames the literati who failed to comprehend the rules of phonology. This is somewhat unfair, since Cheng Ch'iao himself had a defective understanding of phonology and was unable to recognize that the larger problem of transmissibility

Cheng Ch'iao's Understanding of Sanskrit 199

lies in the nature of the Chinese script. For all of his elaborate treatises on the sounds and shapes of Chinese and foreign writing systems, Cheng never came to grips with the basic incompatibility of morphosyllabic writing and precise phonemic analysis. In brief, there is no evidence that Cheng Ch'iao really understood the principle of alphabetical spelling, although he clearly appreciated its effects.

Anyone who reads Cheng Ch'iao's disquisition "On Chinese and Indian Scripts" will certainly have great difficulty making sense of large portions of the text. This is particularly the case when Cheng is discussing specific technical aspects of the Indian alphabet, the reason being that he simply does not command the material he is presenting. One assumes that Cheng purports to offer his reader the Siddham forms of Indian letters, rather than their Brāhmī, Kharoṣṭhī, or, much less, Devanāgarī forms. In truth, most of Cheng's letters are sheer fantasy. It is apparent that he (and his research associates) had only the foggiest idea of what a few of the Siddham letters looked like, let alone understanding anything about Sanskrit language and grammar. Cheng had not the slightest acquaintance with the way Sanskrit words were actually spelled through the combination of consonants and vowels, the constitution of the *varṇapātha* (alphabet), the addition of ligatures to the basic forms of the letters, the construction and role of *akṣara* (syllables), and so forth. Only two or three of the numerous "letters" cited by Cheng in his essay even come close to resembling actual Siddham forms (e.g., 𑖧 > 𑖧 = Devanāgarī य *ya*).[29] I suspect that those who carved the printing blocks for the *T'ung-chih* probably also contributed to the gross errors in Siddham that pervade Cheng's essay. But there is no witness in any of Cheng's writings that he was conversant with Sanskrit (neither the script nor the language). The inability of Cheng Ch'iao to fathom how utterly dissimilar Chinese and Indian scripts really are is borne out by his assertion that the latter include ideograms. In order to reflect Cheng Ch'iao's incapacity to separate semantic content from phonological notation, in my translation I have rendered all sinographs on each occurrence. Because Cheng lacked all sense of genuine phonemics, his efforts to describe consonant clusters fails miserably. In short, "On Chinese and Indian Scripts" falls far short of describing how spelling actually works.

One of the greatest drawbacks in Cheng Ch'iao's analysis is his confusion of language and script. Even though he wrote voluminously on the sound patterns of the Chinese scripts, Cheng did not seem to realize that the most vital element of language is the phonology of speech, and that grammar and lexicon are also essential. Script, on the other hand, possesses a secondary quality in the sense that it depends upon the prior existence of spoken language. The purpose of script is merely to record on a two-dimensional surface the other elements of language. Furthermore, there is no necessary relationship between a given language and a particular script. The Roman alphabet, for example, has been used to write hundreds of different languages from virtually every family and group. Conversely, a single language may, in the course of time, be written in various scripts (e.g., Uighur, which during the last thousand and some years has been written in runes, the Old Uighur script [the precursor of the Mongol and Manchu scripts], the Arabic script, the Cyrillic script, and the Roman alphabet). It is obvious, therefore, that language is primary and that script is secondary.

Nonetheless, Cheng Ch'iao deserves our praise and admiration for striving to grapple with the realities of spelling. In terms of reading psychology, the concept of phonetic spelling is actually rather difficult to grasp because it is so highly abstract. Once the basic concept is understood, however, and the few letters are memorized, it is extremely easy to spell virtually anything that one can say. The situation is quite the opposite with a morphosyllabic script where it is extremely easy to acquire the first twenty or thirty picto-ideographic forms because they are relatively concrete. Subsequently, however, the acquisition of thousands of additional discrete script elements, which do not have a one-to-one correspondence with the words of the spoken language, imposes an enormous burden on the memory of the user. An adult steeped in the upper ranges of literacy in the Chinese morphosyllabic script, Cheng Ch'iao would have faced a nearly insuperable challenge in the acquisition of the fundamental principles of Sanskrit phonetic spelling. These formidable obstacles notwithstanding, it is a tribute to Cheng's intelligence and perceptivity that he was able to see so unmistakably the distinct advantages of an alphabetical script. What is sad is that it took nearly a thousand years before his level of insight was matched again in China.

Notes

1. The best available general study on this script is R. H. van Gulik, *Siddham: An Essay on the History of Sanskrit Studies in China and Japan*, Sarasvati-Vihara Series, 36 (Nagpur: International Academy of Indian Culture, 1956).
2. Jao Tsung-I 饒宗頤, *Chung-Yin wen-hua kuan-hsi shih tun chi, yü-wen p'ien: Hsi-t'an hsüeh hsü-lun* (Papers on the History of Culture Relations between China and India; Language: Introduction to Siddham Studies) 中印文化關係史論集，語文篇——悉曇學緒論, (Hong Kong: Chinese University of Hong Kong Institute of Chinese Studies, 1990).
3. *Writing* (London: Thames and Hudson, 1962).
4. *A Study of Writing* (Chicago: University of Chicago Press, 1963, rev. ed.).
5. See George A. Kennedy, "The Monosyllabic Myth," *Journal of the American Oriental Society*, 71.3 (1951), 161-166, reprinted in Tien-yi Li, ed., *Selected Works of George A. Kennedy* (New Haven: Yale University Far Eastern Publications, 1964), pp. 104-118, and John DeFrancis, *The Chinese Language: Fact and Fantasy* (Honolulu: University of Hawaii Press, 1984), especially chapter 11 (pp. 177-188).
6. Biographical information concerning Teng Su may be found in Ch'ang Pi-te 昌彼得, et al., *Sung-jen chuan-chi tzu-liao so-yin* (Index to Biographical Materials of Sung Figures) 宋人傳記資料索引, 6 vols. (Taipei: Ting-wen, 1975-76), vol. 5, pp. 3734-3735.
7. *Ping-lü chi* (*Ssu-k'u ch'uan-shu chen-pen* [Rare Editions from the Complete Library in Four Divisions] 四庫全書珍本 ed.), 12.27b.
8. Hans Jensen, *Sign, Symbol and Script: An Account of Man's Efforts to Write*, third revised and enlarged edition, translated from the German by George Unwin (New York: G.P. Putnam's Sons, 1969), p. 197.
9. *Sui-shu* (Peking: Chung-hua, 1973), ch. 32, p. 947.
10. See the biography by S. Y. Teng in Herbert Franke, ed. *Sung Biographies*, Münchener Ostasiatische Studien, 16-17 [4 vols.] (Wiesbaden: Franz Steiner, 1976), vol. 16.1, pp. 146-156. An older, simpler account may be found in Herbert A. Giles, *A Chinese Biographical Dictionary* (London: B. Quaritch, 1898; rpt. Taipei: Literature House, 1964), pp. 109-110 (no. 265).
11. For a brief description of Cheng Ch'iao's *T'ung-chih*, see Ssu-yü Teng and Knight Biggerstaff, *An Annotated Bibliography of Selected Chinese Reference Works*, Harvard-Yenching Institute Studies, II (Cambridge,

Massachusetts: Harvard University Press, 1971, third ed.), p. 109 and for the place of this massive work in the tradition of Chinese encyclopedic histories of institutions, see Endymion Wilkinson, *The History of Imperial China: A Research Guide* (Cambridge: Harvard University East Asia Research Guide, 1975), pp. 126ff.

12. Cf. Robert K. Logan, *The Alphabet Effect: The Impact of the Phonetic Alphabet on the Development of Western Civilization* (New York: William Morrow, 1986).
13. See Ch'ien Ya-hsin 錢亞新, *Cheng Ch'iao Chiao-ch'ou lüeh yen-chiu* (Studies on Cheng Ch'iao's "Compendium on Collation") 鄭樵校讎略研究 (Shanghai: Commercial, 1948).
14. *Taisho Tripitaka*, 53(2122). 351bc.
15. Tao-shih has the telltale passage from Seng-yu which begins: "Of old, there were altogether three masters who created writing. The eldest was named Brahmā; his script proceeded to the right. The next was Karoṣṭha; his script proceeded to the left. The youngest was Ts'ang Chieh; his script proceeded downwards...." // 昔造書之主，凡有三人。長名曰梵，其書右行。次名曰佉樓，其書左行。少者倉頡，其書下行。 (T2145[55].46) // I should note that it was not only Tao-shih who copied this misinformation from Seng-yu. We find it being repeated by many later Chinese writers, including Ma Chien-chung 馬建忠 in the second preface to his *Ma-shih wen-t'ung* (Ma's Grammar) 馬氏文通.
16. This is expertly translated and annotated in Arthur E. Link's excellent article entitled "The Earliest Chinese Account of the Compilation of the *Tripitaka*," parts I and II, *Journal of the American Oriental Society*, 81.1 and 81.2 (1961), 87-103 and 281-299. See especially pp. 283-292 which include a detailed examination of Seng-yu's views on translation. Link's study is essential for anyone who wishes to familiarize himself with the early Chinese understanding of Sanskrit. See also the same author's "Shih Seng-yu and His Writings," *Journal of the American Oriental Society*, 80 (1960), 17-43 for a reliable introduction to Seng-yu's life and works. I am grateful to Daniel Boucher for calling my attention to these articles.
17. *Ta hung-lu* 大鴻臚, an old official during the Former Han period, among whose responsibilities was the handling of diplomatic relations with non-Chinese leaders; under him was a Director of Interpreters (*I-kuan ling* 譯官令) who participated in the reception of foreign visitors at court.

18. Literally "turns".
19. The stele bears a panegyric on his own dynasty composed by the First Emperor of the Ch'in 秦始皇帝 on the occasion of ascending Mt. I in Shantung. The calligraphy was by his minister, Li Ssu 李斯.
20. "Squiggles", as it were.
21. This is very nicely put, almost as though Cheng Ch'iao had consciously decided to compose a quotable aphorism.
22. From *T'ung-chih lüeh* (Compendia from the Comprehensive Treatise) 通志畧 (*Kuo-hsueh chi-pen ts'ung-shu* [Basic Sinological Series] 國學基本叢書 ed.), ch. 5, pp. 60-66 (emphasis added). In the complete edition of the *T'ung-chih* published by Commercial Press in 1937, this essay may be found on pp. 510c-511a.
23. The *Shuo-wen chieh-tzu* 說文解字 (Explanation of Simple Characters and Compound Graphs), compiled by Hsü Shen 許慎 in the year 100 BCE, was the first "etymological" dictionary of the Chinese script. To this date, there are still no genuine etymological dictionaries for any of the Sinitic languages.
24. It is highly unlikely that Cheng Ch'iao had any clear conception of "vowels" (my nonce translation of his *mu* 母 ["mother"]) and "consonants" (my nonce translation of his *tzu* 子 ["child"]). Elsewhere ("Compendium on the Six Categories of Sinographs"), pp. 49-51, he treats the *mu* as though they were the *Shuo-wen* radicals (emphasizing their shapes and meanings), the *tzu* as though they were the graphs that are classified under the various radicals (emphasizing their sounds).
25. *Kung* 宮, *shang* 商, *chiao* 角, *chih* 徵, and *yü* 羽 are the five notes of the Chinese pentatonic scale. The two "flats" should be *pien-kung* 變宮 ("modulated *kung*") and *pien-chih* ("modulated *chih*"), but Cheng Ch'iao refers to a *pan-chih* 半徵 ("hemi-chih") and *pan-shang* 半商 ("hemi-shang"). I have partially corrected him in the translation.
26. That is to say, they failed to create a foundation for exact phonological analysis.
27. The *san-shih-liu tzu-mu* 三十六字母 are attributed to the late T'ang monk, Shou-wen 守溫. They are not a syllabary in the strict, technical sense, because the finals are ignored. Rather, it is best to think of the so-called "thirty-six initials" as a fixed group of tetragraphs that were meant to indicate the consonant combinations with which their individual pronunciations began at the time the "syllabary" was established.

28. Adapted from the translation by Victor H. Mair, "Preface to the *Seven Sounds*," *Xin Tang*, 7 (1986), 134-135. The original may be found in *T'ung-chih lüeh*, ch. 5, pp. 67-69 and *T'ung-chih*, p. 513ab.
29. Tansen Sen pointed out to me that several of the letters cited by Cheng Ch'iao may resemble elements of Tamil writing. David Ludden has confirmed the South Indian connection by showing that there are definite resemblances to the Grantha script in particular. The presence of Grantha consonants and vowel-dipthong ligatures (e.g., pa, ka, ve, yai, na, ka, ta, mu, etc.) means that this could not be a mere coincidence. The earliest inscriptions in Grantha (originally intended for writing Sanskrit only, but later, used for a number of indigenous Dravidian languages) date from the fifth-sixth century C.E., but the script is still in use. It is not surprising that Cheng Ch'iao, who was a man of P'u-t'ien in Fukien, would have had contacts with South Indians who came to China by sea. Thus, although he thought he was representing *fan* (Sanskrit, usually in Brahmi script), it was actually some form of Grantha.

CHAPTER 7

BUDDHISM AND THE RISE OF THE WRITTEN VERNACULAR

THE MAKING OF NATIONAL LANGUAGES IN EAST ASIA

Source: Adapted from "Buddhism and the Rise of the Written Vernacular in East Asia: The Making of National Languages," *Journal of Asian Studies* 53.3 (1994): 707-51.

The vast majority of premodern Chinese literature, certainly all of the most famous works of the classical tradition, were composed in one form or another of Literary Sinitic (hereafter LS, *wen-yen* [*-wen*], also often somewhat ambiguously called "Classical Chinese" or "Literary Chinese"). Beginning in the medieval period, however, an undercurrent of written Vernacular Sinitic (hereafter VS, *pai-hua* [*-wen*]) started to develop. The written vernacular came to full maturity in China only with the May Fourth Movement of 1919, after the final collapse during the 1911 revolution of the dynastic, bureaucratic institutions that had governed China for more than two millennia. It must be pointed out that the difference between *wen-yen* and *pai-hua* is at least as great as that between Latin and Italian or between Sanskrit and Hindi. In my estimation, a thorough linguistical analysis would show that unadulterated *wen-yen* and pure *pai-hua* are actually far more dissimilar than are Latin and Italian or Sanskrit and Hindi. In fact, I believe that *wen-yen* and *pai-hua* belong to wholly different categories of language, the former being a sort of demicryptography largely divorced from speech and the latter sharing a close correspondence with spoken forms of living Sinitic. This difference is reflected in the names for these two types of written Sinitic, *wen-yen* literally meaning "literary language" and *pai-hua* meaning "unadorned speech." The problem is that stylists in both the *wen-yen* and *pai-hua* traditions seldom, if ever, employed an unalloyed form of these two types of written Sinitic. Thus, there are varying degrees of mixtures that are loosely characterized as *pan-wen-pan-pai* (semiliterary-semivernacular).

Linguistic data indicate that LS and VS have been distinct systems as far back as they can be traced. This is certainly true from the Warring States period (475–249 B.C.E.) on, but I suspect that eventually we will be able to demonstrate conclusively that LS, starting with its earliest stage in the oracle shell and bone inscriptions (around 1200 B.C.E.), was always so drastically abbreviated and so replete with obligatory nonvernacular conventions used only in writing that it never came close to reflecting any contemporary living variety of Sinitic speech. Naturally, LS must have been founded upon and continuously infused by some variety or varieties of VS, just as written Sumerian (which was likewise "unsayable") must have been based upon a form of the living language of the people of ancient Sumer (cf. DeFrancis 1989:78–79). Yet the disparity between LS and VS is of a wholly different order of magnitude than that between, say, written and spoken English or written and spoken Russian.

An analogy that may be used to illustrate the relationship between LS and VS is that of the relationship between a code or cipher and the natural language upon which it is based, although the difference is not so drastic as it normally is in the latter case where intentional (though strictly principled and hence reversible for a privileged receiver) scrambling may be involved. Or we may describe the radical reduction of VS

Buddhism and the Rise of the Written Vernacular 209

to LS as being somewhat similar to the making of shopping or chore lists and the jotting down of lecture notes that include all sorts of abbreviations and omit auxiliaries, prepositions, endings, and other morphemes that are not absolutely essential. Apart from its being unnecessary for the writer to spell out everything explicitly in detail, early scribes doubtless had added incentives to economize on the time-consuming task of preparing the awkward materials they worked with clay on the one hand and bones and shells on the other—and to be as terse as possible with the complicated, inefficient morphosyllabic symbols of their scripts. After this sort of shorthand got started, it may have seemed the norm for writing. Such drastically pared-down, unnatural (in terms of real [spoken] language) styles would have been fostered and perpetuated by those elite ritual specialists who wished to monopolize their exotic skill. In the case of Sinitic, once such an elliptical system was established, it diverged more and more from the spoken language as the writing remained largely fixed while speech changed over time (DeFrancis 1991). The difference between LS and VS is thus not just a matter of diachronic change, as between Old English and Modern English or between Old Russian and Modern Russian. It is, rather, a distinction between two separately structured linguistic media. As we shall see below, LS and VS coexisted in China for thousands of years. Their maintenance as competing systems was due to support from different social and political constituencies.

Going from LS to VS or in the other direction definitely requires a process of decoding/encoding or translation; witness the burgeoning number of VS translations of LS texts from all ages that are being produced in Taiwan and the People's Republic of China. If LS and VS were merely two variants of the same language, there would be no compelling need to translate the one into the other. The confused notion that LS and VS are simply constituents of a single language is due to their frequent borrowing from and mixing with each other. More of this is done by VS from LS (e.g., *ch'eng-yü* ["set phrases," commonly referred to loosely as "idioms"] whose LS grammar, syntax, and lexicon are noticeably distinct from the VS matrix in which they are implanted) than by LS from VS, since writers of LS tend to be more conscious of maintaining the integrity and purity of their highly mannered style, while writers of VS often aspire to affect an LS aura without really mastering the entire artificial language.

In a stimulating article, "On Representing Abstractions in Archaic Chinese," Henry Rosemont, Jr. (1974) basically concurs with these views on LS when he states that it was not a spoken language but an exclusively written language and hence that it cannot be classified as a natural language. Tsu-Lin Mei (1992a) takes the contrary position that the *Analects,* to a certain extent, reflects spoken language. He sees the best evidence for this in fusion words (or what W.A.C.H. Dobson [1974: 101-2] has called "allegro forms"). Since they can occur only in rapid speech, he regards them as *"prima facie* evidence that the Master did speak in a form pretty close to what was recorded." Indeed, the *Analects* is more vernacular than the *Tso chuan* (*Tso's Chronicle*) in the sense that it uses more grammatical particles, requires more words to say the same thing, etc., and that both are more vernacular than contemporary bronze inscriptions. Nonetheless, I still maintain that all LS texts (including the *Analects* and *Tso's Chronicle*) are dramatically divorced from vernacular speech and represent a separate system of linguistic and orthographic conventions employed solely in writing. The clearest evidence for the separateness of the two systems can be seen in the much higher degree of polysyllabicity of the vernacular, starkly different grammatical structures and usages (see the discussion of *shih* below for one telling example; many others, such as distinctive demonstrative words, the method for handling possessives and relative clauses, different approaches to measure words [also called counters and classifiers], and verbal complements, might be adduced), and the fact that the borrowing back and forth between the two systems is so conspicuous. We shall return to the alleged vernacularity of the *Analects* again under the rubric of *kuan-hua.*

Early Written Vernacular in China

A curious phenomenon about the way the vernacular first comes to be written down in China is that the earliest instances of written VS occur almost exclusively, certainly with absolute and unmistakable predominance, in Buddhist contexts. The most conspicuous examples of this phenomenon are the Tun-huang *pien-wen* (transformation texts: eighth to tenth centuries) that I have worked on for the past two decades (Mair 1983, 1988, 1989; Iriya 1961, 1985) and the recorded sayings of Zen masters referred to as *yü-lu* that date from the period immediately following (Maspero 1914; Kao 1948; Berling 1987). Equally striking is the high proportion of vernacular elements that are present in the earliest translations of Buddhist texts into Sinitic, starting from the second century of the Common Era (C.E.). This has been demonstrated conclusively through the careful research of the eminent Dutch Buddhologist, Erik Zürcher (1977; 1980; 1991), and, following in his footsteps, the young Chinese linguist, Chu Ch'ing-chih (1990).

Chu's study is based on a close reading of all the Chinese Buddhist texts of the early medieval period, by which he intends the Eastern Han, Wei, Chin, and Northern and Southern Dynasties, from about 25-589 C.E. There is an enormous amount of material to be covered—Buddhist scriptures of the early medieval period alone amount to 960 titles in 2,990 scrolls or fascicles composed of roughly 25,000,000 graphs, surprisingly more than the secular native literature from the same period.

Chu richly and conclusively documents a highly significant phenomenon, that medieval Buddhist texts are decidedly more vernacular and colloquial than their non-Buddhist counterparts from the same period. One of the most obvious aspects of Chinese Buddhist texts in comparison with native works is that they contain far more polysyllabic words (particularly disyllabic words), but there are also noticeable syntactic and grammatical differences (cf. Watters's excellent but little known work of 1889, esp. chapters 8 and 9 ["The Influence of Buddhism on the Chinese Language"]). Some of this influence was in direct response to the linguistic features of the Indic (and perhaps Iranian and Tocharian) prototypes for the Chinese translations of Buddhist texts. It is clear, however, that the implantation of Buddhism into the Chinese sociolinguistic body also served to elicit in an active way vernacular, colloquial, and dialectical elements that belonged properly to spoken Sinitic languages but that had been rejected by the indigenous textual tradition as vulgarisms.

I shall give here only two examples in support of Chu's thesis, the first grammatical and the second lexical. *Shih* as the copulative verb shows up in the earliest Buddhist translations (i.e., starting from the second century C.E.) and is quite common in medieval popular Buddhist literature. This is in complete contrast to its use as a demonstrative in LS. Very early use of *shih* as the vernacular copulative has recently been archaeologically confirmed by the discovery of an astronomical text in which it repeatedly and unmistakably occurs in that capacity (cf. Tuan Li-fen 1989). Since this newly found text dates to well before the beginning of the Common Era (from near the beginning of the Western Han [i.e., the early part of the second century B.C.E.]), copulative *shih* can hardly be attributed to the coming of Buddhism. It must, rather, be a feature of the vernacular language that was present very early, perhaps from the start, but that was ignored by LS writers (cf. Cantonese *həi*, which seems, to represent another modern survival of the same vernacular element). This distinctive characteristic of VS (A *shih* B ["A is B"]) which is so apparent even up to the present day, is utterly different from LS, which lacks a copulative verb altogether. Instead, LS employs the nominative sentence structure A B *yeh* ("A [is] B"). It is noteworthy that Ssu-ma Ch'ien's *Records of the Grand Historian* (*Shih-chi*) (c. 90 B.C.E.), which of all LS texts dating to the period before the Common Era has a tendency to admit a few discernable elements from VS, includes a number of instances in which A *shih* B and A B *yeh* are combined, hence A *shih* B *yeh*. Ohta (1958:189) offers an astute analysis of this phenomenon.

Buddhism and the Rise of the Written Vernacular 213

The emergence of the largely polysyllabic VS lexicon is often erroneously explained as the result of the combination of monosyllabic words from LS, as though VS were somehow derived from LS or an attempt to make LS more explicit and understandable when spoken. Conceptually this makes no sense whatsoever, since spoken languages always precede the invention of their written forms. Historically, the alleged derivation of VS from LS is also demonstrably false. In a fuller treatment, I could cite hundreds of instances that show that polysyllabic vocabulary has been a feature of VS from the earliest times that can be attested, but here I shall refer only to one, namely *tao-lu* ("way, road"). *Tao-lu* is a venerable VS word still in use today that is found in a wide variety of pre-Ch'in texts, including the *Tso chuan* (*Tso's Chronicle*) (463 B.C.E.) by Tso Ch'iu-ming (cf. Mair 1990:22–23 for the phonology and philology of this word). The fact that the word *tao-lu* is usually reduced to just *tao* in LS texts shows that the relationship between LS and VS is exactly the opposite of that which is commonly assumed. To wit, where we can test specific instances in the early stages of the formation of LS, it seems to be the result of drastic truncation of VS, including anaphora so extreme that it could not possibly be tolerated in intelligible speech. Of course, once LS was securely established, it became possible to create new polysyllabic (chiefly bisyllabic) words in VS by joining together monosyllabic LS words. But this was a relatively late phenomenon and would have been possible only for those few who were literate in LS. The mass of the population would have continued to use and create polysyllabic words as they always had from the beginnings of the Sinitic language group, i.e., irrespective of the tetragraphic script.

What Zürcher and Chu have both shown clearly is that, from the very beginnings of Buddhism in China, the translated texts of this new religion display a higher degree of vernacular content than do non-Buddhist texts. No other texts from the same period can begin to compare with the early Buddhist translations for the large amount of vernacularisms they contain. Indeed, it is extremely rare in non-Buddhist texts of the same age ever to find even a single unambiguously vernacular usage.

Figure 7. Medieval Vernacular Sinitic written in Tibetan transcription.

Source: Adapted from "Buddhism and the Rise of the Written Vernacular in East Asia: The Making of National Languages," *Journal of Asian Studies* 53.3 (1994): 711. Lines 130-68 of the "Long Scroll" from Tun-huang. Catalogue No. C131 of the Oriental and India Office Collections of the India Office Library. With the permission of the British Library.

Buddhism and the Rise of the Written Vernacular 215

Nonetheless, it must be pointed out that, as the eminent Russian specialist on Medieval Vernacular Sinitic, I. S. Gurevich (1985) has shown, even the Tun-huang *pien-wen* can by no means be said to represent a pure form of VS, inasmuch as they still contain a significant proportion of LS elements. This is probably due to the nature of the sinographic script which is so perfectly well suited to LS but rather inimical to a full representation of any VS language. It should also be mentioned that, once Buddhists had paved the way for the use of a vernacularized written medium, it was tentatively adopted-through emulation-for secular purposes by others who were living in close association with them. Witness the occasional transformation texts, stories, rhapsodies, cantos, and other genres on non-Buddhist subjects that came to be written down at Tun-huang. By the Sung period, it had become acceptable–among certain still mostly nonelite social classes–to employ the written vernacular for historical medleys, love stories, and lyrics.

The evidence for the intimate relationship between Buddhism and the written vernacular in China is so irrefutable, yet so unexpected, that it demands an explanation. Given that the connection is both obvious and uncontested, one might imagine that there would be an easily identifiable set of reasons for this phenomenon. Such, unfortunately, is not the case. The situation is actually quite complex and it is difficult to declare with assurance precisely what it was about Buddhism that proved to be conducive to the adoption of the vernacular as an acceptable written medium. This is all the more remarkable in light of the fact that Chinese literati had always looked down upon any trace of the vernacular in writing as crude and vulgar (*su*). Naturally, like all other vocal human beings, Chinese scholars themselves were forced to use the vernacular in daily conversation, but committing it to writing was an entirely separate matter. On the face of it, the adoption by Chinese Buddhists of written vernacular and Buddhist Hybrid Sinitic (hereafter BHSi) as vehicles for the expression of their faith seems improbable. One would have thought that they would have chosen, instead, LS, since it was uniformly considered by the Chinese elite to be more elegant. Surely straight *wen-yen* would have been more appropriate if one were deliberately searching for a suitable sacred language in which to couch one's scriptures in a new arena of evangelism. Hence, the blatant Buddhist preference for *pai-hua* or *wen-yen* mixed with large chunks of *pai-hua* vocabulary and syntax is puzzling from a conventional point of view.

With time, styles of Buddhist writing in China more nearly approximating LS did develop, especially for those texts that were composed by native authors and were not translated from non-Sinitic languages. To one degree or another, most Buddhist texts that were translated from non-Sinitic languages, particularly those done by non-Chinese individuals, display various types of grammatical and syntactical discrepancies with LS. This is not, of course, to mention the large amounts of translated and transcribed terminology that also stamp BHSi as different from LS.

In the next section, I would like to identify a number of factors peculiar to Buddhism that possibly might have contributed to the acceptance of the vernacular as a workable tool for written expression. Because of the tremendous complexity of this issue, I will refrain from any simple, unidimensional explanation. Starting from the most abstract and general aspects, I shall move to more concrete and specific features that may have fostered the growth of the written vernacular in China.

Buddhism and Language

Buddhism, above all, is a sophisticated religion with an extensive body of doctrine. Perhaps Buddhist teaching contains a core precept that is conducive to the vernacular, a teaching for which there was no parallel in native Chinese traditions, such as Confucianism and Taoism. One that leaps to mind is the notion of *upāya* (*fang-pien*, skillful means). According to this doctrine, believers should use whatever means are appropriate to ensure the salvation of all sorts of living creatures. *Upāya* was not just a rarefied theory, but was actively applied in Buddhist preaching and teaching. In China, for example, lectures for laymen (*su-*

Buddhism and the Rise of the Written Vernacular 217

chiang) were delivered by eminent monks (*kao-seng*) and, upon occasion, by a few who were not so eminent. The notes for some of their lectures have been preserved among the Tun-huang manuscripts as sūtra-lecture texts (*chiang-ching-wen*) and they are quite vernacular in their orientation (Mair 1986). Other literary ramifications of the doctrine of *upāya* are Buddhist parables, apologues, and birth-tales known as *avadāna*, *nidāna*, and *jātaka*. These, too, were much-favored in China and popular with the masses. Vivid descriptions of Buddhist storytelling and lecturing may be found in the *Biographies of Eminent Monks* (*Kao-seng chuan*), travel records of foreigners in China (e.g., *Ennin's Diary*), classical fiction (*ch'uan-ch'i*), Tun-huang texts (e.g., the tale of Hui-yüan [S2144 in the British Library]), anecdotal literature, and other sources.

Buddhism is not only a religion, however, for it also functions as an elaborate philosophical system. Is there anything inherent in Buddhist thought that might sanction the use of the vernacular? Here I am rather skeptical that we can find much that will help us elucidate the mystery of the Chinese Buddhist predilection for the vernacular. My suspicion about the applicability of philosophical premises to our present quandary is based on the fundamental ineffability of Buddhahood and other associated concepts, such as *nirvāṇa*, Already in the Nikāyas (the early Pāli texts) and the Āgamas (a group of texts in the Sanskrit canon that correspond to the Pāli Nikāyas), it is clear that ultimate religious goals are held to lie outside the realm of discourse and, hence, discursive thought. The *Suttanipāta* informs us that the Buddha is beyond the "paths of speech" and in the *Theragāthā* he is described as being inconceivable in visual or auditory images (Gomez 1987:446a). It is a commonplace in Mahāyāna texts that enlightenment is incompatible with words and intellection. The usual formulation is "the way of language is cut off, the workings of the mind are obliterated" (*yuen-yü tao tuan, hsin-hsing ch'u mieh*). See, for example, *Mahāprajñāpāramitopadeśa/Ta chih-tu tun* (*T*25[1509].71c), *Avataṃsakasūtra/Hua-yen ching* (*T*9[278].424c), and **Mahāśamathavipaśyanā* [?]/*Mo-he chih-kuan* (*T*46[1911].59b). Even the Zen masters, whose words are ironically preserved in written vernacular (perhaps one should say, especially the Zen masters), insist on such notions as "transmission from mind to mind" (*i hsin ch'uan hsin*) and "nonestablishment of written words" (*pu li wen-tzu*), which disparage the efficacy of language, especially in its written form, to convey essential truths.

Despite Buddhism's presumed philosophical derogation of language, no religion can survive without sacred texts, and Buddhism definitely produced an abundance of scripture (three huge baskets full!). What is unusual about the Buddhist canon, however, is the pervasive pretense that it has an immediate oral basis. It is remarkable how many works in the Buddhist *Tripiṭaka* begin with the formula *evaṃ mayā śrutam*, Pāli *evaṃ me sutaṃ* ("Thus have I heard," in Sinitic *ju shih wo wen*), or words to that effect. The simulacrum is that of the eminent disciple Ānanda reciting the Buddha's words to the assembled faithful at Rājagṛha after his death. This formula not only stresses the presumed reliability of direct transmission, but also reveals that the Buddhist sūtras were orally conveyed to Ānanda, and thence to the rest of the community. This self-evident mark of oral transmission is like a stamp that authenticates the text that follows. It distinguishes the doctrines of the Buddha from those of teachers who were presumably heretical. Ultimately, then, the entire Buddhist canon—while it clearly represents a large and long scriptural tradition with rules, commentaries, discourses, and exegeses added later —is ostensibly (one might almost say "aggressively") founded upon the spoken word (v. Hinüber 1990:ch. 5). This is also reflected in the large number of East Asian sūtras whose full titles start with the expression *Fo shuo* ("spoken by the Buddha," from Sanskrit *buddhavacana* or *buddhabhāṣita*), even though it would have been impossible for the Buddha to utter all of the words in them, especially those that were originally composed in China, Japan, and Korea! There is even an entire *sūtra* (Pāli *sutta*) entitled the *Itivuttaka*, which means roughly "the speeches beginning with the words 'This was spoken (by the Lord).'" The equivalent Sinitic title *Ju shih yü ching* (Sūtra Spoken Thus). This is the fourth scripture in the *Khuddaka-nikāya* of the Pāli canon. Each section of the sūtra begins *Vuttaṃ hetaṃ bhagavatā vuttam arahatā'ti me sutaṃ* (*Wo wen shih-tsun ying-kung ts'eng ju shih shuo* ["Thus did I hear the worshipful World-Honored speak"]). Interspersed in the text we find such expressions as *iti vuccati* (*ju shih yen* ["said thus"]). At the end of each section occurs the following formula: *Ayaṃ pi attho vutto bhagavatā iti me sutaṃ ti* (*Wo wen shih-tsun shuo tz'u i* ["I heard the World-Honored explain this meaning"], translating the Sinitic text; the Sanskrit has "I also heard..."). The oral affinities of early Buddhist religious texts are underscored by the profession of *bhāṇaka* or *dharma-bhāṇaka*, whose duty it was to declaim them aloud, apparently in a rather entertaining fashion (Hoffman 1990).

With such tremendous emphasis on the presumed orality of the canon, there might have been resistance to rendering it in stilted, "unsayable" LS. I am somewhat dubious, however, that this is a sufficient explanation for the decision to employ large amounts of vernacular in Chinese Buddhist texts. After all, the *Analects* (*Lun-yü*) are famous for the *tzu yüeh* ("the Master said"), which prefaces Confucius's every utterance, but that did not deter their compilers from utilizing LS as the vehicle for conveying his sagely wisdom.

TRANSLATION, LINGUISTICS, AND PSALMODY

It would seem, instead, that the actual process of translation itself had a greater impact on the quality of Chinese Buddhist written language than any ideas about the nature of the canon. The entire enterprise of rendering the Buddhist scriptures and literary texts into Sinitic was begun by foreigners, about a dozen of whom are known for the period from the middle of the second century to the collapse of the Eastern Han dynasty in 220 C.E. Among these individuals were the Parthian prince An (for Arsacid) Shih-kao, who arrived in the capital at Loyang in 148 and was active until around 170; another Parthian, An Hsüan, who was active in Loyang c. 180; the Yüeh-chih (also transcribed as Ju-chih), presumably Kushān, Lokakṣema who worked in Loyang from c. 170-90; another Kushān, Chih Yao, who was active late in the second century; and the Sogdian, K'ang Meng-hsiang, who collaborated with the Indians Chu Ta-li (Mahābala [?]) and Chu T'an-kuo (Dharmaphala [?]) around the turn of the century. These men produced a large amount of material in Sinitic. Applying the most stringent criteria, there are 29 different works in 70 fascicles that still survive, and hundreds of additional titles are attributed to them.

LS is an extremely difficult language to master, not just because of the sinographs but also because it is so terribly allusive, requiring at least ten to fifteen years to gain a modicum of proficiency. In contrast, the spoken Sinitic languages, in part due to their lack of inflection, are relatively easy to acquire through immersion in a Chinese environment, especially if one does not have any severe hangups about the tones. Since these foreign translators usually came to China as adults and often, according to their biographies, quickly plunged into the business of translation, it would have been well-nigh impossible for them to command LS sufficiently well to create passable translations in it. Therefore, it was inevitable that whatever proficiency they acquired in writing Sinitic was bound to be highly contaminated by vernacular elements. Even when the foreign translators relied on Chinese assistants or collaborators to write out their drafts in sinographs, the necessary oral metaphrases that they provided would have had a pronounced tendency to infiltrate the intended LS product.

The result, then, was the peculiar type of BHSi that is so conspicuous in the earliest translations and, indeed, which exists to one degree or another as an acceptable subcategory of LS throughout the history of Chinese Buddhism.

Figure 8. Imperial Decree [of June 17, 1389] to the Buddhist Monk Irinjin Dzangbu (in Tibetan Rin-č'en bTsang-po).

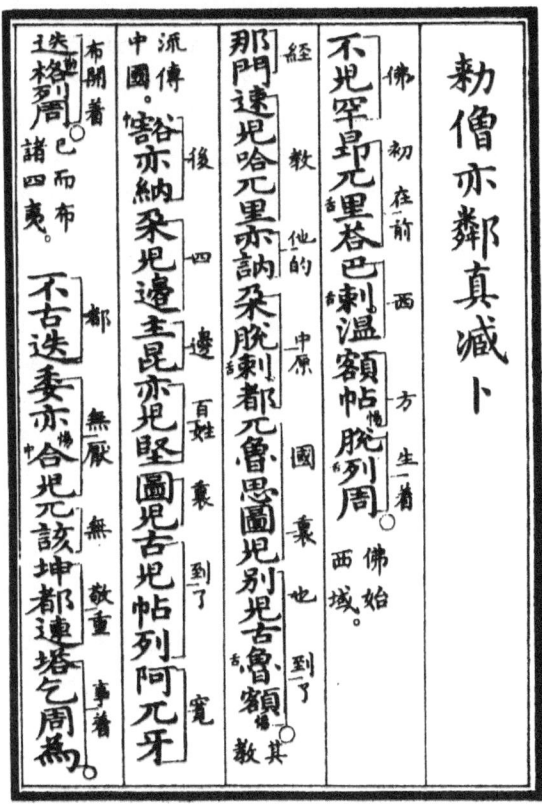

Source: Adapted from "Buddhism and the Rise of the Written Vernacular in East Asia: The Making of National Languages," *Journal of Asian Studies* 53.3 (1994): 715. *Hua-i i-yü* (*Sino-Mongolian Translations*), ed. by Qoninči and Ma Šāīḥ-Muḥammad (1389), 8a. Mongolian text transcribed in sinographs with interlinear phonological notes between graphs and on the left, interlinear vernacular (Early Mandarin) glosses on the right, and vernacular (Early Mandarin) translations at the end of each sentence. Lewicki 1949: 183; Mostaert 1977: 17.

This would also have been the case with the presumably better acculturated translators such as the Tocharian Dharmarakṣa (active c. 265-313), the so-called Bodhisattva of Tun-huang, and Kumārajīva (b. 344 or 350, d. 409 or 413), who was of Indian (Kashmiri) and Tocharian (Kuchan) parentage. These famous pillars of Chinese Buddhism produced an enormous number of Sinitic texts but, whenever precise information concerning their *modus operandi* is available, we find that—more often than not—they worked in teams with Chinese collaborators, sometimes as many as ten people for a single text, or that they simply dictated their translations to Chinese scribes (Fuchs 1930).

The famous late Ch'ing-early Republican "translator" of European and American novels into Sinitic, Lin Shu (1852-1924), was also dependent on oral VS interpretation by others because he knew no Western languages. However, where he was content to paraphrase loosely the secular novels that he rendered into LS, the early Buddhist translators strove to make accurate renditions of the sacred texts with which they were dealing, in spite of the vast dissimilarities between the Sinitic and Sanskritic languages in which they were written.

The special quality of BHSi persists even when learned native Chinese such as Hsüan-tsang (596-664) and I-ching (635-713) later become proficient in Sanskrit by traveling to India and studying there for an extended period of time. The translations they produced upon their return to China were still so heavily influenced by Sanskrit grammar, syntax, and lexicon that they are noticeably distinct from typical LS. I should note, furthermore, that individuals such as Hsüan-tsang and I-ching who acquired the ability to read Sanskrit were extremely rare in China. The majority of Chinese who claimed a knowledge of sacred Buddhist language(s) usually were familiar only with the Siddham script at best (van Gulik 1956).[1] Often their acquaintance with Indic languages was limited to syllabic transcriptions of very short texts in sinographs. Systematic expositions of grammar do not seem to have become available before about the eighteenth century, and even these were disappointingly obscure.

Regardless of how we classify BHSi, however, one thing is clear: the early impetus for" the translation of Buddhist texts into Sinitic came primarily from foreign monks resident 'in China. Indeed, the church at Loyang initially seems to have consisted solely of foreigners and it only gradually came to include a few Chinese (Zürcher 1990; Maspero 1934). Another complicated facet of the early translations is the fact that most of them were done not by Indians, but by Iranian- and Tocharian-speaking individuals. This must have had a great impact on the development of the Chinese Buddhist canon, yet, aside from a few articles by the distinguished Sanskritist and Tocharian specialist Chi Hsien-lin (1947; 1956; 1959; 1990) on very specific terms, this vital issue has scarcely been touched.

John Brough (1961) has highlighted the importance of the northwestern Prākrits (vernaculars) for the early Chinese Buddhist translations. In particular, he makes the case that many of the early Chinese translations of Buddhist texts were done from Prākrits such as Gandhārī rather than from Sanskrit. There is also good evidence from Chinese sources that the Sinitic translation of the *Sūtra of the Wise and the Foolish* (*Hsien-yü ching*) was taken down orally in Khotan by eight monks from western China and compiled by them after they had returned to Qočo (Turfan) (Takakusu 1901; Pelliot 1929).

There must have been a flourishing vernacular Buddhist "literature" (if that is what we may call it; I prefer to refer to nonwritten narrative and dramatic traditions as "dicture") in the **oral** realm in Central Asia before Buddhism was transmitted to China. The paucity of **written** Buddhist texts in the indigenous languages of Central Asia before the seventh century may be due to the perception of adherents of the religion there that scripture should be reserved for the sacred language of Sanskrit. Some evidence for the existence of Buddhist texts in the local languages of Central Asia may be found in the rich tradition of Buddhist narrative art at sites such as Kucha and Bezeklik, several examples of which have extensive narrative inscriptions in Tocharian or other non-Sinitic, non-Indic Central Asian languages, e.g., the exquisite *Mahāprabhāsa avadāna* from the Knights' Cave at Kirish (*Along the Ancient Silk Routes*: 105–6).

We must also remember that, under Indian tutelage, the Tibetans started translating Buddhist texts into their own language by the seventh century. Buddhist Tibetan, while sticking closely to the Sanskrit, is as much Tibetan as the usually quite loose BHSi translations are Sinitic. Furthermore, the Tibetans played a truly major political role in Central Asia just at the time translations of Buddhist texts into Khotanese, Sogdian, and other languages were becoming popular (cf. Beckwith 1987). I suspect that the second vernacular revolution (from around the seventh century), when Buddhist texts were appearing in the indigenous languages of Central Asia, may be related to the wide-ranging activities of the Tibetans there beginning about that time, just as the first "vernacular" revolution (from the second half of the second century), when texts began to appear in BHSi, was most likely due to the sponsorship of Kushan, Parthian, and other Central Asian peoples. The large interval between the two revolutions (nearly half a millennium) would seem to indicate that, while the idea of the translation of Indian Buddhist texts had already been floated by the second half of the second century, sociopolitical circumstances apparently did not permit its realization outside of China until the seventh or eighth century. Hence, in striving to understand the timing of the first and second vernacular revolutions, perhaps we should focus more on geopolitical conditions and less on religious and linguistic criteria.

As a matter of fact, the first "vernacular" revolution was not really vernacular in nature because BHSi is basically LS with some admixtures from VS. This may explain why it was possible for Central Asian monks and missionaries to translate Indian Buddhist texts into BHSi but not into their own vernaculars. In essence, by rendering Sanskrit and Pali texts into BHSi, they were simply transferring scriptures from one sacred

Buddhism and the Rise of the Written Vernacular 225

language into another. Like LS, BHSi was not sayable (i.e., it was nonvernacular) and hence had presented little danger of truly secularizing the sacred Indian texts. The first vernacular Buddhist texts in Sinitic did not appear until the middle of the eighth century (the *pien-wen* [transformation texts]), after the vernacular revolution had already taken place in Central Asian Buddhism. As we have seen above, the *pien-wen* themselves were far from being fully vernacular, though they were decidedly more vernacular than the typical BHSi text, and incomparably more so than all writing in LS.

Above all, it cannot be stressed often enough or strongly enough that our biggest problem in reconstructing the history of Central Asian Buddhism (and virtually everything else about Central Asia) is due to the lack of systematic, scientific archaeological excavation in Sinkiang. Until the Chinese government authorizes and supports more thorough investigations in this region, all that we say about its history must be considered extremely tentative. The notion that Central Asian Buddhists did not create texts in their own languages before the sixth or seventh century, whereas they did so for the Chinese from the second century, may be simply an artifact of preservation or lack thereof (cf. Nattier 1990).

While the repercussions of the Buddhist translation enterprise for language usage in China were undoubtedly enormous, more specific kinds of linguistic expertise were also being transferred. It would not be an exaggeration to state that every major advance in linguistics from the Han period until the advent of Jesuit-inspired evidential learning (*k'ao-cheng-hsüeh*) in the Ch'ing period over 1,500 years later, particularly in phonology, was dependent upon or conditioned by Buddhism in one way or another. Here we need- mention only such momentous developments as the creation of countertormy or cut-and-splice pseudospelling (*fan-ch'ieh*) , generally attributed for the last thousand and more years to the Buddhists, which for the first time enabled Chinese to indicate the pronunciation of unknown graphs fairly unambiguously and analytically (Mair 1992a); the whole system of rhyme classification (*teng-yün*) which laid the foundations of linguistic science in China that are still operative today; and the thirty-six quasiletters (*san-shih-liu tzu-mu*) of the late T'ang monk Shou-wen, inspired by Sanskrit *vyanjanam* ("consonants"), which constituted a sort of abortive alphabet (more accurately termed a "consonantary") for Sinitic (Ni 1948:17). All of this unaccustomed attention to the sounds of spoken language, in contrast to the traditional emphasis of Chinese scholars on the shapes of the written graphs, must have contributed to the legitimation of the vernacular vis-à-vis LS. While the nonphonological aspects of Indian linguistics were not so readily transferable to China, Buddhists were vaguely aware of their importance as subsumed under the general category of *śabda-vidyā*, accurately rendered in Sinitic as "voice-insight" (*sheng-ming*), although the Sanskrit expression refers to grammar and philology as well as phonology. The significance of *śabda-vidyā* for the Indian tradition can be seen by its inclusion among the *pañcā vidyā-sthānāni* (five types of knowledge, Sinitic *wu-ming*), the other four being *hetu-vidyā* (logic, *yin-ming*), *adhyātma-vidyā* (psychology, *nei-ming*), *vyādhi-cikitsā-vidyā* (medicine, *i-fang-ming*), and *śilpa-karmasthāna-vidyā* (arts and crafts, *kung-ch'iao-ming*). Yet we should remember that this kind of linguistic knowledge was restricted to a relatively small group of specialists, so I suspect that it was not the chief reason for the establishment of the written vernacular.

Probably more important in raising the consciousness of some Chinese that the simple sounds of language were just as essential as their elaborate and exalted script, if not more so, was the Buddhist penchant for psalmody. There was no precedent in the indigenous literary and religious traditions for the flood of sacred singing and chanting that engulfed China with Buddhism. The Chinese were completely unprepared for and utterly bedazzled by the meticulousness and seriousness with which their Indo-Iranian teachers delivered their **brahma-pāṭha* (hymns, *fan-pai*), *gāthā* (verses, *chi*), *śloka* (stanzas, *shou-lu*), songs of praise (*sung*), *stotra* (eulogies, *tsan*), *dhāraṇī* (mystical charms and

Buddhism and the Rise of the Written Vernacular 227

prayers, *t'o-lo-ni*), *mantra* (magical formulas and incantations, *man-t'e-lo*), and so forth. *Dhāraṇī*, for example, were thought to be potent only if properly pronounced, hence they were transcribed in their entirety, not translated. Even the mantic recitation of the Buddha's name (*nien Fo*) must have impressed upon the masses the power of the spoken word, although most of the other types of religious utterances listed above were principally the preserve of religious experts. The very real consequences of Indian prosody, as introduced through Buddhism, for even the most celebrated secular verse in China have now been demonstrated by Mair and Mei (1991).

SOCIAL VALUES, INTELLECTUAL HISTORY, AND RELIGIOUS MISSION

So far we have been examining doctrinal, philosophical, intellectual, and technical aspects of Buddhism that may have played a role in the growth of the written vernacular. Perhaps we have overlooked certain social values of Buddhism that might have had an equal or even greater bearing on this question. We must remember that traditional Chinese society, according to Confucian orthodoxy and to a great extent in actuality, was rigidly hierarchical from the family right up to the emperor. The same, of course, was largely true of Hindu society. It is noteworthy that, both in India and in China, at least in the early phases, Buddhism functioned (and perhaps originated) as a means for the individual to escape from the normal societal bonds. Leaving the home (Sanskrit *pravrajyā*; Sinitic *ch'u-chia*) and becoming a monk represented a profound break with the ordinary rules governing social and political intercourse. Even the elder *śreṣṭha*; *chang-che*), the householder *gṛhastha*; *su-jen*), the layman (*upāsaka*; *chü-shih*), and the lay woman (*upāsikā*; *chin-shih-nü*), who never really quit the family, was enjoined to subscribe in his/her daily life to an entirely different set of precepts from those who were completely outside of the Buddhist community. This constituted a dangerously subversive challenge to existing structures and institutions, one that is measurable in economic (Gernet 1956) and demographic (Hartwell and Hartwell 1991a; 1991b) terms, not to mention other indicators.[2] Certainly the Chinese authorities were threatened by encroachments of Buddhist ideology, organizations, and wealth, so much so that they periodically launched massive persecutions against the alien faith—even after it had, as it were, been domesticated. For their part, the more narrowly doctrinaire Confucian literati kept up a vigorous polemical attack almost from the moment Buddhism set foot on Chinese soil, so that there was frequent tension between church and court even when the latter was not burning the temples, melting the statues, confiscating the lands, and defrocking the monks and nuns of the former.

We are slowly gaining a better picture of the true composition of the Buddhist community in China and are finding that it included a high proportion of widows, orphans, and other types of individuals who did not fit within the usual pattern of societal relationships. The composition of the Chinese *saṃgha* may be interpreted as having a bearing on language usage. LS was clearly identified with the literati establishment. The vernacular, on the other hand, served as a more easily acquired tool for written expression of the dispossessed and those who lacked the opportunity or means for the long and tedious education necessary to master the literary language. With these qualities of socially embedded Buddhism in mind, I view the written vernacular as a kind of demotic empowerment. Living in an age of massive manipulation of language for sociopolitical ends, which I have often referred to as "linguistic engineering," I think we can readily appreciate the dramatic consequences of an assertive written vernacular opposing itself to a privileged, hieratic, classical script.[3]

Daniel Gardner (1991) has recently called attention to the importance of the written vernacular in Neo-Confucianism, both for the freer, more inquisitive approach it permitted toward the classics and for allowing the extension of philosophical discourse to a broader segment of the population. Considering the powerful influence of Buddhism on the forma-

Buddhism and the Rise of the Written Vernacular

tion of Neo-Confucian thought and practice, the adoption of the written vernacular as a legitimate form of serious intellectual discussion would seem to be one more example of the radical restructuring of Confucianism brought about by this foreign religion (Angurarohita 1989).

Tsu-Lin Mei has written a lengthy response (1992b) to Gardner that he does not plan to publish. Some of the major points he raises, and which he has authorized me to present here, are:

1. Whereas Gardner stresses the epistemological assumptions of Neo-Confucians concerning the power of mind in every man to comprehend the truth expressed in plain colloquial style, Mei emphasizes the sociolinguistic and historical linguistic background of the development of the written vernacular.

2. In spite of its technical sounding name, *yü-lu* is simply the "transcript" of conversations involving two or more persons in colloquial Sinitic. Its use during the Sung was not just limited to Zen (Ch'an) Buddhists and Neo-Confucians; emissaries on foreign missions also used this form to transcribe what was said during their diplomatic negotiations (e.g., *Shih pei yü-lu* [*Transcripts from a Northern Mission*]), particularly with the Khitans and Jurchens. The rationale for using the vernacular rather than the literary language was that the former medium was capable of recording more accurately what was actually said during the negotiations which, after all, touched upon sensitive matters of national security (Mei 1980).

3. Vernacular short stories and southern dramas (*hsi-wen*) containing colloquial dialogue also make their appearance around the same time (twelfth-thirteenth centuries).

4. The question of timing cannot be limited to the *yü-lu*, but must also be asked about the colloquial diplomatic transcripts and the vernacular literary texts.

5. The most natural context for understanding the origin of Sung colloquial and its use among different social classes is the rise and development of the written vernacular during the late T'ang period. During the T'ang, the ability to compose in the written vernacular was limited to persons (especially individuals with a Buddhist disposition) not belonging to, or marginally belonging to, the elite. The turning point seems to have come in the second half of the eleventh century, and especially during the twelfth, when a substantial number of the bureaucratic elite acquired the ability to write colloquial Chinese. The reason why Confucians did not turn to the colloquial *yü-lu* form prior to the second half of the eleventh century may merely be that they and other members of the elite had not yet mastered the written vernacular, which theretofore had developed in an essentially Buddhist environment.

6. Another factor that has to be taken into account is the spread of literacy. Obviously, the Neo-Confucians' efforts to disseminate their doctrines via the colloquial *yü-lu* would have been in vain if a readership with an adequate degree of literacy had not existed at that time. Victor Mair (1989: 135-39) has shown that low-level literacy was already widespread in the late T'ang period. From previous studies, we know that the invention of printing, the establishment of government schools and private academies (attached to monasteries), and the civil service examination system (particularly at its lowest levels) all promoted literacy. By the Sung, the spread of literacy had become an East Asian phenomenon; the Tangut script and the *chữ nôm* script were both invented during this period in order to write the vernacular languages of the Tanguts and the Vietnamese.

Combining the findings of Gardner and Mei with the comprehensive intellectual history of the period, we may deduce that the gradual adoption of the vernacular for limited purposes during the T'ang and Sung was the result of a complicated adjustment to the norms and values of Buddhist ideology. These norms and values manifested themselves in diverse fields of human endeavor (literature, philosophy, government documents, commentaries for non-Sinitic rulers, etc.), but all of them may be analyzed sociolinguistically as emanating from the fundamentally demotic impulses of the religion.

Another reason for Buddhism to choose the vernacular over the classical may have been its strong missionary zeal. For a religion that wishes to move rapidly into a new area, complex and hard-to-learn written languages like LS are a frustrating obstacle to rapid dissemination of its doctrines. They are, furthermore, usually the jealous possession of an entrenched bureaucratic or priestly elite who would actively oppose the spread of potentially subversive ideologies that are directed toward the populace. One of the major themes in David Diringer's well-known book *Writing* is that "alphabet follows religion." In particular, he shows the close connection between the spread of Buddhism and the creation of written vernaculars from India to Central, Inner, East, South, and Southeast Asia (1962: 148). It would be revealing to make a study of just how many languages in these areas received their first written expression through the activities of Buddhist monks and other types of proselytizers. I suspect that, before the coming of Christianity to this part of the world, aside from a handful of sinographically inspired scripts (most of which are now dead [Tangut, Khitan, Jurchen, Vietnamese, etc.] or dying [Yao, Women's Script/Nü-shu, etc.]) (Zhou 1991; Sofranov 1991; *Sino-Platonic Papers* 31 [October 1991]:29–33), nearly all of the written vernaculars east of the Pamirs to the Pacific Ocean were a direct result of the Buddhist missionary enterprise. Thus, the two great missionary religions, Christianity and Buddhism, together account for the overwhelming majority of Central, Inner, East, South, and Southeast Asian languages that have been committed to writing. The other great religion of conversion, Islam, and the older Semitic faiths account for most of the remainder. The role of Christian missionaries during the nineteenth and twentieth centuries in creating hundreds of written vernaculars throughout the entire world is well known.

The Indian Background

The final characteristic of Buddhism that seems to have lent support for the written vernacular which I wish to examine is a matter of religious policy or practice. As Buddhism swiftly expanded from its original base in Magadha (Rājagṛha, Pāṭaliputra) and gained converts even from among the Brahmans, the founder of the religion was faced with the pressing issue of linguistic usage. Should a single prestige dialect be designated to ensure respect for the Buddha's word? Or should a plurality of language be permitted to enable the unimpeded spread of the *dharma* among those who were not privy to the priestly tongue? Judging from all accounts, the Buddha made the wise decision to allow Buddhist practitioners to transmit his teachings in their own respective languages.[4] This scenario, at any rate, is repeatedly maintained by most extant versions of the *vinaya* (monastic rules) and must represent one of the earliest layers of Buddhist literature.

Since the story is well known, I will simply summarize it here. Two brahman brothers convert to Buddhism and join the *saṃgha*. Having a background in Vedic recitation, they are concerned that other monks of diverse backgrounds will corrupt the Buddha's teachings by reciting them in substandard ways. They go to the Buddha and propose that they standardize his word in *chandas*. Although there are numerous interpretations of the word *chandas,* this presumably signifies mannered, metrical verse and in this context probably just means "Veda," which is how the famous grammarian, Pāṇini (fifth or sixth century B.C.E.) uses it. In any event, the brahman brothers are surely proposing an elite style of delivery for which their training suits them. The Buddha will have none of it. Roundly rejecting them, he emphatically advocates the propagation of his teachings in the vernacular.

The actual history of linguistic usage in Indian Buddhism aside, the Buddha's pronouncement in this celebrated passage stuck. Let us follow it through the *vinaya* of five different schools preserved in the Chinese Buddhist canon. In the Dharmaguptaka recension translated

Buddhism and the Rise of the Written Vernacular 233

by Buddhayasas during the years 410-12, the Buddha calls upon his followers to use "the vernacular languages understood in diverse locales (*pradeśānāṃ prākṛtabhāṣaḥ*) (Lamotte 1958:612) to recite the Buddhist *sūtras*" 國俗言音所解誦習佛經 (*T*22[1428].955a). Although the equivalent sentence is missing in the *vinaya* of the Sarvāstivādins, translated by Puṇyatara, Dharmaruci, and Kumārajīva from 404-9, the same sense is retained in the passage taken as a whole. (*T*23[1435].274a).[5] The Vinayamātṛkā version, translated into Chinese in about 418, expands the passage thus: "You should speak in whatever language all the living beings can obtain enlightenment. For this reason it is called 'doing in accordance with the country'" 隨諸眾生應與何音而得受悟應爲說 之，是故名爲隨國應作 (*T*24[1463].822a). The *vinaya* of the Mahīśāsaka school, translated into Chinese by Buddhajīva in 422-23, only indicates that the Buddha's word should be "recited according to the language of the country'" 隨國音讀誦 (*T*22[1421].174b). Finally, the *Vinayakṣudrakavastu* of the Mūlasarvāstivāda, translated by I-ching in 702 or 703, declares that "there will be no error if one is required to draw out the voice when reciting in the language of a given locale (*pradeśasvara*)" 若方國言音須引聲者作時無犯 (*T*24[1451].232c).[6] There can be little doubt that, no matter which version of the *vinaya* Chinese Buddhists chose to follow, use of the vernacular was approved by the Buddha himself.

It is worth observing that Pāli, the language of the early Buddhist canon, was originally but one of the Prākrits (v. Hinüber 1986). Buddhist Hybrid Sanskrit (BHS), likewise, was actually a Prākrit with augmented elements from Sanskrit (Bender 1991). Aside from being the usual prose dialect of Sanskrit plays, Śaurasenī is a type of Prākrit used in the later Digambara scriptures of the Jains. Māgadhī is another type of Prākrit used in Sanskrit plays, but for persons of still lower rank than those who speak Śaurasenī. Ardha-māgadhī (semi-Māgadhī) is intermediate between Śaurasenī and Māgadhī and is important because it was used in the old Jain writings. Alsdorf (1980) has demonstrated that Mahāvīra (the founder of Jainism) and Śākyamuni Buddha shared certain Māgadhisms (Chi 1959). There are also clear similarities between Old Ardhamāgadhī and the language of the Aśokan pillar inscriptions, which is therefore also referred to as Aśokan Māgadhī. Māhārāṣṭrī or Old Marāṭhī was influential because of its use in the later scriptures of the Śvetāmbaras and in drama. Among the Vibhāṣās, or lesser Prākrits, of which there are many, Saurāṣṭrī is interesting because it contains elements of Scythian dialects (Walker 1968:2.234-35). From this very brief survey of the Prākrits (early Indian vernaculars), it is apparent that they were often used by religions and other social groups who stood outside of the dominant Vedic-Upaniṣadic-Sanskritic culture. Viewed in this light, the Prākrits played the same role in Indian society that BHSi and written VS did in China.

The whole approach to *deśa-bhāṣā*, an expression meaning "language of a country" which can be found already in the *Mahābhārata* (Poona Critical edition, 9.44.98; Calcutta edition, 9.2605; Madras edition, 40.103; Bombay edition, 45.103cd), may have stimulated or reflected the exercise of the vernaculars in India, unlike the attitude toward *fang-yen* (topolect, "the language of a place") (Mair 1991), its parallel in China, which seems to have inhibited their use. There has always been such pronounced official disdain in China for the topolects (in favor of the standard language) that the notion of their being written down is virtually inconceivable. This is in contrast to the situation in India where familiarity with local languages was esteemed. Thus, among the 64 *kalā* (practical skills) cataloged in the *Śaivatantra*, we find *deśa-bhāṣā-(vi)jñāna* ("knowledge of local languages"). This is immediately preceded by *mlecchitaka-vikalpāḥ*, which clearly signifies a babel of foreign tongues, and is followed by *puṣpa-śakaṭikā-nimitta-jñāna*, the ability to understand the omens of heavenly voices. Given such a positive attitude toward the various *deśa-bhāṣā*, with the advent of alphabetic writing it has always been acceptable in India to record many different languages and dialects. Conversely, since any living language in China was perforce merely a topolect, there was an almost insuperable prejudice against the writing down of vernaculars, even the spoken language of the capital.

Buddhism and the Rise of the Written Vernacular

The very notion of the Prākrits (*prākṛta*, literally "made before") as "natural" (i.e., unadorned, unrefined) languages versus Sanskrit (*saṃskṛta*, literally "made together," i.e., refined) as an "artificial" (in the Buddhist context) language differs markedly from the Chinese conception of the various *fang-yen* as vulgar (*su*) and LS as elegant (*ya*). Eventually, however, even the Prākrits became decadent, and by about 550 C.E., various *apabhraṃśa* (deviations) spoken by the *laukika* (commoners) came into existence. We find no mention of *apabhraṃśa* in Vararuci, the oldest Prākrit grammarian who was writing around 579 C.E. (Cowell 1854). Hemacandra (1088-1172), on the other hand, interestingly defines *apabhraṃśa* as Prākrit with additional infusions of popular (*deśī*) speech (Walker 1968:2.233).[7]

Were it not for the permissive Indian attitude toward the vernaculars, we would not have the present situation where there are over a dozen major Indo-Aryan official languages still being spoken *and* written in India, including some such as Hindi, Bengali, Marathi, Gujarati, and Oriya with rich literary traditions. This is not to mention the Dravidian languages such as Tamil, Telugu, and Malayalam, which likewise have long and glorious literary histories. How starkly dissimilar the situation is in China can be seen by the fact that there was not even official recognition of Modern Standard Mandarin (MSM) as an acceptable form of writing until the founding of the Republic of China in the first quarter of this century. The amount of unadulterated writing in the other vernacular Sinitic topolects and languages is so pathetically small as to be virtually nonexistent, except in fairly recent romanized transcriptions (mostly by Christian missionaries and their Chinese followers). Since about the Sung dynasty (960-1279), there was a rather surreptitious tradition of secular vernacular fiction and drama, based largely on the language of the capital. Before that, as I have shown, virtually all vernacular and semivernacular writing was done by Buddhists. And, to this day, it remains almost unthinkable to write down any of the topolects in a relatively integral form, although isolated topolectical expressions are occasionally added to Mandarin texts to give a bit of local flavor. Judging from the overall pattern of the development of the written vernacular in China, I believe we are justified in stating unequivocally that Buddhism was centrally involved in its establishment as a viable mode of expression.

The Concept of "National Language"

One might go even further to say that the whole idea of written national languages in East Asia as founded on the spoken vernaculars may well have been inspired by the Indian concept of *deśa-bhāṣā* introduced by Buddhism. The exact Sinitic equivalent of *deśa-bhāṣā* is *kuo-yü*. Before the coming of Buddhism to China, these two graphs, in the order given, meant only one thing: the title of a book in 21 fascicles traditionally said to have been completed by the historian Tso Ch'iu-ming in the year 469 B.C.E. Naturally, the *Kuo-yü*, like all other pre-Buddhist writing in China, was composed in LS. In this case, the two sinographs designate the individual accounts (*yü*) concerning each of the eight major contending states (*kuo*) that became prominent as the Chou dynasty began to break apart into spheres of influence. After the advent of Buddhism, however, the expression *kuo-yü* began to take on a radically different meaning, namely, the vernacular language belonging to a nation in the sense of a people who saw themselves as a separate politico-ethnic entity.

Perhaps the earliest occurrence of *kuo-yü* that may refer to a vernacular Sinitic topolect (*fang-yen*) is found in a Buddhist context. This is the account of Vighna's translation of the *Fa-chü ching* (*Dhammapada*) in the *Kao-seng chuan* (*Biographies of Eminent Monks*) by Hui-chiao (497-544):

> Vighna (Wei-chih-nan) was originally from India. For generations his family had professed a heterodox way, considering the fire sacrifices (presumably of the *Atharva-veda* or possibly of Zoroastrianism) as the true religion. It so happened that an Indian *śramaṇa* (monk), who was practiced in Hīnayāna ("Lesser Vehicle") and who was proficient in Buddhistic arts, wished to lodge in Vighna's house at nightfall after a long journey. Since

Buddhism and the Rise of the Written Vernacular 237

Vighna's family subscribed to a heterodox way, they were suspicious of Buddhists and made him sleep outside in the open. During the night, the śramaṇa secretly uttered an incantation, causing the fire that was worshipped in Vighna's house suddenly to be extinguished. Thereupon the entire household went out and respectfully invited the śramaṇa to go inside where they made offerings to him. The śramaṇa responded by causing the fire to light again with his incantatory arts. Perceiving that the supernatural power of the śramaṇa surpassed his own, Vighna happily and enthusiastically became an adherent of the Buddhadharma (the Buddhist doctrine).

Consequently, he abandoned his previous faith and left his family (*pravraj*) to follow the Buddhist way. Inducted as a monk by the śramaṇa, he received the teachings of the *Tripiṭaka* (the "three baskets" of the Buddhist canon), wonderful goodness, and the four Āgamas (division of the "Hīnayāna" scriptures). He travelled to many countries, preaching and converting, and all whom he encountered accepted the faith.

In the year 224, with his companion Chu Lü-yen (the surname indicates that he was an Indian), he arrived at Wu-ch'ang (in Hupei province) where he presented the Sanskrit text of the *Dharmapada*,[8] that is, the *Sūtra of Verses on the Dharma*. At that time, the gentlemen of Wu requested that Vighna produce [a Chinese version of] the scripture. But Vighna had not yet mastered the language of the country (*kuo-yü*) so, together with his companion Lü-yen, he translated it into written Sinitic (*Han-wen*). Lü-yen likewise had not mastered spoken Sinitic (*Han-yen*), so there were quite a few deficiencies. Their aim was to preserve the sense of the original, but their style approached plainness.

It was not until the end of the reign of the Chin emperor Hui (r. 290-306) that the śramaṇa Fa-li retranslated it in five scrolls, with the śramaṇa Fa-li writing it down. Their style was somewhat ornate. Fa-li also produced four or so minor scriptures, but most of them were lost during the chaos at the end of the Yung-chia period (307-13).

(*T*50[2059].326bc)

Although this passage is valuable for its early mention of *kuo-yü* with the ostensible meaning of vernacular, it evinces the same sort of confusion between spoken and written language as well as between local and national language that has plagued Chinese linguistics right up to the present day. *Han-yen* and *kuo-yü* both imply spoken language, but *kuo-yü* here seems to indicate the local Nguə (Wu) topolect (for which there never was a full written form until Christian missionaries much later created a romanized alphabet to record different varieties of Nguə speech and to publish religious tracts in them) whereas *Han-yen* would appear to indicate a national *lingua franca*. The relationship between *Han-yen* and *Han-wen* in this passage is unclear, as is the variety of Sinitic upon which they were based. Presumably, however, the basis for *Han-yen* was the standardized speech of the capital used by bureaucrats from around the country to communicate with each other (a precursor of *kuan-hua* or Mandarin)."[9] *Han-wen* must have been a current designation for LS (or, more precisely in this case, its BHSi variant).

It is remarkable that the first clear application of *kuo-yü* with the new meaning of a vernacular belonging to a separate politico-ethnic entity was to the language of a devoutly Buddhist non-Sinitic group of people known as the Tabgatch (T'o-pa in Modern Standard Mandarin transcription) who ruled over north China from 386–534 as the Northern Wei dynasty. These were most likely proto-Mongols (or perhaps a Turkic people) who were responsible for the building of the monumental assemblages of Buddhist sculpture at Yün-kang and Lung-men in north China. In the "Bibliographical Treatise" ("Ching-chi chih") of Chang-sun Wu-chi (d. 659) et al., in the *History of the Sui* (*Sui shu*), part 1, we read that,

> When the Later Wei [i.e., the Northern Wei = Tabgatch] first took control of the Central Plains, all of the commands for the disposition of their armies were given in "barbarian" language (*i-yü*).

Buddhism and the Rise of the Written Vernacular 239

Later, when they had become tainted by Chinese customs (*jan Hua-su*), many of them could no longer understand their own tongue. So they began to teach it to each other, calling it their "national language" (*kuo-yü*).

後魏初定中原，軍容號令，皆疑夷語。後染華俗，多不能通，故錄其本言，相傳教習，謂之「國語」。

(4.32.947)

It is most intriguing that the "Bibliographical Treatise" lists over a dozen works (4.32.935, 945; Dien 1991:55a, 59b n. 87; Ligeti 1970:279-80) on a wide variety of topics written in Tabgatch and *Saerbi (or *Shirvi; Hsien-pei in Modern Standard Mandarin transcription), another powerful, supposedly proto-Mongol, group who were active in north China from the second century on.[10] Unfortunately, none of these books survive, but it would be extremely valuable to know what script(s) they were written in. This tantalizing evidence from the "Bibliographical Treatise" indicates that it was possible to write Tabgatch and *Saerbi centuries before any form of Altaic writing known to modern scholars. What script(s) did the Tabgatch and *Saerbi use? This is a dark mystery whose solution may unfold a new and very important chapter in the history of writing. What is significant for our purposes here, however, is the fact that written Tabgatch and *Saerbi are openly referred to in the "Bibliographical Treatise" as *kuo-yü* or "national languages."

Elsewhere in Chinese historical records, we can find references to such works as *Liao shih kuo-yü* (National Language History of the Khitan) and *Chin shih kuo-yü* (National Language History of the Jurchen). These were presumably histories of the Khitan and Jurchen dynasties that ruled over much of north China during the tenth through twelfth centuries, written in their native Altaic and Tungusic languages. Although these books have also regrettably been lost, scattered inscriptional and documentary instances of writing in these sinographically inspired scripts do survive and scholars are working on their decipherment (Sofranov 1991; Jensen 1969:195–97). It is clear that the earliest usage of the term *kuo-*

yü ("national/vernacular language"), indeed right up to the end of the last dynasty, the Manchu Ch'ing, was almost always in reference to non-Sinitic peoples (Norman 1988:133).

The *History of the Yüan Dynasty* (10.115.2893) records that, in the spare moments when he was not attending to his troops, the great Mongol warrior-prince Kammala (1263-1302, son of Chen-chin ["True Gold"], who was Khubilai's second son) would order one of his trusted advisers to lecture him on the *Tzu-chih t'ung-chien* (*Comprehensive Mirror for Aid in Government*), the quintessential chronologically arranged history of China compiled by Ssu-ma Kuang (1019-86), in the "national language" 以國語講通鑑, meaning Mongolian. Manchu, too, was referred to explicitly in the same fashion. For instance, in Wei Yüan's *Sheng-wu chi* (*Records of Sagely Military Exploits*) (1.9a), we read that "the literary officials were ordered to create a national script on the basis of the national language, using neither Mongol nor Sinitic writing" 命文臣依國語製國俗，不用蒙古，漢字 Even the Vietnamese adopted the notion of a written vernacular with the creation of *quốc ngữ*. As used in Vietnam, *quốc ngữ* seems originally (perhaps as early as the fourteenth century) to have signified the spoken native language as opposed to Sinitic languages. Later, *quốc ngữ* was applied to *chữ nôm* ("script" + "vulgar" = "vernacular writing"), a system for writing Vietnamese involving phonetic use of sinographs and the creation of new, wholly indigenous logographic symbols composed of tetragraphic components. Still later, the term *quốc ngữ* was used to designate the French-sponsored romanized alphabet currently employed by the Vietnamese (DeFrancis 1978:83-87). The notion of *quốc ngữ* as a written national language appears to have been borrowed by Vietnamese refugee intellectuals in Japan from *kokugo* (Modern Standard Mandarin, hereafter MSM, *kuo-yü*).

Buddhism and the Rise of the Written Vernacular

MANDARIN AS *KOINE*

Mandarin is, in effect, the close English translation of the MSM expression *kuan-hua* ("officials' speech") which, in the latter part of the Ch'ing period, was based on the dialect of the capital at Peking and which enabled the bureaucrats from the various parts of China whose native languages were mutually unintelligible to converse with each other. The word "Mandarin" was borrowed into English from Portuguese, which picked it up from Malay *mĕntĕri*. Malay, in turn, acquired the word from Hindi *mantrī*, which is from Sanskrit *mantrin* ("counselor, minister") < *mantra* ("counsel").

The term *kuan-hua* was in use from the Yüan period on and referred to the spoken language of officaldom (*kuan-ch'ang*), which was based on the speech of the capital (mostly Peking from that time till the present; Nanking speech was taken as the standard during the late Ming).[11] There are many records from the Ming and Ch'ing periods that prove that *kuan-hua* was considered to be a prestige supradialect that bureaucrats from all over the empire were forced to learn if they wished to have a successful career. For most of them, this meant acquiring a second spoken language, not merely making minor adjustments in their pronunciation and vocabulary.

The complexion of *kuan-hua* was deliberately changed by reformers around the end of the nineteenth century who wished to make it the *lingua franca* of all China, not just of the officials. Chief among these was Wang Chao (1859-1933), a high-ranking literatus who fled to Japan after the collapse of the Reform Movement of 1898. While there, the Japanese use of their *kana* syllabaries to overcome the difficulties and restrictiveness of the Sinitic script inspired him to devise his own spelling system called *kuan-hua tzu-mu* ("Mandarin letters"). Aside from courageously promoting this enlightened phonetic script during the late Ch'ing-early Republican period, Wang also energetically pushed for the adoption of Mandarin as China's national spoken and written language. The following remarks from the introductory notes to his *Kuan-hua ho-sheng tzu-mu* (*Letters for Combining the Sounds of Mandarin*) serve to illustrate Wang's attitude toward *kuan-hua* and his conscious effort to remold it as a popular language for the whole Chinese nation:

> Because the Chinese characters are difficult to understand, I wish to devise a script based on colloquial Pekingese. To facilitate popular usage, I do not refer to it as colloquial speech but rather as *kuan-hua*. The reason for this is to follow popular custom. North as far as the Amur River, west across the T'ai-hang Mountains to Nanyang and Loyang, south almost to the Yangtze, and east to the ocean: all of the colloquial languages from north to south and from east to west for several thousand tricents [*li*, three hundred paces or about a third of a mile] are more or less mutually intelligible with the language of the capital, but the languages of provinces outside this area are mutually unintelligible. For this reason, it is most convenient to spread the language of the capital. Therefore, I call it *kuan-hua*. By *kuan*, I mean "public"; *kuan-hua* is thus "speech for public use." Its selection is appropriate because it occupies the greatest area and the largest proportion of the population.

Although Wang's explanation of *kuan* is quite different from its original meaning as "[pertaining to the] Mandarin[ate]," the linguistic features of the language in question were essentially the same in both cases. Wang Chao later played a blustery, belligerent role in enforcing northern Mandarin as the standard national language over the other topolects in February 1913, not long after the founding of the Republic of China (Ramsey 1987:7-8).

Kuan-hua corresponds to Jerry Norman's concept of a *koine* (a *lingua franca* developing out of a mixture of other languages) (1988:5, 48, 186f., 246, and 249) which may be traced back as early as the T'ang dynasty.[12] This was a supradialectical form of speech which was normally based on the dialect of Ch'ang-an, Loyang, or K'ai-feng (capitals located along the central part of the Yellow River). The early Sinitic equivalent of the term *koine* is *t'ung-yü* ("common language"; cf. the current name for

Buddhism and the Rise of the Written Vernacular 243

Mandarin in the People's Republic of China, P'u-t'ung-hua ["common speech"]), which dates to around the beginning of the Common Era. Strained attempts have been made to find evidence of such a commonly accepted pattern of speech even in the time of Confucius (551-479 B.C.E.). The usual reference is to *ya-yen* ("elegant language") which occurs in *Analects* 7.18. Much fantastic speculation has been uttered over the passage in question. Aside from the assertion that it demonstrates the existence of Mandarin in the sixth century B.C.E., the passage supposedly also "proves" that there was a connection with the nebulously conceived spoken language of the Hsia dynasty (whose historicity remains to be demonstrated, in spite of wishful thinking to the contrary). To arrive at this forced interpretation, *ya* is conveniently made to be a synonym of Hsia. Such readings are possible only if much violence is done to the original text, which is quite straightforward: "The language that the Master considered elegant is that of the *Odes, History, Arts,* and *Ritual;* these are all written in elegant language" 子所雅言，詩書執（→藝）禮，皆雅言. Judging from the actual texts that have been transmitted to us, it is fairly certain that *ya-yen* is a designation for an early form of LS or, at best, a standard reading pronunciation. In any event, by no means can this sentence be legitimately used to construct a theory of a VS *koine* during the mid-first millennium B.C.E., whatever other data mayor may not be available to construct such a theory.

We must observe that the *koine* did not correspond to the written language of government, which was always LS. Instead, the *koine* constituted the foundation of the emerging written VS. When spoken by individuals from various areas of China outside of the urban centers upon which it was based, the *koine* was heavily affected by local pronunciation, lexicon, and, to a lesser extent, grammar-as is MSM today. The other Sinitic languages essentially remained unwritten and, indeed, "unwritable" because the set of morphosyllabic sinographs (*han-tzu*), though mind-bogglingly enormous, was inadequate to record accurately all the morphemes in the spoken vernaculars. At the same time, there were no conventions in medieval China for the alphabetic or syllabic spelling of connected Sinitic speech.

This situation is very different from that in medieval Europe where Latin was both sayable and writable and hence could serve as a complete vehicle both for the speech and the writing of the educated. Subsequently, just before and during the Renaissance, each national vernacular in Europe took on a life of its own separate from Latin. The development of the written vernaculars in Europe was also facilitated by an alphabet that was capable of recording with ease any variety of spoken language. In contrast, the sinographs inhibited the growth of the individual written vernaculars in China and tended to discourage even the writing of full-fledged Mandarin (it is usually contaminated by LS to one degree or another). Thus there is no flourishing literary tradition for Cantonese, Taiwanese, Shanghaiese, and the other VS languages as there is for French, German, Italian, English, and so forth. At best, there are scattered texts (only an exceeding few of which date from before the late nineteenth century) that include a smattering of elements of the various regional languages embedded in basically Mandarin or semi-Mandarin-semi-LS matrices to provide a bit of "local flavor."

The Japanese Inspiration for *kuo-yü*

It is paradoxical that the Chinese recognized one of their own spoken vernaculars as the basis for a national language (*kuo-yü*) only in this century. This occurred when the government of the Republic of China declared after the May Fourth Movement of 1919 that Mandarin was to be spread throughout all of China as the official language of government and education. The first person known to have used the term *kuo-yü* in reference to a Sinitic language was the scholar and educator Wu Ju-lun. In 1902, Wu went to Japan to observe the educational system there. He was deeply impressed by the success with which the Japanese government had spread the use of the Tokyo dialect as their *kokugo* (i.e., *kuo-*

Buddhism and the Rise of the Written Vernacular 245

yü) (Ramsey 1991). Upon his return to China, Wu began advocating to the Ch'ing government the adoption of Mandarin as a national language. By 1909, various tentative steps had been taken in this direction, but the dynasty collapsed before they became a reality (*Chung-kuo ta paik'e ch'üan-shu,* Yü-yen wen-tzu: 123ab). It remained for the Republic of China, under pressure from progressive intellectuals (Li Chin-hsi 1934), to make official what had slowly been becoming a reality ever since the arrival of Buddhism in China—the acceptance of the vernacular as a legitimate tool for writing.

It is not strange that Wu Ju-lun would have picked up the idea of a *kuo-yü* in Japan, for the Japanese actually had a strong consciousness of possessing a writable vernacular for centuries. *The Tale of Genji* (*Genji monogatari*), for example, was written by the court lady Murasaki Shikibu in the vernacular (with phonetic *kana*) already at the beginning of the eleventh century. (Gender dynamics appear to have been operative in this and similar cases, such as that of the recently discovered Women's Script (Nü-shu) in Hunan. Phonetic scripts for representing the vernacular serve as an empowering counterweight to the male-dominated morphosyllabic [or logographic] sinographs that are so splendidly well-suited for writing LS.) The Japanese preface (dated 1714) to the *Fahua lun-shu* (Commentary on the Lotus Sūtra) by the noted Chinese monk Chi-tsang (fl. 549-69), who was of Parthian descent, states that in preparing the blocks for printing "the national/vernacular language (*kokugo*) has been added at the side" 傍加國語. (*T*40[1818].785a) Regrettably, modern editions have not preserved the running Japanese annotations.

In its earliest Japanese appearances, the term *kokugo* seems to have had more the connotation of "local vernacular" than of an official "national language." In Tokugawa-period Japan, for example, it could even refer to Dutch (Ramsey 1993:3). All of this, plus the distinctly Sinitic ring to the word, recalls the Chinese usage of the term *kuo-yü* to designate spoken vernacular languages as opposed to the customary written language, namely *kanbun* (LS). As we have already seen, it was the Buddhists who introduced this notion to China and it seems to have spread from there to Japan. Only slowly, however, did the idea of Japanese *kokugo* as "local vernacular" become transformed into the status of "national language." Not until around the middle of the nineteenth century did it gradually come to refer specifically to Japanese as the official national language of Japan. Slow as the transformation may have been, vernacular Japanese became the accepted, official language of the people who spoke it long before any variety of VS was sanctioned as the national language of China. It is ironic, in both cases, that the roots of the acceptance of the vernacular as the official language of the country lay in the Indian Buddhist concept of *deśa-bhāṣā*. The seminal importance of Buddhism in the development of written vernacular Japanese during the early Heian (794–898) is recognized by Habein (1984:22) and Miller (1967: 126). The role of Buddhism in the development of the *kana* syllabaries is detailed by Seeley (1991:ch. 4, 59–89), especially in such texts as the *Abidatsuma zōjuron* (*Abhidharmasamuccayavyākhyā*) and *Ōkutsumarakyō* (*Aṅgulimālika-sūtra* or *Aṅgulimālīya-sūtra*), both of which date to around 800 C.E. (also see Miller 1967: 128).

Language Reform in Korea

While, like *kuo-yü* for Mandarin and *quốc ngữ* for Vietnamese, the concept of *kug'o* as the language of a modern Korean nation-state was inspired by Japanese *kokugo*, the Koreans themselves had a tradition of writing in the vernacular that stretched all the way back to the *idu* ("clerk readings") and *hyangch'al* ("local letters") scripts. These depended on either Sino-Korean phonetic or native glosses (similar to Japanese *on* and *kun* readings of sinographs) and are attributed to Sŏl Ch'ong, son of Korea's greatest Buddhist thinker, Wŏnhyo, in the late seventh century. The *hyangch'al*, used exclusively for vernacular songs and poetry (judging from the few surviving specimens), may already have died out before the advent of the Chosŏn (so-called Yi) dynasty in

Buddhism and the Rise of the Written Vernacular 247

1392. The earliest vernacular texts (songs and poems) in Korean literary history are found only in Buddhist sources, and most of them are by Buddhists on Buddhist themes (Lee 1959, 1961). The secular derivative of *hyangch'al—idu*—lasted right down to the nineteenth century, even in spite of the coexistence of the alphabet (Ledyard 1992b).

In 1446 the enlightened King Sejong (1397-1450) promulgated *Hunmin chŏng'ŭm* ("correct sounds for instructing the people," also the title of the book in which the king introduced this new system of writing) as an easily learned phonetic script for Korea.[13] Of course, the elite Chinese-oriented Confucian literati were adamantly opposed to the use of a demotic script like *Hunmin chŏng'ŭm* and gave it the pejorative name *ŏnmun* (vernacular writing, literally "proverbial writing") because it threatened their monopoly on literacy. The Sinitic script, which was the prevailing method for writing in Korea from the end of the seventh century, was clearly the preferred choice of most of the officials. Thus, although *Hunmin chŏng'ŭm* was initially attacked by Korean intellectuals who had a vested interest in the cumbersome sinographs, during the twentieth century it has now become universally accepted in Korea (both north and south) as the standard form of writing called *han'gul* (Korean letters). Since 1948, there has been exclusive use of *han'gul* in the north, and the occasional admixture of sinographs has been steadily decreasing—now dwindled almost to nothing in general public usage (a small group of Sinitically oriented scholars still cling to the Chinese characters stubbornly, if only in a token fashion)—in the south.

The Koreans take great nationalistic pride in *han'gul* as a script that permits them to record accurately the sounds and words of their own language rather than LS or what amounts to various degrees of written creolization (if we may coin a phrase) that resulted when they were forced to rely on the sinographs. Florian Coulmas (1989: 115-17) and Hans Jensen (1969:210-11) describe the contortions that Koreans had to go through when they tried to write their language with sinographs.

King Sejong's own intentions in creating the *Hunmin chŏng'ŭm* are expressed in his preface as follows:

> The speech sounds of our country's language are different from those of the Middle Kingdom and are not confluent with the characters. Therefore, among the stupid [i.e., "common"] people, there have been many who, having something to put into words, have in the end been unable to express their feelings. I have been distressed because of this, and have newly designed twenty-eight letters, which I wish to have everyone practice at their ease and make convenient for their daily use.
>
> (adapted from Ledyard 1966:224)

It is clear that Sejong was deeply concerned about literacy for the common people and that he believed a phonetic script permitting them to write out easily the sounds of their own spoken language would be much more appropriate for that purpose than the clumsy sinographs.

A similar attitude is expressed in Chŏng Inji's postface to the *Hunmin chŏng'ŭm haerye* (Explanations and Examples of the Correct Sounds for Instructing the People), a commentary on the *Hunmin chŏng'ŭm* prepared by a group of scholars commissioned by King Sejong:

> In our Eastern Quarter, ceremonials, music, and literature are comparable to and imitative of those of China, but our local speech and rustic colloquial are not the same. Students of books are troubled by the difficulty of understanding the purport and meaning [of Chinese characters]; those who preside at processes are distressed at the difficulty of the twists and turns [of a legal text]. In olden days, Sŏl Ch'ong of Silla first made the Clerk Readings, and they are practiced in the government offices and among the people to this day. But all of them are used as borrowed characters; some grate on you, others stop you completely. They are not just rustic and crude and unattested; when it comes to the realm of actual speech, not one in a myriad of them is applicable.

Figure 9. Opening page of the preface to *Hunmin chŏng'ŭm* (Corrected Sounds for Instructing the People) by King Sejong (1397-1450).

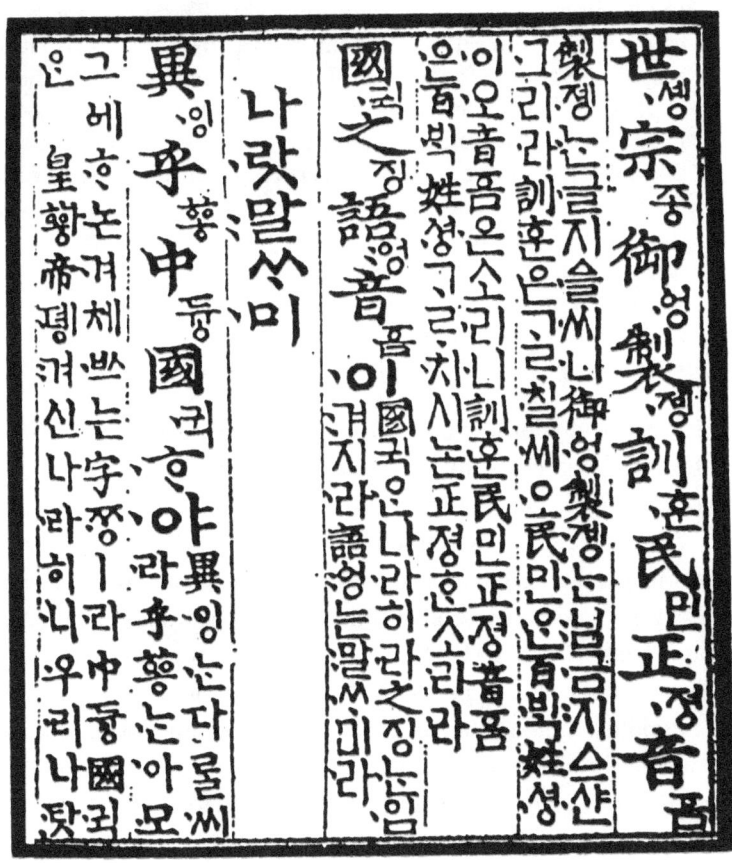

Source: Adapted from "Buddhism and the Rise of the Written Vernacular in East Asia: The Making of National Languages," *Journal of Asian Studies* 53.3 (1994): 733.
Note. It was in this work that the Buddhistically inclined, enlighted ruler formally presented his alphabet for spelling vernacular Korean. National Treasure No. 70, preserved in the Kansong Art Museum. Ch'ŏn 1993:13.

Though only twenty-eight letters are used, their shifts and changes in function are endless; they are simple and fine, reduced to the minimum yet universally applicable. Therefore, a wise man can acquaint himself with them before the morning is over; a stupid man can learn them in the space of ten days. Using these in explaining books, one can know the appropri[e]ties; using these in hearing a litigation, one can grasp the situation. Insofar as the phonology of characters is concerned, clear and eluvial can be distinguished; in matters of music and singing, the twelve semitones may be blended. There is no usage not provided for, no direction in which they do not extend. Even the sound of the winds, the cry of the crane, the cackle of fowl and the barking of dogs-all may be written.

(quoted in Ledyard 1966:257–58)

There can be no doubt that the devisers and advocates of the Korean alphabet were searching for a simple means that would permit their people to express their thoughts and ideas in their own language and that they considered the sinographs to be ill-adapted for that purpose. What is more, the striking formulation of the last sentence manifestly derives from a remarkable expostulation in the preface to the Sung scholar Cheng Ch'iao's (1104-62) *Ch'i-yin lüeh* (*Compendium on the Seven Sounds*) in which he profusely praises the phonological sophistication of Buddhist monks (Mair 1993:338-39). Chŏng Inji and his associates were obviously striving to emulate the flexibility of Indian phonetic writing that was so much admired by Cheng Ch'iao.

It is significant that King Sejong and his wife (d. 1446) were both devout Buddhists and that all except two of the earliest texts written in this new script were Buddhist. The two exceptions are the stultifyingly Confucian *Songs of Dragons Flying through Heaven* (*Yongbi ŏch'ŏn ka*, 1447) and the Sino-Korean glossary entitled *Tongguk chŏng'un*. As literature, the Buddhist works are quite impressive, certainly far superior to the *Songs of the Flying Dragons*. Furthermore, although *Hunmin chŏng'ŭm* (i.e., *han'gul*) is deservedly praised as an ingenious and accurate phonetic script, it was based in part on 'Phags-pa, a Mongolian script devised by a Tibetan lama with that eponym in 1260 to replace the modified old Uighur (< old Syriac < Palmyrene < Aramaic < North Semitic) script that had previously been used to write Mongol (the modified old Uighur script survived as the usual way to write Mongol until the twentieth-century importation of Cyrillic and was later adapted by the Manchus to write their own language). The shapes of the 'Phags-pa letters were inspired by Tibetan letters which themselves were modeled upon Indian Gupta letters. The Tibetan script had been commissioned by the great king Srong-brtsan-sgam-po (ca. 608–50), who is credited with introducing Buddhism to Tibet. It is evident that Khubilai was acting under Buddhist influence when he ordered 'Phags-pa to create a new script for Mongol. The Buddhist impetus, in turn, carried through to King Sejong's *Hunmin chŏng'ŭm*. Also operative was Chinese phonology, in which King Sejong and his closest associates in devising *Hunmin chŏng'ŭm* were quite learned and which, in turn, was based on Indian phonological theories initially brought to China by Buddhist monks during the Han and Six Dynasties periods. It is not surprising, therefore, that Korean Buddhists enthusiastically welcomed the new alphabetic, demotic script as an effective device for the propagation and study of their faith, unlike the elitist, Confucian-minded officials who resolutely resisted it.

A further observation concerning the Buddhist affiliations of phonetic writing in Korea is that *Hunmin chŏng'ŭm* was preceded by an even more explicitly Indian-inspired script, *pŏmsŏ* (= MSM *fan-shu*, "Brahmanic script," probably a form of Siddham). The name, arrangement, and phonological composition of the script all clearly reveal its ultimate Indian origins. *Pŏmsŏ* is still employed today for the transcription of Sanskrit terms in Buddhist ritual texts (Jensen 1969:216).

Figure 10. Opening page of an article on writing from *Hsi-tzu ch'i-chi* (The Miracle of Western Letters) (1605) by the Jesuit priest, Matteo Ricci (1552–1610).

遠	yuèn	任	gín	廣	quām	述	xŭ
擊	xīm	其	Kí'	哉	çāi	文	vên
不	pŏ	憤	fuèn	文	vên	贈	cem̀
相	fiām	悱	fí	字	cù	幼	yeú
閗	vuèn	何	hô	之	cɔ̌y	博	pŏ
而	ſĥ	堪	cán	功	cām	程	chim̀
寓	yú	其	Kî̀	於	yū	子	çù
書	œū	闇	ngɔ̌n	宇	Yù		
以	ì	汝	vén	内	nuí		
通	tūm	手	hû	耶	yê		
即	cié	百	pĕ	世	xí		
兩	leàm	步	pú	無	vû		
人	gîn	之	cɔ̌y	文	vên		
				何	hû		

Source: Adapted from "Buddhism and the Rise of the Written Vernacular in East Asia: The Making of National Languages," *Journal of Asian Studies* 53.3 (1994): 735.

Note. Although Ricci's book was written in Literary Sinitic, it represented the first use of the Roman alphabet to indicate the sounds of a Sinitic language and ultimately led to the creation of convenient methods for writing all of the vernacular languages of China. Published here with the permission of the Vatican Library.

Buddhism and the Rise of the Written Vernacular 253

Ledyard's dissertation (1966) provides a great amount of detailed evidence that Buddhism was indeed a key factor in the creation of the Korean alphabet. For example, he delineates (pp. 261ff.) an alliance between the pro-alphabeticists and Buddhists. He shows, furthermore (p. 267), that many of the earliest compositions using the new alphabet were Buddhist, including a Korean translation of the *Prajñāpāramita-hṛdaya-sūtra* (Heart Sūtra). He also notes (p. 90) that the good king Sejong himself put his alphabet to work by composing odes in Korean on the life and work of the Buddha. It cannot be emphasized too often that Sejong carried out his Buddhist-inspired program of vernacular language reform in the face of fierce opposition from the literati:

> In the last years of his life, Sejong turned more and more to the comforts of Buddhism, and this was tantamount to alienating himself almost completely from the men of his time, whose hatred of that religion bordered on the pathological. But Sejong had actually been sympathetic to Buddhism from early in his reign, and his remonstrators had fought him on this ever since 1426, when they petitioned him to have removed from his throne room a dhāraṇī written on one of the ceiling beams in Siddham letters.
> (Ledyard 1966:90;
> the reference in the last sentence is to *Sejong sillok*,
> November 12, 1426, 34.3a)

But it was not just King Sejong whose Buddhist affinities stimulated him to concrete action aimed at the vernacularization of writing in Korea. Already nine centuries earlier, the Buddhist contributions to the establishment of an authentic Korean literature were absolutely essential:

> The leading role played by Buddhists in the early history of Korean writing must be emphasized.... If what has survived of Silla poetry is any indication, it was Buddhists who wrote most of Silla's native literature. Buddhists preserved it through the Koryŏ period, and Buddhists wrote the biography of Kyunyŏ and the *Samguk yusa* and thus transmitted all we know of that literature to modern times. Even Sŏl Ch'ong, the great expositor of the Chinese

(Confucian) classics, was the son of a Buddhist priest (the famous Wŏnhyo, b. 597), and would have grown up with the concern for the native language shared by his co-religionists. It was no accident that it was a man of this background who should have finally systematized longstanding practices in transcription into a practical way of writing Korean. It was not just in Korea that it was so. The role of Buddhism in the general history of writing in Asia is a story that, when it comes to be written in its entirety, will fill many interesting volumes.

(Ledyard 1966:57)

The role of Buddhism in the rise of printing is another important area of investigation that deserves attention. There is little doubt that printing in East Asia, from its very inception, was primarily a Buddhist phenomenon. In fact, the invention of printing itself may have occurred as an extension of the practice of impressing woodcut engravings of the Buddha's image on silk and paper and of duplicating *dhāraṇī* (charms or prayers, especially as used in Tantrism). Both of these practices were already widespread in China during the seventh century. By the eighth century, millions of *dhāraṇī* were being printed in Japan. For example, between 764 and 770, one million *dhāraṇī* were printed by the order of the empress Shōtoku (d. 769) and were deposited in small stūpas which were distributed to a number of major Buddhist temples (Goodrich 1960: 117). The Buddhist monopoly on the early printing of books proper in Japan is noteworthy:

> Printing after its introduction into Japan (about 740 A.D.) was confined to wealthy Buddhist monasteries until toward the end of the Kamakura period (about 1569) [*sic*] with the result that it was restricted either to Buddhist sutras or Chinese texts. There was very little secular printing in this period from 740 to 1569.
>
> (Peake 1939:58)

The matter of Buddhism's contribution to the history of printing in East Asia, although related to the rise of the written vernacular in the sense that both pertain to the dissemination of learning beyond Confucian literati circles, is a separate question requiring intensive, specialized research of its own. Still, it is significant that this Indian religion had a decisive impact upon both of these fundamentally democratic developments concerning writing in East Asia that occurred at approximately the same time. This naturally leads us to a consideration of the broader issues of the sociology of knowledge, but these unfortunately lie beyond the scope of the present study. For the moment, however, it needs to be pointed out that the legitimization of the vernacular as a written medium, the invention of phonetic syllabaries and alphabets, and the invention of printing are all interrelated phenomena that would appear to stem from the Buddhist missionizing proclivity, namely, the desire to spread the Buddha's *word* as far afield and to as many people, regardless of their background or station, as possible.

Ledyard (1992a) has recently returned to the question of the significance of 'Phags-pa for the creation of *han'gul* in his "The International Linguistic Background of the Correct Sounds for the Instruction of the People."

Along with him, we must make a specific disclaimer that *Hunmin chŏng'ŭm* was not merely a combination of 'Phags-pa orthography and Sino-Indian phonology, but a remarkable creation for which King Sejong personally deserves much credit. Ledyard correctly and perceptively points out the connection between the Korean adoption of vernacular (i.e., native) language as a legitimate medium for writing (as opposed to LS) and the consequent need for a phonetic script with which to represent it. It was this motivation that impelled the king and his associates ingeniously to adapt 'Phags-pa to their own purposes. The *han'gul* alphabet that resulted is marvelously well suited for the phonological representation of Korean and is justly hailed as being perhaps the most logically designed of all alphabets in the world.

Figure 11. A page from *I-mu liao-jan ch'u-chieh* (First Steps in Being Able to Comprehend at a Glance) by Lu Chuang-chang (1854-1928), who had close ties with Christian missionaries.

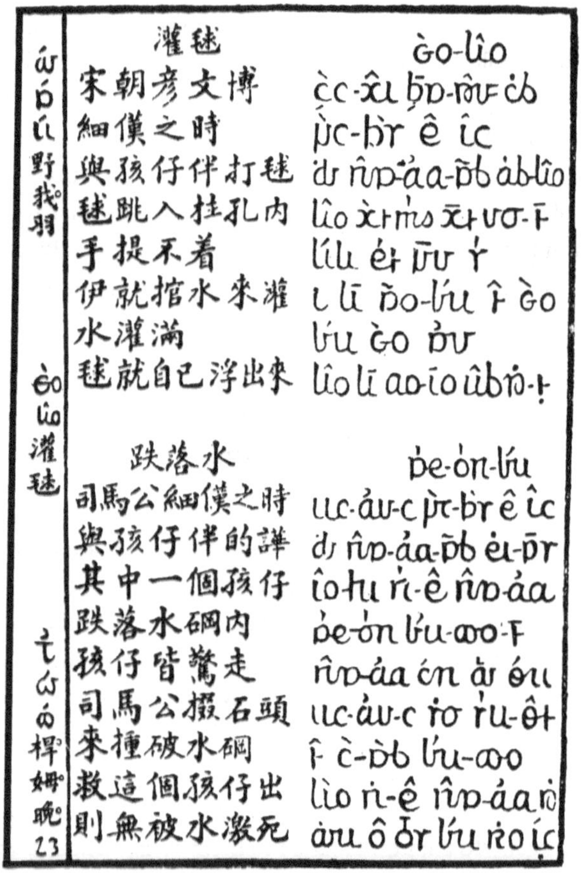
灌毬
宋朝彥文博
細僕之時
與孩仔伴打毬
毬跳入柱孔內
手提不着
伊就搰水來灌
水灌滿
毬就自己浮出來

跌落水
司馬公細僕之時
與孩仔伴的譁
其中一個孩仔
跌落水碙內
孩仔皆驚走
司馬公掇石頭
來摃破水碙
救這個孩仔出
則無被水溺死

Source: Adapted from "Buddhism and the Rise of the Written Vernacular in East Asia: The Making of National Languages," *Journal of Asian Studies* 53.3 (1994): 737.

Note. This is the first work by a Chinese author advocating a system of phonetic spelling for Sinitic languages. It was published in Amoy in 1892 and was keyed to the local Southern Min Language, but Lu contended that his system could be applied to all the living Sinitic vernaculars.

A drawback to the use of *han'gul* became apparent only in this century with the advent of modern information-processing techniques (mechanical and electronic). The tetragraphic (i.e., square) configuration of syllables (originally intended for ease of combination with the sinographs) in the Korean alphabet poses an obstacle to the efficient application of modern information-processing methods that are essentially linear (Chung 1991). There have lately been attempts to rearrange the script in a linear sequence and to mark word boundaries for greater efficiency in information-processing systems (Hannas 1993).

Conclusion

We have seen how, under the probable influence of the Indian concept of *deśa-bhāṣā* brought to China by Buddhism, numerous peoples in East Asia created a whole series of written vernaculars. While Chinese authorities stubbornly resisted recognition of any of their own vernaculars as a national language—probably due to the extremely high prestige and power of LS—the Buddhists used the vernacular liberally in their own writings. Once proffered as a functional alternative written language, use of the vernacular steadily grew until, by the late Ming–early Ch'ing, it is likely that as many books were being printed in vernacular or a heavily vernacularized literary style as in LS, notwithstanding the censure and ridicule of strait-laced scholars. Finally, even the Manchus, who already had their own written national language, which was swiftly dying out because of pervasive sinicization, yielded to the idea that their Sinitic subjects, too, needed a national language keyed to one of the spoken vernaculars. After the agitation of the May Fourth Movement led by progressive Chinese intellectuals and students, many of whom were exposed to radical ideas about language and other aspects of culture and society through the window of Japan, *kuo-yü* was publicly proclaimed the official written language of the nation. This marked the formal end of the multimillennial separation between book language (*shu-mien-yü*) and spoken language (*k'ou-yü*) in China.

That Buddhism played a crucial role in the evolution of the written vernacular throughout East Asia is beyond any doubt. The question remains, however: Which aspect of Buddhism was responsible for these momentous changes? Was there some religious doctrine belonging to Buddhism that fostered the written vernacular? Or was it due to a special Buddhist philosophical principle? Was it the fondness for storytelling, preaching, and public speaking by the early Buddhists in the language of the people? Did the ostensible orality of Buddhist scripture have anything to do with the origins of the written vernacular in China? Was the fact that most of the early translators of Buddhist texts into Sinitic were foreigners with a poor command of the literary language a significant factor? And did the phonological sophistication of Indian linguistical science lend credibility to the spoken vis-à-vis the written? What of the elaborate, rigorously defined Indian traditions of chanting and recitation? And may the social values, institutions, and position of Buddhism have contributed to the rise of the written vernacular? Last but not least, did Buddhist practice have anything to do with the validation of the vernacular? Perhaps I have entirely overlooked some vital facet of Buddhism that contributed to this process. In the end, Buddhist support for the written vernacular may best be identified as a complex combination of diverse factors, all of which were determined by an integrated socioreligious ideology.

Abbreviations

B.C.E.	Before Common Era
BHSi	Buddhist Hybrid Sinitic
BHS	Buddhist Hybrid Sanskrit
C.E.	Common Era
LS	Literary Sinitic

MSM	Modern Standard Mandarin
p.n.	proper name
T	*Taishō Tripiṭaka* (the standard edition of the Chinese Buddhist canon)
VS	Vernacular Sinitic

Table 2a. Glossary (Part 1)

Abidatsuma zōjuron	阿毗達磨雜記論	Abhidharmasamuccayavyākhyā
An Hsüan	安玄	p.n.
An Shih-kao	安世高	p.n.
chang-che	長者	śreṣṭha elder
Chang-sun Wu-chi, "Ching-chi chih"	長孫無忌，經籍志	"Bibliographical Treatise"
Cheng Ch'iao	鄭樵	p.n.
ch'eng-yü	成語	set phrase (so-called "idiom")
chi	偈	gāthā verse
Chi Hsien-lin	季羨林	p.n.
Chi Tsang	吉藏	p.n.
Ch'i-yin lüeh	七音略	Compendium on the Seven Scripts
chiang-ching-wen	講經文	sūtra lecture text
Chih Lou-chia-ch'an	支樓迦讖	p.n.
Chih Yao	支曜	p.n.
Chin shih kuo-yü	金史國語	National Language History of the Jurchen
chin-shih-nü	近事女	upāsikā lay woman
ChŏngInji	鄭麟趾	p.n.
Chou Yu-kuang	周有光	p.n.
Chu Ch'ing-chih	朱慶之	p.n.
Chu Lü-yen	竺律炎	p.n.
Chu Ta-li	竺大力	p.n.
Chu T'an-kuo	竺曇果	p.n.
chū' nôm		Vietnamese vernacular writing
ch'u-chia	出家	pravrajyā, Pali pabbajjā leaving the home (to become a monk)
chü-shih	居士	upāsaka layman
ch'uan-ch'i	傳奇	classical fiction
Chūgokugo rekishi bunpō	中國語歷史文法	A Historical Grammar of Modern Chinese
Chūgokugo shi tsūkō	中國語史通考	A Historical Study of Chinese Language

Source: Adapted from "Buddhism and the Rise of the Written Vernacular in East Asia: The Making of National Languages," *Journal of Asian Studies* 53.3 (1994): 739.

Table 2b. Glossary (Continued)

Chung-kuo ta pai-k'e ch'üan-shu, Yü-yen wen-tzu	中國大百科全書 語言文字	*The Great Chinese Encyclopedia, Language and Script.*
Fa-chü	法巨	p.n.
Fa-chü ching	法句經	*Dhammapada*
Fa-hsien	法顯	p.n.
Fa-li	法立	p.n.
Fa-hua lun-shu	法華論疏	*Commentary on the Lotus Sūtra*
fan-ch'ieh	反切	countertomy; cut-and-splice pseudospelling
fan-pai	梵唄	*brama-pāṭha "Brahmanic" (i.e. Buddhist) hymnody
fan-shu	梵書	Brahmanic script
fang-pien	方便	*upāya* skillful means
fang-yen	方言	topolect
fang-k'uai-tzu	方塊字	tetragraph
Fo-shuo	佛說	*buddhavacana, buddhabhāṣita* spoken by the Buddha; cf. 佛所說 (that which was spoken by the Buddha), 佛言, 佛語, 真佛語 (the true words of the Buddha), 諸佛語言 (the words of the various Buddhas)
"*Fo-tien yü chung-ku Han-yü tz'u-hui yen-chiu*"	佛典與中古漢語 詞彙研究	"A Study of the Relationship between Buddhist Scriptures and the Vocabulary of Middle Sinitic"
həi	系	to be (Cantonese)
Han-erh yen-yü	漢兒言語	the (common) language of the Han people
Han-yen	漢言	spoken Sinitic
Han-wen	漢文	written Sinitic

Table 2c. Glossary (Continued)

Han-tzu	漢字	sinograph ("Chinese character")
Hsi-tzu ch'i-chi	西字奇迹	The Miracle of Western Letters
hsi-wen	戲文	southern drama
Hsien-pei	鮮卑	*Saerbi, *Shirvi
Hsien-yü ching	賢愚經	Sūtra of the Wise and the Foolish
Hsüan-tsang	玄奘	p.n.
Hua-i i-yü	華夷譯語	Sino-Mongolian Translations
Hua-yen ching	華嚴經	Avataṃsakasūtra
Hui-chiao	慧皎	p.n.
Hui-yüan	惠 (→慧) 遠	p.n.
Hunmin chŏng'ŭm	訓民正音	correct sounds for instructing the people
Hunmin chŏng'ŭm haerye	訓民正音解例	Explanations and Examples of the Correct Sounds for Instructing the People
hyangch'al	鄉札	local letters
I-ching	義淨	p.n.
li-du	吏讀	clerk readings
i-fang-ming	醫方明	vyādhi-cikitsā-vidyāsthāna medicine
I hsin ch'uan hsin	以心傳心	transmission from mind to mind
Iriya Yoshitaka	入矢義高	p.n.
i-yü	夷語	"barbarian" language
jan Hua-su	染華俗	tainted by Chinese customs
Ju-chih, see Yüeh-chih		
ju shih wo wen	如是我聞	evaṃ mayā śrutam Thus have I heard; var. 如是聞, 我聞如是, 聞如是, etc.
ju shih yen	如是言	said thus
Ju shih yü ching	如是語經	Sūtra Spoken Thus

Table 2d. Glossary (Continued)

kanbun	漢文	LS as written in Japan
K'ang Meng-hsiang	康孟詳 / 祥	p.n.
Kao Ming-k'ai	高名凱	p.n.
kao-seng	高僧	eminent monk
Kao-seng chuan	高僧傳	Biographies of Eminent Monks
k'ao-cheng-hsüeh	考證學	evidential learning
kokugo	國語	(Japanese) national language
k'ou-yü	口語	spoken language
kuan-ch'ang	官場	officialdom: the Mandarinate
kuan-hua	官話	Mandarin
Kuan-hua ho-sheng tzu-mu	官話合聲字母	Letters for Combining the Sounds of Mandarin
kuan-hua tzu-mu	官話字母	Mandarin letters
kug'o	國語	(Korean) national language
kun	訓	the Japanese reading of a sinograph
kung-ch'iao-ming	工巧明	śilpa-karma-sthāna-vidyā arts and crafts
kuo	國	country, nation
kuo-yü	國語	national (vernacular) language; title of an ancient Chinese historical work
Li Chin-hsi, Kuo-yü yün-tung shih kang	黎錦熙，國語運動史綱	Outline History of the National Language Movement
Li-shih yen-chiu	歷史研究	Studies on History
Liao shih kuo-yü	遼史國語	National Language History of the Khitan
Lin Shu	林紓	p.n.
Lu Chuang-chang, I-mu liao-jan ch'u-chieh	盧戇章，一目了然初階	First Steps in Being Able to Comprehend at a Glance
Lun-yü	論語	Analects

Table 2e. Glossary (Continued)

Lung-men	龍門	place-name
Ma Šāīḥ - Muḥammad	馬沙亦黑	p.n.
man-t'e-lo	曼特羅	*mantra* magical formula or incantation
Mei Tsu-Lin, "San-ch'ao pei-meng hui-pien li te pai-hua tzu-liao," Chung-kuo shu-mu chi-k'an	梅祖麟，三朝北盟會編裡的白話資料，《中國書目季刊》	"Vernacular Materials in the *Compendium of NorthernTreatises of Three Emperors*," *Bibliographic Quarterly*
Mo-he chih-kuan	摩訶止觀	**Mahāśamathavipaśyanā*
nei-ming	內明	*adhyātma-vidyā* psychology
Ni Hai-shu, Chung-kuo p'in-yin wen-tzu kai-lun	倪海曙，中國拼音文字概論	*Introduction to the Chinese Phonetic Script*
Nien Fo	念佛	recite the name of the Buddha
nü-shu	女書	women's script
Ohta [Ōta] Tatsuo	太田長夫	p.n.
Ōkutsumarakyō	央掘魔羅經	*Aṅgulimālika-sūtra* or *Aṅgulimālyā-sūtra*
on	音	Chinese-style phonetic reading of a sinograph used in Japanese
ŏnmun	諺文	vernacular writing
pai-hua[-wen]	白話[文]	written Vernacular Sinitic
pan-wen-pan-pai	半文半白	semiliterary-semivernacular
Pei Wei	北魏	Northern Wei
pien-wen	變文	transformation text
pŏmsŏ	梵書	Brahmanic script (see *fan-shu*)
pu li wen-tzu	不立文字	not to establish written words
p'u-t'ung-hua	普通話	common speech (i.e., Modern Standard Mandarin)
Qoninči	火源潔	p.n.
quốc ngữ	國語	Vietnamese roman alphabet

Table 2f. Glossary (Continued)

san-shih-liu tzu-mu	三十六字母	thirty-six letters
Sejong	世宗	p.n.
Sejong sillok	世宗實錄	Veritable Records of the Reign of King Sejong
Shao-wu	邵武	name of a place in Fukien
sheng-ming	聲明	śabda-vidyā linguistics
shih	是	to be
Shih pei yü-lu	使北語錄	Transcripts from a Northern Mission
shou-lu	首盧	śloka stanza
Shou-wen	守溫	p.n.
shu-mien-yü	書面語	book language
Sŏl Ch'ong	薛聰	p.n.
Ssu-ma Ch'ien, Shih-chi	司馬遷，史記	Records of the Grand Historian
Ssu-ma Kuang, Tzu-chiht'ung-chien	司馬光，資治通鑑	Comprehensive Mirror for Aid in Government
su	俗	vulgar
su-chiang	俗講	lay lecture
su-jen	俗人	gṛhastha householder
sung	頌	song of praise
Sung Lien, Yüan shih	宋濂，元史	History of the Yüan Dynasty
Ta chih-tu lun	大智度論	Mahāprajñāpāramitopadeśa
TakataTokio, "Chibetto moji shosha 'Chōkan' no kenkyū (honbun hen)," Tōhō gakuhō	高田時雄，チベット文字書寫「長卷」の研究 (本文編)，東方學報	"Studies on the 'Long Scroll' inTibetan Transcription (Text)," Journal of Oriental Studies
Ta-luti-ch'üpo-shih lun-wen ts'ung-k'an	大陸地區博士論文叢刊	Mainland Region Doctoral Dissertations Series

Table 2g. Glossary (Continued)

"T'ang-tai ch'an-chia yü-lu so chien te yü-fa ch'eng-fen"	唐代禪家語錄所見的語法成分	"Grammatical Elements Observed in Zen Records of Conversations from the T'ang Period"
tao-lu	道路	way, road
teng-yün	等韻	rhyme classification
t'o-lo-ni	陀羅尼	dhāraṇī mystical charm, prayer
Tongguk chŏng'un	東國正韻	Correct Rhymes of the Eastern Kingdom
T'o-pa	拓 / 托跋	Tabgatch
"Tonkō henbun shū" kōgo goi ho-i	「敦煌變文集」口語語彙補遺	Supplement of Colloquial Expressions in "Tun-huang pien-wen chi"
"Tonkō henbun shū" kōgo goi sakuin	「敦煌變文集」口語語彙索引	Index of Colloquial Expressions in "Tun-huang pien-wen chi"
"Tsai lun yüan-shih Fo-chiao te yü-yen wen-t'i"	再論原始佛教的語言問題	"A Reexamination of the Language Problem of Primitive Buddhism"
"Tsai t'an Fu-t'u yü Fo"	再談浮屠與佛	"More about the Chinese Terms 'Fu Tu' and 'Fo'"
tsan	讚	stotra eulogy
Tso Ch'iu-ming	左丘明	p.n.
Tso chuan	左傳	Tso's Chronicle
"T'u-huo-lo-yü te fa-hsien yü k'ao-shih chi ch'i tsai Chung-Yin wen-hua chiao-liu te tso-yung"	吐火羅語的發現與考釋及其在中印文化交流的作用	"The Tokharian Language: Its Discovery and Decipherment and Its Role in the Cultural Relations between India and China"
Tuan Li-fen, "Tsui-tsao ch'u-hsien hsi-tz'u (shih) te ti-hsia tzu-liao," Yü-wen t'ien-ti	段莉芬，最早出現繫詞「是」的地下資料，語言天地	"The Earliest Excavated Material for the Copula shih," The World of Language and Script

Table 2h. Glossary (Continued)

Tun-huang	敦煌	place-name
t'ung-yü	通語	common language
tzu yüeh	子曰	the master said
Wang Chao	王照	p.n.
Wei Cheng, *Sui shu*	魏徵，隋書	*History of the Sui Dynasty*
Wei-chih-nan	維祇難	Vighna (p.n.)
Wei Yüan, *Sheng-wu chi*	魏源，聖武記	*Records of Sagely Military Exploits*
wen-yen[-wen]	文言[文]	Literary Sinitic
Wo wen shih-tsun shuo tz'u i	我聞世尊說此義	"I heard the World-Honored explain this [meaning]."
Wo wen shih-tsun ying-kung ts'eng ju shih shuo	我聞世尊應供曾如是說	"Thus did I hear the worshipful World-Honored speak."
Wŏnhyo	元曉	p.n.
Wu (Nguə)	吳	p.n.
Wu Ju-lun	吳汝綸	p.n.
wu-ming	五明	*pañcavidyā-sthānāni* five types of knowledge
ya-yen	雅言	elegant language
yeh	也	LS sentence particle
Yen-ching hsüeh-pao	燕京學報	*Yenching Journal*
yin-ming	因明	*hetu-vidyā* logic
yü	語	language
yü-lu	語錄	recorded sayings
Yü-yen yen-chiu	語言研究	*Linguistic Researches*
Yün-kang	雲岡	place-name
yen-yü tao tuan, hsin-hsing ch'u mieh	語言道斷，心行處滅	"The way of language is cut off, the workings of the mind are obliterated."
Yongbi ŏch'ŏn ka	龍飛御天歌	*Songs of Dragons Flying the Heavens*

Table 2i. Glossary (Continued)

Yüeh-chih (also pronounced as Ju-chih)	月氏, var. 月氏, 月支	"Indo-Scythian," more properly Kushān or Kuṣāṇa; perhaps were originally Tocharians

Acknowledgments

Research for the final version of this study, begun a half-dozen years ago, was carried out at the National Humanities Center during the academic year 1991-92. Work at the Center was supported by grants from the National Endowment for the Humanities and the Andrew W. Mellon Foundation. I am grateful to all three of these organizations for providing me the ideal conditions to complete a number of projects. In addition, I would like to thank the following individuals who read this work in one or more of its many previous incarnations: John DeFrancis, Gari Ledyard, S. Robert Ramsey, James Unger, Jan Nattier, Tsu-Lin Mei, Ludo Rocher, Oskar v. Hinüber, T. Griffith Foulk, Stephen F. Teiser, Richard Mather, David Utz, and Linda Chance. While all of them offered helpful comments and useful references, I alone am responsible for any errors of fact and interpretation that remain. The linguists, Chou Yu-kuang, Jerry Norman, W. South Coblin, and Takata Tokio, provided assistance on technical questions, for which I am deeply thankful. Finally, I appreciate the close, critical reading of three anonymous referees for this journal who made several useful suggestions for improvement.

A monographic treatment of this subject, entitled "The Concept of 'National Language' in East Asia and Its Buddhist Beginnings," is forthcoming in *Sino-Platonic Papers*.

Notes

1. Siddham was derived from the Gupta form of the Sanskrit alphabet and was used in East Asian countries for the writing of *dhāraṇīs, mantras,* and other (usually very brief) Buddhist texts.
2. According to the Hartwells, the Buddhist *saṃgha* was perhaps the most egalitarian institution in Sung society. See especially their interesting note and comments on the monk Tsung-ku (database #16548) who was the illiterate son of a Shao-wu (in northwest Fukien) farmer and became the founder of an important Zen temple. Among his friends and disciples were members of some of the most distinguished families of the Sung period.
3. Although those who wrote down early vernacular texts in China were necessarily dependent upon the very script which limited their freedom of expression, they treated it rather casually by using the graphs more for phonetic purposes and less for logographic purposes than was customary in LS. This is evident, for example, in T'ang period transformation texts where homophonic borrowings and "mistakes" routinely occur. // The fundamental nature of the sinographs is still very much in dispute. A few philosophically/theoretically minded scholars continue to insist that the Chinese writing system is pictographic and ideographic, whereas most historically/empirically oriented linguists consider it to function fundamentally as a huge and phonetically imprecise morphosyllabary with conspicuous logographic features (Hansen 1993a, 1993b; Unger 1993). One thing is sure, however, and that is the fact that Chinese characters—unlike the elements of a true syllabary, consonantary, or alphabet which convey only phonetic information—carry both semantic and phonetic weight (albeit limited in both cases).
4. Due to the misleading, if not wholly erroneous, commentary of Buddhaghoṣa *(Cullavagga* 5.33; *Vinaya* ii, 139, 1–16), there has been a small amount of scholarly controversy over whether the Buddha enjoined his followers to use his own native tongue or their own native tongues in spreading the *dharma* (Brough 1980). It would seem that the operative Pāli word *sakāya* (or *sakkāya* = Sanskrit *satkāya),* under the given circumstances, is more apt to function as a third-person reflexive pronoun than as a first-person reflexive. Furthermore, it has not previously been pointed out that the passage in question would seri-

ously contradict itself if we accepted Buddhaghoṣa's explanation ("Lord, here monks of miscellaneous origin are corrupting the Buddha's [i.e., your] words [by repeating them] in your own dialect"[!]). This simply does not make sense. Only when we understand *sakāya* as "their" is the entire passage comprehensible. Cf. Edgerton (1953:1-2) and Lin Li-kouang (1949:216-27). Finally, no one seriously disputes the claim that the Buddha was in favor of the vernaculars at the expense of the classical, priestly language. Of one thing we can be certain, linguistic diversity was present in ancient Buddhism almost from the very beginning of the religion (Bechert 1980: 15).

5. Jan Nattier (1991:3) makes the excellent point that the sentence recommending the use of the vernacular is absent in the Sarvāsrivāda *vinaya*. This was, after all, probably the first sect to abandon the use of Prākrit in favor of elegant, classical Sanskrit. In her words, "It would not be at all difficult to see this absence as a deliberate omission."

6. The quotation given here is preceded by these sentences: "If a *bhikṣu* in reciting a sūtra prolongs the sounds as though he were singing or chanting, that is a mistake. Therefore, a *bhikṣu* should not draw out his voice in song or chant when reciting the sūtras or the *vinaya*. If a *bhikṣu* recites the sūtras and other texts with the sounds of the *chandas*, he will commit a sin by overstepping the law." The quotation is followed by this commentary: "*Chandas* refers to the method of recitation of the brahmans. They prolong the sounds and keep the rhythm by pointing with their finger in the air. The master sings first and the others follow along after him." // I have not been able to locate the equivalent passage in the *vinaya* of the Mahāsaṃghika *(T22[1425].227-549)*, translated by Fa-hsien and Buddhabhadra in 416–18.

7. It is likely, however, that there were already written *apabhraṃśa* by the sixth century (e.g., an inscription of King Dharasena II of Valabhī refers to composition in *apabhraṃśa*) and they may even have existed by the third or fourth century (e.g., certain verses in the fourth act of Kālidāsa's *Vikramorvaśīya*). The bulk of later *apabhraṃśa* literature was mostly Jain works (eighth to twelfth centuries). See *Encyclopaedia Britannica*, 15th ed. (1988), vol. 22, p. 618:2a; vol. 21, p. 50: 1b; and vol. 1, p. 475:3a. Technically speaking, *deśī* is considered to mean language that is "non-derivable from Sanskrit."

8. This should, perhaps, more accurately be thought of as "the Pāli text of the Dhammapada."

Buddhism and the Rise of the Written Vernacular 271

9. In the eleventh chapter of his *Chūgokugo shi tsūkō*, Ohta [Ōta] Tatsuo describes the sporadic rise of *Han-erh yen-yü* (the [common] language of the Han people) as a legitimate mode of expression. He demonstrates not only that the development of the national vernacular was fitful, but that it occurred in the popular realm and that it was counterpoised to the LS of the elite. For an extensive discussion of the term *kuan-hua* and its history, see the next section.
10. It may be more correct to state that Tabgatch was the name of one clan (the royal clan) within the ethnic group known as the *Saerbi or *Shirvi.
11. Paul Yang (1989) has shown that Standard Mandarin of the Ming dynasty was based on the Nanking topolect, not that of Peking, in spite of the fact that the latter city was the primary capital for most of the dynasty. Nanking was the capital during the early Ming (1356–1421) and continued to serve as the secondary capital later.
12. I have benefited much from conversations on this subject with Tsu-Lin Mei who is currently preparing a major study concerning the grammatical influence of the *koine* on the topolects during the T'ang and Sung periods. In it, he will show how the Early Mandarin dialect of the mid-eighth century came to function as a *koine* and how, by the Sung, it had developed as a written vernacular both for popular literature and for limited bureaucratic purposes. Nonetheless, until the turn of the twentieth century, LS remained the sole sanctioned, official medium for writing and there was no conscious attempt to elevate the *koine* to the status of a national language.
13. For an excellent brief account of *Hunmin chŏng'ŭm*, see Ramsey 1992. For more information on the history of *han'gul*, see Gari Ledyard's superb dissertation which, unfortunately, has never been published. I have relied on it heavily for the account of Korean writing presented in these paragraphs.

List of References

Along the Ancient Silk Routes: Central Asian Art from the West Berlin State Museums. 1982. New York: The Metropolitan Museum of Art.

Alsdorf, Ludwig. 1980. "Ardha-Māgadhī." In Heinz Bechert, ed., *Die Sprache der ältesten buddhistischen Überlieferung*, pp. 17-23.

Angurarohita, Pratoom. 1989. "Buddhist Influence on the Neo-Confucian Concept of the Sage." *Sino-Platonic Papers* 10 (June).

Banerjee, Muralydhar. 1931. *The Deśīnāmamālā of Hemacandra. Part I—Text with Readings, Introduction and Index of Words.* Calcutta: University of Calcutta.

Bechert, Heinz, ed. 1980. *Die Sprache der ältesten buddhistischen Überlieferung/The Language of the Earliest Buddhist Tradition.* Symposium zur Buddhismusforschung, II. Abhandlungen der Akademie der Wissenschaften in Göttingen, philologisch-historische Klasse, dritte Folge, Nu. 117. Göttingen: Vandenhoeck and Ruprecht.

Beckwith, Christopher I. 1987. *The Tibetan Empire in Central Asia: A History of the Struggle for Great Power among Tibetans, Turks, Arabs, and Chinese during the Early Middle Ages.* Princeton: Princeton University Press.

Berling, Judith. 1987. "Bringing the Buddha Down to Earth: Notes on the Emergence of *Yü-lu* as a Buddhist Genre." *History of Religions* 27.1 (August): 56-88.

Bender, Ernest. 1991. Personal communications (February).

Bhayani, Harivallabh C. 1966. *Studies in Hemacandra's Deśīnāmamālā.* Parshvanath Vidyashram Research Institute. Varanasi: Banaras Hindu University.

Bond, George. 1982. *The Word of the Buddha.* Colombo: M. D. Gunasena.

Brough, John. 1949-50. "Thus Have I Heard...." *Bulletin of the School of Oriental and African Studies* 13.2:416-26.

———. 1961. "A Kharoṣṭhī Inscription from China." *Bulletin of the School of Oriental and African Studies* 24:517-30, plus 1 plate.

———. 1980. "Sakāya [sic] Niruttiyā: Cauld kale het." In Heinz Bechert, ed., *Die Sprache der ältesten buddhistischen Überlieferung*, pp. 35-42.

Ch'en, Kenneth K. S. 1964. *Buddhism in China: A Historical Survey.* Princeton: Princeton University Press.

Chi Hsien-Lin (also transcribed as Chi Hsian-Lin, Dschi Hiän-Lin, and Ji Xianlin). 1947. "On the oldest Chinese transliterations of the name of Buddha. " *Sino-Indian Studies* 3.1-2 (April and July): 1-9.

———. 1956. "T'u-huo-lo-yü te fa-hsien yü k'ao-shih chi ch'i tsai Chung-Yin wen-hua chiao-liu chung te tso-yung (The Tokharian Language: Its Discovery and Decipherment and Its Role in the Cultural Relations between India and China)." *Yü-yen yen-chiu* (Linguistic Researches) 1:297-307.

———. 1959. "Tsai lun yüan-shih Fo-chiao te yü-yen wen-t'i (A Re-examination of the Language Problem of Primitive Buddhism)." *Yü-yen yen-chiu* (Linguistic Researches) 4:87-105.

———. 1990. "Tsai t'an Fu-t'u yü Fo (More about the Chinese Terms '*Fu Tu*' and '*Fo*')." *Li-shih yen-chiu* (Studies on History) 2:3-11.

Ch'on Hye-Bong. 1993. "Typography in Korea: Birthplace of Moveable Metal Type." *Koreana* 7.2 (Summer):10-19.

Chu Ch'ing-Chih. 1990. "Fo-tien yü chung-ku Han-yü tz'u-hui yen-chiu (A Study of the Relationship between Buddhist Scriptures and the Vocabulary of Middle Sinitic)." Ph.D. diss. Chengtu: Szechwan University, Department of Chinese. Published in Taiwan with the same Chinese title (English title: Study of the relationship between Buddhist scriptures and the vocabulary of medieval Chinese) as part of the *Ta-lu ti-ch'ü po-shih lun-wen ts'ung-k'an* (Mainland Region Doctoral Dissertations Series). Taipei: Wen-chin ch'u-pan-she, 1992.

Chung, Won L. 1991. "Hangeul and Computing." In Victor H. Mair and Yongquan Liu, eds., *Characters and Computers.* Amsterdam, Oxford, Washington, and Tokyo: IOS Press, pp. 146-79.

Chung-kuo ta pai-k'e-ch'üan-shu (The Great Chinese Encyclopedia). *Yü-yen wen-tzu* (Language and Script). Peking and Shanghai: Chung-kuo ta pai-k'e-ch'üan-shu, 1988.

Coulmas, Florian. 1989. *The Writing Systems of the World.* Oxford and Cambridge, Mass.: Basil Blackwell.

Cowell, E. B. 1854. *The Prākṛta-prakāśa, or the Prākṛt Grammar of Vararuchi, with the Commentary (Manoramā) of Bhāmaha*, Calcutta: Punthi Pustak, 1962. First edition, Hertford, 1854; second edition, London, 1868.

Defrancis, John. 1978. *Colonialism and Language Policy in Viet Nam*. Contributions to the Sociology of Language, 19. The Hague: Mouton.

———. 1989. *Visible Speech: The Diverse Oneness of Writing Systems*. Honolulu: University of Hawaii Press.

———. 1991. Letter of March 17.

Dien, Albert. 1991. "A New Look at the Xianbei and their Impact on Chinese Culture." In George Kuwayama, ed., *Ancient Mortuary Traditions of China: Papers on Chinese Ceramic Funerary Sculptures*. Los Angeles: Los Angeles County Museum of Art, pp. 40-59.

Diringer, David. 1962. *Writing*. Ancient Peoples and Places, 25. London: Thames and Hudson; rpt., 1965.

Dobson, W. A. C. H. 1974. *A Dictionary of the Chinese Particles: with a prolegomenon in which the problems of the particles are considered and they are classified by their grammatical functions*. Toronto: University of Toronto Press.

Edgerton, Franklin. 1953. *Buddhist Hybrid Sanskrit Grammar and Dictionary*. 2 vols. New Haven: Yale University Press.

Fuchs, Walter. 1930. "Zur technischen Organisation der Übersetzungen buddhistischer Schriften ins Chinesische." *Asia Major* 6:84-103.

Gardner, Daniel K. 1991. "Modes of Thinking and Modes of Discourse in the Sung: Some Thoughts on the *Yü-lu* ('Recorded Conversations') Texts." *The Journal of Asian Studies* 50.3 (August): 574-603.

Gernet, Jacques. 1956. *Les aspects économiques du Bouddhisme dans la société chinoise du Ve au Xe siècle*. Publications de l'École française d'Extrême-Orient, 39. Saigon: École française d'Extrême-Orient.

Gómez, Louis O. 1987. "Buddhist Views of Language." In Mircea Eliade, ed., *The Encyclopedia of Religion*. New York: Macmillan. Vol. 8, pp. 446-51.

Goodrich, L. Carrington. 1960. "Two Notes on Early Printing in China." In H. L. Hariyappa, ed., *Professor P. K. Gode Commemoration Volume*. Poona Oriental Series, 93. Poona: Oriental Book Agency, pp. 117-20.

Gurevich, I. S. 1985. "Eschë Raz o Byan'ven'... (zametki)." In Akademiya Nauk SSSR, Ordena Trudovogo Krasnogo Znameni Institut Vostokovedeniya, Leningradskoe Otdelenie, *Pis'menn'ie Pamyatniki i Problem'i Istorii Kul'tur'i Narodov Vostoka*. XVIII Godichnaya Nauchnaya Sessiya Io IV AN SSSR (Doklad'i i Soobschenniya, 1983-85), part 3. Moscow: Nauka, pp. 96-101.

Habein, Yaeko Sato. 1984. *The History of the Japanese Written Language*. Tokyo: University of Tokyo Press.

Hannas, William Carl. 1988. "The Simplification of Chinese Character-Based Writing." Ph.D. diss., University of Pennsylvania.

———. 1993. "Korea's Attempts to Eliminate Chinese Characters and the Implications for Romanizing Chinese." Unpublished paper.

Hansen, Chad. 1993a. "Chinese Ideographs and Western Ideas." *The Journal of Asian Studies* 52.2 (May):373-99.

———. 1993b. Reply to J. Marshall Unger. *The Journal of Asian Studies* 52.4 (November):954-57.

Hartwell, Robert M., and Marianne C. Hartwell. 1991a. Executive Finance and State Council, "Notes and Documentation." Philadelphia: electronic database.

———. 1991b. Personal communications (February 18 and 21, 1991).

V. Hinuber, Oskar. 1986. *Das ältere Mittelindisch im Überblick*. Österreichische Akademie der Wissenschaften. Philosophisch-Historische Klasse. Sitzungsberichte. 467. Band. Vienna: Verlag der Österreichischen Akademie der Wissenschaften.

———. 1990. Der *Beginn der Schrift und frühe Schriftlichkeit in Indien*. Abhandlungen der Geistes- und Sozialwissenschaftlichen Klasse, Jahrgang 1989, Nr. 11. Mainz: Akademie der Wissenschaften und der Literatur; Stuttgart: Franz Steiner. Esp. section V (pp. 22-25) on the oral origins of the earliest Buddhist texts.

Hoffman, Frank J. 1990. "Evaṃ me sutaṁ: Oral Tradition in Nikāya Buddhism." Paper presented at the Nineteenth Annual Conference on South Asia, University of Wisconsin-Madison, November 2-4. 34 pages. Published with the same title in a shortened and revised form in Jeffrey R. Timm, ed., *Texts in Context: Traditional Hermeneutics in South Asia*. Albany: State University of New York Press, 1992, pp. 195-219.

Iriya Yoshitaka. 1961. *"Tonkō henbun shū" kōgo goi sakuin* (Index of Colloquial Expressions in *"Tun-huang pien-wen chi"*). Kyoto: privately printed.

———. 1985. *"Tonkō henbun shū" kōgo goi ho-i* (Supplement of Colloquial Expressions in *"Tun-huang pien-wen chi"*), I. Kyoto: privately printed.

Jensen, Hans. 1969. *Sign, Symbol and Script: An Account of Man's Effort to Write*. Third revised and enlarged edition; translated from the German by George Unwin. New York: G. P. Putnam's Sons.

Kajiyama, Y. 1977. "Thus Spoke the Blessed One ..." In Lewis Lancaster, ed., *Prajñāpāramitā and Related Systems: Studies in Honour of Edward Conze*. Berkeley: Regents of the University of California, pp. 93-99.

Kao Ming-K'ai. 1948. "T'ang-tai ch'an-chia yü-lu so chien te yü-fa ch'eng-fen (Grammatical Elements Observed in Zen Records of Conversations from the T'ang Period)." *Yen-ching hsüeh-pao* (Yenching Journal) 34:49-84.

Kim-Renaud, Young-Key, ed. 1992. *King Sejong the Great: The Light of Fifteenth Century Korea*. Washington, D.C.: The International Circle of Korean Linguistics.

Lamotte, Étienne. 1958. *Histoire du bouddhisme indien, des origines à l'ère Śaka*. Bibliothèque du Muséon, 43. Louvain: Publications Universitaires, Institut Orientaliste.

Ledyard, Gari Keith. 1966. "The Korean Language Reform of 1446: The Origin, Background, and Early History of the Korean Alphabet." Ph.D. diss., University of California, Berkeley.

———. 1992a. "The International Linguistic Background of the Correct Sounds for the Instruction of the People." Unpublished paper, 74 pp.

———. 1992b. Letter of October 6.

Lee, Peter. 1959. *Studies in the Saenaennorae: Old Korean Poetry*. Serie orientale Roma, 22. Rome: Istituto italiano per il Medio ed Estremo Oriente.

———. 1961. "The Importance of the Kyunyŏ chŏn (1075) in Korean Buddhism and Literature—Bhadra-cari-praṇidhāna in Tenth-Century Korea." *Journal of the American Oriental Society* 81.4 (December):409-14.

Lewicki, Marian. 1949. *La Langue mongole des transcriptions chinoises du XIVe siècle. Le Houa-yi yi-yu de 1389*. Travaux de la Société des Sciences et des Lettres de Wrocław, ser. A, 29. Wrocław: Nakładem Wrocławskiego Towarzystwa Naukowego.

Li Chin-Hsi. 1934. *Kuo-yü yün-tung shih kang* (Outline History of the National Language Movement). Shanghai: Commercial.

Ligeti, Louis, 1970. "Le Tabghatch, un dialecte de la langue Sien-pi." In Louis Ligeti, ed., *Mongolian Studies*. Bibliotheca Orientalia Hungarica, 14. Amsterdam: B. A. Grüner, pp. 265-308.

Lin, Li-Kouang. 1949. *l'Aide-mémoire de la vraie loi (Saddharma-smṛtyu-pasthāna-sütra): Introduction au compendium de la loi (Dharma-samuc-caya). Recherches sur un Sūtra Développé du Petit Véhicule*. Publications du Musée Guimet, Bibliothèque d'Études, 54. Paris: Librairie d'Amérique et d'Orient Adrien-Maisonneuve.

Mair, Victor H. 1983. *Tun-huang Popular Narratives*. Cambridge: Cambridge University Press.

———. 1986. "Oral and Written Aspects of Chinese Sūtra Lectures (*chiang-ching-wen*)." *Han-hsüeh yen-chiu* (Chinese Studies) 4.2 (cumulative 8) (December): 311-34.

———. 1988. *Painting and Performance: Chinese Picture Recitation and Its Indian Genesis*. Honolulu: University of Hawaii Press.

———. 1989. *T'ang Transformation Texts: A Study of the Buddhist Contribution to the Rise of Vernacular Fiction and Drama in China*. Harvard-Yenching Institute Monograph Series, 28. Cambridge, Mass.: Harvard University Council on East Asian Studies.

———. 1990. "[The] File [on the Cosmic] Track [and Individual] Dough [tiness]: Introduction and Notes for a Translation of the Ma-wang-tui Manuscripts of the Lao Tzu [Old Master]." *Sino-Platonic Papers* 20 (October).

———. 1991. "What Is a Sinitic 'Dialect /Topolect'? Reflections on Some Key Sino-English Linguistic Terms." *Sino-Platonic Papers* 29 (September).

———. 1992a. "Two Papers on Sinolinguistics: 1. A Hypothesis Concerning the Origin of the Term *fanqie* ('Countertomy'); 2. East Asian Round-Trip Words." *Sino-Platonic Papers* 34 (October).

———. 1992b. "Script and Word in Medieval Vernacular Sinitic." *Journal of the American Oriental Society* 112.2:269-78.

———. 1993. "Cheng Ch'iao's Understanding of Sanskrit: The Concept of Spelling in China." *A Festschrift in Honour of Professor Jao Tsung-i on the Occasion of His Seventy-Fifth Anniversary*. Hong Kong: Chinese University of Hong Kong, pp. 331-41.

Mair, Victor H., and Tsu-Lin Mei. 1991. "The Sanskrit Origins of Recent Style Prosody." *Harvard Journal of Asiatic Studies* 51.2 (December):375-470.

Maspero, Henri. 1914. "Sur quelques textes anciens de Chinois parlé." *Bulletin de l'École Française d'Extrême-Orient* 14.4: 1-36. Translated into English as "On Some Texts of Ancient Spoken Chinese" by Yoshitaka Iriya, Ruth F. Sasaki, and Burton Watson. Kyoto: privately circulated, 1954.

———. 1934. "Les origines de la comrnunauté bouddhiste de Lo-yang." *Journal Asiatique* 225 (July-December):87-107.

Mather, Richard B. 1990. "Translating Six Dynasties 'Colloquialisms' into English: *The Shih-shuo hsin-yü*." Paper delivered at the International Conference on the Translation of Chinese Literature, organized by the Department of Foreign Languages and Literature, National Taiwan University, held at the National Central Library (Taipei, Taiwan), November 16-18.

———. 1991. Letter of March 17.

Mel, Tsu-Lin. 1980. "San-ch'ao pei-meng hui-pien li te pai-hua tzu-liao (Vernacular Materials in the Compendium of Northern Treaties of Three Emperors [1117-62])." *Chung-kuo shu-mu chi-k'an* (Bibliography Quarterly) 14.2 (September):27-52.

———. 1992a. Letter of October 8.

———. 1992b. "Vernacular Texts in Historical Context, 750-1200; Some Further Thoughts on the *Yü-lu* Form." Unpublished manuscript, 14 pp.

Miller, Roy Andrew. 1967. *The Japanese Language*. Chicago and London: The University of Chicago Press.

Mostaert, Antoine. 1977. *Le Matérial Mongol du Hua i i iu de Houng-ou* (1389). Edited by Igor de Rachewiltz, with the assistance of Anthony Schönbaum. Mélanges chinois et bouddhiques, 18. Brussels: Institut des Hautes Études Chinoises, 1977.

Nattier, Jan. 1990. "Church Language and Vernacular Language in Central Asian Buddhism." *Numen* 37.2 (December): 195-219.

———. 1991. Letter of March 13.

Ni Hai-Shu. 1948. *Chung-kuo p'in-yin wen-tzu kai-lun* (Introduction to the Chinese Phonetic Script), Shanghai: Shih-tai shu-pao.

Norman, Jerry. 1988. *Chinese. Cambridge Language Surveys.* Cambridge: Cambridge University Press.

Ohta [Ōta] Tatsuo. 1958. *Chūgokugo rekishi bunpō* (A Historical Grammar of Modern Chinese). Tokyo: Kōnan shoin.

———. 1988. *Chūgokugo shi tsūkō* (A Historical Study of Chinese Language). Tokyo: Hakutei sha.

Peake, Cyrus H. 1939. "Additional Notes and Bibliography on the History of Printing in the Far East." *Gutenberg-Jahrbuch*, ed. A. Ruppel. Mainz: Gutenberg-Gesellschaft.

Pelliot, Paul. 1929. "Neuf notes sur des questions d'Asie Central." *T'oung Pao* 26.4-5:201-65.

Pischel, R., ed. 1938. *The Deśināmamālā of Hemachandra.* Second edition by Paravastu Venkata Ramanujaswami. Bombay Sanskrit Series, 17. Bombay: The Department of Public Instruction.

Pye, Michael. 1978. *Skilful Means: A Concept in Mahāyāna Buddhism.* London: Duckworth.

Ramsey, S. Robert. 1987. The Languages of China. Princeton: Princeton University Press.

———. 1991. "The Polysemy of the Term *Kokugo.*" In Victor H. Mair, ed., *Schriftfestschrift: Essays on Writing and Language in Honor of John DeFrancis on His Eightieth Birthday. Sino-Platonic Papers* 27 (August 31):37-47.

———. 1992. "The Korean Alphabet." In Kim-Reynaud, ed., *King Sejong the Great*, pp. 43-50.

———. 1993. "The Japanese Language in Japan." Unpublished manuscript.

Rosemont, Henry, Jr. 1974. "On Representing Abstractions in Archaic Chinese." *Philosophy East and West* 24.1 (January):71-88.

Seeley, Christopher. 1991. *A History of Writing in Japan.* Leiden: E. J. Brill.

Silk, Jonathan A. 1989. "A Note on the Opening Formula of Buddhist *Sūtras,*" *Journal of the International Association of Buddhist Studies* 12.1: 158-63.

Sofronov, M. V. 1991. "Chinese Philology and the Scripts of Central Asia." *Sino-Platonic Papers* 30 (October).

Sung Lien, et al. 1976. *Yüan shih* (History of Yuan Dynasty) 15 vols. Peking: Chung-hua.

Takakusu, J. 1901. "Tales of the Wise Man and the Fool, in Tibetan and Chinese." *Journal of the Royal Asiatic Society of Great Britain and Ireland* (July 15):447-60.

Takata Tokio. 1993. "Chibetto moji shosha 'Chōkan' no kenkyū (honbun hen) (Studies on the 'Long Scroll' in Tibetan Transcription [Text])." *Tōhō gakuhō* (Journal of Oriental Studies) (Kyoto), 65 (March):313-80, plus 13 plates.

Tuan Li-Fen. 1989. "Tsui-tsao ch'u-hsien hsi-tz'u 'shih' te ti-hsia tzu-liao (The Earliest Excavated Material for the Copula *shih*)." *Yü-wen t'ien-ti* [The World of Language and Script] 6 (January): 19-21.

Unger J. Marshall. 1993. Communication to the Editor. *The Journal of Asian Studies*, 52.4 (November):949-54.

Van Gulik, R. H. 1956. *Siddham: An Essay on the History of Sanskrit Studies in China and Japan.* Nagpur: International Academy of Indian Culture.

Walker, Benjamin. 1968. *Hindu World: An Encyclopedic Survey of Hinduism.* 2 vols. New Delhi: Munshiram Manoharlal, 1983. First published by George Allen and Unwin, London.

Watters, Thomas. 1889. *Essays on the Chinese Language.* Shanghai: Presbyterian Mission Press.

Wei Cheng, et al. 1973. *Sui shu* (History of the Sui Dynasty). 6 vols. Peking: Chung-hua.

Wei Yüan. *Sheng-wu chi.* Ssu-pu pei-yao ed.

Wright, Arthur F. 1957. "Buddhism and Chinese Culture: Phases of Interaction." *The Journal of Asian Studies* 17. 1 (November): 17-42.

———. 1971. *Buddhism in Chinese History.* Stanford: Stanford University Press, 1959; rev. ed.

Yang, Paul Fu-Mien. 1989. "The *Portuguese-Chinese Dictionary* of Matteo Ricci: A Historical and Linguistic Introduction." *Proceedings of the Second International Conference on Sinology.* Taipei: Academia Sinica. Vol. 1 of the Section on Language and Script, pp. 191-242.

Zhou, Youguang. 1991. "The Family of Chinese Character-Type Scripts (Twenty Members and Four Stages of Development)." *Sino-Platonic Papers* 28 (September).

Zürcher, E. 1972. *The Buddhist Conquest of China: The Spread and Adaptation of Buddhism in Early Medieval China*. 2 vols. Leiden: E. J. Brill, rpt. with additions and corrections.

———. 1977. "Late Han Vernacular Elements in the Earliest Buddhist Translations." *Journal of the Chinese Language Teachers Association* 12.3 (October): 177- 201.

———. 1980. "Buddhist Influence on Early Taoism." *T'oung Pao* 66.1-3:84-147.

———. 1990. "Han Buddhism and the Western Regions." In W. L. Idema and E. Zürcher, eds., *Thought and Law in Qin and Han China: Studies dedicated to Anthony Hulsewé on the occasion of his eightieth birthday*. Leiden: E. J. Brill, pp. 158-72.

———. 1991. "A New Look at the Earliest Chinese Buddhist Texts." In Koichi Shinohara and Gregory Schopen, eds., *From Benares to Beijing: Essays on Buddhism and Chinese Religion in Honour of Prof. Jan Yün-hua*. Oakville, Ontario: Mosaic, pp. 277-304.

CHAPTER 8

SOUTHERN BOTTLE GOURD (*HU-LU*)

MYTHS IN CHINA AND THEIR APPROPRIATION BY TAOISM

Source: Adapted from "Southern Bottle-Gourd (*hu-lu* 葫蘆) Myths in China and Their Appropriation by Taoism", in *Zhongguo shenhua yu chuanshuo xueshu yantaohui lunwen ji* (Proceedings of the Conference on Chinese Myth and Legend), Taipei: Hanxue Yanjiu Zhongxin, 1996, vol. 1, 185-228.

Gourd symbolism is widespread in Chinese popular religion. In particular, the bottle gourd (or calabash) is used as the sign of herbal doctors, whose putative patron saint was Lü Tung-pin 呂洞賓 ("Cave Guest Lü"), one of the Taoist Eight Transcendents. Li T'ieh-kuai 李鐵拐 ("Iron Crutch Li"), another of the Eight Transcendents, is invariably associated with a bottle gourd. Still another of the Taoist Eight Transcendents, Ho-hsien-ku 何仙姑, plays the *sheng* 笙 ("free-reed mouth organ"), a southern instrument whose most primitive form was made from a bottle gourd. Several of the "Blessed Isles" of the Taoists are thought of as having the shape of a bottle gourd. Gateways, especially those leading to gardens, are often cut in the outline of a bottle gourd. Isolated utopias are frequently described in the imagery of separate, self-contained worlds existing inside of bottle gourds, and sagely Taoist transcendents are said to retreat inside of them. And so forth. The hypothesis of this paper is that all of these and many similar developments in Taoism may be traced back to southern, originally non-Sinitic, cosmogonic and anthropogonic myths having to do with chaos, creation, the flood, and the peopling of the world. In particular, Tai and Tibeto-Burman peoples such as the Dai and the Ne (Modern Standard Mandarin Yi; currently pejorative Lolo) regard the bottle gourd as central to the genesis of the universe and themselves. Philology, comparative mythology, and historical linguistics are used to substantiate this hypothesis.

The bottle gourd belongs to the genus *Lagenaria* (from lagena ["bottle"]) and has the species name *siceraria* (from *sicera* ["drinking vessel"])[1] In other words, its name redundantly tells us that this is a plant which is essentially a drinking vessel. Considering the bottle gourd's shape and one of its most frequent functions, this is an eminently reasonable name.

One form of the Chinese name for *Lagenaria siceraria* hints at essentially the same thing as the English common name and the Latin scientific name. The usual way for writing the Chinese equivalent of "bottle gourd," viz., *hu-lu*, is 葫蘆, but an alternative graphic form for writing the same word is 壺蘆. The first Sinograph used to write this word is based on a picture of a pitcher. Sometimes, because it is a plant that is in question, a grass radical is added, hence 壺蘆. Another early Sinitic word for the bottle gourd designated as *Lagenaria Leucantha* ("bottle" + "white flower" [specifying the color of the characteristic bloom of the bottle gourd]) is simply *hu* 壺, mentioned already in the *Classic of Odes* (*Shih-ching*, ostensibly sixth century BCE, but extant editions date from at least four centuries later) # 154. (Keng, 1974: 401; cf. Bretschneider, 1890–1891: 198–201) These instances show that there was a confusion between or conflation of the words for "pitcher" and "bottle gourd" in the minds of the ancient Chinese who chose this graph to represent the word for the plant.

A third scientific name for the bottle gourd, *Lagenaria vulgaris*, indicates how extremely common this plant was in the tropical and subtropical areas of the world where it normally grew. Because the bottle gourd was both common and possessed of peculiar properties, a great deal of folklore grew up around it. For instance, there is widespread belief among many people in China that their ancestors were born from a gourd. That such beliefs would develop is not surprising since the gourd has a swollen belly like that of a pregnant woman. Furthermore, it contains many seeds which is an obvious sign of its fecundity. We shall see below that such beliefs may be traced to the South, whence the plant itself derived.

The alternative English name for the bottle gourd, namely "calabash," is derived from French *calebasse* < Spanish *calabaza* < Catalan *carabaça* < Arabic *qar'ah yâbisah* ("gourd"+"dry," i.e., "dry gourd"). With this, we may compare Persian *kharbuz* ("melon"). Though Arabic is a Semitic language and Persian is an Indo-European language, the source of both *qar'ah yâbisah* and *kharbuz* must be identical.

The English word "cucumber" is most likely cognate with "gourd," even though their appearance now is quite dissimilar. "Cucumber" was borrowed from Old French *cocombre, coucombre* which, in turn, came from Latin *cucumerem*, accusative of *cucumis* (note the absence of the "b" which entered in the French to ease the assimilation of "m" and "r"). Our word "gourd" comes from French *gourde* (Old French *cöorde*) and ultimately from Latin *cucurbita* which is, without much doubt, related to *cucumis* (the initial *cu-* of these Latin words is a reduplicative syllable). It is difficult, however, to trace the Indo-European word back further than the Latin, which leads me to believe that there is no authentic Indo-European root common to all languages in the family, but rather that words for gourds and related plants were borrowed from elsewhere (see two paragraphs below).

The Chinese words for bottle gourd or calabash, which are Sinographically written in so many different ways (*hu-lu* 葫蘆，胡蘆，胡盧，壺蘆，壺廬，葫蘆，瓠蘆，瓠瓟，瓠㼻, etc.; *p'u-lu* 蒲蘆，蒲盧; *p'iao* 瓢 ("gourd dipper"); *p'ao* 匏; *hu* 瓠), must be transcriptions of an originally non-Sinitic word or words, perhaps in several topolectical forms. The addition of "grass radicals" and "cucurbit radicals" to some of these forms is a transparent attempt to assimilate these borrowings into the writing system. Nonetheless, the individual morphosyllabic graphs of the most common way for writing the word *hu-lu*, viz. 葫蘆("garlic-reed") make no sense as a combination and therefore must have been chosen merely as convenient phonetic representations of a word that was borrowed into Sinitic. The multitude of different Chinese transcriptions of the word for "bottle gourd," in specific, and the various words for different kinds of gourds, in general, were undoubtedly due to the fact that these words were borrowed into Sinitic at different times and places.[2]

I suspect that originally there was one basic world-etymon for "gourd," which sounded roughly like *kwəra* and from which "gourd," "cucumber," "cucurbit," "calabash," *kua* 瓜 (**kwəra*), *hu-lu* 葫蘆 (**ga-rja*), *hu* 壺 (**ga*), *kuo-luo* 果蠃 (**kuajʔ-gruajʔ*), Japanese *kyūri* ("cucumber") etc. are all ultimately derived. Note that there is no known Indo-European root for "gourd" since that language group originated in a cold climate where the cucurbits did not grow naturally. All gourd words in Indo-European and Sinitic languages appear to have been borrowed from language families that originated in tropical and subtropical climates.

Lagenaria siceraria was apparently native to Africa but had already spread to Asia in prehistoric times. (Heiser, 1979: 4) *Tz'u-hai* (Ocean of Phrases) declares (1989: 1576a) that *Lagenaria siceraria* was originally native to India but subsequently cultivated widely in China. *Lagenaria siceraria* must have reached the territory of what is now China as an agricultural crop at a fairly early time since the archaeological site of Hemu-tu village (c. 7000 BP) in Yü-yao County of Chekiang Province has yielded its remains. Pottery from the Pan-p'o site in Shensi, which stretches the plant even farther north beyond its normal natural growing range, includes one vessel that is said to be made in the shape of a bottle gourd.[3] (Simoons, 1991: 174; Wang, 1993: 24; Li, 1984: 59) Carter reasons (1950: 166–167) that *Lagenaria siceraria* was most likely transported to the Americas by the agency of man, perhaps as early as 1000 BCE or before (see also Handy and Handy, 1972: 212–213), although other scholars maintain that gourds reached the Americas by floating there from Africa long before the New World was populated.

The bottle gourd is the plant most often meant when gourds are mentioned without further specification. Its greatest use is as a container for both liquid and dry materials. For that reason alone, it was one of the most important plants for mankind before the development of pottery and basketry. Many primitive (and some not so primitive) peoples still rely heavily on the bottle gourd for containers, vessels, utensils (including dishes, ladles, and spoons[4]) of all sorts. The bottle gourd may also be used for food, floats and rafts, musical instruments (especially rattles, drums, and cordophones), medicine and surgery, art works, attire, pipes, snuffboxes, gunpowder flasks, bombs, penis sheaths, cricket cases, birdhouses, masks, games, charms and amulets, beggars' collection boxes, fishermen's kit boxes, diversionary decoys to attract sharks, child carriers, provision carriers for travellers, ritual summoners of wind and rain, offerings, carved decorations, and for countless other purposes. (cf. Girardot, 1983: 212; Stuart, 1911: 231) Its natural habitat lies in the tropics and subtropics of both the northern and southern hemispheres. However, because of its extreme usefulness to mankind, its range was extended into the temperate zone in some places. In their semiotic study of gourds, Norrman and Haarberg (p. 14) point out that "cucurbits are tropical plants, requiring warmth and humidity to thrive and develop. Thus in the temperate zones of the earth, where summer is something precious, the cucurbits acquire positive connotations from being associated with the summer season."

Already by the time of the earlier chapters of the *Chuang Tzu* (late fourth to mid-second century BCE), the gourd was being mentioned in Taoist literature, not only for its practical functions, but as a means of liberation:

> Master Hui said to Master Chuang, "The King of Wei presented me with the seeds of a large gourd. I planted them and they grew to bear a fruit that could hold five bushels. I filled the gourd with liquid but its walls were not strong enough for me to pick it up. I split the gourd into ladles but their curvature was so slight they wouldn't hold anything. Although the gourd was admittedly of huge capacity, I smashed it to bits because it was useless."

To which Chuang Tzu replies:

> ···Now you, sir had a five-bushel gourd. Why didn't you think of tying it on your waist as a big buoy so that you could go floating on the lakes and rivers instead of worrying that it couldn't hold anything because of its shallow curvature? This shows, sir, that you still have brambles for brains! (Mair, 1994b: 7–8)

Because of the astonishing variety of uses to which the bottle gourd was put by groups of humans living in warmer climates, it is natural that they would be thoroughly familiar with this fantastic plant, that they would reflect upon all aspects of its significance, and that they would ascribe to it powers and meanings that were not limited by its mere physical properties. Through such processes, they devised a set of interwoven myths inspired by the bottle gourd.

In his celebrated essay entitled "Fu-hsi k'ao" (Study of Fu-hsi) 伏羲考 in *Shen-hua yü shih* (Myth and poetry) 神話與詩, Wen Yi-to has collected 49 flood stories from various groups of people in China, most of them located in the south. Wen came to the conclusion that, among all of the vessels used for escaping the flood (drums, buckets, mortars, boxes, vats, beds [!], boats, etc.), the earliest form of escape and the prototype for all of the others is the bottle gourd (*hu-lu*) or, occasionally, some other type of gourd.

The following groups, among many others that could be mentioned (Li, 1984), all possess myths which link their origins to the bottle gourd: Pai 白, Chi-no 基諾, Chuang 壯, Ha-ni 哈尼, La-hu 拉祜, Kao-shan 高山, Miao 苗, Na-hsi 納西, Ne 彞, Nu 怒, Pu-yi 布依, She 畬, Shui 水, Te-ang 德昂, T'ung 侗, Wa 佤, Li 黎, Dai 傣, Yao 瑤, and Ke-lao 仡佬.[5] That so many different groups would have such a distinctive, involved, non-intuitive myth to explain their origins is remarkable and surely points to massive mutual interborrowing. In order to find the probable origin of such myths in China, we should look for their geographic center. It is clearly in the South, among non-Sinitic peoples, that cosmogonic and anthropogonic bottle gourd myths originated.

Eberhard discusses gourd myths among the Yao, Ne (Yi, Lolo[6]), and Dai cultures. (1968: 279–280) He goes on to state that practical objects made of calabash were originally common only in the South (e.g., in Hainan) and that decorated objects made of gourd did not become common in China proper (viz., the north) until the seventeenth century. The various types of cucurbitaceous plants have a southern distribution and are correspondingly very important in southern mythology. Gourds are in general suited for warm climates, so it is natural that they would play a far more prominent role in the autochthonous lore and mythology of the south than in that of the north. T'ao Yang and Mou Chung-hsiu (1990:102–144, 259ff.) also document the vital importance of *hu-lu* in creation myths and myths of ethnogenesis of southern peoples. In Wang Hsiao-lien's comprehensive study of the myths of the peoples of southwestern China, the centrality of the calabash is unmistakable (1992b: *passim*, esp. 393–404 [closing section of the book]). By contrast, his investigation of the myths of northern peoples reveals that rocks and stones occupy a comparable position among them (1992a; 1994: 179–188; cf. Jing Wang, 1992).[7]

Dang Nghiem Van, in a recent study (1993), has gone beyond Wen Yi-to, Eberhard, and other scholars in collecting over 300 myths of a great deluge that is found among virtually every ethnic group in mainland Southeast Asia. Common to many of these myths is the survival of two individuals (usually brother and sister) who consummate an incestuous marriage and give birth to a gourd or a gourd-shaped lump of flesh. The gourd, in turn, is the source of the various ethnic groups in a given locality. Judging from the omnipresent centrality of such myths among mainland Southeast Asian groups and their secondary status in northern Chinese myth cycles, it would seem obvious that they passed from the former to the latter.

The bottle gourd is thought to be the ancestral patriarch of the Ne people and the *hu-lu-sheng* ("bottle gourd mouth organ") produces the music of the ancestral patriarch (more accurately identified as a matri-arch, as we shall soon see). (Liu Hsiao-hsing, 1990) The bottle gourd is seen as a symbol of mother worship and secondarily as a symbol of ancestor worship in general. Some scholars hold that the importance of the bottle gourd in ancestor worship among the southern peoples must reflect the lofty position of women in their primitive, matrilineal societies. (Zixian Li, 1984)

There are also Polynesian myths about the peopling of the world that feature gourds. (Heiser, 1979: 202–204) Similarly, the Wa people of Indochina believe that all sixty races of the world came from a great gourd and that all the animals of the world came from another gourd. (Heiser, 1979: 204–205)

Among all of these peoples, it would appear that nowhere are bottle gourd symbolism and myths more pervasive, prominent, and prevalent than among the Ne. In any event, Ne scholars in the last couple of decades have done yeoman service in collecting and analyzing this lore. As a representative sample of the sort of interpretation that might be carried out for other southern peoples, let us review here some of their findings.[8]

In her *Tao-chia hun-t'un che-hsüeh yü Yi-tsu ch'uang-shih shen-hua* (The Taoist Philosophy of Chaos and the Ne People's Myth of Creation), P'u Chen argues that the Taoist notion of *hun-t'un* ("chaos") 混沌 is related to Ne (i.e., Yi) myths about the creation of the world and the bottle gourd figures prominently in these myths. Her method is not textual, but rather is based on folkloristic and ethnographic materials collected from the people. Through extensive fieldwork, she has intensively studied the oral traditions of the Ne people themselves.

According to P'u Chen, there exists among the Ne a series of interconnected myth systems dealing with Chaos, Creation, and the Flood. All three of these systems have been adapted into Han culture and are known in Modern Standard Mandarin (MSM) as *hun-t'un, k'ai-p'i* 開闢, and *hung-shui* 洪水. How does the bottle gourd (*hu-lu*), which holds such a special position among the Ne, fit into all of this interwoven mythology? The answer is that in the symbolism of the bottle gourd is embraced both the myth of chaos and that of the creation of the world. In other words, for the stage before the creation of the world (*k'ai-p'i t'ien-ti* 開闢天地), the bottle gourd itself symbolizes chaos (*hun-t'un*), but after the creation of the world, the bottle gourd symbolizes the genetrix from which humanity is produced or proliferated. The bottle gourd thus stands for the unity of heaven and humanity (*t'ien-jen he-yi* 天人合一) and is the basis for what P'u Chen calls the "bottle-gourd culture" (*hu-lu wen-hua* 葫蘆文化) of the Ne people and, through them, of the Chinese people as a whole. (see also Liu Yao-han, 1985: 37–46, 99–101, 222–231)

The bottle gourd may also be seen as intimately related to the Ne flood myth. Like a natural sort of Noah's ark, the bottle gourd functions as a vessel that enables a select pair to ride out the flood safely and repopulate the world. Among the Ne people, the flood myth is still a very popular theme, one which is recited widely by young and old alike. There can be no doubt whatsoever that the bottle gourd is crucial to their flood stories. There is a common core to all of the variants of the Ne flood myth collected by P'u Chen in Yunnan, Szechwan, and Kweichow which we shall relate in the following paragraph.

In the distant past, a flood covered the earth and destroyed all the life thereon except for a brother and sister (Apu and Dumu; var. Fu-hsi and Nü-wa). They were directed by the spirit of heaven to enter a bottle gourd so that they could escape the disaster. After the flood receded, the bottle gourd came to rest precariously on a bamboo that was growing from a rocky precipice. Whenever the wind blew, the bottle gourd would wave precariously as though it were about of fall into the yawning abyss. Fortunately, a hawk flew by and grasped the vine-stem[9] of the bottle gourd in its claws. After placing the bottle gourd on a level place at the top of the cliff, the hawk flew away. Thus saved from the flood, the brother and sister repopulated the earth, becoming the ancestors of post-diluvian humanity.

Some of the flood stories current among the Ne people who live in the mountains along the banks of the Chin-sha River 金沙江 preserve only one or two of the three main elements of the myth (bottle gourd, hawk, bamboo) and few preserve all three. The bottle gourd, however, seems to be essential and lies at the heart of the Ne flood myths. The bottle gourd is the most primitive, natural sort of vessel that could be imagined for escaping the flood. No human artifice is required to fashion it. The bottle gourd, symbolizing the genetrix, rescues humanity from the flood and enables humankind—now purified—to reproduce itself.

Thus the bottle gourd is seen as the mother's body and its swollen base is her womb. The Ne have many customs which reflect the identification of the bottle gourd with motherhood. For example, in P'u Chen's own ancestral village in southern Yunnan, there is a marriage custom which goes as follows: when the groom takes the bride to his home, just before they enter the wedding chamber, a bottle gourd filled with ashes is smashed on the ground in front of them. This is to ensure that the newly married couple will soon give birth to children. The gourd symbolizes the maternal body and smashing the gourd causes its fecundity to permeate the bridal chamber. In another Ne village, after her daughter becomes pregnant, a mother is supposed to present her with a bottle gourd that is hung on the wall at the head of her bed to protect the daughter and her child.

P'u Chen has another book, *Chung-hua ch'uang-shih hu-lu: Yi-tsu p'o hu ch'eng-ch'in, hun kuei hu-t'ien* (The Gourd of Chinese Creation: Breaking the Pot to Become Married and the Returning of Souls to Pot-Heaven among the Ne people), which is devoted to the use of the bottle gourd in wedding ceremonies and other important Ne rituals. P'u Chen maintains that the smashing of the gourd, causing the ashes inside to fly up and consecrate the air inside of the bridal chamber, is a key Ne ritual. *Chung-hua ch'uang-shih hu-lu* is about how this unusual ritual came into being, the background and ramifications of the custom of "breaking the gourd and becoming married" (*p'o hu ch'eng ch'in* 破壺成親).

As we have seen, the bottle gourd symbolizes—among many other things—the maternal, fertile body (the womb). It has acquired these connotations in conjunction with its larger cosmogonic and anthropogonic symbolism. That is to say, the bottle gourd symbolizes the womb as productive universe. Inside, it is dark and empty, but all the myriad things are produced from it. In his brilliant study of bottle gourd myths, Lathrap (1977) makes a convincing case that the metaphor of the gourd as universal womb is a pan-tropical myth. Hence, we may conjecture that the Southeast Asian and South Chinese myths of this type may have spread from the homeland of the bottle gourd along with the transmission of the plant. Good evidence that this myth complex may have originated closer to the botanical home of the bottle gourd is found in the ancient Indian epics *Rāmayāna* (I.38) and *Mahābhārata* (III.106, etc.) where Sumati, a wife of King Sagara in Ayodhyâ, gives birth to a gourd from which 60,000 handsome boys emerge! (Eliade, 1949: 260) Chi Hsien-lin (1984: 104) points out that the operative term in the Râmâyana passage is *garbhatumba* which quite literally means "womb-gourd" in

Sanskrit. India also possesses a folk-tale of escape from the deluge in a gourd. (Thompson, 1989: vol. 1, p. 187)

The "bottle-gourd mouth organ" (*hu-lu-sheng*) is the quintessential instrument of the Ne, the Dai, and other South Chinese and Southeast Asian peoples. (*Min-tsu tz'u-tien*, p. 1045b; Miller, 1994: 266) With its numerous bamboo pipes, bamboo (now bronze) reeds, and calabash wind-chest, this instrument and the music it produced were fraught with cosmological significance. Many southern peoples hold the mythical inventor of the bottle-gourd mouth organ to be none other than Nü-wa, their primeval ancestress (subsequently accepted in the same role by mainstream Han culture). (Schafer, 1967: 53, 56, 107, 254–257) In her study of the role of Nü-wa in the myths about the creation of mankind among various southern peoples, Hong Liu stresses (1983: 149) that the bottle-gourd mouth organ "plays an indispensable part in the Miao[10] custom of 'moon dancing' which is held every year in February, and which resembles the ancient ceremony of reveling at the yearly sacrifice to the goddess of marriage."

Mark Bender (1990) has written an interesting paper in which he describes the social setting for the performance of an antiphonal folk epic among the Miao of southeast Kweichow. The epic, entitled *Hxak Hmub*, includes the expected motifs of the flood, the calabash, brother-sister incest, and gourd-like ball of flesh. It is noteworthy that the epic is performed in the context of a festival in which young men energetically play their treasured mouth organs (whose wind-chests were originally made of bottle gourds) as accompaniment for courtship dancing. So characteristic is the bottle gourd of Miao culture that the Chinese frequently referred to some of them as "Bottle-Gourd Miao" (Hu-lu Miao 葫蘆苗). (Hostetler, 1995: 48, 105, 179, 264, 265) To this day, the Chinese still refer to the bottle-gourd mouth organ of the Miao, Ne, Dai, and other southern peoples as *hu-lu-sheng* 葫蘆笙.

It is significant that the bottle-gourd mouth organ eventually becomes the emblem of the only female among the taoist Eight Transcendents,

Ho-hsien-ku 何仙姑. Indeed, Ho-hsien-ku is undoubtedly a transformation of Nü-wa. Her existence among the Eight Transcendents and her identification with the bottle-gourd mouth organ is yet another strong reinforcement of the thesis that there is an inseparable connection between southern, non-Sinitic culture and Taoism. (Werner, 1961: 347–348) I suspect, in fact, that the word *sheng* 笙 itself may be traceable to the Sinitic transcription of some such Southeast Asian word as *khaen* or *khen*, but cannot yet prove it.

The *khaen*, or "free-reed mouth organ" is played throughout almost the whole of Southeast Asia (Laos, Northern Thailand, Upper Burma, South China, and southward to North Borneo). (Baines, 1992: 184) The *sheng* is almost certainly an elaborated, refined, and sophisticated adaptation of the *khaen*. The earliest known archaeologically recovered *sheng* in China is a superb lacquered instrument of gourd and bamboo from the tomb of the Marquis Yi of Cheng dated to the last half of the fifth century BCE (see *Archaeology* [January/February, 1994], pp. 42–51). It is significant that this site, located in Sui-chou (Hu-pei province), belongs to the Ch'u culture which is transitional between north and south and is the cradle of early Taoist thought. The Sinograph for *sheng* does not show up until the time of the small seal script which means that the instrument probably first became well known among the Chinese not much earlier than about the late third century BCE. This is around the same time that we see bottle-gourd themes cropping up in early Taoist literature and probably reflects the achievement of a significantly enhanced level of interaction between northern Chinese and southern non-Chinese peoples.

That the *sheng* is derived from the *khaen* is obvious from the shape of its wind-chest. Whether made of lacquered wood or plated metal, it still retains the shape of a small gourd. This conclusion is assured by the discovery of an unusual mouth organ wind-chest at Stone Stockade Mountain (Shih-chai shan 石寨山) in Yunnan. What is remarkable about this particular wind-chest is that, though made of bronze, it unmistakably bears the shape of a gourd. (Bunker, 1972: section 4 and fig. 10) Furthermore, it dates to the second century BCE and belongs to the non-Sinitic Tien 滇 culture. The Tien were the most powerful sub-tribe of the Mi-mo 靡莫 among the so-called "Southwestern Barbarians" and are clearly related both to the famous Dong-son bronze drum culture of Southeast Asia and to later ethnic groups who succeeded them in the same area of Yunnan. What is most intriguing, both about the Tien culture and about the Dong-son culture, is that art historians and ethnographers have discovered tantalizing linkages in weaponry, armor, bronze technology, cowry hoarding, motifs and designs, etc. with peoples far to the west. This is a topic of extreme importance requiring intensive investigation in a separate paper.

The early assimilation of the mouth organ into transcendental Taoism is evident in such legends as that about Wang-tzu Ch'iao (Chin) 王子喬(晉) in chapter 28 of the *Lieh-hsien chuan* (Biographies of Exemplary Transcendents) 列仙傳 (first century BCE or first century CE [?]), where it is said that "he loved to play the *sheng* with which he produced the cry of the phoenix." 好吹笙作鳳鳴 (Kaltenmark, 1953: 109)

The bottle gourd is prominent among the Ne as the sign of medical practitioners and there are many folk customs among the Ne which relate the bottle gourd to healing. In the end, however, everyone must die, and the bottle gourd even finds a role in Ne beliefs and rituals related to death. According to the Ne, after one dies, his/her soul goes back into the bottle gourd whence it originally came. In many Ne villages, the graves are made in the shape of a bottle gourd. Many "Han" families, particularly in the south, have adopted this originally non-Sinitic custom.

For the Ne, the bottle gourd symbolizes both chaos and the womb: the womb is chaos and chaos is the womb. All of the many other mythic roles of the bottle gourd derive from this fundamental cosmogonic and anthropogonic myth.

Southern Bottle Gourd (*hu-lu*)

What we have learned of the Ne people's attachment to the bottle gourd may also be said, *mutatis mutandis,* of many other southern, non-Sinitic peoples. For example, Li Zixian (1984; 1991: 135–150) has gathered together some of the Dai people's beliefs about the bottle gourd. As with nearly all other Southeast Asian peoples, calabash myths circulate widely among the Dai of Yunnan. Bottle-gourd myths among the Dai (part of the Tai group) consist of three main types: 1. human beings originated from a calabash; 2. the calabash served as a floating vessel to rescue humankind from the Flood; 3. all living plants and animals originated from the calabash. He then summarizes the myths of what he calls the "calabash culture" of numerous other groups in south China under the following three rubrics: 1. humankind is born more or less directly from a bottle gourd; 2. the origination of man from a calabash and the marriage of a brother and sister are condensed into one pattern; 3. the calabash is simply a flood-avoiding vessel for the brother and sister.

The sibling marriage of Fu-hsi and Nü-wa is an important mainstream Chinese myth (Birrell, 1993: 203–204 and *passim*), but it is both more pervasive among southern, non-Sinitic peoples and more tightly integrated in a coherent mythology focusing on the flood, the peopling of the world, and the calabash. One cannot help but gain the impression that the elements of the myth of Fu-hsi and Nü-wa present in the north have been deracinated from their natural environment and not fully absorbed into their alien surroundings. Perhaps one of the reasons Chinese mythology is so "fragmentary" (as numerous scholars studying it have often remarked) is the multiple derivation from diverse, non-Sinitic peoples of many of its major components. This is not, of course, to deny that other factors such as Confucian bias against myth may also have been operative in its fragmentation.

In the collection of stories from Yunnan edited by Lucien Miller, the bottle gourd figures prominently in connection with the flood, brother-sister marriages, and the creation of human beings.[11] For the Chi-no, it is seen as the womb and symbol of the gourd-ancestress, Apierer, who was planted by a twin brother and sister (Mahei and Maniu) after they had survived the flood. (pp. 68–72) The Li-su are represented by a mythic tale of the great flood in which brother and sister escape disaster by floating it out in an enormous gourd. (pp. 79–80) A similar Chuang myth has Fuyi and his sister (clearly related to the Chinese myths of Fu-hsi and Nü-wa) ride out the flood in a gourd as big as a house. (pp. 147–148)

The association of southern peoples with the bottle gourd is so close and so distinctive that the Han Chinese even referred to some of them with that epithet. For instance, "Bottle-Gourd King" (Hu-lu Wang 葫蘆王) was used for the leader of the Wa tribal confederation[12] and the Han Chinese specified the hilly regions where the Wa lived as " Land of the Bottle-Gourd King" (Hu-lu wang ti 葫蘆王地) or "Bottle-Gourd Kingdom" (Hu-lu kuo 葫蘆國). Some Ne settlements were designated by the Han Chinese as "Bottle-Gourd Stockades" (Hu-lu Chai 葫蘆寮) (*Tz'u-hai* (Ocean of Phrases), 1576; Liu, 1990: 32)

The image of the bottle gourd is still highly productive for literature and art among the southern peoples. One of the best known literary works of the Dai is called "Letter in a Bottle Gourd." It is an epic love story linked to historical events of the 1860s.

Much of the southern bottle-gourd symbolism described above that is not absorbed into Chinese mythology is taken up directly into Taoism. The holiest of the holy in the Taoist tradition, Lao Tzu (the Old Master) himself, is associated with the bottle gourd. The Taoist temple at Ch'ing-ch'eng Shan 青城山 (Szechwan) houses the *Tai-shang Lao Tzu Tao-te ching* (Classic of the Way and Integrity of the Supreme Old Master) 太上老子道德經. Accompanying the text are a series of narrative paintings entitled *Lao shih sheng-chi t'u* (Pictures of the Sacred Records of Mr. Old) 老氏聖紀圖. One scene shows Lao Tzu riding an ox, in front of which is an acolyte carrying the Old Master's staff with a bottle gourd. (P'u, 1993b: 88)

Southern Bottle Gourd (*hu-lu*) 299

There is even a Taoist master of sublime profundity who is called Master Bottle/Gourd 壺子. Accounts of him are found in chapter 7 of the *Chuang Tzu* and scattered through chapters 1, 4, and 8 of the *Lieh Tzu* 列子. The *Chuang Tzu* account, one of the most powerful in the book, presents him as a master of nondifferentiation, i.e., of chaos. A curious, but telling, detail of the Hu Tzu legend is that he is once described as looking like "damp ashes" (*shih hui* 濕灰). Speculations abound about the meaning of this characterization, none of which are very convincing. 1 would suggest that it may have something to do with the Ne practice of filling the bottle gourd with ashes in several of the rituals in which it is used. Other suggestive phrases in the *Chuang Tzu* account of Master Hu are that he is "stopped up" (*tu* 杜), that he "flows with the waves" (*yi wei po liu* 以為波流), and so forth. In any event, it would appear that, like the bottle gourd, Master Hu ("Bottle/ Gourd") represents the undifferentiated wholeness of chaos. This is the overall cosmology not only of Hu Tzu, but also of the *Lao Tzu*, the *Lieh Tzu*, and the *Chuang Tzu*.

Many old Taoist texts, some in the Taoist canon and others on stelae, declare that the world can be transported in a gourd. (Stein, 1990: 54) Others view the world, especially ideal, isolated worlds, as gourd-shaped. Taoists often imagine these separate paradises as caves that are difficult to enter because their entrances are narrow and are followed by a passageway like the neck of a bottle. (Stein, 1990: 58–77) Nakano Miyolo has written a fascinating, well documented and profusely illustrated book about Taoist utopias in the shape of bottle gourds. (1991: esp. 215–263 for the parts of Szechwan occupied by the Ne; see also Miura Kunio, 1988, 1984) For Taoists of a more metaphysical stripe, the bottle gourd constituted an entire little universe (*hu-t'ien* 壺天). Those who practiced the "Way of the Great Elixir" (*ta-tan chih tao* 大丹之道) would display a bottle gourd as a sign of their professional commitment and might be referred to as " Sir Bottle Gourd" (*hu-kung* 壺公).

There exists a delightful painting of a "Hu-lu hsien (Bottle-Gourd Immortal)" 葫蘆仙 by the famous fifteenth-century Soochow painter,

Shen Chou 沈周 (1427–1509) (fig. 15). The poem inscribed by the artist reads as follows:

> This carefree immortal, without post or portfolio, makes his home
>   on P'eng-lai Isle and Fang-hu Mountain;
> Thatch-headed, hair a mess, a jolly face is always his.
> You ask how he is endowed with understanding
>   so broad and content;
> It is the bottle gourd—there he preserves his vitality pristine.
>   (translated by Marc F. Wilson in *Eight Dynasties,* p. 191)

This poem and the charming portrait express perfectly the Taoist association of bottle gourds with transcendence.

A quixotic depiction of a full-sized man emerging from a large bottle gourd (Fig. 16) may be found in Wang Shih-chen 王世貞, ed., *Lieh-hsien ch'üan-chuan* (Complete Biographies of Exemplary Transcendents) 列仙全傳 (Ming period woodblock printed book, dated 1598). This scene is based on the legend of Fei Ch'ang-fang 費長房, a market official who lived during the Eastern Han period (25–220). It was said that, upon seeing the bottle gourd of a medicine seller hanging outside the old man's stall, he got the urge to crawl in and did so when the market closed. Fei found the world inside the gourd much to his liking and consequently decide to pursue the Tao 道 ("Way").

We have already observed that the only female among the Taoist Eight Transcendents is indissolubly linked with the bottle gourd by her emblematic mouth organ. Two of the other Eight Transcendents are also associated with the bottle gourd. T'ieh-kuai Li 鐵拐李 ("Iron Crutch Li") carries a bottle gourd from which issues a wisp of *ch'i* ("vapor," "material energy") and the bottle gourd is prominent in the legends which are told about him. (Werner, 1961: 343–344; see also fig. 12) Lü Tung-pin 呂洞賓 ("Cave [!] Guest Lü; 798–?), the presumably late T'ang Taoist master, was honored by the Ch'üan-chen ("Whole Truth") 全真 sect as one of its Northern Five Patriarchs 北五祖. (Werner, 1961: 298, 348–349) Lü Tung-pin was viewed by medical practitioners in traditional China as a sort of patron saint. Here, too, bottle-gourd symbolism is operative, for doctors and pharmacists often hang out a gourd as their sign or they write out in Sinographs the expression " suspend a bottle/gourd to heal the world" (*hsüan hu chi shih* 懸壺濟世). This practice became common throughout most of traditional China, but it derives from a southern belief system. We have already seen how the Ne, for example, believe that the bottle gourd possesses curative powers. It is no accident, therefore, that Ne herbalists frequently carry one or more bottle gourds at their waist in which to store their medicines. The same custom eventually spread to most of traditional China.

Taoist priests, too, often used to hang a gourd from their waists.[13] If one asked them why they do so, one would probably receive a multitude of answers, such as that it symbolizes their healing abilities, paradise, alchemy, longevity, chaos, the genetrix, and so forth. Indeed, different priests would be apt to favor different interpretations, depending on their own predilections and emphases. One thing, however, seems certain: the Taoist's bottle gourd is a clear mark of his ultimately southern, non-Sinitic origins.

The centrality of the gourd is evident in even such esoteric and elaborate Taoist ritual as that employed for the expulsion of the plague. For example, at Wenchow, when the county magistrate wished to submit a memorial confessing his inadequacies (which were presumed to have brought on the plague) to the Emperor of Heaven (T'ien-ti 天帝, most likely the Jade Emperor), the Taoist priests performing the ceremony would ascend a nine-level platform, blowing horns and pacing the Steps of Yü 禹步. Then they would open a gourd out of which poured yellow smoke that set the memorial ablaze and sent it up to heaven. (Katz, 1995: 488)

The bottle gourd has become so thoroughly assimilated to Taoism (or perhaps we should say that Taoism has become so thoroughly assimilated to bottle-gourd culture) that it is a constant metaphor for many aspects of Taoist thought and practice. As we have already seen, it is a perfect symbol of undifferentiated chaos, of Taoistic paradises, and so forth. But the bottle gourd is even more intimately connected with Taoist alchemy, for it can be used to store and mix the magic elixirs which were believed to bestow longevity. (Tai, 1962: 150-151) This led to the Chinese custom of old men wearing it on their backs as charms for longevity. Still today, copper amulets in the shape of a bottle gourd are worn around the neck or wooden ones (preferably made from an old man's coffin) around the wrist. (Williams, 1974: 217; personal observation) Art historians Julia M. White and Emma C. Bunker note (1994: 196) the wide distribution of bottle-gourd-shaped earrings during the Ming period. "Because of the gourd's durability and association with immortality, its shape was often worn as a charm for longevity."

The presumed curative powers of the gourd were of such high repute in old China that its mere shape was thought to protect people from disease:

> The gourd-shell, or a painting of the gourd on wood or paper, or a small wooden gourd, or a paper cut in shape like a perpendicular section of the gourd, or a paper lantern made in shape of a gourd, is in frequent use ... as a charm to dissipate or ward off pernicious influences. Children often wear about their persons a representation or picture of the gourd. The shell of this vegetable is sometimes hung up near the place where the children who have not yet had the small-pox sleep during the last night of the year. This custom is explained by the Chinese by saying that a certain god of the small-pox and measles will "*empty*" the small-pox into the gourd-shell, and not into these children, if he should observe one ready. Afterward, when they break out with the small-pox, they will have it slightly. Some families take a lantern resembling the gourd, and bind it on the neck of each of their children who have not had the small-pox during the last evening of the year, where it is worn until they go to bed.[14] (Doolittle 1865: 315–316)

Here we see a belief that has gone far beyond Taoism and permeated deeply into popular Chinese consciousness and practice. Many people throughout China still subscribe to these Taoistically imbued folk customs.[15] We must remember, however, that the marvelous efficacy of the bottle gourd is ultimately due not to Taoism *per se* but to its roots in southern, non-Sinitic notions of cosmogony and the origins of humanity.

The bottle gourd is such an indispensable part of Chinese life that it has entered into many common expressions and sayings. For example, a *men-hu-lu* 悶葫蘆/胡盧 is a "closed gourd," "a mystery," "something difficult to comprehend." Or consider the saying, *Ta-te hu-lu li tao-ti mai-te shih shen-me yao?* 他的葫蘆裏到底賣的是甚麼藥? ("What trick does he have up his sleeve?"), referring to the mysterious and powerful abilities of the southern healer who has been absorbed into the larger Chinese social fabric. *An-hsia hu-lu fu-ch'i piao* 按下葫蘆浮起飄 means "to solve one problem only to find another cropping up." The expression *chih-siang hu-lu* 吉祥葫蘆 ("bottle gourd of good omen") derives from a custom in which a calabash cut from three-colored paper (red, green, and yellow) is pasted above the door of one's house on the morning of the first day of the fifth month of the year to capture evil spirits which are destroyed when it is taken down and thrown away in the evening. This custom, in turn, led to the notion of *hu-lu wan-tai* 葫蘆萬代 ("bottle gourd for ten thousand generations") which implies that one's family will have offspring and prosperity for a very long time. (*Ts'ai-t'u feng-su*, 1991: 88) Since these sayings were popular during the Ch'ing (Manchu) period in the area of Peking and Tientsin quite apart from Taoism, this is a clear indication of how far north southern ideas about the felicitous power of bottle gourds had reached. It is no accident, then, that the bottle gourd is mentioned in so many of the other articles in this volume (e.g., those by Riftin , Niga [Wei Te-ming], Hsieh Chien, Yang Ju-pin, Lu Yi-lu, and others). Truly, this seemingly odd and unimportant plant serves as a metaphor for life itself and its significance has spread far from the area of its origins.

Lynda Shaffer has written (1994) a stimulating article entitled "Southernization" in which she proposes that a wide spectrum of important cultural influences flowed from South Asia northward during the first millennium of our era and for several centuries thereafter. Much support could easily be garnered for her hypothesis in matters large and small. (Mair, 1988, 1990, 1994a) It would appear that Taoism, both in its transcendental and in its popular guises, is fundamentally a product of this general movement. This is by no means to say that Taoism was solely a product of Southernization, or that Taoism as it developed later in northern China is not a distinctive cultural phenomenon. What is being asserted is the need to be aware of the subtleties of all cultural phenomena. In our estimation, the origins of all cultural phenomena are extremely complex and it is the duty of the scholar to attempt to discover as accurately as possible which are local and which come from elsewhere. Taoism is quintessentially Chinese, but its multiple sources help us to understand what is truly meant by "Chinese."

Jerry Norman and Tsu-Lin Mei (1976) have demonstrated the southern, Austroasiatic roots of several important words that have been borrowed into Sinitic. (see also Norman, 1988: 18) One particularly telling example is that of *chiang* 江, the ancient name of the Yangtze River. The Old Sinitic reconstruction of this hydronym is roughly *krung*. This is clearly congruent with such Austroasiatic forms as Vietnamese sông (< Old Vietnamese *krong*), written Mon *krung*, Brou *kroung*, and Katu *karung*. What is particularly remarkable about *chiang* is that it shows how far north the South actually reached in antiquity. With the expansion of northern Chinese civilization southward, the South has receded, but not without leaving its traces in language, mythology, customs, cooking, and a myriad other phenomena, should one care to look for them. In fact, the southern, originally non-Sinitic, peoples may not have totally withdrawn after all. Ruofu Du, *et al.* (1992) have proven through genetic and surname analysis that there is a dramatic split between north and south China which lies approximately along the Yangtze River.[16] Finger whorl patterns, teeth structure, physical anthropology, and blood types all confirm this radical differentiation between the populations north and south of the Yangtze River. (Turner, 1989; Du and Yip, 1993; Cavalli-Sforza, et al., 1994: 78, 232) My own hypothesis is that Chinese civilization was formed during the Late Neolithic and the Bronze Age through the fusion of three main elements: "Altaic" from the north, Austroasiatic and Austronesian from the south (including, of course, Thai and Miao-Yao [whose phyla are disputed]), and Indo-European from the West. (cf. Chang, 1988). Since 1987, I have been working on a book on this subject (ostensibly and nominally about the origins of the Chinese script but in actuality about the origins of Chinese civilization) which will be published in four volumes in the year 2000.

There can be little doubt that popular Taoism has important southern, originally non-Sinitic linkages. A fuller study would reveal that mystical, intellectual Taoism, as it was adumbrated in the *Tao Te Ching*, the *Chuang Tzu*, the *Huai-nan tzu*, and other works that have been archaeologically recovered in recent decades (Peerenboom, 1993), is also intimately connected with southern traditions.[17] These southern, Taoistic cultural elements stand in contrast with the basically Confucian traditions of the north and with the Buddhist tradition which came into China from the west (also from the southwest and by sea). We have known all along that Chinese thought and religion were composed of these three basic strands—Buddhism, Taoism, and Confucianism. What may not have been so evident is that these three basic strands of Chinese culture possess important, geographic, genetic, linguistic, ethnic, and —consequently—temperamental characteristics. It is only through the interweaving of all three basic strands that Chinese culture as a whole has come into being. Chinese culture, like Chinese civilization, is fundamentally diverse.

From the time of its earliest formation, Chinese civilization has been enriched by elements of culture drawn from the many non-Sinitic peoples living within and around the borders of its expanding territory. Indeed, so fundamental are the non-Sinitic components of Chinese civilization that one may well be inclined to think of it as an amalgamation of other cultures. In this paper, we have seen how a single southern mythopoeic symbol could be absorbed by the dominant (northern) Chinese civilization in amazingly productive and influential ways. As a sort of methodological test-case, we have examined the origin and role of bottle-gourd symbolism and mythology in China in hopes of better understanding the formation and nature of Chinese culture as a whole.[18]

ACKNOWLEDGMENTS

Many thanks to Norman Girardot for letting me peek into his precious gourd box; to Dan Boucher for chasing down the vermilion bird; to Michael Carr for donations of cucurbitic lore from his vast store of Sinographic esoterica; to Stevan Harrell for instructing me in the nuances of Lolo; to Kezia Knauer for encyclopedic knowledge of Late Bronze Age and Iron Age art across the whole of Eurasia; to Carolyn Han for tracking bottle gourd myths, symbols, and stories all the way from Yunnan to Hawaii; to Emma Bunker for her outstanding command of current sources on ancient art and archaeology; to Barry Blakeley for doing more than perhaps any living Sinologist to open up the ancient South to scholars; to Mark Bender for first-hand observations of Ne and Hmong life; to Charles Hartman for bringing together art and poetry in exciting and perceptive fashion; to John Lagerwey for thoughts from the field; to Eugene Anderson for mastery of wisdom about all manner of comestibles from Central Asia to Central America; to Robert S. Bauer for having the vision to see the continuities of language throughout time and space; and, above all, to little Candy Wei for wearing a bottle-gourd amulet and making me wonder why. In spite of all the help they have given me, none of the above named should be held responsible for the infelicities and idiosyncracies of this article, which are attributable solely to the author.

Southern Bottle Gourd (*hu-lu*) 307

Figure 12. T'ieh-kuai Li ("Iron Crutch Li"), one of the Taoist Eight Transcendents.

Source: Adapted from "Southern Bottle-Gourd (*hu-lu* 葫蘆) Myths in China and Their Appropriation by Taoism," *Zhongguo shenhua yu chuanshuo xueshu yantaohui lunwen ji* (Proceedings of the Conference on Chinese Myth and Legend), Taipei: Hanxue Yanjiu Zhongxin, 1996, vol. 1, 224.
Note. Many other Taoist holy men beside T'ieh-kuai Li are depicted bearing a gnarled, knotty staff from which hangs a bottle gourd (e.g., Stein 1990: 100). The staffs symbolize longevity and the gourds symbolize both their curative abilities (because of the medicinal herbs inside) and the utopian worlds of primitive chaos into which they sometimes retreat. (Doré 1915: IX, fig. 148).

308 CHINA AND BEYOND BY VICTOR H. MAIR

Figure 13. Inverted bottle-gourd visage based on the traditional Peking Opera mask of Liu T'ang, known as the "Redhaired Devil."

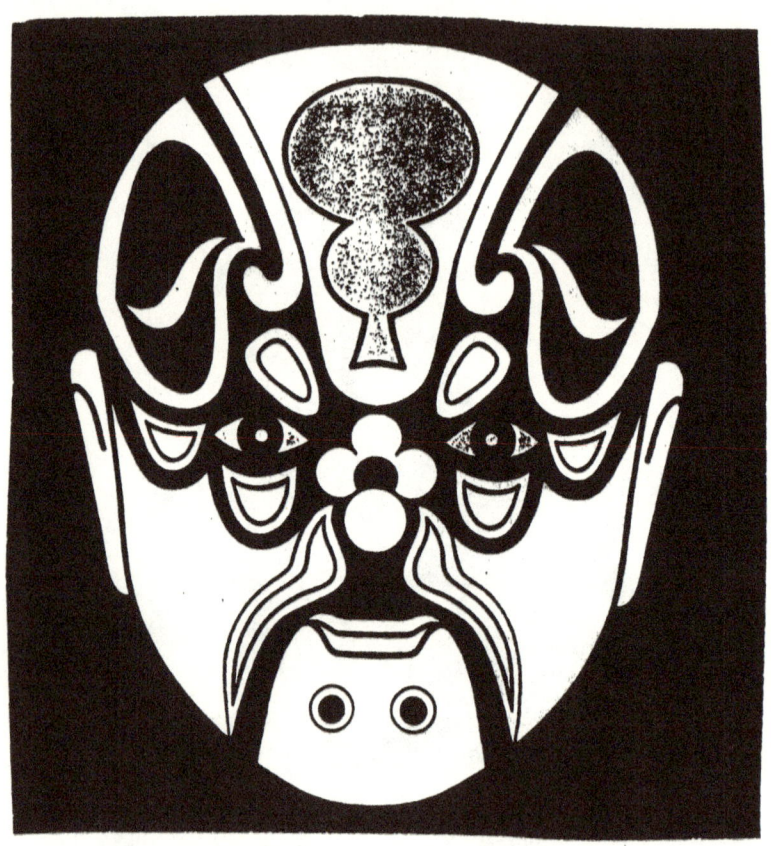

Source: Originally from Girardot, 1983: dust jacket. Adapted from "Southern Bottle-Gourd (*hu-lu* 葫蘆) Myths in China and Their Appropriation by Taoism," *Zhongguo shenhua yu chuanshuo xueshu yantaohui lunwen ji* (Proceedings of the Conference on Chinese Myth and Legend), Taipei: Hanxue Yanjiu Zhongxin, 1996, vol. 1, 225.
Note. This is a good example of the appropriation of an ancient southern symbol by recent, popular northern culture.

Figure 14. A stamp issued by the Republic of China.

Source: Adapted from "Southern Bottle-Gourd (*hu-lu* 葫蘆) Myths in China and Their Appropriation by Taoism," *Zhongguo shenhua yu chuanshuo xueshu yantaohui lunwen ji* (Proceedings of the Conference on Chinese Myth and Legend), Taipei: Hanxue Yanjiu Zhongxin, 1996, vol. 1, 226.
Note. This stamp, issued by the Republic of China, shows beautifully the fundamentally eclectic nature of Chinese culture. The cosmogonic bottle gourd provides the basic shape of the design; it represents the southern, Taoistic component of Chinese culture. The deer symbolizes official emoluments (*lu* 鹿 = *lu* 祿); it represents the northern, Confucian component of Chinese culture.

Figure 15. "The Bottle-Gourd Immortal" by Shen Chou.

Source: From Cleveland Museum of Art, *Eight Dynasties of Chinese Painting*, p. 190, no. 156. Adapted from "Southern Bottle-Gourd (*hu-lu* 胡蘆) Myths in China and Their Appropriation by Taoism," *Zhongguo shenhua yu chuanshuo xueshu yantaohui lunwen ji* (Proceedings of the Conference on Chinese Myth and Legend), Taipei: Hanxue Yanjiu Zhongxin, 1996, vol. 1, 227.

Southern Bottle Gourd (*hu-lu*) 311

Figure 16. Fei Chang-fang inside of his utopian calabash.

Source: Adapted from "Southern Bottle-Gourd (*hu-lu* 葫蘆) Myths in China and Their Appropriation by Taoism," *Zhongguo shenhua yu chuanshuo xueshu yantaohui lunwen ji* (Proceedings of the Conference on Chinese Myth and Legend), Taipei: Hanxue Yanjiu Zhongxin, 1996, vol. 1, 228.
Note. A similar scene may be found in *San-ts'ai tu-hui* (Illustrated Encyclopedia of the Three Realms) 三才圖會. This woodblock print and the painting reproduced in Fig. 16 were called to my attention by Charles Hartman, to whom I am most grateful.

Notes

1. Here I add selected portions of a learned note sent to me by my friend Kezia Knauer on May 2, 1995:

   ···[T]here is no Latin word sicera= "drink ing vessel"; there is, however, a Greek word (I transcribe) sikera= "fermented liquor" (probably of Semitic origin), and—more important—sikys, -os or sikyos, -ou= cucumber (sýkia in modern Greek) and sikýa= bottle-gourd, since Aristotle, HA 616a22 (Lagenaria vulgaris). Latin lagena, or better, lagona, lagoena, laguna, is derived from Greek lágynos, which, in turn, has no known etymology. The Greek word lágynos means a wine bottle in the shape of a bottle gourd—many depictions are known and real examples have been found.... The word traveled along the trade routes across the Alpine passes to southwestern Germany in the early Middle Ages (wine was imported that way): Lägel= "wine cask".

   The Persian word *kharbuz* appears in modern Greek as *karpousi*. The pumpkin, or bottle-gourd, Greek *kolokýnthe*, or *kolokýnte*, Latin *cucumis*, both have no known etymology (probably pre-Indo-Germanic). The best description is in Pliny, *Nat.* 19, 69–74. You probably have heard of Seneca's satire *Apokolokýnthesis* ridiculing the apotheosis of the deceased emperor Claudius. In modem Greek *kolokythia* also means "nonsense".

2. There is great need for a careful listing of gourd words from South China and Southeast Asia. So far, I have only been able to check Chuang equivalents for *hu-lu*. They are *gyoux, hozloz.,* and *lwggyoux.* See Gvangjsih Bouxcuengh Swcigih Saujsu Minz-cuz Yijyenz Vwnzsw Gunghcoz Veijyenzvei Yenzgiusiz, comp., *Sawloih Gun Cuengh (Sinitic-Chuang Glossary)*, p. 108a and Gvangjsih Bouxcuengh Swcigih Saujsu Minzcuz Yijyenz Vwnzsw Gunghcoz Veijyenzvei Yenzgiusiz, comp., *Sawloih Cuengh Gun (Chuang-Sinitic Glossary)*, pp. 429b, 488b. A more thorough comparison of gourd words in other languages and in Old Sinitic reconstructions would surely be revealing but is beyond the scope of this paper and requires separate, linguistic treatment. // The terminology for bottle gourds (which apparently do not grow wild in the Pacific region but are cultivated from seed and hence must have been

introduced by human agency from Southeast Asia during the relatively late peopling of the region) in Hawaiian is extensive. Here I list a few of the more suggestive items for comparative purposes: *hulilau* (broad giant *Lagenaria*), *huewai-puali* (bottle gourd with constriction around the middle), *huewai* ("water bottle" with bulbous base and long, thin neck), *hokeo* (somewhat pear-shaped but with constriction above the middle, used by fishermen to hold their kits and by voyagers as water containers), *hue* (gourd in general; also means "bottle, flask, narrow-necked container"!!). (Handy and Handy, 1972: 213–214)

3. Kominami (1989) has written a scholarly survey of the textual and archaeological sources for gourd-shaped objects in early China. His article also includes a consideration of the ritual meaning of these objects.
4. The shape of the typical Chinese porcelain soup spoon is actually based on that of a section of a bottle gourd with the bottom conveniently flattened for stability when it is set down.
5. All of these names are Modern Standard Mandarin (MSM) transcriptions or other Chinese designations for the groups in question. Although it would be much preferable in other contexts to use the authentic self-references of these groups, because of the audience to which this paper is directed, the Chinese equivalents are employed here.
6. This is one of the self-references of the Ne people. According to the Ne authors cited elsewhere in this paper, it means "tiger" which is their totemic animal. Many villages are called Lolo. Unfortunately, like "oriental," "Eskimo," and other names,"Lolo" is now considered by certain influential groups to be pejorative. Other names for the Ne include Nousu, Ngosu, Asi, Laka , Laulau, Leisu, Mosu, Ne(i)su, No, Norsu, Nosu, Pula, Shani, Lolopo, Lipo, etc. I suspect that Yi is merely the rough MSM transcription of one such native ethnonym as Ne, although the Ne do not have a corresponding term in their own language(s) that includes all of the groups named above. (Yi as a "catch-all" term is not an indigenous usage; rather, like Miao [see note 10], it is a usage imposed by Chinese scholars and bureaucrats.) " Ne" is my attempt to find a name that is as broad as Yi but sounds like a native word.
7. Wang Hsiao-lien (1994: 183) documents the existence of gourd myths among Koreans and Japanese. In the case of Korea, some of the gourd symbolism derives from Indo-Buddhist sources and some is due to being part of the general Chinese *Kulturkreis* which had already absorbed cucurbitic symbolism from the South. In the case of Japan, they derive

from the Southeast Asian component of the culture which is made up mainly of Austronesian, Austroasiatic, Scythian (Iranian), and "Altaic" elements.

8. Since the Ne (a Tibeto Burman group) alone have approximately 7,000,000 population and are one of the biggest so-called "minorities" in China, their influence even today should not be underestimated. Combined with the populations of other Austroasiatic and Tibeto-Burman people in South China who have still not been Sinicized and who still follow their old customs and lore, the significance of myths such as those recounted here for the Ne is by no means negligible.

9. Among some southern peoples, the vine of the bottle gourd is used as a sky-rope to ascend to heaven and thus escape from the flood waters.

10. Miao is the MSM transcription of an ethnonym pronounced variously by natives as Hmong, H'moong, Hmu, Mhong, Hmao, and so forth. It is obvious that the Chinese have simply dropped an important initial phoneme of the name. Although early Chinese descriptions of the Hmong often expatiate upon their name as having to do with "sprouts," that meaning is purely an adventitious artifact of the Sinograph arbitrarily used to write the Sinitic transcription of the ethnonym. The Hmong speak a language that is a branch of the Miao-Yao group within the hypothetical Sino-Tibetan family. Cf. note 6 above.

11. Giradot, *Myth and Meaning*, Appendix 1, offers deluge myths from a number of people of South China and Southeast Asia in which a couple (usually a brother and sister) float to safety in a gourd.

12. The Wa are a Mon-Khmer group within the Austroasiatic family.

13. According to Eberhard (1986: 45-46):

> The bottle-gourd is a typical part of the magician's or the Taoist's paraphernalia. It contains his magic potions and so forth. The story about a Taoist who goes inside a bottle-gourd is well-known; his voice can be heard outside before he emerges. The bottle-gourd is a miniature replica of heaven and earth: in its shape it unites the two. When it is opened, a sort of cloud comes out which can be used to trap demons. Temple paintings depicting the battles between good and evil gods (scenes based usually on the celebrated early 17th-century novel "The Metamorphoses of the Gods" [*Feng-shen yen-yi*]) show the bottle-gourd as an active protagonist on the side of the good, helping them to victory over their evil opponents. A bottle-gourd embellished with arabesques expresses the wish for "Ten thousand generations of sons and grandsons." A bottle-gourd decorated

with arabesques and roses signifies the wish that "Spring may last for ten thousand generations"—i.e., that the recipient family may last forever. On the feast of the summer solstice (the 5th day of the 5th month) a bottle-gourd made of paper is hung up at the gateway into the house.

Scattered reports from informants in the field indicate that some itinerant "Taoists" still carry a bottle gourd with them in their wanderings.

14. Mark Bender (personal communication [May 8, 1995]) speculates that these beliefs may ultimately derive from the "curing" of smallpox vaccine in tenth-century Szechwan. Smallpox scabs from a lightly infected patient were "cured" in some sort of container, then administered on cotton in the mucous membranes of the nose.
15. According to Eugene Anderson (personal communication [May 1, 1995]), thirty years ago when he was working with Hong Kong fishermen, they would put tiny wooden model calabash amulets on their children (usually on bracelets) as symbolic floats (magically protecting the children from falling overboard and drowning). In fact, real-size wooden floats were shaped like gourds. // Similarly, in the old part of Nanning (Kwangsi), a number of houses have large stone decorations in the shape of calabashes on the corners of their roofs (though many of them are now being torn down). This is a clear indication of the apotropaic qualities attributed to the bottle gourd. // A Japanese friend of mine, Takeuchi Tsuguhito 武内紹人, whose house was destroyed in the great Kobe earth-quake of 1995, is rebuilding it with two large bottle gourds (Jap. hyōtan 瓢箪) at either end of the roof to protect it from future disasters.
16. In subtle and not-so-subtle ways, the Chinese north and south of the Yangtze delta viscerally recognize this fundamental distinction without resorting to scientific evidence. Witness the strong prejudice against northern Kiangsu (Su-pei) individuals in Shanghai. Culturally, however, the historical divide between north and south is exceedingly complex. For example, one of the best-known early southern groups was the Ch'u, yet their cosmology and religion show affinities with northern steppe cultures. (Major, 1977) Archaeological evidence is now beginning to show that elements of northern steppe culture had already penetrated south of the Yangtze by the pre-Ch'in period. // Even within a linguistically coherent southern group such as the Ne, there are cultural and historical variations that need to be taken into account. For example, Ne

—being a Tibeto-Burman language—probably came from farther north into southwest China. Perhaps the early Ne peoples themselves adopted calabash myths, along with other elements of southern culture, as they came south down the river valleys off the grasslands. The Nosu of Ta-liang-shan in Szechwan seem to have retained some of the older northern lifestyle and are in many ways very different from the Ne of Yunnan who are in general more "southernized."

17. The institutions, canon, iconography, practices, and doctrines of religious Taoism were strongly influenced by Yoga, Buddhism, and other Indo-Iranian religions, but this is not the place to discuss these matters, adequate coverage of which would require virtually book-length treatment.

18. The same sort of methodology could be applied to countless other facets of Chinese culture. To take the example of another economic plant, tea is usually regarded as a quintessentially "Chinese" drink, yet its native area of production is in the non-Sinitic region of northeastern Assam, northern Burma, and western Yunnan. Tea was scorned as a *man* 蠻 ("barbarian") beverage until well into the T'ang period (618–907 CE) and it was not fully accepted in the north until the Sung period. (Mair, forthcoming) Thus, we can learn much about the history of culture from such seemingly mundane, yet magnificent, plants as tea and the bottle gourd.

References

Backus, Charles
    1981 *The Nan-chao Kingdom and Tang China's Southwestern Frontier.* Cambridge University Press.

Baines, Anthony
    1992 *The Oxford Companion to Musical Instruments.* New York: Oxford University Press.

Bender, Mark
    1990 "'Felling the Ancient Sweetgum': Antiphonal Folk Epics of the Miao of Southeast Guizhou." *Chinoperl Papers*, 15: 27–44.

Berliner, Nancy Zeng
    1986 *Chinese Folk Art: The Small Skills of Carving Insects.* Boston: Little, Brown, and Co.; A New York Graphic Society Book.

Birrell, Anne
    1993 *Chinese Mythology: An Introduction.* With a foreword by Yuan K'o. Baltimore: The John Hopkins University Press.

Bretschneider, E.
    1890–1891 "Botanicum Sinicum: Notes on Chinese Botany, from Native and Western Sources." *Journal of the China Branch of the Royal Asiatic Society*, 25: i–ii, 1–468.

Bunker, Emma C.
    1972 "The Tien Culture and Some Aspects of its Relationship to the Dongson Culture." In Noel Barnard, ed., *Early Chinese Art and Its Possible Influence in the Pacific Basin.* A Symposium Arranged by the Department of Art History and Archaeology, Columbia University, New York City, August 21–25, 1967. 3 vols. New York: Intercultural Arts Press. Vol. 2, pp. 291–328.

Carter, George F.
    1950 "Plant Evidence for Early Contacts with America." *Southwestern Journal of Anthropology.* 6: 161–182.

Cavalli-Sforza, L. Luca, Paolo Menozzi, and Alberto Piazza

    1994 *The History and Geography of Human Genes.* Princeton: Princeton University Press.

Chang, Tsung-tung

    1988 "Indo-European Vocabulary in Old Chinese: A New Thesis on the Emergence of Chinese Language and Civilization in the Late Neolithic Age." *Sino-Platonic Papers,* 7: i+56 pages.

Chi, Hsien-lin 季羨林

    1984 "Kuan-yü hu-lu shen-hua (On Bottle-Gourd Myths)" 關於葫蘆神話. *Min-chien wen-yi chi-k'an* (Collected Papers on Folk Arts) 民間文藝集刊. No. 5. Shang-hai wen-yi ch'u-pan-she.

Cleveland Museum of Art

    1980 *Eight Dynasties of Chinese Painting: The Collections of the Nelson Gallery-Atkins Museum/Kansas City, and the Cleveland Museum of Art.* With essays by Wai-kam Ho, Sherman E. Lee, Laurence Sickman, and Marc F. Wilson. Cleveland: Cleveland Museum of Art, in cooperation with Indiana University Press.

Dang, Nghiem Van

    1980 Cleveland Museum of Art *Eight Dynasties of Chinese Painting: The Collections of the Nelson Gallery-Atkins Museum/Kansas City, and the Cleveland Museum of Art.* With essays by Wai-kam Ho, Sherman E. Lee, Laurence Sickman, and Marc F. Wilson. Cleveland: Cleveland Museum of Art, in cooperation with Indiana University Press.

    1993 "The Flood Myth and the Origin of Ethnic Groups in Southeast Asia." *Journal of American Folklore,* 106 (421): 304–337.

Dingle, Edwin John

    1911 *Borderlands of Eternity.* Embracing "Across China on Foot" Bristol, England: J. W. Arrowsmith; New York: Henry Holt.

Doolittle, Justus

    1865 *Social Life of the Chinese: With Some Account of Their Religious, Governmental, Educational, and Business Customs and Opinions, with Special but not Exclusive Reference to Fuchau.* 2 vols. New York: Harper and Brothers. Taipei: Ch'eng-wen, 1966 rpt.

Doré, Henri

1911–1918 *Recherches sur les Superstitions en Chine.* Variétés Sinologiques No. 44. 18 vols. Shanghai Imprimerie de la Mission Catholique.

Du, Ruofu and Vincent F. Yip

1993 *Ethnic Groups in China.* Peking and China: Science Press.

Du, Ruofu, Yida Yuan, Juliana Hwang, Joanna Mountain, L. Luca Cavalli-Sforza

1992 *Chinese Surnames and the Genetic Differences between North and South China.* Monograph Series Number 5 of *Journal of Chinese Linguistics.*

Eberhard, Wolfram

1968 *The Local Cultures of South and East China.* Translated from the German by Alide Eberhard. Leiden: E. J. Brill. Revised version of *Lokalkulturen im alten china.* Vol. 1. Monograph vol. 3 of *Monumenta Serica,* Peking, 1943. Supplement to *Toung Pao,* 37. Leiden: E. J. Brill, 1943.

1986 *A Dictionary of Chinese Symbols: Hidden Symbols in Chinese Life and Thought.* Translated from the German by G. L. Campbell. London: Routledge and Kegan Paul. Originally published as *Lexikon chinesischer Symbole.* Cologne: Eugen Diederichs, 1983.

Eliade, Mircea

1949 *Traité d histoire des religions.* Paris: Payot.

Girardot, N.J.

1983 *Myth and Meaning in Early Taoism: The Theme of Chaos (hun-tun).* Berkeley: University of California Press. For extensive bibliographical references relating to all aspects of gourds, see pp. 329–387 and 401–409

Gvangjsih Bouxcuengh Swcigih Saujsu Minzcuz Yijyenz Vwnzsw Gunghcoz Veijyenzvei Yenzgiusiz, comp.

1983 *Sawloih Gun Cuengh* (Sinitic–Chuang Glossary). N.p.: Kuangh-hsi min-tsu ch'u-pan-she.

1984 *Sawloih Gun Cuengh* (Sinitic–Chuang Glossary). N.p.: Kuangh-hsi min-tsu ch'u-pan-she.

Handy, E.S. Craighill and Elizabeth Green Handy

1972 With the collaboration of Mary Kawena Pukui. *Native Planters in Old Hawaii: Their Life, Lore, and Environment.* Bernice P. Bishop Museum Bulletin 233. Honolulu: Bishop Museum Press.

Harrell, Stevan, ed.

1995 *Cultural Encounters on China's Ethnic Frontiers.* Seattle: University of Washington Press.

Heiser, Charles B.

1979 *The Gourd Book.* Norman: University of Oklahoma Press.

Hostetler, Laura

1995 "Chinese Ethnography in the Eighteenth Century: Miao Albums of Guizhou Province." University of Pennsylvania Ph. D. dissertation.

Kaltenmark, Max

1953 *Le Lie-sien Tchouan* (Biographies légendaires des lmmortels taoïstes de l'antiquité). Peking: Université de Paris, Publications du Centre d'études sinologiques de Pékin.

Katz, Paul

1995 "Plague God Cults in Late Imperial Chekiang: A Case Study of the Cult of Marshall Wen." In *Si-miao yü min-chien wenhua yen-t'ao-hui lun-wen-chi* (Papers of the Conference on Temples and Popular Culture) 寺廟與民間文化研討會論文集 Taipei: Han-hsüeh yen-chiu chung-hsin. Pp. 459-504.

Keng, Hsuan

1974 "Economic Plants of Ancient North China Mentioned in *Shih Ching* (Book of Poetry)." *Economic Botany,* 28 (October–December): 391–410.

Kominami Ichirô 小南一郎

1989 " Ko-kei no uchû (The Bottle-Shaped Universe)" 壺型の宇宙. *Tôhô gakuho* (Journal of Oriental Studies) 東方學報, 61: 165–221.

Lathrap, Donald W

1977 "Our Father the Cayman, Our Mother the Gourd: Spinden Revisited, or a Unitary Mode for the Emergence of Agriculture in the New World." In *The Origins of Agriculture.* Ed. By Charles A. Reed. The Hague: Mouton. Pp. 713–751.

Li, Tzu-hsien 李子賢

    1991 *Tan-hsün yi-ke shang wei peng-k'uei te shen-hua wang-kuo—chung-hua hsi-nan shao-shu min-tsu shen-hua yen-chiu* (Searching for a Legendary Kingdom that Has Not Yet Collapsed—Studies on the Myths of China's Southwestern Minorities) 探尋一個尚未崩潰的神話王國—中國西南少數民族神話研究. Kunming: Yün-nan ch'u-pan-she.

Li, Zixian

    1984 "On the Dai Calabash Myth." Translated from Chinese by Shin Kun 史昆. *Cowrie, A Chinese Journal of Comparative Literature*, 1.2: 54–64.

Liu, Hong

    1983 "Myths of the Creation of Mankind in Chinese Mythology and the Myths of Nu Gua [*sic*], the Accepted Chinese Creator of Mankind." *Journal of Asian Culture*, 7: 121–151.

Liu, Hsiao-hsing 劉小幸

    1990 *Mu-t'i ch'ung-pai—Yi-tsu tsu-ling hu-lu su yüan* (Worship of the Mother's Body—Tracing the Origins of the Ancestral Bottle Gourd Spirit of the Yi People) 母體崇拜—彝族祖靈葫蘆溯源. Yi-tsu wen hua yen-chiu ts'ung-shu (Studies on the Culture of the Yi People) 彝族文化研究叢書. Kunming: Yunnan jen-min ch'u-pan-she.

Liu, Yao-hao 劉堯漢

    1980 "Chung-hua min-tsu te yüan-shih hu-lu wen-hua (The Primitive Bottle-Gourd Culture of the Chinese People)" 中華民族的原始葫蘆文化. In *Yi-tsu she-hui li-shih tiao-ch'a yen-chiu wen-chi* (Collection of Investigative Research Papers on the History of Ne Society) 彝族社會歷史調查研究文集. Peking: Min-tsu ch'u-pan-she. (not seen)

    1985 *Chung-kuo wen-ming yüan-t'ou hsin-t'an—Tao chia yü Yi-tsu hu yü-chou-kuan* (Investigation into the Origins of Chinese Civilization—Taoism and the Tiger Weltanschauung of the Ne People) 中國文明源頭新探—道家與彝族虎宇宙觀, Kunming: Yünnan jen-min ch'u-pan-she.

Mair, Victor H.

    1984 Review of N. J. Girardot, *Myth and Meaning in Early Taoism*. In *Pacific Affairs*, 57.2 (Summer), 318–319.

1988 *Painting and Performance: Chinese Picture Recitation and Its Indian Genesis.* Honolulu: University of Hawaii Press, 1988.

1990a "[The] File [on the Cosmic] Track [and Individual] Dough [tiness]: Introduction and Notes for a Translation of the Ma-wang-tui Manuscripts of the *Lao Tzu* [*Old Master*]." *Sino-Platonic Papers,* 20 (October). 68 pages.

1990b Tr., annot., and comm. *Tao Te Ching: The Classic Book of Integrity and the Way.* New York: Bantam

1994a "Introduction and Notes for a Complete Translation of the *Chuang Tzu.*" *Sino-Platonic Papers,* 48 (September). xxiv+110 pages.

1994b Tr., annot. and comm. *Wandering on the Way: Early Taoist Tales and Parables of Chuang Tzu.* New York: Bantam.

Forthcoming "The Southern Origins of Tea-drinking in China and Its Late Adoption in the North."

Major, John S.

1977 "Research Priorities in the Study of Ch'u Religion." *History of Religions,* 17 (August): 226–243. *Min-tsu tz'u-tien* (Dictionary of Nationalities) 民族詞典.

1987 Shanghai: Shang-hai tz'u-shu ch'u-pan-she.

Miller, Lucien, ed. and intro.

1994 *South of the Clouds: Tales from Yunnan.* Tr. from Modern Standard Mandarin by Guo Xu, Lucien Miller, and Xu Kun. Seattle: University of Washington Press.

Miura Kunio 三浦國雄

1988 *Chūgokujin no toposu-dōkutsu, fūsui, kochūten* (Topoi of the Chinese) 中國人のトポス—洞窟・風水・壺中天. Tokyo: Heibonsha.

1994 *Ki no Chūgoku bunka – kikō, fūsui, eki* (The Chinese Culture of ch'i-kung, Nourishing Life, Geomancy, and Change) 氣の中國文化—氣功・養生・風水・易. Tokyo: Sogensha.

Nakano Miyiko 中野美代子

1991 *Hyōtan man-yû roku: kioku no naka no chishi* (Record of a Bottle-Gourd Tour: Topography of the Inside of Memory). ひょうたん漫遊録：記憶の中の地誌. Tokyo: Asahi shinbunsha.

Norman, Jerry

1988 *Chinese*. Cambridge: Cambridge University Press.

Norman, Jerry and Tsu-Lin Mei

1976 "The Austroasiatics in Ancient South China: Some Lexical Evidence." *Monumenta Serica*, 32: 274–301.

Norrman, Ralf and Jon Haarberg

1980 *Nature and Language: A Semiotic Study of Cucurbits Literature*. London: Routledge & Kegan Paul.

Peerenboom, R. P.

1993 *Law and Morality in Ancient China: The Silk Manuscripts of Huang-Lao*. Albany: State University of New York Press.

P'u Chen 普珍

1993a *Chung-hua ch'uang-shih hu-lu: Yi-tsu p'o-hu ch'eng-ch'in, hun kuei hu-t'ien* (The Gourd of Chinese Creation: Breaking the Pot to Become Married and the Returning of Souls to Pot-Heaven among the Yi People) 中華創世葫蘆—彝族破壺成親，魂歸壺天. Yi-tsu wen-hua yen-chiu ts'ung-shu (Yi Culture Studies Series) 彝族文化研究叢書. Kunming: Yün-nan jen-min ch'u-pan-she.

1993b *Tao-chia hun-t'un che-hsüeh yü Yi-tsu ch'uang-shih shen-hua* (The Taoist Philosophy of Chaos and the Yi People's Myth of Creation) 道家混沌哲學與彝族創世神話. Yi-tsu wen-hua yen-chiu ts'ung-shu (Yi Culture Studies Series) 彝族文化研究叢書. Kunming: Yün-nan jen-min ch'u-pan-she.

Schafer, Edward H.

1967 *The Vermilion Bird: T'ang Images of the South*. Berkeley and Los Angeles: University of California.

Schuessler, Axel

1987 *A Dictionary of Early Zhou Chinese*. Honolulu: University of Hawaii Press.

Shaffer, Lynda

    1994 "Southernization." *Journal of World History*, 5.1: 1–21.

Simoons, Frederick J.

    1991 *Food in China: A Cultural and Historical Inquiry*. Boca Raton, Ann Arbor, and Boston: CRC Press.

Stein, Rolf A.

    1990 *The World in Miniature: Container Gardens and Dwellings in Far Eastern Religious Thought*. Translated by Phyllis Brooks. Stanford: Stanford University Press, 1990. Originally published in 1987 by Flammarion as *Le monde en petit: jardins en miniature dans la pensée religieuse d ExtrêmeOrient*.

Stuart, G. A.

    1911 *Chinese Materia Medica: Vegetable Kingdom*. Shanghai: American Presbyterian Mission Press.

Tai, Yüan-ch'ang 戴輝長, ed.

    1962 *Hsien-hsüeh t'u-tien* (Dictionary of Transcendent Studies) 仙學辭典. Taipei: Chen-shan-mei ch'u-pan-she.

T'ao, Yang 陶陽 and Mou, Chung-hsiu 牟鐘秀

    1990 *Chung-kuo ch'uang-shih shen-hua* (Creation Myths of China) 中國創世神話. Chung-kuo wen-hua shih ts'ung-shu (Cultural History of China Series) 中國文化史叢書. Taipei: Tung-hua shu-chü.

Thompson, Stith

    1989 *Motif-Index of Folk-Literature: A Classification of Narrative Elements in Folktales, Ballads, Myths, Fables, Mediaeval Romances, Exempla, Fabliaux, Jest-Books and Local Legends*. Revised and enlarged edition. 6 vols. Bloomington: Indiana University Press.

Ts'ai-t'u feng-su tz'u-tien (Color Illustrated Dictionary of Customs) 彩圖風俗詞典

    1991 Shanghai: Shang-hai tz'u-shu ch'u-pan-she.

Turner, II, Christy G.

    1989 "Teeth and Prehistory in Asia." *Scientific American*, 260.2: 88–91.

Tz'u-hai (Ocean of Phrases) 辭海

    1989 3 vols. Shanghai: Shang-hai Tz'u-shu ch'u-pan-she.

Wang Hsiao-lien 王孝廉

    1992a *Chung-yüan min-tsu te shen-hua yü hsin-yang* (Myths and Beliefs of the People of the Central Plains) 中原民族的神話與信仰. *Chung-kuo te shen-hua shih-chieh* (The World of Chinese Myth) 中國的神話世界# hsia-pien (B) 下編. Wen-hua ts'ung shu (Culture Series) 文化叢書, 108. Taipei: Shih-pao wen-hua.

    1992b *Tung-pei, hsi-nan tsu-ch' ün chi ch'i ch'uang-shih shen-hua* (People of the Northeast and Southwest and Their Creation Myths) 東北，西南族羣及其創世神話. *Chung-kuo te shen-hua shih-chieh* (The World of Chinese Myth) 中國的神話世界, shang-pien (A) 上編. Wen-hua ts'ung-shu (Culture Series) 文化叢書, 107. Taipei: Shih-pao wen-hua.

    1994 *Shui yü shui-shen* (Water and Water Deities) 水與水神. Chung-hua min-su wen-ts'ung (Chinese Folklore Series) 中華民俗文叢. Peking: Hsüeh-yüan ch'u-pan-she.

Wang, Jing

    1992 *The Story of Stone: Intertextuality, Ancient Chinese Stone Lore, and the Stone Symbolism, in Dream of the Red Chamber, Water Margin, and Journey to the West.* Durham: Duke University Press.

Wang Shixiang 王世襄

    Shuo hu-lu (The Charms of the Gourd) 說葫蘆. Translated by Hu Shiping 胡世平 and Yin Shuxun 殷書訓. Hong Kong: Next Publication.

Wen Yi-to 聞一多

    1956 *Shen-hua yü shih* (Myth and Poetry) 神話與詩. Peking: Chung-hua shu-chü.

Werner, E. T. C.

    1961 *A Dictionary of Chinese Mythology.* New York: Julian. Originally published by Kelly and Walsh in Shanghai, 1932.

White, Julia M. and Emma C. Bunker

1994 *Adornment of Eternity: Status and Rank in Chinese Ornament.* Denver: Denver Art Museum in association with The Woods Publishing Company.

Williams, C. A. S.

1974 *Chinese Symbolism and Art Mottifs.* Rutland, Vermont: Charles E. Tuttle, third rev. ed. Originally published as *Outlines of Chinese Symbolism and Art Motives.* Shanghai: Kelly and Walsh, 1941.

CHAPTER 9

MA JIANZHONG

AND THE INVENTION OF CHINESE GRAMMAR

Source: Adapted from "Ma Jianzhong and the Invention of Chinese Grammar," *Studies on the History of Chinese Syntax* (*Journal of Chinese Linguistics*, Monograph Series, 10), ed. Chaofen Sun (Stanford, Calif. : *Journal of Chinese Linguistics*, 1997): 5-26.

1. INTRODUCTION

The earliest grammars of Chinese, which started to appear in the first half of the 17th century, were all written by Westerners. It was not until Ma Jianzhong (1845–1900) wrote his *Ma shi wentong* (Ma's Grammar) at the very end of the 19th century that the Chinese themselves started to write their own grammars. A complete translation and analysis of the second preface to Ma's work reveals his motivations and methods, which were strikingly different from those of early Western sinologists. Whereas Ma was concerned entirely with the application of Greek and (mostly) Latin models to Classical Chinese, believing that this systematization would lead to prosperity for his ancient nation, the Westerners focused primarily on the vernaculars as the real, living languages of

China and viewed Classical Chinese almost as an artificial construct that was nonetheless an important repository of the wisdom of the past.

Perhaps what I ought to have written for this symposium was a paper on the extensive syntactical rearrangements and readjustments brought about by the impact of Indo-Iranian languages and Tocharian on Medieval Vernacular Sinitic during the process of translating the Buddhist canon into Chinese. I suspect that some such topic may have been what the organizers of this symposium had in mind when they invited me to attend. Indeed, this is a very important subject to which I have given much thought during the last two decades and more. Unfortunately, that topic is too big to handle adequately at the present time, so I have decided to do something more manageable, namely, to investigate the reasons for the invention of a native grammar of Chinese at the end of the 19th century and the nature of that initial grammar written by a Chinese.

Actually, for those who may—quite justly—have expected me to say something about the study of language in India, because of my background in Indology it is almost impossible for me to avoid doing so, if only by way of comparison with attitudes toward language in China. So I will not totally disappoint them in that respect. However, before plunging into an examination of the first grammar of Chinese written by a Chinese, I need to justify why I am discussing grammar at a conference on syntax.

The reasons are so elementary that I will not spend much time defending myself, except to point out merely that, viewed functionally, syntax is to an isolating language what morphology is to an inflected language. Hence, it is entirely appropriate that conferences such as this on syntax are held for Sinitic instead of conferences on morphology. It is probably no accident that the late, lamented Father Paul Yang did not even include grammar in his classification of Chinese linguistics.[1] Technically speaking, syntax (the juxtaposition of words to form phrases and sentences) is one of the major parts of grammar, the others being—

first and foremost—morphology, phonology, semantics, and etymology. Dionysius Thrax (2nd century B.C.E.), who wrote the first systematic grammar in the Western tradition, dealt only with word morphology; for Dionysius Thrax grammar was tantamount to morphology. It is remarkable that not until Apollonius Dyscolus (2nd century C.E.) was the study of syntax added to grammar. Since the most important part of grammar as conventionally conceived (namely, morphology) is arguably absent in Sinitic languages, as they have evolved under the influence of and are represented in writing by the sinographic script, one might make the claim that, in the strictest sense, the science of grammar as a whole is not applicable to Sinitic, whereas syntax is absolutely crucial for the construction and analysis of Sinitic sentences, particularly as written in the sinographic script.

To be sure, it would be far easier to make a case that, historically, China had already developed its own awareness of syntax by the Song period. Su Shi 蘇軾 (1036–1101) and Yan Yu 嚴羽 (c. 1200–c. 1270) were using the expression *jufa* 句法 with the meaning of "sentence structure," although admittedly it did not become the basis of a rigorous system of syntactical analysis until this century. Conversely, the Sinitic words that we now use for "grammar," *wenfa* 文法 and *yufa* 語法, are essentially calques, what I call "round-trip words." They are "round-trip words" because they started out in China with one set of meanings, then were transported to Japan where—through contact with Western concepts current during the period of "Dutch learning" and the Meiji Restoration—they were invested with an entirely new set of meanings and sent back to China. (Some would argue that the calquing process was simultaneously occurring under missionary influence within China itself and this is true to a certain extent, but it can readily be demonstrated that the vast majority of these new terms were being coined in Japan.[2]) Naturally, there were far more outright neologisms (translations and transcriptions) created to cope with the flood of new terms coming to East Asia from the West, but the calques that I refer to as "round-trip words" constitute a significant subset of the rapidly expanding vocabulary.

2. Historical Background and Translation

There was not a single grammar, not a single compendium of usage for any Sinitic language until the first half of the 17th century when (ironically, but then again, as we shall see, perhaps naturally) Westerners began to compose them. The first that I know of is the *Arte de la Lengua China* by Juan Cobo, O. P. (Ordo Praedicatorum ["Order of Preachers," i.e., the Dominicans]). After that came another by Francisco Diaz O. P. (1606–1646), written in the Philippines around 1641, and so forth.[3] It is curious, but extremely revealing, that these epochal Western grammars were almost all on one or another of the living vernacular languages: Mandarin (especially Nankingese), Min, Shanghainese, Cantonese, etc. The living vernaculars were a subject in which Chinese scholars themselves had shown virtually no interest, except with the intention of occasionally attempting to assimilate isolated elements from them into the literary language

The first grammar of a Sinitic language written by a Chinese was not composed until 1898 (still less than a century ago!) and, even then, this was a grammar of the classical book language as it existed in texts dating back to two thousand and more years before. The author had studied and passed a number of examinations in Paris. Later he went to India and Korea on diplomatic missions; there he also came in contact with foreigners. He was well versed in Latin, Greek, French, and German. His name was Ma Jianzhong 馬建忠 and the title of his book is Ma's Grammar (*Ma shi wentong*[4] 馬氏文通).

It is significant that the author of China's first indigenous grammar was also one of the earliest in a long stream of his countrymen who studied abroad and returned to introduce radically new ideas to their motherland. Ma was from Jiangsu and received his early education in Shanghai. He then went to France in 1876 and, after finishing his education, worked for a while as a translator in the embassy of the Qing (Manchu) government before going back to China where he served as the foreign language secretary of the famous statesman Li Hongzhang

李鴻章. Ma's brother, Ma Xiangbo 馬相伯 (1840-1939), evidently helped him to compile the *Ma shi wentong*, but the extent of the older brother's involvement is not known.

How very different is the situation for India, that other great civilization of Asia! If Sinitic may be said to be the last major group of languages in the world to have grammars compiled for them, Sanskrit was definitely the first. Whereas China had to be reluctantly dragged into the study of grammar by foreigners at the turn of the century, this science had already achieved an extremely sophisticated level over two and a half millennia ago in India. All linguists have heard of the celebrated Indian grammarian Pāṇini (?350-?250 B.C.E.), yet his extremely elegant and exacting sūtras represent merely the culmination of a long and glorious tradition. Pāṇini cites various predecessors and he makes it clear that he was following in their footsteps. Unlike Ma Jianzhong for China, Pāṇini did not invent grammar for India; he simply codified it. The many great grammarians who came after Pāṇini, men like Kātyāyana, Patañjali, and Bhartṛhari, were essentially writing commentaries and subcommentaries on his codification. (It is noteworthy that, like Pāṇini's predecessors[5] and Pāṇini himself, most of these men came from the northwest, but that is the subject of another paper.) There are literally hundreds of other more or less celebrated grammarians in the following centuries who wrote commentaries and subcommentaries on the works of Pāṇini's distinguished successors (Coward and Raja 1990: 439-517 [for those whose dates are more or less known], 517-536 [for those whose dates are unknown]).

Patañjali's rationale for studying grammar is fascinating. The five primary reasons are: 1. to preserve the Vedas, 2. to carry out the contextual modification of Vedic mantras required in the course of certain rituals, 3. because it is ancillary to the Vedas, 4. because it provides brief rules for Brahmans to maintain correct speech forms, 5. to eliminate possible ambiguities. In addition, Patañjali goes on to give other reasons for studying grammar. Among these is to avoid speaking like barbarians (*mleccha*), a major concern of the noble Aryans (Cardona 1988: 631–632, sec. 828; Cardona 1990: 5 and passim on the question of Aryan language).

Whereas grammar was honored as one of the five *vidyas* ("basic types of knowledge") in ancient India, in China language studies were considered to be *xiaoxue* 小學 ("lesser/minor learning"). In India, grammar (*vyākaraṇa*), in the broadest and most comprehensive terms, was an integral and esteemed part of language studies (*bhāṣikā*). In early China, however, language study was almost exclusively lexicographical, witness the seminal *Erya* 爾雅 (Approaching Elegance), *Shiming* 釋名 (Explanation of Terms), and *Shuowen jiezi* 說文解字 (Explanation of Simple and Compound Graphs), all from the centuries just before and after the beginning of the Common Era. It is telling that, even with lexicography, early Chinese scholars were more concerned with the shapes, sounds, and origins of the characters themselves than they were with such fundamental matters as semantics and etymology. In other words, language studies in ancient China, before the arrival of Buddhism when phonology was introduced as an ancillary discipline, were concentrated almost exclusively on the script and not on language per se. Unfortunately, because the standard of analysis was the seal script rather than the oracle bone or bronze forms, much of the value of these old lexicographical works is vitiated.

One might speculate about why the Indians were so well disposed to grammar and why the Chinese were so ill disposed to it. My own interpretation would be that it has something to do with the fact that Sanskrit is one of the most highly inflected languages known to have existed whereas Sinitic (especially in its Classical Chinese form which was the basis for all but the tiniest portion of language studies in premodern China) is perhaps the least inflected language on earth. This presents us with the intriguing prospect that the very enterprise of grammar may be suspect for Chinese, whereas syntax is utterly vital. I have alluded to this predicament in the beginning paragraphs of this paper.

Ma Jianzhong (and many others who came after him) did not realize the dubiousness of the proposition of grammatical science as applied to Sinitic (especially to Literary Sinitic), a dubiousness that apparently accounts for the current and, in my estimation, correct emphasis on syntax among many linguists who specialize in Sinitic. Ma thought that Sinitic was susceptible to full-scale grammatical analysis, just like Latin or Greek. Being the pioneer in linguistic analysis for China that he was, Ma had not reached the stage attained by my colleagues who are participating in this symposium. Yet we should not blame him for that because he was a forerunner and it was upon his shoulders that our work is founded. Thus we should take Ma on his own premises and try to understand how it was that he believed Sinitic really possessed a full-blown grammar.

Before turning directly to Ma's *Grammar*, I have a confession to make. To wit, I have earnestly tried many times to read this "grammar," but I simply cannot make much sense of it. To me, and I suppose that this is true for many others as well (e.g., Tao Kui 陶奎 1916 and Yang Shuda 楊樹達 1929; Yang faults Ma for many careless citations as well as for various types of misinterpretations[6]), the book is largely both impenetrable and incomprehensible. I shudder to think what a nightmare it would be to translate Ma's book into English! In fact, it is highly unlikely that a grammar such as that conceived by Ma Jianzhong could be comprehensible and cogent. In his prefatory essays, however, Ma is quite lucid about his aims for writing the *Grammar* and it is these that will constitute the main object of attention in this paper.

In the "Second Preface" and the "Introduction" to his *Grammar*, Ma lays bare the impetus for his undertaking the unprecedented, unusual task of writing a grammar of Chinese in Chinese and for Chinese readers. This was something completely unheard of for a Chinese and, while Ma with his close missionary connections surely must have been vaguely aware of the many grammars of Sinitic languages that had already been written by Westerners by his time, he makes no mention of them whatsoever and his own grammar is totally different from theirs.

The entire "Second Preface" is worthy of translation for, in it, Ma Jianzhong details his basic ideas about the nature of language and writing. Using non-linguistic and extra-linguistic reasoning, he also justifies why he embarked on the (in hindsight somewhat dubious) project of creating a grammar for Sinitic along the lines of classical Western grammars.

> Master Xun (?314–?217 B.C.E.) said: "That which sets man apart from animals is his ability to group together (*qun* 群)."[7] When the philosopher speaks of "grouping," he is not referring to it strictly in the physical sense. He also implies the ability to group ideas. That whereby the ideas of modern men are grouped is speech (*hua* 話) and that whereby the ideas of modern and ancient men are grouped is writing (*zi* 字). A commentary states: "We call the synthesis of sound and shape a graph (*zi* 字)." The shapes of graphs are made up of strokes that are horizontal and vertical, curved and straight, slanting and upright, above and below, inside and outside, left and right. The sounds of graphs are rising or falling (*yiyang* 抑揚), open or closed (*kaisai* 開塞), tensed or lax (*hesan* 合散),[8] forward or back (*churu* 出入), high or low (*gaoxia* 高下), voiced or unvoiced (*qingzhuo* 清濁). It is impossible to specify all of these permutations.
>
> The only difficulty is that this creature with a round head and rectangular feet—man—is spread over the five continents. His writing is descended from Brāhmī, from Kharoṣṭhī, and from Cang Jie.[9] It goes from left to right, from right to left, or from top to bottom. None of these ways of writing resemble each other and hence their users cannot group together. Even for those whose script derives from a common source, the likelihood of grouping is almost nonexistent because, with the succession of generations, the shapes of their graphs change from round to square or from complicated to simple and the sounds of the graphs change from alveopalatal (*she* 舌) to dental (*chi* 齒) to labial (*chun* 唇) one after another. However, even though speakers of different

languages cannot communicate, the thoughts behind their words can be transmitted by a whole series of translations and retranslations. The sounds and shapes of their writing may be different but, through exegesis, the meanings of their classics can be made widely known.

Now, that which we perceive as dissimilar are these graphs with their various shapes and sounds, all of which are manmade. Yet, from the beginning of time to the present and throughout the universe, whether they be yellow, white, red, or black, all men have been endowed with the capacity to conceive thought in their minds and to convey their thoughts to others. Often have I pondered the evolution of the languages of those countries whose writing is drawn horizontally on parchment, such as Greek and Latin. When I compare texts in these languages, I observe that their graphs (i.e., words) are of different categories and that they are governed by the sentence. There are fixed and unvarying rules for enunciating what is in the mind and for forming one's thoughts. From this, I reasoned that the chief principles regulating our classics, histories, philosophers, and miscellaneous writings would not be dissimilar. Consequently, I applied these common factors to create a similar set of rules for Chinese. That is how this book came into being.

Someone may comment: "Our sons are involved in Western Learning, the more ethereal aspects of which concern the subtleties of life, the relationship between Heaven and Man, the divine and human laws for purifying oneself and the world, as well as the successive changes in government and education from ancient times till the present day, while the more mundane aspects are concerned with the theory and practice of enriching the state and its people, policies for establishing strategic alliances and settling disputes, on down to the manufacture of instruments and observation of phenomena in terms of their measure, number, weight, chemistry, hydraulics, temperature, optics, and electricity. How grand, how vast this all is! In depth, it can measure Hades; in height, it exceeds the Empyrean. Its larger purview embraces the all-pervading ether; its finer focus delves into the infinitely miniscule. There is nothing that it overlooks or that it fails to recognize. Its utility has been proven in the management of resources and the handling of affairs. Its amplitude leaves plenty of room to spare. Now concessions have been granted (to Britain] for the Nanking to Shanghai railroad.[10] We are beset from above and below, surrounded and spied upon by more than a half-dozen other countries. It is a perilous situation! He who recognizes the task at hand considers works that apply Western learning to Confucius and Mencius (i.e., traditional Chinese learning] as deserving only to be rejected. Our sons today concentrate on learning what is necessary to catch up with the times. Why should they waste their spirit and energy on that which others have spurned? If they were to do so, they would grow old without having achieved their aims, and all to what purpose?"

To this my response would be: "There is nothing under heaven that does not partake of the Way and writing is for conveying the Way (*wen yi zai dao* 文以載道). Principles exist in all human minds and writing is for making them clear. Though writing is for conveying the Way, it is not the Way itself; though writing is for making principles clear, it is not the principles themselves. Writing is the means whereby one reaches his goals but it is not the goals themselves. Therefore, the gentleman studies it in order to perpetuate the Way.

"I observe that, in the West, when children enter school, their learning proceeds in an orderly fashion. Before they are fifteen, Western youths are thoroughly practiced in reading and writing. Later, depending on their personal preference, they exert themselves in mathematics, natural science, law, or metaphysics, becoming specialists in a given field. As a result, in their countries there are none who are without learning and everyone studies useful subjects.

"I reckon the number of Chinese youths who can read is quite small and the number who can both read and write is even smaller. Those who learn to write in a timely fashion and use their remaining years to discourse on the Way and elucidate principles for future use do not amount to one in 10,000.[11]

"The Chinese script is constructed of dots and brush-strokes. Although it is difficult in contrast with Western spelling, the word usage and sentence structure of Chinese are easy in contrast with the division into parts of speech in Western writing as well as its habit of inversion to express ideas in a dashing literary style. Western writing is innately difficult, yet it is easy for their youths to learn; Chinese writing is innately easy, but it is difficult for our sons to learn.[12] The reason for this is that Western writing has specific rules. The learner can progress gradually and in an orderly fashion, all the while knowing that there is an endpoint. Although Chinese texts also have implicit rules, no one has gone to the trouble of identifying them through analogy. Consequently, ever since the time when knotted cords were used to keep records, more than four thousand years of wisdom and ability have accumulated, yet every bit of it has dissipated in the writing that is supposed to convey the Way and make principles clear. Hence, there is nothing to convey the Way and no means to make principles clear. Given these circumstances, in a competition with the Westerner who has achieved the Way and elucidated principles, there is no need to declare who is more intelligent or who is superior.

"This book seeks to find in our classical texts those points which are similar or dissimilar to the pre-existent rules of Western writing.[13] It uses circumstantial evidence and copious citations to determine the usages of Chinese writing. Henceforth, when young students enter the classroom, they will be able to learn how to write by following the rules herein. The speed of their accomplishments will not fall behind that of the Westerners. Later on, as they mature in years, as they learn the Way and clarify principles, not only will they become knowledgeable with the Way and principles of Chinese books, relying on this knowledge, they will seek the Way and clarify principles that are conveyed and the principles that are elucidated in Western writing. Nor, by dint of sedulous effort, will it be hard for them to become thoroughly conversant in these matters. Thus, beyond merely serving to group together the thoughts of ancient and modern Chinese whose writing is the same, this book will bring about a great grouping together of the ideas of all those in the world who use their mouths, tongues, dots and brush-strokes to express what is in their minds. Once this happens, all of our tens of millions and hundreds of millions of people will group together their ability and will group together their thoughts for practical use. Then they will be able to group themselves together, rather than being grouped together by some other group. Therefore, the composition of this book may be said to have been undertaken in full awareness of the exigencies of the present moment."

Also important for understanding Ma's motivations in writing his "grammar" and his specific ideas about linguistic analysis is the "Introduction" (*liyan* 例言), of which I here translate the first two-fifths:

The chief purpose of this book is to discuss the clause and the sentence. Clauses and sentences, however, are made up of an assemblage of graphs (i.e., words).[14] A graph must have its proper position in a clause or sentence and, to complement each other, the graphs must fit in various categories. Only after distinguishing the categories of graphs[15] can we proceed to discuss the clause and the sentence. The categories of graphs, the clause, and the sentence—these things were not discussed in ancient books. As a result, there were also no names[16] in ancient times for categories of graphs or for the order of their placement in the phrase and the sentence. When names are not rectified, then language is out of kilter. In the *Analects* (13.3), it is stated: "Would it not be necessary to rectify names?"[17] The topics this book discusses are three in number: 1. rectification of names (i.e., defining terms), 2. categories of graphs (i.e., parts of speech), 3. the clause and the sentence (i.e., syntax).

The ancient classics have been transmitted and recited for thousands of years up to the present day, but the graphs and sentences in them are a vague mass because initially there were no established laws to which one could refer. Still, the same graph or the same sentence might recur in a single book and they might reappear in other books. This makes it feasible to compare extensive citations and corroborating evidence. In accord with what is self-evident, one can then proceed to find wherein they are the same and wherein they differ, after which one can draw up standards that should be explained clearly. It is impossible, nonetheless, that such an exposition can be free of error. So I hope that like-minded individuals will set right the shortcomings of this book in order that it might be brought closer to perfection.

In the West, this book would be called (literally, "named" (*ming* 名) a "grammar" (*gelangma* 葛郎瑪). The sound (*yin* 音) of "grammar" has a Greek source and may be explained as meaning "pattern of graphs" (*xun* 訓), which is to say "formula for learning to write."[18] Each country has its own grammar, the general drift of which resembles the grammars of other countries. Where they differ is in their phonology (*yinyun* 音韻) and the shapes of their graphs (*zixing* 字形).[19] When their young students enter the classroom, they learn how to spell (*qieyin* 切音, literally "cut sounds") first and after that they are instructed in grammar which includes the classification of individual graphs (i.e., the parts of speech for words) and the patterns for putting them together to make sentences. Once they are clear about these matters, they are all able to (read and) write well-ordered prose, after which they go on to learn natural science and mathematics as well as collateral subjects like geography and history. They do all this with lots of energy left to spare.[20] Before they have attained maturity, they are elegantly accomplished.

This book was written in imitation of (Western) grammars.[21] As such, there is a fixed order for the introduction of individual items. Readers of this book who skip ahead even a little will necessarily end up being unable to make any sense of it. If the reader will gradually and in an orderly fashion progress from beginning to end, he will gain a fuller appreciation with each succeeding entry. He will find that not only is this book marvelously handy for his own composition and for learning ancient Chinese writing styles, but he will have the added advantage of a headstart in learning all the ancient and modern literature (literally, *wenzi* 文字 or "scripts") of the West over someone who tries to learn Western writing (*wen* 文) on his own.

Ma Jianzhong had discovered grammar and with it, he thought, the secret of what made the West rich and strong. To tell the truth, I personally think that Ma Jianzhong came just about as close as any of the troubled thinkers of the late Qing and early Republican periods to figuring out the real difference between China and the West, but he was still a long way off.

Ma's paramount concern with bringing wealth and strength to China is evident in his non-linguistic reform writings (Bailey 1996). Between 1878 and 1890, he wrote several essays outlining his plans for economic and administrative reform. Among numerous other proposals for reform, Ma advocated the creation of a specialized and professional diplomatic corps. Viewed in this context of activist reform, Ma Jianzhong's creation of a grammar for Literary Sinitic was but another in a whole series of efforts to improve the material well-being of China.

It was Ma Jianzhong's passionate desire to devise an analogue for Western grammar, thereby enabling China to achieve the wealth and power of the West, that drove him to spend more than ten years bringing together well over 7,000 illustrative sentences (around 300 for *er* 而 alone!) from ancient Literary Sinitic texts and to analyze them according to a complicated set of rules derived from Greek and Latin. The vast disparity between these highly inflected Indo-European languages on the one hand and uninflected Literary Sinitic on the other hand would seem to imply that his enterprise was doomed to failure. And yet we cannot dismiss Ma's "grammar" altogether. In spite of its obvious linguistic deficiencies and its impenetrability as a text for reading, study, and application, as a sort of icon of hope, it has had an enormous inspirational impact on language studies in China. Therefore we are duty bound to take it seriously and must strive to assess its true position and value in the history of Chinese linguistics.

Almost a decade ago, I was a discussant on a panel in Chicago that had to do with the making of Chinese dictionaries for the 1980s. One of the major topics of debate was how to make more explicit the grammatical properties of Mandarin in dictionary entries. On the panel was Wang Huan, one of China's most eminent grammarians. On that occasion, she said something that left me dumbstruck for days. I would like to quote several crucial sentences by Wang Huan. Because I want to be scrupulously exact so as not to misrepresent her in the slightest, I will present her remarks first in the Mandarin in which she uttered them and then give an English translation:

> 我們的語法體系並不盡善盡美，有許多缺點......漢語的語法和詞匯中的許多規律至今還並未挖掘出來......不教外國人，這些規律是不容易發現的。
> *Women de yufa tixi bing bu jin-shan-jin-mei, you xuduo quedian. . . .Hanyu de yufa he cihui zhong de xuduo guilü zhijin hai bing wei wajue chulai.... Bu jiao waiguoren, zheixie guilüshi bu rongyi faxian de.*
> Our grammatical system is by no means perfect; it has lots of defects.... Many rules for the grammar and lexicon of Sinitic to this day have still not been excavated/extracted.... If it weren't for teaching foreigners, it would not be easy to discover these rules. (Mair 1987)

Thus it is evident that the quest to discover Sinitic grammar continues. The quest that Ma Jianzhong began at the end of the 19th century is still not over at the end of the 20th century. The driving force throughout has always been the emulation of foreign grammar.

It was only when 20th-century Chinese linguists turned their attention to the living vernaculars (e.g., the celebrated grammars of Mandarin written by Y. R. Chao and by Li and Thompson as well as the numerous grammars of the other Sinitic languages such as the fine new work of Matthews and Yip for Cantonese) that a genuine approach to grammatical science was made in China.[22] It is significant, moreover, that all of these new grammarians concentrated on the spoken languages themselves instead of being shackled by discussions of the script. Still, because of the very nature of Sinitic languages as they developed under the influence of the Chinese script, it is probably fair to say that most of what passes for grammar even today is actually syntax.

3. Conclusion

I would like to close with a barrage of questions upon which I have often reflected and upon which I invite my readers to ponder. Did Sinitic always have a natural, internal grammar? Or is grammar only being imposed on Sinitic languages by the Indo-European mind?[23] If Sinitic did not have grammar, how could it possibly operate without crippling ambiguity? But if it always had grammar, why didn't any Chinese notice it before Ma Jianzhong? Regardless of whether Sinitic ever had a grammar or not, is there an intrinsic, universal need for all languages to have grammar?[24] Could it be that Sinitic once had grammar but lost it under the impact of the virtually monosyllabic Chinese script? One thing we do know for a palpable certainty, namely, Sinitic languages have to contend with an extraordinarily huge number of discrete graphs—85,000 and growing continuously. If, as I have often claimed, this vast collection of sinographs is by no means coequal to, nor does it adequately represent, any variety of living Sinitic language from an actual speech community (whether past or present, including Pekingese), what then is its relationship to the various Sinitic languages? Finally, did management of this enormous set of mostly morphosyllabic graphs have anything to do with the disinterest of early Chinese thinkers in such abstract, analytical, theoretical matters as grammar and phonology? In any event, if phonological science came to China with medieval Buddhism, then grammatical analysis arrived with the modern West. In contrast, and this is the main point that I wish to make, syntactical concerns would appear to have been a natural development from within—witness the old preoccupation with things like *wenli* 文理 and *jufa* 句法. Maybe Ma Jianzhong need not have felt compelled to invent grammar for China after all. Then again, though, we can sympathize with him for wanting to do so.

ACKNOWLEDGMENTS

I wish to thank my good friend South Coblin for much useful information that has been incorporated into this paper. Takata Tokio has also contributed helpful references, in particular several first editions of early European grammars of Chinese owned by him or purchased by him for the Institute for Research in Humanities (Jinbun Kagaku Kenkyūjo) of Kyoto University. As always, it is I alone who am responsible for the interpretations and views expressed herein.

Notes

1. Yang (1974: 16) contains a short section (2.3) of eleven entries in Chinese, Japanese, and German on the history of grammatical studies in China. It is odd, however, that Yang labels this section "Morphology and Syntax." It is especially curious that Ma Jianzhong's *Grammar* is listed under the section on "Syntax" (5.5) of Archaic Chinese. Indeed, Yang steadfastly refuses to set up a category of "grammar" in his analytical scheme of Chinese linguistics, in spite of the fact that many of the works that he lists under each stage of the development of Sinitic (Archaic, Post-Archaic, Ancient, Medieval, Ancient Mandarin, and Modern) claim to be about grammar.
2. In Kong Yingda's 孔穎達 (574-648) Tang period subcommentary to the *Zuo zhuan* 左傳 (Chronicle of Zuo), *yufa* is used with roughly the meaning of "drift/pattern/thrust of a text/passage." *Wenfa*, on the other hand, originally meant "civil law/rules; method/manner of writing an essay." Both of these terms only came to mean "grammar" in Sinitic languages during this century in emulation of the Japanese calques formed from these terms. See Mair 1992 and, for the relevant citations in Chinese, *Hanyu da cidian* 漢語大詞典 (Great Dictionary of Sinitic) 5.53b, 6.1524b, and 11.223a.
3. For dozens of early Western grammars of Mandarin, Min, Shanghainese, Cantonese, etc., in addition to Literary Sinitic, see Cordier 1906-1907, 3: columns 1650-1683. As samples, I have listed a few of those that I have examined in the bibliography below.
4. By *wentong*, Ma signifies the basic principles for writing clearly and coherently (*tongshun* 通順). Using Ma's rules, one would not commit the error of *wenli bu tong* 文理不通. ("incoherent writing"). It is obvious that, more or less, *wentong* was intended as a neologism for "grammar," but it did not catch on in China. Instead, people preferred the Japanese calques discussed above. Actually, *wentong* is a better neologism for "syntax" than for "grammar" and, if Ma had followed his own intuitions in devising this term instead of being guided by the pre-established dictates of Western grammar, he might have devised a system of rules more suited to the nature of Sinitic languages than what he has bequeathed to us.

5. As for the predecessors to whom Pāṇini refers by name, their names indicate that they all probably came from Central Asia or had very close links to Central Asian Sakas ("Scyths") and other Indo-Aryan/Iranian peoples from the northwest of the South Asian subcontinent: e.g., Śākaṭāyana, Śākalya, Gārgya, Gālava, and Sphoṭāyana.
6. Yang lists ten categories of errors committed by Ma, asserting that he: 1. did not understand theory, 2. did not see clearly, 3. arbitrarily applied rules of foreign grammar to Sinitic, 4. did not realize when the ancients were abbreviating, 5. arbitrarily divided words that should be considered together, 6. did not recognize that ancient writings are sometimes disordered and transformed, 7. misconstrued constructions, 8. wrongly determined parts of speech, 9. did not understand ancient interpretations based on phonology, 10. misread ancient texts. Yang, in turn, has been criticized by others for trying to correct Ma's Latinate grammar with English standards! For Tao Kui's complaints against Ma, see Zhang Wanqi 1987: 3-28.
7. For consistency's sake, I have translated *qun* throughout this preface as "group (together)." While this sometimes leads to a bit of awkwardness, it enables the reader to follow Ma's argument more closely in English. The range of *qun*'s meanings herein actually embraces the following: "communicate," "combine," "link together," "form social or political organizations," and so on.
8. *Kai* and *he* are usually translated as "unrounded" and "rounded" respectively.
9. A strange combination of two historically known early Indian scripts and the name of the supposed mythological creator of writing in China. Without fully understanding his sources, Ma has lifted much of the information in this paragraph from an earlier tradition of writing about the origins of script in China. See Mair 1993.
10. Xiaguan, which is mentioned by Ma in the Chinese text, ultimately became the Nanking terminus of the railway from Shanghai. It had been made a commercial port under the provisions of the treaty of 1858 between China and Great Britain and, in 1897, opened its doors to other nations. The preliminary agreement to build the Shanghai-Nanking Railroad, which was both financed and planned by British interests, was signed on May 13, 1898, the same year that Ma wrote this preface. Because of the first Boer War and the Boxer disturbances, the final agreement between the Chinese government and the British and Chinese Corporation (a British syndicate created by the Hong Kong and

Shanghai Bank together with Messrs. Jardine, Matheson, and Co.) was not concluded until July 9, 1903. The railroad itself was not open to traffic until 1908.

11. Ma's estimate of full literacy in later imperial China is incredibly bleak: one one-hundredth of one percent!
12. Here Ma, like countless others before and after him, makes the fatal (but exceedingly common) error of confusing Sinitic language with Chinese writing. Sinitic languages, in terms of their structure and lexicon, are indeed exceedingly simple and easy to learn, but there is no more difficult system of writing on earth than the sinographs. It is due to this fundamental flaw in his conceptualization that Ma's "grammar" was doomed to failure from its very inception.
13. Ma here openly confesses the flawed premises of his "grammar."
14. Ma does not make a distinction between word and graph, collapsing them both into the single term *zi* 字 (Ma does use *ci* 詞 in his exposition, but for him it means "subject, predicate, object, etc.," i.e., part of a sentence. In actuality, *zi* does not mean "word," a notion attached to *ci* which has only come into being in this century under the impact of modern linguistics.) Since this is a serious defect that vitiates his entire enterprise and still plagues Chinese linguistics to this day, I have chosen not to gloss over it by artificially separating out the two different meanings. Instead, I consistently translate *zi* as "graph" throughout. Fortunately, more and more of the best linguists in China are beginning to comprehend the difference between graph (*zi*) and word (*ci*) in Sinitic languages, although the general public is still hopelessly confused over them.
15. Ma's idea concerning "categories of graphs" is obviously based on the concept of "parts of speech" in Western grammar, yet what a world of difference lies between "graphs" and "speech"!
16. With "names," Ma comes far closer to the notion of "words" than he does with "graphs."
17. Modern critical scholarship holds this question to belong to a late stratum of the *Analects*. Nevertheless, it is clear that Ma is setting up an internal dissonance of great depth in his work by basing it both on the ancient Chinese concept of the "rectification of names" (*zhengming* 正名) and on the classical Western notions of grammar, all the while remaining totally oblivious to the living languages of the Sinitic group. Indeed, the very first chapter of *Ma's Grammar* is entitled *zhengming*, but it is obvious that he wants it to mean "defining terms" instead

of "rectification of names." The latter, however, remains clearly in the background, painting Ma's fundamentally Western project with a hoary Chinese color. Chapters 2-6 deal with what Ma calls "full graphs" (*shizi* 實字) and chapters 7-9 with "empty graphs" (*xuzi* 虛字), that is to say, different categories of content words and particles. Chapter 10 is about *judu* 句讀 ("sentence/clause reading") and is the most important part of the book (Ma himself makes this explicit in his "Introduction" [*liyan* 例言]). Ma advocated determining the part of speech of a word from its meaning. He also believed that the part of speech of a word and its function in a sentence were correlated.

18. The actual etymology of the word "grammar" is Greek *grammatikē* [with -*tekhnē* understood] ("art of letters") < *grammatikos* ("pertaining to letters") < *gramma* ("letter") < *gramein* ("to write") < I-E √ *gerebh* ("to scratch, incise").
19. Ma probably intends by this "the forms of their words," i.e., morphology.
20. Again, Ma fails to realize the enormous burdens placed upon Chinese students in mastering their incredibly complicated script. He attributes the ease and rapidity with which Western students learn to read and write at an advanced level solely to the existence of grammar, whereas the remarkable simplicity of the alphabet is far more responsible for their achievements which seem to have left Ma utterly dazzled.
21. See note 13 above.
22. Norman (1988: 152-154 [7.1]) gives a brief survey of the study of grammar in China. He notes that beginning in the late 1930s a reaction set in against imitative grammar. The leader of this movement was Chen Wangdao, a nativist who wished to reflect the basic nature of Sinitic. It is ironic that all of the members of this group were influenced to one degree or another by Western linguists such as de Saussure, Jespersen, and Bloomfield. Norman describes the impact of structuralism and transformational generative grammar on the development of the study of grammar in China. What started out with a nativist impulse appears to have been swiftly recaptured by Western ideas of grammar, albeit a radically different set than those subscribed to by Ma Jianzhong.
23. With my own ears, I have repeatedly heard Chinese state publicly in classrooms and lecture halls that "Chinese lacks grammar." I have also heard them declare that "China has no religion." Are these statements equally false? Equally true? Is there a common epistemological thread linking both of these declarations?

24. It would seem that parts of speech (nouns, verbs, adjectives, adverbs, etc.) and other basic grammatical features are universal categories, but are they equally applicable to all languages?

References

Abel-Rémusat, J. P. 1822. *Éléments de la grammaire chinoise, ou principes généraux du kou-wen, ou style antique, et du kouan-hoa, c'est-à-dire, de la langue commune généralement usitée dans l'Empire chinois.* Paris: Imprimerie Royale.

Bailey, Paul. 1996. *Strengthen the Country and Enrich the People: The Reform Writings of Ma Jianzhong.* Durham East Asia Series. Richmond, Surrey: Curzon.

Bayer, Theophilus (=Gottlieb) Sigefrid. 1730. *Museum Sinicum: In quo Sinicae Linguae et Litteraturae ratio explicatur.* Petropoli: Typographia Academiae Imperatoriae.

Cardona, George. 1988. *Pāṇini, His Work and Its Traditions: Vol. I: Background and Introduction.* Delhi: Motilal Banarsidass.

———. 1990. "On Attitudes towards Language in Ancient India." *Sino-Platonic Papers,* 15 (January), 19 pages.

Chao, Yuen Ren. 1968. *A Grammar of Spoken Chinese.* Berkeley: University of California Press.

Cordier, Henri. 1904-1908. *Bibliotheca Sinica: Dictionnaire bibliographique des ouvrages relatifs à l'Empire chinois.* 4 vols. Paris: Librairie Orientale & Américaine E. Guilmoto, 2nd ed.

Coward, Harold G., and K. Kunjunni Raja. 1990. *Encyclopedia of Indian Philosophies: The Philosophy of the Grammarians.* Princeton: Princeton University Press.

Edkins, J[oseph]. 1853. *A Grammar of Colloquial Chinese, as Exhibited in the Shanghai Dialect.* Shanghai: London Mission Press.

Endlicher, Stephan. 1845. *Anfangsgründe der Chinesischen Grammatik.* Wien: Carl Gerold. (The *Vorrede* [pp. v-viii] of this book consists of a very brief and incomplete sketch of previous European grammars of Sinitic.)

Fourmont, Stephanus. 1742. *Linguae Sinarum Mandarinicae Hieroglyphicae Grammatica Duplex, Latinè, & cum Characteribus Sinensium, Item Sinicorum Regiae Bibliothecae Librorum Catalogus, Denuò, cum Notitiis amplioribus & Charactere Sinico.* Paris: Joseph Bullot.

Gabelentz, Georg von der. 1881. *Chinesische Grammatik mit Ausschluss der Niederen Stiles und der Heutigen Umgangssprache.* Leipzig: T. O. Wiegel.

Li, Charles N., and Sandra A. Thompson. 1981. *Mandarin: A Functional Reference Grammar.* Berkeley: University of California Press.

Lü Shuxiang 呂叔湘 and Wang Haifen 王海棻, eds. 1986. *Ma shi wentong duben* 馬氏文通讀本 (A Reader of *Ma's Grammar*). Shanghai: Shanghai jiaoyu.

Ma Jianzhong 馬建忠. 1983: *Ma shi wentong* 馬氏文通 (Ma's Grammar). Peking: Shangwu yinshuguan.

Mair, Victor H. 1993. "Cheng Ch'iao's Understanding of Sanskrit: The Concept of Spelling in China." In *A Festschrift in Honour of Professor Jao Tsung-i on the Occasion of His Seventy-Fifth Anniversary.* Editorial Board for the Festschrift, ed. Shatin, New Territories, Hong Kong: Institute of Chinese Studies, Chinese University of Hong Kong. 331-342.

———. 1992. "Two Papers on Sinolinguistics: 1. A Hypothesis Concerning the Origin of the Term *fanqie* ('Countertomy'), 2. East Asian Round-Trip Words." *Sino-Platonic Papers,* 34 (October): 13 pages.

———. 1987. "Discussant's Remarks: Dictionary Panel." *Journal of the Chinese Language Teachers Association,* 22.1 (February): 141-153.

Matthews, Stephen, and Virginia Yip. 1994. *Cantonese: A Comprehensive Grammar.* London: Routledge.

Norman, Jerry. 1988. *Chinese.* Cambridge: Cambridge University Press.

Wang Haifen 王海棻. 1991. *Ma shi wentong ji Zhongguo yufaxue* 馬氏文通及中國語法學 (*Ma's Grammar* and the Study of Chinese Grammar). Hefei: Anhui jiaoyu.

Yang, Paul Fu-mien. 1974. *Chinese Linguistics: A Selected and Classified Bibliography.* Shatin, New Territories, Hong Kong: Chinese University of Hong Kong.

Yang Shuda 楊樹達. 1962. *Ma shi wentong kanwu* 馬氏文通刊誤 (Errors in *Ma's Grammar*). Peking: Zhonghua. 2nd printing, 1983; originally published, 1929.

Zhang Wanqi 張萬起. 1987. *Ma shi wentong yanjiu ziliao* 馬氏文通研究資料 (Research Materials on *Ma's Grammar*). Peking: Zhonghua.

Zhang Xichen 章錫深. 1954. *Ma shi wentong jiaozhu* 馬氏文通校注 (*Ma's Grammar* Collated and Annotated). Peking: Zhonghua. (Based on the work of 1904; 1983 reprint with index.)

Chapter 10

Xie He's "Six Laws" of Painting and Their Indian Parallels

Source: Adapted from "Xie He's 'Six Laws' of Painting and Their Indian Parallels," in *Chinese Aesthetics: The Ordering of Literature, the Arts, and the Universe in the Six Dynasties*, ed. Zong-qi Cai. (Honolulu: Universty of Hawai'i Press, 2004), 81-122.

> *The "Six Laws" [sic] of India and the "Six Laws" of Xie He are actually two unrelated theories.*
> —Jin Ronghua (1984)

> *I feel in my bones that Xie He's "Six Laws" come from India.*
> —Tsu-Lin Mei (ca. 1990)

There is universal agreement that Xie He's 謝赫 " Liu fa" 六法 (Six Laws) constitute the first systematic exposition of painting theory in China.[1] Toward the end of the Tang dynasty, the great art critic and historian Zhang Yanyuan 張彥遠 (ca. 810-880), in his enormously influential *Lidai minghua ji* 歷代名畫記 (A Record of the Famous Painters of Successive Dynasties, ca. 847) makes the Six Laws the centerpiece of his discussion of painting criticism. During the Five Dynasties, Jing Hao 荊浩 (ca. 870-ca. 930) elaborated upon the Six Laws in his "Liu yao" 六要 (Six Essentials). Guo Ruoxu 郭若虛 (eleventh century), begins the chapter entitled "Lun qiyun fei shi" 論氣韻非師 (On Vital Resonance Not Being Teachable) of his *Tuhua jianwen zhi* 圖畫見聞志 (A Record of Things Seen and Heard about Painting) with the seemingly obligatory recitation of the Six Laws. The Song landscape painter Song Zifang 宋子房 was inspired by Xie He's Six Laws to write his own "Liu fa" (Six Laws) and "Liu lun" 六論 (Six Discussions). Also in the Song period, Liu Daochun 劉道醇 (the eleventh-century painting critic) brought out another "Liu yao" (Six Essentials) and a "Liu chang" 六長 (Six Strengths), while a work under the latter title was also issued by the Qing critic Sheng Dashi 盛大士. During the Yuan dynasty Xia Wenyan begins his *Tuhui baojian* 圖繪寶鑒 (The Precious Mirror of Painting) with the words "Xie He says" and then commences immediately with the enumeration of the Six Laws. The editors of the *Qinding siku quanshu zongmu tiyao* 欽定四庫全書總目提要 (Essentials of the General Catalog for the Imperially Commissioned Comprehensive Library in Four Divisions, completed 1781, published 1789), 112, while recognizing that nothing is known of Xie He as a person, close their notice on his *[Gu]hua pinlu* 古畫品錄 (A Record of the Rankings of [Ancient] Painters) by stating that his book is the arbiter for discussions about painting and that the Six Laws from its preface constitute the millennial, immutable standard up to their own day. The term *liufa* was so ubiquitous in later discussions of Chinese art that right through the twentieth century it could be used to signify "painting."[2] Indeed, it would probably not be exaggerating to say, as more than one scholar has put it, that there has been an obsession with Xie He's Six Laws in the evolution of Chinese painting.

Contrasting sharply with the unanimity of opinion that the Six Laws are the fountainhead of all later Chinese art theory and criticism is the virtually universal disagreement concerning two essential matters relating to the terse formulations of Xie He: (1) how to read and understand them, and (2) whether they were based on Indian models. Through a close examination of the relevant texts, this study reveals that the solution to these two problems lies in the realization that they are tightly interwoven. The Six Laws are extremely difficult, almost impossible, to comprehend without taking into account their Indian background. Conversely, once one reads the Six Laws correctly, the one-for-one Indian influence upon them becomes obvious.

We must begin by admitting that we know next to nothing about Xie He, the formulator of the Six Laws. Biographical information concerning the father of Chinese painting theory is virtually nonexistent.[3] Xie He was himself apparently a fashionable court portrait painter of considerable skill but by no means a distinguished artist.[4] Fortunately, there is sufficient internal evidence concerning Xie He's *[Gu]hua pinlu*, in the preface to which the Six Laws appear, enabling scholars to form a broad scholarly consensus that it may be dated to between the years 532 and 549.[5] Given this dire poverty of hard facts about Xie He, it is clear that we cannot rely upon biographical information concerning him to help us solve the thorny problems surrounding his Six Laws. Instead, we will have to concentrate on the philological analysis of the Six Laws and of their Indian counterparts.

Before we embark on our philological quest, it is necessary to observe that the scholarship on the forty-two characters of the terse Six Laws (only twenty-four of which convey substantial meaning) is disproportionately large.[6] On no other subject has so much been said about so little. Considering the Six Laws' seminal importance for the entire history of painting theory and criticism in China, however, this is by no means surprising. In order to proceed as efficiently as possible, we shall not review the host of different opinions concerning the Six Laws. Instead, we shall turn directly to a philological examination of the laws themselves.

Parsing and Punctuating the Six Laws

In their raw form, with Modern Standard Mandarin transcriptions and crude word-for-word English translations, the Six Laws of Xie He are as follows: [see tables 3a and 3b]

The first time that I encountered these Six Laws, my immediate reaction was that they were simply unreadable. In dealing with early Chinese texts, one often encounters awkward formulations, but Xie He's Six Laws are among the most refractory forty-two characters in all of Chinese literature.

For the purpose of our grammatical analysis, let us refer to the components of each of the Six Laws as follows: N = the number that occurs in the initial position; R = the first of the two binomial members constituting the core of the law; S = the second of the two binomial members constituting the core of the law; D = the demonstrative pronoun *shi* ("this"); C = the loose copulative or judgmental particle *ye* at the end of the sentence. Thus each law consists of the following terms or components: NRSDC. (The choice of R and S as mnemonics for the first and second members of the quadrinomial core of each law will be explained below.) The problem confronting the reader of the Six Laws is how to parse their elements in such a fashion that they yield sense. If we strictly adhere to the first order analysis of the grammar as it is presented to us by Xie He, we are compelled to interpret each law as follows: N this is RS (where RS may be R+S, R by means of S, R resulting in S, etc.). Such a formulation, on the very face of it, would be rather ridiculous, for it would have Xie He saying something like N = RS! In other words, it would not make very much sense for Xie He to define a number with two linked binomials, much less to do so emphatically.

Table 3a. The Six Laws of Xie He

N	R		S		D	C
一	氣	韻	生	動	是	也
yi	qi	yun	sheng	dong	shi	ye
one	breath	euphony	be born	move	this	(is)
二	骨	法	用	筆	是	也
er	gu	fa	yong	bi	shi	ye
two	bone	law	use	brush	this	(is)
三	應	物	象	形	是	也
san	ying	wu	xiang	xing	shi	ye
three	(cor)respond	thing	image	form	this	(is)
四	隨	類	賦	彩	是	也
si	sui	lei	fu	cai	shi	ye
four	follow	type	spread	color	this	(is)
五	經	營	位	置	是	也
wu	jing	ying	wei	zhi	shi	ye

Source: Adapted from "Xie He's 'Six Laws' of Painting and Their Indian Parallels," in *Chinese Aesthetics: The Ordering of Literature, the Arts, and the Universe in the Six Dynasties*, 83-4, edited by Zong-qi Cai. Honolulu: University of Hawai'i Press, 2004.

Table 3b. The Six Laws of Xie He (Continued)

five	manage	administer	position	place	this	(is)
六	傳	移	模	寫	是	也
liu	chuan	yi	mo	xie	shi	ye
six	transmit	transfer	model	depict	this	(is)

While the core quadrinomials of each law present their own difficulties (viz., determining the precise semantic content of their rarefied terms and the exact syntactic relationship between their constituent binomials), the primary hurdles that must be surmounted in coping with the very structure of the laws are N and D C. Let us first examine N.

Although the Chinese did have many numbered groupings (e.g., *shi guo* 十過 [ten errors], *shi yi* 十義 [ten moral obligations], *wu chang* 五常 [five constancies], *wu xing* 五行 [five phases; five forms of behavior], *wu biao* 五標 [five markers], *wu du* 五毒 [five vermin], *wu lun* 五倫 [five human relations], and so forth), it was rare in pre-Buddhist times to list sequentially the individual items of such groupings with bulleted numbers in front of each one, especially if they were expressed in whole sentences and not merely individual words.[7] In contrast, numbered lists are extremely common in India. The relative scarcity of numbered lists in early Chinese texts may help to account for Xie He's awkwardness in constructing his Six Laws.

The unfamiliarity of Chinese authors in dealing with numbered lists from India is borne out by their experience with *geyi* 格義 (matching concepts). While modern scholarship has overemphasized the role of *geyi* in the introduction of Buddhism to China far beyond what the available historical data concerning it will allow, a more nuanced examination of that which is actually known about it from contemporary texts is illuminating for our present investigation. Ostensibly, the purpose of *geyi* was for elucidating Buddhist terminology with the help of notions extracted from traditional Chinese thought. It is telling that *geyi* referred especially to numerical categories. Huijiao's 慧皎 (497-554) biography of Zhu Faya 竺法雅 in *Gaoseng zhuan* 高僧傳 (Biographies of Eminent Monks)[8] specifically mentions the notion of *shishu* 事數 (enumeration of items) in connection with *geyi*.[9] Buddhist authors were exceedingly fond of enumerating items relating to often abstruse doctrines, a practice that was challenging to Chinese readers and exegetes. This is vividly brought out in a passage from the fourth chapter, "Wen xue" 文學 (Letters and Scholarship), of *Shishuo xinyu* 世說新語 (New Tales of the World) by Liu Yiqing 劉義慶 (403-444):

> When Yin Hao 殷浩 (306-356) was dismissed and transferred to Dunyang he read a large number of Buddhist sutras, gaining a detailed understanding of them all. It was only when he came to places where items were enumerated (*shishu*) that he did not understand. Whenever he chanced to see a monk he would ask about the items he had noted down, and then they would become clear.[10]

Liu Jun 劉峻 (462-521), in his commentary to this passage, cites several examples of *shishu*: the five personality-components (*wu yin* 五陰, *pañcaskandha*), the twelve entrances (*shier ru* 十二入, *dvādaśāyatana*) the Four Truths (*si di* 四諦, *catvāri ārya-satyāni*), the twelve-fold cycle of dependent origination (*shier yinyuan* 十二因緣, *dvādaśāṅga pratiyasamutpāda*), the five sense-organs (*wu gen* 五根, *pañcendriyāṇi*), the five powers (*wu li* 五力, *pañcabalāni*), the seven degrees of enlightenment (*qi jue* 七覺, *saptabodhyaṅga*), etc. The word *shishu* that Liu Jun is annotating here is a Buddhist technical term indicating the enumeration of affairs, matters, things. It is also referred to as *mingshu* 名數 (enumeration of terms) and *fashu* 法數 (enumeration of dharmas).[11] Many Buddhist texts are largely or almost entirely organized around numbered lists. On the one hand, these seemingly countless numerical schematizations proved extraordinarily troublesome to Chinese who were unaccustomed to them. Yet, on the other hand, various commentators have pointed out that this is one of the major Buddhist contributions to Chinese methods of analysis.[12] Once they became used to it, this manner of explaining Buddhist (and other) ideas was favored particularly by laymen in China, so it is not unexpected that Xie He might have tried his hand at it, even if he had not thoroughly mastered the technique.

Now let us turn to an examination of *shi ye*. The combination *shi ye* is to be found neither in dictionaries of particles nor in comprehensive lexicons with the presumed meaning it has in the Six Laws. Indeed, elsewhere it is uncommon to find *shi ye* occupying the final position at all, especially in sentences that begin with a number. In Sanskrit, however, it is perfectly acceptable to have sentences that end with *eso'sti* ("this is").

Probably because he could not comprehend the Six Laws as they were originally stated by Xie He, Zhang Yanyuan rewrote them as follows in his *Lidai minghua ji*: [see table 4]

Rewritten in this fashion, the Six Laws are relatively easy to read, if not to understand. As a result, virtually all commentators on the Six Laws after Zhang Yanyuan (mis)read them as he did. For our grammatical analysis of the Zhangian reading, we may now add Q = quotational particle. Hence, for each of the Six Laws as rewritten by Zhang Yanyuan, we have N Q R S, which may be interpreted as follows: N (i.e., the N [where N is an ordinal] law) may be stated as R S (where R S may be R +S, R by means of S, R resulting in S, etc.). Reformulated in this manner, while still challenging to the aesthetic exegete, the Six Laws no longer present the formidable obstacles of Xie He's original wording.

Xie He's "Six Laws" of Painting and Their Indian Parallels

Table 4. Six Laws by Zhang Yanyuan

N		R		S	
一	氣	韻		生	動
yi	qi	yun		sheng	dong
one	breath	euphony		be born	move
二	骨	法		用	筆
er	gu	fa		yong	bi
two	bone	law		use	brush
三	應	物		象	形
san	ying	wu		xiang	xing
three	(cor)respond	thing		image	form
四	隨	類		賦	彩
si	sui	lei		fu	cai
four	follow	type		spread	color
五	經	營		位	置
wu	jing	ying		wei	zhi
five	manage	administer		position	place
六	傳	移		模	寫
liu	chuan	yi		mo	xie
six	transmit	transfer		model	depict

Source: Adapted from "Xie He's 'Six Laws' of Painting and Their Indian Parallels," in *Chinese Aesthetics: The Ordering of Literature, the Arts, and the Universe in the Six Dynasties*, 86-7, edited by Zong-qi Cai. Honolulu: University of Hawai'i Press, 2004.

If Xie He had formulated each of his laws as N Q R S D C, they would have been much easier to understand: e.g., "The first is (called) R, that is [defined by] S"; and so forth. As a matter of fact, Liu Xie 劉勰 (ca. 465-ca. 521), in the "Qing cai" 情采 (Aspiration and Embellishment) chapter (the thirty-first) of his *Wenxin diaolong* 文心雕龍 (The Literary Mind and Ornate Rhetoric), which was written not long before Xie He's *[Gu]hua pinlu*, has a numbered list of three sentences where the R binomials (textual form, textual voice, textual mood) are explained by the following S binomials: five colors, five sounds, five emotions (not individually enumerated). That is to say, Liu Xie's three sentences are constructed as N Q R S D C. The addition of the quotative particle after the numeral compels the practiced reader to parse the remaining segment correctly as R S D C. Zhang Yanyuan must have been following some such instinct when he rewrote the Six Laws in the form N Q R S. Unfortunately, by omitting D C at the end, he unwittingly made it inevitable that readers would take RS as a single unit, thus destroying Xie He's original wording. The awkward grammar of Xie He's N R S D C must have thrown Zhang off his stride, since, in section one of the first chapter of *Lidai minghua ji*,[13] where he is discussing the multiple meanings of the word *tu* 圖 (drawing, chart), he three times in succession uses the identical formulation of Liu Xie, viz., N Q R S D C—and few would be apt to misread him here. The acceptability of N Q R S D C is reinforced by its exact recurrence in an essay on calligraphy, "Si ti shu shi" 四體書勢 (The Configuration of the Four Forms of Writing), by the Jin writer Wei Heng 衛恆 (?-291) that is quoted in his *Jin shu* 晉書 (History of the Jin), scroll 36 biography. Wei Heng is enumerating and defining the six different types of Chinese characters (*liu yi* 六義): "The first is called indicative; [the graphs for] 'above' (*shang*) and 'below' (*xia*) are such" (一曰指事上下是也). And so forth. The full complement of N Q R S D C results in a pronounced pause between R and S, such that it is entirely appropriate to mark it with a semicolon or even a period in the English translation. What is most curious (and telling) about Wei Heng's enumeration of the six different types of characters is that he has actually greatly compressed them from their original form in the "Postface" to the *Shuo wen jie zi* 說文解字 (Explanations of Simple and Compound Graphs), by Xu Shen 許慎 (fl. 100-121).[14] Xu Shen's formulation of the six different types of characters was N Q T T P E1 E2 G D C, where T is the binomial term to be defined, P is the nominalizing particle *zhe*, E1 and E2 are quadrinomials that define or explain T, and G is a binomial consisting of two example graphs of the type being defined. Hence, "The first is called 'indicative.' An indicative [is the type of character that] may be understood when seen, may be grasped when inspected. Such are [the graphs for] 'above' and 'below'" (一曰指事指事者視而可識察而可見上下是也). In Xu Shen's original, it is immediately obvious that the full formulation must be broken down into three main syntactic units, viz., N Q T。 T P E1 E2。 G D C。 . Wei Heng's version, N Q R S D C, may be viewed as abbreviated thus: N Q T。 T P E1 E2。 G D C。 , i.e., N Q T。 G D C。 , with T and G being more semantically accurate designators for the central binomials in this particular case than R and S, but playing an identical structural role. Therefore, we have shown that Wei Heng's and Liu Xie's N Q R S D C must be parsed as N Q R。 S D C. Similarly, although less obviously, Xie He's N R S D C should be parsed as N R。 S D C.

Later in his essay, Wei Heng enumerates the six different styles of writing Chinese characters (*liu shu* 六書): "The first is the archaic script; [it] is the writing [that was preserved] in the wall of Confucius's house" (一曰古文孔氏壁中書也). While the structure of the E members of his formulations varies dramatically (including relative markers, conjunctions, and other types of grammatical particles) and is too complicated to discuss in detail here, the other members remain constant, viz., N Q T E C. Note that Wei Heng here omits D, probably because his E are relatively long and complex, varying from three to six characters in length. As a matter of fact, Wei Heng has also borrowed his enumerations and explanations of the *liu shu* wholesale from Xu Shen's "Postface," albeit with mistakes and changes. In Xu Shen's original formulation of the *Liu shu*, the E members vary even more dramatically than they do in Wei Heng's version, ranging in length from four to fifteen (!) characters and with still more complicated internal grammar. Xu Shen once (at the end of his fourth item) omits C, perhaps through sloppiness, but this seems to indicate that when N Q are present, the C is not really necessary, as is borne out by Zhang Yanyuan's rewriting of Xie He's N R S D C as N Q R S. In any event, it is altogether natural not to have D after N Q and, since Q possesses equational qualities of its own, there is a tendency to omit final C when it is present.[15]

Still more transparent than N Q R S D C is R' Q S' C ("R' is [called] S'," where R' is a monomial and S' is either a monomial or a binomial). This exact formulation was, in fact, used twelve times in succession by Xiao Yan 蕭衍 (464-549), a close contemporary of Xie He, at the beginning of his "Guan Zhong You shufa shier yi" 觀鐘繇書法十二意 (Twelve Thoughts on Observing the Calligraphy of Zhong You): "Level is [called] horizontal; upright is [called] vertical" (平謂橫也，直謂縱也).[16]

Another of Xie He's many successors and imitators, Liu Daochun, who was mentioned at the outset, revised the Six Laws even more radically in his "Six Essentials" than Zhang Yanyuan had in his *Lidai minghua ji*: "The first is called vital resonance and / or combined strength (alternatively: combined strength through vital resonance; vital resonance combined with strength; [instilling] vital resonance by combining strength; etc.)" (氣韻兼力一也). Liu Daochun has restructured Xie He's N R S D C as R S N C. Bringing N next to C and omitting both D and Zhang Yanyuan's Q tightens up the syntax considerably, despite the slight oddness of equating R S so emphatically with N.

Such have been the grammatical and syntactical vicissitudes of Xie He's Six Laws during the last millennium and more. It appears that few, if any, of Xie He's successors were satisfied with what he himself had written. Zhang Yanyuan's reformulation as N Q R S, despite its manifest deficiencies, was deceptively easy to read, and it seems to have captured the imagination of art critics, both in China and abroad. Consequently, this is how art historians, theorists, and critics read them for the next twelve hundred years and more. Regrettably, aside from its being patently unfair to rewrite the words of someone who has been dead for centuries (or even the words of someone who is still alive), Zhang Yanyuan's interpretation constitutes a gross misreading of the Six Laws.

Given that Xie He would not intentionally have penned some such nonsense as "N this is R S" for the primary exposition of the aesthetic tenets of painting, he must have meant for his laws to be read differently than the strictest application of grammar would require. Relaxing our grammatical constraints somewhat, we may posit that Xie He looked upon the N members of his laws as indexical tags and that he did not think of them as entering into the grammar of the laws themselves. Hence, (N) R S D C. While R S D C by itself is still slightly unwieldy, it is completely within the realm of grammatical possibility. Naturally, if one insists on treating R S as a tightly bound quadrinomial, R S D C remains nonsensical, because that would be tantamount to saying "this is RS" or "R S is this." Once we insert a syntactical pause between R and S, however, Xie He's laws become instantly intelligible, viz.: R, S D C ("R this is S"). That is to say, R is / means S or R is defined by / as S. As we shall see below, there were sufficiently compelling psychological and linguistic grounds for Xie to adopt such a cumbersome mode for the declaration of his Six Laws. Xie's reasons for choosing inelegant phraseology to launch the aesthetics of painting in China may have been convincing to himself, but others, most notably Zhang Yanyuan, were led seriously astray.

It was only in 1954 that the traditional Zhangian misconstruing of the Six Laws began to unravel. The epochal achievement of apparently being the first person in more than a thousand years to read the Six Laws correctly belongs to William Reynolds Beal Acker.[17] To the best of my knowledge, Acker is the first scholar to go on record, and to do so in a definitive manner, as being in favor of a grammatically stringent reading of the Six Laws as they were originally stated by Xie He. I suspect, however, that Acker's discovery was prompted, or at least partly inspired, by reading the Six Laws in a Japanese fashion (*kundoku* or *kanhun kakikudashi*). He notes[18] that he began his study of the Six Laws in Kyoto as early as 1936. Acker then goes on to state explicitly that the *shi* of each law is equal to Japanese *kore* ("this," "this-like," "such," "just this," "just such," "just-such-as-it-is") and the *ye* of each law is comparable to Classical Japanese *nari* ("is," "be"). Acker's explanation of how he arrived at his new (actually the old and original) reading is both elegant and exacting.[19] It should have been convincing to anyone with a good grounding in the grammar of Literary Sinitic. In fact, Acker's reading of the Six Laws was swiftly approved by Zürcher.[20] In their 1985 collection of translations of Chinese texts dealing with painting, Bush and Shih also adopted the Ackerian interpretation of the Six Laws.[21] The earliest adoption of an Ackerian reading in China known to me occurred in the 1958 Zhonghua reprinting of Yan Kejun's 嚴可均 (1762-1843) *Quan shanggu San Dai, Qin, Han, Sanguo, Liuchao wen* 全上古三代秦漢三國六朝文 (Complete Prose from High Antiquity, the Three Dynasties, Qin, Han, the Three Kingdoms, and the Six Dynasties).[22] The editors added small round circles for punctuation as follows: N R。 S D C。 . While the Zhonghua editors did not set off N and did not use a comma after R, in spite of the fact that they did employ commas sparingly elsewhere in Yan's gigantic collection and should have done so here, the marking of a stop after R was an enormous step forward in rectifying the millennial misreading of Xie's Six Laws.[23] The first concerted effort by a Japanese scholar to promote an Ackerian reading of the Six Laws was that of Nakamura Shigeo 中村茂夫. Nakamura not only provided detailed, extensive annotations for each of the laws, he also translated them into Japanese and offered a punctuated edition of Xie He's text, with the Six Laws being treated thus: N R, S D C。 .[24] Finally, although Acker parsed the Six Laws correctly nearly half a century ago, his grammatical analysis of the text has only recently and gradually begun to win acceptance in China. This is almost entirely due to the awesome reputation of Qian Zhongshu 錢鍾書 (1910-1999), who in 1979—while unleashing a barrage of caustic barbs directed against the muddleheadedness of previous explicators—

punctuated the Six Laws thus: N, R, S D C; (except 。 instead of; for the end of the sixth and final one).²⁵ Qian's reading may be considered an improvement over previous readings in China since it not only marks the extremely important pause between R and S, it also sets aside N. I myself read the Six Laws with syntactic pauses after the first, third, and fifth characters of each line when I initially began my study of them in the late 1970s. Whether or not those who agreed with Acker in correctly dividing the central four characters of each of the Six Laws into two syntactically separate units did so independently, it is to the great and everlasting glory of Acker to have been the first person to have followed the dictates of grammar with regard to the. Six Laws after Zhang Yanyuan's monumental misinterpretation more than a millennium earlier. In any event, there is no longer any excuse for scholars to continue to repeat the misreading of the Six Laws *á la* Zhang Yanyuan.²⁶

Those who persist in a Zhangian reading of the Six Laws are ineluctably ignoring the penultimate character (*shi*) of each line. And yet so deeply entrenched is the customary misapprehension of the laws that even modern Sinologists remain under its spell.²⁷

Because art historians have fallen prey to the "standard" misinterpretation of the Six Laws, not only have they been unable to grasp what Xie He himself meant by them, it has been impossible for them to realize that the Six Laws were not devised out of whole cloth by Xie He, but that they have a precise set of antecedents that will be pointed out in a later section of this chapter.

The failure to parse Xie He's Six Laws correctly has resulted in an incredible array of semimystical gibberish and wildly discrepant translations. The most celebrated translator of Literary Sinitic texts in modern times could come up with no better than a "Pidgin English" (his own characterization) rendering: (1) Spirit-harmony—Life's motion. (2) Bone-means—use brush. (3) According to the object depict its shape. (4) According to species apply colour. (5) Planning and disposing degrees and places. (6) By handing on and copying to transmit designs.²⁸

This is a rather pathetic performance, being not even literally accurate (particularly in the last two laws), but admittedly more honest than padding one's ignorance with fluff. At the other extreme is this "paraphrase" by a well-known art historian who has written more extensively on the Six Laws than any other scholar during the last half century:

> Resonance initiated in the universal, macrocosmic state of energy gives birth to negentropic patterns of assonance, the coming into being of which, in a hierarchy of structural phases, is the nature of existence and life. This is reality. It is also the process by which a work of art comes into being.
> The initiation of activity in macrocosmic potentiality is manifested in microcosmic actuality, the inherent nature and structure of every phenomenon being pressed into its exterior manifestation as a cast vessel receives the form of the master mould. The painter's technique embodies such a process, and his brush is the patterning instrument whereby beauty in materialized form is achieved.[29]

Fortunately, the paraphraser gave up after the first two laws. What we have witnessed here is the complete breakdown of philological rigor in dealing with Xie He's Six Laws. This agonizing frustration over the intractability of the Six Laws did not begin in modern times, but has plagued scholars almost from the day they were first written down.

There is no point in regurgitating all of the turgid twaddle about the Six Laws and the abominable interpretations of them that have been put forth during the course of the last millennium and more.[30] However, for the convenience of nonspecialist readers of this chapter, we here provide a sample series of Zhangian-type mistranslations of the Six Laws:

> The first is called spirit-resonance and / or life-movement.
> (alternatively: life movement through spirit-resonance)
> (alternatively: [instilling] spirit-resonance in engendering vitality), etc.
> The second is called bone-method and / or the use of the brush.
> (alternatively: use of the brush through the bone method)

Xie He's "Six Laws" of Painting and Their Indian Parallels

(alternatively: [relying on] bone method in the use of the brush), etc.

The third is called correspondence to things and / or imaging of forms.

(alternatively: imaging of forms through correspondence to things)

(alternatively: [invoking] correspondence to things in imaging of forms), etc.

The fourth is called accordance to type and / or application of colors.

(alternatively: application of colors through correspondence to type)

(alternatively: [stipulating] accordance to types in the application of colors), etc.

The fifth is called layout and construction and / or placement and positioning.

(alternatively: placement and positioning through layout and construction)

(alternatively: [emphasizing] layout and construction in placement and planning), etc.

The sixth is called transmitting of models and / or reproducing and copying.[31]

(alternatively: reproducing and copying through transmitting of models)

(alternatively: [valuing] transmitting of models by reproducing and copying), etc.

It is clear that a great distance has been traveled from the formulations of Xie He, who lived only a little over three hundred years before Zhang Yanyuan.

In contrast, when we go back to Xie He's original text and force ourselves to read it as the grammar dictates (despite the clumsy syntax), such a procedure yields the following sort of bare bones, literal translation:

1. Vital Resonance, which is the engendering of movement.
2. Bone Method, which is the usage of the brush.

3. Correspondence to the Object, which is the imaging of form.
4. Accordance to Type, which is the application of color.
5. Arrangement and Construction, which is positioning and placement.
6. Transmission and Transfer, which is modeling and depiction.

We next move to a minimally interpretive rendering of the Six Laws, still sticking fairly close to the Chinese text, but attempting to convey what Xie He probably meant when he first coined them:

1. Spiritual nature is (conveyed by) instilling vitality.
2. Inner quality is (suggested through) [skillful] handling of the brush.
3. Correspondence with reality is (achieved through) the representation of forms.
4. Accordance to type is (accomplished by) [subtle] application of colors.
5. Layout and composition are (determined by) [careful] positioning and placement.
6. Similitude and accuracy are (dependent upon) [faithful] modeling and depiction.

We may note that the first pair of laws has to do with metaphysical and aesthetic matters, the second pair with technical skills, and the third pair with pictorial and representational aspects. This pairing of the laws holds an important clue about the origins of the Six Laws, so we shall return to it later in our investigation.

Finally, here are the Six Laws of Xie He as embedded in the context in which they originally appeared, the complete preface to *[Gu]hua pinlu*:

Now, by the ranking of painters is meant the relative superiority and inferiority of all painters. As for painters, there are none who fail to illustrate admonition or show the vicissitudes of human affairs. The desolation of a millennium may be seen as in a mirror by merely spreading out a picture.
Even though painting has its Six Laws, few are able to combine them completely; rather, from ancient times until now each

painter has excelled in one particular branch. What are these Six Laws? First, Vital Resonance, that is, the engendering of movement; second, Bone Method, that is, the usage of the brush; third, Correspondence to the Object, that is, the imaging of form; fourth, Accordance to Type, that is, the application of color; fifth, Arrangement and Construction, that is, positioning and placement; sixth, Transmission and Transfer, that is, modeling and depiction.

Only Lu Tanwei (fifth century) and Wei Xie (fl. late third-early fourth centuries] were thoroughly proficient in all of these. A painter's traces may be skillful or clumsy, but art knows no ancient or modern. Respectfully relying upon remote and recent sources and following their rankings, I have edited and completed the preface and citations. Hence, what is presented does not extend broadly. As for the origins of painting, it is merely reported that it issued from the gods and the transcendents, but none was witness to such.

Though the preface is brief, it is issued in grand, almost cosmic, tones. Xie He is writing from the vantage of a person who is confident that his pronouncements have the weight of the ages behind him.

THE ṢAḍAṄGA (SIX LIMBS) OF INDIAN PAINTING

The striking similarity between Xie He's Six Laws of painting and the Six Limbs of Indian art theory have frequently been noted during the past century, but nearly always rejected as pure coincidence, and never rigorously examined. Indeed, most scholars who raise the possibility of Indian influence on the Six Laws do so only to dismiss it.[32] Given the constant reiteration of the possibility of Indian influence upon the Six Laws, coupled with the automatic denial of any meaningful impact from the Six Limbs, the time is long overdue for the proposition to be thoroughly tested.

It was Abanindranath Tagore (1871-1951; a second cousin of the famous Indian poet and humanist, Rabindranath Tagore [1861-1941]), who not only was the first person in modern times to draw attention to the Six Limbs,[33] but who was also apparently the first person ever to mention Xie He's Six Laws in connection with the Six Limbs. Abanindranath was himself a distinguished artist whose "voluptuous mysticism" set a new trend in modern Indian painting.

While Abanindranath did cite first the Six Limbs and then immediately thereafter the Six Laws in his initial articles on this subject,[34] he did not attempt to correlate them one-for-one, nor did he attempt to fix their dates to determine priority. He merely mentioned that both dealt with rules for painting and both were six in number (not four or five or some other number). In his earliest articles on the subject, Abanindranath did provide some general information about the antiquity of the Six Limbs. He ended them by meekly opining that "our thought of six limbs of painting is purely our own, and is as important as the six Canons of Chinese mentioned by HSIEH HO." In his second set of articles on the subject,[35] Abanindranath actually spent more energy introducing Japanese art and aesthetics on the vague grounds that they preserved ancient traditions better than Chinese art and aesthetics from a comparable period. Naturally, the Japanese evidence is of little value in establishing whether or not the Six Limbs have any relevance for the Six Laws, so we will not dwell upon it. Finally, in his last article and books on the topic, Abanindranath went into erudite detail concerning the philosophical, historical, literary, and aesthetic underpinnings of the Six Limbs, but he did not take up again the question of the relationship between the Six Limbs and the Six Laws. In any event, nowhere in his writings did Abanindranath make a serious, systematic effort to demonstrate that the Six Laws were related to the Six Limbs. He must, however, be credited as the first scholar to note the overall resemblance between the two sets of principles for painting.

The next scholar to mention the Six Limbs and the Six Laws together was Percy Brown, in his popular and long-lasting *Indian Painting* in the Heritage of India series: "... besides the number of laws being the same, there is a certain resemblance in the general intention of both these codes. The Chinese canons, emerging several centuries later, suggest that these were originally borrowed from the much older system of India."[36] Since Brown's suggestion lacked specificity and his handling of dating problems was unsophisticated, his weak assertion of a connection between the Six Limbs and the Six Laws has naturally not found acceptance.

The preeminent modern authority on the philosophical foundations of Indian art theory, the Ceylonese-British scholar Ananda K. Coomaraswamy (1877-1947), who was also highly knowledgeable about the history and principles of Chinese art, rejected an Indian basis for the Six Laws: "These Six Canons have close analogies in Indian theory, but there is no good reason to suppose that they are of Indian origin."[37]

Many scholars who do recognize the possibility of Indian influence on the Six Laws assume that it must have come to China in a Buddhist guise. This is not an unreasonable assumption, considering the massive impact of Buddhism on Chinese culture during the Six Dynasties, the Sui, and the Tang. Certainly, Buddhism was the main vehicle for the transmission of all sorts of Indian cultural elements to China during this period, but it was not the sole vehicle, nor was all that it brought specifically Buddhist in nature (e.g., mathematics, medicine, linguistics, prosody, and countless stories, to name just a few important areas of Chinese culture in which fundamental changes occurred as a result of the importation of Indian ideas and techniques). Scholars who suggest possible Buddhist content in the Six Laws often mention that *suilei* ("according to class or type") refers to a kind of *upāya* ("skill-in-means" or "skillful means") whereby Buddhas and bodhisattvas reveal themselves in varying forms depending upon the need or nature of the beings whom they desire to save. But *suilei* is also used in completely non-Buddhist contexts.[38] Others maintain that the word *fa* of the tide of the Six Laws (*liu fa*) derives from the Buddhist concept of *dharma*, which is translated by *fa* in Chinese, but strictly indigenous meanings of *fa* (laws, regulations, rules, methods, etc.) are actually more suitable than when it is standing in for *dharma* (moral law, doctrine, nature, duty, phenomena or elements [of the universe], truth, justice, virtue, quality, predicate, etc.). Still others invoke the celebrated wall paintings in the caves at Ajaṇṭā (in Hyderabad, northeast of Bombay) as possible sources for the Six Laws. It is true that generations of Buddhist artists worked at Ajaṇṭā, but the wall paintings date from 150 to 650, with only a few from the early period and the vast majority coming after the time of Xie He. Furthermore, even-if the dating of the Ajaṇṭā caves were not a problem, it has never been shown how the principles inherent in the wall paintings there would have been transmitted to China and become known to Xie He in a discrete and codified form. Hence, it is impossible to take seriously a significant direct impact from Ajaṇṭā or other Indian Buddhist wall paintings upon Xie He. Ecke attempts to demonstrate that the sixth of the Six Laws is Buddhist by virtue of the fact that it supposedly has to do with copying, and she believes that transmission of images is an inherent part of Buddhist art.[39] Her argument, however, is exceedingly feeble, while her evidence is largely anachronistic when applied to Xie He. The only other specific claim for a Buddhist link to the Six Laws is that the celebrated layman, Zong Bing 宗炳 (375-443; N.B.: a century before Xie He), is mentioned in the *[Gu]hua pinlu* (first of two individuals in the sixth and last class of painters) as "having an understanding of the Six Laws, but not, after all, possessing the appropriate skill." Furthermore, there is indirect evidence that it may have been Zong Bing who painted an exact copy of the famous "silhouette of the Buddha" from Nāgarahāra on a wall in Master Huiyuan's 慧遠 (334-416) monastery on Mount Lu and that the painting was executed according to certain iconographic rules.[40] Even if we accept the speculative attribution of the painting of the "silhouette of the Buddha," the sum total of the evidence put forward concerning Zong Bing does not amount to a Buddhist basis for the Six Laws. Except for Zong Bing, there are no other individuals with a strong Buddhist background mentioned in the *[Gu]hua pinlu*, and Zong Bing is not the only painter in Xie He's text who is associated with the Six Laws.

Aside from *fa* and *suilei*, it would be difficult to point to anything in the Six Laws themselves that might conceivably have a Buddhist connection, and, as we have seen, even *fa* and *suilei* cannot be certified as definitely Buddhist in this context. There is nothing particularly Buddhist about the Six Limbs, but that does not preclude their having been brought to China along with Buddhism as a kind of cultural baggage. The fact that the *Citralakṣaṇa* (Theory of the Arts) was included in the Tibetan *bStan-'gyur* (Tenjur [Translation of Teachings], the second portion of the Tibetan Buddhist canon) is proof that non-Buddhist Indian aesthetic principles could be conveyed to other cultures via Buddhist intermediaries.[41]

As things now stand, the question of whether or not the Six Limbs and the Six Laws are related is at a standstill. Every weak assertion is matched by a spirited counter assertion.

The only way to solve this scholarly impasse is to examine the Six Limbs as intensively as we have looked at the Six Laws, then combine the results of our parallel investigations. The Six Limbs are spelled out in Yaśodhara's *Fayamaṅgalā* commentary to the famous Indian text on lovemaking, the *Kāma-sūtra* of Vātsyāyana.[42] They occur as a commentarial elaboration upon the word *ālekhyam* (drawing), the fourth in a list of sixty-four arts. Vātsyāyana (also called Mallanāga), the author of the *Kāma-sūtra*, flourished about the fourth century C.E. Yaśodhara, who composed the *Fayamaṅgalā* commentary, lived during the middle of the thirteenth century.

The term *ṣaḍaṅga* itself has a very long history, dating back to the late Vedic period (ca. 800 B.C.E.), where it referred to the six ancillary "limbs" of the Vedas (the oldest sacred texts of the Indian people). From that time on, it was used with reference to all sorts of things that had six parts, six divisions, and so forth. In the tantras (religious writings concerned with mysticism and magic) and elsewhere, it referred especially to the six "active" parts of the body: the head, the two hands, the two feet, and the heart. In the *Kāma-sūtra* itself, *ṣaḍaṅga* is used in the expression *ṣaḍaṅgam amṛtam* (sixfold nectar), which is made up of six elements (butter, honey, sugar, etc.) and which "provides prolonged enjoyment of sex." Here are the Six Limbs in Sanskrit with relevant English translations:

> 1. *rūpa-bhedaḥ* diversity or variety of forms or manifestations
> 2. *pramāṇāni* measurements, scales, standards, ideal proportions
> 3. *bhāva* becoming, being, existence, condition, state, nature, object
> 4. *lāvaṇya* saltiness,[43] beauty, loveliness, charm
> *yojanam* joining, yoking, harnessing, embodying, infusing
> 5. *sādṛśyaṁ* likeness, resemblance, similarity, representation
> 6. *varṇikā-bhaṅga* breaking (down) / bursting / splitting / dividing / analysis of pigments

Several stylistic aspects of the structure of the Six Limbs are worthy of note: the first and last limbs are both compounds; the second and fifth (one from the first and the next to the last) are single words; the third and the fourth (the middle two) are joined by the word *yojana*, which itself means "joining"; the first pair of limbs (one and two) has to do with differentiation of forms and layout; the second pair of limbs (three and four) is concerned with aesthetic elements; and the third pair (five and six) focuses on technical skills. The division of the Six Limbs into three closely linked pairs dealing with different aspects of painting is remarkably similar to the pairing of the Six Laws mentioned above.

A better understanding of the Six Limbs may be gained through the following observations:

> *rūpa-bhedaḥ* (literally "form-distinction") calls for a knowledge of *lakṣaṇas* (characteristic marks of a thing to be represented that distinguish it from others of the same class)
> *pramāṇāni* ("measure") requires a knowledge of *talamāna* or canons of proportion
> *bhāva* ("emotion") signifies the mood of a subject depicted
> *lāvaṇya* ("charm") implies the inner qualities of a figure portrayed

sādṛśyaṁ ("resemblance") refers to visual correspondence (in rhetoric, signifiessimilitude or simulacrum)

varṇikā-bhaṅga ("pigment-analysis") alludes to the proper distribution of colors.

The central concept of Indian aesthetics is *rasa*. The term *rasa* literally means "juice, sap, essence" and is sometimes translated into English as "sentiment." To show how pervasive and unifying *rasa* is, not only in aesthetics, but also in metaphysics, let us examine a few of its usages in various domains. In alchemy, *rasa* basically means "liquid" and implies "element" or "primary form." Among the *rasa* employed in alchemy are various kinds of salts (*lāvaṇa* [N.B.]). In ayurvedic physiology, *rasa* signifies both a bodily substance, such as alimentary juice or chyle, and the distinctive flavor or taste of things: 1. sweet (*madhura*), 2. acid (*āmla*), 3. salt (*lāvaṇa*), 4. pungent (*kaṭu*), 5. bitter (*tikta*), and 6. astringent (*kaṣāya*). These are the *ṣaḍ-vidhaḥ* (the six tastes), whose metaphorical application extends to many other areas of discourse. In philosophy, *rasa* is a subtle substance (one of the *tanmātra*) and the essence of taste. In literature, *rasa* may be used to define the prevailing feeling, tone, or ethos of a work. In this sense, *rasa* is much used by critics of poetry, but it is also frequently employed in discussions of *nāṭya* (dance drama), music, and art. Perhaps the best way to grasp the overwhelming importance of *rasa* in all of the arts is through contemplation of the term *rāsāsvādana,* where the latter part of the compound means "eating with relish, tasting, enjoying." Hence *rāsāsvādana* is the aesthetic experience, and *rasa* is "flavor, savor, quintessence," the substance of the aesthetic experience which is knowable only in the act of "tasting" the work of art in question.

The use of *lāvaṇya* (literally "saltiness," but signifying "charm" in aesthetic terms) in the Six Limbs evokes the whole world of rasa in Indian aesthetics and, beyond that, in metaphysics and associated realms. Its function is analogous to that of *mādhurya* (literally "sweetness," but signifying "grace" in aesthetic terms).[44] Metaphorically speaking, *lāvaṇya* and *mādhurya* connote the aesthetic experience of possessing or sensing "charm," on the one hand and "grace," on the other. It must be pointed out that *lāvaṇya* and *mādhurya* are not surface features but existential attributes.

From this survey of the multiple applications and implications of *lāvaṇya* and *mādhurya*, the unified nature of the arts—indeed of metaphysics, aesthetics, and other realms of thought in India—becomes obvious. Certainly, we find many of the same terms used in Indian painting theory also being used in prosody.[45]

After the sublimely subtle and richly nuanced notion of *rasa*, to which the *lāvaṇya* of the Six Limbs belongs and for which it stands, the next most vital concept in Indian aesthetics is *bhāva* (psychological state, mood). Sometimes thought of as the vehicle for conveying *rasa*, *bhāva* itself is one of the Six Limbs and has already been discussed above where they are first introduced.

Although both rasa and *bhāva* have deep roots in earlier Indian philosophical, religious, and literary texts,[46] their theoretical and practical implications were worked out in elaborate detail by Bharatamuni in chapters 6 and 7 of his celebrated *Nāṭya-śāstra*. The *Nāṭya-śāstra*, an amazingly thorough manual covering all aspects of drama, dates roughly to sometime between about the second century B.C.E. and the second century C.E., and more likely toward the early end of that span, with parts dating still earlier.[47]

It is interesting to note that Bharatamuni, who may be thought of as the historical father of systematic aesthetics in India, uses the notion of Six Limbs. This occurs in *Nāṭya-śāstra*, 7.13, in a discussion of gestures, where he refers to the "six major limbs" (head, hands, breast, sides, waist, and feet) and the "six minor limbs" (eyes, eyebrows, nose, upper lip, lower lip, and chin). Therefore, both the name and the fundamental aesthetic concepts of the Six Limbs are present already before the third century in the *Nāṭya-śāstra*.

It behooves us now to determine whether the aesthetic criteria of the Six Limbs are spelled out in any Indian treatise devoted specifically to painting that dates from a period commensurate with that of Xie He's Six Laws.

The third *khaṇḍa* (section) of the *Viṣṇudharmottara*, one of the dozens of Indian *purāṇas* (the name literally means "ancient"; these are mostly massive collections of lore about the past), consists of the *Citra-sūtra* (Collection of Aphorisms on Painting, chapters 35-43). In his authoritative history of puranic literature, Ludo Rocher states that "the text admits being a compilation of older sources,"[48] and, in her monograph on the *Citra-sūtra*, Stella Kramrisch declares that it is the "earliest exhaustive account of the theory of painting" in India.[49] We will discuss the probable date of the *Viṣṇudharmottara* below, but must first turn our attention to its relevance for the Six Limbs.

It is encouraging to observe that, not only is the elusive term *lāvaṇya* mentioned in the *Viṣṇudharmottara*, it occurs in a context that is peculiarly appropriate for our investigation of the relationship between the Six Limbs and the Six Laws.[50] Furthermore, in the very sentence of the *Viṣṇudharmottara* in which *lāvaṇya* is found, proportionate or appropriate measurement is also mentioned as a criterion for an effective painting. Thus we find the equivalents of two of the Six Limbs (viz., *lāvaṇya* and *pramāṇāni*) in the same sentence of the *Viṣṇudharmottara*, and elsewhere in the text the concerns of the other four are also covered.[51] This lends credence to the existence of the Six Limbs of Indian painting long before Yaśodhara's commentary on the *Kāma-sūtra*.[52]

Since all of the concerns of the Six Limbs are systematically treated in the *Citra-sūtra* of the *Viṣṇudharmottara*,[53] it is essential to determine the approximate date of this crucial text. Alberuni (al-Birūni, 973-1048), the famed Choresmian (Khwarazmian) scientist and scholar, repeatedly cites the *Viṣṇudharmottara* in his *India*.[54] Hence, the *Viṣṇudharmottara* must date to 1030 (when Alberuni's *India* was completed) or earlier. As to the upper limit of the *Viṣṇudharmottara*, it almost certainly falls sometime after the third century, because in *adhyāya* 63.3 mention is made of Udīcyaveṣa and of Aviyāṅga (or Viyāṅga) in the description of the image of Sūrya. These reveal Magian influence that came from Persia around the third century.[55] Thus the date of the *Viṣṇudharmottara* must fall sometime between the third century and 1030. More precise dating of the *Viṣṇudharmottara* is extremely complicated and technical, requiring reference to many relevant Indian authors and texts whose own dates are themselves sometimes difficult to ascertain. Recent scholarly opinion, however, emphasizes a close relationship between specific aspects of the canons of art enshrined in the *Viṣṇudharmottara* and the Gupta age (320-540).[56] More precisely, on the basis of sculptural features referred to in the text, Sivaramamurti detects in the *Citra-sūtra* of the *Viṣṇudharmottara* a period of transition between the art of the Kushans and the Gupta age, thus a time nearer to the fourth century.[57]

Also relevant are the *śilpa-śāstra* ("artisans' manuals") of the fourth to fourteenth centuries. These cover a wide variety of arts, crafts, architecture, and related fields. Again, much of the same aesthetic terminology as that found in the painters' manuals (such as the *Citra-sūtra*) is also employed in the artisans' manuals. In other words, we are dealing with a very old and widespread set of aesthetic standards that find their most succinct expression for painting in the *ṣaḍaṅga*. The Six Limbs are the encapsulation of a huge corpus of Indian texts on aesthetics that are securely grounded in works such as the *Nāṭya-śāstra* (before the third century) and the *Citra-sūtra* (before the sixth century) of the *Viṣṇudharmottara*. Prithvi Kumar Agrawala, who has written a splendid monograph devoted exclusively to the Six Limbs, concludes that they have their origins around the fourth or fifth century (remarking that this is near the time of Xie He) and postulates that they were fully codified sometime during the period between the fifth and the sixth century.[58]

The Six Laws and the Six Limbs Compared

We may open this section of our discussion by revealing why R and S were selected as mnemonics for the first and second binomials, respectively, of each of Xie He's Six Laws. To be blunt, R stands for "Refined" and S for "Simple." The R binomials are uniformly elegant in their diction and relatively recondite in their signification. These are the terms that have required such an enormous expenditure of erudition on the part of scholars for the last thousand and more years in order to explicate them. The S binomials, on the other hand, are straightforward and transparent. Most readers of the Six Laws, even nonspecialists, have little difficulty in apprehending what they mean. Furthermore, whereas nearly all of the R binomials can be found in much earlier literature, the S binomials were either of more recent vintage or were coined by Xie He himself.[59] Now, one may ask, why should Xie He have chosen poetic terminology for the R binomials of his laws and prosaic terminology for their S binomials? On the surface, this seems a most mysterious procedure. When we probe deeper into Xie He's *modus operandi*, his purpose for adopting such an ostensibly curious tactic becomes totally comprehensible. Namely, when Xie He encountered the Six Limbs, for which—as a group—there were no precedents in China, he was forced to come up with more or less nonce translations to convey them. Having a developed sense of *gravitas* with regard to fine writing in Literary Sinitic, he recognized that his direct, *ad hoc* renderings of the Sanskrit terms would not pass muster with the elite of his day, so he reached back into the established lexicon of the literati to find terms that would impress. Having identified six expressions of suitably dignified pedigree and elegant cachet, he proceeded to feign that they were actually the substance of his rules and that he was defining these exquisite expressions with straightforward terminology. What must have happened in reality is exactly the opposite: the substance of the Six Laws lies in the S binomials, whereas the R binomials are elaborate window dressing. Grammatically, of course, the R binomials are primary and the S binomials are secondary, whereas conceptually and derivationally the S binomials are primary and the R binomials are secondary. In other words, by the way he constructs his sentences, Xie He makes it seem as though he is equating the R binomials with the S binomials and thus, in a sense, explaining the R binomials by the S binomials. Whereas, in actuality, Xie He began with the S binomials, which were transparently translations of the Six Limbs (see below), and proceeded to prettify them with the R binomials.

As originally expressed by Xie He, the Six Laws are so notoriously difficult to comprehend that many of the best historians of Chinese art have simply thrown up their hands in despair and are reluctant to discuss them. Indeed, full sense cannot be made of the Six Laws unless they are correctly parsed and unless they are read against their Indian background. The *underlying* concepts are actually largely alien to the Chinese artistic tradition. As such, they have come to make sense in the Chinese context only through a process of reinterpretation and even outright rewriting. What the Six Laws mean now is surely not what they meant when Xie He first wrote them down (or, more cogently, just before he wrote them down in Chinese). One of the main purposes of this study is to make a dedicated effort to understand the Six Laws in the form they took before Zhang Yanyuan tampered with them.

Once we recognize Xie He's *modus operandi,* it is easy to match the S binomials of each of his laws with one of the Six Limbs. Thus, we may arrange the following two tables:

Xie He's "Six Laws" of Painting and Their Indian Parallels 383

Table 5. S binomials of each of his laws with one of the Six Limbs

Six Laws	Six Limbs	Six Limbs	Six Laws
1	3	1	3
2	4	2	5
3	1	3	1
4	6	4	6
5	2	5	2
6	5	6	4

Source: Adapted from "Xie He's 'Six Laws' of Painting and Their Indian Parallels," in *Chinese Aesthetics: The Ordering of Literature, the Arts, and the Universe in the Six Dynasties,* 105, edited by Zong-qi Cai. Honolulu: University of Hawai'i Press, 2004.

The following verbal table makes it easier to see the close parallels between the S binomials of the Six Laws and the Six Limbs: [see table 6]

The identity of the first, third, fourth,[60] fifth, and sixth[61] of the Six Laws with the corresponding members of the Six Limbs is immediately obvious. Only the correspondence between the second of the Six Laws and the fourth of the Six Limbs requires explanation.

Table 6. Parallels between the S binomials of the Six Laws and the Six Limbs

Six Laws	Six Limbs
1. engendering of movement	3. being, becoming, existence
2. usage of the brush	4. charm
3. imaging of form	1. distinguishing of form
4. application of color	6. analysis of color
5. positioning and placement	2. measurements, proportion
6. modeling and depiction	5. likeness, similarity, resemblance

Source: Adapted from "Xie He's 'Six Laws' of Painting and Their Indian Parallels," in *Chinese Aesthetics: The Ordering of Literature, the Arts, and the Universe in the Six Dynasties,* 105, edited by Zong-qi Cai. Honolulu: University of Hawai'i Press, 2004.

While there does seem to be a disparity between "usage of the brush" and "charm," the connection between them becomes evident upon further reflection. We have already explained *lāvaṇya*, the most elusive of the Six Limbs, in some depth above. As for *yongbi*, let us recall that it is equated with *gufa*. Translators are more or less compelled to render *gufa* as "bone method" by the surface semantics of the two constituent graphs, and learned exegetes explain that it has something to do with the quality, of the lines of a painting. This may well be what it has come to mean after a thousand and more years of commentarial overlays and under the impress of the supreme role of brushwork in Chinese painting and in the even more highly esteemed realm of calligraphy. But this is not what *gufa* meant when Xie He adopted the term. *Gufa*—in its original sense—may be somewhat more interpretatively translated as "skeletal makeup / structure." The correctness of this interpretation is confirmed by the synonymous expression *guxiang* 骨相 (skeletal appearance). In other words, the term *gufa* originally referred unmistakably to the inner qualities of a person or animal as seen through their physiognomy. The practice of judging the character, worth, or quality of an individual was actually exceptionally well developed for horses during classical times in China. Applied to human beings, it is also called anthroposcopy, i.e., the art of reading a person's character or foretelling his fate and fortune from the structure of the bones of the head and body. The great Eastern Han rationalist, Wang Chong 王充 (27-ca. 90), has an entire chapter (24, "Guxiang" [On Anthroposcopy]) on this subject in his monumental *Lunheng* 論衡 (Balanced Inquiries).[62]

So what really was the relationship between *gufa* and *yongbi* when Xie He first linked them together for all eternity? Perhaps the corresponding Indian limb can aid in clarifying this perennially puzzling law. It is noteworthy that the earliest Indian treatise on painting, the *Citra-sūtra* of the *Viṣṇudharmottara,* mentions *mādhurya* and *lāvaṇya* together in a discussion focusing on the bodily frame, muscles, and joints.[63] That is to say, as *yongbi* is linked to *gufa* in the Six Laws, so *lāvaṇya* is directly linked to the skeletal fundament of the body in the Six Limbs, thus removing the only possible doubt of a one-for-one correspondence between the Six Laws and the Six Limbs. Superficially, the two terms, *yongbi* and *lāvaṇya,* seem to share very little in common, yet it is possible to discern the type of link between them that Xie He must have had in mind. Because of the exalted place of calligraphy among the arts in China and the strong emphasis on brushwork in painting, it would have been hard (almost impossible) for Xie He to leave the brush out of his canons. Yet, when we take into account the direct relationship between *lāvaṇya* (one of the *rasa*) and the responsibility of the artist to capture the essential, underlying nature of the figure portrayed, that is exactly what transpires in the use of the brush (*yongbi*) to delineate the inner qualities of the person or object being painted.

It is more than curious that Liu Daochun, the eleventh-century painting critic who has twice been mentioned above, in the first of his "Six Strengths" urges the artist to "seek [the power of] the brush through brusqueness" 麤鹵求筆一也 (RSNC).[64] This is obviously a transformation of Xie He's famous second law, the core of which is *gufa yongbi*. Now, although it is almost counterintuitive, the idea that good brushwork is inherent in roughness can be apprehended upon reflection. But what is most strange about Liu Daochun's first strength is that the binomial he uses for brusqueness or roughness, *culu*, has as its second component syllable a graph that signifies saltiness. Of course, exactly mirrors *lāvaṇya*, which, as we have already seen, corresponds to *yongbi* (brushwork). As if this were not cause enough for wonder, the second of Liu Daochun's strengths, "seek 'stuff' through eccentricity" 僻澀求才二也, employs the unusual term *pise*, the second syllable of which means astringency. Along with saltiness, astringency is one of the *ṣaḍvidhaḥ* (six tastes) which play a key role in the discourse of *rasa* in Indian aesthetics. It is so highly improbable for saltiness and astringency to be chosen jointly as metaphors for important elements of painting theory both in India and in China that one feels there must have been some sort of oral transmission concerning them stretching back from Xia Wenyan and Liu Daochun to Xie He and his Indian aesthetic predecessors.

Conclusion

The Six Limbs and the Six Laws are both concerned with basic aspects of painting. The fact that both of the canonical statements of art theory in India and in China are hexapartite already gives cause for suspicion that the two sets of principles may be related. By itself, of course, the hexapartiteness of the Indian and Chinese rules is insufficient to prove that they are linked. However, when we consider that there is a one-for-one correspondence between the Six Limbs and the Six Laws, the odds against their resembling each other so closely purely by coincidence is virtually nil—especially in view of the countless other variables

Xie He's "Six Laws" of Painting and Their Indian Parallels

involved in painting that might have been chosen for emphasis (e.g., shading, contrast, depth, perspective, materials, subjects, and so forth; it is not as though there were only six possible elements in the universe of painting! Why these six and not some other six?). Furthermore, the Six Limbs and the Six Laws date from around the same time and developed in two major cultures that were in intimate, vibrant contact with each other. Thus there are historical grounds for believing that the remarkable resemblances between the Six Limbs and the Six Laws are due to cultural exchange. Finally, it is particularly noteworthy that the Six Laws, which have been seriously misread by their own most ardent advocates, become much more intelligible when interpreted in light of the Six Limbs. As to which set, the Six Limbs or the Six Laws, is more likely to have influenced the other, the answer is plain.[65]

The Six Limbs and the Six Laws correspond closely, not just one-for-one, as we have demonstrated, but pair-for-pair. The central core of the Six Limbs is appropriately the middle pair, viz., *bhāva* (the vehicle of *rasa*, the key concept of Indian aesthetics) and *lāvaṇya* (standing for rasa itself). Only this pair has an extra word (*yojana* [joining, yoking]) added to it, no doubt to emphasize the paramount importance of *bhāva* and *rasa* for art. This central pair represents the purely aesthetic, philosophical, metaphysical, and spiritual aspects of art. *Bhāva* and *rasa* are concerned with the birth of the aesthetic impulse; they precisely mirror the first pair of the Six Laws (engendering of movement [i.e., bringing into being] and usage of the brush to capture the inner qualities of the object portrayed), which were undoubtedly put in the initial position by Xie He to emphasize their essential importance for the conception of art. In terms of Sanskrit stylistics, the central positioning of the key pair of the Six Limbs with the addition of *yojana* to highlight their significance is equivalent to Xie He's opening of the Six Laws with the most important pair.

Moving to the next most salient pair of the Six Limbs, we have *rūpa-bheda* (differentiation of forms) and *varṇikā-bhaṅga* (application of colors), the first and the sixth. This second pair has to do with the technical aspects of painting, how a painting is actually executed. Again, this second pair of the Six Limbs exactly mirrors the second pair of the Six Laws (imaging of forms and application of colors), which is also concerned with the same painterly matters.

In terms of stylistic emphasis (placed between the central core and the exposed first and sixth limbs), the third pair of the Six Limbs is *pramāṇāni* (measurements, placement, proportion) and *sādṛśyaṁ* (visual similarity). This pair is concerned with the pictorial and representational aspects of painting. It should be noted that *pramāṇāni* and *sādṛśyaṁ* are often closely linked in traditional Indian painting theory.[66] Once again, this third pair of the Six Limbs corresponds precisely to the third pair of the Six Laws (positioning and placement; modeling and depiction), both in content and in function. Both third pairs focus on the result or effect of the painting: does it effectively convey to the viewer the overall effect of the object or scene depicted? For both the Six Limbs and the Six Laws, the third pair is concerned with verisimilitude.

With so many precise correspondences in both the form and the content of the Six Limbs and the Six Laws, it is virtually impossible that they are unrelated. If we accept that the Six Laws were actually modeled upon the Six Limbs (and such a conclusion seems inescapable in light of the overwhelming evidence in favor of it), however, this is not to say that the Six Laws are wholly derivative. The situation with the evolution of the Six Limbs into the Six Laws is not unlike that of the transformation of portraits of itinerant Central Asian monks into the standard iconographical form of the famous Tang pilgrim, Xuanzang 玄奘 (596-664). It has been convincingly demonstrated that the early depictions of this iconographical form had nothing whatsoever to do with Xuanzang nor with any other Chinese personage.[67]

Xie He's "Six Laws" of Painting and Their Indian Parallels   389

Figure 17. The Perfect Symmetry of the Six Limbs (Roman numerals) and the Six Laws (Arabic numerals). The central pair is at the top in both cases.

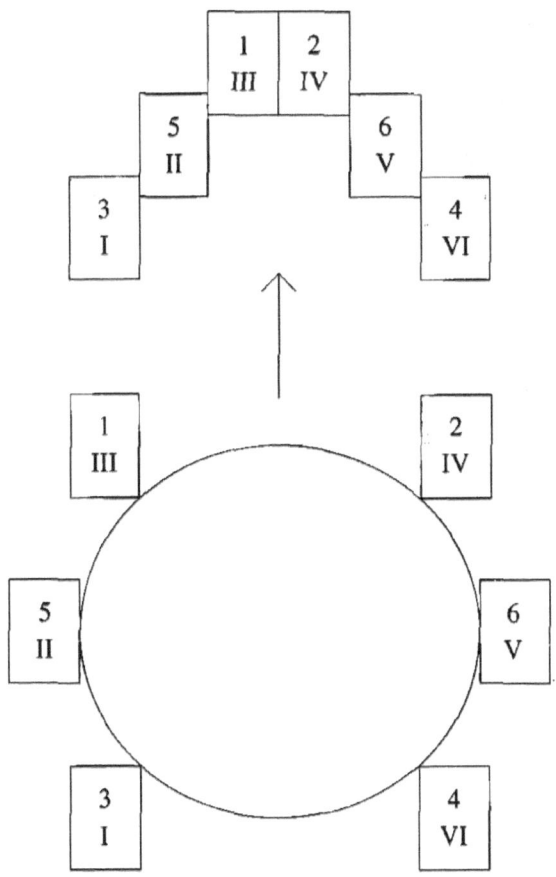

Source: Adapted from "Xie He's 'Six Laws' of Painting and Their Indian Parallels," in *Chinese Aesthetics: The Ordering of Literature, the Arts, and the Universe in the Six Dynasties,* 109, edited by Zong-qi Cai. Honolulu: University of Hawai'i Press, 2004.

Yet, for late Ming, Qing, and modern devotees of the pilgrim, the ubiquitous figure of a walking monk with a basketful of scrolls on his back has truly become Xuanzang. Similarly, in the metamorphosis of the Six Limbs into the Six Laws, the former are now only dimly visible in the latter. As they developed from the sixth century to the present day, the Six Laws truly became an integral phenomenon of Chinese culture and absorbed thoroughly Chinese characteristics. Such is the result of the intricate interplay between external influences and internal dynamics.

The Six Dynasties (220-581) witnessed a sea change in Chinese aesthetics.[68] The culmination was reached in the nearly simultaneous codification and systematization of critical and theoretical approaches to the arts enshrined in Liu Xie's *Wenxin diaolong,* Zhong Rong's 鐘嶸 (469-518) *Shi pin* 詩品 (Rankings of Poets), Yu Jianwu's 庾肩吾 (487-551) *Shu pin* 書品 (Rankings of Calligraphers), and Xie He's *[Gu]hua pinlu.* The radical transformation of theories about literature and art that took place during this period was significantly stimulated by the influx of Indian ideas that came along with the spread of Buddhism and expanding mercantile activity by land and by sea. The identical process that occurred with regard to the evolution of Sanskrit prosodic rules into the standards governing regulated verse in China[69] transpired with the transformation of the Six Limbs into the Six Laws. They started out as a product of India and became a naturalized cultural manifestation of China. Neither the rules governing prosody nor the principles regulating painting were identifiably Buddhist, but they were conveyed to China primarily by Buddhists and were certainly fostered within Chinese Buddhist circles of laymen and monks.[70]

Acknowledgments

Although this is a relatively short paper, there are many friends and colleagues who helped me with it in one way or another. Above all, I wish to thank Ludo Rocher for going over the Sanskrit text of the ṣaḍaṅga with me and for providing key references. I am grateful to Michael Meister for guiding me to the excellent little book on the ṣaḍaṅga by Prithvi Kumar

Xie He's "Six Laws" of Painting and Their Indian Parallels

Agrawala. Daniel Boucher answered questions about Sanskrit grammar, and Fred Smith personally searched the massive lexicographical files of the Deccan College (Pune, India) archives for early occurrences of the term ṣaḍaṅga. Linda Chance clarified specific points about Classical Japanese grammar. Elfriede Regina Knauer answered questions about principles of Greek and Byzantine painting. Alan Berkowitz, Robert Joe Cutter, and Cynthia Chennault kindly confirmed that next to nothing is known about the life of Xie He. Robert Harrist offered valuable help with texts related to calligraphy. Guangda Zhang brought me scholarly publications from the Princeton University library. Michael Puett and Paul Rakita Goldin confirmed my hunches about the relative rarity of numbered lists of sentences in pre-Buddhist Chinese texts. Jidong Yang checked several sources and input characters into the computer. John Kieschnick consulted the Academia Sinica databases for mention of Xie He. Rosalind Bradford and Hsin-Mei Agnes Hsu tracked down bibliographical references and Internet sites. Richard Vinograd shared his perceptive views on key points, and Lothar Ledderose called significant European scholarship to my attention. Audrey Spiro posed intriguing problems raised by my reading of the Six Laws, some of which can only be answered by future research. Members of the audience who heard me deliver an earlier version of this chapter at Columbia University provided much welcome positive feedback. For the magnanimity of all those named above, I am profoundly grateful. Last, but certainly not least, I owe a deep debt to Susan Bush for her tremendous generosity in sharing with me over two decades an abundance of relevant materials and critical insights. Most recently, she helped me visualize the relationship between the Six Limbs and the Six Laws, as depicted in Figure 17 alone. I am responsible for any shortcomings and infelicities that remain.

Epigraphs: Jin Ronghua 金榮華, "Xie He liu fa yu Yindu gudai zhi hua Lun 謝赫六法與印度古代之畫論" *Dalu zazhi* 大陸雜誌 68.4 (1984), 48 (194) of 47-48 (193-194); Tsu-Lin Mei, personal communication.

Notes

1. For a succinct and informative survey of Chinese painting theory and criticism, see the article by Susan Bush in *Encyclopedia of Aesthetics*, ed. Michael Kelly, 4 vols. (New York and Oxford: Oxford University Press, 1998), pp. 368-373. Xie He and his Six Laws are treated at length in the "Introduction" (vol. 1, pp. 3-8) to Osvald Sirén's massive, magisterial *Chinese Painting: Leading Masters and Principles*, 7 vols. (London: Lund Humphries; New York: Ronald Press, 1956-1958) as "the earliest still existing formulation of the essentials of Chinese painting" and "an undercurrent running through all discussions of Chinese painting." Alexander Soper, formerly doyen among historians of Chinese art, devoted an entire article to "The First Two Laws of Hsieh Ho" in *The Far Eastern Quarterly*, 8.4 (August 1949), 412-423, placing them in historical and intellectual context. An idea of how tremendously important the Six Laws are (despite their diminutive size) may be gained by considering that a small handbook covering the whole of Chinese history and culture in 1,500 entries awards Xie He's rules their own place and provides a complete (although slightly incoherent) translation. See Michael Dillon, ed. *China: A Historical and Cultural Dictionary* (Richmond, Surrey: Curzon, 1998), p. 353.
2. *Hanyu da cidian* 漢語大詞典, 2.35b.
3. In his *Zhongguo huaxue zhuzuo kaolu* 中國畫學著作考錄 (Shanghai: Shanghai shuhua chubanshe, 1998), p. 29b, Xie Wei 謝巍 states that Xie He's ancestors had lived at Yangxia 陽夏 (Chen Commandery 陳郡), i.e., (modern Taikang 太康 in Henan Province), but that, after the fall of the Western Jin (317 C.E.), the entire family had moved south where they dwelled at Guiji 會稽 (modern Shaoxing 紹興 in Zhejiang Province). If this were indeed true, it would mean that Xie He was related to the renowned Xie clan, which included among its members the great poet, scholar-official, and defender of lay Buddhism, Xie Lingyun 謝靈運 (385-133). Xie Lingyun was the grandson of the illustrious general, Xie Xuan 謝玄 (343-388), and the older cousin of the poet, Xie Huilian 謝惠連 (407-443). The Xies were the mightiest and wealthiest clan during the second half of the fourth century and the first half of the fifth century. Membership in the Yangxia Xies would have meant that Xie He would have had the sort of heritage that would have given him the oppor-

Xie He's "Six Laws" of Painting and Their Indian Parallels 393

tunity to mingle with high-ranking Buddhist monks who might have communicated various facets of Indian learning to him. Furthermore, Xie Lingyun, Xie Huilian, and two other distinguished members of the family, Xie Zhi 謝穉 (fl. 416-466) and Xie Zhuang 謝莊 (421-466, not long before Xie He's own time), were all known to be skilled artists. See Chen Chuanxi 陳傳席, *Liuchao huajia shiliao* 六朝畫家史料 (Beijing: Wenwu chubanshe, 1990), pp. 182-199. Thus, if Xie He were indeed a member of this outstanding family, which does seem quite probable, then he would not only have had the requisite Buddhist connections for contacts with eminent monks who might have been knowledgeable in the Indian Six Limbs of painting (see below), he would also have possessed the necessary painterly background to take a deep interest in the subject. However, since Xie Wei does not cite the sources for his assertion that Xie He was related to the Yangxia Xies, it would be risky to draw unwarranted conclusions from it.

4. Basic biographical information may be found in the following works: Susan Bush and Hsio-yen Shih, eds., *Early Chinese Texts on Painting* (Cambridge: Harvard University Press, 1985), pp. 23 and 308; Chen Chuanxi, *Shiliao*, p. 255; Chen Chuanxi, *Liuchao hualunyanjiu* 六朝畫論研究 (Taipei: Taiwan xuesheng, 1991), pp. 184-186, 205-206.

5. E. Zürcher, "Recent Studies on Chinese Painting, I," *T'oung Pao* 51(1964), p. 379 (of 377-422); Wang Bomin 王伯敏 ed., *Guhua pinlu; Xu huapin* 古畫品錄; 續畫品錄 (Beijing: Renmin meishu, 1959, 1962), p. 2.

6. John Hay, "Hsieh Ho revisited. Values and history in Chinese painting, II: the hierarchic evolution of structure," *Res* 7-8 (Spring-Autumn, 1984), Appendix, pp. 109-110, plus notes 136-140 (of 102-136), gives bibliographical references to more than two dozen studies of the Six Laws in Western languages, Chinese, and Japanese. See also Hay''s "Values and history in Chinese painting, I: Hsieh Ho revisited," *Res* 6 (Autumn, 1983), 83ff. (of 72-111) for a review of previous scholarship on the Six Laws. Clay Lancaster, "Keys to the Understanding of Indian and Chinese Painting: The 'Six Limbs" of Yaśodhara and the 'Six Principles" of Hsieh Ho," *The Journal of Aesthetics & Art Criticism* 11, no. 2 (December 1952), 100-101, n. 17 (95-104), also provides helpful bibliographical references, especially to earlier studies and translations in Western languages. A valuable study of Xie He's criteria for ranking painters, often overlooked in the English-speaking world, is Dieter Kuhn, "Die Bewertungskriterien im *Ku Hua P'in Lu* des Hsieh Ho, "*Zeitschrift der Deutschen Morgen-*

ländischen Gesellschaft 123, no. 2 (1973), 344-358. Kuhn also provides references to the excellent work of Roger Goepper.
7. There are two such lists, one consisting of six items and the other of seven items, near the beginning of the twenty-fifth chapter ("Anwei 安危" [Security and Danger]) of the *Han Fei Zi* 韓非子 (Master Han Fei) and one such list, consisting of eight items, in the twenty-fifth chapter ("Guyue 古樂" [Ancient Music]) of the *Lüshi chunqiu* 呂氏春秋 (The Springs and Autumns of Lü Buwei). Furthermore, the sections of the *Lüshi chunqiu* demarcate the chapters they contain as follows: *yiyue* 一曰 (the first says [i.e., is], *eryue* 二曰 (the second says), etc.
8. *Taishō Tripiṭaka*, no. 1059, 50.347a.
9. E. Zürcher, *The Buddhist Conquest of China: The Spread and Adaptation of Buddhism in Early Medieval China*, 2 vols. (Leiden: E. J. Brill, 1st ed. 1959; rev. ed., 1972), p. 12; Kenneth K. S. Ch'en, *Buddhism in China: A Historical Survey* (Princeton, N.J.: Princeton University Press, 1964), p. 69; Arthur F. Wright, *Buddhism in Chinese History* (Stanford: Stanford University Press; London: Oxford University Press, 1959), p. 37.
10. Richard B. Mather, trans., *Shih-shuo Hsin-yü: A New Account of Tales of the World* (Minneapolis: University of Minnesota Press, 1976), p. 123.
11. See *Foguang da cidian* 佛光大辭典, 5.4143b and 4.3421a-3422b.
12. For references, see Victor H. Mair, "Buddhism in *The Literary Mind and Ornate Rhetoric*," in *A Chinese Literary Mind: Culture, Creativity, and Rhetoric in* Wenxin diaolong, ed. Zong-qi Cai (Stanford: Stanford University Press, 2001), pp. 251-252, n. 21 (main article is on pp. 63-81).
13. William Reynolds Beal Acker, trans. and annot., *Some T'ang and Pre-T'ang Texts on Chinese Painting* (Leiden: E. J. Brill, 1954), p. 65.
14. See Göran Malmqvist, trans. and annot., "Xu Shen's Postface to the *Shuo Wen Jie Zi*" in *On Script and Writing in Ancient China*, ed. David Pankenier, Skrifter utgivna av Föreningen for Orientaliska Studier, 9 (Stockholm: University of Stockholm, 1974), p. 49 (of 48-53) and K. L. Thern, trans. and annot., "Postface to *Explanation of Simple and Compound Graphs*," in *The Columbia Anthology of Traditional Chinese Literature*, ed. Victor H. Mair (New York: Columbia University Press, 1994), p. 564 (of 562-565).
15. It is possible that Xie He, in formulating his Six Laws, received some sort of influence or inspiration from Xu Shen's lists of six types of characters and six styles of writing, especially as they were rewritten by Wei Heng. But the fact that Xie He's Six Laws have to do with painting, whereas the six types of characters and the six styles of writing are concerned

with script, means that there is virtually no overlap in their contents. If we are looking for a model, we must search within the literature on painting theory. We shall pursue that path throughout the remainder of this chapter.

16. In *Lidai shufa lunwen xuan* 歷代書法論文選 (Shanghai: Shanghai shuhua chubanshe, 1979; 1983), vol. 1 of 2, p. 78.
17. See his landmark book entitled *Some T'ang and Pre-T'ang Texts on Chinese Painting*, p. 4.
18. *Ibid.*, p. xxi.
19. *Ibid.*, pp. xxi-xviii.
20. Zürcher, "Recent Studies," p. 386.
21. Bush and Shin, eds., *Early Chinese Texts on Painting* (Cambridge: Harvard University Press, 1985), p. 40.
22. *Op. cit.*, vol. 3 (of 4), p. 2931a; *Quan Qi wen* (Complete Prose of the Qi Dynasty), 25.7a.
23. The Zhonghua editors deserve special credit for this rectification because Shen Qianyi 沈乾一, a scholar from Wujin 武進, Jiangsu Province, had refrained from marking the stop after R in his 1930 reprinting of Yan's collection, although he did add a brushed *zhu* ⟩ (dot, point), which functioned as a kind of period, after each C. See *Quan Qi wen*, 25.7a in *han* 11, *ce* 45 (from a total of sixty-six threadbound *ce* [fascicles] in sixteen *han* [cases]). Both the 1930 minimally punctuated reprinting and the 1958 partially punctuated reprinting were based on the 1894 woodblock printing by Wang Yuzao 王毓藻 of Huanggang 黃岡, Guangdong. The rough draft of Yan's collection, which was completed in 1836 but never published during his lifetime, may still be found in the Shanghai Library.
24. Nakamura Shigeo 中村茂夫, *Chūgoku garon no tenkai: Shin Tō Sō Gen hen* 中國畫論の展開: 晉唐宋元篇 (Kyoto: Nakayama bunkadō, 1965), pp. 140ff.
25. Qian Zhongshu 錢鍾書, *Guanzhui bian* 管錐篇, 4 vols. (Hong Kong: Zhonghua, 1979), vol. 4, p. 1353. Students of Chinese literature and art are indebted to Ronald Egan for having undertaken the difficult task of translating and annotating Qian's "'Resonance' in Criticism on the Arts," in which his discussion of the Six Laws occurs, and other learned essays from *Guanzhui bian*. See Egan's *Limited Views: Essays on Ideas and Letters by Qian Zhongshu*, Harvard-Yenching Monograph Series (Cambridge: Harvard University Asia Center, 1998), pp. 97-118, especially p. 98.

26. Seven years after Acker's announcement of the proper parsing of the Six Laws, James Cahill launched a determined rebuttal in his "The Six Laws and How to Read Them," *Ars Orientalis*, 4 (1961), 372-381. Motivated by a desire to defend the traditional Zhangian reworking of Xie He's rules, Cahill deployed an impressive array of Sinological and art historical skills. Unfortunately, even such a superlative scholar as Cahill could not rescue a fundamentally flawed reading of the Six Laws, he himself having to admit that his interpretation was fraught with ambiguity and far from definitive.
27. Supposedly authoritative reference works in China continue to treat R S D C as a single unit, being willing to go no further than to separate off the N at the beginning of each law. See, for example, Wu Mengfu 吳孟復, ed., *Zhongguo hua lun* 中國畫論, 2 vols. (Hefei: Anhui meishu chubanshe, 1995), vol. 1, p. 1.
28. Arthur Waley, *An Introduction to the Study of Chinese Painting* (London: Ernest Benn, 1923), p. 72.
29. Hay, "Values and history," p. 135. The author focuses on the first two of Xie He's Laws, but addresses issues that concern all of them.
30. Michael Sullivan, *The Birth of Landscape Painting in China* (Berkeley and Los Angeles: University of California Press, 1962), pp. 106-107, has conveniently assembled four relatively early and influential English translations of the Six Laws that are based on the traditional interpretation. Some of the most distinguished historians of Chinese art, who shall remain nameless, seem to revel in the presumed obscurity of the Six Laws. To be sure, the Six Laws are hard to fathom, but not so hard as they are usually made out to be.
31. One of the most respected historians of Chinese art, who shall remain unidentified, rendered this line as "Transmitting, transferring, copying, writing." Aside from the total disregard for grammar, it is particularly distressing that *xie* has been translated as "writing." *Xie* seldom means "writing" in premodern times, when it is normally interpreted as "unburden, dispel, drain (off), copy, depict," and so forth.
32. Waley, *Introduction*, p. 74: "There is very little resemblance between the two sets of Canons." Acker, *Texts*, p. xlv: "There are some resemblances, but they are not sufficient to establish any direct relation between *these* 'Six Limbs' and the Six Elements." *Zhongguo da baike quanshu; Meishu*, 2 vols. (Beijing: Zhongguo da baike quanshu chubanshe, 1991), vol. 1, p. 467a: "Some Western scholars surmise that the Six Laws of Painting included in the preface to the Chinese [critic] Xie He's *Hua pin* (Rankings

of Painters) (around the fifth century) may possibly have their source in the Six Limbs of Indian Painting. At present, most Chinese scholars take an opposing view to this sort of hypothesis. The two key laws of *gufa yongbi* and *qiyun shengdong* among the Chinese Six Laws are manifestly the products of Chinese traditional painting aesthetics. As for whether or not the Indian Six Limbs and the Chinese Six Laws merely have the same number purely by chance and are mutually unrelated in terms of content, or perhaps the Chinese Six Laws influenced the Indian Six Limbs, deeper research is awaited." Charles Willemen, who is well versed in Buddhist studies, does not even mention the ṣaḍaṅga in his "The Stanza of the Six Rules of Painting," in *Studi in Onore di Lionello Lanciotti*, 3 vols., ed. S. M. Carletti., M. Sacchetti, and P. Santangelo, Dipartimento di Studi Asiatici, Series Minor, 51 (Naples: Istituto Universitario Orientale, 1996), vol. 3, pp. 1413-1429. Heretofore, the most sustained attempt to compare the Six Limbs and the Six Laws was that of Clay Lancaster, "Keys." On the last page of his article, Lancaster even matched up four of the Six Laws with four of the Six Limbs and succeeded in getting two of the pairs (Law 1 and Limb 3, Law 5 and Limb 2) correct. The overall impression one gains from reading Lancaster's article, however, is that he was not at all interested in trying to determine whether or not the two sets of rules may have been related, but only whether by chance they might have shared some of the same concerns. This accounts for his half-hearted and incomplete effort to match the individual items of the two sets. See also Thomas Munro, *Oriental Aesthetics* (Cleveland: The Press of Western Reserve University, 1965), pp. 38-41 and 50-53, who summarizes Lancaster's findings.

33. Abanindranath's rediscovery of the Six Limbs and his mention of the Six Laws were publicized in a series of articles and books published in India and Germany between 1914 and 1922: "Sadanga or the Six limbs of Indian Painting," *The Modern Review*, 15.5; whole No. 89 (May, 1914), 580-581; the same article with the identical title was also published in *Ostasiatische Zeitschrift*, 3 (1914-1915), 103; "Philosophy of the Sadanga or the Six Limbs of Indian Painting," *The Modern Review*, 16.1; whole No. 91 (July, 1914), 102-104; the same article with the identical title was also published in *Ostasiatische Zeitschrift*, 3 (1914-1915), 375-377; "Sadanga or the Six Limbs of Painting," *The Modern Review*, 18.4; whole No. 106 (October, 1915), 337-345; *Sadanga; or The Six Limbs of Painting* (Calcutta: The Indian Society of Oriental Art, 1921); *Sadanga, ou les Six Canons de la Peinture hindoue*, translated from the English by Andrée Karpelès (Paris: Bossard, 1922).

34. "Sadanga or the Six Limbs of Indian Painting" in *The Modern Review* (May, 1914) and in *Ostasiatische Zeitschrift* (1914-1915).
35. "Philosophy of the Sadanga or the Six Limbs of Indian Painting" in *The Modern Review* (July, 1914) and in *Ostasiatische Zeitschrift* (1914-1915).
36. Percy Brown, *Indian Painting*, The Heritage of India Series (Calcutta: The Association Press; London: Oxford University Press, n.d. [probably 1918]), the edition used for this chapter (115 pages); 1927, rev. and enlarged ed.; 1930, 1947, 1953 (132 pages in the later editions).
37. Ananda K. Coomaraswamy, *The Transformation of Nature in Art* (Cambridge: Harvard University Press; New York: Dover, 1934; 1956), p. 20; see also pp. 186-189. In his abundant writings on art history, Coomaraswamy often mentioned parallels between Indian ideas and Chinese concepts. For example, he astutely observed—as have many others—that *qi* 氣 corresponds to Sanskrit *prāṇa* (immanent Breath; to which one might well add Greek *pneuma* and Phoenician and Ugaritic *rḥ*). See *Coomaraswamy: 1, Selected Papers, Traditional Art and Symbolism; 2, Selected Papers, Metaphysics*, ed. Roger Lipsey, Bollingen Series, 89 (Princeton: Princeton University Press, 1977), vol. 1, p. 315. Yet he seldom, if ever, so much as hinted at the possibility of influence from one to the other. Being more of a comparative philosopher than a historian, Coomaraswamy was simply not very concerned with the question of cultural exchange.
38. See *Peiwen yunfu* 佩文韻府 (1711), scroll 63, p. 2443b of the Commercial Press index edition.
39. Tseng Yu-ho Ecke, "A Reconsideration of 'ch'uan-mo-i-hsieh' [*sic*], the Sixth Principle of Hsieh Ho," *Proceedings of the International Symposium on Chinese Painting* (Taipei: National Palace Museum, 1970).
40. See Zürcher, "Recent Studies," p. 390 and Susan Bush, "Tsung Ping's Essay on Painting and the 'Landscape Buddhism' of Mount Lu," in *Theories of the Arts in China*, ed. Susan Bush and Christian Murck (Princeton: Princeton University Press, 1983), p. 143 (of 132-164).
41. Berthold Laufer, *Das Citralakshaṇa*, Dokumente der indischen Kunst, Erstes Heft: Malerei (Leipzig: Otto Harrassowitz, 1913), p, 3, assures us that, despite its inclusion in the *bStan-'gyur*, the *Citralakṣaṇa* "has not the slightest trace of Buddhism. Not once does it mention the name of the Buddha and it lacks all specific Buddhist terms. In the Introduction only brahmanical gods are called upon."
42. Vātsyāyana, *The Kāmasūtra*, with the *Jayamaṅgalā* of Yashodhar, ed. Gosvami Dāmodar Shastri, Kāshi Sanskrit Series (Haridās Sanskrit

Granthamālā), 29 (Benares: Chowkhamba Sanskrit Series Office, 1929), 1.3.16, p. 30. There exists a complete scholarly translation into German by Richard Schmidt, *Das Kāmasūtram des Vātsyāyana; Die Indische Ars Amatoria; Nebst dem Vollständigen Kommentare (Jayamaṅgalā) des Yaśodhara* (Berlin: Hermann Barsdorf, 1907, 1922), p. 45. Unfortunately, Schmidt—apparently inadvertently—skips the third limb of the *ṣaḍaṅga* and commits a serious mistranslation of the sixth limb. Alain Danielou's English translation of *The Complete Kāma Sūtra* (Rochester, Vermont: Park Street Press, 1994) gives only snatches of Yaśodhara's commentary. Regrettably, the *ṣaḍaṅga* is not among the parts that Danielou offers.

43. Even specialists on Sanskrit aesthetics have been puzzled by how a word that basically means saltiness could acquire the derived meanings of beauty, charm, and loveliness. Carl Darling Buck, *A Dictionary of Selected Synonyms in the Principal Indo-European Languages: A Contribution to the History of Ideas* (Chicago and London: University of Chicago Press, 1949), p. 382 (5.81.3), offers a Sanskrit root, *lu*, "cut" (as in *lavaṅga-* the clove [tree]—i.e., something spicy, originally "cutting, sharp") for *lavana-* ("*salt*"), but this seems forced. G. B. Palsule, "A Note on the Word *lāvaṇya*," *Annals of the Bhandarkar Oriental Research Institute*, 32.1-4 (1951), 261-262, attempts to derive *lāvaṇya* from *ramaṇa* (pleasing, charming, delightful), but Manfred Mayrhofer, the preeminent authority on Sanskrit etymology, finds his argument unconvincing. See Mayrhofer's *Kurzgefasstes etymologisches Wörterbuch des Altindischen: A Concise Etymological Sanskrit Dictionary*, 3 vols. (Heidelberg: Carl Winter, Universitätsverlag, 1953-1976), vol. 3, p. 93. In our subsequent investigations of *lāvaṇya*'s usage in various contexts, we shall find that the connection between saltiness and charm is not so far-fetched after all.

44. *Nāṭya-śāstra*, 17.100; 26.34. The *Nāṭya-śāstra* also discusses other aesthetic concepts relevant to the Six Limbs, e.g., *pramāṇa*, 5.179. See Manomohan Ghosh, trans. and annot., *The Nāṭyaśāstra (A Treatise on Ancient Indian Dramaturgy and Histrionics)*, ascribed to Bharata-muni, vol. 1 (chapters 1-27) (Calcutta: Manisha Granthalaya, 1967, rev. 2d ed.), p. 99. The first edition of the second volume is *The Nāṭyaśāstra (A Treatise on Ancient Indian Dramaturgy and Histrionics)*, ascribed to Bharata-muni, vol. 2 (Chapters 28-36), Bibliotheca Indka, Work Number 272, Issue Number 1581 (Calcutta: The Asiatic Society, 1961). See three paragraphs below for the identification and dating of the *Nāṭya-śāstra*.

45. Edwin Gerow, *A Glossary of Indian Figures of Speech* (The Hague, Paris: Mouton, 1971).
46. Prithvi Kumar Agrawala, *Aesthetic Principles of Indian Art: Their Primary Quest and Formation*, Indian Civilisation Series, 21 (Varanasi [Benares]: Prithivi Prakashan, 1980).
47. See Tarla Mehta, *Sanskrit Play Production in Ancient India*, Performing Arts Series, V (Delhi: Motilal Banarsidass, 1995); also Ghosh, *Nāṭyaśāstra*, vol. 1 (rev.), pp. lixff; vol. 2, p. 23.
48. Ludo Rocher, *The Purāṇas*, Fasc. 3 of Vol. II: *Epics and Sanskrit Religious Literature* in *A History of Indian Literature* (Wiesbaden: Otto Harrassowitz, 1986), p. 251.
49. Stella Kramrisch, "*The Vishṇudharmottara* (Part III): A Treatise on Indian Painting and Image-Making," *Journal of the Department of Letters, Calcutta University*, 17 (1924), 2-56. Issued separately as a book with the same title (Calcutta: Calcutta University Press, 1928, 2nd rev. and enlarged ed.), p. 4. For more information concerning the *Viṣṇudharmottara*, see Rocher, *Purāṇas*, p. 252 and Edwin Gerow, *Indian Poetics*, in Jan Gonda, ed., *A History of Indian Literature*, vol. 5, fasc. 3 (Wiesbaden: Otto Harrassowitz, 1977), p. 296.
50. See below at notes 62-64.
51. See, for example, Ananda K. Coomaraswamy, "Viṣṇudharmottara, Chapter XLI" *Journal of the American Oriental Society*, 52.1 (March, 1932), 13-21, esp. pp. 14, 19-20.
52. Tarapada Bhattacharyya, *The Canons of Indian Art, or A Study on Vāstu-vidyā* (Calcutta: Firma KLM, 3d rev. and enlarged ed., 1986; 1st ed., 1947; 2nd ed., 1963), pp. 403-410, discusses the Six Limbs in relation to the *Citra-sūtra* of the *Viṣṇudharmottara* and other early Indian texts on painting. There can be no doubt whatsoever that Yaśodhara was not the originator of the Six Limbs, but that he was merely quoting them in his commentary on the *Kāma-sūtra*.
53. For an exhaustive thesis on the contents of the *Viṣṇudharmottara*, see Priyabala Shah, ed., *Viṣṇudharmottara-purāṇa; Third Khaṇḍa*, Vol. 2: *A Study on a Sanskrit text of Ancient Indian Arts*, Gaekwad's Oriental Series, 130, 137 (Baroda: Oriental Institute, 1961).
54. Georg Bühler, Review of Edward C. Sachau, trans. and annot., *Alberuni's India*, in *Indian Antiquary* (November, 1890), 381-410.
55. Priyabala Shah, ed., *Viṣṇudharmottara-purāṇa; Third Khaṇḍa*, Vol. 1 (Baroda: Oriental Institute, 1958), p. xxvi.
56. *Ibid.*, pp. xxvii-xxviii.

57. C. Sivaramamurti, *Chitrasūtra of the Vishṇudharmottara* (New Delhi: Kanak, 1978), p. 42.
58. Prithivi Kumar Agrawala, *On the ṣaḍaṅga Canons of Painting*, Indian Civilisation Series, 22 (Varanasi: Prithivi Prakashan, 1981), pp. 9, 16.
59. Judging from citations in *Hanyu da cidian*, *Dai Kan-Wa jiten* 大漢和辭典 (Morohashi), *Zhongwen da cidian* 中文大辭典, *Peiwen yunfu*, *Bianzi leibian* 駢字類編, and other comprehensive lexicons of premodern usage, which were checked for all twelve of the binomials in the Six Laws, *qiyun* was a literary term in the Six Dynasties that was probably already in use before Xie He. Certainly *qi* and *yun* separately and in combination with other similarly elegant terms were much favored in Six Dynasties intellectual discourse, while *qi* and *yun* were often employed in the same sentence in close proximity to each other from at least the Jin period. For an extensive, illuminating discussion of *qiyun* (the main topic of the first law), see the chapter by Zong-qi Cai in this volume. There is no doubt whatsoever that *gufa* was very well established in literature by the Western Han period. For example, it is used in Song Yu's 宋玉 "Shennü fu" 神女賦 (Rhapsody on the Goddess) and in Sima Qian's 司馬遷 *Shi ji* 史記 (Records of the Grand Scribe) biography of the Marquis of Huaiyin 淮陰侯. Going back even further is *yingwu*, which was widely used in historical, literary, and philosophical texts from the Warring States and Western Han periods. The next R binomial, *suilei*, was well known in Six Dynasties Buddhism to refer to a kind of *upāya* (skillful means), whereby Buddhas and bodhisattvas reveal themselves differently and express themselves differently to various types of people, but it also occurred in non-Buddhist contexts. The fifth R binomial, *jingying*, was common in literary and historical texts already during pre-Han times for planning and construction, and was taken up by Liu Xie in his *Wenxin diaolong* during the early part of the sixth century to indicate artistic imagination. The last R binomial, *chuanyi*, is an anomaly in that it can not be found anywhere before Xie He. It is possible that *chuanyi* is a *lapsus calami* or that there has been a mistake in textual transmission. We may observe that Zhang Yanyuan has *chuanmo yixie* instead of *chuanyi moxie*, so perhaps he thought that something was wrong with the core of the sentence. On the other hand, Xie He may have fashioned *chuanyi* from many appropriate terms already in common currency, such as *chuanxin* 傳信 (transmit truth), *chuanshen* 傳神 (convey spirit), *yihua* 移畫 (copy a painting; sketch from life), and so forth. In contrast, the first S binomial, *shengdong*, is first used as an

aesthetic term by Xie He. The next S binomial, *yongbi*, was already in use by the middle of the fifth century, but it was not very common and was dictionally not elevated. Although *xiangxing* was in use by the first century B.C.E. ("to represent / image a form"), it did not have a particular meaning for the arts. By the end of the first century C.E., it is used by Xu Shen in the "Preface" to *Shuo wen jie zi* to mean "pictographic" (a type of written character). Both *fucai* and *weizhi* were apparendy coined by Xie He, and *moxie* seems to have come into use only slightly before him. Thus, although a couple of problematic issues remain, the overall nature of the R and S binomials is that the former are older, better established in literary usage, and more refined, while the latter are newer, not common in literary usage, and simpler.

60. It is astonishing that the otherwise astute Acker, *Texts* (p. xlv) goes out of his way to deny that there is anything in the Six Laws corresponding to *varṇikā-bhaṅga* when *fucai* is such a perfect and obvious match.

61. I do not wish to enter into an extended discussion of the traditional understanding of the sixth law, for that would take us too far afield. (See the chapter in this volume by Robert Harrist for a nuanced explanation of different types of tracing and copying [the presumed subjects of the sixth law]). Early Chinese theorists did not make a large distinction between copying from life and copying from models. While recognizing that the sixth law is customarily explained as referring to the copying of ancient models, it is worth pointing out that its constituent terms *(chuanyi, moxie)* and related expressions *(e.g., yixie* 移寫, *yihua* 移畫, *mohua* 摹畫 and so forth) refer not only to the replication of art and calligraphy, but also—and often originally—to painting and drawing from nature. In this sense, depicting something faithfully is to copy from life, as it were. For example, *moxie* can mean either "copy, imitate" or "depict accurately." The latter meaning is clearly intended in Fan Zhen's 范鎮 (1001-1087) *Dongzhai jishi* 東齋記事 (Records of Events from the Eastern Studio), 4 (p. 27, 11. 5-6 in the *Congshu jicheng chubian* 叢書集成初編 edition of the text) where the author mentions two painters from Shu (Sichuan) surnamed Huang who were good at painting birds. From the following sentence, it is obvious that they were painting from life and not copying the works of old masters: "Their family raised many hawks and falcons. They observed the birds' spirited valor in order to accurately depict (*moxie*) it, thus capturing their excellence." Understood in this primary fashion, it is clear that the S binomial of the sixth law corresponds closely to the fifth of the Six Limbs, *sādṛśyaṁ*.

62. See Alfred Forke, trans. and annot., *Lun-hêng; Part 1: Philosophical Essays of Wang Ch'ung; Part 2: Miscellaneous Essays of Wang Ch'ung*, Supplementary volumes to the *Mitteilungen des Seminars für Orientalische Sprachen*, 14 (1907) (New York: Paragon, 1962, rpt.), vol. 1, pp. 304-312.
63. Kramrisch, *The Viṣṇudharmottara*, tr., p. 46, no. 7 (of III.39).
64. Liu Daochun's "Six Strengths" were subsequently taken up by Xia Wenyan (Yuan) in his *Tuhui baojian*, as well as by other art theorists and critics.
65. Xie He seems not to wish to take credit for the invention of the Six Laws: "But while painting has its Six Laws, few are able to combine them all together, and from ancient times until today each painter has excelled in one of the laws." Acker's comments on Xie He's wording are apposite: "The somewhat casual way in which these six elements are introduced here—*'but although there are the six elements of painting'*—rather tends to support the idea that Hsieh Ho is quoting from some earlier work, and is not 'enunciating the Six Canons' for the first time. If he were 'enunciating' anything here one would expect something beginning with a *fu* (Now—) or at any rate a little more emphasis than seems to me to be implied in the *sui hua yu liufa*." *Texts*, p. 4, n. 2, and see also p. xli. Xie He undoubtedly was aware that his Six Laws were derivative.
66. See, for example, Coomaraswamy, *Transformation*, p. 12.
67. See Victor H. Mair, "The Origins of an Iconographical Form of the Pilgrim Hsüan-tsang," *T'ang Studies* 4 (1986), pp. 29-41, plus seven plates.
68. Mair, "Buddhism in *The Literary Mind*," p. 80.
69. Victor H. Mair and Tsu-Lin Mei, "The Sanskrit Origins of Recent Style Prosody," *Harvard Journal of Asiatic Studies* 51, no. 2 (December 1991), pp. 375-470.
70. Years after I had completed this chapter and copy-editing was finished, my good friend in Shanghai Xu Wenkan sent me two articles by the Chinese specialist on Indian philosophy and religion, Jin Kemu 金克木. The first, entitled "Yindu huajia A. Taigeer de meixue sixiang lüeshu" 印度畫家阿·泰戈爾的美學思想略述. In this article, Jin structures his presentation around Abinandranath's disquisitions on the Six Limbs (see note 33), but mentions nary a word about Xie He's Six Laws. The second article, entitled "Yindu de huihua liu zhi he Zhongguo de huihua liu fa" 印度的繪畫六支和中國的繪畫六法, is a superficial introduction to the two sets of rules. Jin dismisses out of hand the probability that they could be related. The most useful part of this article is Jin's discussion of several early Indian Buddhist monk painters who came to China. Both articles

are collected in the author's *Yindu wenhua yulun*—Fanzhu lu ji *bubian* 印度文化餘論—《梵竺廬集補編》 (Beijing: Xueyuan chubanshe, 2002).

CHAPTER 11

HORSE SACRIFICES AND SACRED GROVES

THE NORTH(WEST)ERN[1] PEOPLES OF EAST ASIA

Source: Adapted from "Horse Sacrifices and
Sacred Groves among the
North(west)ern People of East Asia,"
Ouya Xuekan (Eurasian Studies) 6 (2007): 22-53.

INTRODUCTION

Even though the domesticated horse, especially for chariot traction and later for riding, was introduced to the East Asian Heartland (EAH) from abroad during the Bronze Age, the widespread practice of royal and aristocratic horse sacrifice in the EAH is conspicuous to anyone who examines the archeological and historical record. From Shang burials at Anyang to Zhou tombs in Loyang and the tombs of local rulers during the Spring and Autumn and Warring States periods[2], the profligate use of horses for sacrificial purposes is inescapably evident. Clearly the horse meant a great deal to the elites of the EAH, and the consecration of fine victims to the deceased or to heaven was a mark of tremendous respect. For a settled, agricultural people, this obsession with equine oblation seems incongruous, since the horse is customarily associated with mobile, nomadic peoples. (Mair 2005a, 2003; Linduff 2003)

A full discussion of horse sacrifice in the EAH would require monographic treatment. The aim of this study is much more modest. Namely, we begin with a passage from the *Weishu* 魏書 (History of the [Northern] Wei), "Li zhi 禮志 (Treatise on Ritual)," *juan* 108A. Here we learn the important fact that the bodies of the victims were placed on a frame made from a birch tree. More detail containing these ceremonies is provided in a passage from *Hanshu* 漢書 (History of the Western Han [by Ban Gu; 32-92 AD; completed after his death by his sister Ban Zhao; 48?-116?]), "Xiongnu zhuan 匈奴傳 (Monograph on the Xiongnu)," *juan* 94A, which is also found in the *Shiji* 史記 (The Grand Scribe's Records [completed ca. 90 BC by Sima Qian; ca. 145-86 BC]), "Xiongnu liezhuan 匈奴列傳 (Monograph on the Xiongnu)," *juan* 50. The passage in question describes a yearly autumnal gathering of the Xiongnu at a sacred grove in which rituals concerning horses and other domesticated animals took place. From commentaries by Fu Qian 服虔 (2nd c. CE) and Yan Shigu 顏師古 (579-645), we learn that these rituals involved sacrifice and, more importantly, that they were passed down centuries later to the Xianbei (Särbi). Thus the Xianbei inherited at least some of the key traditions of the Xiongnu[3].

Similar practices were continued among many Turkic, Mongolic, and other peoples in South Siberia, Inner Asia, and Central Asia during succeeding centuries up to the present time. But if we search for parallels to the Xiongnu-Xianbei custom of sacrifice of horses in sacred groves, the most plentiful, earlier evidence is to be found among Indo-European (IE) peoples. There are many IE variants of related-rites, but the closest to those carried out at the Xiongnu-Xianbei autumnal sacrifices is that in which the skin of the horse with head and hooves still attached is suspended from a pole or frame over the sacred site of the ritual or, more commonly, only the head and sometimes one or more hooves are deposited on a pole, on the ground, or in the burial chamber.

In this study, our focus is primarily on the disposition of the sacrificial victims. An adequate investigation of the sacrality of the associated trees and groves in which the horse sacrifices under consideration took place would require separate treatment.

Xiongnu and Xianbei Tree Worship and Equine Sacrifice

The standard dynastic histories provide clear records of the sacrificial practices of the Xiongnu and the Xianbei. We will begin with one instance pertaining to the latter:

> 魏先之居幽都也，鑿石為祖宗之廟于烏洛侯國西北。自后南遷，其地隔遠。真君中，烏洛侯國遣使朝獻，云石廟如故，民常祈請，有神驗焉。其歲，遣中書侍郎李敞詣石室，告祭天地，以皇祖先妣配。祝曰："天子燾謹遣敞等用駿足，一元大武敢照告于皇天之靈。自啟辟之初，祐我皇祖，于彼土田。歷載億年，聿來南遷。惟祖惟父，光宅中原。克翦兇丑，拓定四邊。沖人纂業，德聲弗彰。豈謂幽遐，稽首來王。具知舊廟，弗毀弗亡。悠悠之懷，希仰余光。王業之興，起自皇祖。綿綿瓜瓞，時惟多祜。敢以不功，配饗于天。子子孫孫，福祿永延。"敞等既祭，斬樺木立之，以置牲體而還。後所立樺木生長成林，其民益神奉之。咸謂魏國感靈祇之應也。石室南距代京可四千余里。

When the ancestors of the Wei were living in Youdu[4], they chiseled into the rock to make an ancestral temple northwest of the state of Wuluohou[5]. Afterwards, they migrated to the south and were separated by a great distance from that land.

During the Zhenjun reign period (440-451), the state of Wuluohou sent an emissary to pay tribute at court, saying, "the stone temple is as of old. The people often pray there, and the spirits are efficacious."

That same year, [the ruler of the Northern Wei] sent the Vice Director of the Secretariat, Li Chang, to visit the stone chamber, telling him to sacrifice to Heaven and Earth, and to match the august ancestor and ancestress with them. [Li Chang] exclaimed:

"The Son of Heaven, [Tuoba] Tao[6], circumspectly commissioned Chang and others to use a fine horse and a fatted cow to make bold to inform the spirit of August Heaven. Since the beginning of the foundation [of our dynasty], they (i.e., the spirits of Heaven and Earth) have protected our august ancestors in that land. After passing through countless years, then it transpired that [our people] migrated to the south. Thus our ancestors and our fathers have dwelt gloriously in the Central Plains. They have eradicated evil and stabilized the four borders. [We,] the younger (i.e., brash) generations, have arrogated their enterprise, [so that] virtue and fame have not been made manifest."

"How can it be said that you are secluded and remote? Kowtowing, we come [to pay our respects] to the sovereign. We fully realize that the old temple has not been destroyed or demolished. With anxious longing, we hopefully look up to your lingering light. The flourishing of the royal enterprise begins from the august ancestors. Spreading continuously like melon vines, in time there is much blessing. We make bold to sacrifice to Heaven through your (i.e., our ancestors') great accomplishments. May our sons and grandsons prosper forever."

Having completed their sacrifice, Chang and the others cut down a birch tree and erected it [as a frame on which] to place the bodies of the victims, then they returned. Afterwards, the birch tree that they had erected grew into a grove worshipped all the more reverently. Everyone said that this was in response to the stimulation of the gods by the state of Wei. The stone chamber was more than four thousand tricents[7] distant from Daijing ("Replacement Capital") to the south[8].

(*Wei shu, juan* 108A, pp. 2738-2739)

Horse Sacrifices and Sacred Groves

A passage from the "Xiongnu zhuan (Monograph on the Xiongnu)" in the *History of the Han, juan* 94A shows that the Xianbei sacrificial practice described above can be traced back to the Xiongnu:

歲正月，諸長小會單于庭，祠。五月，大會龍城，祭其先、天地、鬼神。秋，馬肥，大會蹛林，課較人畜計。

In the first month of the year, the elders had a small assembly in the shrine of the *chanyu*'s court. In the fifth month they had a major assembly in Dragon City where they sacrificed to their forefathers, Heaven and Earth, the ghosts and spirits. In the autumn when the horses were fat, they had a great assembly at Surrounding (*dai* 蹛) Grove[9] to make an accounting (*ji* 計) of the numbers of people and domesticated animals[10].

(*Han shu, juan* 94A, p. 3752)

The commentaries accompanying this passage make clearer some of the details. Fu Qian explains: "蹛音帶,匈奴秋社八月中皆會祭處也." "*Dai* is pronounced *dai*. It is the place for sacrifice during the eighth month when all the Xiongnu have their autumnal community gathering." (*Ibid.*) The early Tang commentator, Yan Shigu, explains more fully and explicitly:

蹛者，繞林木而祭也。鮮卑之俗，自古相傳，秋天之祭，無林木者尚豎柳枝，眾騎馳繞三周乃止。此其遺法。計者，人畜之數。

Dai means to circle around a grove of trees and sacrifice. The Xianbei custom was passed down from antiquity as an autumnal sacrifice. In places where there is no grove, they still erect a willow branch and gallop around it three[11] times before stopping. This is their inherited practice. *Ji* ("calculate") refers to the numbers of people and domesticated animals.

(*Ibid.*)

Censuses of animals and people, particularly in the autumn, have been common throughout Inner Asian history (e.g., among the Turks, Mongols, and Manchus). (Meserve 2005).

The importance for the Xiongnu of sacrifice in a grove (or around a single tree or pole or branch representing a tree when no grove is available) has been documented by Egami Namio (1948). It is significant that the Manchus, nearly two thousand years later, also felt the need to erect a willow branch (or to find, when possible, a grove of cypress or plant as many as 49 pine trees) as the locus for their sacrificial shrines. (Meng 1959: 314-5, 319-21) Tree cults are common among Inner Asian peoples; while the willow is especially popular, many other types of trees assume cult-status. (Han 1982: esp. 278-87; Meserve 2005). Thus, the kind of tree that serves as the focus of worship is not so important as the sheer fact of there being a tree.

To return to the sacrificial ritual with: which we began, a brief account of the state of Wuluohou 烏洛侯 (a minor tribe in the northern Greater Khingans [Da Xing'an 大興安嶺], said to be over 4,500 li [approximately 1,500 miles] distant from the Northern Wei capital [at that time Pingcheng, in northern Shanxi]) in *Bei shi* 北史 (History of the Northern Dynasties) also mentions the ancestral cave of the Xianbei, but provides some details missing in the passage from the *Wei shu* translated above:

> 太武真君四年來朝，稱其國西北有魏先帝舊墟石室，南北九十步，東西四十步，高七十尺，室有神靈，人多祈請。太武遣中書侍郎李敞告祭焉，刊祝文于石室之壁而還。
> In the fourth year of the Zhenjun reign period of Emperor Taiwu (443), [a mission from the state of Wuluohou] came to have audience. They stated that northwest of their country there was an old, deserted stone chamber of the former rulers of the Wei. It measured 90 paces from north to south, 40 paces from east to west, and 70 *chi*[12] (feet) in height. In the chamber there were spirits, and people often prayed to them. Taiwu sent the Vice Director of the Secretariat, Li Chang, on a mission to inform [the ancestors] and to carry out a sacrifice to them. After engraving the text of an invocation on the wall of the stone chamber, Li Chang returned.
> (*Bei shi, juan* 94, p. 3132)

The historicity of the alleged ancestral cave and the invocation associated with it was dramatically attested in July of 1980 when archeologists discovered an inscription in the Gaxian Cave 嘎仙洞 at 50°38′ north latitude and 123°38′ east longitude. The Gaxian Cave is approximately three miles (ten kilometers) northwest of the administrative center (Alihe Town) of the Oroqen Autonomous Banner, which is located in the northeastern corner of the Inner Mongolian Autonomous Region. Oroqen is probably a derived form of Wuluohou (Middle Sinitic pronunciation *uo-$lâk$-$y\d{o}u$), which further underscores the deep continuity of the cultic and sacrificial practices described in the passages quoted above. The cave is situated 25 meters up on a 100-meter-high granite cliff face. The triangular entrance as twelve meters high and nineteen meters wide, and the cave has a floor area of roughly two thousand square meters. (Mi 1981)

Yang Hong (2002: 27 Fig. 1) has published a photograph of the invocatory inscription in the Gaxian Cave[13], and the text has been transcribed by Mi Wenping (1981: 2). It is located on the western wall, approximately fifteen meters from the entrance. Like the inscription recorded in the *Wei shu* and the *Bei shi*, it is dated to the Zhenjun reign period, specifically the same year (443) as that given in the *Bei shi*. The contents of the inscription are essentially the same as those of the invocation recorded in the *Wei shu*, but with considerable discrepancies. Clearly, though, the text of the invocation recorded in the dynastic histories is somehow closely related to that of the inscription in the Gaxian Cave.

Regardless of the factuality of the events recounted in the inscription (see note 8), it is obvious from the historical record cited above that the Xianbei of the Northern Wei acquired their horse-and-tree ceremony from the Xiongnu of the Han period. In attempting to trace the antecedents of this distinctive ceremony, where does the trail lead us? The answer is unmistakable: to the Indo-Europeans whose origins lay to the west.

Indo-European Parallels

Already in the late Neolithic period, northern European peoples sacrificed horses to rivers. Since the victims were ritually slain with a flint dagger, it is presumed that they were considered to be noble creatures worthy of consecration to the river spirits. (Maringer 1974: 313) It is generally acknowledged that horse sacrifice was practiced already during the common Indo-European period (Koppers 1936: 284-285), and most IE stocks have evidence for the sacrifice of horses[14].

In his survey of the archeological data concerning the ritual treatment of the horse in the Pontic-Caspian region during the putative Proto-Indo-European period, ca. 4000-2500 BC, Mallory (1981) shows that the horse was held in special esteem among the major groups of the Early Kurgan tradition, specifically the Srednii Stog, Yamna (Pit-Grave), and Catacomb-Grave cultures. It is interesting that the deposition of the entire horse is extremely rare in Early Kurgan burials. Generally, only certain parts of the horse's anatomy are placed in the grave or pit. The most frequent deposition is the head (skull, jaw, or teeth), followed by the forelegs or hooves. Other parts of the horse are rarely represented. Furthermore, when more than one part of the horse is found in a burial, it is usually the head and the hooves. In some instances, the arrangement of the horse remains above a burial is in perfect conformity with the head-and-hooves ritual. (*Ibid.*, 213)

The head(s) -and-hooves ritual has been studied in a classic paper by Stuart Piggott (1962)[15]. He begins with an examination of archeological finds uncovered and analyzed by the Danish scholar Ole Klindt-Jensen[16] during excavations of Migration Period sites on the island of Bornholm, which lies close to the southeasternmost tip of Sweden, in particular at the Sorte Muld settlement (in this case the fifth century AD). Following Klindt-Jensen, and moving outward in space and time, Piggott points out that comparable finds of horse skulls and feet (but not other parts of the skeleton), had been made in Danish and German bogs, at least one of which dated to the late Roman Iron Age. Similar deposits accompanied sixth-through eleventh-century burials in Hungary and Transylvania, as well as in South Russia from as early as the fourth century. Klindt-Jensen and Piggott both recognized that all of these finds could only be explained as resulting from rites in which the skin of the sacrificed horse, with head and hoofs still attached, played an essential role. Considering the available historical and ethnographic evidence, much of which is cited in later sections of the present paper, this configuration of skull and hoofs resulted from the practice of eating the flesh of the victim, but leaving its head, complete skin, and hooves intact. This ensemble was then hung on a pole (looking from a distance like an entire horse suspended against the sky) until the skin rotted away, leaving the skull and hooves to fall to the ground. As Piggott astutely closes his virtuosic, well-documented article, "Celtic seer and Siberian shaman had much in common." One cannot but agree with his perception that the widespread adoption of this highly distinctive practice attests to "a loosely-meshed network of contacts over much of Eurasia throughout subsequent[17] prehistory... ." (*Ibid.*, p.111)

The oldest evidence for the head-and-hoof ritual[18] is from the steppe Eneolithic (Copper Age) cemetery at S'ezzh'e (Sezzheye) in the Samara River Valley near Samara (Mallory and Adams 1997: 498b-499a) , east of the Middle Volga, dated to about 5000 BC. (Anthony 2005) This is highly significant, since it stems from the time of the very beginning of the Indo-European people and is located in what the majority of scholars consider to be the IE heartland[19]. The Eneolithic culture along the Middle Volga was succeeded by the Copper / Early Bronze Age culture known as Yamna (c. 3600-2200 BC), which spanned from the Danube to the Urals. Yamna was followed, in turn, by the Early Bronze Age Catacomb Culture (c. 3000-2200 BC) in roughly the same area. Both the Yamna and the Catacomb cultures continued the custom, of burials of heads and hooves of horses with the deceased. (Mallory and Adams 1997: 278b-279b) After these prehistoric instances[20], the practice has continued unabated among IE peoples and spread (as we shall see below) to many other groups with whom the Indo-Europeans came in contact as they traveled across

Eurasia. In short, nothing could be more characteristic of the Proto-Indo-Europeans than the horse, and nothing could be more broadly characteristic of IE cultic practices concerning the horse than the head-and-hooves ritual.

Perhaps the best-known horse sacrifice of antiquity is the Indian *aśvamedha*, whose name preserves well the old IE roots. The first element of the compound is manifestly from IE **ekwo-*("horse"), while the second denotes a sacrificial offering of food and drink, probably related to *mad-*("be drunk, intoxicated; rejoice; enjoy heavenly bliss [said of gods and deceased ancestors]"). It is noteworthy that there is an old Celtic proper name that is undoubtedly cognate with *aśvamedha*, namely ΙΠΡΟΜΙΙDVOS (i.e., *Epomeduos*). The ΙΠΡΟ-(*Epo-*) component of the name reminds us of Greek *hippo-*("horse"), and the *meduos* part is derived from IE **medhu-* and would have indicated a "sweet drink, honey, mead."[21] The early Indo-Europeans were evidently "crazy about horses." (Puhvel 1955) Or, as Mallory (1989: 136) puts it in more linguistically precise terms, "both the Indic and Celtic worlds still preserve the ancient Proto-Indo-European name of a horse-centered ceremony involving intoxication."

The *aśvamedha* was held during the spring in conjunction with the Old Indian inauguration of the king. The *aśvamedha* had a parallel in the Roman *Equus October* (or October Horse) when a stallion from the right side of a winning chariot team was selected for immolation. (Pascal 1981; Hubbell 1928) *Equus October* took place of the Ides (i.e., the fifteenth) of the Roman equivalent of the Old Indian month of *āśvayuja* ("month of the yoked horses," also called Āśvina). The victim was offered to the warrior deity, Mars, and then dismembered, with the head and "tail" (generally thought to be a euphemism for penis), the blood still dripping, being sent to different locations. The ultimate purpose of the *Equus October* was to insure an abundant harvest.

The Indo-Iranian peoples had a particularly close affinity with the horse. (Swennen 2004) Already in the *Ṛgveda*, hymns CLXII and CLXIII are devoted to the horse and its sacrifice[22]. It is particularly noteworthy that the horse is identified with the sun and Agni (fire, but here also functioning as a solar deity), and that the horse is said to draw the chariot of the sun across the sky. The same relationship (sun, horse, chariot) is explicitly embraced among many IE peoples, and there is abundant archeological evidence in support of this tightly knit complex of ideas (see, for example, the discussion of the Trundholm bronze chariot below under "Eurasian Continuities"; cf. Maringer 1981: Figs. 13, 16) from Europe, the Eurasian steppes, and other places where the Indo-Europeans went with their horses and chariots. This sun-horse-chariot symbolism also worked its way into Chinese myth and legend, and this has been perceptively discussed by Snow (2002: *passim*, but especially pp. 35-37).

There are many other crucial details in the Ṛgvedic hymns to the horse, such as its comparison with a deer[23], and the elaborate preparations for cooking it in a cauldron[24], which means that the victim's flesh must have been eaten. For the purposes of our present inquiry, however, let us concentrate only upon verse 6 of hymn CLXII:

> The hewers of the post and those 'who carry it, and those who carve the knob to deck the Horse's stake.... (Griffith, tr., 107b).

There were actually 21 posts (*yūpa*), required for the Ṛgvedic horse sacrifice, and they were made from the wood of six different types of trees. Moreover, special attention was paid to the wooden ring (*caṣāla*) at the top of the *yūpa*. With so many wooden posts surrounding it, the sacrificial horse may be said to have entered an artificial grove.

Despite the extraordinary importance of the *aśvamedha* in ancient India, the horse was not indigenous to the South Asian subcontinent. Because of the subtropical climate, the breeding of horses was seldom successful, hence the need for constant replenishment and revitalization from the lands to the north. The nonindigenousness of the horse in India notwithstanding, this noble animal occupied a central position in the society, religion, and ideology of the Vedic Aryans. (Stutley and Stutley 1984: 24) This would appear to support the argument that the ultimate origins of these cultural attributes lay in the steppes, whence came the tamed (< PIE√*demə*- ["constrain, force, break in"]) horse[25].

The Iranians, the other half of the Indo-Iranian dyad, were masters of the horse. In the early stages, the horse was used mainly for pulling war chariots, but gradually it came to be used for riding as well. This is attested in the *Avesta*, where heroes are described as entering battlefields or sacrificial venues "on horseback" (*Yašt* 5.51, 10.11; *Yasna* 11. 2)

> Horses were also offered to gods, and the Ābān Yašt celebrates many Iranian kings and heroes who sacrificed one hundred horses, one thousand oxen, and ten thousand sheep to Arədvī Sūrā Anāhitā, asking her for special boons. The formula well indicates the value of the horse, and indeed, an Avestan passage records that an excellent (*aγryō.təmō*) horse was worth eight pregnant cows. (Shahbazi 1985-1987: 725a)

Greek historians wrote of horse sacrifice as being a common rite during a Persian monarch's funeral. The Byzantines referred to the worship of a ἔνοπλος ἵππος (literally, "harnessed horse") among the Persians in the 7th century. The Sogdians (Middle Iranian people of Central Asia) observed a special celebration, called the *čahārom*, which centered upon the immolation of a horse, as attested in their art and religious literature. (Compareti 2003: 201)

Herodotus (IV. 72) provides a gruesome, detailed description of the Scythians' voracious appetite for human and equine sacrifice upon the death of one of their kings:

> When a year is gone by, further ceremonies take place. Fifty of the best of the late king's attendants are taken, all native Scythians —for, as bought slaves are unknown in the country, the Scythian kings choose any of their subjects that they like, to wait on them— fifty of these are taken and strangled, with fifty of the most beautiful horses. When they are dead their bowels are taken out, and

Horse Sacrifices and Sacred Groves

the cavity cleaned, filled full of chaff, and straightway sewn up again. This done, a number of posts are driven into the ground, in sets of two pairs each, and on every pair half the felly of a wheel is placed archwise; then strong stakes are run lengthways through the bodies of the horses from tail to neck, and they are mounted upon the fellies, so that the felly in front supports the shoulders of the horse, while that behind sustains the belly and quarters, the legs dangling in midair; each horse is furnished with a bit and bridle, which latter is stretched out in front of the horse, and fastened to a peg. The fifty strangled youths are then mounted severally on the fifty horses. To effect this, a second stake is passed through their bodies along the course of the spine to the neck; the lower end of which projects from the body, and is fixed into a socket, made in the stake that runs lengthwise down the horse. The fifty riders are thus ranged in a circle round the tomb, and so left.

(Herodotus 1942: 318-319)

This is not even to mention the original funeral rites that attended the death of the Scythian king, together with all the sacrifices, of men, women, and horses that occurred during the construction of the tomb and the raising of a vast mound above it[26]. For our purposes, what is most notable about the ceremonies that took place a year after the death of the Scythian king is the extravagant display of sacrificed horses set up on wooden frames.

The sacrifice of horses among the Scythians was by no means restricted solely to the funerals of kings and chieftains. According to Herodotus (IV. 61), the favorite victims of the Scythians were horses, and the Massagetae sacrificed horses to the sun, their only god, "giving to the swiftest of the gods the swiftest of all mortal creatures" (*Ibid.*, I. 216). (Thordarson 1985-87: 731a) Inasmuch as the Scythians and Massagetae were Iranian peoples (and there were others who adhered to similar customs) who roamed the steppes widely from the Black Sea to East Asia during the first millennium BC and the first millennium AD, it is easy to understand how they could have been responsible for transmitting such characteristically Indo-European practices from west to east.

The preponderance of the evidence just cited (and much more could be adduced) indicates clearly that the horse played an important role in Indo-European culture from its inception (von Negelein 1903), and that horse sacrifice was an integral part of the ritual life, of the majority of ancient Indo-European peoples. But what of trees? Did the Indo-Europeans also have a close relationship with trees? And, furthermore, were trees and horses somehow linked in the imagination or psyche of the Indo-Europeans?

The best-known, relatively up-to-date study on this subject is Friedrich (1970). But there have been many other articles and monographs written about the intimate association between Indo-Europeans and trees. For a short, authoritative survey, see Friedrich's articles in Mallory and Adams (1997: 598a-601a and passim), where we find the following perceptive comment:

> To a degree that goes beyond other semantic sets, the arboreal terms and the tree names in particular indicate a relatively strong western-central area that includes Celtic, Italic, Germanic, Baltic and Slavic. Among these Slavic shows the highest rate of mutual correspondence, which may suggest that its ecological area corresponds relatively closely with that of the earliest Indo-Europeans.

As with the horse, so it would appear with trees that the IE homeland may have lain in the region with which the Slavs were most closely related.

The first volume of part I of James George Frazer's celebrated *The Golden Bough* begins with a chapter entitled "The King of the Wood," the first section of which is about Diana and Virbius. (1935 I: esp. 20-21) Virbius was a local, Italian deity worshipped with Diana (Greek Artemis) at the sacred grove of Aricia, and was held to be the presiding genius of the wood and the chase. For some, he was thought of as the sun.

Horse Sacrifices and Sacred Groves

He was, moreover, identified as a reincarnation of Hippolytus, a name obviously derived from the Greek for "horse." According to legend, Hippolytus was a chaste huntsman and a favorite of Artemis. He was slain by horses (his alter egos) and raised from the dead by Æsculapius (the Greek god of medicine), then taken by the goddess to the sacred grove of Aricia in Latium, where he was worshipped as Virbius, a deity of vegetation. Frazer observes that spirits of corn (i.e., grain) are often represented in the form of horses. Thus we see a close interrelationship among horses, the sun, sacred groves, and crops. The second volume of part I of *The Golden Bough* opens with chapter 8, which returns to the theme of the King of the Wood, and, in chapters 9 and 10, Frazer respectively reviews in great detail "The Worship of Trees" and "Relics of Tree-Worship in Modern Europe." With enormous erudition, these themes have been further elucidated by Robert Graves in *The White Goddess* (1948). Mannhardt (1875; 1905) also emphasized the centrality for Northern Europeans of cultic ceremonies held in groves and forests. There can be no mistaking the sacrality of trees, groves, woods, and forests for many ancient and medieval European groups.

The Germanic peoples, in particular, were devoted to trees:

> Germanic cultural fondness for tree symbolism appears to have been widespread, with other, patron trees such as Thor's Oak appearing in surviving accounts (8th century) and Ahmad ibn Faḍlān's account of his encounter with the Scandinavian Rus tribe in the early 10th century, describing them as tattooed from "fingernails to neck" with dark blue "tree patterns." (*Wikipedia*, 5/16/06 2: 31 PM)

It is well known that the Scandinavian peoples were fond of making human sacrifice in sacred bogs. They did not, however, limit themselves to consecrating chosen individuals to the spirits of the bogs, since they also sunk bronze implements and other precious objects in them. What is not so widely known is the fact that they also carried out head-and-hooves rituals above them or in their vicinity. One may still see at Lejre

(Simek 1993: 187-188) in Denmark a stunning reconstruction of such sacrifices, with horse skins (including head and hooves intact) suspended from wooden frames[27]. (Fig. 18) In fact, the set-up is quite similar to that described by Herodotus for the Scythians (see above), with a pole being thrust along the length of the spine to the head of the horse, the skin and legs dangling below, and the pole being suspended from a simple wooden framework.

The sacrificial treatment of the horse in Sweden is documented for the eleventh century by Adam of Bremen[28] in his history (IV. 27):

> It is the custom moreover every nine years[29] for a common festival of all the provinces of Sweden to be held at Uppsala. Kings and commoners one and all send their gifts to Uppsala, and what is more cruel than any punishment, even those who have accepted Christianity have to buy immunity from these ceremonies. The sacrifice is as follows: of every living creature they offer nine head, and with the blood of those it is the custom to placate the gods, but the bodies are hanged in a grove which is near the temple; so holy is that grove to the heathens that each tree in it is presumed to be divine by reason of the victim's death and putrefaction. There also dogs and horses hang along with men. One of the Christians told me that he had seen seventy-two[30] bodies of various kinds hanging there, but the incantations which are usually sung at this kind of sacrifice are various and disgraceful, and so we had better say nothing about them.
>
> (quoted in Davidson 1988: 59)

Adam's Catholic disapprobation notwithstanding, the extreme veneration for groves and the trees within them comes through clearly in this passage. In the sacrifice of men and horses (dogs were particularly important to the Scythians and other Iranian peoples [Mair 1998]), the commonality with Scythian sacrifice is also evident, except that the Scythians—denizens of the steppe—had to resort to posts on which to hang their sacrificial victims, rather than sacred trees. There are, more-over, literary records made by the Vikings themselves which attest to their practice of the peculiar impaling ceremony described for the Scythians and many other Eurasian peoples throughout this study. (Boyle 1963: 207n33; Chadwick 1942: 76)

Jones and Pennick (1995: 139-40) point out that "Ceremonial horse slaughter for a sacral meal of horseflesh was part of northern European Paganism." They go on to explain that the horse was the totemic beast of Woden / Odin, and that the church consequently made determined (but by no means entirely successful) efforts to eradicate it throughout the medieval period and even into early modern times.

The connection between Odin and the horse is cemented through what is the grandest tree of all, Yggdrasill (or Ygdrasil). In Norse mythology, this is the great World Ash Tree whose roots and branches hold together heaven, earth, and hell (indeed, all the nine worlds of Norse cosmology [at the bottom of which lay a spring to water the great tree]) a veritable *axis mundi*[31]. The name is commonly interpreted to mean "Terrible Horse" ("Terrible" being an epithet of Odin), or "The Horse of Ygg (the Ogre)."[32] Yggdrasill was also conceived of as Odin's gallows tree, the gallows being compared to a steed (*drasil*) on which men rode to their death[33].

In his *Germanic Mythology*, the great German philologist and folklorist, Jakob Grimm (1785-1863), provides extensive material that is relevant to the present inquiry:

> In the oldest times chiefly horses seem to have been sacrificed; undoubtedly their flesh was universally eaten before the introduction of Christianity. Missionaries found nothing so repellant about the pagans as the latter not abandoning the killing of horses and enjoying of their flesh. The cutting off of the horse's head, which was not eaten but dedicated to the God, must not be overlooked in this connection.
>
> Among all animal sacrifices, that of the horse was the most noble and the most solemn. Our forefathers had it in common with

> several Slavic and Finnish peoples, with Persians and Indians. The horse was held by them all to be a particularly sacred animal....
>
> A temple is simultaneously a wood. What we think of as a walled building merges, the farther back we go, into a sacred place untouched by human hands, in a grove and enclosed by dense trees. There the God dwells, veiling his form in the rustling foliage of the boughs. There is the place at which the hunter has to present him with the game he has killed and the herdsman his horses, oxen and rams.
>
> Here and there a God may haunt a mountain top, a cave in the rocks, a river. But the solemn general worship by the people had its seat in the grove.
>
> In the course of centuries and until the introduction of Christianity, the custom was served of worshipping the deity in the sacred forests and trees. Among the Saxons and Frisians the worship in the groves lasted far longer. In various parts of Lower Saxony and Westphalia traces of sacred oaks have been preserved until recent times, to which the people showed a half-pagan, half-Christian reverence.
> (Grimm 1997: 10, 12-13 [with minor changes])

Thus we observe among the Indo-Europeans, virtually from the time of their inception, a peculiar concatenation of veneration for horses and for trees. The horsehead-and-hooves ritual, in essence, combines the two forms of worship into a remarkably impressive sacrificial ritual. In its earliest stages, the horsehead-and-hooves ritual was uniquely characteristic of Indo-European peoples. As the Indo-Europeans (and their equestrian arts) spread across Eurasia, however, they carried this distinctive form of sacrificial ceremony (together with other aspects of horse culture) with them, transmitting it to many other groups who were denizens of the steppe.

Horse Sacrifices and Sacred Groves

Eurasian Continuities

At Botai, an Eneolithic site southeast of the Urals in the northern part of Kazakhstan dating to c. 3600-3100 BC, hundreds of thousands of horse bones have been discovered. Aside from being used for consumption, the horse had other functions at Botai. For example, we see an interesting ritual practice involving parts of the horse. The people there buried the tops of horse skulls next to articulated cervical vertebrae in ritual pits around the outside of their houses. The heads pointed to the northeast (spring kill, facing the rising sun), east (probably late summer), or southeast (autumn kill, the most frequent). (Olsen 2005; Olsen 2003: esp. 98a-100b)

Head and neck burials were very common in the Bronze Age in Mongolia. These are often found in association with a particular type of burial complex called a *khirigsuur* (also spelled *khereksur*). This consists of a burial under a large stone mound with a square (or, less often, round) stone enclosure. While there are numerous *khirigsuurs* in Mongolia, we may take the site of Urt Bulagyn (KYR1) as typical, though larger than most. Urt Bulagyn is located in the valley of the Khanuy River, to the north of the Khangay mountain range in Arkhangai Aimag. The central mound has yet to be excavated, but several of the satellite mounds have yielded extremely interesting results. All together, there are approximately 1,750 small mounds around the outside of the rectangular wall made of stones. Concentrated on the eastern and southern sides, each mound typically has a horse head and neck in the center under a pile of stones. All of the horse heads point to the east or southeast (120° or slightly less), in all likelihood a solar orientation. At other *khirigsuurs*, satellite mounds contained various combinations of head, neck, and hoof remains. The orientations of the heads range from east to southeast (around 90° to about 135°. Some of the *khirigsuurs* give evidence of growth and use over an extended period of time. The upper and lower limits of C^{14} dates obtained from *khirigsuurs* in the Khanuy Valley thus far range from 1390 to 680 BC, with the average hovering around 1000 BC. (Olsen 2005; Allard and Erdenebaatar 2005)

It is not surprising that the horse is closely associated with the Sun God in many areas of the Eurasian steppe and beyond. Indeed, one of the most evocative Bronze Age works of art from Northern Europe is the famous Trundholm bronze sun chariot, which dates to c. 1650 BC. The Trundholm sun chariot consists of a model of a horse on four wheels drawing a disk, which is also on wheels (two in this case). The disk is gold-plated on one side, to represent the sun, while the other side may have been meant to represent the moon. The diameter of the disk is 25.9 cm. and the overall length of the entire vehicle is 59 cm. It was recovered from the bog at Trundholm, on the island of Zealand between Jutland (Denmark) and Sweden[34]. (Hammond 1988: 117)

The monumental kurgans at Arzhan (Tuva, Uyuk Valley, in the Altai region of the Russian Federation) provide further insight into the lavish use of horses for sacrifice by peoples of the Eurasian steppe during the first millennium BC. Arzhan kurgan I was constructed during the 9th-8th centuries BC, making it the source of the oldest-known early Scythian artifacts of the Eurasian steppe. It was 4 meters in height and 120 meters in diameter, which gives a good idea of its enormous proportions. Beneath the mound, nearly a hundred wooden burial chambers were arrayed in concentric, interlocking circles around a central tomb. It is estimated that this huge kurgan would have required no less than 1, 500 men to build in a period of seven or eight days. Found within the kurgan were the complete bodies of 160 fully caparisoned horses, plus the remains of 300 additional horses whose flesh had been eaten (Sōma 2005).

Arzhan kurgan II, which yielded massive amounts of golden objects, also belongs to the early Scythian period, although to the latter part of this period— approximately the 7th c. BC. Among the 9, 300 objects recovered from the site by a joint German-Russian team working there from 2000 to 2002, fully 5,700 are made of gold, making it one of the

Horse Sacrifices and Sacred Groves 425

richest archeological inventories ever found in Siberia and the Eurasian steppe. Within the kurgan of Arzhan II, a total of 26 graves have been excavated. For the purposes of our present investigation, the most vital is number 16, significantly positioned in the southeastern sector of the kurgan. In this carefully constructed grave were deposited the remains of 14 horses, complete with bronze bits, cheekpieces, and other fittings, as well as golden ornaments for the mane, and so forth. This grave of elaborately sacrificed horses was covered by a large quantity of massive stone slabs, signaling its special ritualistic importance. (Parzinger 2003; Čugunov 2003)

A little less than a thousand kilometers to the southwest of Arzhan lies the vast complex of cemeteries at Charwighul (Chawuhugou), south of the Tangri Tagh (Tian Shan ["Heavenly Mountains"]) near Khotunsumbul (Hejing), along the north central rim of the Tarim Basin. A typical tomb here is 83M18 in Cemetery I. The main tomb is a stone-lined pit which was covered with massive monoliths and is marked on the surface by a circle of stones. Along the northwestern and western perimeter of the grave were found several ancillary burials, including one with a single horse skull and four thighbones, one with two horse skulls and four hooves, and another one with one horse skull and four hooves, plus the grave of an infant. C14 dates at this cemetery range from 825 ± 80 into 525 ± 80 BC. Charwighul was probably associated with Wusun, or perhaps Scythians, in any event Iranian peoples of some sort. At Zaghunluq, near Chärchän (Qiemo) along the southeastern rim of the Tarim Basin, horse skulls and forelegs are found in burials from a similar time period. At Moron in northern Mongolia, there is a *khirigsuur* known as Ulaan Uushig I, which dates to around the tenth century BC. All along the eastern edge of the site (outside the square enclosure) there are 21 small stone mounds, among which five small pits typically yielded a horse skull, four hooves, and a vertebra. (Sōma 2005)

The ritual practices discussed above in this section all preceded, or were contemporary with, the horse sacrifices of the Xiongnu and Särbi described near the beginning of this paper. The same sorts of treatment of the horse were maintained in Asia during the succeeding centuries. Boyle (1965: 145) recognizes a form of horse sacrifice among the 13th- and 14th- century Mongols "as a late survival of a tradition which goes back to the-great Scythian barrows on the Kuban[35] in the 6th century B.C." The Mongol practice of erecting one or more horse skins over a burial site is documented by travelers from the west: Giovanni da Pian del Carpini, Vincent of Beauvais, Ricoldo da Montecroce, Kirakos of Ganjak, and Ibn-Baṭṭūṭa. As reconstructed from these various sources, the procedure was roughly as follows: "First the horse was ridden around until it dropped of exhaustion; its head was then washed in kumys, its bones and intestines removed and a pole was thrust in at the belly and out through the mouth." (*Ibid.*, p. 147)

It is worth quoting one of these sources in more detail. Here is the testimony of the Franciscan friar Giovanni da Pian del Carpini (ca. 1180-1252), who was the first notable European traveler in the Mongol empire:

> And they bury with him a mare and her foal and a horse with bridle and saddle, and another horse they eat and fill its skin with straw, and this they stick up on two or four poles, so that in the next world he may have a dwelling in which to make his abode and a mare to provide him with milk, and that he may be able to increase his horses and have horses on which to ride[36].

A still more graphic, first-hand account of this peculiar form of ritual as practiced by the Mongols is provided by the Armenian historian Kirakos of Ganjak (1201-1272), who had been captured by the Mongols and forced to serve as one of their secretaries. Writing around 1241, he vividly describes the sacrifice:

> And when they wished to have a memorial of the dead man, they ripped open the belly of a horse and pulled out all the flesh without bones, and then they burnt the intestines and bones and sewed up the skin of the horse as though it had its whole body.

Having sharpened a great pole they thrust it in the belly and pulled it out through the mouth; and thus they raised it up on a tree or some elevated place.

(Boyle 1963: 204-207)

A passage by the Armenian historian Movsēs Dasxurançi (Kalankatuaçi), à propos the mission of the Armeno-Albanian bishop Israyel in 681-682 to the Khazars (or vassals of the Khazars) in Northern Daghestan, reveals deep affinities with the worship of trees and with horse sacrifices among the Northern Europeans discussed earlier in this paper. According to Boyle (1965: 148), Movsēs Dasxurançi states that "this people used to sacrifice horses to oak-trees dedicated to Tengri[37], pouring the animals blood over the trees and suspending their heads and skins from the branches." Boyle goes on to comment that "This is a ritual which survived into modern times amongst the [Finnish and Turkic] forest peoples along the [Middle] Volga." Here I wish to reiterate that the general pattern would appear to be that of a preference for display of the horse's remains in trees, but that where trees were scarce or lacking altogether (as in many parts of the steppe), resort to posts and poles procured from elsewhere was acceptable.

Similar equine sacrificial customs were adopted by the Old Türks of Central and Inner Asia as a crucial component of their burial practices. (Ōsawa 2002) (Fig. 19) Medieval European and Arabian travelers record grave monuments consisting of horse carcasses or horse hides among the Cumans and various Altaic peoples of Central Asia. (Roux 1963: esp. 135ff; Boyle 1965: 145-150; Thordarson 1985-1987; 731a)

During the mid-19th century, at the spring festival Kalmucks in the valley of the Ichurish in the Altai held sacrifices to their deity. The rich gave horses, while the poor offered sheep or goats. The victim was slain and then flayed: its skin was raised on a pole above a framework, placed with its head facing east. The flesh was cooked in a large cauldron, and the tribe held a great feast. (Czaplicka 1914: 304; quoting T. W. Atkinson, *Oriental and Western Siberia* [1858: 382-383])

Radloff (1968 [1893]: 20-25) describes in detail a Siberian horse sacrifice conducted by a shaman, including the words of his chants and songs. In this case too, the pelt of the victim, with head and hooves still attached, is suspended from a long pole. (Fig. 20) Among the Mongol Buryat, the skin and head of a horse are symbolically raised up towards Heaven on a pole during the annual tribal sacrifice. (Chadwick 1942: 76) (Fig. 21) Eliade (1964: 190-97, esp. 192) provides a graphic description of the killing of the sacrificial victim and the display of its pelt and bones on a long pole. (Fig. 22) He also notes that the same ceremony exists among many Altaic tribes and the Teleut, and that the sacrifice of the head and long bones is practiced among Arctic peoples as well (though naturally using reindeer instead of horses).

Finally, Sandor Bökönyi (1978-1979) has documented the vestigial persistence of these rituals in modern Hungary, where horse skulls are mounted on fenceposts.

This has by no means been intended as an exhaustive account of Eurasian horse sacrifice ceremonies, but rather as a representative sampling. One thing that emerges clearly from this survey is the widespread adoption of the head-and-hooves ritual by numerous different groups who lived on the steppe, or who were in close contact, with steppe peoples regardless of ethnic or linguistic affiliation.

Conclusion

It is telling that the major sacrifices of the Xiongnu and Xianbei (as with the Romans and other Indo-Europeans) were in autumn when the horses were at their fattest and healthiest for consumption. The Kazakhs and Mongolians still observe this custom, although the Mongolians do not eat horse very much. The survival of the Xiongnu-Xianbei horse-and-tree ritual may be seen in what the Mongolians still do today. They place a stick in a stone pile (*oboo*, also spelled *obo, obu, obugu, obun, etc.*) and put horse heads, vodka bottles, and other offerings around the base. To decorate and sanctify the "tree," they tie blue prayer scarves onto it. When a traveler comes up to an *oboo*, he or she places a small stone on the pile and walks clockwise around the *oboo* three times[38]. The persistence of ancient Eurasian horse-related customs is also witnessed among Kazakhs who have moved from Mongolia to Kazakhstan. They still put horse skins on sticks, especially if someone is ill. (Olsen 2005)

Human beings engage in animal sacrifice for a variety of reasons: to appease or please the gods, to seek blessings, to avoid disasters, to celebrate good fortune, to mourn the loss of a leader or loved one, and so on. The domestic animals sacrificed include dogs, pigs, chickens, cattle, goats, and sheep. As we have seen, horses were also sacrificed, but it seems as if they were sacrificed less often than the other domestic animals, probably because they were considered to be more valuable and more loved. Thus, when human beings did sacrifice horses, it was often at moments of extraordinary importance, such as the death or coronation of a king or ruler, or at a major (national) festival. The horse sacrifice was the most aristocratic of sacrifices, and it was often carried out in particularly sacred spaces, such as hallowed groves. Furthermore, it was especially among the people of the steppe, above all the Indo-Europeans who domesticated the horse and those who succeeded them (the Xiongnu, the Xianbei, the Mongols, etc.), that horse sacrifice was performed with the utmost solemnity.

ACKNOWLEDGEMENTS

I am grateful to the following friends, colleagues, and students for supplying various types of information or references: David Anthony, Elena Kuzmina, J. P. Mallory, Peter B. Golden, Ruth Meserve, Sandra Olsen, Thomas Barfield, Scott Pearce, Denis Sinor, Ludo Rocher, Elizabeth J. W. Barber, Kathlene Baldanza, Frank Chance, Nicola Di Cosmo, Bryan Miller, Linda Chance, Robert Drews, Sanping Chen, Taishan Yu, Wenkan Xu, Jidong Yang, Matteo Compareti, Takashi Ōsawa, Alban

Kojima, Endymion Wilkinson, Paul Goldin, Takuya Sōma, Min Mao, and Rosalind Bradford. I am also indebted to Suzanne G. Valenstein for asking me a question concerning tree worship that made me think about this topic in the first place.

PICTURES

Figure 18. Reconstruction of a seventh-century (Iron Age) horse sacrifice over a sacred bog at Lejre, Denmark.

Source: "Horse Sacrifices and Sacred Groves among the North(west)ern People of East Asia," *Ou ya Xue kan* (Eurasian Studies) 6 (2007): 51. Nigel Pennick. (Jones and Pennick 1995: 138, Plate 8.1)

Figure 19. Reconstruction of a memorial service among the old Türks of the eastern Altai.

Source: "Horse Sacrifices and Sacred Groves among the North(west)ern People of East Asia," *Ou ya Xue kan* (Eurasian Studies) 6 (2007): 51. (Ōsawa 2002: 200, Fig. 15; after V. D. Kubarev, *Drevnetiurkskie izvaniya Altaya* [Novosibirsk: 1984], 80).

Figure 20. Altaic sacrificial setup with stuffed horse pelt, including head and hooves.

Source: "Horse Sacrifices and Sacred Groves among the North(west)ern People of East Asia," *Ou ya Xue kan* (Eurasian Studies) 6 (2007): 52. (Radloff 1968 [1893] II. 18, Tafel 1)

Figure 21. "Oirot" horse sacrifice.

Source: "Horse Sacrifices and Sacred Groves among the North(west)ern People of East Asia," *Ou ya Xue kan* (Eurasian Studies) 6 (2007): 52. (Boyle 1963: 205) This often reproduced (but seldom accurately attributed) photograph is from an article by Kurt Lubinski entitled "Bei den Schamanen der Ursibirier der Kampf der Sowjetunion gegen den Medizinmann" in the *Berliner Illustrierte Zeitung* (November 25, 1928).

Figure 22. Drawing of a sacrificial scene on a shaman's magic drum from the Altai region.

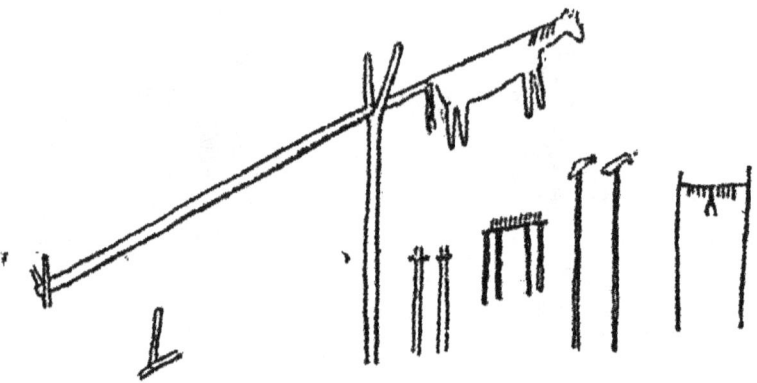

Source: "Horse Sacrifices and Sacred Groves among the North(west)ern People of East Asia," *Ou ya Xue kan* (Eurasian Studies) 6 (2007): 52.
Note. Aside from the horse pelt with head and hooves attached, there is also a rectangular offering table, two stakes with bird figures at the top, a cord with pendant objects, and so forth. (Harva 1938: 564 Abb. 107)

Notes

1. As in previous papers on related themes, by "north(west)ern" I mean both "northern" and "northwestern" (in relation to the East Asian Heartland [EAH]).
2. One extraordinarily large sacrificial horse pit was discovered next to the tomb of Duke Jing 景公 (r. 547-490 BC) of the state of Qi 齊 (at modern Heyatou in Linzi 臨淄, Shandong Province). It is about 200 meters long and contains the skeletons of more than 600 sacrificed horses. (Chang and Xu 2005: 233, Fig. 7.42) The sight of such an enormous number of horses lined up in pairs and stretching into the distance is overwhelming. Clearly the Duke of Qi was striving to make a statement through this grossly prodigal sacrifice. For horse-poor Shandong, the significance of his act is all the more profound. The amount of resources that must have been expended to procure such a vast amount of sacrificial victims is stupendous. It is no wonder that, during the Shang period, the people of the EAH—surely not without envy—referred to certain of their horse-rich nomadic neighbors as *duoma* 多馬 ("[having] many horses").
3. The contentious question of the identity of the Xiongnu 匈奴 is far too complicated to address here. Suffice it to say that the name Xiongnu (Old Sinitic *χiung-no) is clearly related to the ethnonym Hun, since they are equated via Sogdian *xwn* (Hun). The latter occurs in the famous Sogdian letters of the early fourth century (311 AD), which explicitly identify the Xiongnu as *xwn*. (Sims-Williams 1996: 47) This does not, however, mean that the ethnic composition of the Xiongnu and Hun confederations were identical. To be sure, as is natural for highly mobile, clan-based, steppe confederacies, their ethnic makeup was liable to shift in accordance with time and circumstance. Still, while the ethnic composition of the Xiongnu and the Huns may have varied, there is no reason to doubt their fundamental political and cultural identity. (Wright 1997; de la Vaissière 2005). // The role of the Xiongnu has been a major theme of research into the dynamics of the interrelationship between the steppe, nomadic zone and the settled, agricultural zone in East Asian history during the late first millennium BC and early first millennium AD. See Barfield (1989) and Di Cosmo (2002) for two different, yet equally illuminating, approaches to the question.

4. Youdu means roughly "in the northern area where they had gathered"; lit., "secluded capital."
5. A branch of the Xianbei people. As so often happens with words and names transcribed into Sinitic, their name is written in different ways, and they are undoubtedly the same people as the Wuluohun 烏羅渾 (Middle Sinitic pronunciation *'uo-lâ-ɣuən). While modern ethnographers have not made a connection with the tiny (around 7,000 individuals in 1990) minority nationality (shaoshu minzu 少數民族) of today known as the Oroqen (MSM Elunchun 鄂倫春; they are also called variously Chilins, Orochs, Orochels, Orochens, Orochons, Orochans, Oronchans, Orochens, Orochis, Oroquens, Solons, Soluns, and Suluns), there are compelling reasons to link the early medieval Wuluohou / Wuluohun with the Oroqen. Aside from the obvious similarity of their names, the Oroqen live in precisely the same area as did the Wuluohun, namely, in Huma, Xunke, Aihui, and Jiayin counties of Heilongjiang Province and in the Hulun Buir League of the Inner Mongolian Autonomous Region. Their language is Tungusic and is thought by ethnolinguists to be closely related to (perhaps even a dialect of) Evenk. The Oroqen ethnonym is generally interpreted as meaning "mountain people" or "reindeer people (i. e., herders)". For a valuable introduction to the history and ethnography of the Oroqen, together with a helpful bibliography concerning them, see Olson (1998: 267-70). For anthropological (including physical anthropological) data about the Oroqen and photographs of them, see Du and Yip (1993: 39-42). For the folklore of the Oroqen, with due attention to horses, trees, and solar themes, see Stuart and Li (1994).
6. That is, Taiwu Di, the third Northern Wei emperor, 408-452, r. 423-452.
7. Approximately 1, 333 miles. This is a very crude approximation of the actual distance from the far northeastern part of Inner Mongolia, where the Gaxian Cave is located, to Datong in northern Shanxi, where the Northern Wei had its capital until Xiaowendi moved it farther south to Luoyang in the year 493. The actual distance is about 900 miles (roughly 1,400 kilometers).
8. For a detailed historical and political analysis of this and related texts, see Pearce (forthcoming). Most modern scholars hold that the legend of the ancestral cave-shrine of the Northern Wei rulers was concocted by Emperor Taiwu in collusion with his advisers, and perhaps also with the collaboration of the Wuluohu.In any event, the entire episode of the fifth-century discovery of the shrine is deeply revealing of the ethnic complexities and international relations of the time.

9. In accordance with the commentary of Yan Shigu, this might more precisely and felicitously be rendered as "Grove of Circumambulation."
10. The exact same passage (with one tiny exception) occurs in *Shi ji, juan* 110, p. 2892, commentaries on p. 2893. The only difference between the text in the *Han shu* and that in the *Shi ji* is that, for the *long* of Longcheng 龍城 (Dragon City) the latter aberrantly has 蘢城 (City of *Polygonum orientale* [prince's feather]).
11. Many of the old Indo-European horse sacrifices had some noticeable aspect of threeness inherent in them (e.g., the *aśvamedha* [to be described below] lasted three days, the flesh of the horse was offered to three different deities or three estates [as in the Roman *October Equus*, also to be described below], and so forth), and this naturally leads to a consideration of the tripartite nature of society and myth (the so-called "functions") as analyzed by Georges Dumézil (1898-1986) , but a full discussion of this topic lies beyond the scope of the present inquiry.
12. One *chi* among the Northern Wei was equal to 29. 6 cm.
13. In the same article, Yang shows photographs of the inside and outside of the cave, and discusses the art of the Tabgatch Särbi during this period.
14. For a brief but enlightening introduction to horse sacrifice among the early Indo-European peoples, see Mallory (1989:135-37).
15. See also Maringer (1981: 191-192) for additional evidence, references, and penetrating comments on the head-and-hooves ritual.
16. References to the pertinent works of Klindt-Jensen and other scholars may be found in the first half-dozen notes of Piggott's article.
17. By which Piggott means subsequent to the Sub-Mesolithic communities of the early second millennium BC.
18. In the archeological record, the "head and hooves" cult usually shows up as the head and hooves of the animal being found just below the surface of the burial. This, however, reflects what are merely the remnants of the entire skin of the animal with the head and hooves still intact, but all other parts (including flesh and bones) having been removed before display on a wooden frame. After the wood and the skin disappear, all that is left are the head and the hooves.
19. See, for example, Maringer (1981: 177), who holds that "[t]he domesticated horse emerged in the wooded steppe north of the Caspian and Black Seas" at a time (early fifth millennium BC) and presumably place that were essentially coterminous with the rise of the Indo-European peoples.

20. See Piggott (1962) for many more examples of prehistoric sites where horse-hide (i.e., heads and hooves) burials occurred.
21. As has often been remarked, the most widely accepted early borrowing from IE into Sinitic is the word for "honey" (Modern Standard Mandarin mì 蜜): Common Tocharian *myit* > Old Sinitic *mit, Middle Sinitic, *mjit (Carling 2005: 55). Cf. modern English "mead," Sanskrit *madhu*, Avestan *maδu-* ("alcoholic beverage"), Greek *methy* ("wine"), Old Church Slavonic *medu*, Lithuanian *medus*, Old Irish *mid*.
22. Horse sacrifice is also the subject of the 14th book of the epic *Mahābhārata*, the Āśvamedhika *parvan*, in which Yudhiṣṭhira performs the *aśvamedha* after he is crowned emperor.
23. In *Ṛgveda*, Book 1, CLXIII, the sacrificed horse is explicitly compared to a deer. The horse is even said to have horns!

> Verse 9: "Horns made of gold hath he."
>
> Verse 11: "Thy horns are spread abroad in all directions."
>
> (tr. Griffith)

Commentators have engaged in the wildest contortions and circumlocutions (the "horns" [śṛṅga] actually signify hairs of the mane, the hoofs, etc.) in their vain efforts to explain these ostensibly odd formulations. In my opinion, when properly set in the context of the ultimate ancestry of the authors of the *Ṛgveda*, the description of the horse as a deer is not so strange after all. As I shall explain momentarily, there is good reason to believe that the Aryans truly possessed a deep memory of an intimate, primordial association with the deer, specifically the reindeer. // The latter verse (11) especially sounds more like it is describing the antlers of a deer rather than the horns of a bovine or ovicaprid. The fact that, in this verse, the word for "horn" is in the plural rather than the dual is not probative against an interpretation of the appendages as antlers, since the latter have a multiplicity of spreading branches that do seem to go "in all directions." In any event, the Ṛgvedic cervidization of the horse reminds-one of Scythian steppe art (e.g., at the Iron Age "[ca. 5 c. BC] site of Pazyryk in the Altai Mountains), where horses were often outfitted to resemble deer. What possible rational explanation could there be for this seemingly bizarre custom? I believe that it was because humans most likely first domesticated (herded, yoked, and rode) reindeer—which are far more placid than horses (personal observation of large, diffuse

Horse Sacrifices and Sacred Groves 439

herds at close range in the far north of Sweden), and only then domesticated the horse by analogy based on their experience with reindeer. Hence, the horse may be thought of as a sort of surrogate reindeer. // According to this theory, human beings who had become acculturated to the reindeer during the latter stages of the Pleistocene would have migrated southward (with the retreat of the glaciers) during the early stages of the Holocene. As they did so, however, they would gradually have moved out of the range of the reindeer and into the habitat of the horse. This theory, which I am only able to sketch briefly here, accords well with the old notion of a northern origin of the Aryans, although —in my estimation—the boreal antecedents of the Aryans would have had to go back beyond their own inception to the very beginnings of the Indo-Europeans. Indeed, I hypothesize that it was the domestication of the horse itself, modeled on the deep familiarity of their forefathers with the reindeer during the first portion of the Holocene, that enabled the emerging Indo-Europeans to tame the horse, and that this very act —which took place in the southern Urals was the defining moment of their birth as a distinct cultural and linguistic entity. I include language as an essential criterion because that is, after all, the touchstone for a family such as Indo-European, but also because the rising Indo-Europeans would naturally have required a fresh vocabulary and mode of expression to accord with-their new environment and, above all, their intensely symbiotic relationship with the horse.

24. Note the importance of such vessels for the peoples of the steppe. The cauldron also figured prominently in the Irish analogue to the aśvamedha. (Mallory and Adams 1997: 278a; Mallory 1989: 136)
25. For the northern origins of the Aryans, see note 23. The situation with regard to the horse is similar for China, though yet more attenuated, undoubtedly as a result of East Asia being even farther from the homeland of the domesticated horse than South Asia. (Mair 2005a: 217n89)
26. Those familiar with the Shang royal burials at Anyang will immediately recognize the striking resemblance they bear to Scythian royal burials as evidenced in Historical descriptions and through archeological evidence. Since the Scythians (first millennium BC), however, came after the time of the Shang royal burials (12th c. BC), the obvious similarity must be due to derivation from an earlier ancestral culture.
27. See "Lejre Experimental Centre: Sacrificial Bog" on the Web for striking color photographs of such sacrifices.

28. Adam of Bremen was a renowned church historian in whose works, among many other interesting things, is to be found the first mention of Vinland, the part of North America reached by Leif Eriksson (fl. ca. 1000).
29. The custom of performing such *blót* ("blood sacrifices") every nine years must have been common throughout Scandinavia, since it was also observed at Lejre, among other places. (Davidson 1988: 59) // Our Modern English word "blessing" is derived from Old English *blœdsian, blēdsian, blētsian* ("to bless, wish happiness, consecrate") < Germanic **blōdan* ("blood"). Hence *blœdsian* literally means "sprinkle (i.e., consecrate) with blood". (*The American Heritage Dictionary of the English Language*, 4th ed., 2000: 196b)
30. Seventy-two is a Eurasian mystical number, not to be taken literally. (Mair 2005a: 70-72)
31. Belief in a Tree of Life or Pillar of the World is widely distributed among many peoples in Eurasia and northeast Africa. (Holmberg 1922-23) In Chinese myth there is a tree in the far west called the Ruo 若木 whose foliage emits a reddish light that illuminates the earth, this is most likely a mythological explanation for the glow of sunset. Additionally, some scholars view the Ruo as a cosmic tree or the tree of life. See "The Classic of the Great Wildnerness: the North" in *Shanhai jing* 山海經 (The Classic of Mountains and Seas). (Birrell 1999: 188) The Ruo tree also occurs several times in the southern songs known as *Chu ci* 楚辭 (Elegies of Chu), namely "Li sao 離騷" (Encountering Sorrow), "Tian wen 天問" (Heavenly Questions), and "Jiu zhang 九章" (Nine Declarations). (Hawkes 1959: 28, 49, 78) The Ruo tree in the far west is matched by the Fusang 扶桑 tree, whence the sun rises, in the east.
32. There are alternative, though less convincing, explanations for the name (e. g., "yew-column").
33. Odin is said to have spent nine nights hanging from Yggdrasill in order to discover the secret runes. In Old Norse poetry (the Eddas), the gallows are sometimes described as "horse of the hanged."
34. Maringer (1981: 191) mentions a similar find from Tågeborgshövden, Sweden.
35. The Kuban River flows northwest from the Caucasus to the Black and Azov Seas.
36. John of Piano Carpini, "History of the Mongols," in Christopher Dawson, *The Mongol Mission* (New York: Sheed and Ward, 1955), pp. 12-13, as cited in Elliott (1999: 51n61).

37. Also spelled Tängri, this is the Turkic celestial deity still worshipped by many peoples in Central and Inner Asia.
38. Cf. at note 11 above.

Bibliography

Allard, Francis, and Diimaajav Erdenebaatar. 2005. "Khirigsuurs, ritual and mobility in the Bronze Age of Mongolia."*Antiquity*, 79: 547-563.

Anthony, David. 2005. Personal communication. April 6.

Barfield, Thomas J. 1989. *The Perilous Frontier: Nomadic Empires and China.* Cambridge, Massachusetts and Oxford: Blackwell; rpt. 1992.

Bökönyi, Sandor. 1978-79. "Eine Analogie der Arpadenzeidichen Sitte: aufgespiesste Pferdeköpfe in nahostlichen Dörfern." *Mitteilungen des Archäologischen Instituts der Ungarischen Akademie des Wissenschaften* (Budapest), 8-9: 161-164, Taf. 393-394.

Boyle, John Andrew. 1965. "A Form of Horse Sacrifice amongst the 13th-and 14th-Century Mongols." *Central Asiatic Journal.* 10: 145-150.

---. 1963. "Kirakos of Ganjak on the Mongols." *Central Asiatic Journal*, 8: 199-214.

Carling, Gerd 2005. "Proto-Tocharian, Common Tocharian, and Tocharian on the value of linguistic connections in a reconstructed language." Appendix to Mair 2005b: 47-71.

Chadwick, N. Kershaw. 1942. *Poetry and Prophecy.* Cambridge: Cambridge University Press.

Chang, Kwang-chih, and Xu Pingfang. 2005. *The Formation of Chinese Civilization: An Archaeological Perspective. The Culture and Civilization of China.* New Haven and London: Yale University Press.

Compareti, Matteo. 2003. "The Last Sasanians in China." *Eurasian Studies*, 11/2: 197-213.

Čugunov, Konstantin V., Hermann Parzinger, and Anatoli Nagler. 2003. "Der skythische Fürstengrabhügel von Aržan 2 in Tuva: Vorbericht der russisch-deutschen Ausgrabungen 2000-2002." Deutsches Archäologisches Institut, Eurasien-Abteilung. *Eurasia Antiqua*, 9: 113-162.

Czaplicka, M. A. 1914. Aboriginal Siberia: *A Study in Social Anthropology.* With a Preface by R. R. Marett. Oxford: Clarendon; rpt. Oxford University Press, 1969.

Davidson, H. R. Ellis. 1988. *Myths and Symbols in pagan Europe: Early Scandinavian and Celtic Religions.* Syracuse: Syracuse University Press.

Di Cosmo, Nicola. 2002. *Ancient China and Its Enemies: The Rise of Nomadic Power in East Asian History.* Cambridge, New York: Cambridge University Press.

Du Ruofu and Vincent F. Yip. 1993. *Ethnic Groups in China.* Beijing, New York: Science Press.

Eberhard, Wolfram. N. d. The Eberhard Collection of North and West Tribes (on IBM punch cards). Housed in the Research Institute for Inner Asian Studies (RIFIAS) at Indiana University.

Egami Namio 江山波夫. 1948. "Xiongnu de jisi 匈奴的祭祀 (Xiongnu Sacrifice)."In Liu Junwen 劉俊文, ed., *Riben xuezhe yanjiu Zhongguo shi lunzhu xuanyi* 日本學者研究中國史論著選譯 (Selected Translations of Research on Chinese History by Japanese Scholars). Vol. 9. *Minzu jiaotong* 民族交通 (Communication of Peoples). Huang Shumei 黃舒眉, tr. Beijing: Zhonghua shuju. Pp. 1-36.

Eliade, Mircea. 1964. *Shamanism: Archaic Techniques of Ecstasy.* Translated from the French by Willard R. Trask. Bollingen Series LXXVI. New York: Pantheon. Originally published as *Le Chamanisme et les techniques archaïques de l'extase* (Paris: Librairie Payot, 1951).

Elliott, Mark C. 1999. "Manchu Widows and Ethnicity in Qing China." *Comparative Studies in Society and History,* 41. 1: 33-71.

Frazer, James George. 1935. *The Golden Bough: A Study in Magic and Religion.* Part I. *The Magic Art and the Evolution of Kings.* 2 vols. New York: Macmillan. 3rd ed.

Friedrich, Paul. 1970. *Proto-Indo-European Trees: The Arboreal System of a Prehistoric People.* Chicago: University of Chicago Press.

Graves, Robert. 1948. *The White Goddess: A Historical Grammar of Poetic Myth.* New York: Noonday Press (Farrar, Straus, and Giroux). Rev. and enlgd. ed. 1966.

Griffith, Ralph T. H. 1889. *Hymns of the Ṛgveda.* 2 vols. Delhi: Munshiram Manoharlal, rpt.

Grimm, Jakob. 1997. *Germanic Mythology.* Translated from the German by Vivian Bird. Mankind Quarterly Monograph Series, 7. Washington, DC: Scott-Townsend.

Hammond. 1988. *Past Worlds: The Times Atlas of Archaeology.* Maplewood, New Jersey: Hammond.

Han Rulin 韓儒林. 1982. "Tujue Menggu zhi zuxian chuanshuo 突厥蒙古之祖先傳說 (Legends Concerning the Ancestors of the Turks and the Mongols). In the author's *Qionglu ji: Yuan shi ji xibei minzu shi yanjiu* 穹廬集: 元史及西北民族史研究 (Yurt Collection; Studies on the History of the Yuan and of the Peoples of the Northwest). Shanghai: Shanghai Renmin Chubanshe. Pp. 274-95.

Harva, Uno. 1938. *Die religiösen Vorstellungen der altaischen Völker.* FF Communications, No.125. Helsinki: Suomalainen Tiedeakatmia.

Herodotus. 1942. *The Persian Wars.* George Rawlinson, tr. New York: Random House.

Holmberg, Uno (Uno Harva). 1922-1923. *Der Baum des Lebens.* Annales Academiae Scientiarum Fennicae / Suomalaisen Tiedeakatemian Toimituksia. Ser. B.,Vol. XVI, No. 3. Helsinki: Suomalainen Tiedeakatemia.

Hubbell, Harry M. 1928. "Horse Sacrifice in Antiquity." *Yale Classical Studies,* 1: 181-192.

Jones, Prudence, and Nigel Pennick. 1995. *A History of Pagan Europe.* London and New York: Routledge.

Koppers, Wilhelm. 1936. "Pferdeopfer und Pferdekult der Indogermanen: Eine ethnologisch-religionswissenschafdiche Studie." In Koppers, ed., *Die Indogermanen- und Germanenfrage: Neue Wege zu ihrer Lösung.* Wiener Beiträge zur Kulturgeschichte und Linguistik, IV. Salzburg-Leipzig: Anton Pustet. Pp. 279-411.

Levine, Marsha, Colin Renfrew, and Katie Boyle, eds. 2003. *Prehistoric Steppe Adaptation and the Horse.* McDonald Institute Monographs. Cambridge: McDonald Institute for Archaeological Research, University of Cambridge.

Linduff, Katheryn M. 2003. "A Walk on the Wild Side: Late Shang Appropriation of Horses in China." In Levine, Renfrew, and Boyle 2003: 139-162.

Mair, Victor H. 2005a. "The North (west) ern Peoples and the Recurrent Origins of the Chinese State." In Joshua A. Fogel, ed. *The Teleology of the*

Modern Nation-State: Japan and China. Philadelphia: University of Pennsylvania Press. Pp. 46- 84, 205-217.

---. 2005b. "Genes, Geography, and Glottochronology: The Tarim Basin during Late Prehistory and History." In Karlene Jones-Bley, Martin E. Huld, Angela Della Volpe, and Miriam Robbins Dexter, ed., *Proceedings of the Sixteenth Annual UCLA Indo-European Conference.* Los Angeles, November 5-6, 2004. Journal of Indo-European Studies Monograph Series, No. 50. Washington: Institute for the Study of Man. Pp. 1-46.

---. 2003. "The Horse in Late Prehistoric China: Wresting Culture and Control from the 'Barbarians.'" In Levine, Renfrew, and Boyle 2003: 163-187.

---. 1998. "Canine Conundrums: Eurasian Dog Ancestor Myths in Historical and Ethnic Perspective." *Sino-Platonic Papers,* 87: 1-74.

Mallory, J. P. 1989. *In Search of the Indo-Europeans: Language, Archaeology and Myth.* London and New York: Thames and Hudson.

---. 1981. "The Ritual Treatment of the Horse in the Early Kurgan Tradition." *The Journal of Indo-European Studies,* 9.3-4 (Fall/Winter): 205-226.

Mallory, J. P. and D. Q. Adams, eds. 1997. *Encyclopedia of Indo-European Culture.* London and Chicago: Fitzroy Dearborn.

Mannhardt, Wilhelm. 1875-1877; 1905. *Wald- und Feldkulte.* 2nd edition, W. Heuschkel, ed. 2 vols. Berlin: Gebrüder Borntraeger.

Maringer, Johannes. "The Horse in Art and Ideology of Indo-European Peoples." *The Journal of Indo-European Studies,* 9.3- 4 (Fall/Winter): 177-204.

---. 1974. "Fluβopfer und Fluβverehrung in vorgeschichtlicher Zeit." *Germania,* 52.2: 309-318.

Meng Sen 孟森. 1959. "Qing dai tangzi suo si Deng jiangjun kao 清代堂子所祀登將軍考 (An Investigation of the Shrines for the Worship of General Deng)." In the author's *Ming-Qing shi lunzhu jikan* 明清史論著集刊 (Collected Publications of Studies on Ming-Qing History). Beijing: Zhonghua shuju. Pp. 311-323.

Meserve, Ruth. 2005. Personal communication. January 28.

Mi Wenping 米文平. 1981. "Xianbei shishi de faxian yu chubu yanjiu 鮮卑石室的發現與初步研究 (A Preliminary Study of the Discovery of the

Stone Caves of the Xianbei Nationality)." *Wenwu* 文物 (Cultural Relics), 2: 1-7.

von Negelein, Julius. 1903. *Das Pferd im arischen Altertum.* Teutonia, 2. Königsberg i. Pr.: Gräfe & Unzer.

Olsen, Sandra. 2005. Personal communication. February 2.

---. 2003. "The Exploitation of Horses at Botai, Kazakhstan." In Levine, Renfrew, and Boyle 2003: 83-103.

Olson, James S. 1998. *An Ethnohistorical Dictionary of China.* Westport, Connecticut: Greenwood.

Ōsawa Takashi 大沢孝. 2002. "Kodai Türuku-kei yūbokumin no maisōgirei ni okeru dōbutsu kugi-sekijin ishikakoi iseki ni okeru kanren ibutsu o chūshin ni 古代テュルク系游牧民の埋葬儀礼における動物供牺一石人・石囲い遺跡における関連遺物を中心に (Animal Sacrifices as Burial Ceremony among Ancient Turkic Nomadic Peoples: Especially Based on the Sites with Stone Statues and Stone Circles)." In Konagaya Yūki 小長谷有紀, ed., *Kita Ajiya ni okeru hito to dōbutsu no aida* 北アジアにおける人と動物のあいだ (The Relationship between the Peoples of Northern Asia and Animals). Tokyo: Tōhō shoten. Pp. 159-206.

Parzinger, Hermann. 2003. "Le Tumulus funéraire d'un Prince Scythe d'Arzan 2 dans la Région de la Touva (Russie)." *Comptes Rendus, Académie des Inscriptions et Belles-lettres,* April-June: 975-995.

Pascal, C. Bennett. 1981. "October Horse." *Harvard Studies in Classical Philology,* 85: 261-291.

Pearce, Scott. Forthcoming. "The Tabgatch Origin Myths."

Piggott, Stuart. 1962. "Heads and Hoofs."*Antiquity,* 36: 110-118.

Puhvel, Jaan. 1955. "Vedic *aśvamedha* and Gaulish *IIPOMIIDVOS.*" *Language,* 31.3: 353-354.

Radloff, Wilhelm (Vasilii Vasil'evich Radlov). 1968. *Aus Sibirien: Lose Blätter aus meinem Tagebuche.* Oosterhout (the Netherlands): Anthropological Publications. Originally published in 2 vols, by T. O. Weigel at Leipzig in 1893.

Roux, Jean-Paul. 1963. *La mort chez les peoples altaïques anciens et médiévaux d'après les documents écrits.* Paris: Adrien-Maisonneuve.

Shahbazi, A. Sh. 1985-87. "Asb ('horse'): i. In Pre-Islamic Iran." *Encyclopaedia Iranica.* Ehsan Yarshater, ed. Vol. II. London and New York: Routledge & Kegan Paul. Pp. 724b-730b.

Simek, Rudolf. 1993. *Dictionary of Northern Mythology.* Tr. Angela Hall. Woodbridge, Suffolk: D. S. Brewer. First published in 1984 as *Lexicon der germanischen Mythologie* (Stuttgart: Alfred Kröner).

Sims-Williams, Nicholas. 1996. "The Sogdian Merchants in China and India." In Alfredo Cadonna and Lionello Lanciotti, eds., *Cina e Iran: Da Alessandro Magno alla Dinastia Tang.* Orientalia Venetiana, V. Florence: Leo S. Olschki. Pp. 45-67.

Snow, Justine T. 2002. "The Spider's Web. Goddesses of Light and Loom: Examining the Evidence for the Indo-European Origin of Two Ancient Chinese Deities." *Sino-Platonic Papers,* 118 (June): 1-75, plus 1 color plate and 1 black-and-white plate.

Sōma, Takuya. 2005. "Horse Sacrificial Customs; Altay Mountain Areas." Presentation before the International Turfan Symposium. Turfan, Xinjiang. August 25-29.

Stuart, Kevin and Li Xuewei, ed. "Tales from China's Forest Hunters: Oroqen Folktales." *Sino-Platonic Papers,* 61 (December): i-iv, 1-59.

Stutley, Margaret and James. 1984. *Harper's Dictionary of Hinduism: Its Mythology, Folklore, Philosophy, Literature, and History.* San Francisco: Harper & Row.

Swennen, Philippe. 2004. *D'India Tištrya: Portrait et évolution du cheval sacré dans les mythes indo-iraniens anciens.* Publications de l'Institut de civilisation indienne, Fascicule 71. Paris: Collège de France.

Thordarson, F. 1985-1987. "Asb ('horse'): ii. Among the Scythians." *Encyclopaedia Iranica.* Ehsan Yarshater, ed. Vol. II. London and New York: Roudedge & Kegan Paul. Pp. 730b-731b.

de la Vaissière, Étienne. 2005. "Huns et Xiongnu." *Central Asiatic Journal,* 49.1: 3-26.

Xinjiang Wenwu Kaogu Yanjiu Suo 新疆文物考古研究所 (Xinjiang Institute of Cultural Relics and Archeology). 1999. Wang Mingzhe 王明哲 (nominal editor), Lü Enguo 呂恩國 (actual editor). *Xinjiang Chawuhu Daxing shizu mudi fajue baogao* 新疆察吾呼一大型氏族墓地發掘報

告 (Xinjiang Charwighul—A Large-scale Clan Cemetery Excavation Report). Beijing; Dongfang chubanshe.

Yang Hong. 2002. "An Archaeological View of Tuoba Xianbei Art in the Pingcheng Period and Earlier." *Orientations*, 34.5 (May): 27-33.

Chapter 12

What Is *Geyi*, After All?

Source: Adapted from "What Is *geyi*, After All?" in *Philosophy and Religion in Early Medieval China*, ed. Alan Kam-leung Chan and Yuet Keung Lo (Albany: State University of New York Press, 2010), 227-264.

TEXTS

A constant theme of nearly all introductory and general expositions of the history of Buddhism, be they composed in the East or in the West, be they presented in the classroom or in written works, is that the presumed translation technique of *geyi* 格義 played a central role in the transmission and assimilation of Indian Buddhism in China during its earliest phases. According to this scenario, *geyi* (usually rendered in English as "matching concepts" or "matching meanings") served to pair Sanskrit Buddhist terms with Sinitic Daoist terms. The ubiquity of this explanation in textbooks, handbooks, encyclopedias, Web-based resources, articles, monographs, and so on is astonishing when one begins to look at the historical evidence used to support it: there is next to nothing.

In this chapter, it will be shown that *geyi*, as now understood, is a thoroughly modern construction. The first thing that must be done is to gather all of the available references to geyi, both inside and outside the Buddhist canon, then translate and annotate each one of these references in context. From this investigation, it emerges clearly that *geyi* had nothing whatsoever to do with translation, but that it was instead a highly ephemeral and not-very-successful attempt on the part of a small number of Chinese teachers to cope with the flood of numbered lists of categories, ideas, and so forth (of which Indian thinkers were so much enamored) that came to China in the wake of Buddhism.

A secondary aspect of this inquiry is to demonstrate how what was originally an exegetical technique of circumscribed application and limited duration developed into a key element of Chinese Buddhist historiography. It will be possible to trace the growth of *geyi* from an inefficacious interpretive strategy into a supposed translational method and philosophical approach that occurred during the course of the last century. This delineation, however, is essentially a side issue. The main purpose of this study is simply to set the record straight about what *geyi* really was and was not at the time of its actual existence. In the process of doing so, new materials that have heretofore never been cited in the protracted discussions on *geyi* will be introduced, and old sources will be revisited and thoroughly scrutinized.

Fundamental Semantics

Starting from the second half of the twentieth century and still adhered to today, the standard English translation of *geyi* is "matching concepts" or "matching meanings." This rendering conforms well with the scenario of *geyi* as an essential component of the means whereby Indian Buddhist texts were translated into Chinese. Unfortunately, "matching meanings/concepts" is an inaccurate rendition of *geyi*. There is no serious problem with the second syllable ("meanings" or "concepts"), but rendering *ge* as "matching" falls wide of the mark.

The fact that *ge* is written with a wood radical gives us a hint of its basic denotation, viz., lattice, which signifies a structure of crossed wooden strips arranged to form a pattern of rectangular, square, or diagonal open spaces between the lines. From this is derived the notion of *gezi* 格子 ("square" or "checked"), as in *gezi zhi* 格子紙 (the sort of paper on which one writes *hanzi* 漢字 ["sinograms"]). In linguistics, *ge* can refer to grammatical case, and *ge* is also used in some advanced types of mathematical logic, geometry, set theory, algebra, and combinatorial mathematics where it renders the English term *lattice*. Another telling term formed with *ge* as a constituent morpheme is *gelü* 格律. This is a technical term in traditional Chinese poetics that refers to such aspects of verse as the number of syllables per line, antithesis, parallelism, and rhyme. These poetic features are governed by prosodic rules that can be thought of as determined by the *gezi*-like structure of Chinese regulated verse.

Perhaps the easiest way to think of how these fundamental facets of *ge* relate to the problem of *geyi* is to visualize a set of pigeonholes and contemplate its function as a device for the classification of discrete items. From classification, it is only a short step to categorization, which is precisely what the *ge* of *geyi* signifies.

Axel Schuessler states that the graph *ge* 格 was used to write at least three different Sinitic etyma meaning "rack," "tree branch," and "to come, go to" (the latter originally written without the wood radical).[1] The first and second etyma evidently have to do with wood (as signified by the radical), and the first provides the basis for the evolved meanings of "lattice," etc.

In *Hanyu da cidian* 漢語大詞典 (4.989b–991a), the graph 格 has four different Modern Standard Mandarin (MSM) pronunciations (*gé, luò, gē, hè*, plus an additional two embedded pronunciations [*lù, hé*]) with a total of forty-two (38+2+1+1) definitions. *Hanyu da zidian* 漢語大字典 (2.1203b-1205a) gives the same four MSM pronunciations (plus the same two additional embedded pronunciations) for a total of thirty-three (29+2+1+1) definitions. Despite the plethora of definitions for this single graph, neither of these authoritative works offers a justification for rendering it as "matching" (the closest they come is "to oppose [an enemy]," but that is too remote to justify translating *geyi* as "matching meanings").

Most dictionaries of Modern Chinese (i.e., MSM) give some or all of the following definitions for *ge* alone, and more or less in the order listed:[2] square/compartment/check/chequer (formed by crossed lines); lattice, grid; division; standard, pattern, rule; character, manner, style; impede, obstruct, resist, bar (designated by some dictionaries as a literary usage); hit, beat, fight; investigate, examine; case (grammatical). The majority of these meanings can be directly or indirectly derived from the basic idea of a compartmentalized wooden framework in which sections are blocked off. No dictionaries, whether of Literary or Modern Chinese, give "matching" or "pairing" as a definition for *ge*. There is thus no lexicographical warrant for the currently ubiquitous translation of *geyi* as "matching meanings." We must conclude, therefore, that "matching" is simply an *ad hoc*, unsubstantiated rendering of the graph devised by modern scholars perplexed by its occurrence in the shadowy expression *geyi*.

The present investigation emphasizes philology over philosophy, particularly since many researchers leap into the *geyi* fray as though it were strictly a matter of intellectual history and without taking into serious account the very difficult linguistic problems surrounding this vexed term. Our inquiry needs to be solidly based on the available evidence, so the first order of business is to take stock of all the relevant texts in which the term *geyi* appears. Primary Evidence In actuality, it might be better to label this section "Lack of Primary Evidence," because there is not much. One would think that, for such an allegedly vital translation technique as *geyi*, which supposedly enabled Buddhism to gain a foothold in China during the Eastern Han period and succeeding age, it would be unmistakably prominent in texts from the second century and later. If that is what one assumes, one will be sadly disappointed. In the whole of the Buddhist canon, the term *geyi* occurs fewer than two dozen times, and many of these instances are repetitions of each other. Thus far, I have not been able to find a single instance of *geyi* anywhere in the Daoist canon, including compendia such as Wushang biyao 無上秘要 (Essentials of unsurpassed arcana; around 580), *Daojiao yishu* 道教義樞 (The pivotal meaning of Daoist doctrine; early eighth century), and *Yunji qiqian* 雲笈七籤 (Cloudy Bookcase with Seven Labels; ca. 1028). Nor is *geyi* to be found anywhere in the massive twenty-five official histories. Similarly, it is not in *Zizhi tongjian* 資治通鑑 (Comprehensive mirror for aid in government; 1084) or *Xu Zizhi tongjian* 續資治通鑑 (Comprehensive mirror for aid in government, continued; 1801). There is not a single occurrence of *geyi* in the entirety of the massive *Gujin tushu jicheng* 古今圖書集成 (Assemblage of books and illustrations past and present; 1728). There are no independent instances of *geyi* in the enormous *Siku quanshu* 四庫全書 (Complete writings in the four repositories; 1771-1781) or in the comprehensive CHANT (CHinese ANcient Texts) database maintained by the Chinese University of Hong Kong.[3] It would appear that, after a few fleeting mentions during the Wei-Jin period (late third to fourth centuries), the term *geyi* was almost totally obliterated from Chinese intellectual discourse and consciousness until the twentieth century.[4]

Significantly, *geyi* does not appear in *Shishuo xinyu* 世說新語 (A new account of tales of the world; ca. 430) by the Liu-Song prince, Liu Yiqing 劉義慶 (403-444). If *geyi* were a notable feature of Eastern Jin intellectual life, it would almost certainly have been mentioned in *Shishuo xinyu*. Therefore, it is crucial to determine precisely what *geyi* did imply during the short span of time when it was current among a small group of Buddhist teachers.

The primary and single most important document for the study of the history of *geyi* is the biographical account of Zhu Faya 竺法雅 (latter half of the third century and the first half of the fourth century, i.e., the Western Jin [265-316] and the early part of the Eastern Jin [317-420]). Since, in the lengthy debates on the subject, it has never been rendered in its entirety, it will be worth the effort to provide an integral translation with extensive annotation.

> (Zhu)[5] Faya[6] was a man of Hejian.[7] He was of a staid, tolerant disposition. As a youth, he excelled at non-Buddhist[8] studies, and when he grew up he became proficient in Buddhist doctrine.[9] The sons of gentry families all attached themselves to him and requested that he teach them. At that time, the adherents who followed him were uniformly well-versed in secular works, but did not yet excel in Buddhist principles. Consequently, (Zhu Fa)ya, with Kang[10] Falang and others, correlated the enumerations of items *(shishu* 事數) in the sutras with non-Buddhist writings[11] as instances of lively[12] explication; this was called "categorizing concepts" *(geyi)*. Thereupon, Vībhū (?), Tanxiang,[13] and others also debated over the categorized concepts in order to instruct their disciples. (Zhu Fa)ya's manner was unrestrained and he excelled (in getting at)the crux (of the matter). He alternately lectured on secular works and Buddhist sutras. With Dao'an and Fatai,[14] he often explained the doubtful points they had assembled, and together they exhausted the essentials of the sutras.
> 法雅，河間人，凝正有器度。少善外學，長通佛義。衣冠士子咸附諮稟。時依門徒并世典有功，未善佛理。雅乃與康法朗等以經中事數擬配外書，為生解之例，謂之格義。乃毘浮、曇相等，亦辯格義以訓門徒。雅風采灑落，善于樞機。外典佛經遞互講說，與道安、法汰每披釋湊疑，共盡經要。
> Later, he established a monastery at Gaoyi,[15] where he tirelessly taught a *saṅgha*-fellowship of more than a hundred. One of (Zhu Fa)ya's disciples, Tanxi, emulated his master in excelling at discourse, and was honored by Shi Xuan, heir apparent to the throne of the Latter Zhao (319-351).
> 後立寺於高邑，僧眾百餘，訓誘無懈。雅弟子曇習祖述先師，善於言論，為偽趙太子右(石)宣所敬云。[16]

What Is *Geyi*, After All? 455

A key to understanding this much-discussed, but poorly understood, text is the expression "enumeration of items" *(shishu)* that occurs in the middle of it. There are several reasons why a thorough comprehension of *shishu* is crucial in this investigation, among them the fact that it is characterized as a type of explication (not translation) and, still more vitally, because it is directly related to *geyi*. Fortunately, we have a roughly contemporaneous, authoritative definition of *shishu* in the form of a passage in the fifty-ninth section of the "Wen xue" 文學 (Letters and scholarship) chapter of *Shishuo xinyu* and a valuable commentary on it by the Liang scholar and bibliophile, Liu Jun 劉峻 (*zi* Xiaobiao 孝標, 462-521). Before presenting the passage in question, it should be noted that *Shishuo xinyu* is celebrated for its intimate familiarity with the intellectual, religious, and social life of the Eastern Jin, the very period in which *geyi* abruptly arose and rapidly disappeared.

> When Yin Hao[17] was dismissed and transferred to Dongyang,[18] he read a large number of Buddhist sutras, gaining a detailed understanding of them all. It was only when he came to places where items were enumerated that he did not understand. [Afterwards,] when he met a monk, he asked about [the items] he had noted down, and then they were all resolved.
> 殷中軍被廢，徙東陽，大讀佛經，皆精解；唯至事數處不解。遇見一道人，問所籤，便釋然。[19]

Liu Jun's commentary on this passage gives a half-dozen specific examples of exactly what *shishu* signified:

> *Shishu* means categories such as: the Five Personality components/aggregates (*pañcaskandha*),[20] the Twelve Entrances (*dvādaśāyatanāni*),[21] the Four Truths (*catvāri ārya-satyāni*),[22] the Twelve Links of Dependent Origination (*dvādaśaṅga pratītyasamutpāda*)[23], the Five Sense-organs (*pañcendriyāni*),[24] the Five Powers (*pañca balāni*),[25] and the Seven Factors of Enlightenment (*sapta bodhyangāni*).[26]
> 事數謂若五陰、十二入、四諦、十二因緣、五根、五力、七覺之屬。

Aside from all of this invaluable testimony from *Shishuo xinyu* and its main commentary, it is also pertinent to note that *shishu* may be equated with *fashu* 法數 (which is linked to Sanskrit *dharma-paryāya* ["formulaic terms of the dharma," usually translated in Chinese as *famen* 法門 and generally signifying "text/discourse on dharma"] in the *Mahāvyutpatti* [see below]) or *mingshu* 名數 ("Buddhist terms that begin with a number," i.e., numerical groups of related items).[27] These are numerical categories of Buddhist doctrine such as the three realms, five *skandhas*, five regions, four dogmas, six paths, twelve *nidānas*, etc.[28] Equipping ourselves with unequivocal information about *shishu*, we can feel a much greater degree of confidence in our comprehension of *geyi*.

It is obvious that *shishu* was a Buddhist technical term of the time and that people were well aware of precisely what it signified when they employed it. Since *shishu* unmistakably means the enumeration of items or matters pertaining to Buddhist doctrine, then we may conclude that *geyi* (which is equated with *shishu* in the biographical sketch of Zhu Faya) was not a translation technique at all but an exegetical method, and that it was by no means restricted exclusively to drawing upon Daoist texts for its non-Buddhist (i.e., non-Indian, non-Indic) comparanda. The *raison d'être* of *geyi* was its dedication to the explication of the countless (!) lists of complicated technical terms that are so characteristic of Indian philosophy, but which are so rare in traditional (i.e., pre-Buddhist) East Asian thought. In short, *geyi*'s fundamental purpose was the correlation of lists of enumerated Buddhist concepts with presumably comparable lists of notions extracted from non-Buddhist works. The inherent fallacy of such an approach is manifest in the contradiction between the ubiquity of such lists (often lengthy) in Buddhist texts and their rarity (usually very short) in non-Buddhist texts. There clearly were not enough numbered lists in non-Buddhist texts to go around!

One can easily imagine why the *shishu* would have given Chinese Buddhists of the late third and early fourth centuries so much trouble. Everywhere one turns in Indian philosophy and practice, and that

What Is *Geyi*, After All?

includes Buddhist philosophy and practice, there are longer and shorter lists of technical terms to contend with. The individual terms by themselves are often difficult enough to comprehend. When they are bundled together in groups, they become all the harder to grasp. For those like the early Chinese Buddhists of the Jin period, whose native traditions of thought and praxis were unaccustomed to drawing up such lists of complicated terminology, the experience of encountering the *shishu* must have been mind-numbing. No wonder that even someone such as Yin Hao, who dedicated the last years of his life to Buddhism, would be stymied by the *shishu*.

In a word, *geyi* was no more or no less than an ephemeral, abortive attempt on the part of Zhu Faya and a few of his close associates to ease the frustration their students felt upon encountering the *shishu*. *Geyi* was a short-lived phenomenon, as it was roundly repudiated by the very next generation of Chinese Buddhist teachers under the leadership of Dao'an 道安 (312-385). Thus, *geyi* lasted for no more than a generation and it was restricted to a very small group of persons who experimented with it unsuccessfully for a limited, specific purpose: to lessen the burden of Chinese Buddhists in dealing with numerical lists of concepts and terms.

For someone who is unfamiliar with the pervasive propensity for Indian (and especially Buddhist) philosophers and religionists to resort to drawing up numbered lists for purposes of analysis and teaching, a glance at the *Mahāvyutpatti*, a Sanskrit-Tibetan lexicon of the early ninth century, should suffice to arrive at an appreciation of this aspect of Indian and Buddhist thought. *Mahāvyutpatti* contains 9,565 items classified according to 277 different categories. There are, for example, eighty epithets of the Buddha, eighteen types of emptiness, and eight kinds of mundane dharmas. Some of the categories have hundreds of entries.

The lexicographical compilation of numbered lists of technical terms began long before the *Mahāvyutpatti*. The *Kośa* of Nāgārjuna (fl. late second century CE) was written in Pali and consists of sections such as the following:

CXXXII The threefold (fruit of) work.
CXXXIII The three kinds of magic.
CXXXIV The eight untimely ways of being born.[29]

Under each section, the various items referred to are listed.

The Indian (and Buddhist) delight in such numbered lists proved to be a nightmare for their Chinese followers. Indeed, a major source of the tension over the issue of Sinicization versus Indianization (i.e., adaptation and flexibility versus authority and faithfulness) derived from having to deal with a flood of bewildering Sanskrit technical terminology. Grouping these unfamiliar terms into numbered categories only made them all the more forbidding.

It is significant that the Chinese translation of Sāṃkhya (or Sāṅkhya) was simply *shu* 數,[30] since Sāṃkhya is the Indian philosophical tradition whose name has been variously defined as "enumeration," "investigation," "analysis," viz., "of the categories [N.B.] of the phenomenal world."[31] Further indication of the importance of numerical categorization for Buddhist thought in particular and for Indian philosophy in general are the *shulun* 數論 ("numerical treatises"). These were the *śāstras* of the Sarvāstivādins and were also a method of Sāṃkhya philosophy whereby all concepts were placed within twenty-five categories.

Another way to comprehend the meaning of *shu* for early Chinese Buddhists is to consider the term *chanshu* 禪數 (literally, "Chan/Zen Numbers"). It occurs in Dao'an's preface to the *Anban shouyi jing* 安般守意經 (*Ānāpana-smṛti-sūtra*), translated by An Shigao 安世高, and refers to the enumerated categories concerning *dhyāna* ("meditation, concentration") (*T.55* [2145] 43c20). The *Ānāpana-smṛti-sūtra* is an Abhidharma scripture, and An Shigao—the first major translator of Buddhist texts into Chinese—was a specialist in Abhidharma ("higher doctrine," i.e., the scholastic analysis of religious teachings), who concentrated on the translation of meditation texts.[32] Inasmuch as Abhidharma is permeated with lists of concepts and is particularly devoted to exposition by division and subdivision, we can see how pervasive this challenging aspect of Buddhist doctrine was for the Chinese right from the very beginning.

In sum, the *shu* of *shishu* means "(analytical) enumerative categories." *Shishu*, then, indicates "enumerative categories (or categorized enumeration) of things/items, i.e., (technical) terms." Therefore, *geyi*—which is explicitly defined by Huijiao 慧皎 ([497-554] in the biography of Zhu Faya) as the correlation of *shishu* from Buddhist scriptures with comparable material from non-Buddhist (not necessarily Daoist) sources—has to do with enumerated categories of technical matters. This is the most authoritative explanation of *geyi* from the earliest source in which it was mentioned. Since *geyi* was such a short-lived phenomenon (it was already rejected by Dao'an by the middle of the fourth century in his conversation with Sengxian [see below] and was only initiated earlier in the same century by Zhu Faya and his associates),[33] it did not have time to develop into something more elaborate or important, as is often imagined by modern interpreters.

Much has been made of the fact that Huiyuan 慧遠 (334-416), the important precursor of the Pure Land schools of Buddhism and Dao'an's chief disciple, on one occasion referred to the early Daoist thinker, Zhuangzi:

> When he was twenty-four (357 CE), Huiyuan began to lecture. Once there was a guest who, listening to Huiyuan's lecture, raised objections about the concept of ultimate reality.[34] The discussion went back and forth for quite some time, with the guest becoming all the more confused. Thus, Huiyuan drew upon a concept from *Zhuangzi* as an analogy. Thereupon, the deluded one came to understand. After that, Dao'an especially permitted Huiyuan not to abandon secular writings.
> 年二十四便就講說。嘗有客聽講，難實相義，往復移時，彌增疑昧。遠乃引《莊子》義為連類。於是惑者曉然。是後安公特聽慧遠不廢俗書。(*GZ 6, T.50* [2059] 358a11-14)

The rather awkward wording of the last part of the final sentence implies that it was normal "to abandon secular writings," while the first part indicates that Huiyuan was given a special privilege in this regard, whereas other disciples were most likely encouraged to concentrate exclusively on Buddhist texts. Regardless of what one may think of Huiyuan's invocation of the *Zhuangzi* in this particular instance, it is irrelevant to the question of *geyi*, which—as we have seen unmistakably above—is a separate matter. Furthermore, by the time of Huiyuan's allusion to *Zhuangzi* (in the year 357), Dao'an had already repudiated *geyi*, as is evident in the following paragraph. Therefore, the frequent citation of this passage from Huiyuan's biography in support of the allegation that *geyi* was a technique used by Buddhists for borrowing from Daoism is completely fallacious.

When Dao'an was living together with Sengxian 僧先 (or Sengguang 僧光)[35] on Feilong Shan ("Flying Dragon Mountain")[36] around 349,[37]

> [Dao]'an said, "The old 'categorized concepts' *(geyi)* of the past was often at odds with Buddhist principles." "We ought to analyze [the texts] carefreely,"[38] said Sengxian. "How are we permitted to dispute our predecessors?" (Dao)'an said, "In spreading and praising the [Buddhist] principles and doctrines, we should make them fitting and proper. When dharma-drums[39] compete to resound, what [does it matter who comes] first [and who comes] later?"
> 安曰：「先舊格義於理多違。」先曰：「當分折逍遙，何容是非先達？」安曰：「弘贊理教，宜令允愜，法鼓競鳴，何先何後？」(*GZ 5, T.50* [2059] 355a25-28)

Judging from this brief and somewhat enigmatic exchange with Sengxian, Dao'an was opposed to *geyi* because it distorted Buddhist teachings. Furthermore, he did not stand in awe of *geyi* simply because a few earlier teachers had employed it for a brief spell.

What Is *Geyi*, After All? 461

Another monk from Henan who criticized *geyi* was Sengrui 僧叡 (352-436) in his *Pimoluojieti jing yishu xu* 毘摩羅詰堤經義疏序 (Preface to a commentary on the *Vimalakīrti-sūtra*):

> Since the Wind of Wisdom fanned eastward and the Word of the Dharma flowed forth in song, although it may be said that there were places [set up] for lecturing, the categorizing of concepts [employed in them] was pedantic and at odds with the original [sense of the Indian texts being discussed]; the Six Schools [of Prajñāpāramita] were biased and did not touch [the truth]. As for the fundamental doctrine of the emptiness of nature *(prakānti-śūnyata)*,[40] examined from the vantage of today, it comes closest to grasping the actuality [of Prajñāpāramita].
> 自慧風東扇，法言流詠以來，雖曰講肆，格義迂而乖本，六家偏而不即。性空之宗，以今驗之，最得其實然。
> (*CSJ4, T.55* [2145] 59a1-4)

It is evident that, approximately a century after its rise and demise, the opposition to *geyi* had been cemented among the most important Buddhist exponents of the age. By the end of the fourth century and the beginning of the fifth century, *geyi* had already long since ceased to exist as a functioning device, and—even in memory—it was thought of with opprobrium. Certainly there were none at this time who advocated, much less adopted, *geyi*.

A text that is often cited in discussions of *geyi* is the following passage from the "Yuyi lun" 喻疑論 (Treatise on the clarification of doubts) by Huirui 慧叡,

a disciple of the renowned Kumārajīva (344/350-409/413; arrived in Chang'an in 401):

> At the end of the Han and the beginning of the Wei (i.e., ca. 220 CE), the chancellor of Guangling and the chancellor of Pengcheng joined the Order, and both were able to maintain the great light [of the Doctrine].[41] The worthies who sought the essence [of Buddhist ideas] for the first time had fixed lecturing places. But

> they puffed up [their lectures] with copious concepts and made them pedantic with their paired explanations.
> 漢末魏初，廣陵、彭城二相出家，並能任持大照。尋味之賢始有講次，而恢之以裕義，迂之以配說。(*CSJ* 5, *T.55* [2145] 41b10-12)

It is only the Ming edition of the text that has the variant *geyi* for *yuyi* 裕義 (not to be confused with the title of the treatise). The earlier, majority reading of *yuyi*, however, fits better because it complements *hui* 恢 ("extensive, vast," translated here as "puffed up"). This reading also goes well with the following, parallel clause, which seems to be criticizing circuitous redundancy and repetition. Consequently, this passage most likely has nothing to do with *geyi*. However, even if we adopt the late variant, this passage would have to be said to display a decidedly negative attitude toward *geyi*. Furthermore, we must note that it dates to roughly two centuries after the time that it is commenting upon.[42]

From Sengyou's 僧佑 (445-518) biography of Kumārajīva himself we have the following telling and oft-repeated passage:

> Since the Great Law covered the east, beginning in [the time] of Emperor Ming (58-75) of the [Later] Han and passing through the Wei (220-265) and the Jin (265-420), the [translated] *sūtras* (scriptures) and *śāstras* (treatises) that were produced gradually became numerous. Yet the [translations] produced by Zhi (Qian) and Zhu (Fahu)[43] mostly [were plagued by] stagnant wording[44] and categorized concepts.
> 自大法東被始於漢明，歷涉魏晉經論漸多，而支、竺所出多滯文格義。(*CSJ* 14, *T.55* [2145] 101b13-15; copied [with a couple of minor variants] in *GZ* 2, *T.50* [2059] 332a27-28)

Judging from its parallelism with *zhi*, *ge* here was probably intended to mean "obstruct, block, confine, restrict," and so forth. Yet, even in this case it may be said to function as an extension of the basic meaning of "compartment(alize)."

Although Sengyou, the compiler of *CSJ*, uses *geyi* to chastise translators that he clearly disapproves of, he seems to have only a vague understanding of the term, since it originally was not a translation technique but a method of exegesis (one that was, furthermore, restricted to the explication of numbered lists). As a matter of fact, Sengyou's complaint against Zhi Qian 支謙 (fl. 220-252) and Dharmarakṣa (Zhu Fahu 竺法護, ca. 233-310) was almost certainly derived from Sengzhao's 僧肇 (374-414) *Weimojie jing xu* 維摩詰經序 (Preface to the *Vimalakīrti-sūtra*), where the wording is as follows: "detested (translations) produced by Zhi and Zhu as causing principles to stagnate in their texts (理滯於文), and often feared that abstruse precepts (i.e., Buddhist doctrines) would founder at the hands of the translators," with no allusion to *geyi* (*CSJ* 8, *T.55* [2145] 58b9-10). The addition of *geyi* to *zhiwen* 滯文 as another supposed defect of the translations of Zhi Qian and Dharmarakṣa was thus due to Sengyou, writing approximately a century after Sengzhao, and more than a century and a half after the time of Zhu Faya, apparently the chief exponent of *geyi*.

Sengyou's censure of the translations of Zhi Qian and Dharmarakṣa as being *zhiwen geyi* is repeated verbatim by the following:

>Daolang 道朗 (Eastern Jin) *CSJ 14, T.55* (2145) 101b13-15[45]
>Huixiang 慧祥 (fl. 667) *T.51* (2067) 15b9-10
>Daoshi 道世 (d. 683) *T.53* (2122) 474b6-17
>Zhisheng 智昇 (ca. 669-740) *T.55* (2154) 514c13-15
>Yuanzhao 圓照 (fl. 778) *T.55* (2157) 811c3-4

None of these authors add anything that would help us better comprehend the nature or significance of *geyi*. The last-named author, a specialist in *vinaya*, elsewhere uses the expression *geyi* for the literal signification of its two graphs and not in the specialized technical sense that it had during the early Jin period (viz., explaining the *shishu* ["enumerations of items"]): "Was it only because he categorized the concepts of the nine divisions that he was renowned?" 豈惟格義九轍，獨擅名哉—referring to an analytical approach said to have been devised by Kumārajīva's disciple Sengrui 僧叡, who consequently came to be known as the Nine Divisions Dharma Master 九轍法師, although this method was actually created by an earlier Wei-Jin period monk named Daorong 道融 and that it only came to be attributed to Sengrui through confusion *(T.55* [2157] 895c9).

The versatile and prolific monk Daoxuan 道宣 (596-667), compiler of *Xu gaoseng zhuan* 續高僧傳 (Further biographies of eminent monks) and *Guang hongmingji* 廣弘明集 (Expanded collection for the propagation of the light), twice mentions *geyi* in the context of textual obfuscation (*T.40* [1804] 97b10; *T.45* [1895] 840a8). It would appear that Daoxuan viewed *geyi* as a faulty type of explication, although he too provided no details concerning the way it operated. Elsewhere, he states unmistakably that Dao'an strove to extirpate the *geyi* of the past and to open up spiritual principles (*shenli* 神理) for the future (*T.50* [2060] 548b2).

The leader of the Three Treatises (*Sanlun* 三論) School, Jizang 吉藏 (born into a family of Parthian origin, 549-623), four times repeats the identical set of paired clauses: "Categorized concepts were pedantic arid went against the fundament; the Six [Prajñā] Schools were biased and off the mark" (格義迂而乖本，六家偏而未即) (*T.42* [1824] 4c11, 29a7-8; *T.42* [1825] 174a12-13, 183a2). Jizang twice prefaces these remarks with reference to the flourishing of lecture sites for the propagation of Buddhism and once mentions that all of this took place before the advent of Kumārajīva, who translated the three *śāstras* that formed the basis for Jizang's brand of Madhyamaka. While it is evident that Jizang was dissatisfied with *geyi*, as he was with the Six *Prajñā* Schools of the Eastern Jin period, he does not provide any specific information that would indicate how it functioned.

In his syncretic volume entitled *Beishan lu* 北山錄 (A record of North Mountain), the late Tang monk, Shenqing 神清 (d. ca. 820), repeated from *GZ 4* the account of Zhu Faya resorting to *geyi* in his lectures (*T.52* [2113] 595a7-9). Shenqing makes, however, a couple of curious —and revealing—modifications. Where the original text reads "endeavored to correlate the enumerations of items (*shishu*) in the sutras with non-Buddhist writings as instances of lively explication; this was called 'categorizing concepts (*geyi*),'" Shenqing writes, "endeavored to discuss Confucian writings (*rushu* 儒書) with the classifications of concepts in the sutras as instances of lively explication; this was called *geyi*." Further, in the next sentence, Shenqing writes that this was done "to instruct their students" (*menxue* 門學) instead of "to instruct their disciples" (*mentu* 門徒), and completely omits the clause about Vibhū (?), Tanxiang, and the others. The story about Zhu Faya must have seemed altogether strange and distant to Shenqing and his eleventh-century commentator, Huibao 慧寶, who made no attempt to clarify this opaque passage.

A Buddhist lexicon from the first half of the eleventh century alludes to *geyi* in such an oddly garbled fashion that the compiler, Daocheng 道誠 (fl. 1019), seems to have been confused about its true meaning. To show how badly rewritten this entry of the lexicon is, it will be useful to cite the relevant portions of the original account on which it was based: 法雅⋯少善外學，長通佛義。衣冠士子咸附諮稟⋯。以經中事數擬配外書。為生解之例，謂之格義⋯ (*T.*50 [2059] 347a18-22; translated in full above). In the eleventh-century lexicon, this admittedly somewhat difficult passage is corrupted as follows: 擬書。高僧法雅。善內外學。多俗士咨稟。以經義難解雅。將比擬外書為生解之。例謂之挌義 (*T.*54 [2127] 294a16-18). The compiler manifestly was oblivious of the actual meaning of the reference to *geyi* in the passage concerning Zhu Faya from the *GZ*, so it would be futile to make a serious translation of his entry on *nishu* 擬書. Instead, I shall attempt to replicate its effect in English, warts and all (and ignoring the gross mispunctuations of the *T.* editors):

> Matched writings. The eminent monk Faya excelled at Buddhist and non-Buddhist studies. Many lay scholars requested that he teach them. Given that the meanings in the sutras were difficult to explain, Faya matched them with [those] in non-Buddhist litera-

ture in order to provide instances of lively explications. This was called "striking concepts."

Even if we grant that 挌義 in the lexicon is simply a typographical error for 格義,⁴⁶ Daocheng has glossed over an essential component (*shishu* 事數) of the original. Perhaps the best light we can put on this corrupted passage is that Daocheng was intentionally attempting to emend (and thus [in his mind] to improve) the original wording of the latter phrase, which has indeed befuddled all scholars who have confronted it. However, in substituting *yi nan jie* 義難解 for *shishu*, Daocheng has eviscerated the passage, leaving it limp and lifeless.

In a short essay on friendship, the Ming monk, Rujin 如卺 (fl. 1470-1489), quotes the Sengxian passage from *GZ 5* without elaboration and seemingly without a clear understanding of the issues involved, no doubt because he was separated by so many centuries from the time when Huijiao originally wrote it (ca. 530) (*T.45* [2023] 1047a1).

The much vexed term *geyi* occurs a total of twenty-three times⁴⁷ in the entire Buddhist canon. All of the relevant occurrences in *T.* are cited and discussed in this chapter. There are no other pertinent texts containing *geyi* outside of *T.* that are not simply copies of passages in it.

It is clear from the above-cited evidence that *geyi* was a method for coping with the Indian proclivity for numerical lists of ideas and concepts. From its few occurrences in the Buddhist canon, it is evident that *geyi* was an abortive exegetical method, not a vital translation technique or essential philosophical principle. The main reason we know about *geyi* at all is because the celebrated Eastern Jin monk Dao'an, rightly so, criticized it as ineffective. After the meager series of texts cited above, there is no significant mention of *geyi* until the twentieth century, when it is miraculously revived by modern historians and made to play a key role in the early development of Buddhism in China.

What Is *Geyi*, After All?

Secondary Evolution

The overwhelming majority of the modern translations and interpretations of *geyi* are partially or totally false. Only a few accurately relate even a portion of what *geyi* really was. Since the vast preponderance of these modern definitions, when measured against the historical data, are self-evidently incorrect, it will not be necessary to comment on them individually. Instead, I will merely cite a few of the more representative figures who have been influential in making the obscure notion of *geyi* into the unjustifiably key term in Buddhist studies that it has become.

So far as I have been able to determine, the first modern scholar to resurrect *geyi* was the celebrated historian, Chen Yinke. Not only was he the one to rescue *geyi* from its richly deserved obscurity, it was he who established the basic nature of the discourse that would be used to discuss it by nearly all scholars who followed in his wake. Chen's groundbreaking study of *geyi* was buried in his tour de force investigation of the little-known figure, Zhi Mindu 支愍度:

> During the Jin era, the scholars who engaged in Pure Conversation (*qingtan* 清談) mostly favored strained comparisons *(bifu* 比附) between Buddhist texts and non-Buddhist writings. What is more, among the monks there was a concrete method called *geyi*. Although the term *geyi* is seldom seen in written records, it was prevalent for a period, and its influence on contemporary thought was profound. . . .[48]

One wonders, if *geyi* is "seldom seen in written records," what evidence Chen can adduce to buttress his bald assertion that it had a profound influence on contemporary thought. A careful reading of his article on the subject reveals that there is precious little, and that most of what he has to say about *geyi* is sheer speculation. Chen's grasping at straws in his allegations of the importance of *geyi* may be seen in a complex case that he adduces near the end of one of his lectures on the subject.[49] He begins with the Zhulin 竹林 ("Bamboo Grove") of India,[50] to which he adds the mysterious *zuozhe qi ren* 作者七人 ("seven men who acted"—Chen does not tell us who they are) of the *Analects* (14.37). According to Chen this yields the celebrated Zhulin Qi Xian 竹林七賢 ("Seven Sages of the Bamboo Grove"), the lively group of third century bohemian, nonconformist intellectuals, poets, musicians, and tipplers who gathered in the environs of Luoyang. He then proceeds to note that the eclectic Jin poet and thinker,[51] Sun Chuo 孫綽 (314-471), compared the Tianzhu Qi Seng 天竺七僧 ("Seven Monks of India") to the Chinese "Seven Sages of the Bamboo Grove." Chen's discussions of *geyi* are filled with this sort of unbridled attribution of practically any syncretic tendencies to this elusive snark. What is still more remarkable, however, is that a scholar of Chen's stature would claim that, not only did *geyi* remain a powerful intellectual force through the Six Dynasties, but Northern Song Neo-Confucianism itself was an outgrowth of *geyi*![52] He even goes on to assert that *geyi* was an essential component for the whole of the history of Chinese philosophy. Given Chen Yinke's enormous prestige, it is not surprising that his uncharacteristically poorly substantiated article and lectures on *geyi* set the tone for all discussions of this topic for the next seven decades.

Chen's lead was taken up in a hugely influential article on *geyi* by Tang Yongtong that was first issued in an English translation by M. C. Rogers: " 'Ko' [*Ge*], in this context, has the meaning of 'to match' or 'to measure'; 'yi' means 'name,' 'term' or 'concept'; 'Ko-yi' [*Geyi*] is (the method or scheme of) matching ideas (or terms), or 'the equation of ideas.'"[53] This short passage is shot through with contradictions. For instance, how can *yi* mean both "name" and "concept" in the same context? Even more damning, how can *ge* simultaneously mean both "to match" and "to measure"? (In the term *geyi*, *ge* actually means neither.) And how does one arrive at Tang's double definition for *geyi* as a whole from the ambivalent parts with which he asserts it is constituted? Elsewhere in the same article, Tang states that *geyi* means "the equation of concepts,"[54] but this is not very illuminating or philologically exact either. Matters did not improve when Tang's article on *geyi* was translated into Chinese,[55] for several mistakes were introduced in the process and errors that were originally in Tang's English version remain uncorrected.⁵⁶ Tang's understanding of *geyi* here (in his 1950 article) is consistent with his interpretation in his *History*: "What is *geyi*? *Ge* means 'to measure, estimate, evaluate' (*liang* 量). It is a method of comparing and matching with Chinese thought to cause people to understand Buddhist writings easily."⁵⁷

Among the many bizarre twists in the saga of *geyi* is the development of what Japanese specialists refer to as *kakugi Bukkyō* 格義佛教 ("*geyi* Buddhism"). Here we have the reification of a hypothetical construct that never existed in historical reality, but one that—once born—takes on a life of its own and becomes a cornerstone in studies of the history and thought of Chinese Buddhism, especially among Japanese scholars, but also among Chinese and Western scholars who appear to have been influenced by them,⁵⁸ with countless disquisitions being written on the nature and impact of what is essentially an imaginary phenomenon.

One of the first Japanese scholars to use the expression "*geyi* Buddhism" was Tsukamoto Zenryū. Section 5 of chapter 1 of his *Shina Bukkyō shi kenkyū* is entitled "Kakugi Bukkyō no Tō Shin seidan shakai e no tenkai" 格義佛教の東晉清談社會への展開 (The unfolding of *geyi* Buddhism toward a society of pure conversation during the Eastern Jin).⁵⁹ The previous section offers an even more dubious proposition, that of "Daoistic Buddhism" (*Dōkyōteki Bukkyō* 道教的佛教),⁶⁰ since Daoist religion was hardly well enough established before the Eastern Jin (the period to which Tsukamoto is here referring) to have subsumed or significantly colored Buddhism. Unfortunately, Tsukamoto's notion of *Dōkyōteki Bukkyō* is adopted by later proponents of *kakugi Bukkyō* as a staple for Wei-Jin intellectuals and promoted as a parallel system that circulated among the people.⁶¹

Tsukamoto and other advocates of *geyi* as a vital factor in the early development of Chinese Buddhism connect the "Dark/Abstruse/Mysterious/Metaphysical Learning" (*xuanxue* 玄學) of the Wei-Jin period with *prajñā* studies, asserting that the latter were carried out under the aegis of the former. Quite the contrary, it might much more forcefully be argued (in terms of chronology and content) that it was Buddhism (in particular *prajñā* and *abhidharma* studies) that provided the new leaven in the batter of existing Chinese thought (chiefly Confucian and Daoist philosophy [not yet fully elaborated religion]) that led to the ferment which resulted in *xuanxue*.

America's major introduction to *geyi* is to be found in the enormously influential *A History of Chinese Philosophy* by Fung Yu-lan: "Such use of Taoist terminology to explain Buddhist concepts was known at the rime as *ko yi* 格義 or the 'method of analogy' (lit., 'extending the idea')."[62] Here we have two incompatible renderings of *geyi* in the same sentence. On the next page, Fung expresses his indebtedness to Chen Yinke.[63] Whether directly derived from Chen or not, neither of Fung's definitions is satisfactory in terms of the available primary evidence.

Relying on Fung Yu-lan is another important Chinese scholar of the mid-twentieth century, Kung-chuan Hsiao, who makes the following unverifiable claim about *geyi*: "At the time there were many who discussed Buddhism in terms drawn from the *Chuang Tzu* (*Zhuangzi*); that process was called 'ko-yi' (格義, or 'matching of terms')."[64] In the index-glossary, Hsiao gives a totally different and completely idiosyncratic, self-contradictory definition for *geyi*: "'invoking the meaning', a method of matching terms used in translating Buddhist writings into Chinese."[65]

Also influenced by Chen Yinke and Tang Yongtong was Arthur Link who, in 1957, began a long series of articles in which he focused on issues that revolved around the problem of *geyi*, which he initially defined as " 'matching meanings', a method whereby Chinese terms and concepts (chiefly Taoist) were paired with analogous Indian terms and ideas."[66]

The next American scholar to address the matter of *geyi* was Arthur Wright. In his short, but widely read, volume on *Buddhism in Chinese History*, he rendered the term as "matching concepts" and stated that

What Is *Geyi*, After All? 471

"([t]his device, which was prevalent in the second and third centuries, was probably favored in the oral exposition of Buddhist teachings."[67] Aside from the fact that there is no indisputable evidence for *geyi* until the fourth century, Wright's characterization of this technique is so ambiguous as to be of little value. He is to be credited, however, for recognizing that numerical groupings played a part in *geyi*.

In his *Source Book*, Wing-tsit Chan defines *geyi* as "the practice of 'matching concepts' of Buddhism and Taoism, in which a Buddhist concept is matched with one in Chinese thought. Thus *tathatā* (thusness, ultimate reality) was translated by the Taoist term 'original non-being' (*pen-wu* [*benwu*], pure being)."[68] For all intents and purposes, this description of *geyi* is completely erroneous.

Kenneth Ch'en's explanation, which is based heavily on the 1950 article of Tang Yongtong, has been particularly damaging because his book has been, and still is, so widely used in introductory courses concerning Chinese Buddhism. Ch'en describes *geyi* as "the method of matching the meaning. This, method was used especially by the translators of the Prajñā sutras for the purpose of making Buddhist thought more easily understood by the Chinese."[69] Many other scholars followed Ch'en in rendering *geyi* as "matching the meaning."[70] Lai spells out his definition more fully: "match Buddhist and Taoist concepts."[71] Robert Shih gives two idiosyncratic renderings of *geyi* in his French translation of GZ: "rendait inexactement [le sens]" and "interprétation par analogie."[72]

A typical description of *geyi* during the seventies is that given by Hurvitz and Link:

> Prior to Tao-an's time it had been popular to explain Buddhist works by a method of exegesis called *ko yi* 格義, "matching meanings." This meant that the Indian terms and concepts in a systematic fashion were explained via Chinese terms and concepts. In general, the texts used for this purpose were the *Lao tzu* 老子, the *Yi ching* 易經, and the *Chuang tzu* 莊子. Though this was a

definite step forward in the earlier period, when it was devised as a technique of analysis and exegesis of the foreign texts, it later became a crutch and a hindrance to a correct understanding of the Buddhist concepts. Tao-an came to understand that this method of "matching meanings" frequently did injustice to the Indian texts, and it is characteristic of his great originality that, despite its traditional and almost universal acceptance by his contemporaries, he nevertheless abandoned it.[73]

Very little, if any, of this elaborate scenario can be substantiated by the meager textual evidence concerning *geyi* that is available.

Closer to the truth of the matter is Zürcher, who states that *geyi* is "elucidating Buddhist terms, notably numerical categories (*shu*), with the help of notions extracted from traditional Chinese philosophy."[74] Elsewhere, however, he follows the crowd in translating *geyi* as "matching the meanings."[75]

Tsukamoto states that, when Buddhism was first introduced to China, it was received as a sort of "Taoistic" religion, and then passed to the stage of *geyi*.[76] His translator, Hurvitz, leaves the term unrendered here, but Tsukamoto explains it as signifying the interpretation of Buddhist doctrine "by resort to the ideas of *Lao-tzu* and *Chuang-tzu*." In discussing the account of Zhu Faya in *Biographies of Eminent Monks*, Tsukamoto identifies *geyi* as an exegetical method, and here (1: 294) Hurvitz offers the unusual translation of "investigating the Doctrine" for this poorly understood term, although he also renders it as "matching the categories" on the very same page. A few pages later (1: 297), Tsukamoto characterizes *geyi* as a "method of interpreting the Buddhist scriptures through the mediation of classic Chinese ideas." He goes on to cite Dao'an's preface to An Shigao's translation of Saṃgharakṣa's *Yogācārabhūmi-sūtra* (*Xiuxing daodi jing* 修行道地經) and his subcommentary to Kang Senghui's 康僧會 (fl. 247, d. 280 [var. 276]) commentary to An Shigao's translation of *Ānāpāna-smṛti-sūtra* (*Anban shouyi jing*) to show that, in the early stage of his career, Dao'an often utilized terms and ideas derived from the *Laozi*, *Zhuangzi*, and *Yijing*, which were

What Is *Geyi*, After All? 473

fashionable in the *xuanxue* of the times (viz., the Wei and Western Jin periods). Tsukamoto concludes (1: 299) that "the propagation of Buddhism in keeping with 'dark learning' is just another name for *ko yi* Buddhism . . . ," a gigantic leap of faith that I am unable to follow. Yet another inexplicable rendering of *geyi* is given by Hurvitz at p. 305: "seeking the meaning." While Hurvitz's notes (1: 577-79 [n. i-al]), drawing heavily on the scholarship of Arthur Link, ably and conclusively document the Buddhist use of terminology from *Laozi*, *Zhuangzi*, and the *Yijing*, the presumed connection with *geyi* is not demonstrated. Tsukamoto proceeds to describe (1: 309, cf. 248) *geyi* as "a movement whose aim was, through the intermediacy [*sic*] of the ideas of *Lao-tzu*, *Chuang-tzu*, and *the Canon of Changes*, to enable the Chinese to understand the Indian Buddhist scriptures."

A curious facet of Tsukamoto's treatment of *geyi* is embodied in the following passage (1: 284, cf. 294 and 575, n. bw):

> an appeal to the knowledge of traditional Chinese ideas, e.g., the equation of the Five Precepts *(wu jie* 五戒, *pañca śīlāni)* with the Five Norms *(wu chang* 五常) for the purpose of propagating the scriptures among Chinese intellectuals—a style of learning known in the history of Chinese Buddhism as *ko yi*.

While this seems entirely reasonable and in line with the close connection between *geyi* and *shishu* analyzed above, the alleged equation between *wu jie* (*pañca śīlāni*) and *wu chang* is not attested among early texts referring to *geyi*.[77] Even if it were so attested, it would show how hopelessly facile and unilluminating the attempt to match up one of the countless Indian lists of technical terms with one of the few Chinese lists was.

Table 7. Comparison between *wu jie* (*pañca śīlāni*) and *wu chang*.

pañca śīlāni	*wu chang*
abstinence (virati) from taking of animate life (*prāṇtipāta*)	humanity (*ren* 仁)
taking of anything not freely given by the possessor (*anattādāna*)	justice (*yi* 義)
violation of the code of sexual behavior obtaining in one's own society (*kāmamithyācāra*)	propriety (*li* 禮)
lying (*mṛṣāvāda*)	wisdom (*zhi* 智)
taking of alcoholic drink (*maireya-madyapāna-surā*)	faith (*xin* 信)

Source: Adapted from "What Is *geyi*, After All," in Alan Kam-leung Chan and Yuet Keung Lo, ed., *Philosophy and Religion in Early Medieval China* (Albany: State University of New York Press, 2010), 246.

Tsukamoto's readiness to expand the applicability of *geyi* is apparent in a subsection entitled "'Ko yi' Translation" (1: 301-306) and in his use of the expression *"ko yi* Buddhism" (1: 333). This he defines (2: 679, cf. 431) as "a device resorted to by all of his (i.e., Dao'an's) contemporaries, that of interpreting the Buddhist scriptures in terms of the Chinese classics and of traditional Chinese ideas." Such a characterization grossly overrates the actual importance of *geyi*. Tsukamoto becomes further ensnarled in the labyrinthine coils of the *geyi* trap when he claims (2: 705), without any factual grounding, that it is "the method that consisted of understanding, or of expounding, the Prajñāpāramitā by resort to 'dark learning,' i.e., to a set of ideas claiming descent from Lao-tzu and Chuang-tzu. . . ." We are provided (2: 709, cf. 1:297 and

2: 712 and 803) yet another definition of our elusive term: "'investigating the meaning' *(ko yi,* that is, of interpreting and explaining the translated scriptures through the intermediacy [*sic*] of words and ideas indigenous to the Chinese tradition)." Finally, Tsukamoto avers (2: 796) that Buddhist scholarship of Dao'an's time was called *geyi* and consisted of "understanding and explaining the Buddhist scriptures in terms of Chinese literature...."

Confusion and imprecision concerning *geyi* persisted with Ren Jiyu's pronouncements on this subject:

> As for Dao'an and others using the words of Lao-Zhuang and Dark Learning in their prefaces for sutras and such compositions to explain Buddhist doctrines, this is also *geyi*. If this foreign religion, Buddhism, wanted to sink its roots solidly in China, it would have been difficult for Chinese to understand and accept it had they not resorted to *geyi*.[78]

Such sweeping assertions are unsupported by the actual textual evidence for *geyi*. But still more outlandish interpretations of *geyi* continue to abound, of which I shall mention only Peng Ziqiang's "Subjectively Retelling."[79]

In contrast, Robert Sharf is to be commended for his skeptical approach to *geyi* as a significant phenomenon in Chinese Buddhist history. He realizes that it is—at best—a hermeneutic strategy, and evinces a critical attitude toward modern scholarly interpretations of this vastly overrated teaching technique,[80] even going so far as to refer to it as a "red herring."[81]

A soberer approach is reflected in the studies of early Buddhist translation procedures carried out by Jan Nattier. In them, we learn what actually transpired when Sanskrit texts were converted into Chinese scriptures, instead of what some imaginary *geyi* technique demanded. For instance, Nattier refers to what she calls "Chinese cultural calques." These are "translations that make no attempt to reflect the etymology of the Indian term, but instead employ what was viewed as a suitable counterpart in Chinese."[82] The examples she gives are telling:

> *āraṇya* ("forest, wilderness" → *shan ze* 山澤 ("mountain and marsh")
> *kṣatriya* ("warrior, aristocrat") → *junzi* 君子 ("gentleman")
> *arhat* (worthy one, person who has attained the ultimate goal of *nirvāṇa* → *zhenren* 真人 ("perfected one")
> *niraya* ("hell, nether regions") → *taishan* 太山 ("Mt. Tai")
> *nirvāṇa* ("awakening; the unconditioned [*asaṃskṛta*] state") → *wuwei* 無為 ("inaction, unmade")
> *cakravartin* ("wheel-turning [king], universal ruler") → *feixing huangdi* 飛行皇帝 ("flying emperor")

By no means can all of these terms, even by the remotest stretch of the imagination, be characterized as "Daoist." Indeed, if one were pressed to denominate their intellectual-religious orientation, they may be classified as variously belonging to Confucian, Daoist, popular, and whimsical outlooks. Even *wuwei,* which *geyi* enthusiasts constantly invoke as one of their favorite examples of an early Buddhist borrowing of "Daoist" terminology, was certainly not restricted to Daoist texts, but was used more broadly by Confucians and others as well.[83] There is no question that *nirvāṇa/nibbāna* was occasionally rendered as *wuwei* in early Buddhist translations,[84] yet there is no indication that this was part of a systematic, conscious policy to appropriate Daoist terminology that was allegedly known as *geyi*. Furthermore, *wuwei* is used to render more than a half-dozen different Sanskrit terms,[85] and the negative *wu* is used at the beginning of more than two thousand words translated from Sanskrit.[86] It would be ludicrous to insist that any Buddhist text that uses the terms *wu* or *wuwei* be branded as Daoistic simply because they also occur in Daoist texts.

It is often alleged by *geyi* enthusiasts that, since early translators such as Lokakṣema (支婁迦讖, fl. ca. 180-189) and Zhi Qian 支謙 (220-252) (in their translations of the *Aṣṭasāhasrikā-prajñāpāramitā-sūtra*) used *benwu* 本無 ("fundamental nothingness; original nonbeing") to translate *tathatā* ("thusness"), they were emulating Laozi and Zhuangzi. But Laozi never used the expression *benwu*, and it is quite a stretch to claim —as some do—that this is the sort of language Laozi might have used. In the *Zhuangzi*, the graphs *ben* and *wu* occur in succession three times, but never as a technical term, only with the meaning "there originally was no X."[87] One might just as well assert that using *benwu* for *tathatā* was an innovative effort on the part of the early translators (in particular, Lokakṣema) to come up with a suitable functional equivalent of *tathatā*, especially when they were as yet unequipped to devise more philologically exact renderings. But even if we accept that *benwu* is a Daoist technical term (a proposition of which I remain dubious [*contra* Wing-tsit Chan[88] and countless others]), there is no justification for citing the rendering of *tathatā* ("thusness") by *benwu* as an instance of *geyi*, since *benwu* is nowhere even remotely associated with *geyi*. Although the use of *benwu* for *tathatā* is a favorite example of supposed "*geyi* translation," it is entirely spurious, as is the very concept of *geyi* translation itself.

What this sample of Buddhist terminology shows unmistakably is that early translators of Indian texts into Chinese creatively used the entire inventory of Literary Sinitic (LS), picking and choosing from what was available to convey as best they could the ideas and images of this alien religion. There is no evidence whatsoever that indicates that they favored Daoist terminology over any other sector of the whole lexicon of LS. In fact, some early translators, especially Lokakṣema, Zhi Qian, and Kang Senghui, avoided indigenous terminology as much as possible, resorting to transcription instead. This is in contrast to individuals (actually a team) such as An Xuan 安玄 (fl. 181) and Yan Fotiao 嚴佛調 (fl. 181-188), who tended to translate names and terms rather than transcribe them.[89] Yet even the latter (those who preferred translation over transcription) were not demonstrably partial to Daoist terminology.

Conclusion

Though *geyi* is enshrined in modern scholarship as a cardinal principle of early Buddho-Daoist interactions, in terms of what actually transpired in history it was but a brief, insignificant episode. With regard to the question of the transmission of Buddhism from India to China, it was by no means an essential mechanism for its early assimilation. Although (according to the modern doctrine of *geyi*) it is commonly asserted that, when Buddhism arrived in China during the Eastern Han period, it instinctively turned to Daoism for its technical terminology and other religious attributes, what actually transpired is more nearly just the opposite. Namely, Buddhism came to China as an already highly sophisticated religion with an extensive corpus of texts, an elaborate system of thought, complex institutional structures, and an advanced tradition of artistic representation. Conversely, it was at this very same time (around the second century CE) that Daoist religion began to take shape. Consequently, Daoism was in no position to serve as a model for the development of Buddhism in China. In other words, we may say that Daoism as a formal, organized religion with a body of texts, monastic rules and institutions, nascent iconography, and set of ritualized practice was to a large extent a response to the advent of Buddhism. But that is a large and daunting topic that I hope will someday merit an international conference or several panels of its own. Surely, the whole issue of Buddho-Daoist interactions deserves to be worked out in much more detail, specificity, and accuracy than heretofore.

In the meantime, the erroneous understanding of *geyi* distorts both the history of Buddhism and of Daoism individually, especially the former. It is enough that countless innocent students are led astray by erroneous definitions and specious accounts of *geyi* in otherwise generally reliable reference books, textbooks, and monographs. Perhaps worst of all, pseudo-*geyi* has spawned an entire industry of fake philosophizing about the intellectual history of China, particularly that of the period of the Northern and Southern Dynasties (or Six Dynasties) that followed the Han. *Geyi Fojiao* or *kakugi Bukkyō* ("*geyi* Buddhism") is a purely modern notion, but it is projected back nearly two thousand years, as though "matching concepts" were the defining characteristic of the first stage of Buddhism in China. It would be easy to cite dozens of wildly imaginative articles that make pseudo-*geyi* the linchpin of their recondite ruminations on *xuanxue*, which is surely already a difficult enough subject of its own without having to get mixed up with a chimera such as pseudo-*geyi*.[90] Many of these studies frankly admit, moreover, that they are working with extended (*yinshen* 引伸) interpretations of *geyi*, and go so far as to declare that *geyi* was a method of comparative philosophy operative throughout Chinese history after the advent of Buddhism.[91] All of these overblown theses built upon pseudo-*geyi* and its extended variations are empty and ahistorical.

Ito's 1996 article is a handy survey of Chinese and Japanese scholarship on *geyi*. The author declares:

> For my own part, I basically wish to adopt the interpretation of *geyi* put forward by Chen Yinke and other Chinese researchers. In addition to this, I characterize the indigenous thought of China that played such a decisive role especially in *geyi*-based Buddhism, namely, Lao-Zhuang thought, as the "philosophy of *dao-li*," and defining *geyi* as the comprehension and interpretation of Buddhism on the basis of this philosophy of *dao-li*. I refer to all forms of Buddhism based on this *geyi*-conditioned understanding as "*geyi*-based Buddhism."[92]

This is a prime example of *geyi*ism run amok. From a failed exegetical technique of little consequence, *geyi* has mushroomed into a colossal, chimerical congeries of Daoistic Buddhisms premised on a nebulous "philosophy of *dao-li* 道理." We must resist the temptation to dehistoricize the limited textual record available to us and to stray so far from the results of disciplined philological inquiry concerning it.

In sum, it is vital to recognize that the comparanda of *geyi* were not Buddhist and Daoist terms for purposes of translation,[93] but numerical lists of Buddhist and non-Buddhist terms for purposes of explanation. Furthermore, *geyi* lasted for but a brief moment in the history of Buddhism, and was almost totally unknown outside of the handful of its practitioners. In a comprehensive, detailed history of the development of early Chinese Buddhism, *geyi* deserves to be mentioned, but not as the centerpiece that modern scholarship has made of it.

Abbreviations

Table 8. Abbreviations

CSJ	*Chu sanzang jiji* 出三藏記集 (Collected notes on the production of the *Tripiṭaka*).
GZ	*Gaoseng zhuan* (Biographies of Eminent Monks).
HDC	*Hanyu da cidian* 漢語大詞典 (Unabridged Dictionary of Sinitic).
j.	*juan* 卷 ("scroll, fascicle, chapter").
MSM	Modern Standard Mandarin.
n.	Note.
SQ	(*Qinding*) *Siku quanshu* 欽定四庫全書 (Imperially Commissioned Complete Writings in the Four Repositories). 1,500 vols. Shanghai guji reprint (1987).
T	*Taishō shinshū daizōkyō,* 大正新脩大藏經, 100 vols. The standard modern edition of the Chinese Buddhist canon, edited by Takakusu Junjirō 高楠順次郎 and Watanabe Kaigyoku 渡辺海旭. Tokyo: The Taishō Issaikyō Kankōkai, 1922-1934. The form of reference for this work is *T.50* (2059) 347a18-27, where 50 is the volume number, 2059 is the text number, 347 is the page number, "a" is the register, and 18-27 are the lines quoted.

Source: Adapted from "What Is *geyi*, After All," in Alan Kam-leung Chan and Yuet Keung Lo, ed., *Philosophy and Religion in Early Medieval China* (Albany: State University of New York Press, 2010), 251.

Acknowledgments

So many people have helped me in so many ways during the prolonged course of the writing of this chapter that I almost feel as though what started as a personal quest gradually became a collaborative enterprise. Daniel Boucher, Josh Capitanio, and Jidong Yang were responsible for the computer searches that provided the hard data for my analysis. This trio also provided much other expert assistance and good advice. Denis Mair photocopied important materials and mailed them to me when I was on leave in distant places, and Jidong Chen went out of his way to track down an important article at a critical moment. Seishi Karashima and the keenly interested members of his "clubs" in Tokyo participated in informed discussions on various aspects of *geyi*, and lively audiences at Princeton University, UCLA, the Swedish Collegium for Advanced Study in the Social Sciences, and a panel at the Fourth International Convention of Asia Scholars in Shanghai organized by Alan K. L. Chan and Yuet-Keung Lo all offered valuable feedback. Several years ago, Jan Nattier kindly sent me two of her unpublished papers on early Chinese Buddhist translation procedures and later made many helpful suggestions for improvement of the final draft. Nathan Sivin and Paul Goldin offered incisive philological comments on *shishu*. Takata Tokio and Kajiura Susumu made it possible for me to use the splendid resources of the library of the Institute for Research in Humanities (Jinbun Kagaku Kenkyūjo) of Kyoto University, while Silvio Vita and Antonino Forte made available the holdings of the Italian School for Oriental Studies' in Kyoto, as did François Lachaud those of the French Institute for Far Eastern Research, also m Kyoto. Among those who generously supplied scholarly references are Jens Braarvig, John Kieschnick, James Benn, Funayama Toru, Stefano Zacchetti, Timothy Barrett, Antonello Palumbo, Stephen Bokenkamp, Charles Muller, Jinhua Chen, Huaiyu Chen, Whalen Lai, Ronald Egan, and Alban Kojima. Finally, I am grateful to Li-ching Chang for serving as a sounding board during the three decades of this chapter's gestation and always being ready to proffer sensible advice. Naturally, I alone, bear full responsibility for the views expressed herein.

Notes

1. Axel Schuessler, *Etymological Dictionary of Old Chinese* (Honolulu: University of Hawaii Press, 2006), under *gé, gè*.
2. Among the dozens of dictionaries consulted are the following authoritative standard sources: *Xiandai Hanyu cidian* 現代漢語詞典 (5th ed.; to save space, I do not give complete publication data (place, publisher, etc.) for well-known works); *Xinhua zidian* 新華字典 (10th ed.); *New Age Chinese-English Dictionary* (Beijing: Commercial Press, 2000); *ABC Chinese-English Comprehensive Dictionary* (Honolulu: University of Hawaii Press, 2003).
3. In the whole of the enormous *SQ*, there are only seven occurrences of *geyi*, and not one of them meaningfully enlarges our understanding of the development of Buddhism during the late Han, Wei-Jin period beyond what can be learned from the sources gathered in the "Primary Evidence" section of this chapter. I have very carefully read all of the passages in *SQ* that contain *ge* and *yi* in immediate succession and have determined that they are all "false hits" (in that they should be separated by a period or comma), repetitions of one of the primary sources already discussed, or irrelevant to the problem of Buddho-Daoist interaction during the late Han, Wei-Jin period. Vol. 851. Wang Guanguo 王觀國 (an author of the Zhao Song period [960-1279]), *Xuelin* 學林 (Grove of learning; a lexicographical, philological study), 5.18a (p. 125a): false hit. Vol. 1021. Zhang Yushu 張玉書 (1642-1711) et al., (*Yuding*) *Peiwen yunfu* 御定佩文韻府 ([Imperially commissioned] treasury of rhymes (from the studio of), esteem for literature; a huge lexicon first published in 1711, with a supplement in 1720), 63/8.34a (p. 379b): a repetition of the *Fayuan zhulin* passage to be discussed shortly. Vol. 709. Wu Ruyu 吳如愚 (fl. 1238), *Zhun zhai zashuo* 準齋雜說 (Miscellaneous discussions from the Studio of Standards; a collection of essays on Neo-Confucian topics), A5b (p.709a): "the meaning of *ge*" (which is here defined as *zheng* 正 ["correct, upright"]). Vol. 1253. Cheng Minzheng 程敏政 (1445-ca. 1499), *Huangdun wenji* 篁墩文集 (Collected prose from the Bamboo Grove Mound; miscellaneous essays on topics of interest to literati), 53.4a (p. 245b): "the meaning of *jiushe ge* 九射格 (a target used in drinking games that is divided into nine compartments)." Vol. 1400. Mei Dingzuo 梅鼎祚 (1549-1615), *Shiwen ji* 釋文紀 (Records of Buddhist writings), 11.9b

(p. 608b): copies Sengrui's comments discussed below. Vol. 1401. *Ibid.*, 16.6b (p. 73a), copies Huirui's comments discussed below. Vol. 1474. Hu Wenxue 胡文學 (fl. 1660), *Yongshang qijiu shi* 甬上耆舊詩 (A collection of poems from the elders of Ningbo), 29.2a (p. 562a): false hit. Guoxue baodian 國學寶典 has a total of nine occurrences of *geyi*, of which six may be traced back to *T*. Of the remaining three, one is from Wang Qinruo 王欽若 et al., ed., Cefu yuangui 冊府元龜 (Outstanding models from the storehouse of literature [1013]), j. 337 where the two graphs mean something entirely different from the geyi of early Buddhism ("repository of principles for the categories of commendation" [*xunge yifu* 勳格義府]), another is from the Confucian scholar Chen Hu's 陳瑚 (1613-1675) Yiguan wenda 一貫問答 (Questions and answers on the one thread that ties everything together), 1, where it occurs with yet another meaning in the clause *you ge jun xin zhi ge yi* 有格君心之格義 ("has the meaning of ge in the expression *ge jun xin* ['examine' the mind of the sovereign]"). The third occurrence is from a reference in a twentieth-century journal entitled *Guoxue jin lun* 國學今論 to Chen Yinke's article discussed below. Similar observations may be made about the even fewer instances of *geyi* in the CHANT database and in other major electronic resources consulted during the preparation of this chapter.

4. It is noteworthy that *geyi* is generally not mentioned in Buddhist dictionaries and encyclopedias compiled before around the sixties of the twentieth century. For instance, it is not to be found in Ding Fubao 丁福保 ed., *Foxue da cidian* 佛學大辭典 (1925) or William Edward Soothill and Lewis Hodous, comps., *A Dictionary of Chinese Buddhist Terms with Sanskrit and English Equivalents and a Sanskrit-Pali Index* (1937). In many cases, major non-Buddhist reference works from the sixties and later still do not mention *geyi*. It is missing from Morohashi Tetsuji 諸橋轍次, ed., *Dai Kan-Wa jiten* 大漢和辭典 (1955-1960; rev. 1966-1988; enlarged 1984-1986) and Luo Zhufeng 羅竹風, ed., *Hanyu da cidian* 漢語大詞典 (1986-1994). Other dictionaries from which *geyi* is absent are the following: *Bol'shoi Kitaisko-Russkii Slovar'*, 4 vols. (1983-1984); *Grand dictionnaire Ricci de la langue chinoise*, 7 vols. (2001); Herbert Giles, *A Chinese-English Dictionary* (1892, 1912); *Mathews' Chinese-English Dictionary* (1931; 1975); *Gwoyeu tsyrdean* 國語辭典 (1937 and later editions). Even the largest available dictionaries for the study of Daoism do not have entries for geyi, e.g., *Daojiao da cidian* 道教大辭典 (1994) and *Zhonghua daojiao da cidian* 中華道教大辭典 (1995). All of this goes to show that, properly speaking, *geyi* was not recognized as

worthy of inclusion in general reference works and, indeed, in specialized works for the study of Buddhism and Daoism. It was only from the seventies and later that *geyi* began to be common in reference works for the study of Buddhism and occasionally in general reference works. The otherwise usually reliable *Foguang da cidian* 佛光大辭典 (1988), edited by Ciyi 慈怡, has a fairly lengthy entry on *geyi* (vol. 5, p. 4143bc), the first part of which I shall translate here as typical of the sort of thing that started to show up after the seventies:

> To explain Buddhist principles through Daoist or (other) non-Buddhist ideas. When Buddhism was first transmitted to the east, intellectuals often were receptive to it because of its resemblance to Lao-Zhuang thought. By Wei-Jin times Lao-Zhuang thought was even more often used to explain the principle of emptiness in *prajñā*. The intellectual fashion of this transitional period was called *geyi*. Representative figures of the times were the Seven Sages of the Bamboo Grove. Buddhism was thus influenced by the fashion of the Pure Conversationalists (to talk about) the principle of emptiness in Lao-Zhuang. Without exception, Buddhist lectures and commentaries on Buddhist texts all regularly cite terms from Lao, Zhuang, and *Yijing* (The Book of Changes). In later times, aspects of the Buddhist dharma were also forcefully compared to Confucian thought, and this too can be considered as a type of *geyi*.

Though the second long paragraph of the entry is more believable (inasmuch as it is devoted to citing specific texts in which the term *geyi* actually occurs), most of what is said in the first paragraph (quoted here) is pure fantasy. The dictionary declares that it has based its entry on Tang Yongtong, *Wei-Jin Nanbeichao Fojiao shi*, ch. 9. Tang's interpretation of *geyi* will be discussed below. The entry on *geyi* in the widely respected *Bukkyōgo daijiten* 佛教語大辭典 (1975) edited by Nakamura Hajime 中村元 (vol. 1, 174d) says essentially the same thing as does the Foguang dictionary, but uses only two sentences and is less elaborate in its presentation: "Matching non-Buddhist religious concepts to Buddhist technical terms in order to understand Buddhism. When Buddhism was first transmitted to China, it was the scholarly fashion to explain the emptiness of *prajñā* by analogy to Lao-Zhuang thought." The general indebtedness to Tang Yongtong is inescapable. By the eighties and nineties, this type of misinformation about *geyi* had managed to seep into such reputable reference tools as the last printed edition (1974,1988: 6.778a) and the

What Is *Geyi*, After All?

online version of the *Encyclopaedia Britannica* and *Routledge Encyclopedia of Philosophy* (1998). Similarly, the 1999 edition of *Cihai* 辭海, vol. 3, 3506b defines *geyi* thus:

> A method for explaining Buddhist sutras during the Wei-Jin period. At that time, when Buddhist sutras had only recently been transmitted to China, in order to make it easier to propagate them, some Buddhist scholars invariably used indigenous concepts and vocabulary from Chinese philosophy (chiefly Lao-Zhuang philosophy) to carry out strained comparisons and explanations. They believed that they could thereby "measure" the texts of the sutras and clarify the principles in them, hence the name [*geyi*].

The signature of Tang Yongtong is also evident in this entry, particularly in the interpretation of *ge* 格 as "measure" (*liangdu* 量度). But the ultimate indebtedness to Chen Yinke is inescapable as well, especially in the use of the expression "strained comparisons" (*bifu*). A refreshing, recent counterexample to all of this attention paid to *geyi* is the *Encyclopedia of Buddhism*, Robert E. Buswell Jr., editor in chief, 2 vols. (Macmillan Reference USA. New York, Detroit: Thomson Gale, 2004), which declines to award it an entry. However, in his article on China in this encyclopedia (143a), Mario Poceski states: "A case in point is the putative method of 'matching the meaning' (*geyi*), which involved pairing key Buddhist terms with Chinese expressions primarily derived from Daoist sources."

5. Missing in some editions of the text, the surname Zhu 竺 is short for Tianzhu 天竺 (a Sinitic transcription of Sindhu). Zhu does not always indicate Indian ancestry, since (in the case of monks) it can also serve as a "lineage surname," i.e., an indication of ethnikon borne by the monk's master rather than of his own ethnic heritage.
6. The name literally means "Dharmic Elegance."
7. There is still a county of this name in central Hebei, approximately 150 km south of the center of Beijing.
8. Literally, "external" (*wai* 外).
9. Literally, "ideas," "meanings," or "concepts" (*yi* 義).
10. The name signifies Sogdian parentage. He was from Zhongshan 中山, a little over one hundred km to the west of Hejian.
11. By which Huijiao 慧皎 (497-554; compiler of *GZ*, the text being quoted here) must mean "with (comparable enumeration of items) in non-Buddhist writings."

12. None of the scholars who have studied this passage have come up with a satisfactory interpretation of the phrase *sheng jie zhi li* 生解之例. A possible alternative to the novel attempt given in my translation is "examples for generating understanding."
13. The precise identification of these individuals is not known, but they were most likely followers of Zhu Faya and Kang Falang.
14. Dao'an is the famous fourth-century cleric about whom we will have much more to say below; nothing more is known about Fatai.
15. Apparently 130 km to the southwest of Zhongshan.
16. *GZ* 4, *T*.50 (2059) 347a18-27. Subsequent citations from the *Taishō* will be given in the text.
17. Yin Hao 殷浩 (306-356) is referred to in the text as *zhongjun* 中軍 ("[Generalissimo of the] Central Army"), a post he assumed in 350. For failure in a military campaign (352-353) to recover the north, he was dismissed and exiled to western Zhejiang, where he spent the last three years of his life immersed in the study of Buddhist scriptures. See Richard B. Mather, trans. and annot., *Shih-shuo Hsin-yü: A New Account of Tales of the World* (Minneapolis: University of Minnesota Press, 1976), 604, for a short biographical sketch.
18. The commandery in western Zhejiang to which Yin Hao was exiled.
19. Cf. Mather, *Shih-shuo Hsin-yü*, 123; Chinese text in Zhang Yongyan 張永言, ed., *Shishuo xinyu cidian* 世說新語辭典 (Chengdu: Sichuan renmin, 1992), 643.
20. These are the five components that are said to constitute the pseudo-personality: 1. the physical body; form or sensuous quality *(rūpa)*, 2. sensation, reception, feeling *(vedanā)*, 3. thought, perception; conceptualization *(samjñā)*, 4. action; mental acts *(karma* or *saṃskāra)*, 5. consciousness; cognition *(vijñāna)*.
21. The six sense-fields/organs *(sadindriyāni)* and their corresponding objects of perception/cognition: 1. the eyes *(caksus)* and 2. visible sights *(rūpa)*, 3. the ears *(śrota)* and 4. sounds *(śabda)*, 5. the nose *(ghrāṇa)* and 6. smells *(gandha)*, 7. the tongue *(jihvā)* and 8. taste *(rasa)*, 9. the tactile body *(kāya)* and 10. tangible objects *(spraṣṭavya)*, 11. the mind *(manah)* and 12. mental data *(dharma)*.
22. These are the Four Noble Truths that form the core of Buddhist religion: 1. life is flawed/unsatisfactory, i.e., suffering *(duhkha)*, 2. the arising *(samudaya)* of suffering is due to craving, 3. there can be cessation *(nirodha)* of suffering, 4. there is a way *(mārga)* (viz., the Eightfold Path) to the cessation of suffering.

23. These twelve *nidānas* (contributory causes/conditions) are: 1. spiritual ignorance (*avidyā*), 2. blind volition (*saṃskāra*), 3. consciousness (*vijñāna*), 4. mental functions and the formation of physical elements (*nāma-rūpa*), 5. the six sense-organs (*ṣaḍ-āyatana*), 6. contact with external objects (*sparśa*), 7. sensations/perceptions (*vedanā*), 8. craving/ desire for pleasure (*tṛṣṇā*), 9. grasping what one craves/desires (*upādāna*), 10. the state of existing (*bhava*), 11. birth (*jāti*), 12. old age and death (*jarā-maraṇa*).
24. These are the same as the six sense-organs (*ṣaḍ-indriya*) listed above in note 21, minus the last, viz., "mind" (*manaḥ*).
25. These are the five positive powers, each of which overcomes its opposite negative tendency: 1. faith (*śraddhā*) overcomes false beliefs, 2. energy (*vīrya*) overcomes slothfulness, 3. mindfulness (*smṛti*) overcomes forgetfulness, 4. concentration (*samādhi*) overcomes distractedness, 5. transcendental insight (*prajñā*) overcomes ignorance.
26. They are: 1. mindfulness (*smṛti*), 2. investigation of the elements of empirical reality (*dharma-pravicaya*), 3. energetic exertion (*vīrya*), 4. rapture (*prīti*), 5. lightness, i.e., repose (*praśabdhi*), 6. concentration (*samādhi*), 7. indifference (*upekṣā*).
27. *Foguang da cidian* (1988), 4.3421c-3422a.
28. Soothill and Hodous, *A Dictionary of Chinese Buddhist Terms* (1937), 270a.
29. Kasawara Kenjiu, annot., F. Max Müller and H. Wenzel, ed. *Buddhist Technical Terms: An ancient Buddhist text ascribed to Nāgārjuna* (Delhi: Orient, n.d.), 66.
30. Wogihara Unrai (Ogiwara Unrai) 荻原雲來 and Tsuji Naoshirō 辻道四郎, eds., *Kan'yaku taishō Bon-wa daijiten* (漢譯對照)梵和大辭典 (Tokyo: Suzuki gakujutsu zaidan, 1968), 471a, 1457a.
31. Margaret Stutley and James Stutley, *Harper's Dictionary of Hinduism: Its Mythology, Folklore, Philosophy, Literature, and History* (San Francisco: Harper and Row, 1984), 264a.
32. An Shigao was a Parthian who arrived in Luoyang in 148 CE. His surname is a truncated form of the Chinese transcription of the dynastic name Arsacid. T'ang Yung-T'ung (Tang Yongtong 湯用彤), "On 'Ko-Yi,' the Earliest Method by which Indian Buddhism and Chinese Thought were Synthesized," translated by M. C. Rogers, in *Radhakrishnan: Comparative Studies in Philosophy Presented in Honour of His Sixtieth Birthday* (London: George Allen and Unwin, 1950), 280-83 (full essay, 276-86), provides an excellent account of An Shigao's affinity for Abhidharma and the vital role of categories therein. Anyone who wishes to

have a deeper understanding of the significance of enumeration (*shu*) in early Chinese Buddhism leading up to the time of Zhu Faya would profit from reading this account by Tang. See also Arthur E. Link, "Biography of Shih Tao-an," *T'oung Pao*, 46.1-2 (1958): 9, n. 4 (full essay, 1-48). In short, Abhidharma was extraordinarily fond of enumerations and exposition by division and subdivision.

33. There is no evidence that *geyi* existed or was practiced before the time of Zhu Faya.
34. *Shixiang* 實相 (*dharmatā, dharma-svabhāva, naya, bhūta-naya, lākṣanika, svabhāva-lakṣana*). For references, see Zhu Qingzhi 朱慶之 and Mei Weiheng 梅維恆 (Victor H. Mair), eds., *Diyuan Yunlai (Ogiwara Unrai) Hanyi duizhao Fan-He da cidian Hanyici suoyin* 荻原雲來《漢譯對照梵和大辭典》漢譯詞索引 (Alphabetical index to the Chinese translations in the Sanskrit-Japanese Dictionary [with Parallel Chinese Translations] of Ogiwara Unrai) (Chengdu: Ba-Shu, 2004), 255a; cf. n. 30 above.
35. The complete biography (*T.50* [2059] 355a.18-29) of Sengxian is translated by Link, "Biography of Shih Tao-an," 42-44.
36. In Yongshi County, modern Hebei.
37. Tang, "On 'Ko-Yi'," 284, mistakenly writes 394. There is also an error in his footnote 2 on the same page which states that the following passage is from *Taishō*, Vol. 50, p. 33 (instead of p. 355).
38. The expression *xiaoyao* 逍遙 here does not refer to the first chapter in *Zhuangzi* ("Xiaoyao you" [Carefree wandering]), as some interpreters have assumed. Already by the Han, *xiaoyao* (in various sinographs forms) was used to indicate an unrestrained, happy attitude. It is particularly interesting to note that it was sometimes used to indicate a more relaxed approach to life in contrast to lectures and study as, for example, in "Chi she fu" 馳射賦 (Rhapsody on mounted archery) by the Han writer, Ying Yang 應瑒 (d. 217): "On a fine day in sunny spring, in my spare time from lectures and study, I am carefree (*xiaoyao*) in the courtyard, take pleasure in riding and archery" (see *HDC* 11.366ab). Indeed, no less a giant of Buddhist translation than Kumārajīva undertook some of his work in the Xiaoyao Yuan 逍遙園 ("Carefree Garden") of Chang'an (see his biography in *GZ 14*; *T.55* [2145] 101b.16).
39. Sanskrit *dharma-dundubhi* or *dharmarbheri*, here signifying Buddhist monks in their capacity as preachers of the Dharma.
40. Realized by Sengrui's teacher, Dao'an.

What Is *Geyi*, After All? 491

41. My translation of this sentence is indebted to Erik Zürcher, *The Buddhist Conquest of China: The Spread and Adaptation of Buddhism in Early Medieval China*, 2 vols. (Leiden: E. J. Brill, 1972), 328, n. 56. Zürcher points out that "[t]he chancellor of Guangling" (in the vicinity of modern Jiangdu 江都 county northeast of Nanjing, between Yangzhou and Taizhou in Jiangsu province) must refer to Zhai Rong 笮融, although, strictly speaking, at that moment this post was occupied by another magistrate, viz., Zhao Yu 趙昱 "[T]he chancellor of Pengcheng" 彭城 (the region north of the Huai River, in eastern Henan, southern Shandong, and northern Jiangsu) in 194 CE was Xue Li 薛禮, who appears to have been associated with Zhai Rong, though nothing is known about his alleged Buddhist sympathies.
42. If, as the totality of evidence would seem to indicate, Zhu Faya was the chief proponent and probable initiator of *geyi* during the first half of the fourth century, then the ca. 220 date of the passage from the "Yuyi lun" under discussion makes the late *geyi* variant all the more suspect.
43. The text says merely Zhi-Zhu 支竺, which is an abbreviated reference for Yuezhi 月支 (through a process of historical description, this name often used to be rendered as "Indo-Scythian," but the precise ethnicity and linguistic affiliation of this important Central Asian group are still being debated; hence I shall leave it untranslated) and Tianzhu (signifying "Indian"). The phrase is that of Sengzhao who, in his preface to the *Vimalakīrti-sūtra* (*T.55* [2145] 58b.9-10), originally used it to designate Zhi Qian (fl. 220-252) and Zhu Fahu (i.e., Dharmarakṣa, who is said in traditional biographies to have been a descendant of the Yuezhi). See Robert Shih, trans. and annot., *Biographies des moines éminents (Kao seng tchouan) de Houei-kiao*. Bibliothèque du *Muséon*, vol. 54 (Louvain: Institut Orientaliste, 1968), 74n56. For a detailed study of the translation techniques of this period, see Daniel J. Boucher, "Buddhist Translation Procedures in Third-Century China: A Study of Dharmarakṣa and His Translation Idiom" (PhD dissertation, University of Pennsylvania, 1996). Boucher points out (p. 8) that it was particularly Zhi Qian and Dharmarakṣa who preferred to translate proper names and technical terms rather than transcribe them, in contrast to the style of Lokakṣema (Zhiloujiachen 支婁迦讖, fl. 180-189), who, however, was also a Yuezhi. The gist of Sengzhao's critique of the style of Zhi Qian and Dharmaraksa as *zhiwen geyi*, then, would seem to be that they erred in overly Sinicizing or indigenizing their translations, presumably at the expense of faithfulness to the Indic originals. In any event, there can be no doubt

that *zhiwen geyi* is a pejorative stigmatization of the translation style of Zhi Qian and Zhu Fahu.

44. For a note on the origin and significance of this expression, see Shih, *Biographies des moines éminents*, 74, n. 57, who points out that it may ultimately derive from Dao'an's preface to the *Moheboluoruoboluomi jing chao* 摩訶鉢羅若 [sic] 波羅蜜經鈔 (Extracts from the *Mahāprajñāpāramitā-sūtra*), in which Dao'an states, "Whenever I come to a stagnant sentence (*zhi ju* 滯句) or a passage where the beginning and the ending are obscured, I set the scroll aside and think deeply, regretting that I never met such men as Dharmarakṣa and Mokṣala" (*CSJ* 8; *T*.55 [2145] 52b.11-13). The text only says "Hu gong Chaluo" 護公叉羅, but most likely is an abbreviated reference to the Gansu Yuezhi Zhu Fahu 竺法護 and the Khotanese Wuchaluo 無叉羅 (var. Wuluocha 無羅叉), both of whom produced *Prajñāpāramitā* translations in the latter part of the third century (286 and 291 respectively).

45. To save space, for texts that are not discussed in depth, I only give the *Taishō* reference, and not the titles of the individual texts themselves.

46. But we should not overlook the fact that 搨 and 格 are interchangeable in one of the many senses of the former, viz., "to strike, hit" (though, of course, not in all senses).

47. Or twenty-five if two questionable variants are included. In addition, *ge* and *yi* occur next to each other, but not as a technical term related to the problem under discussion here, in *T.38* (1779) 799c23 (by Zhiyuan 智圓 [976-1022]) and *T.40* (1805) 353B13-15 (by Yuanzhao 元照 [1048-1116]).

48. Chen Yinke 陳寅恪, "Zhi Mindu xueshuo kao" 支愍度學說考, in *Guoli Zhongyang Yanjiuyuan Lishi Yuyan Yanjiusuo jikan* 國立中央研究院歷史語言研究所集刊 (Bulletin of the Institute of History and Philology of Academia Sinica), *Wai bian* 外編 (Extra series), 1, *Qingzhu Cai Yuanpei xiansheng liushiwu sui lunwen ji* 慶祝蔡元培先生六十五歲論文集 (Beiping: Zhongyang Yanjiuyuan, 1933, 1935), 6. Reprinted in Chen Yinke wenji 陳寅恪文集, 2, *Jinmingguan conggao* 金明館叢稿 (Shanghai: Shanghai guji, 1980), 141-67.

49. Chen Yinke, "Qingtan wu guo (fu 'geyi')" 清談誤國(附"格義"), in Wan Shengnan 萬繩楠, ed., *Chen Yinke Wei Jin Nanbeichao shi jiangyan lu* 陳寅恪魏晉南北朝史講演錄 (Hefei: Huangshan, 1987), 63-64 (full essay, 45-64).

50. In his identification of cultural parallels as constituting instances of *geyi*, Chen Yinke apparently does not distinguish between alleged Buddhist borrowing of Daoist terms and Daoist borrowing of Buddhist terms, for

surely in this instance a supposedly Daoist group has been modeled on an Indian topos, inasmuch as Zhulin 竹林 is the Chinese translation of the celebrated Venuvana ("Bamboo Grove") or Karaṇḍa-venuvana, a monastery park near the city of Rājagṛha that was donated to Śākyamuni by King Bimbisāra (or, according to another account, by the elder Karaṇḍa).

51. Sun Chuo was fond of Confucianism, Daoism, and Buddhism, as is evident in his "Yu Dao lun" 喻道論 (A treatise on analogies of the Way), which is contained in *Hongmingji* 弘明集, 3, in *T.52* (2102) 16b7-17c25.
52. Chen Yinke, "Zhi Mindu xueshuo kao," 10.
53. Tang Yongtong, "On 'Ko-Yi,'" 277-78 (see note 32 above).
54. *Ibid.*, 276.
55. Tang Yongtong, "Lun 'geyi'—zui zao yi zhong ronghe Yindu Fojiao he Zhongguo sixiang de fangfa" 論「格義」—最早一種融合印度佛教和中國思想的方法, translated from English (Tang 1950) to Chinese by Shi Jun 石峻, in *Lixue, Foxue, Xuanxue* 理學・佛學・玄學 (Beijing: Beijing daxue, 1991), 282-94. This has also been collected in *Tang Yongtong quanji* 湯用彤全集 (The complete works of Tang Yongtong), vol. 5 (Shijiazhuang, Hebei: Hebei renmin, 2000), 231-42. The original Chinese draft on which Rogers based his English translation has not, to the best of my knowledge, been found.
56. See, for example, those mentioned in note 32 above.
57. Tang Yongtong, *Han Wei Liang Jin Nanbeichao Fojiao shi* 漢魏兩晉南北朝佛教史 (A History of Buddhism during the Han, Wei, Two Jin, and Northern and Southern Dynasties), 2 vols. (Beijing: Zhonghua, 1983; originally published by Shangwu in 1936-38), 168 (171 in the 1936 edition). Or *geliang* 格量, as on p.170 (173).
58. For example, Kobayashi Masayoshi 小林正美, "'Kakugi Bukkyō' kō"「格義仏教」考, in Takasaki Jikidō 高崎直道 and Kimura Kiyotaka 木村清孝, eds., *Shin Bukkyō no kōryū: Higashi Ajiya no Bukkyō shisō II* 新仏教の興隆：東アジアの仏教思想 II, Higashi Ajiya Bukkyō 東アジアの仏教, 3 (Tokyo: Shunjūsha, 1997), 293-303. Also see Hayashima Kyōshō 早島鏡正 and Takasaki Jikidō, eds., *Bukkyō-Indo shisō jiten* 仏教・インド思想辞典 (Tokyo: Shunjūsha, 1987), 54b-55b (Hirai Shun'ei 平井俊栄); and Whalen Lai, "Limits and Failure of *ko-i* (Concept-Matching) Buddhism," *History of Religions*, 18.3 (February 1979): 238-57.
59. Tsukamoto Zenryū 塚本善隆, *Shina Bukkyō shi kenkyū: Hokugi hen* 支那佛教研究：北魏篇 (Kyoto: Kōbundō, 1942), 25-34.
60. *Ibid.*, 18-25.

61. For example, Kameta Shigeo 鎌田茂雄, *Chūgoku Bukkyō shi* 中国仏教史, Iwanami zensho 岩波全書, 310 (Tokyo: Iwanami, 1978, rpt. 1979), 32.
62. Fung Yu-lan, *A History of Chinese Philosophy, vol. II: The Period of Classical Learning (from the Second Century B.C. to the Twentieth Century C.E.)*, trans. Derk Bodde (Princeton: Princeton University Press, 1953), 241.
63. *Ibid.*, 242, n. 1.
64. Kung-chuan Hsiao, *A History of Chinese Political Thought, vol. I: From the Beginnings to the Sixth Century C.E.*, trans. F. W. Mote (Princeton: Princeton University Press, 1979), 657, n. 110.
65. *Ibid.*, 741a.
66. Arthur E. Link, "Shyh Daw-an's Preface to Sangharaksa's *Yogācārabhūmi-sūtra* and the Problem of Buddho-Taoist Terminology in Early Chinese Buddhism," *Journal of the American Oriental Society* 77 (1957), 4, n. 11 (full essay, 1-14); cf. Link, "Biography of Shih Tao-an,"45.
67. Arthur F. Wright, *Buddhism in Chinese History* (Stanford: Stanford University Press, 1959), 37.
68. Wing-tsit Chan, trans. and comp., *A Source Book in Chinese Philosophy* (Princeton: Princeton University Press, 1963), 336. For further discussion of *benwu*, see below near the end of this section at n. 87.
69. Kenneth K. S. Ch'en, *Buddhism in China: A Historical Survey* (Princeton: Princeton University Press, 1964), 68-69.
70. For example, Itō Takatoshi, "The Formation of Chinese Buddhism and 'Matching the Meaning' (*geyi* 格義)," trans. Rolf W. Giebel, *Memoirs of the Research Department of the Tōyō Bunko (The Oriental Library)*, No. 54 (1996): 69, passim (full essay, 65-91).
71. Whalen Lai, "Limits and Failure of *ko-i* (Concept-Matching) Buddhism," 238.
72. Robert Shih, *Biographies des moines éminents*, 74 and n. 57.
73. Leon N. Hurvitz, and Arthur E. Link, "Three Prajñāpāramitā Prefaces of Tao-an," *Mélanges de Sinologie offerts à Monsieur Paul Demiéville*, vol. II, Bibliothèque de l'Institut des Hautes Études Chinoises, XX (Paris: Presses Universitaires de France, 1974), 406 (full essay, 403-70).
74. Erik Zürcher, *The Buddhist Conquest of China*, 12.
75. *Ibid.*, 294.
76. Tsukamoto Zenryū, *A History of Early Chinese Buddhism: From Its Introduction to the Death of Hui-yüan*, translated by Leon Hurvitz, 2 vols. (Tokyo, New York, San Francisco: Kodansha International, 1985; originally published in Japanese as *Chūgoku Bukkyō tsūshi* 中國佛教通史,

vol. 1 [Shunjūsha, 1979]), 1:248. Subsequent citations from this work will be given in the text.

77. So far as I am aware, this pairing off of the Buddhist *wu jie* with the non-Buddhist *wu chang* did not occur until the *Tiwei Bolijing* 提謂波利經 (Sutra of Trapusa and Bhallika), written by the Northern Wei (386-535) monk Tanjing 曇靜 sometime between 454 and 464. See Tang Yongtong, "On 'Ko-Yi'," 285-86. Furthermore, there is no indication that Tanjing, in comparing the Buddhist Five Precepts with the non-Buddhist Five Norms, was conscious of engaging in *geyi*. Indeed, there is no reason why he should have been aware of *geyi* because it had been defunct for more than a century, and it was of limited circulation even during its supposed heyday (first half of the fourth century).

78. Ren Jiyu 任繼愈, *Zhongguo Fojiao shi* 中國佛教史, 3 vols. (Beijing: Zhongguo shehui kexue, 1981, 1985, 1988), 201.

79. From the English title of Peng Ziqiang 彭自強, "Cong '*geyi*' dao '*deyi*': Fojiao Boruoxue yu Wei-Jin Xuanxue jiaorong de zhuxian" 從「格義」到「得意」：佛教般若學與魏晉玄學交融的主線 (From "Ge-yi [Subjectively Retelling]" to "De-yi [Objectively Understanding]": Interference between Prajñāpāramitā Study and Metapisics [sic] in the Wei-jin [sic] Period), *Foxue yanjiu* 佛學研究 8 (1999): 90-99.

80. Robert H. Sharf, *Coming to Terms with Chinese Buddhism: A Reading of the Treasure Store Treatise*, Studies in East Asian Buddhism, 14 (Honolulu: Kuroda Institute; University of Hawaii Press, 2001), 5, 10, 11, 97-99, 288 n. 12, 309 n. 56.

81. *Ibid.*, 97.

82. Jan Nattier, "Beyond Translation and Transliteration: A New Look at Chinese Buddhist Terms," unpublished paper delivered at the annual meeting of the Western Branch of the American Oriental Society, Portland (October 16, 2004), 10.

83. For a note on the Confucian *wuwei*, as it occurs in *Analects* 15.5, see E. Bruce Brooks and A. Taeko Brooks, *The Original Analects: Sayings of Confucius and His Successors* (New York: Columbia University Press, 1998), 131. To gain an appreciation of the broad usage of the term *wuwei* among various schools and in various texts (e.g., *Laozi*, *Zhuangzi*, *Huainanzi* 淮南子, *Li ji* 禮記, *Chunqiu fanlu* 春秋繁露, etc.), see *HDC* 7.138ab.

84. See Stefano Zacchetti, "An early Chinese translation corresponding to Chapter 6 of the *Peṭakopadesa*; An Shigao's *Yin chi ru jing* T 603 and its Indian original: a preliminary survey," *Bulletin of the School*

of *Oriental and African Studies*, 65, no. 1 (2002): 87 (full essay, 74-98) for some precisely documented examples. In truth, however, *wuwei* eventually came to be used as a translation for a number of other Sanskrit terms whose meanings it more nearly fits: *asaṃskṛta, akṛta, anadhvan, anabhisaṃskāra, anabhisaṃskṛtava, anutpāda, asaṃskāra, asaṃskṛtatva, asaṃskṛta-dharma, asaṃskṛta-pada, asaṅga, nisprapañca*. See Hirakawa Akira 平川彰, *Bukkyō kanbun daijiten* 佛教漢梵大辭典 (Tokyo: Reiyukai, 1997), 776ab.

85. Zhu Qingzhi and Mei Weiheng (Victor H. Mair), *Diyuan Yunlai* (see note 34 above), 310b. For notes on the Daoist *wuwei* and its parallels in various Sanskrit concepts, see Victor H. Mair, trans. and ed., *Tao Te Ching: The Classic Book of Integrity and the Way* (New York: Bantam, 1990), 138, 142.

86. Zhu Qingzhi and Mei Weiheng, Diyuan Yunlai, 302a-314c.

87. In the hundreds of occurrences of *ben wu* that are to be found in texts dating from the Pre-Qin period to the Six Dynasties, it is only in Buddhist texts that it fuses as *benwu* to become a technical term meaning "fundamental nothingness" or "original nonbeing." There simply is no correlation between Daoist texts and *benwu* as a technical term. Furthermore, its chief function during the Eastern Jin was as an effective synonym for *prajñā*, but it also was used at various times to render the following Sanskrit terms: *abhūta, amūla, apūrva, tathatā*, and *śūnya*. Thus, far from being a Daoist technical term borrowed by Buddhism, *benwu* was created by the Buddhists themselves.

88. Wing-tsit Chan, *Source Book*, 336.

89. Jan Nattier, "How to Do Things with Translations: Methodological Reflections on Working with Early Chinese Buddhist Texts," unpublished paper delivered at the annual meeting of the American Academy of Religion, Toronto (November 25, 2002); also personal communications, December 13, 2004 and October 11, 2007.

90. For example, Zhou Daxing (Chow Ta-hsing) 周大興, "Ziran huo yinguo—cong Dong-Jin Xuan-Fo zhi jiaoshe tan qi" 自然或因果—從東晉玄佛之交涉談起, *Zhongguo wenzhe yanjiu jikan* 中國文哲研究集刊 (Bulletin of the Institute for Literature and Philosophy) 22 (March 2003): 91-126.

91. Liu Lifu 劉立夫, "Lun geyi de benyi ji qi yinshen" 論格義的本義及其引伸, *Zongjiao xue yanjiu* 宗教學研究 2 (2000): 76-82.

92. Itō Takatoshi, "The Formation of Chinese Buddhism and 'Matching the Meaning' (*geyi* 格義)," 74.

93. It is an article of faith among even otherwise respectable historians of Chinese Buddhism that *geyi* was an essential translation technique. For example, see Kenneth Ch'en, *Buddhism in China*, 68-69; Charles D. Orzech, *Politics and Transcendent Wisdom: The Scripture for Humane Kings in the Creation of Chinese Buddhism* (University Park: The Pennsylvania State University Press, 1978), 170-71.

Index

Abanindranath Tagore, 371–372, 397
Abhidharma, 458, 470, 489–490
Acker, William Reynolds Beal, 146, 365–366, 394
Advanced Scholars, 2, 6, 9–10, 18, 27
aesthetics, xx, 353, 357, 361, 365, 372, 377–378, 380, 383–384, 386–387, 389–390, 392–393, 397, 399
Akkadian, 164
Altai mountains, 161, 438
Amoyese, 186
Amplified Instructions, 53–54, 57–59, 61–66, 68–70, 78–79, 82, 85–87, 89
Andronovo culture, 161
An Shigao 安世高, 458, 472, 489, 495
An Xuan 安玄, 477
Anyang, 158–159, 162, 164, 175, 405, 439
Aramaic, 163, 177, 251
Arzhan Kurgan, 424
aśvamedha, 414–415, 437–439

Babylonian, 163, 177, 181
Bactrians, 158
baihua (*pai-hua*), 150, 207–208, 216
barbarian, 188, 238, 316
bhāva, 376, 378, 387, 489

bian wen (*bian-wen/pien-wen*) 變文 (transformation texts), xvii, 93–96, 107, 109, 113–114, 116, 118–119, 121–122, 124, 132–133, 135, 137, 145, 147, 150–151, 211, 215, 225, 269
Bo/Bai Juyi (Po Chü-i) 白居易, 14, 16, 25, 29, 33
Botai, 423
"bottle-gourd mouth organ" (*hulu sheng, hu-lu-sheng*), 290, 294–295
Brahmi, 188, 199, 205, 334
Bronze Age, xxii, 177, 183, 305–306, 405, 413, 423–424
burial, 169–170, 405, 407, 412–413, 423–427, 437–439

Catholic, 187, 420
Cantonese, 50, 58, 173, 186, 212, 244, 330, 341, 344
Caucasoid, 155–156, 164, 166
Central Asia, xix, xxii, 102, 116, 121, 129, 134, 153, 161, 169–171, 183, 223–225, 306, 345, 406, 416, 427
chanshu 禪數, 458
Chao Yen-wei 趙彥衛, 5, 26–27
chariot, 15, 160–161, 170, 172, 175, 183, 405, 414–416, 424
Chen Yinke, 467–468, 470, 479, 485, 487, 492–493

children, 10, 46–47, 50–51, 60, 66, 68–69, 100, 204, 287, 292–293, 302, 315, 336
Chinese characters, 84, 116, 173, 242, 247–248, 269, 362–363
Chinese civilization, 89, 122–124, 162, 166, 172, 182, 198, 304–306
Chinese drama, 128–130, 148
Chinese linguistics, 151–152, 238, 327–328, 340, 344, 346
Chinese script, 180, 187–188, 190, 196, 199–200, 204, 305, 337, 342
Classic of Filial Piety, 41
colloquialism, 41–43, 45, 49–50, 55, 57, 59, 64, 67, 70, 81, 85–86, 95, 112, 130–131, 211–212, 229–230, 242, 248
Communism, 124
Confucian, xx, 25, 40–41, 70, 74–76, 81, 83, 90, 189, 198, 227–229, 247, 250–251, 254, 297, 305, 309, 465, 470, 476, 484–486, 495
Confucius, 81, 125, 198, 219, 243, 336, 363, 495
corruption, 1, 11, 24
Cross Potent, 165–166, 180, 182
cultural borrowing, xvii, 121–124, 127, 137
cultural influence, 123, 146
cultural product, 124
Cyrillic, 200, 251

Daoan (Tao-an) 道安, 79, 81, 94, 114, 153, 190, 203, 213, 217, 298–299, 303, 345, 471–472, 490, 494, 496
Daocheng 道誠, 465–466
Daoshi (Tao-shih) 道世, 81, 114, 153, 190, 203, 291, 298, 300, 303, 463, 490, 494

Daoxuan 道宣, 464
deity, 71, 179, 414–415, 418–419, 422, 427, 437, 441
Deng Su (Teng Su) 鄧肅, 187–188, 202
Denmark, 412, 420, 424, 430
deśa-bhāṣā, 234, 236, 246, 257
Devanāgarī, 135, 199
Dharmarakṣa, 97, 222, 463, 491–492
Dialect, 49–50, 56–58, 79, 132, 232–233, 241–242, 244, 270–271, 436
Direct Explanation, 41, 54–56, 59–64, 79, 86, 88
Dunhuang (Tun-huang), xix, 93–96, 105, 107–110, 112–116, 119, 121, 126, 132, 145–146, 149, 151, 211, 214–215, 217, 222

East Asian Heartland (EAH), 405–406, 435
East–West interaction, 117, 155, 169–170, 172, 182, 198, 242, 329, 405, 410, 418, 430–435, 440, 449
Eastern Han period, 132, 211, 219, 300, 385, 453, 478
Egypt, 163, 181
Eight Transcendents, 283, 294–295, 300, 307
Elaboration, 84
Elamite, 164
Emperor of Heaven (Tian di, T'ien-ti, 天帝, most likely the Jade Emperor), 301
En-shou, 45, 47–48, 85, 146
Equus October, 414
Erya (Erh-ya) 爾雅 (Approaching Elegance), 332
etoki, 124

Index   501

Eurasia, xxii, 158, 161, 182, 306, 405, 413–415, 421–425, 428–434, 440
Europoid. *See* Caucasoid
examination system, 1, 3, 11, 13, 26–27, 230

fashu 法數, 359, 456
figurine, 155–156, 164, 166, 176
filial piety, 40–42, 48, 56, 63, 67, 74, 97, 99
Five Dynasties, 8, 11, 30, 121, 128, 150, 354
Fu Qian, 406, 409
Fukien, 52, 56, 189, 205, 269
Fung Yu-lan, 470, 494
Fuxi (Fu-hsi), 32–33, 148, 192–193, 288, 292, 297–298

Gansu (Kansu), 35, 93, 121, 162, 198, 492
Gaxian Cave, 411, 436
Germanic, 312, 418–419, 421, 440
Germanic Mythology, 421
Germany, 124, 169, 177, 202, 244, 312, 330, 344, 397, 399, 412, 421, 424
geyi 格義, xviii, 358–359, 449–457, 459–482, 484–487, 490–492, 494–497
Gobi desert, 162
gold, 15, 21, 116, 154, 174, 240, 418–419, 424–425, 429, 438
Great Khitan script, 188
Greek, 118, 163–165, 169, 178, 181–182, 312, 327, 330, 333, 335, 339–340, 347, 391, 398, 414, 416, 418–419, 438
Grimm, Jakob, 421
guo yu (*kuo-yü*), 32, 148, 150–152, 179, 236–240, 244–246, 257

guxiang 骨相, 385

Han Yu (Han Yü) 韓愈, 3, 5, 14–15, 17, 22, 27–28, 32, 36–37
hanzi (*han-tzu*) 漢字, 185–186, 243, 451
Hindu, 131–132, 227
historical linguistics, 132, 173, 183, 284
Hittite, 158
Hokkienese, 186
Hu Shi (Hu Shih), 109, 124–125, 131, 150
Hu Xiansu (Hu Hsien-su) 胡先驌, 129
Hulu Xian (Hu-lu hsien) (Bottle-Gourd Immortal) 葫蘆仙, 299, 310
Hunmin chŏng'ŭm, 247–251, 255, 271
hyangch'al, 246–247

Illustrated Explanations, 45–48, 79, 83
India, xvii, xix, 116, 121–122, 124, 126, 128–131, 134, 137, 145–148, 150, 153, 163, 179, 202, 214, 222, 227, 231, 234–236, 286, 294, 328, 330–332, 353, 358, 372–373, 378–379, 386, 390–391, 397–398, 400, 415, 467–468, 478
Indian influence, 123, 128–131, 137, 145, 148, 152–153, 355, 371, 373
Indo-European, 133, 160, 165, 168–173, 182–183, 285–286, 305, 340, 342, 399, 406, 412–414, 418, 422, 437, 439
Indo-Iranian, 147, 163, 170, 183, 226, 316, 328, 414, 416
Indonesia, 124, 145

Inner Asia, 406, 427, 441
Iranian, xvii, 116, 118, 147, 160, 162–165, 169–172, 177–179, 183, 212, 223, 226, 314, 316, 328, 345, 414, 416–417, 420, 425

Japan, 91, 147, 185, 202, 218, 240–241, 244–246, 254, 257, 313, 329
jiang yuan (*chiang-yüan*) 講院, 105
jiangjing wen (*chiang-ching-wen*) 講經文 (sūtra lectures), xvii, 93–96, 105, 107–108, 110, 112–113, 115, 119, 217
jinshi (*chin-shih*) 進士 (Advanced scholar), 2, 9, 19, 23, 25, 53, 57, 227
Jogīmāra cave of Rāmgarh, 127
Jurchen, 187–188, 231, 239

kakugi Bukkyō 格義佛教, 469, 479
Kang Senghui, 472, 477
Kangxi (K'ang-hsi) Emperor, xvi, 7, 28, 32–33, 35, 39–40, 42–43, 48, 52, 55, 61, 80–82, 84, 137, 149, 153, 202, 289
Kharoṣṭhī, 199, 334
Khitan, 188, 231, 239
khirigsuur, 423, 425
Khotanese, 104, 133, 152, 171, 224, 492
koine, 241–243, 271
kokugo, 240, 244–246
Korea, 185, 198, 218, 246–247, 251, 253–254, 313, 330
Kumārajīva, 132, 222, 233, 461–462, 464, 490
kurgans, 412, 424–425

Latin, 163–164, 169, 207–208, 244, 284–285, 312, 327, 330, 333, 335, 340
lāvaṇya, 376–379, 384–387, 399
Laozi, 472–473, 477, 495
Li Chao 李肇, 3, 25–26, 33–34
Link, Arthur, 470, 473
literary influence, 124, 130
Literary Sinitic, xvii, 207, 252, 258, 333, 340, 344, 366–367, 381, 477
Little Khitan script, 188
Liu Daochun, 354, 364, 386, 403
liu fa (*liu-fa*) 六法 (Six Canons), 126, 372–373, 397, 403
Liu Jun 劉峻, 359, 455
Liu yu (*Liu-yü*) (Six Maxims), 27, 42–43, 68, 70, 82, 84, 88
Liu yu yan yi (*Liu-yü yen-i*) (Elaboration of the Hortatory Edict of Six Maxims), 43, 84
Lokakṣema 支婁迦讖, 220, 476–477, 491
Lü Dongbin (Lü Tung-pin) 呂洞賓, 283, 300
Lu Yu 陸游, 5–6, 26, 28–29, 31–32, 35–36, 44, 82, 85, 148, 150, 152, 202–203, 211, 229–230, 237, 283, 307–311, 394, 398
Luoyang (Lo-yang), 132, 152, 482

Ma Jianzhong (Ma Chien-chung) 馬建忠, xvii, 203, 327, 330–331, 333–334, 340–342, 344, 347
Ma shi wentong (*Ma shih wen t'ung*) 馬氏文通, xvii, 327, 330–331
mādhurya, 377–378, 385
mage, 160, 163, 176, 180
Mahāvyutpatti, 456–457

Index 503

Manchu, 44, 53, 59, 84, 169, 200, 240, 303, 330
Mandarin, xvii, 49–50, 54, 56, 59, 69, 84, 163, 165, 173, 221, 235, 238–246, 259, 271, 284, 291, 313, 330, 341, 344, 356, 438, 451
Massagetae, 417
mingshu 名數, 359, 456
Modern Standard Mandarin, 163, 173, 235, 238–240, 259, 284, 291, 313, 356, 438, 451
Mongolian, 41, 53, 169, 198, 200, 221, 238–240, 251, 409, 411, 423, 425–426, 428–429, 436, 440

nan xi (*nan-hsi*) 南戲 (southern drama), 129–130, 148
Nattier, Jan, 268, 270, 475, 482, 495–496
nāṭya-śāstra, 378, 380, 399
Neolithic, 169, 182, 305, 412
Norse, 169, 421, 440
Nüwa (Nü-wa), 289, 292, 294–295, 297–298

Old Persian, 155, 157, 159–160, 163–168, 171–172
Old Sinitic, 155, 157, 159–160, 165–173, 183, 304, 312, 435, 438
Old Uighur, 150, 200, 251

paganism, 176, 421–422
Pāṇini, 232, 331, 345
Patañjali, 331
patronage, 2, 12–13, 23, 25, 36, 127, 130, 283, 301, 419
Pekingese, 242, 342
Persia, 164, 174, 380

Persian, 102, 155, 157, 159–160, 163–168, 171–172, 174, 285, 312, 380, 416
phonetic, 131, 177, 186, 188–189, 198, 200–201, 203, 240–241, 245–248, 250–251, 255–256, 269, 286
poetry, xx, 1, 5–6, 13–14, 17–21, 33–34, 36, 153, 246, 253, 288, 306, 377, 440
prajñā, 150, 464, 469–471, 486, 489, 496
Prakrit, 132, 149, 152, 177, 223, 233–235, 270
presentation scroll, 4, 19, 21
Protestant, 54, 187
Proto-Indo-European, 169, 171, 412, 414

Rasa, 377–378, 385–387, 488
reincarnation, 68, 419
Ricci, Matteo, 187, 252, 485
ritual, 8, 70, 114, 162, 164–165, 168, 171, 176, 179, 209, 243, 251, 287, 293, 296, 299, 301, 313, 331, 406, 410, 412–414, 418–419, 422–423, 425–428, 437
Roman alphabet, 200, 252
Romanization, 173, 186–187

sacred bogs, 412, 419, 424, 430, 439
Ṣaḍaṅga (Six Limbs), xviii, 126, 146, 371–373, 375–391, 393, 396–403
Saka, 156, 171, 174
Sakas, 156, 160, 163, 345
Samara, 413

Sanskrit, xvii, 34, 99, 104, 115–117, 126, 128–134, 147–152, 171, 177, 185–187, 190–191, 199, 201–203, 205, 207–208, 217–219, 222–224, 226–227, 233, 235, 237, 241, 251, 258, 269–270, 294, 331–332, 360, 376, 381, 387, 390–391, 398–400, 403, 438, 449, 456–458, 475–476, 485, 490, 496
Sanskrit plays, 128–129, 233
Saubhikas, 124
Scandinavia, 419, 440
Schafer, Edward, 136, 294
Scythian, 127, 158, 170, 174, 234, 314, 416–417, 420–421, 424–426, 438–439, 491
Scythians, 158, 170, 174, 416–417, 420–421, 425, 439
Sengrui 僧叡, 461, 464, 485, 490
Sengyou (Seng-yu) 僧佑, 14, 32, 190–191, 203, 236, 462–463, 491
Shakespeare, 124
shaman, 162–163, 176–177, 180, 413, 428, 434
Shen Kuo (Shen Kua) 沈括, 135, 153
Shenqing 神清, 464–465
Sheng yu guang xun (*Sheng-yü kuang-hsün*) (Amplified Instructions on the *Sacred Edict*), 52, 54, 59, 62–63, 66, 69, 82, 85, 88
Shiming (*Shih ming*) 釋名 (Explanation of Terms), 36, 332
shishu 事數, 359, 454–457, 459, 463, 465–466, 473, 482
Shouwen (Shou-wen) 守溫, 85, 134, 146, 148, 204, 226

Shuowen jiezi (*Shuo wen chieh tsu*) 說文解字 (Explanation of Simple and Compound Graphs), 332, 394
Siberia, 162, 406, 413, 425, 427–428
Siddham, 134, 185, 199, 202, 222, 251, 253, 269
silk, xxii, 169, 173, 224, 254
Sinitic, xvii, xix, 155, 157, 159–160, 165–173, 180, 183, 186–187, 191, 204, 207–209, 211–216, 218–220, 222–227, 229, 231, 235–238, 240–245, 247, 252, 256–259, 284, 286, 289, 295–297, 301, 303–305, 312, 314, 316, 328–334, 340–342, 344–347, 366–367, 381, 411, 435–436, 438, 449, 451, 477, 487
Sino-Tibetan, 186, 314
Sinograph, 185–187, 190–191, 199, 204, 220–222, 236, 240, 243–248, 250, 257, 269, 284, 295, 301, 314, 342, 346, 490
Six Maxims, 68, 70, 82, 84, 88
Soushen ji (*Sou-shen chi*) 搜神記, 110
Southeast Asia, 147, 231, 290, 293–297, 312–314
Southern Bottle-Gourd (*hulu*, 283–284, 286, 289–291, 293–294, 303, 307–312
storytellers, 75, 80, 90, 100
Sun God, 424
Sweden, 412, 420, 424, 439–440, 482
syntax, 133, 209, 216, 222, 327–329, 332–333, 338, 342, 344, 364, 369
Syrian, 163

T'ang Gleanings, 2, 18, 32, 34–35
Taiwan 32, 96, 100, 108
Taiwanese, 186, 244

Index

Talmudic Hebrew, 163
Tang Yongtong, 468, 470–471, 486–487, 489, 493, 495
temple, 15, 71–73, 81, 127–128, 130, 148, 156, 178, 228, 254, 269, 298, 314, 407–408, 420, 422
Teng Su 鄧肅, 187–188, 202
tetragraphs, 137, 185–187, 190, 204
Tianzhu Qi Seng 天竺七僧 ("Seven Monks of India"), 468
Tian Shan (Tangri Tagh, Heavenly Mountain), 425
Tieguai Li (T'ieh-kuai Li) 鐵拐李 ("Iron Crutch Li"), 283, 300, 307
Tocharian, 133, 149, 158, 170, 177, 183–184, 212, 222–224, 328, 438
transformation text, xvii, 83, 93–96, 107–109, 111, 113–116, 118–119, 121–122, 124, 132–133, 135, 137, 145, 147, 150, 204, 211, 215, 225, 269
Tripiṭaka, 191, 203, 218, 237, 259, 394
Tsukamoto Zenryū, 469, 472–475, 493–494
T'ung-chih 通志, 89, 189, 199, 202, 204–205

Uighur(s), 90, 100–101, 149–150, 200, 251
upāya (*fangbian*), 216
Urals, 161, 413, 423, 439
Urt Bulagyn, 423

Vietnam, 185, 240
view of history, 122–123
village lectures (*xiang yue, hsiang-yüeh*), 44, 57, 68, 81–83, 88, 113, 151

Vimalakīti, xvii, 93–97, 100–101, 103–108, 110, 112–114, 116–117, 119, 217–218, 223, 237, 245–246, 253, 270, 375, 379–380, 385, 399–400, 458, 461, 463, 472, 476, 491–492, 494–495
Viṣṇudharmottara, 379–380, 385, 400

Wang Huan, 341
wayang bëbër, 124
wen yi zai dao (*wen i tsai tao*) 文以載道, 336
wenfa (*wen-fa*) 文法, 329, 344
wenli (*wen-li*) 文理, 342, 344
wenyan (*wen-yen*), 207–208, 215–216
Western Regions, 135–137, 150, 188, 193, 195, 197
Westerner, 327, 330, 334, 337
women, xxii, 18, 47, 60, 66, 81–82, 103–104, 116, 149, 227, 231, 245, 285, 290, 294, 300, 341, 417
Wright, Arthur, 470
Wu-sun, 158
Wuluohou, 407, 410–411, 436

Xianbei (Särbi), 406–407, 409–411, 425, 428–429, 436–437
Xiang Da (Hsiang Ta), 116, 137, 146
xiaoxue (*Hsiao-hsüeh*) 小學 ("lesser/minor learning"), 48, 332
Xie He (Hsieh Ho) 謝赫, xviii, 126, 353–358, 360–372, 374, 379–387, 389–394, 396, 398, 401–403
Xinjiang (Sinkiang), 127, 149, 225
Xiongnu (Huns), 158, 406–407, 409–411, 425, 428–429, 435
Xu Dishan (Hsü Ti-shan), 128, 148

xuanxue 玄學, 469–470, 473, 479, 493
Xuanzong (Hsüan-tsung) 玄宗, 2, 28, 90, 134, 153

Yan Fotiao 嚴佛調, 477
Yan Shigu, 406, 409, 437
yangban xi (*yang-pan-hsi*) 樣板戲, 123
yazuo wen (*ya-tso-wen*) 押座文 (seat-settling texts), 110
Yongzheng (Yung-cheng) Emperor, 52–53, 68, 85
yufa (*yü-fa*) 語法, 329, 341, 344
yuyi 裕義, 461–462, 491

Zarathustra, 164, 178
Zhang Yanyuan, 353, 360–362, 364–365, 367–369, 382, 396, 401

Zheng Zhenduo (Cheng Chen-to) 鄭振鐸, 128, 130, 148
Zhi Mindu 支愍度, 467, 492–493
Zhi Qian 支謙, 406, 462–463, 476–477, 491–492
Zhou Yiliang (Chou I-liang) 周一良, 94, 113, 118, 132, 151
Zhouyuan (Chou-yüan), 16, 27, 29, 31, 34, 148, 151, 155, 157, 166, 173–176
Zhu Faya 竺法雅, 359, 454, 456–457, 459, 463–465, 472, 488, 490–491
Zhuangzi (Chuang-tzu) 莊子, xviii, 110, 288, 299, 305, 459–460, 470–474, 477, 490, 495
Zhulin Qi Xian 竹林七賢 ("Seven Sages of the Bamboo Grove"), 468, 486
Zoroastrianism, 162, 177–179, 236

www.ingramcontent.com/pod-product-compliance
Lightning Source LLC
Chambersburg PA
CBHW021349290426
44108CB00010B/169